A SURVEY
OF BASIC
ACCOUNTING

THE ROBERT N. ANTHONY/WILLARD J. GRAHAM SERIES IN ACCOUNTING

A SURVEY
OF BASIC
ACCOUNTING

R. F. Salmonson, Ph.D., CPA
Professor Emeritus
Michigan State University

James Don Edwards, Ph.D., CPA
J. M. Tull Professor of Accounting
University of Georgia

Roger H. Hermanson, Ph.D., CPA
Ernst & Whinney Alumni Professor
Research Professor of Accounting
Georgia State University

1985   Fourth Edition

RICHARD D. IRWIN, INC.   Homewood, Illinois   60430

ISBN 0-256-03203-3

Library of Congress Catalog Card No. 84–081128

Printed in the United States of America

1 2 3 4 5 6 7 8 9 0 K 2 1 0 9 8 7 6 5

Dow Jones-Irwin—
a division of Richard D. Irwin, Inc.—has developed
Personal Learning Aids (PLAIDS)
to accompany texts in this subject area.
Copies can be purchased through your bookstore
or by writing PLAIDS,
1818 Ridge Road, Homewood, IL 60430

PREFACE

This fourth edition of *A Survey of Basic Accounting* is designed for use by those who wish to obtain a basic understanding of financial and managerial accounting. Accounting topics are introduced and discussed on the assumption that the reader has no prior knowledge of accounting.

We have sought in this book to introduce topics in a manner that emphasizes the output of the accounting process. While some attention is directed toward procedures and techniques used to accumulate accounting information, the major emphasis is on the content of accounting reports and on the interpretation and possible uses of this information.

This fourth edition has been thoroughly updated and substantially revised. A new introduction to the text appears in this edition. The first 12 chapters are devoted to a discussion of topics that relate largely to the determination and reporting of net income and financial position and to the basic theory underlying the financial statements of business corporations. Here again we have deliberately sought to emphasize certain subject matter because we believe that knowledge of it is crucial in gaining an understanding of financial accounting and financial reporting. For example, we direct attention to the alternative approaches to accounting for inventories and plant assets since these approaches may produce substantially different measurements of net income and of financial position. We also discuss such matters as the theory underlying accounting statements, the appraisal of financial position and the adequacy of earnings, stockholders' equity, debt financing and investments, changes in financial position, and inflation accounting. We omit largely procedural matters, such as payroll accounting and specialized journals.

The remaining eight chapters deal with topics that are likely to be of concern to management in directing the internal affairs of a business. The topics discussed include income determination, cost concepts, and cost systems in manufacturing operations; responsibility accounting and segment analysis; the budget; cost-volume-profit analysis; short-term decisions; tax considerations; and capital budgeting. We believe that knowledge of the topics included is essential to every reader who aspires to an executive position in business if he or she expects to understand accounting reports, to plan and control the operations of a business, and to communicate with other executives. Appendix A covers the increasingly important topic of international accounting and is a new feature of this edition.

We have designed this text for use in a one-term survey-of-accounting course. It will provide students who have no prior knowledge of accounting with the background necessary for further courses dealing with the accumulation, interpretation, and use of accounting information.

Various approaches may be taken in using this book in a one-quarter or a one-semester course. For a primarily "financial" course, one could focus attention on the first 12 chapters. If management accounting is to be emphasized, one could cover Chapters 1–4 and then concentrate on the last eight chapters. Alternatively, a balanced approach could be taken by covering all the chapters or by covering selected chapters from both groupings.

Questions, exercises, and problems are provided at the end of each chapter in sufficient quantity for use in classroom discussion and for assignment as homework. An instructor's manual and a combination study guide and work papers booklet for students are available. The student booklet has been strengthened considerably with the addition of from 15–25 multiple choice questions with answers and explanations for each chapter.

We are indebted to a number of members of the faculties of our respective universities for helpful comments on the organization and content of this book. In addition, we would like to acknowledge specifically the assistance of Martin A. Bubley, Northern Illinois University; V. Bruce Irvine, University of Saskatchewan; Gerald L. Johnson, California State University, Fresno; Larry N. Killough and Rosalind Cranor, both of Virginia Polytechnic Institute and State University; Richard D. Lamb, University of New Hampshire; Lawrence Rittenberg, University of Wisconsin; Deborah A. Wheless, University of Alabama; and Donald L. Wilson, University of Georgia.

Barbara Howard and Dianne Hermanson provided capable and efficient service in typing the manuscript. But we, of course, bear full responsibility for any deficiencies in the text.

R. F. Salmonson
James Don Edwards
Roger H. Hermanson

CONTENTS

variances. *Overhead variances.* Goods completed and sold. Investigating variances from standard. Disposing of variances from standard. Appendix.

INTRODUCTION: THE ACCOUNTING ENVIRONMENT

Many decisions are made daily in our society that have economic consequences, such as whether our savings should be invested in a savings account, in government bonds, or in shares of stock issued by business corporations. We may feel that our savings can be quite safely invested in a savings account or a government bond, but we are far less certain about the outcome of an investment in shares of stock. To make an informed decision, we need information about the economic activity of corporations that issue such shares. It is at this point that accounting enters the picture, since accounting is a primary source of information on economic activity.

Economic activity includes the production, exchange, and consumption of scarce goods and is found everywhere in our society. Accounting is nearly as extensive. Accounting is needed to show what activity was accomplished at what cost. This statement is true whether resources are used by individuals, business firms, or not-for-profit entities such as churches, units of government, and hospitals. Although accounting is used in all types of organizations, attention in this text will center on accounting and reporting by business firms.

ACCOUNTING DEFINED

Accounting *is the process used to measure and report relevant financial information regarding the economic activity of an organization or unit.* [1] This information is stated in monetary terms.

When people first study accounting, they often confuse it with bookkeeping. Bookkeeping involves the recording of business activities and is a very mechanical process. Accounting includes bookkeeping but goes well beyond it. Accountants prepare financial statements; conduct audits; design accounting systems; prepare special studies, forecasts, and budgets; do income tax work; and analyze and interpret financial information.

In performing their work, accountants *observe* the economic scene and *select* (or identify) those events they consider evidence of economic activity, such as the purchase and sale of goods and services. Then these events are *measured* in financial terms and *recorded* to provide a permanent history of the financial activities of the organization. In order to *report* upon what has happened, accountants *classify* their measurements of recorded events into meaningful groups and *summarize* these measurements to avoid excessive detail. Finally, accountants may be asked to *interpret* the contents of their statements and reports. Interpretations involve explanations of the uses, meanings, and limitations of accounting information.

Accounting may also be defined as an *information system* designed to provide, through financial statements, relevant financial information. In designing this system, accountants keep in mind the types of users of the information (for example, owners and creditors) and kinds of decisions users make which require financial information. Usually, information provided by accounting relates to the economic resources owned by an organization, claims against these resources, changes in both resources and claims, and results of using these resources for a given period of time.

EMPLOYMENT OPPORTUNITIES IN ACCOUNTING

In our society, accountants typically are employed in (1) public accounting, (2) private industry, or (3) the not-for-profit sector. Within each of these areas, specialization is possible; an accountant may, for example, be considered a professional in auditing, systems development, budgeting, or cost or tax accounting.

Public Accounting

To become a **certified public accountant (CPA),** a person must pass a national examination prepared and graded by the **American Institute of Certified Public Accountants (AICPA)**—the accounting equivalent of the American Bar Association or American Medical

---

[1] A complete discussion of the objectives of financial reporting is contained in FASB, *Statement of Financial Accounting Concepts No. 1,* "Objectives of Financial Reporting by Business Enterprises" (Stamford, Conn., 1978). Further reference will be made to this FASB Statement in Chapter 12.

Association. After passing the CPA examination and meeting certain other requirements (such as work experience), an individual may be licensed by a state to practice as a certified public accountant. As an independent professional accountant, a CPA may offer clients auditing, management advisory, and tax services. Clients may be business firms, individuals, or not-for-profit organizations.

Auditing. When a business seeks a loan or wants to have its securities traded on a stock exchange, it is usually required to provide statements on its financial affairs. Users of financial statements may accept and rely upon them more freely when they are accompanied by an **auditor's opinion (or report).** The auditor's opinion pertains to the fairness of the statements.[2] In order to have the knowledge necessary for an informed opinion, the CPA conducts an audit (examination) of the accounting and related records and seeks supporting evidence from external sources.

Management advisory services. Often from knowledge gained in an audit, CPAs offer suggestions to their clients on how to improve operations. CPAs may be engaged to provide a wide range of management advisory services, many of which tend to be accounting related. For example, services may include the design and installation of an accounting system or services in the areas of electronic data processing (computers), inventory control, budgeting, or financial planning.

Tax services. CPAs also provide expert advice for the preparation of federal, state, and local tax returns to determine the proper amount of taxes due. Because of high tax rates and complex tax laws, tax planning is of equal importance. Proper tax planning requires that the tax effects of business decisions be known and considered before the decisions are made.

Private (Industrial) Accounting

Accountants employed by a business are referred to as private, industrial, or management accountants. A private business may employ only one accountant, or several, who may or may not be CPAs. Management accountants may possess a CMA rather than (or in addition to) a CPA designation. A Certificate in Management Accounting (CMA) is issued to persons who have passed an examination prepared and administered by the Institute of Management Accounting (IMA). The IMA was established by the National Association of Accountants, which is an organization for accountants primarily employed in private industry.

Management accountants may specialize in providing certain services. For example, they may be concerned with recording events

---

[2] For an example of an actual auditor's opinion, see Appendix B at the end of the text. Included in Appendix B is a complete set of financial statements of the type often presented to external users by a major corporation.

and transactions and with preparing financial statements. Alternatively, they may be engaged in accumulating and controlling the costs of goods manufactured by their employer. Still others may be specialists in budgeting—that is, in the development of financial plans relating to future operations. Many private accountants become specialists in the design and installation of systems for the processing of accounting data. Others are internal auditors and are employed by a firm to see that its policies and procedures are adhered to in its departments and divisions. These latter individuals may earn the designation, Certified Internal Auditor (CIA), granted by the Institute of Internal Auditors.

Accounting in the Not-for-Profit Sector

Many accountants, including CPAs, CMAs, or CIAs, are employed by not-for-profit organizations, including governmental agencies at the federal, state, and local levels. The governmental accountant is likely to be concerned with the accounting for and control of tax revenues and their expenditure. Accountants are also employed by governmental agencies whose function is the regulation of business activity—for example, the regulation of public utilities by a state public service commission.

Some accountants are also employed in the academic part of the profession. Here attention is directed toward teaching accounting, researching the uses and limitations of accounting data, and improving accounting information and the theories and procedures under which it is accumulated and communicated.

THE NEED FOR ACCOUNTING INFORMATION: THE DECISION-MAKING PROCESS

The need for accounting information in making economic decisions has been noted, but little has been said about the decision-making process. Basically, as shown in Illustration 0.1, any decision-making process involves (1) recognition of the existence of a problem, (2) determination of alternative courses of action considered solutions to the problem, (3) prediction of the possible outcome of each alternative, (4) selection of the preferred outcome as determined by refer-

Illustration 0.1
A MODEL OF THE DECISION-MAKING PROCESS

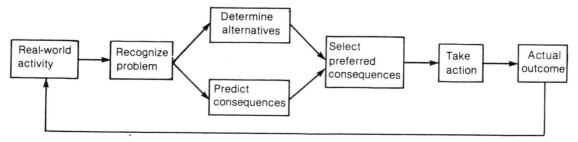

ence to the decision maker's personal preferences or previously set goals, and (5) implementation of the alternative chosen.

A problem is caused, at least in part, by events occurring in the world of human activity and scarce resources. Existence of the problem must then be recognized or there can be no decision. The nature of the problem must be understood so that alternatives, which are possible solutions to the problem, can be determined. The list of alternatives should be complete so the best solution may be found.

To determine the best solution, the consequences of each alternative must be predicted. Still, different decision makers may make different decisions even though they predict the same consequences from the same alternatives. This is so because different individuals have different preferences and every consequence may have multiple dimensions.

Implementing a decision causes new events to occur. New problems will arise that will, in turn, bring about a recycling of the whole process.

As a practical illustration, assume that a bank has received requests for loans from Company X and Company Y. The bank has a problem in that limited funds are available for loans. It is in doubt as to which loan will meet its objectives relative to risk, interest earnings, use of the money, date of repayment, ability to repay, and similar matters.

To solve the problem, the bank gathers information that helps it to *predict the outcome of granting each loan.* The predicted outcome of each loan is based on such factors as the rate of interest that can be charged, how the money will be used, and when it will be repaid. Projected results of the alternatives are compared with set objectives of the bank, and a decision is reached. This decision may be influenced by the personal preferences of the banker making the loan. The banker may conclude that as far as the bank is concerned, a loan to X does not differ significantly from a loan to Y. The banker may, however, have a strong preference for loaning money to X because X intends to acquire pollution control equipment, while Y intends to acquire new smelting equipment.

Having made the decision, the bank's position with its environment is now changed. New problems will arise requiring new information and future decisions.

In predicting the outcome of granting each of the above loans, the bank relied, in part, upon accounting information. Virtually every attempt to predict the future involves a review of the past. So in making its predictions, the bank relied upon the accounting records of the past financial activities of each company.

External Users

The bank attempting to decide whether to loan money to Company X or Company Y is considered an external user of accounting information. External users and the types of questions they want answered can be classified as follows:

1. **Owners (stockholders) and prospective owners.** Has the firm had satisfactory income from its total investment? Should an ownership interest be acquired in this firm? Should an existing ownership be increased, decreased, or retained at its present level? Can the firm install costly pollution control equipment and still remain profitable?

2. **Creditors and lenders.** Should a loan be granted to the firm? Will the firm be able to pay its debts as they become due?

3. **Employees and their unions.** Does the firm have the ability to pay increased wages? Is the firm financially able to provide permanent employment?

4. **Customers.** Will the firm survive long enough to honor its product warranties?

5. **Governmental units.** Is the firm (a public utility) earning a fair profit on its capital investment? How much in taxes does the firm pay?

6. **The general public.** Is the firm selling desired products and services at reasonable prices?

Most of the information needs of the above users are met by providing a set of general-purpose financial statements. These statements are the end product of a process known as financial accounting.

Financial accounting. Financial accounting provides statements that describe a firm's financial position, changes in this position, and results of operations (profitability). Many companies publish these statements in an **annual report.** This report contains the auditor's opinion as to the fairness of the financial statements, as well as other information about the company's activities, products, and plans.

Financial accounting information is historical in nature, being a report of what has happened. Because interfirm comparisons are often made, the information supplied must conform to certain standards or principles, called **generally accepted accounting principles (GAAP).**

Internal Users

Accounting information is also used by people within an organization to make decisions. For example, a business manager may have to decide whether to begin offering a new line of merchandise. The decision process employed within a company is the same decision process employed by users outside an organization. Internal decisions can be classified into four major types:

1. **Financing decisions**—deciding what amounts of capital are needed and whether it is to be secured from owners or creditors.
2. **Resource allocation decisions**—deciding how the total capital of a firm is to be invested, such as the amount invested in machinery.
3. **Production decisions**—deciding what products are to be produced, by what means, and when.
4. **Marketing decisions**—setting selling prices and advertising budgets; determining where a firm's markets are and how they are to be reached.

Managerial accounting provides information for such management decisions.

Managerial accounting. Managerial accounting provides special analyses and other information for internal purposes. The information ranges from the very broad (long-range planning) to the quite detailed (why costs varied from their planned levels). The information must meet two tests: it must be useful, and it must not cost more to gather than it is worth. Managerial accounting information generally relates to a part of a firm such as a plant or a department because this is where most decisions are made. It is used to measure the success of managers in, for example, controlling costs and is used to motivate these managers to help a firm achieve its goals. It is forward-looking, often involving planning for the future, while financial accounting information is generally a reflection of past occurrences.

It would be a mistake to assume that a clear-cut distinction can be drawn between financial accounting information and managerial accounting information. Managers are keenly aware of the fact that their jobs may depend upon how the figures appear in the annual report. Also, much of what is called managerial accounting information is first accumulated in an accounting system designed with financial reporting in mind.

Although accounting information is essential in the management of not-for-profit as well as profit-oriented organizations, primary attention in this text is devoted to business (that is, for-profit) organizations.

THE DEVELOPMENT OF FINANCIAL ACCOUNTING STANDARDS

As noted previously, financial statements a business issues to external parties must conform to certain standards. These generally accepted accounting principles have been developed largely by accounting practice or have been established by an authoritative body. Brief mention is made at this point of four of the prominent accounting authorities.

American Institute of Certified Public Accountants (AICPA)

The AICPA has been the dominant factor in developing accounting standards in the United States over the past half century. In a 20-year period ending in 1959, its Committee on Accounting Procedure issued 51 *Accounting Research Bulletins* recommending certain principles or practices. From 1959 through 1973, the committee's successor, the **Accounting Principles Board (APB),** issued 31 *Opinions* which CPAs generally were *required* to follow. These bulletins and opinions dealt with controversial issues. Through its monthly magazine *(Journal of Accountancy),* research division, and other divisions and committees, the AICPA continues to influence the development of accounting standards and practices.

Financial Accounting Standards Board (FASB)

The APB was replaced in 1973 with a new, independent, seven-member, full-time **Financial Accounting Standards Board (FASB).** The FASB has issued numerous *Statements of Financial Accounting Standards* and *Interpretations* of those statements. The FASB is now widely accepted as the major influence in the private sector in the development of new financial accounting standards.

U.S. Securities and Exchange Commission (SEC)

Created under the Securities and Exchange Act of 1934, the **Securities and Exchange Commission (SEC)** administers a number of important acts dealing with the interstate sale of securities. The SEC has the power to prescribe in detail accounting practices to be followed by companies required to file financial statements with it, which includes virtually every major U.S. business corporation. Nonetheless, the SEC has adopted a policy of working closely with the accounting profession, especially the FASB, in the development of accounting standards.

American Accounting Association (AAA)

Consisting largely of college professors and instructors of accounting, the **American Accounting Association (AAA)** has sought to encourage research and study at a theoretical level into the concepts, standards, and principles of accounting. The AAA publishes statements on topical matters and supports the research efforts of individuals. In recent years, its quarterly magazine, *The Accounting Review,* has provided a principal outlet for research studies on accounting topics.

This text outlines the fundamentals of financial accounting with the student in mind who will pursue accounting as a career. Even if you decide not to become an accountant, you will find your knowledge of accounting useful in whatever business career you follow.

SUMMARY

Accounting is a systematic or organized means of gathering and reporting information on economic activity. The information provided, together with other information, is used by many external and internal parties, for a wide range of decisions.

An accountant may be employed in public, private, or governmental accounting and may be a specialist in one of many fields of expertise such as auditing, budgeting, systems development, taxation, or financial reporting.

Internally, accounting information is used by various levels of management personnel. External users include actual and potential stockholders and creditors and their professional advisers, employees and their unions, customers, suppliers, governmental agencies, and the public at large.

Organizations influential in the development of accounting standards include the AICPA, FASB, SEC, and AAA.

QUESTIONS

1. Define accounting. What does the term *relevant* mean when speaking of accounting information? Give an example of relevant information.

2. What is the relationship between accounting as an information system and economic resources?

3. What is a CPA? What are some of the services usually provided by a CPA?

4. What is the role of the accountant in private industry? What are some of the services provided by the industrial accountant?

5. How does accounting information usually enter into the decision-making process?

6. Name four organizations that have played or are playing an important role in the development of accounting standards. Describe each briefly.

1 ACCOUNTING— A SOURCE OF FINANCIAL INFORMATION

FORMS OF BUSINESS ORGANIZATIONS

There are three basic forms of organization for a business enterprise. They are the **single proprietorship, partnership,** and **corporation.** Accounting serves all forms of business organizations, but this book will use the corporation in its illustrations of basic accounting concepts. The corporation is the most significant in terms of volume of business. Virtually the same accounting concepts, however, apply to all three forms of organization.

Single proprietorship. A **single proprietorship** is *an unincorporated business owned by an individual and often managed by that same individual.* Many individuals in small service-type businesses (such as physicians, lawyers, barbers, and electricians) and retail establishments (such as clothing stores, antique shops, and novelty stores) do business as single proprietorships. There are no legal formalities in organizing such a business, and usually only a limited amount of money is required to begin operations. There is no legal distinction between the business and its owner, since the owner is responsible for both personal and business debts. However, there is an accounting distinction. The financial activities of the business, such as selling services to the public, are kept separate from the personal financial activities, such as making a payment on an auto used exclusively for nonbusiness purposes. The business is considered an **entity** separate from the owner.

Partnership. A **partnership** is *a business owned by two or more persons* *associated as partners* and is often managed by those same persons. The partnership is created by an agreement setting forth the terms of the partnership. Preferably, the agreement should be in writing, but it may be oral. Included in the agreement will be such things as the initial investment of each partner, duties of each partner, means of dividing income (profits) or losses between the partners each year, and settlement to be made upon the death or withdrawal of a partner. A partnership often evolves out of one or more single proprietorships. For instance, Mr. X and Ms. Y, both CPAs, may each operate single proprietorships. Each sees the need to have another CPA to serve clients during vacations. Also, there may be a need to combine their strong points (X is a tax person, and Y is an auditor) to improve service to their clients. They may decide to combine their single proprietorships into a partnership. Partnerships, like single proprietorships, are commonly found in the service and retail fields.

Corporation. A **corporation** *is a business that may be owned by a few persons or by thousands of persons and is incorporated under the laws of one of the 50 states.* A corporation often is managed by persons other than the owners, although major owners sometimes serve as officers (managers) of the corporation. Ownership in a corporation is divided into units known as shares of stock. Thus, the owners are called stockholders or shareholders. Ownership interest is easily transferred by selling one's shares of stock to another person. Organized exchanges (such as the New York Stock Exchange) exist for this purpose. Corporations may evolve from single proprietorships or partnerships, although sometimes they are formed directly. The corporate form is more likely to appear where substantial money is needed to start the business, a wide range of talents is needed to manage the business, and the owners desire to limit their personal liability for debts. Unlike the single proprietorship and partnership forms, the corporation is a separate *legal entity* from its owners. The owners are *not* personally responsible for the debts of the corporation beyond the amount they have invested in the corporation.

FINANCIAL STATEMENTS OF BUSINESS ENTERPRISES

Although a modern business firm has many objectives or goals, the two primary objectives of every business firm are *profitability* and *solvency.* Unless a firm can produce satisfactory income (profit) and pay its debts when they are due, any other objectives a firm may have will never be realized simply because the firm will not survive. The financial statements that reflect a firm's solvency (the balance sheet), its profitability (the income statement), and its changes in retained earnings (the statement of retained earnings) are illustrated and discussed below. A fourth financial statement, the statement of changes in financial position, is discussed in Chapter 10.

The Balance Sheet

The **balance sheet** (often called the **statement of financial position**) shows the assets, liabilities, and stockholders' equity of a business firm at a specific moment in time. The balance sheet is like a still photograph; it only captures reality for a particular point in time.

Assets are things of value; they constitute the resources of the firm. They have value to the firm because of the uses to which they can be put or the things that can be acquired by exchanging them. In Illustration 1.1, the assets of the Ross Company, which performs delivery services, amount to $38,700. The assets consist of cash, **accounts receivable** (amounts due from customers for services previously rendered), delivery equipment, and office equipment.

Illustration 1.1

ROSS COMPANY
Balance Sheet
July 31, 1986

Assets		Liabilities and Stockholders' Equity	
Cash	$15,500	Liabilities:	
Accounts receivable	700	Accounts payable	$ 600
Delivery equipment	20,000	Notes payable	6,000
Office equipment	2,500	Total liabilities	$ 6,600
		Stockholders' equity:	
		Capital stock	$30,000
		Retained earnings	2,100
		Total stockholders' equity	$32,100
		Total liabilities and stock-	
Total assets	$38,700	holders' equity	$38,700

Liabilities are the debts owed by a firm. Typically, they must be paid at certain known moments in time. Ross Company's liabilities consist of **accounts payable** (amounts owed to suppliers for previous purchases) and **notes payable** (written promises to pay a specific sum of money) totaling $6,600.

The Ross Company is a corporation. It is customary to refer to the owners' interest in a corporation as **stockholders' equity.** Ross Company's stockholders' equity consists of $30,000 paid for shares of capital stock and retained earnings of $2,100. **Capital stock** shows the amount of investment in a corporation by its owners. **Retained earnings** generally consists of the accumulated income of the corporation minus dividends distributed to stockholders. All of these items will be discussed in detail later in the text. At this point, simply note that the balance sheet heading includes the name of the organization and the title and date of the statement. Also note that the dollar amount of the total assets is equal to the claims on (or interest in) those assets.

The Income Statement

The purpose of the **income statement** (often called the **earnings statement**) is to report the profits of a business organization for a stated period of time. In accounting, profits are measured by comparing revenues generated in a given period with expenses incurred to produce those revenues. **Revenues** are the inflows of assets from the sale of products or the rendering of services to customers. **Expenses** are the sacrifices made or the costs incurred to produce revenues. Expenses are measured by the assets surrendered or consumed in serving customers. If revenues exceed expenses, **net income** results. If the reverse is true, the business is said to be operating at a **net loss.** Illustration 1.2 contains the income statement of the Ross Company for the month of July 1986.

Illustration 1.2

ROSS COMPANY		
Income Statement		
For the Month Ended July 31, 1986		
Service revenues . . .		$5,700
Expenses:		
Wages	$2,600	
Rent	400	
Gas and oil	600	
Total expenses . .		3,600
Net income		$2,100

The income statement shows that revenues (or delivery fees) of $5,700 were generated by serving customers during the month. Expenses for the month totaled $3,600, resulting in net income for July of $2,100. The major difference in the heading of the income statement from that of the balance sheet is that it expresses a period of time covered rather than a specific date or point in time.

The Statement of Retained Earnings

The purpose of the **statement of retained earnings** is to explain the changes in retained earnings that occurred between two balance sheet dates. Usually, these changes consist of the addition of net income (or deduction of net loss) and the deduction of dividends. Dividends are the means by which a corporation rewards its stockholders for providing it with investment funds. A **dividend** is a payment (usually of cash) to the owners of the business. It is a distribution of income to the owners rather than an expense of doing business. Since it is not an expense, it does not appear on the income statement.

The effect of a dividend is to reduce cash and retained earnings by the amount paid out. In effect, the income (earnings) is no longer "retained" but has been passed on to the stockholders (owners). And, of course, earning a return in the form of dividends is one of the primary reasons why people organize corporations.

The statement of retained earnings for the Ross Company for the month of July 1986 is quite simple (see Illustration 1.3). Since the company was organized on June 1 and did not earn any revenues or incur any expenses during June, the beginning retained earnings balance on July 1 is zero. Net income for July of $2,100 would be added. Since no dividends were paid, the $2,100 would be the ending balance.

Illustration 1.3

ROSS COMPANY
Statement of Retained Earnings
For the Month Ended July 31, 1986

Retained earnings, July 1	–0–
Add: Net income for July . . .	$2,100
Retained earnings, July 31 . . .	$2,100

To provide a more effective illustration, assume that the Ross Company's net income for August was $1,500 (revenues of $5,600 less expenses of $4,100) and that the company declared and paid dividends of $1,000. Its statement of retained earnings for August would be as shown in Illustration 1.4.

Illustration 1.4

ROSS COMPANY
Statement of Retained Earnings
For the Month Ended August 31, 1986

Retained earnings, July 31	$2,100
Add: Net income for August	1,500
Total	$3,600
Less: Dividends	1,000
Retained earnings, August 31 . . .	$2,600

THE FINANCIAL ACCOUNTING PROCESS

We have introduced three principal financial statements: the balance sheet, income statement, and statement of retained earnings. Attention is now directed to the process of accumulating the data to include in the financial statements.

The Accounting Equation

In the balance sheet presented in Illustration 1.1, total assets of the Ross Company were equal to total liabilities plus stockholders' equity. Another way of stating this relationship is that the assets of a business are equal to the equities in those assets; that is, **Assets = Equities.** Assets have already been defined simply as things of value. They are further defined as those economic resources which are owned by a business and which can be measured. All desired things, except those available in unlimited quantity without cost or effort, are economic resources.

Equities are interests in, or claims upon, assets. For example, assume that you purchased a new automobile for $10,000 by withdrawing $1,000 from your savings account and borrowing $9,000 from your credit union. Your equity in the automobile is $1,000 and that of your credit union is $9,000. The $9,000 can be further described as a **liability.** Your $1,000 equity could be described as the **owner's equity** or interest in the asset. Since, in the case of a corporation, the owners are stockholders, the basic **accounting equation** becomes:

$$\text{Assets} = \text{Liabilities} + \text{Stockholders' equity}$$

Resources, or assets, must always be provided by someone—either a creditor or an owner (stockholder); therefore, this equation must always be in balance.

The right side of the above equation is also looked upon in another manner—namely, it shows the sources of the existing group of assets. Thus, liabilities are not only claims against assets; they are also sources of assets. In a corporation, all assets are provided by either creditors (liability holders) or owners (stockholders).

As a business engages in economic activity, the dollar amounts and composition of its assets, liabilities, and stockholders' equity change. But the equality of the basic equation always holds true.

Accounting Assumptions

Some underlying assumptions or concepts are used by the accountant in recording business transactions. A **transaction** is an event that affects the assets, liabilities, stockholders' equity, revenues, and/or expenses of an entity. Most transactions are the result of exchanges between entities. Our society is characterized by exchange. That is, the bulk of goods and services are exchanged rather than consumed by their producers. Exchange transactions provide much of the raw data entered into the accounting system. There are several reasons why this is true. First, an exchange is an observable event providing evidence of activity. Second, an exchange takes place at an agreed-upon price, and this price provides an objective measure of the economic activity that has occurred.

Before transactions can be recorded, however, certain basic accounting assumptions must be made. For instance, the data gathered in an accounting system are assumed to relate to a specific business firm or entity. This **entity** is deemed to have an existence separate and apart from its owners, creditors, employees, and other interested parties. Also, every transaction has a two-sided, or dual, effect upon each of the parties engaging in it; this is referred to as **duality.** Consequently, if information is to be complete, both sides or effects of every transaction must be included in the accounting system. Economic activity is initially recorded and reported in terms of a common unit of measure—the dollar. This is referred to as **money measurement.** Since most of the numbers entered in an accounting system are the bargained prices of exchange transactions, the result is that most assets (excluding cash and receivables) are recorded and reported at their acquisition costs. (**Cost** refers to the amount of cash or resources given up to acquire some desired thing.)

Unless strong evidence exists to the contrary, the accountant assumes that the entity will *continue* operations into the indefinite future. This is referred to as the **continuity (going-concern)** assumption. Consequently, assets that will be used up or consumed in future operations need not be reported at their current **liquidation values** (the amount that could be received from their sale). The underlying assumptions or basic concepts of accounting will be discussed further in Chapter 12.

Transaction Analysis

Since each transaction that affects a business entity needs to be recorded in the accounting records, the analysis of transactions is an important part of financial accounting. To illustrate the analysis of transactions and their effects upon the basic accounting equation, the activities of the Ross Company that led to the statements in Illustrations 1.1, 1.2, and 1.3 are presented below. The numbers 1a, 2a, and so on refer to the summary of transactions found in Illustration 1.5.

1a. Investment of owners' capital. Assume that Ross Company was organized as a corporation on June 1, 1986. In its first transaction it issued shares of **capital stock** to John Ross for $30,000 cash. The transaction increased the assets (cash) of the Ross Company by $30,000 and increased its equities (the capital stock element of stockholders' equity) by $30,000. Consequently, the transaction yields a basic accounting equation containing the following:

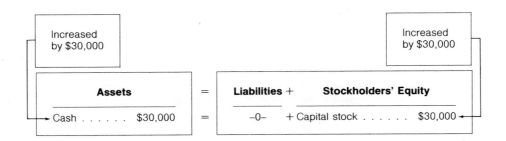

2a. Borrowing of money. As its second transaction, the company borrowed $6,000 from Mrs. Ross' father, giving its written promise to repay (called a *note payable*) the amount within one year. The basic equation after the effects of this transaction is:

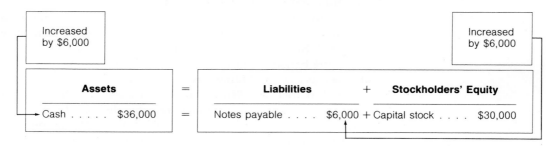

3a. Purchase of assets for cash. As its third transaction, the Ross Company spent $20,000 for three delivery trucks and $1,500 for some office equipment. In this transaction, the Ross Company received delivery equipment priced at $20,000 and office equipment priced at $1,500. It gave up cash of $21,500. This transaction does not change the totals in the basic equation; it merely changes the composition of the assets. The equation is now as follows:

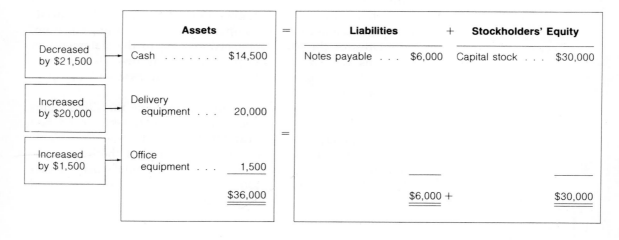

4a. Purchase of an asset and incurring a liability. In its fourth transaction in June, the Ross Company purchased an additional $1,000 of office equipment, agreeing to pay for it within 10 days after it receives a bill from the supplier. This transaction increases liabilities in the form of *accounts payable* by $1,000. (If merely an order for the equipment had been placed, no transaction would be recorded since the exchange had not yet been completed.) The items making up the totals in the accounting equation now appear as follows:

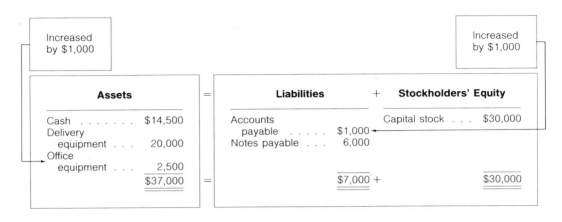

5a. Payment of an account payable.   Next, the company paid the $1,000 balance due on the purchase of the office equipment. This transaction reduced cash by $1,000 and reduced the debt owed to the equipment supplier by $1,000. Thus, assets and liabilities are both decreased by $1,000. After this transaction, the totals in the accounting equation are as follows:

Decreased by $1,000				Decreased by $1,000
Assets	=	**Liabilities**	+	**Stockholders' Equity**
Cash $13,500		Accounts payable . . . . $ –0–		Capital stock . . . $30,000
Delivery equipment . . . 20,000		Notes payable . . 6,000		
Office equipment . . . 2,500				
$36,000	=	$6,000 +		$30,000

A summary of transactions prepared for the month of June appears in Illustration 1.5 in accounting equation form. You can see how the totals at the bottom tie into the balance sheet shown in Illustration 1.6. The balance sheet in Illustration 1.6 is dated June 30, 1986. These totals become the beginning totals for the month of July 1986.

Illustration 1,5
SUMMARY OF TRANSACTIONS

ROSS COMPANY
Summary of Transactions
Month of June 1986

Trans-action	Explanation	Cash	Accounts Receiv-able	Delivery Equip-ment	Office Equip-ment		Accounts Payable	Notes Payable	Capital Stock
			Assets			*=*	*Liabilities*	*+*	*Stockholders' Equity*
	Beginning balances	$ –0–	$–0–	$ –0–	$ –0–	=	$ –0–	$ –0–	$ –0–
1a	Owner invested cash	+30,000							+30,000
		$30,000				=			$30,000
2a	Borrowed money	+ 6,000						+6,000	
		$36,000				=		$6,000 +	$30,000
3a	Purchased equip-ment for cash	–21,500		+20,000	+1,500				
		$14,500		$20,000	$1,500	=		$6,000 +	$30,000
4a	Purchased equip-ment on account				+1,000		+1,000		
		$14,500		$20,000	$2,500	=	$1,000	$6,000 +	$30,000
5a	Paid an account payable	–1,000					–1,000		
	End-of-month balances	$13,500		$20,000	$2,500	=	$ –0–	$6,000 +	$30,000

Illustration 1.6
BALANCE SHEET

ROSS COMPANY
Balance Sheet
June 30, 1986

Assets		Liabilities and Stockholders' Equity	
Cash	$13,500	Liabilities:	
Delivery equipment	20,000	Notes payable	$6,000
Office equipment	2,500	Total liabilities	$ 6,000
		Stockholders' equity:	
		Capital stock	30,000
Total assets	$36,000	Total liabilities and stockholders' equity	$36,000

Revenue and Expense Transactions

Thus far all transactions have consisted of exchanges or acquisitions or assets either by borrowing or by owner investment. This procedure was used so that you could focus on the accounting equation as it relates to the balance sheet. But a business is not formed merely to hold present assets. Rather, *a business seeks to use its assets to generate greater amounts of assets.* A business increases its assets by providing goods or services to customers. The expectation is that the value of the assets received from customers will exceed the cost of the assets consumed in serving them. The assets received are usually in the form of cash or accounts receivable.

Assume that the company engaged in the following transactions in July 1986.

1b. Earning of revenue for cash. Delivery services are performed for Ross' customer for $4,800 cash. The cash balance increases by $4,800, and the stockholders' equity increases by $4,800 because revenues increase stockholders' equity.

Including the effects of the revenue transaction upon the financial status of the Ross Company yields the following basic equation:

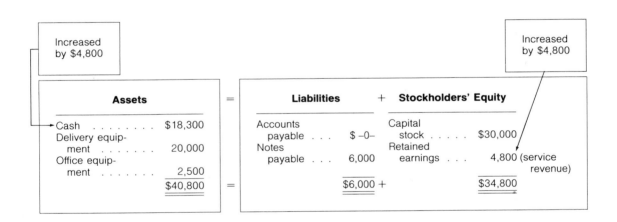

Note that the increase in stockholders' equity brought about by the revenue transaction is recorded as a separate item, "Retained earnings." It cannot be recorded as capital stock. No additional shares of stock were issued. The expectation is that revenue transactions will yield net income. If net income is not distributed to stockholders, it is in fact retained. Later chapters will show that because of complexities in handling large numbers of transactions, revenues will be shown as affecting retained earnings only at the end of an accounting period. The procedure presented above is a shortcut used to explain why the accounting equation remains in balance.

2b. Earning of revenue on account. As its second transaction in July, the Ross Company performs services for a customer who agrees to pay $900 at a later date. The transaction consists of an exchange of services for a promise by the customer to pay later. It is similar to the preceding transaction in that stockholders' equity is increased because revenues have been earned. It differs because cash has not been received. A different asset, or item of value has been received. This is the claim upon the customer—the right to collect from him or her at a later date. Technically, such claims are called **accounts receivable.** The important point is that accounting recognizes such claims as assets and records them. (If merely an *order* for service had been received, but the service had not yet been performed, no transaction would be recorded since the revenue would not have been earned.) The accounting equation, including this item, is as follows:

3b. Collection of an account receivable. Assume that $200 is collected from a customer who purchased services "on account." The transaction consists of the giving up of a claim upon the customer in exchange for cash. The effects of the transaction are to increase cash by $200 to $18,500 and to decrease accounts receivable by $200 to $700. Note that this transaction consists solely of a change in the composition of the assets, not of an increase in assets resulting from the generation of revenue.

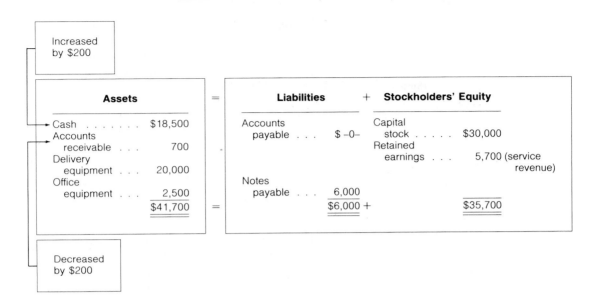

4b. Payment of wages. The payment of wages of $2,600 consists of an exchange of cash for employee services. Typically, the employee services will have already been received by the time payment is made (at week's end or month's end). Thus, the accountant treats the transaction as a decrease in an asset (cash) and a decrease in stockholders' equity because an expense has been incurred.

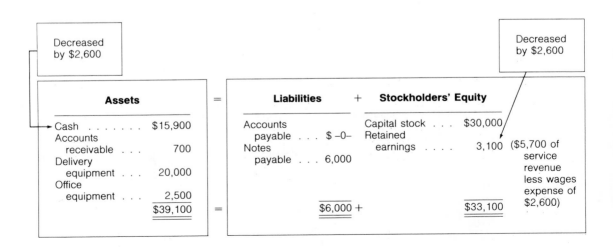

5b. *Payment of rent.* The Ross Company paid cash of $400 as rent for office space in July. This transaction causes a decrease in the asset, cash, of $400 and a similar decrease in stockholders' equity. Including all of the above items in our accounting equation, it now reads:

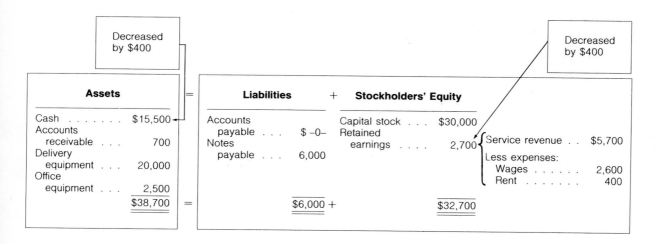

6b. *Incurring gas and oil expense.* The company received a bill for gasoline and oil used during the month in the amount of $600. This transaction involves an increase in a liability, accounts payable, and a decrease in stockholders' equity because of the incurrence of an expense. The accounting equation of the Ross Company now reads:

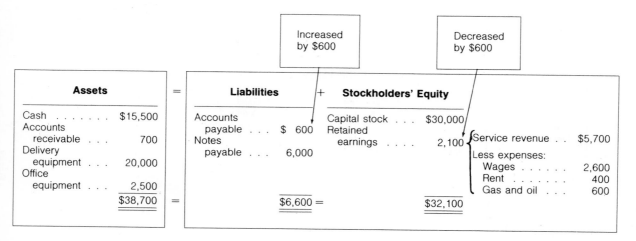

Illustration 1.7
SUMMARY OF TRANSACTIONS

ROSS COMPANY
Summary of Transactions
Month of July 1986

Trans-action	Explanation	Cash	Accounts Receivable	Delivery Equipment	Office Equipment	=	Accounts Payable	Notes Payable	+	Capital Stock	Retained Earnings	
	Beginning balances (Illustration 1.5)	$13,500	$-0-	$20,000	$2,500	=	$-0-	$6,000	+	$30,000	$-0-	
1b.	Earned service revenue and received cash	+4,800									+4,800	(service revenue)
		$18,300		$20,000	$2,500	=		$6,000	+	$30,000	$4,800	
2b.	Earned service revenue on account		+900								+ 900	(service revenue)
		$18,300	$900	$20,000	$2,500	=		$6,000	+	$30,000	$5,700	
3b.	Collected cash on account	+200	−200									
		$18,500	$700	$20,000	$2,500	=		$6,000	+	$30,000	$5,700	
4b.	Paid wages	−2,600									−2,600	(wages expense)
		$15,900	$700	$20,000	$2,500	=		$6,000	+	$30,000	$3,100	
5b.	Paid rent	−400									−400	(rent expense)
		$15,500	$700	$20,000	$2,500	=		$6,000	+	$30,000	$2,700	(gas and oil expense)
6b.	Received bill for gas and oil used						+600				−600	
	End-of-month balances	$15,500	$700	$20,000	$2,500	=	$600	$6,000	+	$30,000	$2,100	

$38,700 $6,600 $32,100

Illustration 1.8
BALANCE SHEET

ROSS COMPANY
Balance Sheet
July 31, 1986

Assets

Cash	$15,500
Accounts receivable	700
Delivery equipment	20,000
Office equipment	2,500
Total assets	**$38,700**

Liabilities and Stockholders' Equity

Liabilities:
Accounts	$ 600
Notes payable	6,000
Total liabilities	$ 6,600

Stockholders' equity:
Capital stock	$30,000
Retained earnings	2,100
Total stockholders' equity	$32,100

Total liabilities and stockholders' equity	$38,700

Illustration 1.9
INCOME STATEMENT

ROSS COMPANY
Income Statement
For the Month Ended
July 31, 1986

Service revenue		$5,700
Expenses:		
Wages	$2,600	
Rent	400	
Gas and oil	600	
Total expenses		3,600
Net income		$2,100

Summary of Transactions

The effects of all of the preceding transactions on the assets, liabilities, and stockholders' equity of the Ross Company in the month of July are summarized in Illustration 1.7. This summary shows how the basic equation of Assets = Equities is subdivided into three major elements of financial accounting: **assets, liabilities,** and **stockholders' equity.** The ending balances in each of the columns in Illustration 1.7 are the dollar amounts in Illustration 1.8 and those reported earlier in the balance sheet in Illustration 1.1. The itemized data in the Retained earnings column are the revenue and expense items in Illustration 1.9 and those reported earlier in the income statement in Illustration 1.2. The beginning balance in the Retained earnings column ($0) plus net income for the month ($2,100) is equal to the ending balance in retained earnings ($2,100) as shown earlier in Illustsration 1.3.

DIVIDENDS PAID TO OWNERS

We have seen that stockholders' equity is increased by capital contributed by the stockholders and by revenues earned through operations. We also saw that stockholders' equity is decreased by expenses incurred in producing revenues. Withdrawals of cash or other assets in the form of dividends also reduce stockholders' equity. Thus, if the owners receive a dividend in the form of cash, the effect would be to reduce cash and stockholders' equity by that amount. It would reduce the retained earnings part of stockholders' equity. This amount is not an expense but is instead a distribution of income.

SUMMARY

The three basic forms of business organization are the single proprietorship, partnership, and corporation. This book uses the corporation in its illustrations of accounting concepts.

The end products of the financial accounting process are the balance sheet, income statement, statement of retained earnings, and statement of changes in financial position. Discussion of the statement of changes in financial position is deferred until Chapter 10.

Most of the information reported in these statements is found originally in the transactions entered into by an entity. These transactions are analyzed and their effects recorded as increases or decreases in assets, liabilities, stockholders' equity, revenues, and expenses—the five basic elements of accounting. The framework for analysis is the basic equation of Assets = Equities, expanded to Assets = Liabilities + Stockholders' equity. Revenues and expenses will create income (or loss) which affects the Retained Earnings account and, therefore, stockholders' equity.

QUESTIONS

1. Accounting has often been called the language of business. In what respects would you agree with this designation? How might it be argued that it is deficient?

2. Define asset, liability, and stockholders' equity.

3. How do liabilities and stockholders' equity differ? In what respects are they similiar?

4. How do accounts payable and notes payable differ? How are they similar?

5. Define revenue. How is revenue measured?

6. Define expense. How is expense measured?

7. What is a balance sheet? This statement generally seeks to provide information relative to what aspect of a business?

8. What is an income statement? This statement generally provides information on what aspect of a business?

9. What information does the statement of retained earnings provide?

10. What is a transaction? What use does the accountant make of transactions? Why?

11. What is the accounting equation? Why must it always balance?

12. Give an example from your personal life that you believe illustrates your use of accounting information in reaching a decision.

EXERCISES

1. Give examples of transactions that would have the following effects upon the elements in a firm's accounting system:
   a. Increase cash; decrease some other asset.
   b. Decrease cash; increase some other asset.
   c. Increase an asset; increase a liability.
   d. Increase an expense; decrease an asset.
   e. Increase an asset other than cash; increase revenue.
   f. Decrease an asset; decrease a liability.

2. Assume that retained earnings increased by $12,000 from June 30, 1985, to June 30, 1986. A cash dividend of $1,000 was declared and paid during the year.
   a. Compute the net income for the year.
   b. Assume that expenses for the year were $30,000. Compute the revenue for the year.

3. On December 31, 1985, Star Company had assets of $360,000, liabilities of $260,000, and capital stock of $80,000. During 1986, it earned revenues of $120,000 and incurred expenses of $90,000. Dividends declared and paid amounted to $8,000.
   a. Compute the company's retained earnings on December 31, 1985.
   b. Compute the company's retained earnings on December 31, 1986.

4. For each of the happenings below, determine if it has an effect upon the basic elements of accounting. For those that do, present an analysis of the transaction showing clearly its two sides or dual nature.

  a. Purchased equipment for cash, $600.

  b. Purchased a truck for $7,000, payment to be made later in the month.

  c. Paid $200 cash for the current month's utilities.

  d. Paid for the truck purchased in *(b)*.

  e. Employed Jack Lovgren as a salesperson at $1,500 per month. He is to start work next week.

  f. Signed an agreement with a bank in which the bank agreed to lend the company up to $125,000 any time within the next two years.

5. Which of the following transactions results in an increase in an expense? Why?

  a. Cash of $40,000 was paid to employees for services received during the month.

  b. Cash of $200,000 was paid to acquire land.

  c. Paid a $20,000 note payable. No interest was involved.

6. At the start of a year, a company had liabilities of $18,000 and capital stock of $50,000. At the end of the year, retained earnings amounted to $45,000. Net income for the year was $15,000, and $5,000 of dividends were declared and paid. Compute retained earnings and total assets at the beginning of the year.

7. Selected data for the Denver Company for the year 1986 are as follows (including all income statement data):

Revenue from services rendered on account.	$ 55,000
Revenue from services rendered for cash	15,000
Cash collected from customers on account	42,000
Stockholders' equity, January 1, 1985	80,000
Expenses incurred on account	30,000
Expenses incurred for cash	20,000
Dividends declared and paid	5,000
Capital stock issued for cash	10,000
Stockholders' equity, December 31, 1986.	105,000

Compute net income for 1986.

8. Indicate the immediate amount of change (if any) in the stockholders' equity balance based on each of the following transactions:

  a. The owner invested $30,000 cash in the business by purchasing capital stock.

  b. Land costing $5,000 was purchased by paying cash.

  c. The company performed services for a customer who agreed to pay $8,000 in one month.

  d. Paid wages for the month, $7,200.

  e. Paid $1,500 on an account payable.

9. Martin Company, engaged in a service business, completed the following selected transactions during the month of July 1986.

  a. Purchased office equipment on account.

  b. Paid an account payable.

c. Earned service revenue on account.

d. Borrowed money by signing a note at the bank.

e. Paid wages for month to employees.

f. Received cash on account from a charge customer.

g. Received gas and oil bill for month.

h. Purchased a truck for cash.

i. Paid a cash dividend.

Using a tabular form similar to that used in Illustration 1.7, indicate the effect of each transaction on the equation using (+) for increase and (−) for decrease. No dollar amounts are needed, and you need not fill in the Explanation column.

10. The column totals of a summary of transactions for the Stillwagon Company as of December 31, 1986, were as follows (listed in alphabetical order):

Accounts payable	$15,000
Accounts receivable . . .	30,000
Capital stock	50,000
Cash	20,000
Land	80,000
Notes payable	10,000
Retained earnings	?

Prepare a balance sheet.

11. Assume that the following items made up the total of the $80,000 ending balance in the Retained earnings column in the summary of transactions for the Trask Company for the month of July 1986:

Wages expense	$20,000
Service revenue	40,000
Gas and oil expense . . .	4,500
Rent expense	8,000
Dividends paid	5,000

Prepare an income statement for the month of July 1986.

12. Given the following facts, prepare a statement of retained earnings for the Kent Company for the month of August 1986:

Balance in retained earnings at end of July, $40,000
Dividends paid in August, $15,000
Net income for August, $25,000

PROBLEMS

1–1. Hunt Company completed the following transactions in September 1986:

Transactions:

Sept. 1 The company was organized and received $20,000 cash from the issuance of capital stock.

　 5 The company bought equipment for cash at a cost of $5,400.

　 7 The company performed services for a customer who agreed to pay $2,000 in one week.

　 14 The company received the $2,000 from the transaction of September 7.

Sept. 20 Equipment which costs $800 was acquired today; payment was postponed until September 28.
  28 $600 was paid on the liability incurred on September 20.
  30 Employee services for the month, $700, were paid.
  30 Placed an order for new equipment advertised at $5,000.

Required:

Prepare a summary of transactions (see Illustration 1.7) for the company for the above transactions. Use money columns headed— Cash, Accounts Receivable, Equipment, Accounts Payable, Capital stock, and Retained earnings. Determine balances after each transaction to show that the basic equation balances.

1–2. The Springfield Company completed the following transactions in June 1986:

Transactions:

June 1 The company was organized and received $40,000 cash from the issuance of capital stock.
  4 The company paid $32,000 cash for equipment.
  7 The company borrowed $6,000 cash from one of its suppliers by giving two notes, one for $2,700 and the other for $3,300. Neither note bears interest.
  9 Cash received for services performed for a customer, $3,000.
  12 Employee wages were paid in cash, $2,100.
  18 Services performed for a customer who agreed to pay within a month amounted to $3,600.
  25 The company paid the $2,700 note of June 7th.
  30 Employee wages of $2,550 were paid in cash.
  30 An order was received from a customer for services to be performed tomorrow, which will be billed at $2,000.

Required:

a. Prepare a summary of transactions (see Illustration 1.7). Include money columns for—Cash, Accounts receivable, Equipment, Notes payable, Capital stock, and Retained earnings.
b. Prepare a balance sheet as of June 30, 1986.

1–3. The following transactions are for the Daniels Company:

Transactions:

May 1 Paid May rent on the parking structure, $10,000.
  8 Received cash from James Company for parking services provided for its employees, $4,840.
  15 Received cash from James Company for week's parking services, $6,040.
  15 Wages paid for first half of May, $2,400.
  17 Received cash for shares of capital stock issued, $5,000.
  19 Paid advertising expenses for May, $800.
  22 Received cash from James Company for week's parking services, $7,920.
  31 Wages paid for last half of May, $3,000.
  31 Cash received from James Company for nine days' parking services, $7,040.
  31 Purchased motorized sweeper to clean parking structure, $6,000 cash.

Required:

Prepare an income statement for the month of May 1986.

1–4. Following are summarized transaction data for the Ewing Company for the year ending June 30, 1986:

Rent revenue from building owned	$320,000
Building repairs	10,000
Building cleaning, labor cost	11,200
Property taxes on the building	7,620
Insurance on the building	4,800
Commissions paid to rental agent	12,000
Legal fees (for preparation of tenant leases) . .	4,600
Heating	10,500
Electricity	17,100
Cost of new awnings installed	12,400

Of the $320,000 of rent revenue above, $20,000 was not collected in cash until July 5, 1986.

Required:

Prepare an income statement for the year ended June 30, 1986.

1–5. The following data are for the Davis Corporation:

DAVIS CORPORATION
Balance Sheet
October 1, 1986

Assets

Cash	$34,000
Accounts receivable	3,000
Total assets	$37,000

Liabilities and Stockholders' Equity

Accounts payable	$ 9,000
Capital stock	22,000
Retained earnings	6,000
Total Liabilities and Stockholders' Equity . . .	$37,000

Transactions:

Oct. 1 The account payable owed as of October 1 ($9,000) was paid.
 1 The company paid rent for the premises for October, $3,200.
 7 The company received cash of $700 from Thomas Company for parking by its employees during the week.
 10 The company collected an account receivable of $2,400.
 14 Cash received from Thomas Company for parking by its employees was $1,100.
 15 Parking revenue earned but not yet collected from a fleet customer was $500.
 16 The company paid wages of $400 for the period October 1–15.
 19 The company paid advertising expenses of $200 for October.
 21 Cash received from Thomas Company for parking service was $1,200.
 24 The company incurred miscellaneous expenses of $140, which will be due November 10.
 31 Cash received from Thomas Company for parking services $1,400.
 31 The company paid wages of $500 for the period October 16–31.
 31 A bill was sent to a large customer for parking services for October, $3,600.
 31 Paid cash dividends of $4,000.

Required:

a. Prepare a summary of transactions (see Illustration 1.7) using column headings as given in the above balance sheet.

b. Prepare an income statement for October 1986.

c. Prepare a statement of retained earnings for October 1986.

d. Prepare a balance sheet as of October 31, 1986.

1–6. Given below are balance sheets for May and June and the income statement for June of the Harris Company:

HARRIS COMPANY
Balance Sheets

	May 31, 1986	June 30, 1986
Assets		
Cash	$20,000	$14,000
Accounts receivable	–0–	8,000
Land	12,000	12,000
Total assets	$32,000	$34,000
Liabilities and Stockholders' Equity		
Liabilities	$ 8,000	$ 4,000
Capital stock	20,000	20,000
Retained earnings	4,000	10,000
Total liabilities and stockholders' equity	$32,000	$34,000

HARRIS COMPANY
Income Statement
For the Month Ended June 30, 1986

Revenue from services rendered		$32,000
Expenses:		
Salaries	$16,000	
Supplies bought and used	8,000	24,000
Net income		$ 8,000

A cash dividend of $2,000 was declared and paid in June.

Required:

State the probable causes of the changes in each of the balance sheet accounts from May 31 to June 30, 1986.

1–7. Upon graduation from high school, Wayne Burke went to work for a builder of houses and small apartment buildings. During the next six years, Wayne earned a reputation as an excellent employee—hard working, dedicated, and dependable—and as a very capable all-around employee in the light construction industry. He could handle almost any job requiring carpentry, electrical, or plumbing skills.

Wayne then decided to go into business for himself under the name of Burke's Repair Shop, Inc. He invested cash, some power tools, and a used truck in his business. He completed many repair and remodeling jobs for both homeowners and apartment owners. The demand for his services was so large that he had more work than he could handle. He operated out of his garage which he had converted into a shop, adding several new pieces of power woodworking equipment.

Two years after going into business for himself, Wayne is faced with a decision of whether to continue in his own business or to accept a position as construction supervisor for a home builder. He has been offered an annual salary of $35,000 and a package of "fringe benefits" (medical and hospitalization insurance, pension contribution, vacation and sick pay, and life insurance) worth approximately $5,000 per year. The offer is very attractive to Wayne. But he dislikes giving up his business since he has thoroughly enjoyed "being his own boss," even though it has led to an average workweek well in excess of the standard 40 hours.

Wayne now comes to you for assistance in gathering the information needed to help him make a decision. Adequate accounting records have been maintained for his business by an experienced accountant.

Required:

Indicate the nature of the information Wayne needs if he is to make an informed decision. Pay particular attention to the information likely to be found in the accounting records for his business that would be useful. Does the accounting information available enter directly into the decision? Explain. Would you expect that Wayne could sell his business assets for more or less than their recorded amounts? Why?

2

THE BASIC ACCOUNTING SYSTEM

THE ACCOUNT

In Chapter 1, the effects of transactions were shown as increases or decreases in the elements of the basic accounting equation. This approach was adopted solely as a means of affording easy understanding of some basic relationships. It is far too cumbersome to be used in actual practice since even a small business enters into a huge number of transactions every week, month, or year.

A business may engage in thousands of transactions. To guide future actions, data in these transactions must be classified and summarized. The task is great. Still, the accountant's task is made somewhat easier by the fact that most business transactions are repetitive in nature. They can be classified into groups having common characteristics. For example, there may be thousands of receipts or payments of cash. As a result, a part of every transaction affecting cash may be recorded and summarized in one account. An *account* is a storage unit used to classify and summarize money measurements of business activity of a similar nature. An account will be established whenever the data to be recorded in it are believed to be useful to some party having a valid interest in the business. Thus, every business will have a Cash account in its accounting system simply because knowledge of the amount of cash owned is useful information. An account title should indicate, as concisely as possible, the item of information being accumulated within it.

An account may take on a variety of forms, from a printed

format in which entries are written by hand to an invisible encoding on a piece of magnetic computer tape. Every account format must provide for increases and decreases and computation of a balance.

The number of accounts in a given accounting system will depend upon the information needs of those interested in the business. The primary requirement is that each account provide useful information. Thus, one account may be established for cash rather than separate accounts for cash in the form of coins, cash in the form of currency, and cash in the form of deposits in banks, simply because the amount of cash may be useful information while the form of cash usually is not important.

The T-Account

The way an account functions may be shown by use of a T-account. It is used in texts for illustrative purposes only (it is not a replica of a form of account actually used in business). A *T-account* resembles the letter T. The name of the item accounted for (such as cash) is written across the top of the T. Increases are recorded on one side and decreases on the other side of the vertical line of the T.

Recording changes in assets and equities. Increases in *assets* are recorded on the left side of the account, decreases on the right side. The process is reversed for *equities* so that increases are recorded on the right side and decreases on the left side. Thus, a corporation would record the receipt of $10,000 for shares of its capital stock as follows (the figure in parentheses refers to the number of the transaction and ties the two sides of the transaction together):

Cash		Capital Stock	
(1)　　10,000			(1)　　10,000

The transaction involves an increase in the asset, cash, which is recorded on the left side of the Cash account, and an increase in stockholders' equity in the form of capital stock, which is recorded on the right side of the Capital Stock account.

Because liabilities are a subset of equities, changes in them are recorded in the same manner as for equities—increases on the right side, decreases on the left side.

To help remember which side of a T-account increases in assets and equities are shown on, simply remember the accounting equation given in the last chapter, Assets = Equities. Increases in the T-accounts are shown for each element on the same side that the element appears in the accounting equation. Assets appear on the left side of the equation, and increases in assets appear on the left side of the T-account. The opposite is true for equity items.

Recording changes in expenses and revenues. To understand the logic behind the recording of changes in expense and revenue accounts, recall that all expenses and revenues could be recorded directly in the Retained Earnings account, as was shown in Chapter 1. Since Retained Earnings is an equity account, increases are shown on the right side of the T-account and decreases are shown on the left side. Expenses and revenues are significant amounts to a business organization, so rather than place all of these changes within the Retained Earnings account, separate accounts are maintained for each expense and revenue item. The recording rules for expenses and revenues are as follows:

1. Since expenses decrease stockholers' equity (and decreases in stockholders' equity are recorded on the left side of a T-account), it follows that increases in expenses should be recorded on the left side of a T-account. Therefore, increases in expenses are recorded on the left, decreases in expenses on the right.
2. Similarly, since revenues increase stockholders' equity (and increases in stockholders' equity are recorded on the right side), it follows that increases in revenues should be recorded on the right side, decreases on the left side.

Thus, the payment of $600 of cash to employees as wages (transaction 2) would be recorded as follows:

Cash			Wages Expense		
	(2)	600	(2)	600	

A collection of $1,000 of cash from customers for services rendered (transaction 3) would be recorded in the following manner:

Cash			Service Revenue		
(3)	1,000			(3)	1,000

Recording changes in dividends. Since dividends decrease stockholders' equity, the Dividends account is treated similarly to expense accounts: Increases are shown on the left side and decreases on the right side. Thus, the payment of a $2,000 cash dividend (transaction 4) would be recorded as follows:

Cash			Dividends		
	(4)	2,000	(4)	2,000	

At the end of the accounting period, the balances in the expense, revenue, and Dividends accounts are transferred to the Retained Earnings account. This transfer occurs only after the information in these accounts has been used to prepare the income statement. This step is discussed and illustrated in the next chapter.

Debits and credits. The accountant uses the term ***debit*** in lieu of saying "place an entry on the left side of the account" and *credit* for "place an entry on the right side of an account." Debit (abbreviated Dr.) means simply left side; credit (abbreviated Cr.), right side. A *debit entry* is an entry on the left side of an account, while a *credit entry* is an entry on the right side of an account.

Note that since assets and expenses are increased by debits, these accounts normally have *debit* (or left side) *balances.* Conversely, liability, stockholders' equity, and revenue accounts are increased by credits and normally have *credit* (or right side) *balances.*

The balance of any account is obtained by summing the debits to the account, summing the credits to the account, and subtracting the smaller sum from the larger. If the sum of the debits exceeds the sum of the credits, the account has a debit balance. For example, the Cash account below has a debit balance of $8,400, computed as total debits of $11,000 less total credits of $2,600:

(Dr.)		Cash		(Cr.)
(1)	10,000	(2)		600
(3)	1,000	(4)		2,000
Bal.	8,400			

Similarly, the following Accounts Payable account has a credit balance of $3,000:

(Dr.)	Accounts Payable		(Cr.)
	10,000		7,000
			6,000
		Bal.	3,000

For the most part, amounts entered into the accounts are found in the transactions entered into by the business. Business transactions are first analyzed to determine the effects (increase or decrease) that they have upon the assets, liabilities, stockholders' equity, revenues, expenses, or dividends of the business. Then these increases or decreases are translated into debits and credits. For example, an increase in an asset is recorded as a debit in the proper asset account. (A synonym for "debit an account" is *"charge* an account.") When an asset account is debited, there may be any of five credits:

1. Another asset account may be credited (decreased).
2. A liability account may be credited (increased).
3. A stockholders' equity account may be credited (increased).
4. A revenue account may be credited (increased).
5. An expense account may be credited (decreased).

This double-entry procedure keeps the accounting equation in balance. Every transaction can be analyzed similarly into debits and credits, always of equal amounts.

The rules of debit and credit (rules of **double entry**) may be presented in account form as follows:

Debits	Credits
1. Increase assets.	1. Decrease assets.
2. Decrease liabilities.	2. Increase liabilities.
3. Decrease stockholders' equity.	3. Increase stockholders' equity.
4. Increase dividends.	4. Decrease dividends.
5. Decrease revenues.	5. Increase revenues.
6. Increase expenses.	6. Decrease expenses.

These rules may also be summarized as shown below. Note the treatment of expense and Dividends accounts as if they were merely subsets of the debit side of the Retained Earnings account. Increases in expenses and dividends do tend to reduce what would otherwise be a larger growth in Retained Earnings; and if expenses and dividends are reduced, Retained Earnings will increase. The exact reverse holds true for revenues.

$$\text{Assets} = \text{Liabilities} + \text{Stockholders' equity}$$

Asset Accounts		=	Liability Accounts	+	Stockholders' Equity Accounts	
Debit	Credit		Debit	Credit	Debit	Credit
+	−		−	+	−	+
Increases	Decreases		Decreases	Increases	Decreases	Increases

Expense Accounts and Dividends Account		Revenue Accounts	
Debit	Credit	Debit	Credit
+	−	−	+
Increases	Decreases	Decreases	Increases

THE LEDGER

Accounts are classified into two general groups: (1) balance sheet accounts or **real accounts** (assets, liabilities, and stockholders' equity); and (2) the income statement accounts or **nominal accounts** (revenues and expenses). Balance sheet accounts are called *real* accounts since they are *not* subsets or subdivisions of any other account.

Income statement accounts are called *nominal* accounts because they *are* merely subsets of the Retained Earnings account. The *accounts are collectively referred to as the **ledger,*** whether kept in a bound volume, handwritten in loose-leaf form, or magnetically encoded on plastic computer tape.

The list of the names of the accounts is known as the **chart of accounts.** Each account typically has an identification number as well as a name. For example, assets might be numbered from 100 to 199, liabilities from 200 to 299, stockholders' equity items from 300 to 399, revenues from 400 to 499, and expenses from 500 to 599. (Although any logical numbering may be used, the accounts usually appear in this order in the ledger.) The accounts would then be arranged in numerical sequence in the ledger. The use of account numbers helps to identify and locate accounts when recording data.

Having completed this introduction to accounts and the recording process, attention is now directed to the journal and to journal entries as the means whereby data are entered into an accounting system.

THE JOURNAL

Under double-entry accounting, every business transaction has a dual effect on the accounts of the business entity. With the rare exception of transactions such as an exchange of land for land, every recorded business transaction will affect at least two ledger accounts. Since each ledger account shows only the increases and decreases in the item for which it was established, the entire effects of a single business transaction will not appear in any one account. For example, the Cash account contains only data on changes in cash and does not show the exact accounts credited for receipts of cash or the exact accounts debited for cash disbursements.

Therefore, if transactions are recorded directly in the accounts, it is difficult to see the entire effect of any transaction upon an entity by looking at the accounts. To remedy this deficiency, the accountant employs a book or a record known as a journal. A *journal contains a chronological record of the transactions of a business.* Because each transaction is initially recorded in a journal before being entered in the ledger, a journal is called a book of **original entry.** Here every business transaction is analyzed for its effects upon the entity. These effects are expressed in terms of debit and credit—the inputs of the accounting system.

The functions and other advantages of using a journal are summarized below. The journal:

1. Sets forth transactions of each day.
2. Records transactions in chronological order.

3. Shows the analysis of each transaction in terms of debit and credit effects.
4. Supplies an explanation of each transaction.
5. Serves as a source for future reference to accounting transactions.
6. Removes lengthy explanations from the ledger accounts.
7. Makes posting the ledger at convenient times possible.
8. Assists in keeping the ledger in balance.
9. Aids in tracing errors.
10. Promotes the division of labor (for example, one person may enter the journal entries and another may post them).

The general journal. The general journal is illustrated and discussed in this chapter. It is the most commonly used form of journal. The term *general* means all-purpose or for recording all types of transactions. Other types of special-purpose journals, however, also may be used. These are discussed in the Appendix to Chapter 7. As shown in Illustration 2.1, a general journal contains the following columns:

Illustration 2.1

GENERAL JOURNAL — Page 1

Date		Account Titles and Explanation	Post. Ref.	Debit	Credit
1986 Jan.	1	Cash	100	5 0 0 0	
		Capital Stock	300		5 0 0 0
		Capital stock issued for cash.			
	5	Office Equipment	110	1 2 0 0	
		Accounts Payable	201		1 2 0 0
		Equipment purchased for the office on			
		account.			

1. **Date column.** The first column on each general journal page is for the date. For the first journal entry on a page, the year, the month, and the day are entered here. For other entries on that page, only the day of the month is shown unless the month changes.

2. **Account Titles and Explanation column.**   The names of the account to be debited, the account to be credited, and the explanation are given in this column. The debit is shown on the first line, and the credit is shown on the following line, indented to the right. The explanation of the transaction appears on the line(s) below the transaction, indented halfway between the debit and credit entry.

3. **Posting Reference (Post. Ref.) column.**   This column shows the account number of the account that has been debited or credited. For instance, the number 100 in the first entry means that the Cash account number is 100. No number appears in the column until the information is posted to the appropriate ledger account.

4. **Debit column.**   This column shows the monetary amount of the debit; it is on the same line as the name of the account debited.

5. **Credit column.**   This column shows the monetary amount of the credit; it is on the same line as the name of the account credited.

A blank line separates the entries for individual transactions.

Journalizing

Journalizing is the process of entering a transaction in a journal. Information to be journalized originates on source materials or documents such as invoices, cash register tapes, timecards, and checks. The activity recorded on these documents must be analyzed to determine whether a recordable transaction has occurred. If so, the specific accounts affected, the dollar amounts of the changes, and the direction of the changes (whether increases or decreases) must also be determined. Then all of these changes must be translated into terms of debits and credits and entered in the journal.

A *journal entry* is the entire analysis of a business transaction, including when it occurred, what accounts were affected (debited or credited), and what the amount of the increase or decrease was. The explanation of a journal entry should be complete enough to fully describe the transaction and to prove the entry's accuracy and at the same time be concise. If a journal entry is self-explanatory, the explanation is often omitted in practice.

Compound Journal Entries

The analysis of a transaction often shows that more than two accounts are directly affected. In such cases, the journal entry involves more than one debit and/or credit. Such a journal entry is a ***compound journal entry.*** An entry with one debit and one credit is a simple journal entry.

As an illustration of a compound journal entry, assume that Beck Company purchased $8,000 of machinery from Taylor Company, paying $2,000 cash with the balance due in 30 days. The journal entry for Beck is as follows:

Machinery 8,000
    Cash 2,000
    Accounts Payable, Taylor Company 6,000
    Machinery purchased from Taylor Company, Invoice
    No. 42.

POSTING

In a sense, a journal entry is a set of instructions. It directs the entry of a certain dollar amount as a debit in a specific account. It also directs entry of a certain dollar amount as a credit in a specific account. The carrying out of these instructions is known as posting. *Posting is the process of transferring information recorded in the journal to the proper place in the ledger.* In Illustration 2.2, the first entry directs that $10,000 be posted as a debit to the Cash account and as a credit to the Capital Stock account. (The arrows in the illustration show how these amounts have been posted to the correct accounts.) The three-column balance type of account is shown in this illustration and is the more common form of ledger account. In contrast to the two-sided T-account format shown so far, the three-column format has columns for debit, credit, and balance. One advantage of this form is that the balance of the account is shown after each item has been posted.

Postings to the ledger accounts may be made (1) at the time the transaction is journalized; (2) at the end of the day, week, or month; or (3) as each journal page is filled. The time of posting is determined by such things as the need for ledger account balances to be completely up to date, type of accounting system in use, number of people working in the accounting area, and number of business transactions recorded.

Cross-Indexing

The number of the ledger account to which the posting was made is placed in the *Posting Reference (Post. Ref.) column* (sometimes called Folio column) of the journal (see the arrow from Account No. 100 to the debit in the entry in the general journal). The number of the journal page *from* which the entry was posted is placed in the Post. Ref. column of the ledger account (see the arrow from page 1 in the general journal to GJ1 in the Post Ref. column of the general ledger). The date of the transaction is also shown in the general ledger (see the arrows from the date in the general journal to the dates in the general ledger). Posting is always *from* the journal *to* the ledger account. *Cross-indexing is the placing of the account number in the journal and the placing of the journal page number in the ledger account,* as shown in Illustration 2.2.

Illustration 2.2

	GENERAL JOURNAL				Page 1

Date	Account Titles and Explanation	Post. Ref.	Debit	Credit
1986 May 1	Cash	100	1 0 0 0 0	
	Capital Stock	300		1 0 0 0 0
	Cash invested in the business.			

GENERAL LEDGER

Cash   *Account No. 100*

Date	Explanation	Post. Ref.	Debit	Credit	Balance
1986 May 1	Sale of Capital Stock	GJ1	1 0 0 0 0		1 0 0 0 0 Dr.

Capital Stock   *Account No. 300*

Date	Explanation	Post. Ref.	Debit	Credit	Balance
1986 May 1	Cash from owner	GJ1		1 0 0 0 0	1 0 0 0 0 Cr.

Cross-indexing aids the tracing of any recorded transaction, either from the journal to the ledger or from the ledger to the journal. Cross-reference numbers should not be placed in the Post. Ref. column of the journal until the entry is posted; thereafter, the presence of cross-reference numbers indicates that the entry has been posted.

An understanding of the posting and cross-indexing process can be obtained by tracing the entries from the journal to the ledger. The ledger accounts might not contain explanations of all the entries since the explanations can be obtained from the journal.

THE ACCOUNTING SYSTEM ILLUSTRATED

Presented below is an illustration of an accounting system that might be employed by a small decorating service company, the Morgan Company. The company's balance sheet at December 31, 1985, is as follows:

MORGAN COMPANY
Balance Sheet
December 31, 1985

Assets		Liabilities and Stockholders' Equity		
Cash	$15,000	Liabilities:		
Accounts receivable	4,500	Accounts payable		$ 2,000
Furniture and equipment	6,000	Stockholders' equity:		
Office fixtures	10,000	Capital stock	$30,000	
		Retained earnings . .	3,500	
		Total stockholders' equity		33,500
		Total liabilities and		
Total assets	$35,500	stockholders' equity . .		$35,500

The balance sheet reflects ledger account balances as of the close of business on December 31, 1985. These are, of course, the opening balances on January 1, 1986, and are shown as such in the illustrated ledger accounts. The furniture, equipment, and office fixtures were purchased on December 31, 1985.

The Morgan Company's chart of accounts is as follows:

	Account No.	Account Title
Assets	100	Cash
	101	Accounts Receivable
	103	Furniture and Equipment
	104	Office Fixtures
Liability	200	Accounts Payable
Stockholders' equity	300	Capital Stock
	301	Retained Earnings
	302	Dividends
Revenue	400	Service Revenue
Expenses	500	Advertising Expense
	501	Sales Expense
	502	Rent Expense
	504	Supplies Expense
	505	Miscellaneous Expense

Now assume that the following is a complete list and analysis of the transactions entered into by the Morgan Company in January 1986.

1. Jan. 2   Paid January rent for office, $1,000.

(Dr.)	**Rent Expense**	(Cr.)
1986		
Jan. 2	**1,000**	

An expense, rent expense, is increased (debited); and an asset, cash, is decreased (credited) by $1,000.

(Dr.)	**Cash**	(Cr.)
1986		1986	
Beg. bal.	15,000	**Jan. 2**	**1,000**

2. Jan. 3   Purchased additional office furniture for cash, $1,500.

(Dr.)	**Furniture and Equipment**	(Cr.)
1986		
Beg. bal.	6,000	
Jan. 3	**1,500**	

One asset, furniture and equipment, is increased (debited); and another asset, cash, is decreased (credited) by $1,500.

(Dr.)	**Cash**	(Cr.)
1986		1986	
Beg. bal.	15,000	Jan. 2	1,000
		3	**1,500**

3. Jan. 4   Received a $200 invoice from the Burk Agency for planning January's advertising.

(Dr.)	**Advertising Expense**	(Cr.)
1986		
Jan. 4	**200**	

An expense, advertising is increased (debited); and a liability, accounts payable, is increased (credited) by $200.

(Dr.)	**Accounts Payable**	(Cr.)
		1986	
		Beg. bal.	2,000
		Jan. 4	**200**

Sometimes prepaid expenses such as advertising, insurance, rent, and supplies are bought and will be fully used up within the current accounting period as in the first and third entries above. For instance, the company may buy supplies during the first part of the month that it intends to fully consume during that month. If supplies will be fully consumed during the period of purchase, it is best to debit Supplies Expense rather than an asset account such as Supplies on Hand, at time of purchase. This same advice applies to insurance and rent. If insurance is purchased that will be fully consumed during the current period, Insurance Expense rather than Prepaid Insurance should be debited at the time of purchase. If rent is paid that applies only to the current period, Rent Expense rather than Prepaid Rent should be debited at the time of payment. Following this advice simplifies the procedures at the end of the accounting period, as illustrated in the next chapter.

4. Jan. 6   Paid a $2,000 account payable.

(Dr.)	**Accounts Payable**		*(Cr.)*
1986		1986	
Jan. 6	**2,000**	Beg. bal.	2,000
		Jan. 4	200

(Dr.)	**Cash**		*(Cr.)*
1986		1986	
Beg. bal.	15,000	Jan. 2	1,000
		3	1,500
		6	**2,000**

A liability, accounts payable, is decreased (debited); and an asset, cash, is decreased (credited) by $2,000.

5. Jan. 8   Paid the $200 advertising bill received on January 4.

(Dr.)	**Accounts Payable**		*(Cr.)*
1986		1986	
Jan. 6	2,000	Beg. bal.	2,000
8	**200**	Jan. 4	200

(Dr.)	**Cash**		*(Cr.)*
1985		1985	
Beg. bal.	15,000	Jan. 2	1,000
		3	1,500
		6	2,000
		8	**200**

A liability, accounts payable, is decreased (debited); and an asset, cash, is decreased (credited) by $200.

6. Jan. 9   Purchased, for $200 cash, supplies to be used in January.

(Dr.)	**Supplies Expense**		*(Cr.)*
1986			
Jan. 9	**200**		

(Dr.)	**Cash**		*(Cr.)*
1986		1986	
Beg. bal.	15,000	Jan. 2	1,000
		3	1,500
		6	2,000
		8	200
		9	**200**

An expense, supplies expense, is increased (debited); and an asset, cash, is decreased (credited) by $200.

7. Jan. 10   Received $4,500 cash on an account receivable.

(Dr.)		Cash		(Cr.)
1986		1986	
Beg. bal.	15,000	Jan. 2	1,000
Jan. 10	**4,500**	3	1,500
		6	2,000
		8	200
		9	200

(Dr.)		Accounts Receivable		(Cr.)
1986		1986	
Beg. bal.	4,500	**Jan. 10**	**4,500**

An asset, cash, is increased (debited); and another asset, accounts receivable, is decreased (credited) by $4,500.

8. Jan. 15   Performed services on account for a customer, $7,600.

(Dr.)		Accounts Receivable		(Cr.)
1985		1985	
Beg. bal.	4,500	Jan. 10	4,500
Jan. 15	**7,600**		

(Dr.)		Service Revenue		(Cr.)
		1985	
		Jan. 15	**7,600**

An asset, accounts receivable, is increased (debited); and a revenue, service revenue, is increased (credited) by $7,600.

9. Jan. 17   Paid a miscellaneous expense, $1,000.

(Dr.)	Miscellaneous Expense		(Cr.)
1986		
Jan. 17	**1,000**	

(Dr.)		Cash		(Cr.)
1986		1986	
Beg. bal.	15,000	Jan. 2	1,000
Jan. 10	4,500	3	1,500
		6	2,000
		8	200
		9	200
		17	**1,000**

An expense, miscellaneous expense, is increased (debited); and an asset, cash, is decreased (credited) by $1,000.

10. Jan. 23   Received a $300 invoice from the *New York News* for advertising in the first half of January.

(Dr.)	**Advertising Expense**	(Cr.)
1986		
Jan. 4	200	
23	**300**	

An expense, advertising expense, is increased (debited); and a liability, accounts payable, is increased (credited) by $300.

(Dr.)	**Accounts Payable**		(Cr.)
1986		1986	
Jan. 6	2,000	Beg. bal.	2,000
8	200	Jan. 4	200
		23	**300**

11. Jan. 31   Performed services on account, $3,000.

(Dr.)	**Accounts Receivable**		(Cr.)
1986		1986	
Beg. bal.	4,500	Jan. 10	4,500
Jan. 15	7,600		
31	**3,000**		

An asset, accounts receivable, is increased (debited); and a revenue, service revenue, is increased (credited) by $3,000.

(Dr.)	**Service Revenue**		(Cr.)
		1986	
		Jan. 15	7,600
		31	**3,000**

12. Jan. 31   Paid salaries of $7,800 for the month.

(Dr.)	**Salaries Expense**	(Cr.)
1986		
Jan. 31	**7,800**	

An expense, salaries expense, is increased (debited); and an asset, cash, is decreased (credited) by $7,800.

(Dr.)	**Cash**		(Cr.)
1986		1986	
Beg. bal.	15,000	Jan. 2	1,000
Jan. 10	4,500	3	1,500
		6	2,000
		8	200
		9	200
		17	1,000
		31	**7,800**

13. Jan. 31 Paid a cash dividend to stockholders, $2,000.

(Dr.)	**Dividends**		(Cr.)
1986			
Jan. 31	**2,000**		

(Dr.)	**Cash**			(Cr.)
1986		1986		
Beg. bal.	15,000	Jan. 2	1,000	
Jan. 10	4,500	3	1,500	
		6	2,000	
		8	200	
		9	200	
		17	1,000	
		31	7,800	
		31	**2,000**	

A stockholders' equity account, Dividends, is increased (debited); and an asset, cash, is decreased (credited) by $2,000. Remember that dividends reduce the amount of Retained Earnings—which carries a credit balance—so dividends are debited for increases.

The T-accounts shown in the list of transactions were used only for analysis purposes. In the accounting records, the transactions would first be entered in a journal and then posted to a ledger.

The transactions presented have been entered in the general journal of the Morgan Company for January 1986. Remember that the Posting Reference column normally would not be filled in until after the entries have been posted to the ledger.

Date		Account Titles and Explanation	Post. Ref.	Debit	Credit
1986 Jan.	2	Rent Expense	502	1 0 0 0	
		Cash	100		1 0 0 0
		Rent for January 1986.			
	3	Furniture and Equipment	103	1 5 0 0	
		Cash	100		1 5 0 0
		Purchased additional furniture.			
	4	Advertising Expense	500	2 0 0	
		Accounts Payable	200		2 0 0
		Advertising expense on account.			
	6	Accounts Payable	200	2 0 0 0	
		Cash	100		2 0 0 0
		Payment on account.			
	8	Accounts Payable	200	2 0 0	
		Cash	100		2 0 0
		Paid invoice of January 4.			
	9	Supplies Expense	504	2 0 0	
		Cash	100		2 0 0
		Supplies purchased and used.			
	10	Cash	100	4 5 0 0	
		Accounts Receivable	101		4 5 0 0
		Collection on account.			
	15	Accounts Receivable	101	7 6 0 0	
		Service Revenue	400		7 6 0 0
		Performed services on account.			
	17	Miscellaneous Expense	505	1 0 0 0	
		Cash	100		1 0 0 0
		Paid other selling expenses.			
	23	Advertising Expense	500	3 0 0	
		Accounts Payable	200		3 0 0
		Advertising expense on account.			

GENERAL JOURNAL   *Page 2*

Date		Account Titles and Explanation	Post. Ref.	Debit	Credit
1986 Jan.	31	Accounts Receivable	101	3 0 0 0	
		Service Revenue	400		3 0 0 0
		Performed services on account.			
	31	Salaries Expense	501	7 8 0 0	
		Cash	100		7 8 0 0
		Paid salaries for January.			
	31	Dividends	302	2 0 0 0	
		Cash	100		2 0 0 0
		Paid a dividend to stockholders.			

Posting the journal entries to the ledger produces the following accounts for the Morgan Company. Be sure to trace the posting of at least a few of the journal entries to make sure you understand how it was done.

GENERAL LEDGER

Cash   *Account No. 100*

Date		Explanation	Post. Ref.	Debit	Credit	Balance
1986 Jan.	1	Balance				1 5 0 0 0 Dr.
	2		GJ1		1 0 0 0	1 4 0 0 0 Dr.
	3		GJ1		1 5 0 0	1 2 5 0 0 Dr.
	6		GJ1		2 0 0 0	1 0 5 0 0 Dr.
	8		GJ1		2 0 0	1 0 3 0 0 Dr.
	9		GJ1		2 0 0	1 0 1 0 0 Dr.
	10		GJ1	4 5 0 0		1 4 6 0 0 Dr.
	17		GJ1		1 0 0 0	1 3 6 0 0 Dr.
	31		GJ2		7 8 0 0	5 8 0 0 Dr.
	31		GJ2		2 0 0 0	3 8 0 0 Dr.

GENERAL LEDGER *(continued)*

Accounts Receivable   Account No. 101

Date		Explanation	Post. Ref.	Debit	Credit	Balance
1986 Jan.	1	Balance				4 5 0 0 Dr.
	10		GJ1		4 5 0 0	– 0 – Dr.
	15		GJ1	7 6 0 0		7 6 0 0 Dr.
	31		GJ2	3 0 0 0		1 0 6 0 0 Dr.

Furniture and Equipment   Account No. 103

Date		Explanation	Post. Ref.	Debit	Credit	Balance
1986 Jan.	1	Balance				6 0 0 0 Dr.
	3		GJ1	1 5 0 0		7 5 0 0 Dr.

Office Fixtures   Account No. 104

Date		Explanation	Post. Ref.	Debit	Credit	Balance
1986 Jan.	1	Balance				1 0 0 0 0 Dr.

Accounts Payable   Account No. 200

Date		Explanation	Post. Ref.	Debit	Credit	Balance
1986 Jan.	1	Balance				2 0 0 0 Cr.
	4		GJ1		2 0 0	2 2 0 0 Cr.
	6		GJ1	2 0 0 0		2 0 0 Cr.
	8		GJ1	2 0 0		– 0 –
	23		GJ1		3 0 0	3 0 0 Cr.

GENERAL LEDGER (continued)

Capital Stock   Account No. 300

Date		Explanation	Post. Ref.	Debit	Credit	Balance
1986 Jan.	1	Balance				3 0 0 0 0 Cr.

Retained Earnings   Account No. 301

Date		Explanation	Post. Ref.	Debit	Credit	Balance
1986 Jan.	1	Balance				3 5 0 0 Cr.

Dividends   Account No. 302

Date		Explanation	Post. Ref.	Debit	Credit	Balance
1986 Jan.	31		GJ2	2 0 0 0		2 0 0 0 Dr.

Service Revenue   Account No. 400

Date		Explanation	Post. Ref.	Debit	Credit	Balance
1986 Jan.	15		GJ1		7 6 0 0	7 6 0 0 Cr.
	31		GJ2		3 0 0 0	1 0 6 0 0 Cr.

Advertising Expense   Account No. 500

Date		Explanation	Post. Ref.	Debit	Credit	Balance
1986 Jan.	4		GJ1	2 0 0		2 0 0 Dr.
	23		GJ1	3 0 0		5 0 0 Dr.

Salaries Expense   Account No. 501

Date		Explanation	Post. Ref.	Debit	Credit	Balance
1986 Jan.	31		GJ2	7 8 0 0		7 8 0 0 Dr.

GENERAL LEDGER *(concluded)*

Rent Expense   *Account No. 502*

Date		Explanation	Post. Ref.	Debit	Credit	Balance
1986 Jan.	2		GJ1	1 0 0 0		1 0 0 0 Dr.

Supplies Expense   *Account No. 504*

Date		Explanation	Post. Ref.	Debit	Credit	Balance
1986 Jan.	9		GJ1	2 0 0		2 0 0 Dr.

Miscellaneous Expense   *Account No. 505*

Date		Explanation	Post. Ref.	Debit	Credit	Balance
1986 Jan.	17		GJ1	1 0 0 0		1 0 0 0 Dr.

Control of the Recording Process

Earlier in the chapter, it was stated that accountants record increases in assets, expenses, and dividends as debits and increases in equities and revenues as credits. It would be possible to devise a scheme whereby all accounts were increased by entries on the debit side. At the end of any given period, then, all accounts would have positive debit balances. Under such a scheme, however, accountants would not know whether the basic equation of Assets = Equities was being maintained in the records. Furthermore, a valuable automatic check for arithmetic errors would be missing. If accountants wished to check upon the arithmetic accuracy of their work, they would have to repeat virtually every step in the initial recording process. Fortunately, there is an easier way.

Increases in assets, expenses, and dividends are recorded as debits and increases in equities and revenues as credits. This yields two sets of accounts—those with debit balances and those with credit balances. If the totals of these two groups are equal, the accountant has *some* assurance that the arithmetic part of the recording process has been properly carried out. The double-entry system of accounting requires that debits must equal credits in the entry to record every transaction. This equality of debits and credits for each transaction will always hold because both sides of every transaction are recorded. It is the equality of debits and credits, not of increases and decreases, that provides the important control device. If every transaction is recorded in terms of equal debits and credits, it follows that the total of the debit-balanced accounts must equal the total of the credit-balanced accounts.

THE TRIAL BALANCE   The arithmetic accuracy of the recording process is generally tested by preparing a trial balance. A **trial balance** is a listing of the accounts and their debit or credit balances. The trial balance for the Morgan Company is shown in Illustration 2.3. Note the listing of the account titles on the left (account numbers could be included, if desired), the column for debit balances, the column for credit balances, and the equality of the two totals.

Illustration 2.3
A TRIAL BALANCE

MORGAN COMPANY
Trial Balance
January 31, 1986

	Debits	Credits
Cash	$ 3,800	
Accounts receivable	10,600	
Furniture and equipment	7,500	
Office fixtures	10,000	
Accounts payable		$ 300
Capital stock		30,000
Retained earnings		3,500
Dividends	2,000	
Service revenue		10,600
Advertising expense	500	
Salaries expense	7,800	
Rent expense	1,000	
Supplies expense	200	
Miscellaneous expense	1,000	
	$44,400	$44,400

Any inequality in the totals of the debits and credits columns would automatically signal the presence of an error. To find the cause of such an error, the accountant should work backwards through the accounting process by performing the following steps:

1. Re-add the trial balance.
2. Compare the trial balance figures with the account balances, and determine if the account balances are in the appropriate money columns.

3. Verify the balance of each ledger account.
4. Verify postings to the ledger.
5. Verify journal entries.
6. Review the transactions.

The equality of the two totals does not mean that the accounting has been error free. Serious errors may still have been made. Such errors might include the complete omission of an important transaction or the recording of an entry in the wrong account (for example, the recording of an asset as an expense, or vice versa). In these instances, the trial balance would have equal debit and credit totals but would be incorrect.

A trial balance may be prepared at any time—at the end of a day, a week, a month, a quarter, or a year. Typically, one is prepared whenever financial statements are to be prepared. Thus, the trial balance provides a listing of the accounts for statement preparation. A trial balance that is out of balance will also indicate the period in which an error was made.

FINANCIAL STATEMENTS

The financial statements desired by the management of the Morgan Company are presented in Illustrations 2.4, 2.5, and 2.6. As shown by the income statement in Illustration 2.4, the company showed net income of $100.

Illustration 2.4
AN INCOME STATEMENT

MORGAN COMPANY
Income Statement
For Month Ended January 31, 1986

Revenues:		
Service revenue		$10,600
Expenses:		
Advertising expense	$ 500	
Salaries	7,800	
Rent expense	1,000	
Supplies expense	200	
Miscellaneous expense . . .	1,000	10,500
Net income		$ 100

In Illustration 2.5, the net income is added to the beginning balance in retained earnings. Then the dividends are deducted from that total to arrive at the ending balance in retained earnings. This ending balance of retained earnings appears in the balance sheet in Illustration 2.6, along with the ending balances in the other balance sheet accounts.

Illustration 2.5
A STATEMENT OF RETAINED EARNINGS

MORGAN COMPANY
Statement of Retained Earnings
For Month Ended January 31, 1986

Retained earnings, December 31, 1985 . .	$3,500
Add: Net income for January	100
Total	$3,600
Less: Dividends	2,000
Retained earnings, January 31, 1986 . . .	$1,600

Illustration 2.6
A BALANCE SHEET

MORGAN COMPANY
Balance Sheet
January 31, 1986

Assets

Cash		$ 3,800
Accounts receivable		10,600
Furniture and equipment		7,500
Office fixtures		10,000
Total assets		$31,900

Liabilities and Stockholders' Equity

Liabilities:		
Accounts payable		$ 300
Stockholders' equity:		
Capital stock	$30,000	
Retained earnings	1,600	
Total stockholders' equity		31,600
Total liabilities and stockholders' equity . . .		$31,900

The financial accounting process once again is back to its end products, the financial statements. Thus far, the accounting process has been shown to consist of (1) analyzing economic activity, (2) journalizing transactions, (3) posting to ledger accounts, (4) preparing a trial balance, and (5) preparing financial statements.

SUMMARY

This chapter introduced the basic components of an accounting system and the manner in which data are entered in the system.

An account is a means employed to classify and summarize changes in assets, liabilities, stockholders' equity items, revenues, expenses, and dividends. By agreement, asset, expense, and dividend accounts are increased by entries on the left side of the account (called the debit side) and decreased by entries on the right (credit) side. Liability, stockholders' equity, and revenue accounts are increased by entries on the credit side and decreased by entries on the debit side. As a result, assets, expenses, and dividends usually have debit balances, and the others usually have credit balances.

Recording increases and decreases in accounts in a manner that provides two groups of accounts—those with debit balances and those with credit balances—gives an automatic check upon the arithmetic accuracy of the accounting process.

Collectively, the accounts are referred to as the ledger. The chart of accounts is a list of the names and numbers of the accounts in an accounting system.

All data are entered in an accounting system by means of a journal, which is a chronological record of business transactions analyzed in terms of debit and credit. Business activity is analyzed and certain transactions are recorded in the journal in a process known as journalizing. The amounts journalized are then posted to the accounts. A trial balance is a listing of all of the accounts in the ledger together with their debit or credit balances which, in total, must be equal. Then, financial statements can be prepared.

QUESTIONS

1. Define debit and credit. Name the types of accounts that are:
   a. Increased by debits.
   b. Decreased by debits.
   c. Increased by credits.
   d. Do you think this system makes sense? Can you conceive of other possible methods for recording changes in accounts?

2. Describe a ledger and a chart of accounts. How do these two compare with a book and its table of contents?

3. Why are expense and revenue accounts used when all revenues and expenses could be shown directly in the Retained Earnings account?

4. What types of accounts appear in the trial balance? What are the purposes of the trial balance?

5. You have found that the total of the debits column of the trial balance of the Burns Company is $100,000 while the total of the credits column is $90,000. What are some of the possible causes of this difference?

6. Store equipment was purchased for $1,500. Instead of debiting the Store Equipment account, the debit was made to Delivery Equipment. Of what help will the trial balance be in locating this error? Why?

7. Differentiate between the trial balance, chart of accounts, balance sheet, and income statement.

8. A student remembered that the side toward the window in the classroom was the debit side of an account. The student took an examination in a room where the windows were on the other side of the room and

became confused and consistently reversed debits and credits. Would the student's trial balance have equal debits and credits totals? If there were no existing balances in any of the accounts to begin with, would the error prevent the student from preparing correct financial statements? Why?

9. Are the following possibilities conceivable in an entry involving only one debit and one credit? Why?

   a. Increase a liability and increase an expense.

   b. Increase an asset and decrease a liability.

   c. Increase a revenue and decrease an expense.

   d. Decrease an asset and increase another asset.

   e. Decrease an asset and increase a liability.

   f. Decrease a revenue and decrease an asset.

   g. Decrease a liability and increase a revenue.

10. Describe the nature and purposes of the general journal. What does "journalizing" mean? Give an example of a compound entry in the general journal.

11. Describe the act of posting. What difficulties could arise if no cross-indexing existed between the general journal and the ledger accounts?

12. Which of the following cash payments would involve the recording of an expense? Why?

   a. Paid vendors for office supplies previously purchased on account.

   b. Paid an automobile dealier for a new company auto.

   c. Paid the current month's rent.

   d. Paid salaries for the last half of the current month.

EXERCISES

1. Below is a diagram of the various types of accounts. Indicate where pluses (+) or minuses (−) should be inserted to indicate what effect debits and credits have on each account.

Asset Accounts		= Liability Accounts		+ Stockholders' Equity Accounts	
Debit	Credit	Debit	Credit	Debit	Credit

Expense Accounts and Dividend Accounts		Revenue Accounts	
Debit	Credit	Debit	Credit

2. What debit and credit would be required for each of the following transactions?

   a. Cash was received for services performed for a customer, $800.

   b. Services were performed for a customer on open account, $1,400.

3. Give the entry required for each of the following transactions:

a. Capital stock was issued for $100,000 cash.

b. Purchased machinery for cash, $30,000.

4. Using T-accounts, show how the following transactions would be recorded.

a. Capital stock was issued for $20,000.

b. Wages for the period were paid to employees, $2,500.

c. Services were performed for a customer on account, $4,000.

5. Give the journal entry required for each of the following transactions:

a. Capital stock was issued for $25,000.

b. A $15,000 loan was arranged with a bank. The bank increased the company's checking account by $15,000 after management of the company signed a written promise to return the money in 30 days.

c. Cash was received for services performed for a customer, $400.

d. Services were performed for a customer on account, $600.

6. Explain each of the sets of debits and credits existing in the accounts below. There are 10 transactions to be explained. Each set is designated by the small letters to the left of the amount. For example, the first transaction is the issuance of capital stock for cash and is denoted by the letter *(a)*.

Cash

(a)	35,000	(e)	25,000
(d)	300	(f)	100
		(g)	600
		(i)	5,000
Bal.	4,600		

Delivery Fee Revenue

	(c)	300
	(j)	2,350
	Bal.	2,650

Accounts Receivable

(c)	300	(d)	300
(j)	2,350		
Bal.	2,350		

Rent Expense

(f)	100

Land

(b)	25,000
(i)	5,000
Bal.	30,000

Delivery Expense

(h)	200

Accounts Payable

(e)	25,000	(b)	25,000
		(h)	200
		Bal.	200

Salaries Expense

(g)	600

Capital Stock

(a)	35,000

7. Assume that the ledger accounts given in Exercise 6 are those of the Conrad Company as they appear at December 31, 1986. Prepare the trial balance as of that date.

8. Prepare the income statement for 1985 and the balance sheet as of the end of 1985 assuming that the data given in Exercise 6 are for the Conrad Company.

9. Prepare journal entries to record each of the following transactions for the Tom King Company. Use the letter of the transaction in place of the date. Include an explanation for each entry.

a. Capital stock was issued for cash, $80,000.

b. Purchased delivery equipment on account, $50,000.

c. Earned (but did not yet receive) delivery fee revenue, $1,000.

d. Collected the account receivable for the delivery fee, $1,000.

e. Paid the account payable for the delivery equipment purchased, $50,000.

f. Paid utilities for the month in the amount of $500.

g. Paid salaries for the month in the amount of $1,500.

h. Incurred delivery expenses in the amount of $400, but did not yet pay for them.

i. Purchased more delivery equipment for cash, $10,000.

j. Performed delivery services for a large retail store on account, $5,000.

10. Using the data in Exercise 9 record the transactions in T-accounts. Write the letter of the transaction in the T-account before the dollar amount. Determine a balance for each account.

11. Using your answer for Exercise 10, prepare a trial balance. Assume the date of the trial balance is March 31, 1985.

12. Give the entry (without dollar amounts) of a transaction that would involve the following combinations of types of accounts:

a. An asset and a liability.

b. An expense and an asset.

c. A liability and an expense.

d. Stockholders' equity and an asset.

e. Two asset accounts.

f. An asset and a revenue.

13. Ray Braxton owns and manages a bowling center called Tri-Angle Lanes. He also maintains his own accounting records and was about to prepare financial statements for the year 1986. When he prepared the trial balance from the ledger accounts, the total of the debits column was $814,800 and the total of the credits column was $812,800. What are the possible reasons why the totals of the debits and credits are out of balance? How would you proceed to find the error?

PROBLEMS

2–1. The Cole Company had the following transactions in August 1986:

Transactions:

Aug. 1 Issued capital stock for cash, $15,000.
  3 Borrowed $5,000 from the bank on a note.
  4 Purchased a truck for $5,300 cash.
  6 Performed services for a customer who promised to pay later, $3,600.
  7 Paid employee wages, $700.
  10 Partial collection was made for the services performed on August 6, $800.
  14 Supplies were purchased for use this month, $500. They will be paid for next month.
  17 A bill for $100 was received for gas and oil used to date.
  25 Services were performed for a customer who paid immediately, $4,500.
  31 Paid employee wages, $1,500.
  31 Paid dividend, $400.

Required:

    a. Open T-accounts for the Cole Company and enter therein transactions given. Place the date of each transaction in the account.

    b. Prepare a trial balance as of August 31, 1986.

2–2. The Robin Company had the following transactions for July 1986.

Transactions:

July 2 Cash of $5,000 was received for capital stock issued to the owners.
  3 The company paid rent for July, $250.
  5 Office furniture was purchased for $3,000 cash.
  9 A bill for $500 for advertising for July was received and paid.
  14 Cash of $700 was received for services to a customer.
  15 Wages of $200 for the first half of July were paid in cash.
  20 The company sold services on account to a customer, $400. The account is to be paid August 10.
  22 Office furniture was acquired on account from the Mason Company; the price was $400.
  30 Cash of $2,250 was received for services to a customer.
  31 Wages of $200 for the second half of July were paid in cash.

Required:

    a. Open proper T-accounts for the Robin Company and enter therein the transactions given. Place the date of each transaction in the accounts.

    b. Prepare a trial balance as of July 31, 1986.

2–3. Presented below are the transactions of the Tate Company (partially summarized for the sake of brevity) for the month of March 1986.

Transactions:

a. The company was organized and issued capital stock for cash of $60,000.
b. Paid $1,800 as the rent for March on a completely furnished building.
c. Paid cash for delivery trucks, $35,000.
d. Paid $750 as the rent for March on two forklift trucks.
e. Paid $400 for supplies received and used in March.
f. Performed delivery services for a customer who promised to pay $15,000 at a later date.
g. Collected cash of $12,000 from a customer on account (see [f] above).
h. Received a bill for $300 in advertising in the local newspaper in March.
i. Paid cash for gas and oil consumed in March, $96.
j. Paid $1,400 to employees for services provided in March.

k. Received an order for services at $10,000. The services will be performed in April.

l. Paid cash dividend, $2,000.

Required:

Prepare the general journal entries that would be required to record the above transactions in the records of the Tate Company.

2–4. The trial balance prepared as of the end of the Guyson Company's calendar-year accounting period is as follows:

GUYSON COMPANY
Trial Balance
December 31, 1986

	Debits	Credits
Cash	$ 8,000	
Accounts receivable	25,000	
Land	73,000	
Accounts payable		$ 18,000
Notes payable		20,000
Capital stock		26,000
Retained earnings, January 1, 1986		15,800
Service revenue		66,000
Rent expense	2,400	
Supplies expense	1,400	
Advertising expense	2,000	
Salaries expense	34,000	
	$145,800	$145,800

Required:

a. Prepare an income statement for the year ended December 31, 1986.

b. Prepare the statement of retained earnings for the year ended December 31, 1986.

c. Prepare the balance sheet as of December 31, 1986.

2–5. Remco, Inc., was organized July 1, 1986. The following account numbers and titles constitute the chart of accounts for the company:

Account No.	Account Title
101	Cash
102	Accounts Receivable
111	Office Equipment
112	Cleaning Equipment
113	Service Truck
221	Accounts Payable
222	Notes Payable
331	Capital Stock
332	Retained Earnings
333	Dividends
441	Cleaning Service Revenue
551	Salaries Expense
552	Insurance Expense
553	Service Truck Expense
554	Rent Expense
555	Utilities Expense
556	Cleaning Supplies Expense

Transactions for July are:

Transactions:

July 1 The company issued $60,000 of capital stock for cash.
5 Office space was rented for July, and $1,200 cash was paid for the rental.
8 Desks and chairs were purchased for the office on account, $6,000.
10 Cleaning equipment was purchased for $8,400; a note was given, to be paid in 30 days.
15 Purchased a service truck for $36,000, paying $24,000 cash and giving a 60-day note to the dealer for $12,000.
18 Paid for cleaning supplies received and already used, $600.
23 Received $3,600 cash from a customer as cleaning service revenue.
27 Insurance expense for July was paid, $900 cash.
30 Paid for gasoline and oil used by the service truck in July, $120.
31 Billed a customer for cleaning services rendered, $8,400.
31 Paid salaries for July, $10,800.
31 Paid utilities bills for July, $1,100.
31 Paid cash dividend, $2,000.

Required:

a. Prepare ledger accounts for all of the above accounts except Retained Earnings.

b. Journalize the transactions given for July 1986.

c. Post the journal entries to the ledger accounts.

d. Prepare a trial balance as of July 31, 1986.

2–6. Moss Company is a lawn care company. Thus, it earns its revenue from sending its trucks to customers' residences and certain commercial establishments to care for lawns and shrubbery. Moss Company's trial balance at the end of the first 11 months of the year is presented below.

MOSS COMPANY
Trial Balance
November 30, 1986

Account No.	Account Title	Debits	Credits
1	Cash	$ 49,160	
2	Accounts receivable	52,400	
11	Office equipment	5,600	
12	Trucks	68,600	
21	Accounts payable		$ 22,400
31	Capital stock		20,000
32	Retained earnings, January 1, 1985		20,360
40	Lawn care revenue		180,000
41	Shrubbery care revenue		67,340
51	Salaries expense	43,900	
52	Chemical supplies expense	49,600	
53	Advertising expense	12,200	
54	Truck operating expense	14,600	
55	Rent expense	10,000	
56	Office Supplies expense	800	
57	Telephone and utilities expense	1,540	
58	Customer entertainment expense	1,700	
		$310,100	$310,100

Transactions for December are:

Transactions:

Dec. 2 Paid rent for December, $2,000.
  5 Paid an account payable of $22,400.
  8 Paid advertising for the month of December, $800.
  10 Purchased a new office desk on account, $700.
  13 Purchased $160 of office supplies for December use on account.
  15 Collected cash from a customer on account, $47,200.
  20 Paid for customer entertainment, $50.
  24 Collected $4,000 from a customer on account.
  26 Paid for gasoline used in the trucks in December, $180.
  28 Billed a commercial customer for services; lawn care, $31,500, and shrubbery care, $21,500.
  30 Paid for December chemical supplies, $13,200.
  31 Paid December salaries, $10,200.
  31 Paid a $2,000 dividend. (The Dividends account is #33.)

Required:

 a. Open three-column ledger accounts for each of the accounts in the trial balance under the date of December 1, 1986. Place the word *Balance* in the explanation space of each account.

 b. Prepare general journal entries for the transactions given below for December 1985.

 c. Post the journal entries to the general ledger accounts.

 d. Prepare a trial balance as of December 31, 1986.

 e. Prepare an income statement for the year ended December 31, 1986.

 f. Prepare a statement of retained earnings for the year ended December 31, 1986.

 g. Prepare the balance sheet as of December 31, 1986.

2–7. A friend of yours, Frank Lane, is quite excited over the opportunity he has to purchase the land and several miscellaneous assets of the Farley Bowling Lanes Company for $125,000. Frank tells you that Mr. and Mrs. Farley (the sole stockholders in the company) are moving due to Mr. Farley's ill health. The annual rent on the building and equipment is $18,000.

  Mr. Farley reports that the business earned a profit of $25,000 in 1986 (last year). Frank believes that an annual profit of $25,000 on an investment of $125,000 is a really good deal. But before completing the deal, he asks you to look it over. You agree and discover the following:

 1. Mr. Farley has computed his annual profit for 1986 as the sum of his cash dividends plus the increase in the Cash account: dividends of $15,000 + increase in Cash account of $10,000 = $25,000 profit.

 2. As buyer of the business, Frank will take over responsibility for repayment of a $100,000 loan (plus interest) on the land. The land was acquired at a cost of $208,000 seven years ago.

 3. An analysis of the Cash account shows the following for 1986:

Rental revenues received		$140,000
Cash paid out in 1986 for:		
Wages paid to employees in 1986	$80,000	
Utilities paid for 1986	6,000	
Advertising expenses paid	5,000	
Supplies purchased and used in 1986 . . .	8,000	
Interest paid on loan	6,000	
Loan principal paid	10,000	
Cash dividends	15,000	130,000
Increase in cash balance for the year		$ 10,000

4. You also find that the annual rent of $18,000 and a December utility bill of $1,000 and an advertising bill of $1,500 have not been paid.

Required:

a. Prepare a written report for Frank giving your appraisal of the offer to sell the Farley Bowling Lanes Company. Comment on Mr. Farley's method of computing the annual "profit" of the business.

b. Include in your report an approximate income statement for 1986.

3

ADJUSTING ENTRIES AND COMPLETION OF THE ACCOUNTING CYCLE

THE NEED FOR ADJUSTING ENTRIES

The income statement of an entity for a certain period should report all of the entity's revenues for the period and all of the expenses incurred to generate those revenues. It if does not, it is incomplete, inaccurate, and may be misleading to users. Similarly, a balance sheet that does not report all of an entity's assets, liabilities, and stockholders' equities at the end of a period may also be misleading.

Some relatively small business firms, such as those engaged in rendering services, may account for their revenues and expenses on a cash basis. The **cash basis of accounting** means that, in most instances, expenses and revenues are not recorded until cash is paid out or received. Thus, for example, services rendered to clients in 1985 for which cash was collected in 1986 would be treated as 1986 revenues. Similarly, expenses incurred in 1985 that were paid for in 1986 would be treated as 1986 expenses. Because of potential mismatching of revenues and expenses, the cash basis of accounting is generally considered deficient. It is acceptable only in those circumstances where its results approximate those obtained under the accrual basis of accounting.

The **accrual basis of accounting** recognizes revenues when sales are made or services are rendered, whether or not cash has been received. Expenses are recognized as incurred, whether or not cash has been paid out. The accrual basis is more generally accepted than the cash basis because the accrual basis provides a better measure of an entity's income due to proper *matching* of revenues and expenses.

Since interested parties seek timely information, periodic financial statements must be prepared. In order to prepare such statements, the accountant must arbitrarily divide an entity's life into time periods and attempt to assign economic activity to specific periods. An **accounting period** may be one month, one quarter, or one year long. An accounting period of one year is called an **accounting year** or fiscal year. A **fiscal year** is any 12 consecutive months; it may or may not coincide with the **calendar year,** ending on December 31. Periodic reporting necessitates the preparation of adjusting entries.

Adjusting entries record economic activity that has taken place, but which has not yet been recorded. Some economic activity may be continuous in nature, such as the use of supplies during a month. It is not feasible to make an entry each time a pencil or pen is taken from a supply cabinet for use. The use of one pencil is hardly a recordable event. However, by the end of the month, many supplies have been used and it is then feasible to record their usage. Adjusting entries update certain account balances to record such continuous, previously unrecorded activities. Many adjusting entries are based in part upon estimates of future events. Estimation is necessary in order to provide timely information to users of financial statements.

Adjusting entries must be prepared whenever financial statements are to be prepared. Thus, if monthly financial statements are prepared, monthly adjusting entries are required. By custom, and in some instances by law, business firms report to their stockholders at least annually. Thus, adjusting entries will be required to be made at least once each year.

CLASSES OF ADJUSTING ENTRIES

Adjusting entries can be grouped into two broad classes. One class, **deferred items,** consists of those entries that relate to data previously recorded in the accounts. Adjusting entries in this class normally involve moving data from asset and liability accounts to expense and revenue accounts. (Sometimes the direction is reversed.) The two types of adjustments within this deferred items class are asset/expense adjustments and liability/revenue adjustments.

The other major class of adjusting entries, **accrued items,** consists of entries relating to activities on which no data have been previously recorded in the accounts. These entries involve the initial recording of assets and liabilities and the related revenues and expenses. The two types of adjustments within this accrued items class are asset/revenue adjustments and liability/expense adjustments. Illustration 3.1 shows the two major classes—deferred items and accrued items—and the four types of adjusting entries.

Illustration 3.1
CLASSES OF ADJUSTING ENTRIES

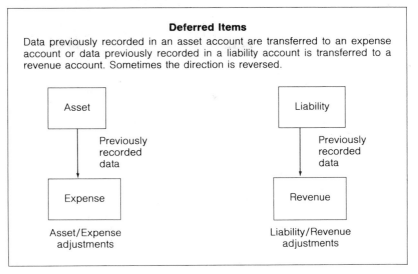

Deferred Items

Data previously recorded in an asset account are transferred to an expense account or data previously recorded in a liability account is transferred to a revenue account. Sometimes the direction is reversed.

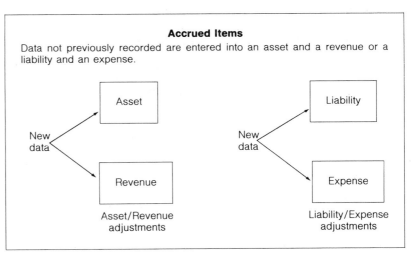

Accrued Items

Data not previously recorded are entered into an asset and a revenue or a liability and an expense.

ADJUSTMENTS FOR DEFERRED ITEMS

The two types of adjustments within the deferred items class are prepaid expenses and unearned revenues. Prepaid expense (asset/expense) adjustments are discussed first.

Asset/Expense Adjustments—Prepaid Expenses and Depreciation

A **prepaid expense** is an asset awaiting assignment to expense. An adjusting entry for a prepaid expense involves recognition of the complete or partial expiration of the ability of such an asset to render future services because it has been used in generating current revenues. This makes the asset less valuable to its owners. Because of its relative importance, several examples of this type of adjusting entry are presented below.

Prepaid insurance. When the premium on an insurance policy is paid in advance of the period covered by the policy, an asset is created. With the passage of time, the value of this asset expires and part of its cost becomes an expense. To illustrate, advance payment of the $7,200 premium on a one-year insurance policy that covers the period from August 1, 1986, to July 31, 1987, creates an asset called prepaid (or unexpired) insurance. An asset exists because benefits—insurance protection—will be received in the future. *The future services that an asset can render are what make the asset "a thing of value" to a business.* The journal entry to record this transaction is:

```
1986
Aug.  1   Prepaid Insurance   .   .   .   .   .   .   .   .   .   .   7,200
              Cash   .   .   .   .   .   .   .   .   .   .   .                  7,200
              To record payment in advance of annual insur-
              ance premium.
```

There are two accounts that relate to insurance, Prepaid Insurance (an asset) and Insurance Expense. After posting this entry, the Prepaid Insurance account has a $7,200 debit balance and the Insurance Expense account has a zero balance:

(Dr.)	**Prepaid Insurance**	*(Cr.)*	*(Dr.)*	**Insurance Expense**	*(Cr.)*
1986 Aug. 1	7,200		Bal.	–0–	

If the company making this insurance payment has a calendar-year accounting period and records adjusting entries only at the end of the year, by December 31 a part of the period covered by the insurance policy has expired. Therefore, a part of the **service potential** (or benefits embodied in the asset) also has expired. The asset now provides less future benefits than when acquired, and this reduction of the asset's ability to provide services must be recognized. The cost of the services used up is treated as an expense. Since the policy provides the same services for every month of its one-year life, it seems logical to assign an equal amount of the initial cost to each month. Thus, with 5 of the 12 months of coverage provided by payment of the premium having elapsed, $\frac{5}{12}$ of the annual premium is charged to expense on December 31. The journal entry and the accounts after posting appear as follows:

| Adjustment 1— |
| Insurance |

```
1986
Dec. 31   Insurance Expense   .   .   .   .   .   .   .   .   .   .   .   .   3,000
              Prepaid Insurance   .   .   .   .   .   .   .   .   .   .   .              3,000
              To record expense for five months, August 1 to
              December 31, 1986.
```

In T-account format, the accounts would appear as follows after posting the two entries:

(Dr.)	Prepaid Insurance				(Cr.)	
1986			1986			Decreased
Aug. 1 Purchased for cash	7,200		Dec. 31 Adjustment	3,000		by $3,000
Bal. after adjustment	4,200					

	(Dr.)	Insurance Expense		(Cr.)
Increased by $3,000	1986			
	Dec. 31 Adjustment	3,000		

The three-column ledger accounts after posting the two entries above appear as follows:

Prepaid Insurance   *Account No. 103*

Date		Explanation	Post. Ref.	Debit	Credit	Balance
1986 Aug.	1	Purchased on Account	GJ63*	7 2 0 0		7 2 0 0 Dr.
Dec.	31	Adjustment	GJ75*		3 0 0 0	4 2 0 0 Dr.

Insurance Expense   *Account No. 504*

Date		Explanation	Post. Ref.	Debit	Credit	Balance
1986 Dec.	31	Adjustment	GJ75*	3 0 0 0		3 0 0 0 Dr.

* Note: These posting references are assumed.

Before the adjusting entry was made, the entire $7,200 was a prepaid expense (an asset). The adjusting entry transferred $3,000 of the $7,200 to insurance expense. The insurance expense of $3,000 is reported in the income statement for the year ended December 31, 1986, as one of the expenses incurred in generating that year's revenues. The remaining amount of the prepaid expense, $4,200, is reported on the balance sheet as an asset. The $4,200 prepaid expense is a measure of the cost of the remaining asset, prepaid insurance. Prepaid insurance is an asset because it provides future benefits; in this case, there is insurance coverage for 7 more months.

In initially recording the purchase of the $7,200 of insurance, the accountant could have followed an alternative procedure. The debit could have been to Insurance Expense rather than Prepaid Insurance as shown below. If this were the case, the adjusting entry would have been a debit to Prepaid Insurance (setting up the asset on the books) and a credit to Insurance Expense for $4,200 (reducing the period's expense). This would have resulted in a balance of $4,200 in the asset account and $3,000 in the expense account as shown in the T-accounts below. Thus, the end result is the same either way, and either method is correct. The adjusting entry, however, will depend on which account was originally debited for the prepayment. This same comment applies to many of the other adjustments that are illustrated in this chapter.

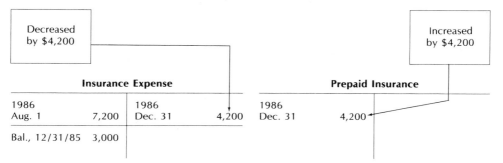

Prepaid rent. Prepaid rent is another example of the continuous incurrence of an expense that results from using up a previously recorded asset. When rent is paid in advance for any substantial period of time, the prepayment is debited to the Prepaid Rent account (an asset) at the date it is paid. Because the benefits resulting from the expenditure are yet to be received, the expenditure creates an asset. Services from the facilities being rented are received *continuously* through time. The expense is incurred *continuously* as time elapses. An entry could be made frequently, even daily, to record the expense incurred. But typically the entry is not made until financial statements are to be prepared. At that time, an entry is made transferring the cost of that portion of the asset that has expired from the asset account to an expense account.

The measurement of rent expense usually presents no problems. Generally, the rental contract specifies the amount of rent per unit of time. If the contract states an annual rental, $\frac{1}{12}$ of this annual rental is charged to expense each month. This may be the case even though there are varying numbers of days in some months. Normally, the variations are not considered significant enough to be taken into consideration.

To illustrate, assume that rent was paid in advance in the amount of $12,000 on September 1, 1986, for one year beginning on that date. The entry made at that time was:

```
1986
Sept. 1   Prepaid Rent  . . . . . . . . . . . .   12,000
              Cash  . . . . . . . . . . . . .              12,000
          To record advance payment of one year's
          rent.
```

The two accounts relating to rent are Prepaid Rent and Rent Expense. After this entry has been posted, the Prepaid Rent account has a $12,000 balance and the Rent Expense account has a zero balance:

(Dr.)	**Prepaid Rent**	*(Cr.)*	*(Dr.)*	**Rent Expense**	*(Cr.)*
1986 Sept. 1 12,000			Bal. –0–		

Assuming the company has a calendar-year accounting period ending December 31, 1986, an adjusting entry must be prepared. Since one third of the period covered by the prepaid rent (4 of 12 months) has elapsed, one third of the $12,000 of prepaid rent is charged to expense. The required adjusting entry and the accounts after posting appear as follows:

<table>
<tr><td>Adjustment 2—
Rent</td><td>

```
1986
Dec. 31   Rent Expense  . . . . . . . . . .   4,000
              Prepaid Rent  . . . . . . . . .          4,000
          To record rent expense for four months.
```

</td></tr>
</table>

The T-accounts would appear as follows after posting the adjusting entry:

(Dr.)	**Prepaid Rent**	*(Cr.)*	
1986 Sept. 1 Cash paid 12,000	1986 Dec. 31 Adjustment 4,000		Decreased by $4,000
Bal. after adjustment 8,000			

(Dr.)	**Rent Expense**	*(Cr.)*
1986 Dec. 31 Adjustment 4,000		

(Increased by $4,000)

The $4,000 rent expense would appear in the income statement for the year ended December 31, 1986. The remaining $8,000 of prepaid rent is reported as an asset in the balance sheet for December 31, 1986.

Supplies on hand. Every business uses assets referred to as supplies in its operations. Supplies may be classified as office supplies (paper, stationery, carbon paper, pencils) or selling supplies (gummed tape, string, paper bags or cartons, wrapping paper) or, possibly, as cleaning supplies (soap, disinfectants). Supplies are frequently bought in bulk. The asset may be called **supplies on hand** or **supplies inventory.**

To illustrate, on December 4, 1986, a company purchased supplies for $1,400 and recorded the transaction as follows:

```
1986
Dec. 4   Supplies on Hand   . . . . . . . . . .   1,400
             Cash   . . . . . . . . . . . . .                1,400
         To record the purchase of supplies for future use.
```

After this entry has been posted, the Supplies on Hand account shows a debit balance of $1,400 and the Supplies Expense account has a zero balance as shown:

(Dr.)	**Supplies on Hand**	(Cr.)	(Dr.)	**Supplies Expense**	(Cr.)
1986 Dec. 4	1,400		Bal.	–0–	

An actual physical inventory (a count of the supplies on hand) at the end of the month showed that only $900 of supplies were on hand. Thus, $500 of supplies must have been used in December. An adjusting journal entry is required to bring the accounts to their proper balances. The entry recognizes the reduction in the asset and the incurrence of an expense through the using up of supplies. From the information given, the asset balance should be $900 and the expense incurred, $500. By making the following adjusting entry, the accounts will be adjusted to those balances:

Adjustment 3— Supplies

```
1986
Dec. 31   Supplies   . . . . . . . . . . . . . . .   500
              Supplies on Hand   . . . . . . . . . .          500
          To record supplies used during December.
```

The T-accounts after posting the entry would appear as follows:

(Dr.)			**Supplies on Hand**			(Cr.)	
1986 Dec. 4	Cash paid	1,400	1986 Dec. 31	Adjustment	500 ◄	Decreased by $500	
Bal. after adjustment		900					

	(Dr.)	**Supplies Expense**	(Cr.)
Increased by $500	1986 → Dec. 31 Adjustment 500	

While the entry to record the usage of supplies could be made when the supplies are issued from the storeroom, it is usually not worth the cost to account so carefully for such small items each time they are issued.

Supplies expense will appear in the income statement. Supplies on hand will be reported as an asset in the balance sheet.

Sometimes prepaid expenses such as insurance, rent, supplies, and advertising are bought and fully used up within one accounting period (usually one month or one year). If so, it is easier to debit an expense rather than an asset at the time of purchase. This procedure avoids having to make an adjusting entry at the end of the accounting period.

Depreciation. Depreciation is another example of the continuous incurrence of an expense that results from the gradual using up of a previously recorded asset. Assets such as buildings, machinery, and equipment will not continue to provide benefits or services indefinitely. Wear and tear resulting from their use will eventually cause them to be disposed of. The overall period of time involved in using up such assets is, however, less definite than in the case of an insurance premium or prepaid rent. The life of such assets (called **depreciable assets**) must be estimated in advance by the accountants or managers of a business.

In addition to estimating the life of a depreciable asset, the accountant must estimate the **scrap** (or salvage) **value** that the asset may have at the time of disposal in the future. For example, if you plan to dispose of your car three years after you purchase it, you can estimate the "trade-in" value that it will have at that time. Trade-in value is very similar to scrap value. The difference between the cost of an asset and its estimated scrap value is sometimes referred to as an asset's **depreciable cost.** This difference is the net cost of using the asset during its **useful life.**

Even though depreciable assets involve the use of estimates (for scrap value and life), the pattern of incurring an expense because of the expiration of service potential of an asset is basically the same as it was for a prepaid insurance premium. The cost of the asset less its scrap value is divided by the estimated number of years of life to find the amount of asset cost to be charged as an expense to each time period. **Depreciation expense** is the cost of a depreciable asset assigned to any time period. **Depreciation accounting** is the process of allocating the cost of a depreciable asset over the time periods assumed to benefit by that asset's usage.

The method of depreciation presented here is known as straight-line depreciation. (Other methods are discussed in Chapter 10.) The three factors involved in the computation of depreciation are:

1. Asset cost.
2. Estimated useful life.
3. Estimated scrap value.

The **depreciation formula** is as follows:

$$\text{Annual depreciation} = \frac{\text{Cost} - \text{Estimated scrap value}}{\text{Number of years of useful life}}$$

If a depreciable asset is used for less than a full annual period, only a fraction of the annual cost should be assigned to the expense account. In other words, if the asset has only been used for three months of a year, only $3/12$ (or $1/4$) of the annual amount should be recorded as an expense in that year.

Depreciation is sometimes expressed as an annual percentage rate determined by dividing the annual amount of depreciation by the cost of the asset. For instance, $1,000 ÷ $10,000 = 10$ percent depreciation rate.

The accumulated depreciation account. The amount of an asset that expires in a period is not credited directly to the asset account itself but to an account called Accumulated Depreciation. The **Accumulated Depreciation account** is a type of contra account. A **contra account** is an account that is directly related to another account, but it carries the opposite type of balance. The accumulated depreciation account is a **contra asset account.** Since assets generally carry debit balances, a contra asset carries a credit balance.

Why is a contra asset account used to account for depreciation? Asset accounts such as prepaid insurance or rent may be credited directly when their values expire due to their short-term nature and the fact that it is known exactly what periods of time are benefited by them. Depreciable assets, on the other hand, require the use of estimates for both life and scrap value. Therefore, the recorded amounts of depreciation are really quite tentative. To provide more complete information on the balance sheet, depreciable asset accounts are shown at their original acquisition cost and the related accumulated depreciation is shown separately. The difference between the cost and the accumulated depreciation for any depreciable asset is called **book value,** or the cost not yet allocated as an expense. The balance in the accumulated depreciation account increases each year by the amount of depreciation recorded. Eventually, the accumulated depreciation account reaches the amount originally calculated as the depreciable cost of the asset.

Depreciation accounting illustrated. To illustrate the accounting for depreciation, assume that at December 31, 1986, a company owns one delivery truck that cost $9,200. The truck was purchased on

January 1, 1986. It is expected to have a useful life of five years; scrap value is estimated at $1,200. Therefore, the depreciation expense for one year equals ($9,200 − $1,200) ÷ 5, or $1,600. This amount of depreciation expense is allocated to 1986.

Depreciation for 1986 is recorded by the following entry:

<table>
<tr><td>Adjustment 4— Depreciation</td><td>1986
Dec. 31   Depreciation Expense—Delivery Truck   . . .   1,600
         Accumulated Depreciation—
         Delivery Truck   1,600
        To record the depreciation expense for the
        year.</td></tr>
</table>

The T-accounts would appear as follows after posting the adjusting entry:

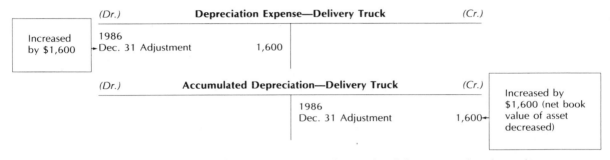

(Dr.)   **Depreciation Expense—Delivery Truck**   *(Cr.)*

Increased by $1,600

1986
Dec. 31 Adjustment   1,600

(Dr.)   **Accumulated Depreciation—Delivery Truck**   *(Cr.)*

1986
Dec. 31 Adjustment   1,600

Increased by $1,600 (net book value of asset decreased)

The ledger accounts involving the delivery truck, after adjustment, will appear as follows:

Delivery Truck   *Account No. 130*

Date		Explanation	Post. Ref.	Debit	Credit	Balance
1986 Jan.	1	Purchased one truck	GJ8	9 2 0 0		9 2 0 0

Accumulated Depreciation—Delivery Truck   *Account No. 131*

Date		Explanation	Post. Ref.	Debit	Credit	Balance
1986 Dec.	31	Adjustment	GJ14		1 6 0 0	1 6 0 0

Depreciation Expense—Delivery Truck   *Account No. 418*

Date		Explanation	Post. Ref.	Debit	Credit	Balance
1986 Dec.	31	Adjustment	GJ14	1 6 0 0		1 6 0 0

In the balance sheet at December 31, 1986, the asset accounts include the following:

Assets

Delivery truck	$9,200	
Less: Accumulated depreciation—delivery truck	1,600	$7,600

The portion of the cost of the asset not yet charged to expense at the end of the first year is $7,600. Since expected scrap value is $1,200, only $6,400 is expected to be charged to expense in future years. Since another $1,600 of depreciation would be recorded at the end of each of the next four years, the balance sheet at the end of the fifth year would show the following:

Assets

Delivery truck	$9,200	
Less: Accumulated depreciation—delivery truck	8,000	$1,200

Depreciation expense is reported in the income statement with all other expenses.

Liability/Revenue Adjustments— Unearned Revenues

The second type of adjusting entry under deferred items are those involving unearned revenues. An adjustment involving unearned revenues covers those situations where the customer has transferred assets, usually cash, to a company prior to the receipt of merchandise or services. When assets are received before being earned, a liability called **unearned revenue** is created. Such receipts are debited to Cash and credited to a liability account called Unearned Fees, Revenue Received in Advance, Advances by Customers, or some similar title. The seller is obligated either to provide the goods or services or return the customer's money. By providing the merchandise or performing the services, revenue is earned and the liability is canceled.

Advance payments are received for many items such as delivery services, tickets, rent, and magazine or newspaper subscriptions. While only advance receipt of delivery fees will be illustrated and discussed, the other items are treated similarly.

Unearned delivery fees. On December 7, a company received $4,500 from a customer in payment for future delivery services. The entry was recorded as follows:

1986			
Dec. 7	Cash	4,500	
	Unearned Delivery Fees		4,500
	To record the receipt of cash from a customer in payment for future delivery services.		

The two T-accounts relating to delivery fees are Unearned Delivery Fees (a liability) and Delivery Service Revenue. These accounts appear as follows after this entry has been posted.

(Dr.) **Unearned Delivery Fees** *(Cr.)*	*(Dr.)* **Delivery Service Revenue** *(Cr.)*
1986 Dec. 7 4,500	Bal. –0–

The liability established when the cash was received will be converted into revenue as the delivery services are performed. An adjusting entry is required in order to recognize the earning of revenue and the reduction of the related liability. Assuming that one third of the delivery services paid for in advance have been performed by the end of December, the required adjusting entry is:

| Adjustment 5— Previously unearned revenue | 1986
Dec. 31   Unearned Delivery Fees 1,500
           Delivery Service Revenue   1,500
           To transfer a portion of delivery fees from the
           liability account to the revenue account. |

The T-accounts would appear as follows after the adjusting entry has been posted:

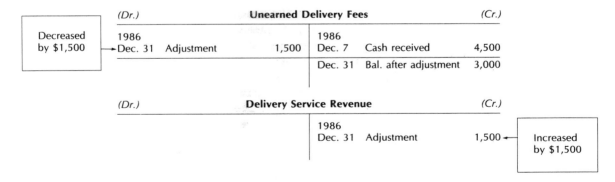

Decreased by $1,500	*(Dr.)*	**Unearned Delivery Fees**	*(Cr.)*	
	1986 Dec. 31 Adjustment 1,500		1986 Dec. 7 Cash received 4,500	
			Dec. 31 Bal. after adjustment 3,000	

(Dr.)	**Delivery Service Revenue**	*(Cr.)*	
		1986 Dec. 31 Adjustment 1,500	Increased by $1,500

Delivery service revenue is reported in the income statement for 1986. The $3,000 balance in the Unearned Delivery Fees account is reported as a liability in the balance sheet. In 1987, the $3,000 will be earned and transferred to a revenue account.

ADJUSTMENTS FOR ACCRUED ITEMS

The two types of adjustments within the accrued items class are accrued assets and accrued liabilities. Accrued assets are discussed first.

Asset/Revenue Adjustments— Accrued Assets

Accrued assets are those assets that exist at the end of an accounting period but have not yet been recorded. They represent rights to receive payments that are not legally due at the balance sheet date. At the end of an accounting period, any such rights must be recognized by preparing an adjusting entry. An example of this type of adjustment includes revenues earned that have not been billed or collected.

Interest revenue. The interest received periodically on investments such as bonds and savings accounts is literally earned moment by moment. Rarely is payment of the interest made on the last day of the accounting period. Thus, the accounting records normally will not show the amount of interest revenue earned nor the total assets owned by the investor unless an adjusting entry is made. An entry at the end of the accounting period is needed that debits a receivable account (an asset) and credits a revenue account to record the asset owned and the interest earned.

For example, assume that a company deposits some money in a savings account. The interest is received twice a year on May 1 and November 1 in the amount of $1,800 on each date. Interest, then, is being earned at the rate of $300 per month ($1,800 ÷ 6). If the account was opened on May 2, 1986, Interest Revenue is credited with the $1,800 of cash received on November 1. At December 31, 1986, an additional two months' interest has been earned, although no money will be received until May 1, 1987. An entry must be made to show the amount of interest earned and the asset (the right to receive this interest) at December 31, 1986. The entry to record the accrual of interest revenue is:

Adjustment 6—Interest	Accrued Interest Receivable 600	
	Interest Revenue	600
	To record two months' interest revenue.	

The T-accounts relating to interest would appear as follows:

Accrued Interest Receivable

Increased by $600	1986 Dec. 31 Adjustment 600	

Interest Revenue

	1986 Nov. 1 Cash received 1,800	
	Bal. before adjustment 1,800 Dec. 31 Adjustment 600	Increased by $600
	Bal. after adjustment 2,400	

The $600 debit balance in Accrued Interest Receivable is reported as an asset in the December 31, 1986, balance sheet. The term **accrued** refers to a claim that comes into existence over time. The claim accumulates gradually with the passage of time. the $2,400 credit balance in Interest Revenue is the interest earned during the year. Recall that *under accrual basis accounting, it does not matter whether cash was collected during the year or not.* The interest revenue earned is reported in the income statement for the year.

   Unbilled service fees.   Services may be performed for customers in one accounting period while the billing for those services is in a different accounting period. Assume a company performed $1,000 of delivery services on account for clients in the last few days of December. Because it takes time to do the paper work, the clients will be billed for the services in January. The necessary adjusting entry at December 31, 1986, is:

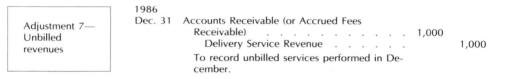

> Adjustment 7—
> Unbilled
> revenues

	1986		
	Dec. 31	Accounts Receivable (or Accrued Fees Receivable)	1,000	
		Delivery Service Revenue		1,000
		To record unbilled services performed in December.		

After posting the adjusting entry the T-accounts will appear as follows:

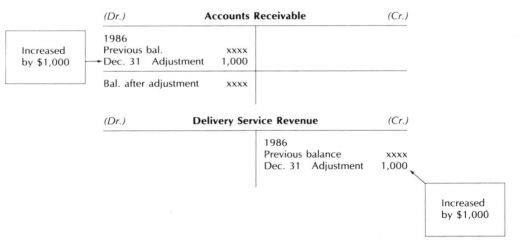

(Dr.)   **Accounts Receivable**   (Cr.)

> Increased
> by $1,000

1986
Previous bal.   xxxx
Dec. 31   Adjustment   1,000

Bal. after adjustment   xxxx

(Dr.)   **Delivery Service Revenue**   (Cr.)

1986
Previous balance   xxxx
Dec. 31   Adjustment   1,000

> Increased
> by $1,000

   The delivery service revenue will appear in the income statement, and the accounts receivable will appear in the balance sheet.

Liability/Expense Adjustments— Accrued Liabilities

Accrued liabilities are those liabilities that exist at the end of an accounting period, but that have not yet been recorded. They represent obligations to make payments that are not legally due at the balance sheet date. At the end of an accounting period, any such obligations and the related expenses must be recognized in an adjusting entry. Accrued salaries, for example, are accrued liabilities that require adjustment.

Salaries. The recording of the payment of employee salaries (or wages) usually involves a debit to an expense account and a credit to cash. Unless salaries are paid on the last day of the accounting period for a pay period ending on that date, an adjusting entry will be required to record any salaries incurred but not yet paid.

Assume that a company paid $3,600 of salaries on Friday, December 27, 1986, to cover the first four weeks of December. The entry made at that time was:

```
1986
Dec. 27   Salaries Expense  . . . . . . . . . .  3,600
                Cash   . . . . . . . . . . . . .        3,600
          Paid salaries for the first four weeks of Decem-
          ber.
```

If salaries are $3,600 for four weeks, they are $900 per week. Assuming a five-day workweek, daily salaries are $180. Since the last day of December 1986 is a Tuesday, the expense account does not show salaries earned by employees for the last two days of the month. Nor does the account show the employer's obligation to pay these salaries. The accounts pertaining to salaries appear as follows before adjustment:

(Dr.)	**Salaries Expense**	*(Cr.)*	*(Dr.)*	**Accrued Salaries Payable**	*(Cr.)*
1986 Dec. 27	3,600			Bal.	–0–

The following adjusting entry is needed on December 31:

Adjustment 8— Accrued salaries

```
1986
Dec. 31   Salaries Expense  . . . . . . . . . .  360
                Accrued Salaries Payable  . . . . . . .       360
          To accrue two days' salaries that were earned but
          are unpaid.
```

The two accounts involved appear as follows after adjustment:

(Dr.)		**Salaries Expense**		*(Cr.)*
1986 Dec. 27		3,600		
Dec. 31	Adjustment	360		
Bal. after adjustment		3,960		

Increased by $360

(Dr.)		**Accrued Salaries Payable**		*(Cr.)*
			1986 Dec. 31	Adjustment	360

Increased by $360

The debit in the adjusting journal entry brings the month's salaries expense up to its correct $3,960 amount for income statement purposes. The credit records the $360 salary liability to employees. The accrued salaries payable is shown as a liability in the balance sheet.

Failure to prepare proper adjusting entries causes net income to be in error. The following diagram shows the effect on net income of failing to record each of the major types of adjusting entries:

Failure to Recognize	Effect on Net Income	Effect on Balance Sheet Items
1. Consumption of the benefits of an asset (prepaid expense).	Overstates	Overstates assets Overstates retained earnings
2. Earning of previously unearned revenues.	Understates	Overstates liabilities Understates retained earnings
3. Accrual of assets.	Understates	Understates assets Understates retained earnings
4. Accrual of liabilities.	Overstates	Understates liabilities Overstates retained earnings

This chapter has discussed and illustrated many, but not all, of the typical adjusting entries that companies must make at the end of an accounting period. Other types of adjusting entries are covered in later chapters.

CLOSING ENTRIES

One step remains in our illustration of the financial accounting process—a step known as "closing the books." As illustrated, after adjusting entries have been prepared and posted, the accounts contain basically two types of information: (1) information relating to the activities for the period just ended (reported in the income statement) and (2) information on financial condition (reported in the balance sheet).

The first type of information is found in the expense and revenue accounts. As already indicated, these accounts are temporary subdivisions of the Retained Earnings account. They help the accountant fulfill a most important task—the determination of periodic net income. But after the financial statements for the period have been prepared, these temporary accounts have served their purpose. They must now be brought to a zero balance, or "closed," to use accounting jargon. In this way, information pertaining to the next period can be gathered in them.

The balance in each expense and revenue account is transferred to an account called Income Summary. This is a **clearing** account used only at the end of the accounting period. It summarizes the expenses and revenues for the period, with the difference between these two being either net income or a net loss. Since revenue accounts have credit balances, they are debited and Income Summary credited. Conversely, expense accounts have debit balances, so they are credited and Income Summary debited. The Income Summary now contains either a debit (net loss) or a credit (net income) balance; it is then debited or credited to bring it to a zero balance. Retained Earnings is credited or debited to keep the entry in balance. With the making of this last entry, the books are closed. Note carefully that only expense and revenue accounts and the Income Summary account are closed. If dividends are recorded by debiting Retained Earnings and crediting Cash, no closing entry for that item is required. But, if dividends are recorded by debiting a separate Dividends account and crediting Cash, the Dividends account must be credited and Retained Earnings debited as part of the closing process.

The closing process, using T-accounts and assuming there is net income for the period, is as shown below.

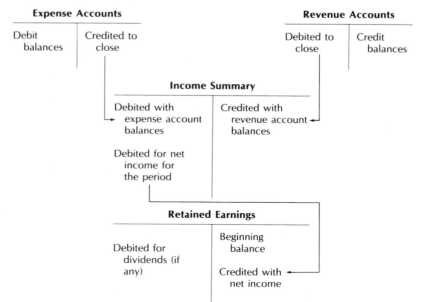

Assume the income statement shown in Illustration 3.2 is for a company called Jane's, Inc. The accounts to be closed are all of the expense and revenue accounts shown in the income statement.

Illustration 3.2

JANE'S, INC.
Income Statement
For the Year Ended December 31, 1986

Sales		$145,000
Expenses:		
Salaries	$75,000	
Advertising	5,000	
Utilities	8,000	
Rent	12,000	
Payroll taxes expense	6,000	
Insurance	2,000	
Supplies	9,000	
Depreciation expense—Equipment	4,000	
Depreciation expense—Fixtures	2,000	
Miscellaneous	1,000	
Total expenses		124,000
Net income		$ 21,000

In journal form, the closing entries for Jane's, Inc. would read:

Sales	145,000	
Income Summary		145,000
To close the Sales revenue account.		
Income Summary	124,000	
Salaries Expense		75,000
Advertising Expense		5,000
Utilities Expense		8,000
Rent Expense		12,000
Payroll Taxes Expense		6,000
Insurance Expense		2,000
Supplies Expense		9,000
Depreciation Expense—Equipment		4,000
Depreciation Expense—Fixtures		2,000
Miscellaneous Expense		1,000
To close the expense accounts for the year.		
Income Summary	21,000	
Retained Earnings		21,000
To close net income for the year to Retained Earnings.		

When the entries are posted, each of the company's expense and revenue accounts will be reduced to a zero balance. Thus, they are ready to accumulate data on the operations for the year 1987. Note that Retained Earnings will have the same balance that it would have if all expenses and revenues had been entered directly in it. But the use of expense and revenue accounts permits classification of these elements and makes them readily available for reporting in the income statement.

The Use of a Worksheet

The appendix to this chapter describes and illustrates how a worksheet could have been used in the above example involving Jane's, Inc. The use of such a worksheet is optional but often helpful.

The Financial Accounting Process Summarized

The steps involved in the operation of an accounting system are often referred to collectively as the accounting cycle. These steps include:

1. Journalizing transactions (and other events) in the journal.
2. Posting journal entries to ledger accounts.
3. Taking a trial balance of the accounts.
4. Journalizing the needed adjusting entries.
5. Posting the adjusting entries to the accounts.
6. Preparing the financial statements.
7. Journalizing the closing entries.
8. Posting the closing entries to the accounts.

THE CLASSIFIED BALANCE SHEET

An **unclassified balance sheet** has only major categories labeled assets, liabilities, and stockholders' equity. A **classified balance sheet** subdivides at least some of the three major categories in order to provide useful information for interpretation and analysis by users of financial statements.

An example of a classified balance sheet is given in Illustration 3.3. It contains major categories of assets and liabilities. Accounts are then classified into these major categories. Notice that assets appear above liabilities and stockholders' equity in the Illustration. This vertical format is as appropriate as the horizontal format for either a classified or unclassified balance sheet. The horizontal format has assets on the left side and liabilities and stockholders' equity on the right side.

Included below are definitions and illustrations of accounts to be included under each major classification.

Current Assets

Current assets are cash and other assets that will be converted to cash or used up during a relatively short period of time, usually a year or less. Current assets are normally listed in the order of liquidity (how readily they can be converted to cash).

The current assets commonly found in a service-type business are as follows:

Cash includes deposits in banks available for current operations at the balance sheet date, plus cash on hand consisting of currency,

Illustration 3.3
A CLASSIFIED BALANCE SHEET

WEST CORPORATION
Balance Sheet
June 30, 1986

Assets

Current assets:

Cash		$ 40,000	
Accounts receivable		55,000	
Notes receivable		15,000	
Prepaid insurance		2,000	
Total current assets			$112,000

Property, plant, and equipment:

Land		$114,000	
Building	$300,000		
Less Accumulated depreciation	100,000	200,000	
Store equipment	$ 75,000		
Less: Accumulated depreciation	15,000	60,000	
Office equipment	$ 18,000		
Less: Accumulated depreciation	6,000	12,000	
Total property, plant, and equipment			386,000
Total assets			$498,000

Liabilities and Stockholders' Equity

Current liabilities:

Accounts payable		$ 25,000	
Notes payable		6,000	
Accrued wages payable		800	
Unearned subscriptions revenue		1,100	
Total current liabilities			$ 32,900

Long-term liabilities:

Notes payable, 10%, due in 1997			150,000
Total liabilities			$182,900

Stockholders' equity:

Capital stock		$250,000	
Retained earnings		65,100	
Total stockholders' equity			315,100
Total liabilities and stockholders' equity			$498,000

undeposited checks, drafts, and money orders. Normally, cash is the first current asset to appear in a balance sheet.

An **account receivable** is an amount owed to a concern by a customer (debtor). The account receivable arises when a service (or merchandise) is sold and cash is not received immediately. Normally, no written evidence of indebtedness is given by the customer except by affixing his or her signature to the sales invoice or delivery ticket.

A **note** is an unconditional written promise to pay a definite sum of money at a certain or determinable date, usually with interest at a specified rate. A note is a *note receivable* on the balance sheet of the enterprise to which the note is given and is a *note payable* on the balance sheet of the promisor. A note receivable arises *(a)* when a sale is made and a note is taken from the customer, *(b)* when a customer gives a note for an amount due on open account, or *(c)* when money is loaned and a note is received as evidence.

Prepaid expenses are items that have been paid for in advance of their usage. Such items will be used up during the next accounting period. If they were not paid for in advance, they would require the disbursement of cash in the following period.

Property, Plant, and Equipment

Property, plant, and equipment are types of assets acquired for use in a business rather than for resale. Property, plant, and equipment also are termed *plant assets* or *fixed assets.* They are called fixed assets because they are to be used for long-term purposes. Several of the more common types of property, plant, and equipment are described below:

Land is ground upon which the business buildings of the enterprise are located.

Buildings that appear in the property, plant, and equipment section of a balance sheet are quarters used to carry on the business; buildings owned as investments are not included as plant assets.

Machinery is heavy equipment used in manufacturing a product or performing a service for a customer. This item is not included in Illustration 3.3.

Store equipment, or **store fixtures,** includes items such as showcases, counters, tools, chairs, and cash registers.

Office equipment, or **office fixtures,** includes items such as file cabinets, calculators, typewriters, computers, desks, and chairs.

Delivery equipment is utilized primarily in making deliveries to customers. This item is not included in Illustration 3.3.

Accumulated depreciation is a contra asset account to depreciable assets such as buildings, machinery, and equipment. It shows total depreciation taken to date on the assets.

Current Liabilities

A **current liability** is a debt—usually due within one year—the payment of which normally will require the use of current assets. Examples of current liabilities follow:

Accounts payable are amounts owed to creditors for items purchased from them. In the balance sheet, accounts payable are shown in one amount, which is the sum of the individual accounts payable.

Notes payable are unconditional written promises to pay a certain sum of money at a definite future date. The notes may arise from borrowing money from a bank, the purchase of assets, or the giving of a note in settlement of an account payable. Notes payable to banks are known as *nontrade notes;* those arising from purchases are known as *trade notes.* Generally, only notes payable due in one year or less are included as current liabilities.

Accrued wages payable are amounts owed to employees for services rendered but for which payment has not been made at the balance sheet date. The wages have not been paid at the balance sheet date because they are not due until later.

Unearned revenues (revenues received in advance) result when payment is received for goods or services before it is earned, such as in a subscription to a magazine. They represent a liability to return the asset received or to perform the agreed services or other contractual requirements, usually within the succeeding accounting period.

Long-Term Liabilities

Long-term liabilities are those not due for a relatively long period of time, usually more than one year. It is a good policy to show maturity dates in the balance sheet for all long-term liabilities.

Notes payable with maturity dates at least one year beyond the balance sheet date are long-term liabilities.

Stockholders' Equity

This section shows the owners' interest (equity) in the business. This interest is equal to the amount contributed plus the income left in the business.

Capital stock shows the capital paid into the company as the owners' investment.

Retained earnings show the cumulative income of the company less the amounts distributed to the owners in the form of dividends.

SUMMARY

Adjusting entries are made to include information on economic activity that has occurred but has not been recorded. They fall into two major classes; namely, those involving deferrals and those involving accruals.

Specific types of adjustments involving deferrals are for (1) asset/expense and (2) liability/revenue items. Adjustments involving accruals are for (3) asset/revenue and (4) liability/expense items. In (1), the adjustment involves recognition of an expense as a result of the using up of a previously recorded asset; examples include insurance, rent, supplies, depreciation, and advertising. In (2), the adjustment involves recognition of the earning of revenue and the cancellation of a liability by providing services for which customers pay in advance; examples include delivery services, tickets, rent, and subscriptions. In (3), the adjustment involves recognition of the growth of an asset as a result of the rendering of services to customers; examples include interest and various kinds of services. In (4), the adjustment involves recognition of an expense and the corresponding obligation to pay as a result of the receipt of services;

examples include salaries and interest. In all cases, adjusting entries involve changing account balances at the end of the period from what they presently contain to what they should contain for proper financial reporting.

At the end of the accounting period, after financial statements have been prepared, the expense and revenue accounts are closed. The closing process brings all the revenue and expense accounts to zero balances to be ready to receive information on the next period's activities.

A classified balance sheet shows the assets divided into categories such as current assets and property, plant and equipment. The liabilities are divided into current and long-term categories.

APPENDIX

THE WORKSHEET FOR A SERVICE COMPANY

In manually operated accounting systems containing large numbers of accounts, the accounting activities to be completed at the end of a financial reporting period may be organized and handled more efficiently through use of a worksheet. A worksheet is simply a sheet of paper containing a number of columns and lines for recording account titles, item descriptions, and dollar amounts. Since it is used internally only, it can take on a variety of forms. But to be of any real value, it will, as a minimum, contain columns for an unadjusted trial balance, adjusting entries, an income statement, and a balance sheet. An expanded version of a worksheet is presented in Illustration 3.4 and discussed below.

The Unadjusted Trial Balance Columns

Instead of preparing a separate trial balance, the open accounts in the ledger (assumed for Jane's, Inc.) are entered in the first pair of columns titled Unadjusted Trial Balance in the worksheet for the year ended December 31, 1986. The columns are summed, and the equality of the debits and credits in the ledger is shown by entering the totals ($187,000) immediately after the last item in the trial balance.

The Adjustments Columns

In the next pair of columns, all of the adjustments required to bring the accounts up to date prior to the preparation of financial statements are entered. The adjustments for Jane's, Inc. are assumed to be based on the following data:

a. An inventory taken at year-end shows supplies on hand with a cost of $3,000.

Illustration 3.4

JANE'S, INC.
Worksheet
For the Year Ended December 31, 1986

	Unadjusted Trial Balance		Adjustments*		Adjusted Trial Balance		Income Statement		Statement of Retained Earnings		Balance Sheet	
	Dr.	Cr.	Dr.	Cr.	Dr.	Cr.	Dr.	Cr.	Dr.	Cr.	Dr.	Cr.
Cash	5,000				5,000						5,000	
Supplies on hand	12,000			(a) 9,000	3,000						3,000	
Prepaid insurance	4,000			(b) 2,000	2,000						2,000	
Equipment	40,000				40,000						40,000	
Fixtures	20,000				20,000						20,000	
Accounts payable		2,000				2,000						2,000
Capital stock		30,000				30,000						30,000
Retained earnings, 12/31/85		10,000				10,000				10,000		
Dividends	2,000				2,000				2,000			
Sales		145,000				145,000		145,000				
Salaries expense	72,000		(e) 3,000		75,000		75,000					
Advertising expense	5,000				5,000		5,000					
Utilities expense	8,000				8,000		8,000					
Rent expense	12,000				12,000		12,000					
Payroll taxes expense	6,000				6,000		6,000					
Miscellaneous expense	1,000				1,000		1,000					
	187,000	187,000										
Supplies expense			(a) 9,000		9,000		9,000					
Insurance expense			(b) 2,000		2,000		2,000					
Depreciation expense—equipment			(c) 4,000		4,000		4,000					
Accumulated depreciation—equipment				(c) 4,000		4,000						4,000
Depreciation expense—fixtures			(d) 2,000		2,000		2,000					
Accumulated depreciation—fixtures				(d) 2,000		2,000						2,000
Accrued salaries payable				(e) 3,000		3,000						3,000
			20,000	20,000	196,000	196,000	124,000	145,000				
Net income for 1986							21,000			21,000		
							145,000	145,000		31,000		
Retained earnings, December 31, 1986									29,000			29,000
									31,000	31,000	70,000	70,000

* These are keyed to the adjustments described in the chapter on pages 92–94.

b. The $4,000 balance in the Prepaid Insurance account represents the premium paid for insurance coverage for the years 1986 and 1987.

c. The equipment was acquired on January 1, 1986, and has an estimated useful life of 10 years with no scrap value.

d. The fixtures were acquired in January 1, 1986, and have an estimated useful life of 10 years with no scrap value.

e. There are $3,000 of unpaid salaries at year-end.

One advantage of a worksheet is that it assembles all of the accounts in one place, where they may easily be studied to determine the need for possible adjustment. As a result, entries are not likely to be overlooked.

After all of the adjusting entries are entered in the Adjustments columns, the two columns are totaled and their equality is noted as a partial check of the arithmetic accuracy of the work completed thus far.

The Adjusted Trial Balance Columns

After the adjustments have been entered, the adjusted balance of each account is determined and entered in the Adjusted Trial Balance columns.

Note carefully how the rules of debit and credit determine whether an entry increases or decreases the balance in the account. For example, Supplies on hand has a debit balance of $12,000 which is decreased by a credit of $9,000 to a total of $3,000—the correct balance for financial reporting purposes.

The balances in the Adjusted Trial Balance columns are summed. The equality of the accounts with debit balances and those with credit balances is noted as a check upon the arithmetic accuracy of the work completed.

The Income Statement Columns

All of the accounts in the Adjusted Trial Balance columns that will appear in the Income Statement (the expense and revenue accounts) are now extended into the Income Statement columns—revenues as credits, expenses as debits. Each column is subtotaled, revealing revenues (credits) of $145,000 and expenses (debits) of $124,000. This means that the net income for the period amounted to $21,000. This amount is entered in the debit column to bring the two column totals into agreement. Note the similarity of the debit here to the debit in the Income Summary account to close or transfer net income to the Retained Earnings account. A net loss would, of course, be recorded in the opposite manner—that is, as a credit.

The Statement of Retained Earnings Columns

These columns contain the items that appear in the statement of retained earnings, namely: the $10,000 beginning balance of retained earnings as a credit, the $21,000 net income for the period as a credit, and the $2,000 of dividends as a debit. The columns are subtotaled, and the difference between the two subtotals, the ending balance of retained earnings, $29,000, is entered in the debit column in order to bring the two column totals into balance.

The Balance Sheet Columns

All of the asset, liability, and stockholders' equity accounts are extended into the Balance Sheet columns—assets as debits and the others as credits. Note that the ending $29,000 balance in Retained Earnings is carried into the credit column. Once again, to check the arithmetic accuracy of the work completed, the columns are totaled and their agreement is noted.

The Completed Worksheet

Some accountants, in completing a worksheet, enter brief explanations keyed to the adjusting entries in the lower left-hand corner of the worksheet. Such a practice is useful for complicated adjustments, but is not necessary for the relatively routine adjustments illustrated here.

When the worksheet has been completed, all of the information needed to prepare the financial statements is readily available. It need only be recast into a more formal format.

Note, also, that it would be a relatively routine matter to journalize the adjusting and closing entries in the journal and then post them to the accounts. The adjusting entries can be readily prepared from information in the Adjustments columns and closing entries from the items in the Income Statement columns. But, since financial statements can be prepared from the worksheet, such entries are not likely to be entered formally in the journal and posted to the accounts at any time other than at the formal annual closing of the books. Thus, one of the real advantages of using a worksheet is that (monthly or quarterly) financial statements can be prepared without going through the work of journalizing and posting adjusting and closing entries.

The worksheet is a very convenient tool that assists in completing the accounting tasks at the end of the accounting period. While its use is optional, it is almost always used by accountants.

QUESTIONS

1. Why are adjusting entries necessary? Why not treat every cash disbursement as an expense and every cash receipt as a revenue when the cash changes hands?

2. Give an example of each of the following:
   a. Equal growth of an expense and a liability.
   b. Earning of revenue that was previously recorded as unearned revenue.

c. Equal growth of an asset and a revenue.

d. Equal growth of an expense and decrease in an asset.

3. "Adjusting entries would not be necessary if the cash basis of accounting were followed (assuming no mistakes were made in recording cash transactions as they occurred). Under the cash basis, receipts that are of a revenue nature are considered revenue when received, and expenditures that are of an expense nature are considered expenses when paid. It is the use of the accrual basis of accounting, where an effort is made to match expenses incurred against the revenues they created that makes adjusting entries necessary." Do you agree with this statement? Why?

4. Why don't accountants keep all the accounts at their proper balances continuously throughout the period so that adjusting entries would not have to be made before financial statements are prepared?

5. Identify the two major classes of adjusting entries and identify the types of adjusting entries that are included in each.

6. A fellow student makes the following statement: "It is easy to tell whether a company is using the cash or accrual basis of accounting. When an amount is paid for future rent or insurance services, a firm that is using the cash basis will debit an expense account while a firm that is using the accrual basis will debit an asset account." Is the student correct?

7. You notice that the Supplies on Hand account has a debit balance of $2,700 at the end of the accounting period. How would you determine the extent to which this account needs adjustment?

8. It may be said that some assets are converted into expenses as they expire and that some liabilities become revenues as they are earned. Give examples of asset and liability accounts for which the statement is true. Give examples of asset and liability accounts to which the statement does not apply.

9. What does the term *accrued liability* mean?

10. What is meant by the term *service potential?*

11. Give the depreciation formula for straight-line depreciation.

12. When assets are received before they are earned, what type of account is credited? As the amounts are earned, what type of account is credited?

13. The accountant often speaks of expired costs. Do costs literally expire?

14. What does the word *accrued* mean? Is there a conceptual difference between interest payable and accrued interest payable?

15. It is more difficult to match expenses incurred with revenues earned than it would be to match expenses paid with revenues received. Do you think that the effort is worthwhile?

16. What are the closing entries? In general, why must they be made?

17. How is a classified balance sheet different from an unclassified balance sheet?

18. (Based on the Appendix.) Describe the purposes for which a worksheet is prepared.

EXERCISES

1. a. A one-year insurance policy is purchased on August 1 for $1,200 and the following entry is made at that time:

Prepaid insurance	. . . .	1,200
Cash	. . . .	1,200

What adjusting entry is necessary at December 31, the end of the accounting year?

b. Give the adjusting entry that would be necessary if the entry to record the purchase of the policy on August 1 had been:

Insurance Expense	. . . .	1,200
Cash	. . . .	1,200

c. Show by the use of T-accounts that the end result is the same under either *(a)* or *(b)*.

2. Assume that rent of $7,200 was paid on September 1, 1986, to cover a one-year period from that date. Prepaid Rent was debited. If financial statements are prepared only on December 31 of each year, what adjusting entry is necessary on December 31, 1986, to bring the accounts involved to their proper balances?

3. If in Exercise 2 Rent Expense had been debited on September 1, 1986, what adjusting entry would have been necessary on December 31, 1986?

4. At December 31, 1986, an adjusting entry was made as follows:

Rent Expense	. . . .	2,000
Prepaid Rent	. . . .	2,000

You know that the gross amount of rent paid was $6,000, and it was to cover a one-year period. Determine:

a. The opening date of the year to which the $6,000 of rent applies.

b. The entry that was made on the date the rent was paid.

5. Office supplies were purchased for cash on May 2, 1986, for $1,600. Show two ways in which this entry could be recorded, then show the adjusting entry that would be necessary for each, assuming that $400 of the supplies remained at the end of the year.

6. Assume that a company acquires a building on January 1, 1986, at a cost of $500,000. The building has an estimated useful life of 40 years and an estimated scrap value of $100,000. What adjusting entry is needed on December 31, 1986, to record the depreciation for the entire year 1986?

7. A building is being depreciated by an amount of $14,000 per year. You know that it had an original cost of $155,000 and was expected to last 20 years. How must the $14,000 have been determined?

8. On September 1, 1986, the Rand Company received a total of $30,000 as payment in advance for a number of one-year subscriptions to a monthly magazine. By the end of the year, one third of the magazines paid for in advance had been delivered. Give the entries to record the receipt of the subscriptions fees and to adjust the accounts at December 31 assuming annual financial statements are prepared at year-end.

9. Guilty and Innocent, a law firm, performed legal services in late December 1986 for clients. The $12,000 of services will be billed to the clients in January 1987. Give the adjusting entry that is necessary on December 31, 1986, if financial statements are prepared at the end of each month.

10. Grill Company incurs sales salaries at the rate of $1,000 per day. The last payday in January is Friday, January 27. Salaries for Monday and Tuesday of the next week have not been recorded or paid as of January 31. Financial statements are prepared monthly. Give the necessary adjusting entry on January 31.

11. State the effect that each of the following would have on the amount of annual net income reported for 1986 and 1987.

   a. No adjustment was made for accrued salaries of $900 as of December 31, 1986.

   b. The collection of $800 for services yet unperformed as of December 31, 1986, was credited to a revenue account and not adjusted. The services are performed in 1987.

12. A firm borrowed $20,000 on November 1. By December 31, $200 of interest had been incurred. Prepare the adjusting entry required on December 31.

13. After adjustment, selected account balances of the Sleepy Campground are:

	Debits	Credits
Retained earnings		$40,000
Campsite rental revenue		60,000
Salaries expense	$21,000	
Depreciation expense	4,000	
Utilities expense	13,000	
Dividends	2,000	

In T-account format, give the entries required to close the books for the period. Enter the above balances in the accounts before doing so. Key the postings from the first closing entry with the number (1), the second with the number (2), and so on.

PROBLEMS

3–1. The following data pertain to the Kraft Company:

Account Title	Trial Balance	Information for Adjustments
Case 1: Equipment	$40,000	The equipment has an estimated useful life of five years and an estimated scrap value of $10,000.
Accumulated Depreciation— Equipment	6,000	
Case 3: Salaries Expense	1,500	Unpaid salaries incurred amounts to $200.
Case 3: Prepaid Insurance	8,400	Of the prepaid insurance in the trial balance, only $2,200 is for additional protection after December 31.

Required:

For each of the cases:

a. Prepare the adjusting journal entry, dating it December 31, 1986.

b. Set up ledger accounts showing debit, credit, and balance. Enter balances as given, if any, and post the adjusting entries made in part *(a)*.

c. State the correct figures for the balance sheet. Show related accounts in each case as they should appear on that statement.

d. State the correct figures for the income statement.

3-2. The trial balance of the Pinkus Company at December 31 of the current year includes, among other items, the following account balances:

	Debits	Credits
Prepaid insurance	$ 3,648	
Buildings	79,000	
Accumulated depreciation—buildings		$15,800
Salaries expense	55,000	
Prepaid rent	12,000	

Additional data:

a. The debit balance in the Prepaid Insurance account is the advance premium for one year from September 1 of the current year.

b. The buildings are expected to last 25 years with no scrap value expected.

c. Salaries accrued and payable at December 31 amount to $3,200.

d. The debit balance in Prepaid Rent is for a one-year period that started March 1 of the current year.

Required:

Prepare the adjusting journal entries at December 31.

3-3. Among the account balances shown in the trial balance of the Jackson Company at December 31 of the current year are the following:

	Debits	Credits
Office supplies on hand	$ 1,740	
Prepaid insurance	2,400	
Buildings	42,000	
Accumulated depreciation—buildings		$9,750

Additional data:

a. The inventory of supplies on hand at December 31 amounts to $300.

b. The balance in the Prepaid Insurance account is for a two-year policy taken out June 1 of the current year.

c. Depreciation for the buildings is based on the cost shown in the Buildings account, less scrap value estimated at $4,500. When acquired, the lives of the buildings were estimated at 50 years each.

Required:

a. Prepare the adjusting journal entries at December 31.

b. Open ledger accounts for each of the accounts involved, enter the balances as shown in the trial balance, post the adjusting entries, and calculate balances.

3–4. The reported net income amounts for the Adams Company were: 1986, $80,000; and 1987, $95,000. *No* annual adjusting entries were made at either year-end for any of the transactions given below:

Transactions:

a. A building was rented on April 1, 1986. Cash of $24,000 was paid on that date to cover a two-year period. Prepaid Rent was debited.

b. The balance in the Office Supplies on Hand account on December 31, 1986, was $4,000. An inventory of the supplies on December 31, 1986, revealed that only $2,500 were actually on hand at that date. No new supplies were purchased during 1986. At December 31, 1987, an inventory of the supplies revealed that $500 were on hand.

c. A building costing $500,000 and having an estimated useful life of 40 years and a salvage value of $100,000 was put into service on January 1, 1986.

d. Services were performed for a customer in December 1986. The $15,000 bill for these services was not sent until January 1987. The only transaction that was recorded was a debit to Cash and a credit to Service Revenue when payment was received in January.

Required:

Calculate the correct net income for 1986 and 1987. In your answer start with the reported net income amounts. Then show the effects of each correction (adjustment) using a plus or a minus to indicate whether reported income should be increased or decreased as a result of the correction. When the corrections are added to or deducted from the reported net income amounts, the result should be the correct net income amounts. The answer format should be as follows:

Explanation of Corrections	*1986*	*1987*
Reported net income	$80,000	$95,000
To correct error in accounting for:		
a. Prepaid rent:		
Correct expense in 1986	− 9,000	
Correct expense in 1987		− 12,000

3–5. The Sancho Company occupies rented quarters on the main street of the city. In order to get this location, it was necessary for the company to rent a store larger than needed, so a portion of the area is subleased (rented) to Fredrick's Restaurant. The partial trial balance of the Sancho Company as of December 31, 1986, is as follows:

SANCHO COMPANY
Partial Trial Balance
December 31, 1986

	Debits	Credits
Cash	$40,000	
Prepaid insurance	5,700	
Store equipment	44,000	
Accumulated depreciation—store equipment		$ 4,800
Notes payable		10,000
Service revenue		300,000
Supplies expense	5,400	
Rent expense	7,200	
Store salaries expense	49,000	
Rent revenue		2,200

Data to be considered:

a. Wages of the store clerks amount to $180 per day and were last paid through Wednesday, December 27. December 31 is a Sunday. The store is closed Sundays.

b. An analysis of the Store Equipment account disclosed:

Balance, January 1, 1986		$32,000
Addition, July 1, 1986		12,000
Balance, December 31, 1986, per trial balance		$44,000

The company estimates that all equipment will last 20 years from the date it was acquired and that the scrap value will be zero.

c. The store carries one combined insurance policy which is taken out once a year effective August 1. The premium on the policy now in force amounts to $3,600 per year.

d. Unused store supplies on hand at December 31, 1985, have a cost of $360.

e. December's rent from Fredrick's Restaurant has not yet been received, $200.

Required:

Present the period-end entries required by the statements of fact presented above. Show your calculations of the amounts as explanations of your entries.

3–6. On June 1, 1986, Jeff Hanley opened a swimming pool cleaning and maintenance service business, Hanley Company. He vaguely recalled the process of making journal entries and establishing ledger accounts from a high school bookkeeping course he had taken some years ago. At the end of June, he prepared an income statement for the month of June, but he had the feeling that he had not proceeded correctly. He contacted his brother, Jay, a recent college graduate majoring in accounting, for assistance.

Jay immediately noted that his brother had kept his records on a cash basis, so he set about to bring the books to a full accrual basis.

Transactions:

June 1 Received cash of $9,000 from a motel chain in exchange for service agreements to clean and maintain their pools for the months of June, July, August, and September.

  5 Paid rent for automotive and cleaning equipment to be used during the period June through September, $2,000. The payment covered the entire period.

  8 Purchased a two-year liability insurance policy effective June 1 for $2,640 cash.

  10 Received an advance of $2,500 from a Florida building contractor in exchange for an agreement to help service pools in his housing development during the months of October through May.

  16 Paid wages for the first half of June, $2,800.

  17 Paid $120 for advertising to be run in a local newspaper for two weeks in June and four weeks in July.

  19 Paid the rent of $4,000 under a four-month lease on a building rented and occupied on June 1.

  26 Purchased $1,800 of supplies for cash. (Only $300 of these supplies were used in June.)

  29 Billed a customer for services rendered, $4,200.

  30 Unpaid employee services received in the last half of June amounted to $2,600.

  30 Received a bill for $200 for gas and oil used in June.

Required:

  a. Prepare the entries for the transactions as Jeff must have recorded them under the cash basis of accounting.

  b. Prepare the necessary adjusting entries as Jay must have prepared them to bring the books to a full accrual basis of accounting.

  c. Calculate the change in the net income for June brought about by changing from the cash to the accrual basis of accounting.

3–7. The balances of all of the Paul Company accounts as of June 1, 1986, were as follows:

Cash	8,400	Accounts payable	4,000
Accounts receivable	8,600	Capital stock	12,000
		Retained earnings	1,000

The transactions (and certain other data) for the company for June were as follows:

  (1) Services rendered to a customer for cash, $8,000; on account, $16,000.

  (2) Paid rent for the six months ending November 30, $6,000. (Record entire amount as prepaid rent.)

  (3) Purchased equipment for cash, $9,600.

  (4) Supplies purchased on account, $1,600.

  (5) Received cash on account from a customer, $22,000.

  (6) Made payment on account to a supplier, $2,800.

  (7) Employee services received, $15,000; cash paid to employees, $13,000.

  (8) Paid utility bill of $400.

  (9) Paid dividend to stockholders, $600.

(10) Equipment has an expected life of four years. It was acquired early in the month.

(11) Adjust for prepaid rent that has expired.

(12) Of the supplies purchased in (4), $1,400 were used by the end of the month.

Required:

    a. Set up T-accounts and record the above data, including the beginning balances given above. (Ignore any possible federal income taxes.)

    b. Prepare an income statement for the month of June.

    c. Prepare a balance sheet as of June 30, 1986.

    d. Enter in the T-accounts the closing entries that would be required if June 30, 1986, is the end of the accounting period. (Key these entires *a, b,* and *c* in the T-accounts.)

3–8. Randy Hall, president and sole stockholder of Hall's Service, Inc., prepared the following income statement for the company's second month of operations, May 1986.

Service revenues		$10,000
Wages	$5,600	
Oil and gasoline used . . .	1,000	
Other expenses	1,400	8,000
Net income		$ 2,000

In preparing the above income statement, Randy merely looked at the checkbook and treated deposits of receipts from customers as revenue and checks drawn in payment for expenses as the expenses for the month. Further analysis shows that, of the $10,000 collected from customers in May, $1,200 was for services rendered in April. Services were rendered in May for which customers were billed $1,400, none of which was paid by the end of May. The $5,600 of wages paid included wages of $1,600 earned by employees in April. Wages earned in May but not paid by the end of May amounted to $600. A bill for $200 for gasoline and oil used in May remains unpaid at the end of May. The expenses shown above do not include depreciation on the equipment owned, which has a cost of $240,000 and an estimated life of 10 years.

Required:

    Prepare a corrected income statement for May for Hall's Service, Inc.

3–9. You are given the following adjusted balances for the Isaac Company.

ISAAC COMPANY
Adjusted Trial Balance
December 31, 1986

	Debits	Credits
Cash	$ 58,600	
Accounts receivable	24,000	
Accrued interest receivable	200	
Notes receivable	10,000	
Prepaid insurance	1,200	
Supplies on hand	900	
Land	16,000	
Buildings	95,000	
Accumulated depreciation—buildings		$ 20,000
Office equipment	14,000	
Accumulated depreciation—office equipment		4,000
Accounts payable		19,000
Accrued salaries payable		4,250
Accrued interest payable		450
Notes payable (due 1989)		32,000
Capital stock		60,000
Retained earnings		21,400
Dividends	20,000	
Commissions and fees revenue		186,260
Advertising expense	7,000	
Commissions expense	37,720	
Travel expense	6,440	
Depreciation expense—building	4,250	
Salaries expense	44,200	
Depreciation expense—office equipment	1,400	
Supplies expense	1,900	
Insurance expense	1,800	
Building repair expense	950	
Utilities expense	1,700	
Interest expense	900	
Interest revenue		800
	$348,160	$348,160

Required:

    a. Prepare the closing journal entries.

    b. Prepare a classified balance sheet.

3–10. (Based on the appendix). The trial balance and additional data given below are for the Wright Company:

WRIGHT COMPANY
Trial Balance
December 31, 1986

	Debits	Credits
Cash on hand and in bank	$ 35,320	
Accounts receivable	69,760	
Notes receivable	85,000	
Stores supplies on hand	1,200	
Store equipment	44,000	
Accumulated depreciation—store equipment		$ 8,800
Accounts payable		39,400
Notes payable		12,000
Capital stock		150,000
Retained earnings		10,820
Service revenue		288,680
Interest revenue		500
Interest expense	300	
Sales salaries	69,200	
Advertising	39,000	
Store supplies expense	1,480	
General office expense	4,940	
Fire insurance expense	2,400	
Office salaries	40,400	
Officers' salaries	80,000	
Legal and auditing expenses	5,000	
Telephone and telegraph	2,400	
Rent expense	28,800	
Dividends	1,000	
	$510,200	$510,200

Additional data as of December 31, 1986:

a. Fire insurance unexpired, $700.

b. Store supplies on hand, $850.

c. Prepaid rent expense (store only), $3,500.

d. The store equipment has a 10-year estimated life with no scrap value.

e. Accrued sales salaries, $2,000.

f. Accrued office salaries, $1,500.

Required:

a. Prepare a 12-column worksheet for the year ended December 31, 1986. (See chapter appendix for an illustration.)

b. Prepare the December 31, 1986, closing entries, in general journal form.

4 SALES, COST OF GOODS SOLD, AND INVENTORIES

As already noted, accountants seek to fulfill one of their most important tasks—the measurement of periodic net income—through a process of matching revenues and expenses by time periods. This chapter discusses accounting for the major source of revenue for most business firms—sales of a product—and a major element of expense—cost of the goods sold.

Attention is focused on cost of goods sold not only because it is a relatively large expense but, as we shall see, because measures of its periodic amount may differ, depending on which of several alternative accounting methods is used.

SALES, COST OF GOODS SOLD, AND GROSS MARGIN

Accounting for Sales Revenue

The revenue of a company engaged in selling merchandise is typically recorded at the time of the completion of the sale (which is assumed to occur when the goods are delivered) and at the price agreed upon in the sales contract. Thus, a sale of a machine on account at a price of $3,000 would be recorded when the machine was delivered as follows in journal entry and T-account form:

(a) Accounts Receivable 3,000
        Sales 3,000
    To record sales on account.

Accounts Receivable		Sales	
(a) 3,000			(a) 3,000

Recording revenue at the time of sale is usually considered appropriate because (1) the revenue has been earned, that is, the seller has completed its part of the contract; (2) the revenue is readily measurable—the actual selling price is known; (3) legal title to the goods has passed to the buyer; and (4) the revenue has been realized—a valid asset has been received in an exchange with an outsider. Furthermore, the actual sale of the goods may be the critical event in a series of events that end in a sale. As a practical matter, revenue from the sale of goods is usually recorded when the goods are delivered in a valid sales transaction. But goods delivered on a consignment basis should not be recorded as sold. Here the goods remain the property of the shipper until they are sold by the party to whom they are consigned—the consignee.

Cost of Goods Sold— Perpetual Procedure

Firms securing revenue from the sale of goods usually keep a supply of such goods on hand which is called merchandise inventory. If prior to the above sale the seller had purchased three identical machines on account at a price of $1,800 each, this purchase transaction would, under what is known as **perpetual inventory procedure,** be recorded as follows:

(b) Merchandise Inventory 5,400
        Accounts Payable   5,400
     To record purchase on account.

Merchandise Inventory		Accounts Payable	
(b) 5,400			(b) 5,400

Merchandise inventory is a current asset account, and accounts payable is a current liability. Under perpetual procedure, a second entry is required at the time of sale to record the **expense** incurred as a result of transferring an asset, part of the inventory, to the customer:

(c) Cost of Goods Sold 1,800
        Merchandise Inventory   1,800
     To record cost of merchandise sold.

Merchandise Inventory		Cost of Goods Sold	
(b) 5,400	(c) 1,800	(c) 1,800	

The $1,800 in the above entry would be secured from supporting records called **stock cards** or **perpetual inventory cards.** These records show the dates, quantities, and prices of goods received and goods issued, and the quantities and prices of the goods on hand at any given time.

Assume that $500 of other expenses were incurred in the week ending July 18, 1986, in which the above sale was the company's only sale. The income statement for the week would be as follows:

Sales	$3,000
Cost of goods sold	1,800
Gross margin	$1,200
Other expenses	500
Net income	$ 700

The difference between sales and the cost of goods sold is called **gross margin** or **gross profit,** and the relationship between the gross margin and sales is often expressed as a percentage called the gross profit or gross margin rate—40 percent in this instance ($1,200 ÷ $3,000).

Perpetual inventory procedure is widely used in companies that sell merchandise of high individual unit value, such as furs, jewelry, and autos. Because each unit has a high value, management finds it especially useful to know which merchandise is selling and which is not. Promotional activity and purchasing can be planned. Also, inventory shortages can be determined by comparing amounts shown on perpetual records with physical counts of the items on hand. Thus, the benefits derived from keeping detailed perpetual records often exceed the cost of maintaining such records.

Cost of Goods Sold— Periodic Procedure

On the other hand, companies that sell goods with low unit values, such as greeting cards, nuts and bolts, and pencils, may find it too costly to maintain perpetual records for their merchandise. Such companies use **periodic inventory procedure.** Under this procedure, inventory is not updated in the accounts after every purchase and sale. Rather, the proper inventory balance is determined and recorded only after a physical count is taken of the goods on hand and the goods are properly priced. Such physical counts are usually taken once a year at a minimum. And the cost of goods sold is determined only after the physical inventory has been taken.

The Purchases account. Under periodic procedure, merchandise acquisitions are recorded in a separate Purchases account. A purchase of $40,000 of goods on account would then be recorded as follows:

(a)	Purchases	40,000	
	Accounts Payable		40,000
	Purchases of merchandise on account.		

Purchases		Accounts Payable	
(a)	40,000	(a)	40,000

The cost of the goods sold in any period is then determined as follows:

Merchandise inventory (at beginning of period)
+ Purchases for the period
= Cost of goods available for sale; this sum
− Ending inventory (goods on hand not sold)
= Cost of goods sold (the expense for the period)

The computation of the cost of the goods sold can be included in the income statement, if desired, as shown in Illustration 4.1. Future examples will illustrate this periodic procedure only.

Illustration 4.1

X COMPANY
Partial Income Statement
For the Month Ended July 31, 1986

Sales		$50,000
Cost of goods sold:		
Inventory, July 1	$15,000	
Purchases	40,000	
Cost of goods available for sale	$55,000	
Less: Inventory, July 31	22,000	
Cost of goods sold		33,000
Gross margin		$17,000

Returns and Allowances

Whenever goods are sold, some of them may be returned by the buyer to the seller for any of a variety of reasons. For example, assume that goods have been sold to a buyer on account in the amount of $5,000. This transaction was recorded as a debit to Accounts Receivable and a credit to Sales of $5,000 by the seller, and as a debit to Purchases and a credit to Accounts Payable of $5,000 by the buyer. Now goods with a sales price of $400 are returned. The entry on the seller's books would be:

(a) Sales Returns and Allowances 400
      Accounts Receivable 400
    To record return of goods by customer.

Sales Returns and Allowances		Accounts Receivable		
(a) 400		Bal. 5,000	*(a)*	400

The entry on the buyer's books would be:

(b) Accounts Payable 400
      Purchase Returns and Allowances 400
    To record return of goods to supplier.

Purchase Returns and Allowances		Accounts Payable			
		(b)	400	Bal.	5,000
(b)	400				

The seller has credited the customer's account because the return has reduced the customer's obligation to pay. The customer (buyer) debited the vendor's account because the return reduced its obligation to the seller.

Occasionally, concessions will be granted from the originally agreed-upon price of a sale of merchandise because of blemishes, defects, or damage. Such price concessions are recorded in the same manner as returns.

Because sales returns and allowances represent actual cancellations of all or a part of a sale, they theoretically could be recorded directly as debits in the Sales account. For similar reasons, purchase returns and allowances could be recorded as credits in the Purchases account. But, returns and allowances are likely to be significant information to management and others, since the handling of returns can be costly to both buyers and sellers. Returns and allowances amount to as much as 15 percent of sales in some businesses; they are, therefore, recorded in separate accounts (called contra accounts) and often reported separately as deductions from sales and purchases to arrive at net sales and net purchases in the income statement.

Cash Discounts

Frequently, when goods are sold on a credit basis, the buyer is permitted to pay an amount less than the full invoice price of the goods if payment is made within a stated period of time. Thus, an invoice might state credit terms of "2/10, n/30"[1] (read as 2 10, net 30), which means that a 2 percent discount can be deducted from the total price of the goods if the invoice is paid within 10 days of the invoice date, and the gross amount is due within 30 days from date of purchase.

The gross price method. The transaction may be recorded at the $1,000 gross invoice price. If so, the payment within the discount period, under terms 2/10, n/30, would be recorded as follows:

Seller's Books

(a)	Accounts Receivable	1,000	
	Sales		1,000
	To record sales on account.		
(b)	Cash	980	
	Sales Discounts	20	
	Accounts Receivable		1,000
	To record receipt of payment within discount period.		

---

[1] Some students believe the terms should read 2/10, g/30, since the *gross* amount is due in 30 days. But we will use the conventional terms, 2/10, n/30.

Accounts Receivable				Sales		
(a)	1,000	*(b)*	1,000		*(a)*	1,000

Cash		Sales Discounts	
(b)	980	*(b)*	20

Buyer's Books

```
(c) Purchases  . . . . . . . . . . . . . . .   1,000
        Accounts Payable  . . . . . . . . . .          1,000
    To record purchase on account.

(d) Accounts Payable  . . . . . . . . . . . .   1,000
        Cash  . . . . . . . . . . . . . . . .            980
        Purchase Discounts  . . . . . . . . .             20
    To record payment made within discount period.
```

Purchases			Accounts Payable		
(c)	1,000		*(d)*	1,000	*(c)* 1,000

Cash			Purchase Discounts	
Bal.	xxx	*(d)* 980	*(d)*	20

The Sales Discounts and Purchase Discounts accounts are also contra accounts to the Sales and Purchases accounts, respectively. This treatment reflects the preferred theoretical view that such discounts are adjustments of recorded revenue and cost.

The net price method. An alternative, seldom used method, consists of recording purchases at net invoice price (net of discount) and isolating in a separate account any discounts not taken. To illustrate, assume that a $1,000 invoice, terms 2/10, n/30, is recorded at net invoice price ($980) and is paid after the discount privilege period has expired. The required entries on the buyer's books are:

```
(a) Purchases  . . . . . . . . . . . . . . .   980
        Accounts Payable  . . . . . . . . . .         980
    To record purchase of merchandise at net invoice
    price.

(b) Accounts Payable  . . . . . . . . . . . .   980
    Purchase Discounts Lost  . . . . . . . . .    20
        Cash  . . . . . . . . . . . . . . . .         1,000
    To record payment of invoice after discount period
    had expired.
```

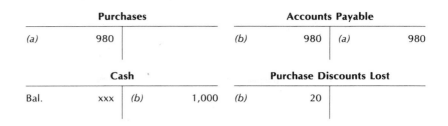

Purchases		Accounts Payable		
(a) 980		*(b)* 980	*(a)*	980

Cash		Purchase Discounts Lost	
Bal. xxx	*(b)* 1,000	*(b)* 20	

This procedure, in effect, applies the principle of management by exception by drawing attention to the exception rather than the routine, that is, to discounts *not* taken. Well-run businesses seldom fail to take all discounts offered simply because of the relative cost involved. For example, failure to take a 2 percent discount under credit terms of 2/10, n/30 is the equivalent of paying 2 percent for 20 days since the account is due 20 days after the discount period expires. Two percent for 20 days is equivalent to an annual rate of interest of 36 percent.

Transportation-In

The cost a buyer incurs to have merchandise delivered is part of the total cost of the goods. But because the total freight costs incurred may be significant information, the receipt of a freight bill usually results in an entry debiting Transportation-In and crediting Accounts Payable.

The partial income statement shown in Illustration 4.2 illustrates the financial reporting of returns, allowances, discounts, and transportation-in.

Adjusting and Closing Entries

The data in Illustration 4.2 can be used to show the adjusting and closing entries required in the accounts of a merchandising firm. First, an entry is needed to accumulate in one account (Cost of Goods Sold) all of the costs relating to the goods that were available for sale. Thus, the existing balances in the inventory, transportation-in, and the purchase-related accounts are transferred to the Cost of Goods Sold account as follows:

Cost of Goods Sold	85,000	
Purchase Returns and Allowances	5,000	
Purchase Discounts	1,000	
Purchases		60,000
Transportation-In		3,000
Inventory		28,000

The Cost of Goods Sold account (which started with a zero balance) now contains the cost of the goods available for sale. But not all of the goods have been sold. An inventory of $21,000 remains

Illustration 4.2

FICTITIOUS COMPANY
Income Statement
For the Year Ended December 31, 1986

Sales			$100,000
Less: Sales returns and allowances . .		$ 4,000	
Sales discounts		1,000	5,000
Net sales			$95,000
Cost of goods sold:			
Inventory, January 1		$ 28,000	
Purchases	$60,000		
Less: Purchase returns and			
allowances	$5,000		
Purchase discounts . . .	1,000	6,000	
Net purchases		$54,000	
Transportation-in		3,000	57,000
Cost of goods available			
for sale		$ 85,000	
Less: Inventory, December 31 . . .		21,000	64,000
Gross margin			$31,000
Operating expenses:			
Administrative expenses		$ 6,000	
Selling expenses		9,000	15,000
Net income			$16,000

on hand. This must be set up as an asset and deducted from the balance in the Cost of Goods Sold account, which leads to the following entry:

Inventory	21,000	
Cost of Goods Sold		21,000

Now the revenue and revenue contra accounts can be closed to Income Summary:

Sales	100,000	
Sales Returns and Allowances		4,000
Sales Discounts		1,000
Income Summary		95,000

The Cost of Goods Sold account would be closed in an entry involving a debit to Income Summary and a credit to Cost of Goods Sold, as follows:

Income Summary	64,000	
Cost of Goods Sold		64,000

The operating expenses would be closed in an entry involving a debit to Income Summary and a credit to the various expense accounts, as follows:

Income Summary	15,000	
Administrative Expenses		6,000
Selling Expenses		9,000

The net income of $16,000 would be closed to Retained Earnings, as follows:

Income Summary 16,000
    Retained Earnings   16,000

Worksheet. The appendix to this chapter illustrates a worksheet that may be used in preparing adjusting entries, closing entries, and the financial statements for a merchandising company.

BAD DEBTS

A seller doing business on a credit basis faces the virtual certainty that some customers' accounts will ultimately prove uncollectible. For example, assume that, because of past experience, a seller expects to collect only $95,000 out of $100,000 of accounts receivable outstanding at year-end. Normally, this would require the following entry:

Bad Debts Expense		Allowance for Doubtful Accounts	
(a) 5,000		*(a)* 5,000	

This entry serves two purposes: (1) uncollectible accounts are charged as an expense in the year the sale giving rise to them was made; that is, a proper matching results when, say, uncollectible accounts arising from credit sales made in 1986 are charged as an expense in 1986, (2) the accounts receivable at year-end are properly valued at their **net realizable value**—the amount of cash expected to be collected.

The Bad Debts Expense account is shown as an operating expense in the income statement. The Allowance for Doubtful Accounts is a contra account (reduction account) to Accounts Receivable and is credited rather than crediting Accounts Receivable directly because it is not known at this time which customers' accounts will actually prove uncollectible. The $100,000 of accounts receivable and the related allowance for doubtful accounts of $5,000 are reported as follows in the current assets section of the balance sheet:

Accounts receivable $100,000
Less: Allowance for doubtful accounts 5,000 $95,000

Estimation Methods

There are two basic methods of estimating the amount of bad debts to be charged to a given accounting period.

Percentage of sales method. The **percentage of sales method** involves calculating the amount that has proven uncollectible from credit sales in previous years. The ratio of uncollectible accounts to credit sales is then used in estimating the amount for the bad debts adjusting entry. If cash sales are small or are a fairly constant percentage of total sales, the entry may be based on total net sales.

To illustrate, assume that the Boulder Company has found that 1 percent of its net sales is uncollectible. On the basis of this experience, each period the company may charge an amount equal to 1 percent of the net sales for the period to Bad Debts Expense and add a like amount to the Allowance for Doubtful Accounts. If net sales for 1986 are $400,000, the entry will read:

```
Bad Debts Expense  . . . . . . . . . . . . .  4,000
    Allowance for Doubtful Accounts  . . . . . .          4,000
    To record bad debts expense.
```

Assuming that the gross (total) amount of accounts receivable is $100,000 and there was no previous balance in the allowance account, net accounts receivable would appear as follows on the balance sheet:

```
Accounts receivable  . . . . . . . . . . . . .  $100,000
Less: Allowance for doubtful accounts  . . . . . . .     4,000    $96,000
```

Sometimes the Allowance for Doubtful Accounts account has a balance before adjustment. Under the percentage of sales method, any existing balance in the allowance account will *not* influence the size of the bad debts adjusting entry.

This method is theoretically preferable because it bases the estimate of expense solely on the sales revenue of the same period and gives a more precise matching of expense and revenue than the alternative method.

Percentage of accounts receivable method. The **percentage of accounts receivable method** is designed to adjust the Allowance for Doubtful Accounts balance to a certain percentage of accounts receivable. It may use one overall percentage or may use a different percentage for each age category of receivable. To illustrate the use of one overall percentage, assume that on the basis of past experience the Fox Company estimates that 5 percent of its outstanding receivables of $100,000 as of December 31, 1986, will ultimately prove to be uncollectible. The Allowance for Doubtful Accounts already has a *debit* balance of $1,000. The journal entry to adjust the balance in the allowance account to its required $5,000 ($100,000 × 0.05) *credit* balance is as follows:

```
Bad Debts Expense  . . . . . . . . . . . .  6,000
    Allowance for Doubtful Accounts  . . . . . .          6,000
    To adjust allowance for possible uncollectible accounts.
```

In T-account form, the effect of this entry can be shown as follows:

Bad Debts Expense		Allowance for Doubtful Accounts		
Dec. 31 Adjustment 6,000		Beg. bal. 1,000	Dec. 31 Adjustment 6,000	
			Bal. after adjustment 5,000	

Thus, the percentage of accounts receivable method requires that you (1) determine what the balance of Allowance for Doubtful Accounts should be and (2) determine the amount that needs to be recorded in a journal entry to bring the account to this required credit balance.

Aging schedule. Alternatively, an **aging** schedule may be used to apply a different percentage for each age category of receivable. An aging schedule is presented in Illustration 4.3, showing how the age of each customer's account is determined. As can be seen from Illustration 4.3, under this method the age of the accounts is the basis for estimating uncollectibility. For example, only 1 percent of the accounts not yet due (sales made less than 30 days prior to the end of the accounting period) is expected to be uncollectible. At the other extreme, 50 percent of all accounts 91 to 180 days past due is expected to become worthless. The journal entry amount is still affected by the amount already in the allowance account prior to adjustment. For instance, Illustration 4.3 shows that $33,150 is needed in the allowance account. If the account has a credit balance of $5,000 before adjustment, the adjusting entry would be made for $28,150.

Illustration 4.3
ACCOUNTS RECEIVABLE AGING SCHEDULE

ROGERS COMPANY
Analysis of Accounts Receivable
December 31, 1986

Customer	Debit Balance	Not Yet Due	Number of Days Past Due			
			1–30	31–60	61–90	91–180
X	$ 8,000					$ 8,000
Y	16,000		$ 12,000	$ 4,000		
Z	4,000				$ 800	3,200
All others	800,000	$560,000	200,000	20,000	5,000	15,000
Totals	$828,000	$560,000	$212,000	$24,000	$5,800	$26,200
Estimated uncollectible percentage		1%	5%	10%	25%	50%
Amount uncollectible	$ 33,150	$ 5,600	$ 10,600	$ 2,400	$1,450	$13,100

Subsequent write-offs. Later, when an account is determined to be uncollectible, an entry is made debiting the Allowance for Doubtful Accounts and crediting Accounts Receivable. Note that this entry has no effect on net income or on the valuation of the accounts receivable. The expense and the reduced valuation for the asset were recognized when the adjusting entry for estimated uncollectibles was made. The write-off entry merely gives recognition to an event that was anticipated when the allowance was established.

If, by chance, an error was made in writing off an individual customer's account (as shown by the collection of the account), an entry is made debiting Accounts Receivable and crediting the Allowance for Doubtful Accounts. Then the cash collection is recorded as a debit to Cash and a credit to Accounts Receivable.

INVENTORY MEASUREMENT

A crucial step in the determination of net income is the measurement of the ending inventory of the period. This is true not only because it affects net income but also because it affects measurements of current assets, total assets, gross margin, retained earnings, and total stockholders' equity. How this happens will be explained later when questions of what to include as part of the cost of the inventory and which of several measurement methods should be used are discussed.

The Basic Rule

Chapter 4 of *Accounting Research Bulletin 43* states that "the primary basis of accounting for inventories is cost" and further stipulates that "a departure from the cost basis . . . is required when the utility of the goods is no longer as great as" their cost. Thus, inventories are usually reported in the balance sheet at a dollar amount described as *cost or market, whichever is lower.*

In applying this general or basic rule, several problems exist. As discussed below, these include:

1. What costs should be included as part of the cost of the inventory?
2. What is the cost of the inventory when goods have been purchased at different unit costs?
3. What constitutes evidence of a decline in the utility of goods, and how is it measured?

Inventory Cost— Possible Inclusions

In principle, the cost of inventory includes all costs incurred, directly or indirectly, to acquire the goods and place them in position and condition for sale. Thus, cost includes the net invoice price of the goods plus insurance in transit; transportation charges; receiving, handling and storage costs; and duties. But, as a practical matter, these related costs are often omitted from inventory cost because (1) they are not material in amount relative to the total cost of the goods purchased, or (2) there is no easy way to allocate these costs to individual units of merchandise. Also, because they are immaterial, purchase discounts are on occasion not deducted from the invoice price in determining inventory cost.

Inventory Costing Methods

As already indicated, the cost of goods available for sale (beginning inventory plus purchases) must be apportioned between ending inventory and cost of goods sold. But how are these costs to be apportioned when goods have been acquired at different unit costs? For example, suppose that at the beginning of a month a retailer has three units of a product on hand, one acquired at $10, another at $11, and the third at $12. Suppose that during the month two units were sold. What is their cost? Is it $21, the cost of the first and second units? Or $22, the cost of the first and third units? Or $23, the cost of the second and third units? Or should it be $22 determined as two units at an average cost of $11? Four inventory costing methods have been developed to solve this type of problem. They are: (1) specific identification, (2) first-in, first-out (FIFO), (3) last-in, first-out (LIFO), and (4) weighted average. The cost-flow assumption used does not necessarily have to match the physical flow of the goods.

The data in Illustration 4.4 are assumed for the beginning inventory, purchases, and sales of a given product in order to illustrate the application of these four inventory costing methods.

The total goods available for sale consisted of 80 units with a total cost of $854. Of the units available, 60 were sold, producing sales revenue of $940, and 20 units were left on hand in inventory. Our task now is to apportion the $854 between cost of goods sold (an expense) and ending inventory (an asset).

Specific identification. This method calls for the assignment of a known actual cost to a particular identifiable unit of product. The specific product involved is usually identifiable through the

Illustration 4.4
INVENTORY, PURCHASE, AND SALES DATA: PRODUCT X, MODEL 12

Beginning Inventory and Purchases				Sales			
Date	Number of Units	Unit Cost	Total Cost	Date	Number of Units	Price	Total
1/1 inventory . .	10	$10.00	$100.00	3/8	10	$15.00	$150.00
3/2	10	10.40	104.00	7/5	10	15.00	150.00
5/28	20	10.50	210.00	9/7	20	16.00	320.00
8/12	10	11.00	110.00	11/27	20	16.00	320.00
10/12	20	10.90	218.00				
12/21	10	11.20	112.00				
Total	80		$854.00		60		$940.00

use of a serial number plate or an identification tag. The method is quite appropriately applied when large, readily identifiable units of product such as automobiles are purchased and sold.

To illustrate, assume that the 20 units of product on hand at the end of the year in Illustration 4.4 are definitely known to consist of 10 from the August 12 purchase and 10 from the December 21 purchase. The ending inventory then is shown in Illustration 4.5.

Illustration 4.5
ENDING INVENTORY UNDER SPECIFIC IDENTIFICATION

From Purchase of—	Number of Units	Cost Each	Total Cost
August 12	10	$11.00	$110.00
December 21	10	11.20	112.00
Total	20		$222.00

The cost of the ending inventory of $222 would be deducted from the total cost of goods available for sale of $854 to get the cost of goods sold of $632.

The specific identification method results in the cost of goods sold and the inventory being stated in terms of the actual cost of the actual units sold and on hand. Thus, costs are matched against revenues with a high degree of precision. The method is used most logically to account for "big ticket" items, such as autos and trucks, because each unit tends to be unique. Also, the selling price of such items tends to be based on a markup over a specifically identified cost.

The method is criticized by some because it may result in two identical units of product being included in the inventory at different prices even if they have the same utility because they are identical. But supporters would contend that this is entirely logical and consistent with the cost basis of asset measurement. The method is also criticized by some as theoretically unacceptable because income may be manipulated when it is used. If higher income is desired, ship the units with the lower cost. If lower income is desired, ship the high-cost units.

But the major deficiency in the specific identification method is that it is simply too costly and too time consuming to apply in many situations. This would be true where large quantities of many different types of products with low unit costs are purchased and sold.

First-in, first-out (FIFO). Effective merchandising policy usually calls for moving the oldest goods first, if at all possible. In many businesses, the actual physical flow of goods *is* first-in, first-out to avoid substantial losses from spoilage, as in the case of dairy products and fresh produce.

The application of the FIFO method results in the latest costs being included in inventory, while the older costs are charged to cost of goods sold. The method may be applied even in those circumstances in which goods do not flow in a first-in, first-out manner.

FIFO applied under periodic procedure.   Under the FIFO method, the 20 units in ending inventory would be priced as shown in Illustration 4.6.

Illustration 4.6
FIFO COST OF ENDING INVENTORY UNDER PERIODIC PROCEDURE

From Purchase of—	Number of Units	Unit Price	Total Cost
December 21	10	$11.20	$112.00
October 12	10	10.90	109.00
Total	20		$221.00

The ending inventory includes the costs of the latest purchases, and the balance of the cost of the goods available for sale (consisting of older costs) is charged to cost of goods sold. The ending inventory is $221, and this sum will be deducted from the total cost of goods available for sale of $854 to get the cost of goods sold of $633.

Last-in, first-out (LIFO).   Under LIFO, the cost of the last goods purchased is charged against revenues as the cost of the goods sold, while the inventory is composed of the costs of the oldest goods acquired. Tax regulations provide that LIFO may be used for tax purposes only if it is used in general financial reports. Although the costs of the goods purchased are assumed to flow in a last-in, first-out manner, this does not necessarily mean that the goods physically flow in this manner.

In order to determine the cost of the ending inventory, list the goods in the beginning inventory and continue listing subsequent purchases until enough units have been listed to equal the number in the ending inventory. Illustration 4.7 shows the determination of the ending inventory for the data listed in Illustration 4.4.

Illustration 4.7
LIFO COST OF ENDING INVENTORY

From Purchase of—	Number of Units	Unit Cost	Total Cost
Beginning inventory	10	10.00	$100.00
March 2	10	10.40	104.00
Total	20		$204.00

The cost of the ending inventory of $204 would be deducted from the cost of the goods available for sale of $854 to show a cost of goods sold of $650. Note that in this example the costs charged against revenues as the cost of the goods sold are all fairly current or recent costs while the inventory consists of a March 2 cost and the cost of the beginning inventory that may actually have been incurred many years ago.

FIFO and LIFO compared. Much has been written in recent years concerning the relative merits of FIFO and LIFO. LIFO's appeal can be tied directly to the long-run tendency toward rising prices experienced in this country since the early 1930s. An example will make this point clear.

Suppose that Company A has one unit of a given product on hand that cost $10. The unit is sold for $15, other expenses of sale amount to $3.50, the tax rate is 50 percent, and the unit is replaced for $11 prior to the end of the accounting period. Under FIFO accounting, net income is computed as follows:

Net sales	$15.00
Cost of goods sold	10.00
Gross margin	$ 5.00
Expenses	3.50
Net operating margin	$ 1.50
Federal income taxes (50 percent rate)	0.75
Net income	$ 0.75

According to the above schedule the company is selling this product at a price sufficient to produce net income. But consider the following:

Cash secured from sale	$15.00
Expenses and taxes paid ($3.50 + $0.75)	4.25
Net cash available from sale	$10.75
Cash spent to replace unit sold	11.00
Additional cash that was required to replace inventory	$ 0.25

Thus, Company A, which is reporting net income, finds itself unable to replace its inventory without securing additional cash. But note what happens when LIFO is used as the method of inventory pricing:

Net sales	$15.00
Cost of goods sold	11.00
Gross margin	$ 4.00
Expenses	3.50
Net operating income	$ 0.50
Federal income taxes	0.25
Net income	$ 0.25

The 25 cents of net income is matched by an increase in cash that is available for distribution as dividends or for other purposes:

Cash secured from sale	$15.00
Expenses and taxes ($3.50 + $0.25)	3.75
Net cash available from sale	$11.25
Cash spent to replace unit sold	11.00
Cash available for dividends (or other uses)	$ 0.25

Because the unit sold was replaced before the end of the year, the effect of using LIFO increased cost of goods sold $1.00 ($11.00 — $10.00). This, in turn, reduced taxable income by $1.00 and, with a 50 percent tax rate, reduced federal income taxes by 50 cents. Some of LIFO'S popularity is due to its ability to minimize current tax payments in periods of rising prices, which is what has occurred in our economy over recent years.

But LIFO is supported on theoretical grounds in that it tends to match current revenues and current costs. The income statement reports sales and the most recent costs of making those sales when LIFO is used. Thus, the income reported reflects operating results and does not include gains from holding inventory in periods of rising prices—"inventory profits," as they are called. The inventory profit in the above example was $1—the difference between the cost to replace the unit sold at the time of sale ($11) and its actual cost ($10). LIFO is also supported by accountants who believe that selling prices are most likely to be based on replacement cost and that LIFO cost most closely approximates replacement cost.

On the other hand, FIFO advocates point out that LIFO matches the cost of *un*sold goods (because goods usually move in a first-in, first-out manner) against sales revenue. LIFO also tends to yield an inventory amount that, after a period of rising prices, is substantially below the inventory's current replacement cost. The net income reported under LIFO can also be manipulated to a certain extent by purchasing, or not purchasing, goods near the end of the accounting year when unit costs have changed. If smaller income is desired, increase the amount of purchases at current high costs, and, under LIFO, these high costs will be charged to cost of goods sold. If higher income is desired, delay making purchases and charge to cost of goods sold some of the older, lower costs in inventory.

Weighted average method. Under this method the total number of units purchased plus those on hand at the beginning of the year is divided into the total cost of the purchases plus the cost of the beginning inventory in order to derive a weighted average unit cost. This unit cost is then multiplied by the number of units in the ending inventory to arrive at the cost of the inventory. Illustration 4.8 shows the application of this procedure.

Illustration 4.8
APPLICATION OF WEIGHTED AVERAGE METHOD

Purchase Date	Number of Units Purchased	Unit Cost	Total Cost
1/1 inventory	10	$10.00	$100.00
3/2	10	10.40	104.00
5/28	20	10.50	210.00
8/12	10	11.00	110.00
10/12	20	10.90	218.00
12/21	10	11.20	112.00
Total	80		$854.00

Weighted average unit cost is $854 ÷ 80, or $10.675.
Ending inventory, then, is $10.675 × 20 . . . . 213.50
Cost of goods sold $640.50

Differences in cost methods summarized. Illustration 4.9 summarizes the cost of goods sold, ending inventories, and gross margins that will result from the application of the same data to the four basic cost methods of pricing ending inventory.

Illustration 4.9
SUMMARY OF EFFECTS OF EMPLOYING DIFFERENT INVENTORY METHODS WITH SAME BASIC DATA

	Specific Identification	FIFO	LIFO	Weighted Average
Sales	$940.00	$940.00	$940.00	$940.00
Cost of goods sold:				
Beginning inventory	$100.00	$100.00	$100.00	$100.00
Purchases	754.00	754.00	754.00	754.00
Cost of goods available for sale	$854.00	$854.00	$854.00	$854.00
Ending inventory	222.00	221.00	204.00	213.50
Cost of goods sold	$632.00	$633.00	$650.00	$640.50
Gross margin	$308.00	$307.00	$290.00	$299.50

Note that each of the above methods produces a different inventory measurement and gross margin. As might be expected, since the trend of prices was upward during the period, LIFO shows the highest cost of goods sold and the lowest gross margin.

Which is the "correct" method? All of the above methods are considered acceptable, and no one of them can be considered the only "correct" one. Each method is attractive in particular circumstances. The application of LIFO results in matching current cost with current revenue and makes it more likely that any net income reported can be distributed as dividends without impairing the level of operations. LIFO is actually a partial answer to the problems encountered in accounting under inflationary conditions.

LIFO also reduces the amount of taxes currently payable under these conditions.

On the other hand, LIFO often charges against revenues the cost of goods *not* sold. And it permits manipulation of net income simply by changing the time at which additional purchases of merchandise are made. If precision in the matching of *actual historical cost* with revenue is desired, FIFO or specific identification are preferred. But income may also be manipulated under the specific identification method, as it may be under the simple weighted average method. Under the latter method the purchase of a large amount of goods at a relatively high price after the last sale of the period will change the average unit cost of the goods charged to the Cost of Goods Sold account. Only under FIFO is the manipulation of income *not* possible. But because net income under this method in periods of rising prices may have to be reinvested in inventory in order to maintain a given level of sales volume, this income is considered fictitious by many accountants and dubbed "paper profits."

There is also some evidence to suggest that companies have changed their method of inventory measurement simply to conform with other companies in their industry. And further, a company may employ different methods for different inventories.

Inventories at Less than Cost

As already noted, Chapter 4 of *Accounting Research Bulletin 43* requires a departure from the cost basis for inventories when the utility of the goods is less than their cost. Such loss of utility may be evidenced by damage or obsolescence or by a decline in the selling price of the goods.

Net realizable value. Damaged, obsolete, or shopworn goods are not to be carried in inventory or reported in the financial statements at an amount greater than their net realizable value. Net realizable value is defined as estimated selling price less costs to complete and dispose of the goods. For example, assume that an auto dealer has on hand one auto that has been used as a demonstrator. The auto was acquired at a cost of $7,200 and had an original sales price of $8,400. But, because it has been used and it is now late in the model year, the net realizable value of the auto is estimated at:

Estimated selling price	$7,000
Estimated maintenance and selling costs	600
Net realizable value	$6,400

The auto would be written down for inventory purposes from $7,200 to $6,400. In this way, the $800 would be treated as an expense in the period in which the decline in utility took place. If net realizable value exceeds cost, the item would of course be carried at cost. Accountants generally frown upon recognizing revenues before goods are sold.

Inventories at Cost or Market, Whichever Is Lower

Pricing inventories at the lower of cost or current market price has a long history of acceptance in accounting. The method is based, in part, upon the assumption that, if the purchase price in the market in which the firm buys has fallen, the selling price has fallen or will fall. This is not always a valid assumption.

The term **market** as used in this context means replacement cost in terms of the quantity usually purchased. In the application of the method, it is still necessary to determine cost (by either the specific identification, FIFO, LIFO, or average method).

The method uses market values only to the extent that these values are less than cost. If the inventory at December 31, 1986, has a cost of $20,000 and a market value of $21,000, this increase in market value is not recognized. To do so would be to recognize revenue prior to the time of sale.

On the other hand, if market value is $19,400, the inventory may be written down to market value from cost and a $600 loss recognized since the inventory has lost some of its revenue-generating ability. Thus, the entry made anticipates a reduced selling price when the goods are actually sold.

Application of the method. As shown in Illustration 4.10, the lower-of-cost-or-market method may be applied to each item in the inventory, to each class in the inventory, or to the total inventory. Each method of application is considered acceptable, although tax regulations require application to individual items whenever feasible.

Illustration 4.10
APPLICATION OF LOWER-OF-COST-OR-MARKET METHOD

Item and Class	Quantity	Unit Cost	Unit Market	Total Cost	Total Market	Lower of Cost or Market By Classes	Lower of Cost or Market By Units
Class A							
A1	100	$8.00	$6.90	$ 800	$ 690		$ 690
A2	200	5.00	4.25	1,000	850		850
				$1,800	$1,540	$1,540	
Class B							
B1	500	3.00	3.40	$1,500	$1,700		1,500
B2	300	4.00	3.90	1,200	1,170		1,170
				$2,700	$2,870	2,700	
				$4,500	$4,410	$4,240	$4,210

The inventory in Illustration 4.10 could be reported at $4,210, $4,240, or $4,410, and each of these measurements referred to as the lower of cost or market. When applied to each individual item, all possible losses are consistently anticipated. But this may be unduly conservative, since the inventory may be written down even though there has been an actual increase in its total market value.

Gross Margin Method of Estimating Inventory

The gross margin method is an estimating procedure used to approximate the amount of an inventory for the following purposes:

1. To obtain an inventory at the end of each month of a fiscal period except the last. The inventory cost so computed is used in the monthly financial statements.
2. As a method of verifying a previously determined ending inventory amount.

The gross margin method is based on the assumption that the **rate** of gross margin realized is highly stable from period to period; the method is satisfactory only if this assumption is correct.

To illustrate the gross margin method of computing the inventory, assume that the Sweet Company has for several years maintained a rate of gross margin on sales of 40 percent. From this fact and the data given below, the approximate inventory of December 31, 1986, may be determined as shown in Illustration 4.11.

Inventory, January 1, 1986	$ 30,000
Purchases of merchandise in 1986 . . .	390,000
Sales of merchandise in 1986	600,000

Because the gross margin method is based on the assumption that the gross margin rate in the **current** period is the **same** as in prior periods, which, of course, may not be true, it is generally not an accurate enough method to be used for the year-end financial

Illustration 4.11
COMPUTATION OF THE INVENTORY, DECEMBER 31, 1986

Inventory, January 1, 1986		$ 30,000
Purchases		390,000
Cost of merchandise available for sale . .		$420,000
Less estimated cost of sales:		
Sales	$600,000	
Gross margin (40% of $600,000) . . .	240,000	
Estimated cost of sales		360,000
Inventory, December 31, 1986		$ 60,000

statements. One of the other methods described in this chapter should be used, preferably in conjunction with a physical inventory.

The Retail Method of Estimating Inventory

The retail method is used by a wide variety of companies that sell goods directly to the ultimate consumer. In such companies, each item of merchandise is usually marked or tagged with its retail or selling price. The result is that the goods are referred to and inventoried at their retail prices.

In skeletal form, the retail method consists first of determining the ending inventory at retail prices:

> Beginning inventory at retail prices
> + Purchases at retail prices
> = Goods available for sale at retail prices; this sum
> − Sales (which are, of course, at retail prices)
> = Ending inventory at retail prices

In order to convert the ending inventory at retail prices to cost, the relationship between cost and retail prices must be known. This requires that information on the beginning inventory and purchases be accumulated so that goods available for sale can be expressed in terms of **cost** and **retail prices.** Transportation-in is added to beginning inventory and net purchases in the cost column. This cost/retail price ratio is then applied to sales to determine cost of goods sold and to the ending inventory at retail to reduce it to cost. This procedure is shown in Illustration 4.12.

Illustration 4.12
INVENTORY CALCULATION USING THE RETAIL METHOD

	Cost	Retail Price
Inventory, January 1, 1986	$ 12,000	$ 20,000
Purchases, net	115,000	200,000
Transportation-in	5,000	–0–
Cost/retail price ratio:		
$132,000/$220,000, or 60%	$132,000	$220,000
Cost of goods sold and sales (cost is 60% of retail)	111,600	186,000
Inventory, January 31, 1986 (cost is 60% of retail)	$ 20,400	$ 34,000

The $186,000 on the line entitled "Cost of goods sold and sales" is the amount of sales in the department for the month of January and is taken from the accounting records. The $111,600 is the cost of goods sold during the month, found by applying the cost/retail price ratio of 60 percent to the sales of $186,000. Deducting these two amounts, $111,600 and $186,000, from the $132,000 and $220,000 amounts on the preceding line—goods available for sale at cost and at retail—gives the January 31, 1986, inventory for the department at cost and at retail.

SUMMARY

Revenue generated by the selling activities of a business is usually recorded when the goods are delivered with the intent of making a sale. At that time, the revenue is measurable and has been earned and realized.

The major expense incurred in making sales to customers—the cost of the merchandise delivered—may be recorded at the time of sale (perpetual procedure) or at the end of the period (periodic procedure). The difference between sales revenue and the cost of the goods sold is called gross margin. Merchandise delivered may be returned or price concessions may be granted for any of a number of reasons. These returns and allowances are adjustments of recorded revenues or purchases and are recorded in separate contra accounts. Cash discounts are viewed and recorded similarly.

To obtain a proper matching of expense and revenue and to report a proper valuation for accounts receivable, the estimated uncollectible accounts arising from a year's sales are charged to bad debts expense and credited to an allowance for doubtful accounts.

Inventory cost theoretically includes the net invoice price of the goods and the cost of transportation-in, insurance in transit, receiving, handling, storage, and duties. As a practical matter, invoice cost alone is often used.

The cost of the inventory may be determined by attaching known invoice costs to specifically identified goods or by assuming a pattern of cost flows—FIFO, LIFO, or average. Each method will yield different reported amounts for inventory and net income. Management faces the task of choosing the method it will use, and this choice may be influenced by many factors including the methods employed by other members of the industry. Generally, the method chosen will be used over a period of years because generally accepted accounting principles prohibit indiscriminate switching between methods. Such switching would open the door to manipulation of reported net income and would yield information lacking in consistency between years.

Generally accepted accounting principles usually require the writedown from cost to market value (replacement cost) of those goods for which selling prices have fallen or are expected to fall before the goods are sold. Damaged, obsolete, or shopworn goods should be inventoried at their net realizable value, if less than cost.

Inventories can, if necessary, be estimated by using the gross margin method or the retail inventory method.

APPENDIX

THE WORKSHEET FOR A MERCHANDISING COMPANY

The appendix in Chapter 3 illustrated the basic structure of a worksheet. It was prepared for a company providing services.

The purpose of this appendix is to show how a worksheet would be prepared for a merchandising company (see Illustration 4.13). The example is simplified to focus on the merchandise-related accounts.

The accounts which appear in the trial balance of a merchandising company that do not appear in the trial balance of a service company are Merchandise Inventory, Sales, Sales Returns and Allowances, Sales Discounts, Purchases, Purchase Returns and Allowances, Purchase Discounts, and Transportation-In. The balances in the Merchandise Inventory account (representing the beginning inventory), the Purchases account, and all of the purchase-related accounts (such as Transportation-In, Purchase Discounts, and Purchase Returns and Allowances) are transferred to the Cost of Goods Sold account in entry (a) in the worksheet. The entry made consists of debits to Cost of Goods Sold, Purchase Discounts, and Purchase Returns and Allowances; and credits to Merchandise Inventory, Purchases, and Transportation-In. The ending inventory (assumed to be $8,000) is established by debiting Merchandise Inventory and crediting Cost of Goods Sold in entry (b) in the worksheet. All of these debits and credits should appear in the Adjustments columns of the worksheet.

All revenue accounts in the worksheet are carried to the credit Income Statement column. All revenue contra accounts and all expense accounts, including the Cost of Goods Sold account, are carried to the debit Income Statement column.

The amount needed to balance the Income Statement columns is the net income or net loss amount for the period. It is carried to the credit (or debit, if loss) Statement of Retained Earnings column.

The beginning balance in retained earnings is carried to the credit Statement of Retained Earnings column. The dividends balance is carried to the debit Statement of retained Earnings column. The amount needed to balance the Statement of Retained Earnings columns is the ending retained earnings balance. It is carried to the credit Balance Sheet column.

All assets are carried to the debit Balance Sheet column. All liabilities and stockholders' equity items are carried to the credit Balance Sheet column.

Illustration 4.13

HUNTLEY RETAIL STORE, INC.
Worksheet
For the Month Ended January 31, 1986

Acct. No	Account Titles	Unadjusted Trial Balance Debit	Unadjusted Trial Balance Credit	Adjustments Debit	Adjustments Credit	Adjusted Trial Balance Debit	Adjusted Trial Balance Credit	Income Statement Debit	Income Statement Credit	Statement of Retained Earnings Debit	Statement of Retained Earnings Credit	Balance Sheet Debit	Balance Sheet Credit
1	Cash	18,663				18,663						18,663	
3	Accounts receivable	1,880				1,880						1,880	
4	Merchandise inventory, Jan. 1	7,000			(a) 7,000								
6	Accounts payable		700				700						700
7	Capital stock		15,000				15,000						15,000
8	Retained earnings		10,000				10,000				10,000		
9	Sales		13,600				13,600		13,600				
10	Sales returns and allowances	20				20		20					
11	Sales discounts	44				44		44					
12	Purchases	6,000			(a) 6,000								
13	Purchase returns and allowances		100	(a) 100									
14	Purchase discounts		82	(a) 82									
15	Transportation-in	75			(a) 75								
16	Sales salaries	650				650		650					
17	Rent expense	150				150		150					
18	Dividends	5,000				5,000				5,000			
		39,482	39,482										
	Cost of goods sold			(a) 12,893	(b) 8,000	4,893		4,893					
	Merchandise inventory, Jan. 31*			(b) 8,000		8,000						8,000	
				21,075	21,075	39,300	39,300	5,757	13,600				
	Net income for January							7,843			7,843		
								13,600	13,600	5,000	17,843		
	Retained earnings									12,843			12,843
										17,843	17,843	28,543	28,543

* If desired, the $8,000 in the Adjustments column may be placed on the same line as the $7,000 beginning inventory figure.

QUESTIONS

1. State several of the advantages of recording revenue at the time a credit sale is made. State one disadvantage of this practice.

2. Explain how perpetual procedure affords control over inventory.

3. Explain the meaning of the phrase "to take a physical inventory."

4. Why does an understated ending inventory understate net income (before income taxes) by the same amount?

5. In what respects are a purchase return and a purchase allowance similar? How do they differ?

6. What kind of an account is Sales Returns and Allowances? Why is such an account used?

7. Conceptually, what should the cost of inventory include?

8. What is the effect of a failure to include the cost of transportation, insurance in transit, and other handling and receiving costs in inventory?

9. What are the two basic ways of determining the necessary amount of the adjusting entry for bad debts expense?

10. Show how reported net income can be manipulated by a company using LIFO in pricing its inventory. Why is the same manipulation not possible under FIFO?

11. In what three ways can the lower-of-cost-or-market method of inventory measurement be applied?

12. Under what operating conditions will the gross margin method of computing an inventory produce approximately the correct amounts?

EXERCISES

1. **a.** The Young Company purchased merchandise from the Metro Company on account and, before paying its account, returned damaged merchandise with an invoice price of $900. Assuming use of periodic inventory procedure, prepare entries on both firms' books to record the return.

   b. Prepare the necessary entries, assuming that the Metro Company granted an allowance of $300 on the damaged goods instead of accepting the return.

2. The Drew Corporation purchased goods for $6,000 on June 14 under the following terms: 2/10, n/30. The bill for the freight amounted to $150 and was paid in cash on June 14. Assume that the invoice was paid within the discount period, and prepare all of the entries required on Drew's books under the gross price method.

3. The accounts of the Pond Company as of December 31, 1986, show Accounts Receivable, $180,000; Allowance for Doubtful Accounts, $1,000 (credit); Sales, $1,080,000; and Sales Returns and Allowances, $20,000. Prepare journal entries to adjust for possible uncollectible accounts under each of the following assumptions:

   a. Bad debts expense are estimated at one half of 1 percent of net sales.

   b. The allowance is to be increased to 3 percent of accounts receivable.

4. On April 1, 1986, Doran Company, which uses the allowance method of accounting for uncollectible accounts, wrote off Bill Combs' account receivable of $352. On December 14, 1986, the company received a check for that amount from Combs marked "in full of account." Prepare the necessary entries for all of the above.

5. Compute the required size of the Allowance for Doubtful Accounts account for the following receivables:

Accounts Receivable	Age (Months)	Estimated Percentage Uncollectible
$100,000	Less than 1	5
40,000	1 to 3	20
20,000	3 to 6	30
5,000	6 to 12	60
1,000	12 and over	90

6. The Grosse Company inventory records show:

Inventory:		
Jan. 1		500 units at $6.00 = $3,000
Purchases:		
Feb. 14		300 units at $5.40 = $1,620
Mar. 18		800 units at $5.25 = $4,200
July 21		600 units at $5.70 = $3,420
Sept. 27		600 units at $5.40 = $3,240
Nov. 27		200 units at $5.85 = $1,170
Dec. 31 Inventory		800 units

a. Present a short schedule showing the measurement of the ending inventory using the LIFO method.

b. Repeat using the FIFO method.

7. The Miller Company's inventory of a certain product consisted of 8,000 units with a cost of $14 each on January 1, 1986. During 1986, numerous units of this product were purchased and sold. Also, during 1986 the purchase price to Miller of this product fell steadily until at year-end it was $10. The inventory at year-end consisted of 12,000 units. State which of the two methods of inventory measurement, LIFO or FIFO, would have resulted in the higher reported net income and explain briefly.

8. The following inventory data are for the Davis Company for 1986:

Jan.	1	Inventory, 100 units at $40 = $4,000.
Jan.	31	January sales were 20 units.
Feb.	28	February sales totaled 30 units.
Mar.	1	Purchased 50 units at $42.
Aug.	31	Sales for March through August were 40 units.
Sept.	1	Purchased 10 units at $48.
Dec.	31	September through December sales were 55 units.

Determine the cost of the December 31, 1986, inventory and the cost of goods sold for 1986, using the weighted average method.

9. Jimmy's Furniture Store has a stereo on hand at year-end that cost $400 and that it expected to sell for $600. But, since the stereo has been used as a display model, the estimated selling price is now only $350. Estimated reconditioning costs and selling commission amount to $50. At what dollar amount should this set be included in the year-end inventory? Why?

10. Your assistant prepared the following schedule to assist you in pricing the inventory under the lower-of-cost-or-market method applied on an item basis. What is the dollar amount of ending inventory?

Item	Count	Unit Cost	Unit Market	Total Cost	Total Market
A ..	200	$18.00	$17.00	$ 3,600	$ 3,400
B ..	200	8.00	9.00	1,600	1,800
C ..	600	6.00	6.00	3,600	3,600
D ..	1,000	10.20	10.40	10,200	10,400
				$19,000	$19,200

11. Richie Company follows the practice of taking a physical inventory at the end of each calendar-year accounting period to establish the ending inventory amount for financial statement purposes. Its financial statements for the past few years indicate a normal gross margin of 20 percent. On July 25 a fire destroyed the entire store building and contents. The records were in a fireproof vault and are intact. These records through July 24 show:

Merchandise inventory, January 1 . .	$ 25,000
Merchandise purchases	675,000
Purchase returns	7,500
Transportation-in	42,500
Sales	775,000
Sales returns	25,000

The company was fully covered by insurance, and it asks you to determine the amount of its claim for loss of merchandise.

12. Using the retail inventory method, determine the ending inventory at cost from the following:

	Cost	Selling Price
Beginning inventory . .	$105,000	$ 195,000
Purchases	954,000	1,584,000
Purchase returns . . .	12,000	22,500
Sales		1,224,000
Sales returns		6,000
Transporation-in	6,900	

PROBLEMS

4–1. Erickson Company, which uses periodic inventory procedure, purchased merchandise as follows:

(1) $10,000 from Lunt Company, terms 2/10, n/30

(2) $8,000 from Andrews Company, terms 2/10, n/30

The Lunt invoice was paid within the discount period. The Andrews invoice was paid late.

Required:

    a. Prepare journal entries for the above transactions, assuming that the invoices were originally recorded at their gross invoice amounts.

    b. Post the entries to T-accounts.

    c. Repeat **a** and **b,** assuming that the invoices were originally recorded at their net invoice amounts.

4–2. Following are selected, summarized transactions of the Drake Company (which uses periodic inventory procedure) for the year 1986:

    (1) Sales on account, $500,000; terms 2/10, n/30.

    (2) Sales returns and allowances totaled $10,000.

    (3) Customers remitted $392,800 in settlement of $400,000 of accounts after taking discounts offered.

    (4) Purchases on account, $400,000; terms 2/10, n/30.

    (5) Purchase returns and allowances amounted to $12,000.

    (6) Transportation-in costs incurred on account, $16,000.

    (7) Payments on account, $353,200, in settlement of $360,000 of invoices for merchandise after taking discounts offered.

    (8) Bad debts are estimated at 1 percent of sales, less sales returns and allowances.

Required:

    a. Prepare journal entries for the above transactions using the gross price method (omit explanations).

    b. Post the entries to T-accounts.

    c. Assume that the inventory was $44,000 on January 1 and $72,000 on December 31 and that operating expenses and taxes amount to $70,000—including bad debts expense. Prepare an income statement for the year which includes the gross margin determination.

4–3. The following inventory data are for the Green Corporation for January:

    Jan. 1   Inventory on hand cost, $2,000

           12   Purchased on account from the Beatle Company goods costing $12,000; terms 2/10, n/30.

           12   Paid transportation on goods purchased, $1,000 cash.

           15   Returned to the Beatle Company goods costing $2,000.

           21   Paid the Beatle Company the amount due.

           25   Sale on account was $14,000; terms n/30.

           31   Partial collection of $6,000 was made on the receivable resulting from the sale.

    The inventory on hand on January 31 cost $5,000. The operating expenses for the month were $4,000.

Required:

    a. Prepare journal entries to record the transactions for the month of January using the gross price method (omit explanations).

b. Post the entries to T-accounts.

c. Determine the cost of goods sold in January.

d. Determine the gross margin for January.

e. Prepare an income statement for January.

4–4. Presented below are selected accounts of the Hertha Company as of December 31, 1986. Prior to closing the accounts, the $3,000 account of Pond Company is to be written off (this was a credit sale of February 12, 1986).

Accounts receivable	$ 240,000
Allowance for doubtful accounts . .	4,000 Dr.
Sales	1,120,000
Sales returns and allowances . . .	20,000

Required:

a. Prepare journal entries to record the above and to record the bad debts expense for the period, assuming the estimated expense is 2 percent of net sales.

b. Give the entry to record the estimated expense for the period if the allowance is to be adjusted to 5 percent of outstanding receivables instead of as in (a) above.

4–5. The Butler Company began business on July 1, 1985, selling a single product. For the year ending June 30, 1986, 15,000 units were sold at $20 each. Purchases consisted of 10,000 units on July 1 at $8 and 10,000 units on December 18 at $10. Jim Johnson, the accountant for Butler Company, prepared the following income statement for the year ended June 30, 1986, for presentation to the board of directors:

Sales	$300,000
Cost of goods sold	135,000
Gross margin	$165,000
Expenses	80,000
Net income before taxes . .	$ 85,000

At the board meeting, members of the board questioned Jim's use of the average cost method in determining the cost of goods sold and the cost of the ending inventory. One member indicated a preference for LIFO; another preferred FIFO; and yet another asked about the effects of using FIFO or LIFO and the direction of price changes. The board directed Jim to prepare the information desired by the various members and to report at the afternoon meeting of the board.

Required:

a. Using the above information, prepare two income statements similar to the one given, one using FIFO and the other using LIFO, for presentation to the board. Assume that Butler Company uses periodic inventory procedure.

b. Repeat a, using all of the same information, except assume that the July 1 purchases cost $10 each, while the December purchases cost $8 each.

c. What facts are revealed by the statements in *a* and *b* that should be brought to the board's attention?

4–6. The Crissy Corporation was organized on January 1, 1984, to sell a product whose resale price reacts promptly to changes in cost. Unit prices rose during the three years ended December 31, 1986. Selected data for 1984–86 follow:

Year Ended December 31	Inventory FIFO	Inventory LIFO	Annual Data Purchases	Annual Data Sales
1984	$3,200	$2,400	$14,400	$16,200
1985	4,000	2,800	12,000	19,000
1986	6,600	4,000	14,800	16,400

Required:

a. Compute the gross margin for each of the three years under FIFO and under LIFO.

b. Comment on your answer to *a*.

4–7. Following are data relating to the beginning inventory and purchases of the Ralph Company for the year 1986:

Jan. 1 inventory . . .	2,800 @	$4.20
Purchases:		
Feb. 2	2,000 @	4.00
Apr. 5	4,000 @	3.48
June 15	2,400 @	3.40
Sept. 20	2,800 @	3.20
Nov. 28	3,600 @	3.60

A physical count showed 4,400 units on hand at the end of the year.

Required:

Compute the cost of goods sold and the cost of the ending inventory under each of the following methods: *(a)* FIFO, *(b)* LIFO, and *(c)* weighted average.

4–8. The following data are related to the beginning inventory and purchases of the Swiss Corporation for 1986.

Jan. 1 inventory . . .	1,000 @ $4.00	$ 4,000
Purchases:		
Mar. 2	2,000 @ 4.10	8,200
June 5	5,000 @ 4.20	21,000
Aug. 12	2,000 @ 4.30	8,600

The Swiss Corporation sold 8,000 units at $10 each during 1986.

Required:

Compute the cost of the ending inventory, the cost of goods sold, and the gross margin under each of the following methods: *(a)* FIFO, *(b)* LIFO, and *(c)* weighted average.

4–9. Given below are data relating to the December 31, 1986, inventory of the Land Company:

Item		Quantity	Unit Cost	Unit Market
1	. . .	1,500	$4.00	$3.80
2	. . .	3,000	3.20	3.60
3	. . .	1,000	3.00	3.20
4	. . .	2,500	5.60	5.00
5	. . .	2,000	5.00	5.20
6	. . .	500	3.60	3.20

Required:

    a. Compute the ending inventory, applying the lower-of-cost-or-market method to the total inventory.

    b. Repeat *a*, applying the method to individual items.

    c. What would be the effect on net income before income taxes of using the method applied to individual items rather than to total inventory?

4–10. You are the chief accountant of the Beacham Hardware Store, and your assistant has been applying the lower-of-cost-or-market method on an item basis to your company's December 31, 1986, inventory. Your assistant brings the following data to your attention:

Item	Units	Unit Cost
Product R: This item has been selling extremely well. Its retail price was recently raised 20 percent because replacement cost increased from $200 to $220 per unit	10	$200
Product S: The retail price of this item has been reduced because of a lack of demand. The cost to replace this item has also been reduced—from $60 to $50	40	60
Product T: The units on hand of this item are obsolete and damaged to such an extent that it will cost more to repair them than they can be sold for after repair	4	25
Product U: The cost of replacing this item has dropped 5 percent, but Beacham has a contract to sell all of these items at their regular selling price, which includes normal markup	100	10
Product V: This item is being discontinued. Its sales price is expected to be reduced from $50 to $25, with disposal costs of $2 each expected	50	50
Product W: This item was shipped to Beacham by Abrams on a consignment basis, with Beacham to pay only for units sold	20	75
Remainder: No problems encountered. Their dollar amount at lower of cost or market is $28,000.		

Required:

    a. Compute the cost or market dollar amount, whichever is lower, for the ending inventory. State the amount assigned to each of the above items separately.

    b. For the six items above, state the reason for the unit dollar amount you assigned in *a*.

4–11. The accountant for the Wilson Company prepared the following schedule of the company's December 31, 1986, inventory, and used the lower of total cost or total market in determining the cost of the goods sold for the year.

Item	Quantity	Unit Cost	Unit Market	Total Cost	Total Market
A	. . . 4,000	$6.00	$6.00	$24,000	$24,000
B	. . . 3,000	4.00	3.60	12,000	10,800
C	. . . 6,000	2.00	1.60	12,000	9,600
D	. . . 8,000	1.00	1.20	8,000	9,600
				$56,000	$54,000

Required:

a. State whether the method used is an accepted way of applying the lower-of-cost-or-market method.

b. Compute the dollar amount of the inventory under an alternative way of applying this method.

c. What would be the effect on net income before taxes of using the alternative method?

d. If the 3,000 units of product B are obsolete and shopworn so that they can be sold for an estimated $2 each, less total delivery charges of $75, at what amount should they be included in inventory?

4–12. Rex Company recently asked Durant Company to sell merchandise to Rex on a credit basis. Durant asked for current financial statements before making a decision. Rex does not wish to incur the cost of taking a physical inventory, which it normally takes only at the end of its accounting year, December 31. Financial statements for the previous three years ending on December 31, 1985, show that Rex has consistently earned a gross margin on net sales of 40 percent. The accounts show, for the seven months ending on July 31, 1986, the following:

Expenses	$ 328,000
Sales	1,257,000
Purchases	726,000
Purchase returns	6,000
Sales returns	37,000
Inventory, January 1, 1986 . .	92,000

Required:

a. Indicate in general terms how the cost of an inventory can be estimated for interim periods.

b. Estimate the July 31, 1986, inventory of Rex.

c. Prepare an income statement for Rex for the seven months ended July 31, 1986.

d. Upon what factor used in preparing the income statement in *c* does the accuracy of the statement depend very heavily? Explain.

4–13. (Based on the chapter appendix).

Required:

From the following trial balance and supplementary information, prepare:

a. A 12-column worksheet for the year ended December 31, 1986. (See chapter appendix for illustration of form.)

b. The required closing entries.

Supplementary data:

(a) The building is to be depreciated at the rate of 2 percent per year.

(b) Depreciate the store fixtures 10 percent per year.

(c) The Allowance for Doubtful Accounts is to be increased by one half of 1 percent of net sales. (Round amount to nearest full dollar.)

(d) Accrued interest on notes receivable is $150.

(e) Accrued interest on the mortgage note is $250.

(f) Accrued sales salaries are $700.

(g) Prepaid insurance is $200.

(h) Prepaid advertising is $500.

(i) Included in the cash on hand is a worthless check for $25 which was cashed for a former employee in 1986.

(j) Cost of merchandise inventory on hand December 31, 1986, is $27,750.

WELLS COMPANY
Trial Balance
December 31, 1986

	Debits	Credits
Cash	$ 8,600	
Accounts receivable	41,250	
Allowance for doubtful accounts		$ 850
Notes receivable	3,750	
Merchandise inventory, January 1, 1986	20,800	
Land	30,000	
Building	55,000	
Accumulated depreciation—building		16,500
Store fixtures	27,800	
Accumulated depreciation—store fixtures		5,560
Accounts payable		18,950
Mortgage note payable		25,000
Capital stock		50,000
Retained earnings		35,090
Sales		275,750
Sales returns and allowances	1,000	
Sales discounts	1,850	
Purchases	156,450	
Purchase returns and allowances		700
Purchase discounts		1,300
Transportation-in	3,650	
Sales salaries	32,000	
Advertising expense	6,000	
Transportation-out	2,300	
Officers' salaries	37,000	
Insurance expense	1,450	
Interest revenue		200
Interest expense	1,000	
	$429,900	$429,900

5 INTERNAL CONTROL AND THE CONTROL OF CASH

This chapter covers internal control in general and the control of cash. Internal control is covered first. Various aspects involving the control of cash are covered including the control of receipts and disbursements, bank reconciliation statements, payroll checking accounts, petty cash funds, a voucher system, and certain other matters.

INTERNAL CONTROL

A system of internal control includes all the procedures and actions taken by an organization to (1) protect its assets against theft and waste, (2) ensure compliance with company policies and federal law,[1] (3) evaluate the performance of personnel in all parts of the company to promote efficiency of operations, and (4) ensure accurate and reliable operating data and accounting reports. The system provides direction to all activity within the organization and ensures that all units are functioning as intended.

Various aspects of internal control are dealt with throughout the text. For instance, Chapter 4 dealt with merchandise transactions

---

[1] In December 1977 the Foreign Corrupt Practices Act of 1977 went into effect. Under this law all companies in the United States (as well as their officers, directors, agents, employees, and stockholders) are prohibited from bribing foreign governmental or political officials. Also, publicly-held corporations are required to meet certain requirements concerning internal control and record keeping.

and mentioned some of the control documents that are used. Control documents that are used include:

1. Purchase requisition—a form sent by a department manager to the purchasing department requesting that department to purchase various items that are needed.
2. Purchase order—a form used by the purchasing department to order items from another company.
3. Invoice—an itemized statement (or bill) sent by the supplier of goods or services to the purchaser of those goods or services. It is considered to be a purchase invoice to the purchaser and a sales invoice to the seller.
4. Receiving report—a form prepared by the receiving department showing the description, quantity, and condition of items received.

A copy of each of these documents is sent to the accounting department. As a group, the documents serve as authorization to pay the invoice. In the absence of these documents, the company might fail to pay a legitimate invoice, might pay fictitious invoices, or might pay certain invoices more than once. Purchase requisitions, purchase orders, invoices, and receiving reports should be serially numbered for greater control. Additional coverage of the control aspects of the payment of invoices is contained in the voucher system discussion later in this chapter. Various other procedures for protecting cash are also discussed later in this chapter. Control aspects concerning other assets are discussed in later chapters.

Some features of organization and some broad policies and procedures that lead to a strong system of internal control include:

1. Those responsible for safeguarding an asset should *not* maintain the accounting records for that asset. Also, the responsibility for related transactions should be divided between individuals so that the work of one serves as a check on the other. In this way, collusion between at least two parties would be necessary to steal assets and cover up the theft in the accounting records.
2. Complete and accurate accounting records should be maintained on a current basis. Inadequate records serve as an invitation to theft by dishonest employees.
3. Whenever possible, responsibilities should be assigned and duties subdivided in such a way that only one person is responsible for a given function or asset. Then, if a shortage occurs, responsibility cannot be denied and blamed on someone else.
4. Employees should be rotated in their job assignments when possible. Mere knowledge that this will be done may discourage certain employees from engaging in long-term schemes to steal from

the company. Also, if such theft does occur, the scheme may be uncovered by the employee who is later rotated into a job. Related to job rotation is the requirement that all employees take an annual vacation. Many schemes that have been used by employees to steal from their company will collapse if not attended to on a daily basis.

5. Where feasible, devices such as check protectors (which perforate the amount of a check into the check), cash registers, and time clocks should be used to record amounts in such a way that employees cannot alter them.

6. An internal auditing function should be performed, especially in large, complex companies. The internal auditing staff investigates operating efficiency throughout the company. The staff is constantly alert for breakdowns in the system of internal control and makes recommendations for improvement of the system.

7. Honest, competent employees should be hired and then trained concerning internal control procedures. They should be made to understand the importance of following the procedures.

8. In spite of all the above features, it is impossible to construct a foolproof internal control system. If collusion among dishonest employees exists, the system can be beaten. Therefore, it is advisable to carry adequate casualty insurance on assets and to carry fidelity bonds on employees who handle cash and other negotiable assets. With these coverages the company can recover at least a portion of any loss from the insurance or bonding company.

THE CONTROL OF CASH

The Nature of Cash

Cash includes currency, coins, negotiable instruments (such as checks, bank drafts, and money orders), amounts in checking or savings accounts at a bank, and demand certificates of deposit at a bank. Cash does *not* include such items as postage stamps, IOUs, and notes receivable. Cash is usually divided into cash on hand and cash in banks. But in financial reporting these are combined into one amount and reported as "cash."

Many business transactions involve cash. Also, cash is the most useful item for someone to steal since it can be used to obtain anything else. Therefore, management must keep close control over cash and account for it carefully.

The objectives of management in regard to cash are:

1. Account for all cash transactions accurately so that management will have correct information regarding cash.

2. Make sure there is enough cash to pay bills as they come due.

3. Avoid holding excessive amounts of idle cash which could be invested in productive assets to increase earnings.

4. Prevent the loss of cash by theft or fraud.

Most of a firm's cash transactions involve a bank checking account. The firm deposits its daily receipts into a checking account and writes checks on that account to pay its bills. Periodically, the firm's account and the bank's account are reconciled to make sure that no errors have been made. Therefore, in this chapter, significant attention is given to the checking account portion of cash. But first we examine the procedures used to control cash receipts and cash disbursements to prevent error, theft, and fraud.

Controlling Cash Receipts

From the moment cash is received until it is deposited in the bank, it should be completely safeguarded. While cash is of no more importance than inventory, it is sometimes more easily stolen. This is because it can be concealed and because each separate unit of money is not readily identifiable since serial numbers generally are not recorded.

The methods used to control cash receipts vary with each business. Therefore, the following description of the internal control of cash receipts may be varied in practice to suit the individual needs of each business. A few basic principles for controlling cash receipts follow.

1. A record of all cash receipts should be prepared as soon as the cash is received. Most thefts of cash receipts occur before a record is made of them. Once a record has been made, improper uses are more readily traceable.

2. All cash receipts should be deposited intact in the bank, preferably on the next business day or in the bank's night depository on the same day. Cash disbursements should not be made from cash receipts but only by check or from petty cash funds. In many retail stores, refunds for returned merchandise are made from the cash register. If this practice is followed, refund tickets should be prepared.

3. The person who handles the cash receipts should not record them in the accounting records, and the company accountant should not have access to the cash receipts.

4. If possible—and it is possible in all but small concerns—the internal function of receiving cash should be separated from the internal function of disbursing cash.

Controlling Cash Disbursements

The procedures for controlling cash disbursements are:

1. With the exception of petty cash disbursements, all disbursements should be by check. No cash receipts should be disbursed.

2. All checks should be prenumbered—consecutively—and all should be controlled and accounted for.

3. Preferably, two signatures should appear on all checks.

4. If possible, the person who approves payment should not be one of the persons who signs the checks.

5. Each check should be supported by approved invoices or approved vouchers (authorizations to draw the checks).

6. The person authorizing the disbursement of cash should be certain that payment is in order and that it is made to the proper payee.

7. Invoices and vouchers should be indelibly stamped "paid," together with the date and the check number. This minimizes duplicate payments of a debt.

8. The person signing the checks should not have access to returned checks paid by the bank.

9. The bookkeeper should obtain the bank statement and the paid checks and prepare the bank reconciliation statement.

10. All voided and spoiled checks should be retained and mutilated to prevent their unauthorized use.

The Bank Checking Account

A bank must account to its depositors for all funds received from and spent for them. Certain business papers are involved.

The signature card.   A bank requires a new depositor to complete a signature card giving the signatures of the persons authorized to sign checks on the account. The signature card is retained at the bank to identify the signatures as they appear on returned checks drawn on the bank.

Bank deposit tickets.   When a deposit is made in the bank, the depositor prepares a deposit ticket. Deposit tickets come in many forms, but all of these include the name of the account, the account number, the amount of cash deposited, and a listing of the checks deposited. In modern machine-based bank accounting systems, each depositor is given a number of deposit tickets imprinted with the depositor's name and account number. When making a deposit, the depositor receives a machine-imprinted receipt showing the date and the amount of the deposit.

The bank check.   There are three parties to every bank check transaction: (1) the depositor issuing the check; (2) the bank on which the check is drawn; and (3) the party to whose order the check is made payable.

A check is a written order on a bank to pay a specific sum of money to a designated party (called the payee) or to his or her order. It is signed by the person issuing the check.

The type of check generally used by modern business firms is prenumbered when printed. It is prepared in sets of an original and as many copies as are needed. The lower section of the check is known as a **remittance advice** and is detached prior to the depositing of the check. The remittance advice contains information explaining the check.

The checking account statement. The bank furnishes each checking account depositor with a **bank statement,** one form of which is shown in Illustration 5.1. It is usually issued once each month.

The bank statement shows *(a)* each deposit made during the period, *(b)* each check which cleared during the period, and *(c)* a daily balance of the account whenever it changes. Any debit memoranda (amounts deducted from the account, such as service charges) and credit memoranda (amounts added to the account, such as the proceeds of notes collected for the depositor by the bank) will also be shown.

The deposit tickets for deposits made during the month and the checks paid by the bank during the month will also be returned to the depositor with the bank statement.

Reconciling the bank statement and Cash account balances. The balance shown by the bank statement will usually differ from the balance for the same date in the depositor's ledger account for cash in bank. The reasons for this difference include:

1. Items that cause a larger balance to be shown on the bank's statement than in the depositor's ledger account.
   a. Checks issued by the depositor that are still outstanding; the payees have not presented the checks to the bank for payment.
   b. Deposits made in the depositor's account by the bank for which entries have not been made on the depositor's books. For example, the bank may collect a note for the depositor, add it to the depositor's balance, and advise the depositor of the collection immediately; the depositor may not yet have recorded the amount in its accounting records.
2. Items that cause a smaller balance to be shown on the bank's statement than in the depositor's ledger account:
   a. Deposits recorded on the depositor's books that are in transit (have not yet been recorded by the bank). They are picked up as deposits on the next period's bank statement.
   b. Bank charges for services rendered by the bank to the depositor that have been deducted from its bank balance but have not been credited to cash on the books of the depositor. Notice of these deductions is included with the bank statement in the form of debit memoranda. Examples of these deductions are service charges for checks and deposits (when the daily balance in an account is below the minimum required by the bank) and charges for collecting notes.
   c. Deductions for NSF (not sufficient funds) checks. These are

Illustration 5.1 BANK STATEMENT

C&S

THE CITIZENS AND SOUTHERN NATIONAL BANK
ATLANTA, GEORGIA 30302   491-0000

Account Number	**Date of Statement**
023-45-678	2/28/86

Branch Number
09

ABC COMPANY
123 PRYOR STREET
ATLANTA, GEORGIA 30301

Statement Summary

Ending Balance Previous Statement		Total Amount Deposits and Credits		Total Amount Checks and Debits		Balance as of Statement Date
10,500.00	+	159,207.52	—	153,435.12	=	16,272.40

Checks and Debits				Deposits and Credits	Date	Balances
					JAN 31	10,500.00
2,100.00	1,500.75	700.00	NF	6,500.50	FEB 1	12,699.75
75.00	150.28			7,200.22	2	19,674.69
280.50	420.31	600.00		6,200.00	5	
				7,500.00 CM		32,073.88
410.40	270.27	20.00	SC	8,100.00	6	39,473.21
340.30	560.73	14,000.00		4,700.76	7	29,272.94
70.85	105.67	5,000.00	DM	5,800.00	8	29,896.42
530.62				6,100.50	9	35,466.30
710.57	15,500.20			10,200.25	12	29,455.78
840.61	10,961.75	625.40		9,400.40	13	26,428.42
660.83	12,200.00			8,300.60	14	21,868.19
214.14	46.27	10,500.00	DM	8,800.70	15	19,908.48
380.00	8,200.50			7,300.35	16	18,628.33
210.76	10,200.00			7,700.14	19	15,917.71
465.98				6,700.16	20	22,151.89
715.00	68.20	9,472.50		8,200.25	21	20,096.44
840.50	642.10 NF	9,300.00		9,100.41	22	18,414.25
965.45	8,700.00			9,300.37	23	18,049.17
5,210.33	877.50	962.15		8,900.89	26	19,900.08
762.87	7,481.50			5,600.60	27	17,256.31
910.74	7,628.40	45.19		7,600.42	28	16,272.40

Symbols SC Service Charge. NF Charge for Check on not-sufficient funds. DM Debit Memo. CM Credit Memo. R Reversal of Posted Amount. BP Batch Posted

Member FDIC

checks that the depositor received from customers. When such a check arrived at the bank that was ordered to pay the funds, there were insufficient funds to cover it. Since the customer has not satisfied the debt, the company needs to reestablish the account receivable.

Also, errors may be made by either the bank or the depositor. As a result of these various items, neither the bank statement nor the depositor's ledger account may show the exact expendable balance of cash that should appear in the balance sheet. Correcting entries to reflect items 1*(b)*, 2*(b)*, and 2*(c)* and depositor errors (if any) should be made in the depositor's records.

The bank reconciliation statement. A bank reconciliation statement is prepared to explain the difference between the cash balance on the books and on the bank statement. Both the bank statement balance and the balance in the Cash ledger account are adjusted to the true balance of expendable cash that should appear on the balance sheet as shown in Illustration 5.2.

Illustration 5.2
BANK RECONCILIATION STATEMENT

ATLANTA COMPANY
Bank Reconciliation Statement
August 31, 1986

Balance per bank statement, August 31, 1986	$23,195.85	Balance per ledger, August 31, 1986		$22,009.85
Add: Deposit in transit	1,057.05	Add: Note collected by bank		800.00
	$24,252.90			$22,809.85
Less: Outstanding checks	1,645.55	Less: Bank charges	$ 2.50	
		NSF check	200.00	202.50
Adjusted balance, August 31, 1986	$22,607.35	Adjusted balance, August 31, 1986		$22,607.35

The first step in preparing the reconciliation statement is to examine the bank statement and the debit and credit memoranda, if any, returned with the statement. The depositor's accounting records should be examined to see if the items referred to in these memoranda have been recorded. If they have not, they must be added to or deducted from the balance in the Cash account, as shown by the adjustments for $800 for the note collected, $2.50 for bank service charges, and $200 for the NSF check in Illustration 5.2.

The second step is to sort the canceled checks returned by the bank into numerical order. The outstanding checks are identified by a process of elimination. The numbers of the checks which have cleared and been returned by the bank are compared with the numbers of the checks issued. Tick marks (✓) are used in the books to indicate those returned. The checks issued for which no canceled checks have been returned from the bank are the outstanding checks. Checks outstanding at the start of the month that have cleared the bank during the month may be traced to the reconciliation statement prepared at the end of the preceding month. Any checks outstanding at the end of the preceding month that have not yet been returned during the current month are, of course, still outstanding at the end of the current month.

The next step in preparing the reconciliation statement is to see if there are any deposits in transit to the bank. The receipts for the last day of the month might have been deposited in the night depository box at the bank. Thus, they would be reported as a deposit by the bank as of the next day. The debits to the Cash account can be traced to the individual deposits per the bank statement.

Deposits in transit and outstanding checks, together with the bank service charges indicated on the bank statement, will often account entirely for the difference between the balance in the bank statement and the balance in the Cash account. Any omissions and errors in the depositor's books are corrected by proper entries. These entries should be made prior to the preparation of the financial statements. If any errors made by the bank are discovered in preparing the reconciliation statement (such as charging a check against the wrong account), they should be called to the attention of the bank.

To illustrate the preparation of a bank reconciliation statement, assume that the bank statement of the Atlanta Company at August 31, 1986, showed a balance of $23,195.85; the Cash account balance of the depositor at the same date was $22,009.85. By comparing the canceled checks returned by the bank with the accounting records, the following checks were found to be outstanding at the end of the month:

Check No.	Amount
556	$ 840.00
570	354.25
571	451.30
	$1,645.55

An examination of the debit and credit memoranda returned with the bank statement reveals a credit memorandum showing that the bank had collected a customer's note for the Atlanta Company and had credited the amount collected, $800, to the company's account. (A credit memorandum is evidence of an addition to a depositor's account which arises from a transaction other than a normal deposit.) For this service, the bank charged the Atlanta Company $2.50 and so advised the company by including a debit memorandum for that amount with the canceled checks returned on August 31, 1986. There was another debit memorandum in the amount of $200 for an NSF check received from Rook Company on August 10 and deposited on that date.

A tracing of the deposits shown in the accounting records to the bank statement revealed that cash receipts for August 31, $1,057.05, did not appear as a deposit on that date. Examination of the deposit ticket showed that the bank recorded the deposit on September 1.

The statement reconciling the balance per the bank statement with the balance per Cash account as of August 31, 1986 (Illustration 5.2) shows that the cash available for immediate disbursement is not $22,009.85 or $23,195.85, but $22,607.35. Consequently, the following journal entries must be prepared and posted:

Cash	800.00	
Notes Receivable		800.00
To record note collected by bank.		
Bank Service Charges	2.50	
Cash		2.50
To record bank collection charges.		
Accounts Receivable (Rook Company)	200.00	
Cash		200.00
To record NSF check which was deducted from our account.		

Entries such as these are only made for the reconciling items affecting the balance per ledger. No entries are made for items affecting the balance per bank statement.

The income statement for the period ended August 31, 1986, should include the expense of $2.50. The balance sheet as of August 31, 1986, should show a cash balance of $22,607.35.

When more than one checking account is maintained by a company, each account must be reconciled separately with the bank statement covering the amount.

Certified checks. Because a check may not be paid when it is presented to the bank upon which it is drawn, a payee may demand that the check be certified. A certified check is a regular check drawn by a depositor and taken by the depositor to his or her bank for certification. The bank will stamp "certified" across the face of the check and insert the name of the bank and the date; the certification will be signed by a bank official. The bank will do this only after determining that the depositor's balance is large enough to cover the check, and the check will be deducted from the depositor's balance immediately. The check then becomes a liability of the bank. For this reason, it usually will be accepted without question.

Transfer bank accounts. A company operating in many widely scattered locations and having accounts with many local banks must use special procedures to avoid accumulating too much idle cash. One such procedure involves the use of special-instruction bank accounts. Transfer accounts are set up in the local banks. These banks automatically transfer to a central bank (by wire or bank draft) all amounts on deposit in excess of a stated amount (which may be zero). In this way funds not needed for local operations are quickly sent to the company's headquarters, where they can be invested.

Payroll Checking Accounts

Many firms maintain a separate payroll bank account, especially when many employees are paid by check. In general, a payroll checking account is used in the following fashion. Before each payday, the net payroll is computed, a check is drawn on the general commercial bank account for that amount, and the check is deposited in the payroll bank account. Individual payroll checks are issued to the employees. When these are cashed they are cleared against the payroll bank account.

The use of a payroll bank account has the following advantages:

1. A distinctive payroll check form may be used, with spaces provided on an attached apron for the amounts of gross earnings, the various payroll deductions, and the net cash paid.
2. Payroll checks, identifiable as such, are easily cashed by employees.
3. The work of reconciling the bank balances may be divided among employees. One check is drawn against the general commercial bank account. The hundreds or thousands of payroll checks issued each payday are drawn on the payroll bank account. Occasionally, payroll checks are lost or negotiated many times before clearing the bank. Including these items in the payroll reconciliation simplifies the reconciliation of the general Cash account.
4. Only one authorization is prepared, calling for one check drawn against the general commercial bank account; therefore, payroll checks are issued without separately prepared and signed authorizations.
5. The individual payroll checks need not be entered in the regular cash disbursements record; the payroll check numbers are inserted in the payroll journal or record, and a repetition of the entering of the checks is avoided.

Frequently $1,000 or more is deposited to the payroll account over and above immediate payroll needs. Thus, during the period between regular payroll dates there will be a balance available for such payroll checks as may be issued for advances to employees or for final pay upon termination of employment.

Cash Short and Over

Occasionally, errors are made in returning change to customers. In these cases the amount of cash will be short of, or in excess of, the amount shown by the total of a cash register tape or an adding machine tape total of sales slips for a day.

Assume that a store clerk accidentally shortchanges a cash customer to the extent of $1. Total cash sales for the day were $704.50. At the end of the day, the total actual cash will be $1 over the sum of the sales tickets or the total of the cash register tape. The journal entry to record the day's business is as follows:

Cash	705.50	
Sales		704.50
Cash Short and Over		1.00

The Cash Short and Over account is a miscellaneous expense (debit balance) or revenue (credit balance) account. It is credited if the cash received is greater than the correct amount and debited if the cash received is less than the correct amount. The balance of the account at the end of the period will be treated as an "other expense" or "other revenue."

The Petty Cash Fund

While it is desirable that all disbursements be made by check, most concerns find it convenient to make certain small payments in cash. Disbursements for delivery charges, postage stamps, taxi fares, supper money for employees working overtime, and other small items usually require a small amount of cash on hand.

To permit such small disbursements to be made in cash and at the same time to maintain adequate control over these disbursements, firms often establish a petty cash fund of some round dollar amount such as $50 or $100. One individual in the company is placed in charge of the fund and is responsible for the entire sum.

Petty cash funds are almost always maintained on an **imprest** basis. This means that only periodically is the petty cash fund reimbursed out of general cash. At that time, the expenses that have been paid out of petty cash are recorded. All future discussion will assume the establishment and maintenance of petty cash funds on this basis.

When the petty cash fund is established, a check is prepared, payable to the order of the person who is to be the petty cash cashier, and an entry is made as follows:

Petty Cash Fund	100	
Cash		100
To record drawing a check to establish a petty cash fund of $100.		

The fund should be large enough to take care of petty cash disbursements for a reasonable period of time, for example, one month. The check is cashed, and the fund is now ready to make disbursements.

A **petty cash voucher** (Illustration 5.3) should be prepared for each disbursement from the petty cash fund. If the person receiving the cash can furnish an invoice, it should be stapled to the petty cash voucher. The petty cash cashier is accountable at all times for cash and petty cash vouchers totaling to the amount of the fund.

Illustration 5.3
PETTY CASH VOUCHER

RECEIVED OF PETTY CASH

No. 359 DATE June 29, 1986

DESCRIPTION OF ITEM / SERVICE PURCHASED	AMOUNT
Freight on parts	2 27
CHARGE TO ACCOUNT 27 Local Cartage, Inc. **TOTAL**	

RECEIVED BY *Ken Black* APPROVED BY O.E.S.

TOPS FORM 3008 LITHO IN U.S.A.

Replenishing the fund. Whenever the balance in the petty cash fund is at a relatively low level, it is replenished. A check is drawn, payable to the cashier of the fund in an amount that will bring the cash in the fund back up to the original fund balance. Various expense accounts (and occasionally other accounts) are debited for the proper amounts and cash is credited for the difference between the original fund balance and the actual amount of cash presently in the fund. Sometimes it is necessary to debit or credit Cash Over and Short to make the entry balance.

To illustrate, assume that when summarized, the vouchers in a given fund show petty cash fund expenditures of $22.75 chargeable to Transportation-In, $50.80 for postage stamps, and $19.05 chargeable to Delivery Expense, for a total of $92.60. A check in that amount would be drawn, payable to the cashier of the fund, and it would be charged to the accounts indicated above. The entry would read:

Transportation-In	22.75
Stamps and Stationery	50.80
Delivery Expense	19.05
Cash	92.60

To record check drawn to replenish petty cash fund.

After the check for $92.60 has been endorsed and cashed, the amount of cash in the fund is at the established amount, $100. After the petty cash vouchers have been audited (by someone other than the custodian of the fund) and approved and the fund has been replenished, the vouchers should be stamped or mutilated so that they cannot be reused.

Generally, the Petty Cash account is debited only when the fund is created or increased in size and credited only when the fund is discontinued or decreased in size. But at the end of the accounting period (assume it is December 31) it is necessary to bring all expenses for the period into the accounts for income determination purposes and for proper balance sheet reporting. This must be done even if the fund is not replenished at that time. Therefore, at the end of the year, if the fund contains $80 of cash and vouchers totaling $20, the following entry should be made:

Dec. 31	Various expense accounts (itemized)	20	
	Petty Cash		20

The amount of the entry is for the total of the expense vouchers in the petty cash fund. The $80 petty cash balance would be reported as part of the total representing all of the company's cash balances.

Assuming that $10 in additional expenditures have been paid out of the petty cash fund prior to January 10, the journal entry to record its replenishment on that date would read as follows:

Jan. 10	Various expense accounts (itemized)	10	
	Petty Cash	20	
	Cash		30

The above entry restores the petty cash fund to its original $100 balance.

The Voucher System for Controlling Disbursements

In very small companies where the owner has an intimate knowledge of all transactions and personally signs all checks, there need be no great concern over the proper handling of cash disbursements. In larger companies where the owners or top-management people have no direct part in the payment process, close control over this function should be provided via a formalized system of internal control.

With a voucher system, internal control over cash disbursements is achieved in the following way. Each transaction that will involve the payment of cash is entered on a voucher. A voucher is a form with spaces provided for data concerning the liability being set up (such as invoice number, invoice date, creditor's name and address, description of the goods or services, terms of payment, and amount due). It also has spaces for the signatures of those approving the obligation for payment. The voucher usually forms a "jacket" for the invoice and other supporting documents. Each voucher goes through a rigorous process of examination and eventual approval or disapproval. By the time a voucher is approved for payment, one can be quite certain that the liability for payment is legitimate, since various persons have attested to the propriety and accuracy of the claim.

After a voucher has bene approved, it is returned to the accounting department and the proper accounts to be debited and credited are noted on the voucher. After a final review by an authorized person, the proper entry is made in the voucher register (debiting an expense or other type of account and crediting Vouchers Payable) and the voucher is filed in the unpaid voucher file. In a voucher system the file of unpaid vouchers serves as the subsidiary accounts payable ledger. When payment is made, an entry is recorded in a check register debiting Vouchers Payable and crediting Cash. The voucher is then moved from the unpaid vouchers file to the paid vouchers file.

The system of internal control is enhanced by a separation of duties. For instance, the person or persons who authorize the incurrence of liabilities should not also prepare and distribute checks. The receipt of assets or services resulting from a liability incurrence must be acknowledged and approved by (a) the receiving department or (b) others who do not have authority to prepare and distribute checks. The persons who have authority to sign checks should do so only when approved vouchers authorizing each check are presented. The possibilities of errors and of recording unauthorized liabilities or cash disbursements are minimized thereby.

SUMMARY

A system of internal control includes all the procedures and actions taken (1) to protect the company's assets against theft and waste, (2) to ensure compliance with company policies and federal law, (3) to evaluate the performance of personnel, and (4) to ensure accurate and reliable operating data and accounting reports.

Information on cash position and cash movement supplied by the accounting system is used by management in fulfilling its cash management function and by outsiders in appraising the overall financial position of a business firm.

Adequate control over receipts and disbursements is necessary to protect cash. Defalcations that involve stealing cash when it is flowing in or out of the business are quite numerous.

The balance on the monthly bank statement showing the activity in a checking account will usually differ from the balance shown in the ledger account. The usual causes of this difference are outstanding checks, deposits in transit, and bank service charges which have not been recorded by the depositor. A statement should be prepared reconciling these differences. An entry is often needed to record items uncovered in reconciling the two amounts.

A company operating in many widely scattered locations may establish transfer accounts in local banks which require the immediate forwarding by the bank of any funds in excess of a stated amount to a central bank. There the funds can be quickly invested if they are not needed for other purposes.

Control over payroll checks is often established, at least in part, through use of a separate payroll checking account. The location of errors is also facilitated if the possible thousands of payroll checks are not intermingled with other checks in one account.

Management may use a petty cash fund for small expenditures of cash. A voucher system may be used to provide close control over cash disbursements.

QUESTIONS

1. What purposes does a system of internal control accomplish?

2. Identify some features which, if present, would strengthen the internal control system.

3. What are the four objectives sought in effective cash management?

4. Cite some essential features in a system of internal control over cash receipts.

5. The bookkeeper of a given company was stealing remittances received from customers in payment of their accounts. To cover the theft, the bookkeeper made out false credit memoranda indicating returns and allowances made by or granted to the customers. What feature of a system of internal control, if operative, would have prevented this defalcation?

6. Cite some essential features in a system of internal control over cash disbursements.

7. The difference between a company's Cash ledger account balance and the balance in the bank statement is usually a matter of timing. Do you agree or disagree? Why?

8. Why might a company's management wish to determine the cash position daily?

9. Explain how the use of transfer bank accounts can bring about effective cash management.

10. Indicate the manner in which a payroll bank account is operated.

11. Indicate the method of operation of an imprest petty cash fund and the advantages obtained through its use. Be sure to indicate exactly how control is effected through the use of the imprest system.

12. Describe how the use of a voucher system provides close control over cash disbursements.

EXERCISES

1. The Garber Company's Cash account balance was $140,350 at the end of August. The bank statement showed a balance of $137,200 for the same date. Checks outstanding totaled $42,000, and deposits in transit totaled $61,000. If these are the only pertinent data available to you, what was the correct amount of cash against which the Garber Company could have written checks as of the end of August?

2. From the following data, prepare a bank reconciliation statement and determine the correct available cash balance for the Burk Company as of October 31, 1986:

Balance per bank statement, October 31, 1986	$9,316
Ledger account balance	7,352
Note collected by bank not yet entered in ledger	2,000
Bank charges not yet entered by Burk Company	12
Deposit in transit	1,120
Outstanding checks:	
No. 527	256
No. 528	192
No. 529	480
No. 531	168

3. From the following information for the Higgins Company:

a. Prepare a bank reconciliation statement as of September 30, 1986.

b. Give the necessary journal entries to correct the Cash account.

Balance per bank statement, September 30, 1986 . . .	$32,600
Ledger account balance as of September 30, 1986 . .	29,300
Note collected by bank	2,000
Bank charges	20
Deposits in transit	1,848
NSF check deposited and returned	168
Check of Brent Company deducted in error	100
Outstanding checks	3,436

4. As of March 1 of the current year the Davis Company had outstanding checks of $30,000. During March the company issued an additional $114,000 of checks. As of March 31 the bank statement showed that $102,000 of checks had cleared the bank during the month. What is the amount of outstanding checks as of March 31?

5. The Crowe Company's bank statement as of August 31, 1986, shows total deposits into the company's account of $51,340 and a total of 14 deposits. On July 31 deposits of $2,700 and $2,100 were in transit. The total cash receipts for August amounted to $52,750, and the company's records show 13 deposits made in August. What is the amount of deposits in transit at August 31?

6. On August 31, 1986, the Dudley Company's petty cash fund contained:

Coin and currency	83.00
IOU from office boy	10.00
Vouchers covering expenditures for:	
Postage	40.00
Taxi fares	17.00
Entertainment of a customer	46.00

The Petty Cash account shows a balance of $200. If financial statements are prepared for each calendar month, what journal entry is required on August 31?

7. Use the data in Exercise 6 above. If the fund were replenished on August 31, 1986, what journal entry would be required? Which of the accounts debited would not appear in the income statement?

8. You are the chief accountant of the Custer Company. An invoice has just been received from the Dunlop Company in the amount of $4,000, with terms of 2/10, n/30. List the procedures you would follow in processing this invoice up through the point of filing it in the unpaid vouchers file.

PROBLEMS

5–1. The bank statement for the Holley Company's general checking account with the First National Bank for the month ended August 31, 1986, showed an ending balance of $10,618, service charges of $20, an NSF check returned of $420, and the collection of a $2,000 note plus interest of $20. Further investigation revealed that a wire transfer of $3,600 from the bank account maintained by a branch office of the company had not been recorded by the company as having been deposited in the First National Bank account. In addition, a comparison of deposits with receipts showed a deposit in transit of $4,200. Checks outstanding amounted to $2,012, while the cash ledger balance was $6,626.

Required:

a. Prepare a bank reconciliation statement for the Holley Company account for the month ended August 31, 1986.

b. Prepare all necessary journal entries.

5–2. The bank statement for Fulmer Company's account with the First National Bank for the month ended April 30, 1986, showed a balance of $21,772. On this date the company's Cash account balance was $19,054. Returned with the bank statement were (1) a debit memo for service charges of $20, (2) a debit memo for a customer's NSF check of $200, and (3) a credit memo for a $4,400 wire transfer of funds on April 14 from the State Bank, the local bank used by the company's branch office. Further investigation revealed that outstanding checks amounted to $2,600, the cash receipts of April 30 of $3,242 did not appear as a deposit on the bank statement, and the canceled checks included a check for $820 (drawn by the president of the company to cover travel expenses on a recent trip) which the company has yet to record.

Required:

    a. Prepare a bank reconciliation statement for the month ended April 30, 1986.

    b. Prepare any necessary journal entries.

5–3. The following data pertain to the Grant Company:

    (1) Balance per the bank statement dated June 30, 1986, is $40,760.

    (2) Balance of the Cash in Bank account on the company books as of June 30, 1986, is $11,980.

    (3) Outstanding checks as of June 30, 1986, are $20,000.

    (4) Bank deposit of June 30 for $3,140 was not included in the deposits per the bank statement.

    (5) The bank had collected a $30,000, 6 percent, 30-day note and the interest of $150, which it credited to the Grant Company account. The bank charged the company a collection fee of $20 on the above note.

    (6) The bank erroneously charged the Grant Company account for a $14,000 check of the Brant Company. The check was found among the canceled checks returned with the bank statement.

    (7) Bank service charges for June, exclusive of the collection fee, amounted to $100.

    (8) Among the canceled checks was one for $690 given in payment of an account. The bookkeeper had recorded the check at $960 in the company records.

    (9) A check of Mr. Crosley, a customer, for $4,200, deposited on June 20, was returned by the bank marked NSF. No entry has been made to reflect the returned check on the company records.

    (10) A check for $1,680 of Mr. Moran, a customer, which had been deposited in the bank, was erroneously recorded by the bookkeeper as $1,860.

Required:

    Prepare a bank reconciliation statement as of June 30, 1986. Also prepare any necessary adjusting journal entries.

5–4. The following data pertain to the Flores Company. The reconciliation statement as of June 30, 1986, showed a deposit in transit of $2,700 and three checks outstanding:

No. 553	. . .	$1,200
No. 570	. . .	2,200
No. 571	. . .	1,600

During July the following checks were written and entered in the Cash account:

No. 572	. . .	$1,500	No. 578	. . .	$2,300
No. 573	. . .	1,650	No. 579	. . .	2,820
No. 574	. . .	2,820	No. 580	. . .	360
No. 575	. . .	1,270	No. 581	. . .	4,854
No. 576	. . .	2,526	No. 582	. . .	4,800
No. 577	. . .	1,690	No. 583	. . .	1,848

As of July 31, all of the checks written, except No. 578, had been mailed to the payees. Check No. 578 was kept in the vault pending receipt of a statement from the payee. Four deposits were made at the bank as follows:

July 7	. . .	$15,000
14	. . .	19,200
14	. . .	11,400
28	. . .	13,800

The bank statement, which was received on August 2, correctly included all deposits and showed a balance as of July 31 of $50,520. The following checks were returned: Nos. 570, 571, 572, 573, 574, 575, 576, 577, 580, and 581. With the paid checks there were three debit memoranda for:

(1) Fee of $8 for the collection on July 30 of a $2,200 noninterest-bearing note payable to the Flores Company for which a credit memorandum was enclosed.
(2) Monthly service charge of $10.
(3) Payment of a $1,500 noninterest-bearing note of the Flores Company.

The bank statement included a credit for $6,000 dated July 29. The bank telephoned the company on the morning of August 3 to explain that this credit was in error because it represented a transaction between the bank and the Florist Company.

The balance in the Cash account on the books of the Flores Company as of July 31 is $30,870.

Required:

Prepare a bank reconciliation statement for the Flores Company as of July 31, 1986. Also prepare any necessary adjusting entries.

5–5. The following information is taken from the books and records of the Massey Company:

Balance per bank statement, July 31, 1986	$45,778
Balance per ledger, July 31, 1986	46,484
Collections received on the last day of July and debited to Cash in Bank on books but not entered by bank until August	10,624
Debit memo for customer's check returned unpaid (uncollectible check is on hand, but no entry for the return has been made on the books)	1,000
Debit memo for bank service charge for July	30
Check issued but not paid by bank	10,068
Credit memo for proceeds of a note receivable which was left at the bank for collection but has not been recorded on the books as collected ($16 of this is interest revenue)	1,600
Check for an account payable entered on books as $960 but issued and paid by the bank in the correct amount of $1,680.	

Required:

Prepare a bank reconciliation statement and the necessary journal entries to adjust the accounts.

5–6. The following data for March 1986 are summarized from the accounts of Hall Company. The accountant also acts as cashier.

Cash Receipts			Cash Disbursements		
Mar. 2	. . .	$2,200	Check No. 911	. . .	$1,768
4	. . .	6,400	No. 912	. . .	2,452
5	. . .	2,600	No. 913	. . .	2,916
11	. . .	5,600	No. 914	. . .	1,776
13	. . .	7,000	No. 915	. . .	3,228
14	. . .	8,400	No. 916	. . .	4,800
19	. . .	2,000	No. 917	. . .	7,600
20	. . .	1,600	No. 918	. . .	5,400
27	. . .	120	No. 919	. . .	1,500
29	. . .	740	No. 920	. . .	1,400

At March 1 the checks outstanding were:

No. 209	. . .	$ 180
No. 792	. . .	3,200
No. 796	. . .	1,116
No. 910	. . .	2,524

There were no deposits in transit. The balance of the Cash in Bank account per books was $30,700 at March 31. The bank statement for the month of March is as follows:

BANK STATEMENT

Date	Checks	Deposits	Balance
Mar. 1			34,000
3		2,200	36,200
4	1,768		
4	2,452		31,980
6		9,000	40,980
9	3,228		
9	1,776		35,976
16		21,000	56,976
19	4,800		
19	5,400		46,776
24		3,600	50,376
25	1,116		
25	2,524		46,736
26	7,600		
26	2,000 NSF		37,136
27	2,000 DM		35,136
29		760	35,896
31	8 DM		35,888

The debit memoranda (DM) are for the payment of a company note and for the monthly service charge.

Required:

    a. Prepare a bank reconciliation statement as of March 31, 1986.

    b. Journalize the entry or entries necessary to correct the books.

    c. Comment on the company's control of cash receipts.

5–7. Keller Company uses an imprest payroll checking account, with a $2,000 balance. This balance is used for payroll advances and to pay employees whose services are terminated between payroll payment dates. Following are selected transactions of the First Company during 1986:

June 15 Payroll department determines that the payroll and payroll deductions for the first half of the month of June are:

Office salaries		$ 50,000
Sales salaries and commissions		82,000
Sales office salaries		40,000
		$172,000
Payroll deductions:		
Federal income taxes withheld	$22,000	
FICA taxes withheld	4,000	
Community Fund contributions withheld . .	6,000	32,000
Net payroll		$140,000

    17 A check in the amount of the net payroll is drawn on the general checking account and deposited in the payroll checking account.

    20 Payroll checks are issued.

    24 One employee's services are terminated. The salary of this office employee for the partial period is $600, and the only deduction is for $90 of income taxes to be withheld. A payroll check is issued. (Hint: What entry did you make for the payroll checks issued for the payroll for the first half of June?)

The bank statement for the payroll account shows a balance of $2,701.26. Checks outstanding are for $556.50 and $654.76.

Required:

a. Prepare general journal entries to record those transactions which would be formally recorded in the records of the Keller Company.

b. Determine the actual (not the book) balance in the payroll checking account at June 30. Why is it not the imprest balance of $2,000?

c. Prepare a bank reconciliation statement for the payroll checking account as of June 30, 1986.

5–8. Following are selected transactions of the Shell Company during 1986:

Mar. 1 Established a petty cash fund of $1,000 which will be under the control of the assistant office manager and is to be operated on an imprest basis.

Apr. 3 Fund is replenished on this date. Prior to replenishment, the fund consisted of the following:

Coin and currency	$569.16
Payroll check issued by Shell Company to part-time office boy, Keri Kerr,	
properly endorsed by Kerr	56.96
Petty cash vouchers indicating disbursements for:	
Postage stamps	140.00
Supper money for office employees working overtime	48.00
Office supplies	43.60
Window washing service	80.00
Flowers for wedding of employee	20.00
Flowers for hospitalized employee	20.00
Employee IOU	20.00

The employee's IOU is to be deducted from his next paycheck.

Required:

Present journal entries for the above transactions.

5–9. The following data pertain to the petty cash fund of the Longhorn Company:

Nov. 2 A $800 check is drawn and cashed, and the cash is placed in the care of the assistant office manager to be used as a petty cash fund maintained on an imprest basis.

Dec. 17 The fund is replenished. An analysis of the fund shows:

Coins and currency	. . . . .	$196.54
Petty cash vouchers for:		
Delivery expenses	. . . . . .	231.30
Freight-in	. . . .	348.16
Postage stamps purchased	. .	20.00

31 The end of the accounting period falls on this date. The fund was not replenished. Its contents on this date consist of:

Coins and currency	. . . .	$669.40
Petty cash vouchers for:		
Delivery expenses	. . . .	42.20
Postage stamps	. . . . .	48.40
Employee's IOU	. . . . .	40.00

Required:

Present journal entries to record the above transactions.

6 PLANT ASSETS: ACQUISITION AND DEPRECIATION

Business assets are commonly classified as current or noncurrent assets, depending upon the amount of time that is expected to expire before they are converted into cash, consumed, or used up in the operations of the business. For many businesses, the noncurrent category of assets consists largely of plant assets (property, plant, and equipment), natural resources, and intangible assets. This chapter is the first of two on this important accounting and business topic. The acquisition of plant assets and their depreciation will be covered in this chapter.

NATURE OF PLANT ASSETS

The term **plant assets** refers to tangible long-lived assets (assets whose useful lives are expected to exceed more than one period) obtained for use in business operations instead of for resale. Land, buildings, machinery, delivery equipment, and office equipment are typical examples of plant assets.

To be properly classified as a plant asset, an asset must be used in the production or sale of another asset or service. For example, a delivery truck or equipment held for sale by a dealer is classified as inventory, whereas the same truck or equipment used in producing or selling a product is classified as a plant asset. Once an asset is retired from service and held for sale or left idle, the asset is no longer classifiable as a plant asset.

Plant assets can be viewed as consisting of bundles of service potential that are consumed or used up over a period of time. For instance, a new delivery truck may represent 100,000 miles of transportation service. Likewise, a new building may represent 40 years of housing service. To match the revenues and the related expenses of a period as accurately and logically as possible, it is necessary to measure the part of the service potential of plant assets that expired during the period. While it is often difficult to determine the exact length of these assets' useful lives, some estimate must be made so that the amount of expense (the amount of the service expired) may be determined.

Types of Plant Assets

Plant assets can be broadly classified as land and depreciable property. Since land does not deteriorate with age or use, it is not depreciable. Farmland is an exception to this rule because it may lose its fertility or suffer from erosion.

All other plant assets are depreciable property. Their usefulness is reduced through wear and tear, or obsolescence.

The Cost of Plant Assets

Plant assets are usually recorded at cost. Cost includes all normal, reasonable, and necessary outlays to obtain and get the asset ready for use, such as invoice price, installation costs, and transportation. Traffic tickets or fines that must be paid as a result of hauling machinery to a new plant are not part of the cost of the machinery. Likewise, if the machinery is dropped and damaged while being unpacked, the cost of repairing the damage is not included in the cost of the machinery.

Land and land improvements. The cost of land includes the purchase price; the option cost; real estate commissions; the cost of title search; fees for recording the title transfer; unpaid taxes assumed by the purchaser; the cost of surveying, clearing, grading, and landscaping; and local assessments for sidewalks, streets, sewers, and water mains. Sometimes land purchased as a building site contains an old building that must be removed. In such cases, the entire purchase price should be debited to the Land account. The Land account should also be debited for the cost of removing the old building, less any proceeds received from the sale of salvaged materials.

As stated above, land purchased as a building site is considered to have an unlimited life and is therefore not depreciable. But land improvements such as driveways, fences, parking lots, lighting systems, and sprinkler systems have limited lives and are therefore depreciable. Hence, the costs of land and land improvements should be recorded in two separate accounts.

Building. If a building is purchased, its cost includes the purchase price, the costs of repairing and remodeling the building for the purposes of the new owner, unpaid taxes assumed by the purchaser, legal costs, and real estate brokerage commissions. When land and buildings are purchased together, the total cost should be divided so that separate ledger accounts may be established for land and for buildings. An appraisal may be done by a competent appraiser and is needed in order to have a dollar amount on which to base the depreciation charges for the building.

If a building is constructed, the cost may be more difficult to determine. But its cost usually includes payments to contractors, architects' fees, building permits, taxes during construction, salaries of officers supervising construction, insurance during construction, and interest during construction. Miscellaneous revenues earned during construction reduce the cost of the building. For instance, if one floor is rented for some special purpose during construction the proceeds reduce the cost of the building.

To illustrate, assume that Collins Company purchased an old farm on the outskirts of Bridgeport, Connecticut, as a factory site. The company paid $300,000 for this property. In addition, the company agreed to pay taxes of prior years (called back taxes) of $12,000. Attorneys' fees and other legal costs related to the purchase of the farm amounted to $1,800. The farm buildings were demolished at a net cost of $20,000 (the cost of removal less the salvage value), and a building was constructed at a cost of $400,000. Building permits and architects' fees totaled $30,000. Interest incurred on a construction loan was $900. Finally, the company paid an assessment of $12,000 to the city for water mains, sewers, and street paving. The costs of the land and factory building are computed as follows:

	Land	Building
Cost of factory site	$300,000	
Back taxes	12,000	
Attorneys' fees and other legal costs	1,800	
Demolition	20,000	
Factory construction		$400,000
Building permits and architects' fees		30,000
Interest during construction		900
City assessment	12,000	
	$345,800	$430,900

All of the costs relating to the purchase of the farm and the razing of the old buildings are assignable to the land account because none of the old buildings purchased with the land are to be used. The real goal was to purchase the land, but the land was not available without taking the buildings also.

Instead of the situation described above, suppose that through a remodeling program one or more of the existing buildings had been adapted for use by Collins Company. Then it would have been necessary to determine what part of the cash purchase price of the farm, the back taxes, and the legal fees was allocable to such buildings and what part of the acquisition cost and the remodeling cost would be included in the cost of the new factory. These costs would have been allocated on the basis of appraised values. For instance, assume that the land was appraised at three fourths of the total value and the buildings at one fourth. Then three fourths of the acquisition cost would have been assigned to the land and one fourth to the buildings. The appraised values of any buildings to be demolished are added to the appraised value of the land in determining the allocation.[1]

Machinery.   If machinery is purchased, its cost includes the net invoice price, transportation charges, insurance in transit, the cost of installation, the costs of any attachments or accessories, testing costs (if any), and other costs needed to put it into condition and location for use. If a company builds a machine for its own use, the cost includes material, labor, and an amount equal to the increase in factory costs caused by the construction of the machine. This cost of the machine should be recorded in the Machinery account (even if it is less than what the company would have paid if it had purchased the machine) since it represents resources sacrificed to acquire the machine.

To illustrate, assume that after pricing machinery of the type needed, the Dension Company decided to build its own machine. The cost of construction was $40,000. The shipping point price of a similar machine purchased from the usual source is $43,000, and transportation charges to the Dension Company's plant amount to another $1,000. The machine should be recorded in the accounts at $40,000—the amount of resources sacrificed to acquire it.

Delivery equipment.   The cost of delivery equipment includes all costs necessary to place the equipment in use. Included in the cost are the net invoice purchase price, transportation charges, the cost of accessories, and special paint and decoration costs.

Office equipment.   The cost of office equipment includes the net invoice purchase price and all costs necessary to place the equipment in condition and location for use.

Noncash Acquisitions and Gifts of Plant Assets

Plant assets are usually acquired by purchase for cash or on account. They may also be acquired through an exchange for securities or other assets or as gifts. When plant assets are acquired under these conditions, it is necessary to determine the amount at which they should be initially recorded. Several possible bases may be used, such as fair market value, appraised value, and book value.

---

[1] Some accountants merely ignore the appraised values of any buildings to be destroyed in determining the allocation.

Fair market value. If noncash assets are received in an exchange for securities or other noncash assets having a known market value, the cost of the assets received is considered equal to the fair market value of the securities or assets given up. If the securities or assets given up do not have a known market value, the cash purchase price at which the assets received **could** have been acquired should be used as the cost of the acquired assets. This same cost would also be considered the amount received for the securities or assets given up.

Appraised value. Noncash assets are sometimes acquired as gifts. Although these assets do not cost the recipient anything, they are usually recorded in the accounts. If similar assets are not regularly traded and a market value cannot be determined for them, they may be recorded at an appraised value determined by a professional appraiser or by management.

Book value. The book value of an asset given up is an acceptable basis for measuring a newly acquired asset only if a better basis is not available. This statement is true even if some cash is given or received in the exchange. The cost of an old asset is usually a poor and misleading indication of the economic importance of a new asset. When assets are received in a noncash exchange, it is the accountant's job to find the best measure of their value. The general rule followed is to use the fair market value of the assets received or of the assets given up, whichever is more clearly evident.

DEPRECIATION OF PLANT ASSETS

Depreciation in accounting is an estimate, usually expressed in terms of cost, of the amount of an asset's service potential that expired in a given period. Major causes of depreciation are physical deterioration, inadequacy for future needs, and obsolescence.

Physical deterioration results from use, wear and tear, and the action of the elements. Even if a good maintenance and repair policy is in effect, a plant asset will eventually have to be discarded. If a company grows more rapidly than anticipated, existing plant assets may become inadequate. In such a case, the company will not be able to meet all of the demands for its product or service. Obsolescence refers to the process of becoming out of date or obsolete. A machine may be in excellent physical condition yet also be obsolete because more efficient, economical, and higher quality machines have become available. A good example of this would be in the computer industry. Computers generally become obsolete before they physically wear out. Both inadequacy and obsolescence are difficult to predict, but they must be taken into consideration in depreciation accounting.

Depreciation accounting distributes in a systematic and rational manner the cost of a depreciable plant asset, less its salvage value, over the asset's estimated useful life. *Thus, depreciation is a process of cost allocation and not of valuation.* Depreciation is recorded by debiting the depreciation expense account and crediting the accumulated depreciation account. The later accounting treatment of the amounts of depreciation recorded depends upon the type of services which the asset provides. If the services received are classified as selling or administrative, the depreciation is usually expensed in the period recognized. If manufacturing services are received, the depreciation may be treated as a part of the manufacturing cost. In such an instance, it attaches to the units of product as part of the cost of the asset, inventory, and becomes an expense (as part of the cost of goods sold) only when the manufactured goods are sold to customers. The depreciation recorded on one asset may be considered part of the cost of another—for example, when a truck is used in the construction of a building.

Depreciation is one of the costs of operating a business. The cost of plant assets is recovered from customers by charging them enough for the product to cover all expenses, including depreciation. But note that the charge to expense by itself is not sufficient evidence that the cost has been recovered. Costs are recovered only when total revenue is at least equal to total expenses, which, of course, is the normal situation for firms that remain in business.

Factors affecting depreciation estimates. To estimate periodic depreciation the following three factors must generally be considered:

1. Cost.
2. Estimated salvage value. Salvage or scrap value is the amount estimated to be recoverable (less disposal cost) on the date that the asset will be disposed of or retired.
3. Estimated useful life. This may be expressed in years, months, working hours, or units of production.

There are several methods of computing depreciation. When evaluating the various depreciation methods, it is important to remember the main causes of depreciation—physical deterioration, inadequacy, and obsolescence. These three factors should be taken into consideration in estimating salvage value and useful life as well as in selecting the appropriate depreciation method. For example, a machine may be capable of producing units for 20 years, but it is expected to be obsolete in 6 years. Thus, its estimated useful life is 6 years, not 20 years.

DEPRECIATION METHODS

The depreciation methods illustrated here are for financial reporting purposes. At one time, these same methods could be used for tax purposes. In 1981, a significant change in the tax laws occurred that allows very fast write-offs of depreciable assets for tax purposes. A discussion of depreciation for tax purposes is beyond the scope of this text.

Straight-Line Depreciation

The straight-line method assigns the same dollar amount of depreciation to expense each period. Under this method the passage of time is considered to be the main factor in allocating cost. The method assumes that wear, obsolescence, and deterioration of the plant assets are directly proportional to elapsed time. This assumption may not be true.

This formula for computing depreciation under the straight-line method is:

Depreciation per period

$$\frac{\text{Depreciation}}{\text{per period}} = \frac{(\text{Cost} - \text{Estimated salvage value})}{\text{Number of accounting periods in estimated life}}$$

To illustrate, for a machine costing $54,000 with an estimated life of 10 years and an estimated salvage value of $4,000, the depreciation per year is ($54,000 — $4,000) ÷ 10, or $5,000. The schedule in Illustration 6.1 presents the annual depreciation entries, the balance in the accumulated depreciation accounts, and the book (or carrying) value of this machine.

Illustration 6.1
DEPRECIATION SCHEDULE—STRAIGHT-LINE METHOD

End of Year	Depreciation Expense Dr.; Accumulated Depreciation Cr.	Total Accumulated Depreciation	Book Value (cost — accumulated depreciation)
			$54,000
1	$ 5,000	$ 5,000	49,000
2	5,000	10,000	44,000
3	5,000	15,000	39,000
4	5,000	20,000	34,000
5	5,000	25,000	29,000
6	5,000	30,000	24,000
7	5,000	35,000	19,000
8	5,000	40,000	14,000
9	5,000	45,000	9,000
10	5,000	50,000	4,000*
	$50,000		

* Estimated salvage value.

The entry to record depreciation at the end of year 1 is:

```
Depreciation Expense—Machinery  . . . . . . . . .  5,000
    Accumulated Depreciation—Machinery   . . . .          5,000
  To record depreciation on machinery for year 1.
```

Depreciation expense is shown on the income statement, while accumulated depreciation is shown on the balance sheet as a deduction from the Machinery account. The balance in the accumulated depreciation account continues to grow year by year as shown in Illustration 6.1. The book value of the machinery at any point in time is equal to cost minus accumulated depreciation.

Units-of-Production Depreciation

If usage is the main factor causing the expiration of the asset, depreciation may be based on physical output. The depreciation charge per unit of output may be found by dividing the original cost of the asset, less any salvage value, by the estimated number of units to be produced during the asset's life. The periodic depreciation is then obtained by multiplying the rate per unit by the actual number of units produced during the period.

To illustrate, assume that on April 1, 1986, Lee Company purchased a machine at a total cost of $54,000. The machine is expected to have a 10-year useful life and a $4,000 salvage value. It is estimated that the machine will produce 5 million units of product throughout its useful life. The depreciation charge per unit of product produced is one cent, computed as follows:

$$\text{Depreciation per unit of product} = \frac{(\text{Cost} - \text{Estimated salvage value})}{\text{Estimated units of production}}$$

$$= \frac{(\$54,000 - \$4,000)}{5,000,000} = \$0.01$$

The formula for calculating total depreciation for a period is:

$$\text{Depreciation for the period} = \text{Depreciation per unit} \times \text{Number of units}$$

Thus, if the machine produces 100,000 units in 1986, the depreciation charge under the units-of-production method will be $1,000 ($0.01 × 100,000). Similarly, if 250,000 units are produced in 1987, the depreciation charge will be $2,500 ($0.01 × 250,000).

Accelerated Depreciation

Accelerated depreciation methods permit larger amounts of depreciation to be recorded in the earlier years of an asset's life than in the later years. There is theoretical support for these methods. Their use seems especially appropriate when the service-rendering or revenue-producing ability of the asset declines over time, when the value of the asset declines more in the earlier years and less in the later years of its life, and when repairs and other maintenance costs increase over time.

Double-declining-balance method of depreciation. Under this method the straight-line rate of depreciation is doubled, and the doubled rate is applied to the declining balance of the asset—

its net book value. Salvage value is ignored in the calculation but serves as a base below which the asset should not be depreciated. The formula for the double-declining-balance method is:

$$(\text{Cost} - \text{Accumulated depreciation}) \times \left(\frac{100\%}{\text{Useful life}} \times 2\right)$$

Illustration 6.2 gives an example of an asset costing $54,000 with an estimated life of 10 years and a salvage value of $4,000. In this example, the 10 percent straight-line rate of depreciation (100 percent ÷ 10 years = 10 percent per year) is doubled, giving a depreciation rate of 20 percent.

Illustration 6.2
DOUBLE-DECLINING-BALANCE METHOD DEPRECIATION SCHEDULE

End of Year	Depreciation Expense Dr.; Accumulated Depreciation Cr.		Total Accumulated Depreciation	Book Value
				$54,000.00
1	$10,800.00	(20% of $54,000)	$10,800.00	43,200.00
2	8,640.00	(20% of $43,200)	19,440.00	34,560.00
3	6,912.00	(20% of $34,560)	26,352.00	27,648.00
4	5,529.60	(20% of $27,648)	31,881.60	22,118.40
5	4,423.68	(20% of $22,118.40)	36,305.28	17,694.72
6	3,538.94	(20% of $17,694.72)	39,844.22	14,155.78
7	2,831.16	(20% of $14,155.78)	42,675.38	11,324.62
8	2,264.92	(20% of $11,324.62)	44,940.30	9,059.70
9	1,811.94	(20% of $9,059.70)	46,752.24	7,247.76
10	1,449.56*	(20% of $7,247.76)	48,201.80	5,798.20

* This amount could be $3,247.76 so as to reduce the book value down to the estimated salvage value of $4,000 if the salvage value is still expected to be $4,000. Also in practice, the amounts in this schedule would undoubtedly be rounded.

When the double-declining-balance method is used to compute the annual depreciation amount, the annual amount is allocated to the months within the year on a straight-line basis. For example, the depreciation per month in the first year for the asset in Illustration 6.2 is $900 ($10,800 ÷ 12). In the second year, it is $720 ($8,640 ÷ 12) per month.

Sum-of-the-years'-digits depreciation. This method also producers larger depreciation charges in the early years of an asset's life. The years of estimated life of an asset are added together and used as the denominator in a fraction. The number of years of life remaining at the beginning of the accounting period is the numerator. Cost, less estimated salvage value, is then multiplied by this fraction to compute the periodic depreciation. The formula for the sum-of-the-years'-digits method is:

$$(\text{Cost-salvage value}) \times \frac{\substack{\text{Remaining useful life as of} \\ \text{beginning of period}}}{\text{Sum-of-the-years'-digits}}$$

This method is illustrated below for a plant asset that costs $54,000 and has an estimated useful life of 10 years and a salvage value of $4,000.

Sum-of-the-years' digits: $1 + 2 + 3 + 4 + 5 + 6 + 7 + 8 + 9 + 10 = 55$

Depreciation:

Year 1:	10/55 of $50,000	9,091
Year 2:	9/55 of $50,000	8,182
Year 3:	8/55 of $50,000	7,273
Year 4:	7/55 of $50,000	6,364
Year 5:	6/55 of $50,000	5,455
Year 6:	5/55 of $50,000	4,545
Year 7:	4/55 of $50,000	3,636
Year 8:	3/55 of $50,000	2,727
Year 9:	2/55 of $50,000	1,818
Year 10:	1/55 of $50,000	909
Total depreciation		$50,000

At the beginning of Year 1 there are 10 years of life remaining. Thus, the ratio used to compute the depreciation charge for Year 1 is 10/55.

The mathematical formula for finding the sum-of-the-years' digits for any given number of periods is:

$$S = \frac{n(n + 1)}{2},$$

where S is the sum-of-the-years' digits and n is the number of periods in the asset's life. Thus, the sum-of-the-years' digits for 10 years is 55, computed as follows:

$$\frac{10(10 + 1)}{2} = \frac{110}{2} = 55$$

Depreciation on Assets Acquired or Retired during an Accounting Period

When plant assets are acquired or retired during an accounting period, depreciation is usually computed to the nearest month. Thus, an asset purchased on or before the 15th day of the month is treated as if it had been purchased on the first of the month. An asset purchased after the 15th day of the month is treated as if it had been purchased on the 1st day of the following month. For instance, assume that a company that operates on a calendar year accounting period acquired a machine on March 14, 1986. The machine has a $52,000 cost, a $4,000 salvage value, and a 10-year estimated useful life. Under the straight-line method, the depreciation expense for 1986 would be $4,000 ($48,000 × 0.10 × 10/12). But if the machine had been purchased on March 16, the straight-line depreciation expense for 1986 would be $3,600 ($48,000 × 0.10 × 9/12).

When the double-declining-balance method is used the procedure is quite simple. For example, assume that a machine is acquired on July 1, 1986. The machine has an $80,000 cost, a $2,000 salvage value, and a 10-year estimated useful life. Double-declining-balance depreciation is used. For the year ending December 31, 1986, the depreciation expense is $8,000 ($80,000 × 0.20 × 1/2). The 1987 depreciation expense would be $14,400, computed as follows:

$$(\$80,000 - \$8,000) \times 0.20 = \$14,400$$

But when the sum-of-the-years' digits method is used, the computation is more complex. Assume that an asset with a cost of $17,000, a salvage value of $2,000, and an estimated five-year life is acquired on July 1, 1986. Depreciation for 1986 is:

$$(\$17,000 - \$2,000) \times 5/15 \times 1/2 = \$2,500$$

Depreciation for 1987 is:

$$
\begin{array}{ll}
(\$17,000 - \$2,000) \times 5/15 \times 1/2 = & \$2,500 \\
(\$17,000 - \$2,000) \times 4/15 \times 1/2 = & \underline{2,000} \\
\text{Total} & \underline{\underline{\$4,500}}
\end{array}
$$

Notice that the depreciation for 1987 includes one half of the first year of life of the asset and one half of the second year of its life.

Revisions of Life Estimates

When it is found that the estimate of the life of an asset is incorrect, the annual depreciation charge under the straight-line method may be changed as follows: the net book value (less salvage) of the asset at the beginning of the current period is divided by the estimated number of life periods remaining. The result is the revised annual depreciation charge applicable to the current and succeeding years.

For example, assume that a machine cost $60,000 and that it has an estimated salvage value of $6,000 and an estimated useful life of eight years. At the end of the fourth year of the machine's life, the balance in its accumulated depreciation account is $27,000. At the beginning of the fifth year, it is estimated that the asset will last six more years (the salvage value remains at $6,000). The revised annual depreciation charge is $4,500 [($60,000 − $27,000 − $6,000) ÷ 6].

Depreciation on the Financial Statements

When depreciation is recorded, a depreciation expense account is debited.[2] The depreciation expense appears in the income statement

---

[2] We have already noted that, in some instances, the depreciation recorded on one asset may be recorded as part of the cost of acquiring another asset, such as when a truck is used in constructing a building.

as one of the expenses of generating revenue. The periodic depreciation is credited to an accumulated depreciation account. The accumulated depreciation account is used so that the original cost of the asset will continue to be shown in the asset account. The ratio of the accumulated depreciation account to the asset's cost may give a hint as to the age of the asset. The total cost and accumulated depreciation will be shown separately on the balance sheet as follows:

Plant, property, and equipment:

Store equipment	$ 24,000	
Less: Accumulated depreciation	4,000	$ 20,000
Building	$200,000	
Less: Accumulated depreciation	40,000	160,000
Land		80,000
Total plant, property, and equipment . .		$260,000

The presentation of cost less accumulated depreciation may give the reader of financial statements a better understanding of the condition of a company's assets than does the mere presentation of undepreciated cost. For instance, it is one thing to report $200,000 of assets with $120,000 of accumulated depreciation and quite another to report $80,000 of new assets.

Some readers of financial statements mistakenly assume that the amount of accumulated depreciation represents funds available for replacing old assets with new assets. But accumulated depreciation is simply a measure of the cost of the portion of the asset that has expired and been charged to depreciation expense. Accumulated depreciation has a credit balance and is a contra asset account. An informed reader should realize that cash is required to replace assets and that the amount of cash a company owns is shown as a current asset on its balance sheet. There is no cash represented in the Accumulated Depreciation account.

Measurement of Plant Assets on the Balance Sheet

As stated above, plant assets are reported on the balance sheet at their undepreciated cost (cost less accumulated depreciation). The going concern concept is the justification for reporting undepreciated cost instead of market values. Under the **going concern concept,** it is assumed that the company will remain in business and will continue to use the plant assets in business operations instead of selling them. Thus, market values are not reported in the primary financial statements. Furthermore, the accounting requirement of **realization** does not allow recording market prices greater than cost until the asset is sold. It is also not proper to recognize a loss by writing down the asset to a market value lower than cost if the cost of the asset is expected to be fully recovered from the future revenues that the asset will produce.

SUBSEQUENT EXPENDITURES ON PLANT ASSETS

It is often necessary to make expenditures for plant assets at times other than the time when they are acquired. The accounting treatment of such expenditures may consist of charging the amount to (1) an asset account, (2) an accumulated depreciation account, or (3) an expense account.

Expenditures that are added to the asset account or charged to the accumulated depreciation account are often called **capital expenditures.** These expenditures increase the net book value of the plant assets. On the other hand, expenditures recorded as expenses are called **revenue expenditures** because they help to produce revenues in the current period. The differences between these two are developed below.

Expenditures Capitalized in Asset Accounts

Expenditures for new or used assets, additions to existing assets, and betterments or improvements to existing assets are called capital expenditures. They are properly chargeable to asset accounts because they add to the service-rendering ability of the assets. For example, assume that a used press cost the Day Company $50,000 in cash plus $900 in transportation costs, both of which were properly recorded in the company's Machinery account.

The Day Company then spent $7,900 to recondition the press and $1,700 to install it. These expenditures should also be charged to the Machinery account. They are part of the total costs incurred to obtain the services from the press throughout its entire life. They are capital expenditures.

Betterments are increases in the **quality** of the services an asset provides. For example, the air conditioner installed in an auto which did not have one previously is a betterment, and the cost should be debited to the asset account.

Expenditures Capitalized as Charges to Accumulated Depreciation

Occasionally, expenditures are made on a plant asset that extend its life or increase the **quantity** of output expected beyond the original estimate but not the quality of the services it produces. Because they will benefit future periods, these expenditures are properly capitalized. But because there is no visible, tangible addition to or improvement of the assets, such expenditures are often charged to the accumulated depreciation account. The expenditures are viewed as canceling a part of the accumulated depreciation.

Expenditures for major repairs that do not extend the life of the asset are also often charged to accumulated depreciation (which increases future depreciation charges). This avoids the distortion of net income that might result if such expenditures were expensed in the year incurred. In this way the cost of major repairs is spread over a number of years.

To illustrate, assume that after operating its press for four years, the Day Company spent $7,500 to recondition it. The effect of the reconditioning is to increase the life of the press to a total of 14 years from an original estimate of 10 years. The journal entry to record the major repair is:

```
Accumulated Depreciation—Machinery   . . . . . . .  7,500
    Cash (or Accounts Payable)   . . . . . . . .          7,500
    Cost of reconditioning press.
```

When it was acquired, the press had an estimated life of 10 years with no expected salvage value. At the end of the fourth year, the balance in its Accumulated Depreciation account under the straight-line method is $24,200 [($60,500 ÷ 10) × 4]. After the $7,500 debit to the Accumulated Depreciation account, the balances in the Asset account and its related Accumulated Depreciation account are:

```
Cost of press   . . . . . . . . . .  $60,500
Accumulated depreciation   . . . . .   16,700
Net book value (end of four years)   . .  $43,800
```

The remaining book value of $43,800 is divided equally among the 10 remaining years in amounts of $4,380 per year under the straight-line method. The effect of the expenditure, then, is to increase the carrying amount of the asset by reducing its contra account, accumulated depreciation.

If the expenditure did not extend the life of the asset but, because of its size, was still charged to accumulated depreciation, the $43,800 would be spread over the remaining six years of life. The annual charges would be $7,300 ($43,800 ÷ 6) under the straight-line method.

Expenditures Charged to Expense

Recurring expenditures that neither add to the service-rendering abilities of the asset nor extend its life are treated as expenses. Thus, regular maintenance (lubricating a machine) and ordinary repairs (replacing a broken fan belt) are expensed immediately as revenue expenditures. For example, if the Day Company spends $380 to repair the press after using it for some time, the journal entry is:

```
Maintenance Expense   . . . . . . . . . . . . . . .  380
    Cash  . . . . . . . . . . . . . . . . . . . . . .          380
    To record payment of repair cost on press.
```

SUMMARY

Noncurrent assets are those assets which are used in a business for an extended time period. The assets represent packages of service potential which are expected to yield future positive benefits. Non-current assets are usually referred to as plant assets. These assets may be divided into items which do not expire, for example, land used for a plant site, and assets which lose their service potentials over time, such as equipment. Proper accounting calls for allocating the costs of the assets for which service potentials expire to the periods benefiting from their use. Such allocation is referred to as depreciation of plant assets.

The proper method for allocating the cost of an asset to the periods benefited will depend on many factors including the nature of the revenue patterns, the expected useful life of the asset, and the maintenance policy of the firm. There are three main approaches to allocating the cost of an asset: (1) the straight-line method, in which the cost of the asset less its salvage value is allocated in equal amounts to each year of the expected life of the asset; (2) the units-of-production method, in which the cost allocated to each year is based upon the number of units produced; and (3) two accelerated methods (double-declining-balance and sum-of-the-years'-digits), in which decreasing portions of the cost are allocated to each year. Plant assets are generally reported on the balance sheet at cost less accumulated depreciation.

Expenditures made on plant assets after their acquisition may be either capital expenditures (capitalized) or revenue expenditures (expensed). Expenditures for new or used assets, additions to existing assets, and betterments or improvements are called capital expenditures. Capital expenditures are debited to the asset account if they increase the service-rendering ability of the asset or to the accumulated depreciation account if they simply extend the life of the asset. Expenditures recorded as expenses, such as regular maintenance and ordinary repairs, are called revenue expenditures.

QUESTIONS

1. What is the main distinction between inventory and plant assets?

2. Which of the following items are properly classifiable as plant assets on the balance sheet?

   a. Advertising to inform the public about new energy-saving programs at a manufacturing plant.

   b. A truck acquired by a manufacturing company to be used to deliver the company's products to wholesalers.

   c. An automobile acquired by an insurance company to be used by one of its salespersons.

   d. Adding machines acquired by an office supply company to be resold to customers.

   e. The cost of constructing and paving a driveway which has a useful life of 10 years.

3. In any exchange of noncash assets, the accountant's task is that of finding the most appropriate valuation to assign to the assets received. What is the general rule for determining the most appropriate valuation in such a situation?

4. Why should periodic depreciation be recorded on all plant assets except land?

5. Howard Company is offered $200,000 for a tract of land carried in its accounts at $80,000. Should it accept the offer? Why or why not?

6. Define the terms **inadequacy** and **obsolescence** as used in accounting for plant assets.

7. What four factors must be known in order to compute depreciation on a plant asset?

8. What is the sum-of-the-years' digits for a machine that has an estimated useful life of nine years?

9. The Lloyd Company has just acquired new factory machines and is trying to determine which depreciation method to use. List the relative merits of using each of the following methods:

   a. Straight-line.

   b. Units-of-production.

   c. Accelerated.

10. What does the balance in the accumulated depreciation account represent? Can this balance be used to replace the related plant asset?

11. What is the justification for reporting plant assets on the balance sheet at undepreciated cost rather than market value?

12. Distinguish between capital expenditures and revenue expenditures.

13. For each of the following, state whether the expenditure made should be charged to an expense, an asset, or an accumulated depreciation account:

    a. Cost of installing air-conditioning equipment in a car that previously did not have air conditioning.

    b. Painting of an owned factory building every other year.

    c. Cost of replacing the roof on a 10-year-old building which was purchased new and has an estimated total life of 40 years. The replacement did not extend the life beyond the original estimate.

    d. Cost of repairing an electric motor.

EXERCISES

1. Cole Company recently bought a plot of land for $100,000 for construction of a new warehouse. Legal fees connected with the transaction were $1,100. Back taxes on the property amounted to $4,000, for which Cole Company assumed the liability. Demolition costs incurred to raze (destroy) the old warehouse on the property were $4,500. What is the cost of the land?

2. Porter Company acquired real property consisting of a tract of land and two buildings for $160,000 cash. The company intended to raze (destroy)

the old factory building and to remodel and use the old office building. To allocate the cost of the property acquired, the company had the property appraised. The appraised values were: land, $60,000; factory building, $60,000; and office building, $80,000. The factory building was demolished at a net cost of $8,000. The office building was remodeled at a cost of $16,000. The cost of a new identical office building was estimated to be $90,000. Present a schedule or schedules showing the determination of the amounts at which the assets acquired should be carried in the Porter Company accounts. Show calculations.

3. Dwight Company purchased an earthmover for $10,000, less a 2 percent cash discount. One of the company's employees drove the equipment to the company's storage lot. The company was fined $200 because the employee had failed to obtain a permit to drive the equipment on city streets. Break-in and testing costs totaled $1,000. What is the cost of the equipment?

4. The Roy Company purchased some office furniture on March 1, 1985, for $3,100 cash. Cash of $50 was paid for freight and cartage costs. The furniture is being depreciated over a four-year life under the straight-line method, assuming $150 of salvage value. The company employs a calendar-year accounting period and records depreciation for the full month in which an asset is installed. On July 1, 1986, $20 was spent to refinish the furniture. Prepare journal entries for the Roy Company to record all of the above data, including the annual depreciation adjustments, through 1986.

5. Keller Company purchased a new machine on January 2, 1985, at a cash cost of $60,000. The machine is estimated to have a life of five years, with no salvage value at the end of that time. If federal income taxes are levied at a rate of 50 percent of net income, how much would the income taxes payable for the years 1985 and 1986 be reduced if the company could choose the double-declining-balance method of computing depreciation rather than the straight-line method?

6. Coker Company acquired equipment costing $30,000 on April 1, 1985. The equipment has an estimated salvage value of $2,000 and an estimated useful life of seven years. The machine is being depreciated using the sum-of-the-years'-digits method. Compute the depreciation for the years ended December 31, 1985 and 1986.

7. On January 2, 1985, a new machine was acquired for $50,000. The machine has an estimated salvage value of $2,000 and an estimated useful life of 10 years. The machine is expected to produce a total of 500,000 units of product throughout its useful life. Compute depreciation for 1985 and 1986 using each of the following methods:

a. Straight-line.

b. Units-of-production (assume that 30,000 and 50,000 units were produced in 1985 and 1986, respectively).

c. Double-declining-balance.

d. Sum-of-the-years'-digits.

8. The Hart Company acquired a delivery truck on January 2, 1985, for

$14,000. The truck has an estimated salvage value of $750 and an estimated useful life of eight years. The truck is being depreciated on a straight-line basis. At the beginning of 1988, it is estimated that the truck has a remaining useful life of seven years. What are the depreciation charges for 1985 and for 1988?

9. Classify each of the following as either a capital expenditure or an expense:

a. Painting of office building at a cost of $400. The building is painted every year.

b. Addition of a new plant wing at a cost of $100,000.

c. Expansion of a paved parking lot at a cost of $60,000.

d. Replacement of a stairway with an escalator at a cost of $16,000.

e. Lubricating a machine at a cost of $200.

f. Replacing a broken fan belt at a cost of $150.

PROBLEMS

6–1. Lewis Company purchased land and a building having appraised values of $120,000 and $200,000, respectively. The terms of the sale were that Lewis would pay $163,000 in cash and assume responsibility for a $100,000 mortgage note, $5,000 of accrued interest, and $12,000 of unpaid property taxes. Lewis intends to use the building as an office building.

Required:

Prepare a journal entry to record the purchase.

6–2. The Meers Company purchased a two-square-mile farm from its owner under the following terms: cash paid, $202,500; mortgage note assumed, $100,000; and accrued interest on mortgage note assumed, $2,500. The company paid $23,000 for brokerage and legal services to acquire the property and secure clear title. It planned to subdivide the property into residential lots and to construct homes on these lots. Clearing and leveling costs of $9,000 were paid. Crops on the land were sold for $6,000. A house on the land, to be moved by the buyer, was sold for $2,100. The other buildings were razed at a cost of $4,000, and salvaged material was sold for $4,200.

Approximately six acres of the land were deeded to the township for roads, and another 10 acres were deeded to the local school district as the site for a future school. After the subdivision was completed, this land would have an approximate value of $3,200 per acre. The company secured a total of 1,200 salable lots from the remaining land.

Required:

Present a schedule showing in detail the composition of the cost of the 1,200 salable lots.

6–3. Hazel Company planned to erect a new factory building and a new office building in Atlanta, Georgia. Preliminary studies showed two possible sites as available and desirable. Further studies showed the second site to be preferable. A report on this property showed an appraised value of $300,000 for land and orchard and $200,000 for a building.

After considerable negotiation the company and the owner reached the following agreement. Hazel Company was to pay $260,000 in cash, assume a $150,000 mortgage note on the property, assume the accrued interest on the mortgage note of $3,200, and assume unpaid property taxes of $12,000. Hazel Company paid $33,000 cash for brokerage and legal services in acquiring the property.

Shortly after acquiring the property, Hazel Company sold the fruit on the trees for $4,400, remodeled the building into an office building at a cost of $64,000, and removed the trees from the land at a cost of $15,000. Construction of the factory building is to begin in a week.

Required:

Prepare schedules showing the proper valuation of the assets acquired by the White Company.

6–4. When you were hired as manager of the Ivy Street Company on January 1, 1986, the company bookkeeper gave you the following information regarding one of its equipment accounts (in T-account form):

Equipment—Machine C

1985			1985		
Jan. 1	Disposition cost of Machine B	1,000	Jan. 1	Cash from sale of Machine B	800
1	Material used in building Machine C . . .	30,000	Dec. 31	Depreciation on Machine C for year ended 12/31/85 (10% of $56,000)	5,600
1	Labor used in building Machine C	20,000			
1	Cost of installing Machine C	3,800			
1	Net income from building Machine C rather than purchasing it . . .	3,000			

Required:

Construct the theoretically correct equipment account for Machine C.

6–5. The Morton Company has the following entries in its Building account:

1985		*Debits*
May 5	Cost of land and building purchased	$400,000
5	Broker fees incident to purchase	18,000
1986		
Jan. 3	Contract price of new wing added to south end of building	110,000
15	Cost of new machinery, estimated life ten years	400,000
June 10	Real estate taxes for six months ended 6/30/86	9,000
Aug. 10	Cost of parking lot for employees in back of building . . .	12,400
Sept. 6	Replacement of broken windows	400
Oct. 10	Repairs due to regular usage	4,600

1985		Credits
Dec. 31	Transfer to Land account, as per allocation of purchase cost authorized in minutes of board of directors	60,000
1986		
Jan. 5	Proceeds from lease of second floor for six months ended 12/31/85	10,000

The original property was acquired on May 5, 1985. The Morton Company immediately engaged a contractor to construct a new wing on the south end of the building. While the new wing was being constructed, the company leased the second floor as temporary warehouse space to the Joy Company. During this period (July 1 to December 31, 1985) the company installed new machinery costing $400,000 on the first floor of the building. Regular operations began on January 2, 1986.

Required:

a. Compute the correct balance for the Building account as of December 31, 1986. The building is expected to last 40 years. The company employs a calendar-year accounting period.

b. Prepare the necessary journal entries to correct the records of the Morton Company at December 31, 1986. No depreciation entries are required.

6–6. The Neal Company's fiscal year ends May 31. The company has its own fleet of delivery vehicles. Included are the following:

Description	Date Acquired	Cost	Expected Life	Expected Salvage Value
Sedan No. 3 . . .	June 1, 1984	$16,000	4 years	$2,400
Truck No. 2 . . .	June 1, 1980	24,000	100,000 miles	2,000
Truck No. 5 . . .	Jan. 1, 1986	56,000	150,000	5,600
Trailer No. 8 . . .	Apr. 1, 1983	32,000	400,000	–0–

Speedometer readings at May 31 show the following:

	1985	1986	Total Mileage for Year Ended May 31, 1986
Sedan No. 3 . . .	15,000 miles	28,000 miles	13,000 miles
Truck No. 2 . . .	120,000	150,000	30,000
Truck No. 5 . . .	0	20,000	20,000
Trailer No. 8 . . .	50,000	75,000	25,000

Required:

Set up schedules showing in full detail the amount of depreciation to be recorded for the year ended May 31, 1986, on each of the above assets. Use the straight-line method for Sedan No. 3 and the units-of-production (number of miles driven) method for the other vehicles.

6–7. Crawford Company acquired a machine on July 1, 1985, at a cash cost of $48,000 and immediately spent $2,000 to install it. The machine was estimated to have a useful life of eight years and a scrap value of $3,000 at the end of this time. It was further estimated that the machine would produce 500,000 units of product during its life. In the first year, the machine produced 100,000 units.

Required:

Prepare journal entries to record depreciation for the fiscal year ended June 30, 1986, if the company used:

a. The straight-line method.

b. The units-of-production method.

c. The double-declining-balance method.

d. The sum-of-the-years'-digits method.

6–8. Garland Company acquired equipment on January 2, 1986, at a cash cost of $250,000. Transportation charges amounted to $2,000, and installation and testing costs totaled $8,000. The equipment was damaged while being installed, and the cost of repairing the damage was $1,000.

The equipment was estimated to have a useful life of nine years and a salvage value of $4,000 at the end of its life. It was further estimated that the equipment would be used in the production of 640,000 units of product during its life. During 1986, 142,000 units of product were produced.

Required:

Prepare journal entries to record depreciation for the year ended December 31, 1986, if the company used:

a. The straight-line method.

b. The units-of-production method.

c. The double-declining-balance method.

d. The sum-of-the-years'-digits method.

6–9. Norcross Company purchased a machine on January 2, 1984, at an invoice price of $62,600. Transportation charges amounted to $700, and $1,500 was spent to install the machine. The costs of removing an old machine to make room for the new one amounted to $600; $200 was received for the scrapped material from the old machine.

Required:

a. State the amount of depreciation that would be recorded on the machine for the first year on the straight-line basis, on the double-declining-balance basis, and on the sum-of-the-years'-digits basis, assuming an estimated life of eight years and no salvage value.

b. Give the journal entry needed at December 31, 1986, to record depreciation, assuming a revised total life expectancy of 12 years for the machine. Assume that depreciation has been recorded through December 31, 1985, on a straight-line basis.

6–10. The Nill Corporation acquired a new computer on July 1, 1985. The computer had an invoice price of $72,000, but the company received a 3 percent cash discount by paying the bill at the date of acquisition. While transporting the computer to its new location, a Hill employee was fined $200 for speeding. Hill paid the fine. Installation and testing costs totaled $7,104. The computer is estimated to have a $2,800 salvage value and a seven-year useful life.

Required:

    a. Prepare the journal entry to record the acquisition of the computer.

    b. Prepare the journal entry to record depreciation for 1985 under the double-declining-balance method.

    c. Assume that at the beginning of 1988 it is estimated that the computer will last another six years. Prepare the journal entry to record depreciation for 1988. Assume that depreciation has been recorded through 1987 on a straight-line basis and that the expected salvage value remains at $2,800.

6–11. A machine belonging to the Dewey Company that cost $30,000 has an estimated life of 20 years. After 10 years, an extremely important machine part, representing about 40 percent of the original cost, is worn out and replaced. The replacement cost is $9,000, and the useful life of the new part is the same as the remaining useful life of the machine.

Required:

    a. Prepare journal entries to record the replacement of the old part with the new part. Assume that depreciation has already been brought up to date.

    b. Compute the annual depreciation charge after replacement, using the straight-line method.

6–12. Jarvis Company purchased a machine at a cash cost of $70,000. An electric motor was purchased for cash and attached to the machine at a total cost of $52,000. The machine was installed in a production center on the first floor at a cost of $16,000 on July 1, 1985. Its estimated life was 15 years, with no salvage value expected. On July 1, 1990, the machine and motor unit was moved from its first-floor location to the second floor and the entire unit was installed at a cost of $32,000. The estimated life of the unit in its second-floor location is 10 years, with no salvage value expected.

Required:

    Compute the depreciation charge for the year ending June 30 1991, using the straight-line method.

7

PLANT ASSET DISPOSITIONS; NATURAL RESOURCES AND INTANGIBLE ASSETS

In the preceding chapter, the discussion focused on certain aspects of accounting for plant assets, such as determining the cost, estimating the depreciation, and distinguishing between capital and revenue expenditures. This chapter will examine accounting for (1) plant assets at their time of disposition and (2) natural resources and intangible assets.

DISPOSITION OF PLANT ASSETS

Plant assets eventually wear out, become inadequate, or become obsolete and must be sold, retired, or traded in on new assets. Upon disposition of a plant asset, the asset's cost and accumulated depreciation must be removed from the accounts.

Sale of Plant Assets

When a plant asset is sold, there may be a gain or a loss on the sale. The gain or loss is determined by comparing the asset's book value (cost less accumulated depreciation) and its sales price. If the sales price is greater than the asset's book value, there is a gain. If the sales price is less than the asset's book value, there is a loss. Of course, if the sales price is equal to the asset's book value, there is no gain or loss.

To illustrate accounting for the sale of a plant asset, assume that equipment costing $30,000 and having accumulated depreciation of $12,000 is sold for $20,000. A gain of $2,000 is realized, as computed below:

Equipment cost	$30,000
Accumulated depreciation	12,000
Book value	$18,000
Sales price	20,000
Gain realized	$ 2,000

The journal entry to record the sale is:

```
Cash  . . . . . . . . . . . . . . . . .   20,000
Accumulated Depreciation—Equipment  . . . . .   12,000
    Equipment  . . . . . . . . . . . .                30,000
    Gain on Sale of Plant Assets  . . . . . . .        2,000
    To record sale of equipment at a price greater than
    book value.
```

The gain of $2,000 is reported on the income statement under Other Revenue. If the equipment is sold for $16,500, a loss of $1,500 ($18,000 book value — $16,500 sales price) is realized, and the journal entry to record the sale is:

```
Cash  . . . . . . . . . . . . . . . . .   16,500
Accumulated Depreciation—Equipment  . . . . .   12,000
Loss on Sale of Plant Assets  . . . . . . . .    1,500
    Equipment  . . . . . . . . . . . .                30,000
    To record sale of equipment at a price less than book
    value.
```

The loss of $1,500 is reported under Other Expenses on the income statement.

If the equipment is sold for $18,000, there is no gain or loss and the journal entry to record the sale is:

```
Cash  . . . . . . . . . . . . . . . . .   18,000
Accumulated Depreciation—Equipment  . . . . .   12,000
    Equipment  . . . . . . . . . . . .                30,000
    To record sale of equipment at a price equal to book
    value.
```

Accounting for Depreciation to Date of Disposition

When a plant asset is sold or otherwise disposed of, it is important to record the depreciation to the date of the sale or disposition. For example, if an asset were sold on July 1 and depreciation was last recorded on December 31, depreciation for six months (January 1 to June 30) should be recorded. If depreciation is not recorded for that period, operating expenses will be understated and the gain on the sale of the asset understated or the loss overstated.

To illustrate, assume that on August 1, 1986, Ray Company sold a machine for $1,500. The machine cost $12,000 and is being depreciated at the rate of 10 percent per year. As of December 31, 1985, after adjustment, the machine's accumulated depreciation account had a balance of $9,600. Before recording a gain or loss, an entry should be made to record depreciation for the seven months ended July 31, 1986:

Depreciation Expense	700	
Accumulated Depreciation—Machinery		700

To record depreciation for seven months ($12,000 × 0.10 × 7/12).

Now, the $200 loss on the sale can be computed as shown below:

Machine cost	$12,000
Accumulated depreciation ($9,600 + $700)	10,300
Book value	$ 1,700
Sales price	1,500
Loss realized	$ 200

The journal entry to record the sale is:

Cash	1,500	
Accumulated Depreciation—Machinery	10,300	
Loss on Sale of Plant Assets	200	
Machinery		12,000

To record sale of machinery at a price less than book value.

Retirement of Plant Assets without Sale

When a plant asset is retired from productive service, it is necessary to remove the asset's cost and accumulated depreciation from the plant asset accounts. For example, Hayes Company should make the following journal entry when it retires a fully depreciated machine that cost $15,000 and had no salvage value:

Accumulated Depreciation—Machinery	15,000	
Machinery		15,000

To record the retirement of a fully depreciated machine.

Occasionally a plant asset is continued in use after it has been fully depreciated. In such a case, the asset's cost and accumulated depreciation should *not* be removed from the accounts until the asset is sold, traded, or retired from service. But depreciation should not continue to be recorded on a fully depreciated asset. The purpose of depreciation accounting is to charge a plant asset's cost to expense. Thus, the total depreciation expense can never exceed the plant asset's cost.

Sometimes a plant asset is retired from service or discarded before it is fully depreciated. If the asset is scrapped for salvaged materials—even though the materials will not be sold immediately—the value of the scrap materials should be debited to a Salvaged Materials account. To illustrate, assume that a machine with an original cost of $7,000 and accumulated depreciation of $6,200 is retired and that the scrap value of the machine is estimated at $375. The journal entry to record the retirement is:

Salvaged Materials	375	
Accumulated Depreciation—Machinery	6,200	
Loss on Retirement of Plant Assets	425	
Machinery		7,000

To record retirement of machinery.

Destruction of Plant Assets

Plant assets are sometimes damaged in accidents or destroyed by fire, flood, storm, or other casualties. Losses are normally incurred in such situations. For example, assume that an uninsured building costing $40,000 with accumulated depreciation of $12,000 is completely destroyed by fire. The journal entry is:

```
Fire Loss  . . . . . . . . . . . . . . . .   28,000
Accumulated Depreciation—Building  . . . . . .   12,000
    Building  . . . . . . . . . . . . . .             40,000
        To record fire loss.
```

If the building were insured, only the net fire loss in excess of the amount to be recovered from the insurance company would be debited to the Fire Loss account. To illustrate, assume that in the example above the building was partly insured and that $22,000 was recoverable from the insurance company. The journal entry is:

```
Receivable from Insurance Company  . . . . . .   22,000
Fire Loss  . . . . . . . . . . . . . . . .    6,000
Accumulated Depreciation—Building  . . . . . .   12,000
    Building  . . . . . . . . . . . . . .             40,000
        To record fire loss and amount expected to be recov-
        ered from insurance company.
```

EXCHANGES OF PLANT ASSETS

Certain plant assets such as automobiles, trucks, and office equipment are often acquired by trading in an old asset. In such cases, a trade-in allowance is usually granted on the old asset and the balance of the price is paid in cash. The accounting problem is to determine the amount at which the new asset is to be recorded and the amount of gain or loss, if any, to be recognized on the exchange. The general rule is that the asset received should be recorded at its fair value (its cash price). The cash price may be stated or it may have to be determined by adding the cash paid and the fair market value of the old asset traded-in. For instance, assume the cash price of the new asset is not given. The new asset is acquired by paying $5,000 cash plus trading in an old asset with a fair market value of $1,000. The cash price of the new asset is $6,000, ($5,000 + $1,000). The fair value of the asset received may differ from its list price or "sticker" price (as for new automobiles). The list price is irrelevant. The "price" of an asset is its cash price. Any trade-in allowance on the old asset is deducted from the cash price to find the amount of cash that must be paid.

Exchanges of Dissimilar Assets

When dissimilar assets (such as a factory machine and a delivery truck) are exchanged, both gains and losses are recognized. The new asset is recorded at its fair value, its cash price, which is equal to the fair value of the old asset at the time of the exchange plus the amount of cash paid. To illustrate, assume that an old factory machine is exchanged for a new delivery truck. The machine cost $40,000, has a related accumulated depreciation balance of $33,000, and a fair market value of $3,000. The truck has a cash price of $50,000. The truck is acquired by trading the machine and paying $47,000 cash. A $4,000 loss is realized on the exchange as computed below:

Machine cost	$40,000
Accumulated depreciation	33,000
Book value	$ 7,000
Fair market value of old asset	3,000
Loss realized	$ 4,000

Notice that the trade-in allowance is $3,000, ($50,000 − $47,000), since it is the difference between the cash price and the cash paid. (Sometimes the trade-in allowance is stated in terms of the list price, but we will not use that concept in this text.) The journal entry to record the exchange is:

Delivery Truck ($47,000 + $3,000)	50,000	
Accumulated Depreciation—Factory Machinery	33,000	
Loss on Exchange of Plant Assets	4,000	
Factory Machinery		40,000
Cash		47,000

To record loss on exchange of dissimilar plant assets.

The fair value of the new truck is $50,000, the sum of cash paid plus the fair value of the old machine.

To illustrate the recognition of a gain on the exchange of dissimilar plant assets, assume that the fair value in the above illustration was $8,000 instead of $3,000 and that $42,000 was paid in cash. The gain would be $1,000 ($8,000 fair value less $7,000 book value). The journal entry to record the exchange would be:

Delivery Trucks ($42,000 + $8,000)	50,000	
Accumulated Depreciation—Factory Machinery	33,000	
Factory Machinery		40,000
Cash		42,000
Gain on Exchange of Plant Assets		1,000

To record gain on exchange of dissimilar plant assets.

Exchanges of Similar Assets

When similar assets (such as an old delivery truck and a new delivery truck) are exchanged, *losses are recognized but gains are not recognized.* If a loss is indicated on an exchange of similar assets, the new asset is recorded at its fair value, its cash price, and the loss *is* recognized. But, if a gain is indicated on an exchange of similar assets, the new asset is recorded at the sum of the cash paid and the book value of the old asset, and the gain is not recognized.

To illustrate accounting for exchanges of similar assets, assume that $47,000 cash and delivery truck 1, which cost $40,000, has a related accumulated depreciation balance of $33,000, and has a fair value of $3,000, are exchanged for delivery truck 2, which has a cash price of $50,000. A loss of $4,000 is realized on the exchange, as computed below:

Cost of delivery truck 1	$40,000
Accumulated depreciation	33,000
Book value	$ 7,000
Fair market value of old asset ($50,000 − $47,000)	3,000
Loss on exchange of plant assets	$ 4,000

The journal entry to record the exchange is:

Delivery Trucks (2) ($47,000 + $3,000)	50,000	
Accumulated Depreciation—Delivery Trucks	33,000	
Loss on Exchange of Plant Assets	4,000	
Delivery Trucks (1)		40,000
Cash		47,000
To record loss on exchange of similar plant assets.		

Notice that an exchange of similar plant assets is recorded just like an exchange of dissimilar plant assets, provided that a loss occurs on the exchange.

In the preceding example, assume that delivery truck 1 (which has a fair value of $8,000) and $42,000 cash were given in exchange for delivery truck 2. A gain of $1,000 is indicated on the exchange, as computed below:

Cost of delivery truck 1	$40,000
Accumulated depreciation	33,000
Book value	$ 7,000
Fair market value of old asset ($50,000 − $42,000)	8,000
Gain indicated	$ 1,000

The journal entry to record the exchange is:

Delivery Trucks (2) ($42,000 + $7,000)	49,000	
Accumulated Depreciation—Delivery Trucks	33,000	
Delivery Trucks (1)		40,000
Cash		42,000
To record exchange of similar plant assets.		

Notice that a gain is *not* recognized on the exchange of similar assets. The new asset is recorded at the book value of the old asset ($7,000) plus the amount of cash paid ($42,000). Thus, the gain is used to reduce the recorded cost of the new asset. Also observe that the cost basis of the new delivery truck is equal to its cash price of $50,000 less the $1,000 gain. The $49,000 cost basis of the delivery truck is used in recording depreciation on the truck and in determining any gain or loss on its disposition.

The justification for not recognizing gains on exchanges of similar plant assets is that "revenue should not be recognized merely because one productive asset is substituted for a similar productive asset but rather should be considered to flow from the production and sale of the goods or services to which the substituted productive asset is committed."[1] In effect, the gain on exchanges of similar plant assets is realized in the form of increased net income because of smaller depreciation charges on the newly acquired asset. In the preceding example, depreciation is less if it is based on the $49,000 cost basis of the truck than if it is based on the $50,000 cash price of the truck. Thus, net income is larger.

Tax Rules and Plant Asset Exchanges

The Internal Revenue Code does not allow recognition of gains or losses for tax purposes when **similar productive assets** are exchanged. For tax purposes, the cost basis of the new asset is the book value of the old asset plus any additional cash paid. The additional cash outlay is called "boot."

Accounting principles and income tax laws agree on the treatment of gains, but they disagree on the treatment of losses. Thus, the previous example involving a $4,000 loss on the exchange of delivery trucks (see page 192) must be recorded as follows for tax purposes:

Delivery Trucks (2) ($47,000 + $7,000)	54,000	
Accumulated Depreciation—Delivery Trucks . . .	33,000	
Delivery Trucks (1)		40,000
Cash		47,000
To record exchange of similar plant assets for tax purposes.		

Because of the differences between accounting principles and income tax laws, two sets of records must be kept if a **material loss** occurs on an exchange of similar plant assets. One set of records will be based on the accounting valuation of the new asset (fair value of the old asset plus cash paid) and will be used in determining net income for financial reporting purposes. The second set of records will be based on the tax basis of the new asset (book value of the old asset plus cash paid) and will be used in determining the "depreciation" deduction for tax purposes.

Under the accounting principle of materiality, two sets of records do not have to be kept if the loss on the exchange is immaterial. In the case of an immaterial loss, the new asset can be recorded at the book value of the old asset plus the amount of cash paid for both tax purposes and financial reporting purposes. For example,

---

[1] APB, "Accounting for Nonmonetary Transactions," *APB Opinion No. 29* (New York: AICPA, 1973), par. 16.

assume that a company that earns $1 million suffers a $25 loss on an exchange of plant assets. In relation to $1 million, $25 is considered immaterial. Thus, the company can record the newly acquired asset at the sum of the book value of the old asset and the amount of cash paid. Only one set of records is required.

SUBSIDIARY PLANT ASSET RECORDS

Most business firms maintain an asset account and a related accumulated depreciation account in the general ledger for each major class of plant asset—buildings, factory machinery, office equipment, delivery equipment, and store equipment. In addition, many firms use subsidiary plant asset ledgers or record cards to maintain better control over plant assets. Each subsidiary record card contains detailed information about a single item of property, such as a desk or a typewriter.

The balance in the general ledger control account for each major class of plant asset should equal the total of the amounts shown on all the subsidiary record cards for that class of plant asset. Each time a plant asset is acquired, exchanged, or disposed of, an entry should be posted to both a general ledger control account and an appropriate subsidiary record card.

NATURAL RESOURCES

Mines, quarries, oil reserves, gas deposits, and timber stands are known as **natural resources** or **wasting assets.** In their natural state, they represent inventories of raw materials that will be consumed or exhausted through extraction or removal of their physical properties. But on the balance sheet, natural resources are classified as a separate group of noncurrent assets under a heading such as "Timber stands" or "Oil reserves."

Natural resources should be recorded in the accounts at the cost of acquisition plus the cost of development. They should be reported on the balance sheet at total cost less accumulated depletion.

Depletion is the exhaustion of a natural resource. It results from the physical removal of part of the resource. The amount of depletion that is recognized in a period is an estimate of the cost of the amount of the resource which is removed during the period. It is recorded by debiting the depletion account and by crediting either the resource account directly or an accumulated depletion account. This depletion cost is combined with other mining or removal costs to determine the total cost of the resource mined. This total cost is then divided between the cost of goods sold and the inventory of ore on hand according to the amount of ore sold. Thus, it is possible that all, some, or none of the depletion recognized in a period will be expensed in that period. The part not considered an expense will be part of the cost of a current asset—inventory.

Depletion charges may be computed by dividing the total cost of the property by the estimated number of units—tons, barrels, or board feet—in the property. For example, assume that, in 1986, $900,000 was paid for a mine estimated to contain 900,000 tons of ore. The unit depletion charge is $1 per ton ($900,000 ÷ 900,000 tons). If 100,000 tons of ore were mined in 1986, the depletion charge is 100,000 × $1, or $100,000. The journal entry to record the depletion charge is:

```
Depletion  . . . . . . . . . . . . . .   100,000
    Accumulated Depletion—
        Mineral Deposits  . . . . . . . . . .           100,000
    To record depletion for 1986.
```

The Mineral Deposits account also may be credited directly. The Depletion account contains the material cost of the ore mined; it is combined with labor and other mining costs to arrive at the total cost of the ore mined. This total cost is then allocated to cost of goods sold and inventory.

To illustrate, assume that in addition to the $100,000 depletion cost, mining labor costs totaled $300,000 and other mining costs (such as depreciation, property taxes, supplies, and power) totaled $80,000. The total cost of mining 100,000 tons of ore in 1986 is $480,000. Therefore, the cost per ton is $4.80 ($480,000 ÷ 100,000). If 80,000 tons were sold in 1986, the income statement would show cost of ore sold at $384,000 ($4.80 × 80,000), and the balance sheet would show inventory of ore on hand (a current asset) at $96,000 ($4.80 × 20,000). The balance sheet would also report the cost less accumulated depletion of the natural resource as follows:

```
Mineral deposits  . . . . . . . . . . . .   $900,000
Less accumulated depletion  . . . . . . . .    100,000   $800,000
```

It is often necessary to revise the depletion charge per unit when evidence indicates that the original estimate of the number of units in the property was wrong. When a change in estimate occurs, the unallocated cost is spread over the estimated remaining units. Referring to the above example, assume that in 1987 it is estimated that there are 1 million tons (instead of 800,000 tons) of ore remaining in the mine. The depletion charge per ton for 1987 would then be $0.80, or [($900,000 − $100,000) ÷ 1,000,000].

Depreciation of Plant Assets on Extractive Industry Property

Depreciable plant assets erected on extractive industry property are depreciated in the same manner as other depreciable assets. If such assets will be abandoned when the natural resource is exhausted, they should be depreciated over the shorter of *(a)* the life of the physical asset or *(b)* the life of the natural resource. In some cases, the periodic depreciation charge is computed on the basis of the units of mineral or other resource extracted.

To illustrate, assume that a building costing $310,000 and having an estimated physical life of 20 years and an estimated salvage value of $10,000 is constructed at the site of a mine. The mine is estimated to contain 1 million tons of ore and is expected to be completely exhausted within 10 years. During the first year of the building's life, 150,000 tons of ore are mined. Since the life of the mine (10 years) is shorter than the life of the building (20 years), the building should be depreciated over the life of the mine—that is, 10 years. If the depreciation charge is based on the units of ore mined, the depreciation charge for the first year is $45,000, as computed below:

$$\text{Depreciation} = (\text{Cost} - \text{Salvage value}) \times \frac{\text{Units mined}}{\substack{\text{Total units in mine at} \\ \text{time of acquisition}}}$$

$$= (\$310,000 - \$10,000) \times \frac{150,000}{1,000,000}$$

$$= \$45,000$$

INTANGIBLE ASSETS

Intangible assets arise from (1) superior entrepreneurial capacity or management know-how—**goodwill;** and (2) exclusive privileges granted by governmental authority—**trademarks, patents, copyrights,** and **franchises.** These intangible assets have no physical characteristics. They have value because they give business advantages or exclusive privileges and rights to their owners.

All intangible assets are nonphysical, but not all nonphysical assets are classified as intangible assets. For example, accounts receivable and prepaid expenses are nonphysical, but they are classified as current assets. Thus, intangible assets are both nonphysical and noncurrent.

Intangible assets are initially recorded at their cost of acquisition. Some companies may have extremely valuable intangibles such as trademarks that were acquired at little or no cost. Nonetheless, intangible assets should be reported on the balance sheet only if they were acquired at a cost.

Intangible assets are usually classified as follows:

1. Those that are specifically identifiable and can be acquired individually as well as in groups, such as patents, trademarks, and franchises.

2. Those that are not individually identifiable and can be acquired only as part of a group of assets. Because they cannot be identified individually, they are often lumped together and called goodwill.

Amortization of Intangible Assets

All intangible assets are subject to amortization. Amortization is similar to the depreciation of plant assets and the depletion of natural resources and is an estimate of the services or benefits received from an intangible asset in a given period. Amortization is recorded by debiting an amortization expense account and crediting the intangible asset account or an accumulated amortization account.

In general, intangible assets should be amortized over the shorter of their expected economic life or their legal life. *Opinion No. 17* of the Accounting Principles Board requires that an intangible asset acquired after October 31, 1970, be amortized over a period of not more than 40 years. Straight-line amortization must be used unless another method can be shown to be superior.

Patents

A patent is a right granted by a government which gives the owner of the patent the exclusive right to manufacture, sell, lease, or otherwise benefit from the patent. The real value of a patent lies in its ability to produce income. The legal life of a patent is 17 years. Protection under the patent starts at the time of application for the patent and lasts for 17 years from the date it is granted.

A patent that is purchased should be recorded in the Patents account at cost. The cost of successfully defended patent infringement suits should also be charged to the Patents account.

The cost of a purchased patent should be amortized over the shorter of 17 years or its estimated useful life. If a patent cost $40,000 and is to be amortized over a useful life of 10 years, the journal entry to record the amortization at the end of each year is:

```
Patent Amortization Expense  . . . . . . . . .  4,000
    Patents    . . . . . . . . . . . . . . .          4,000
        To record patent amortization.
```

If, after a few years, the patent becomes worthless, the unamortized balance should be charged to expense and, if material in amount, it should be set forth separately in the income statement.

Copyrights

A copyright gives its owner an exclusive right protecting writings, designs, and literary productions from being illegally reproduced. A copyright has a life equal to the life of the creator plus 50 years. Since most publications have a limited life, it is advisable to charge the cost of a copyright against the first edition published through charges to expense over the period of its publication.

Franchises

A franchise is a contract, usually between a government agency and a private company (generally a public utility). A franchise gives the company certain rights, ranging from rights of a nominal nature to the right of complete monopoly; it also places certain restrictions on the company, especially regarding rates charged. If periodic payments to the grantor of the franchise are required, they should be debited to a Franchise Expense or Rent Expense account. If a lump-sum payment is made to obtain the franchise, the cost should be amortized over the shorter of the useful life of the franchise or 40 years.

Goodwill

Goodwill is best viewed as an intangible value attached to an entity that results primarily from the skill of its management. A firm may be continuously generating goodwill. That goodwill may be represented by a superior marketing organization, product reputation, marketing channels, technical know-how, and astute management. Such factors, though, are hard to identify and value. Thus, the value of goodwill is often described as the value of the entity over the sum of the fair values of its net individually identifiable assets. Goodwill arises because management has the ability to use the resources of the entity to produce an above-average rate of earnings per dollar of investment. Thus, proof of the existence of goodwill is found in the ability to generate superior or above-average earnings.

A goodwill account will appear in the records only if goodwill has been bought and paid for in cash or other property of the purchaser. Goodwill cannot be purchased by itself. An entire business or a part of it must be purchased to obtain the accompanying intangible asset, goodwill.

To illustrate, assume that Company A purchases all the assets of Company B. These assets consist of accounts receivable, inventories, land, buildings, equipment, and patents. Company A pays Company B $600,000 cash and assumes responsibility for $300,000 of debts owed by Company B. With assumed market values (not costs from B's books) as follows, the intangible value attached to B and purchased by A is $75,000:

Cash paid		$600,000
Liabilities assumed		300,000
Total price paid		$900,000
Less fair market values of individually identifiable assets:		
Accounts receivable	$100,000	
Inventories	90,000	
Land	150,000	
Buildings	250,000	
Equipment	200,000	
Patents	35,000	825,000
Goodwill		$ 75,000

The $75,000 is called goodwill and is recorded in a Goodwill account; it is treated in this way because it is difficult to identify the specific reasons for the existence of goodwill. The reasons might include a good reputation, product leadership, valuable human resources, and a good information system.

Amortization of goodwill. Goodwill cannot be amortized in determining taxable income. But current accounting practice requires the amortization of goodwill over a period not to exceed 40 years. The reasoning behind this requirement is that the value of the purchased goodwill will eventually disappear. Other goodwill may be generated in its place, but the organization is not equipped to value the regenerated goodwill. If Company A in the above example decided that the goodwill attached to Company B would last 10 years, it would make annual adjusting entries debiting Goodwill Amortization Expense and crediting Goodwill for $7,500.

Leases and Leaseholds

A lease is a contract by which the person acquiring the lease (the lessee) makes payments to the person granting the lease (the lessor) in exchange for the right to use property for the amount of time stated in the lease.

Under certain circumstances, a lease transaction may be regarded as a purchase and should be recorded as one. This type of lease is called a capital lease.

If a lease does not meet the criteria for a capital lease, it is called an operating lease. An operating lease is not shown on the lessee's books unless an initial lump-sum payment is made when the lease is signed. An advance payment is recorded in a Leasehold account and is amortized over the life of the lease by a debit to Rent Expense and a credit to Leasehold. Straight-line amortization is commonly used.

Leasehold improvements. If the lessee improves the leased property, these improvements will usually become the property of the lessor after the lease has expired. Improvements are assets and should be debited to a Leasehold Improvements account. The useful life of the leasehold improvements to the lessee is the shorter of the life of the improvements or the life of the lease; hence, this is the period over which the cost of the leasehold improvements should be spread. To illustrate, assume that on January 2, 1986, Y leases a building for 25 years under a nonrenewable lease at an annual rental of $20,000 payable on each December 31. Y immediately incurs a cost of $80,000 for improvements to the building, which are estimated to have a life of 40 years. The $80,000 should be amortized over 25 years, since the period of the lease is shorter than the life of the improvements and Y will not be able to use the improvements beyond the life of the lease. If only annual statements are prepared, the following journal entries will properly record the expense for the year ended December 31, 1986:

```
Rent Expense (or Leasehold
  Improvement Expense)  . . . . . . . . . .  3,200
    Leasehold Improvements  . . . . . . . .         3,200
  To charge off 1/25th of $80,000.

Rent Expense  . . . . . . . . . . . . . .  20,000
  Cash  . . . . . . . . . . . . . . . .         20,000
  To record annual rent of $20,000.
```

The total rental expense is $23,200 per year.

Although leaseholds are intangible assets, leaseholds and leasehold improvements are ordinarily shown in the plant assets section of the balance sheet.

RESEARCH AND DEVELOPMENT COSTS

Prior to 1975, research and development costs were often capitalized as intangible assets when future benefits were expected from their incurrence. Since it was often difficult to determine the costs applicable to future benefits, many firms expensed all such costs as they were incurred. Other firms capitalized those costs that related to proven products and expensed the rest as incurred. As a result of these varied accounting practices, the Financial Accounting Standards Board ruled that all research and development costs other than those directly reimbursable by government agencies and others must be expensed at the time they are incurred. Immediate expensing is justified on the grounds that the amount of costs applicable to the future cannot be measured with any high degree of precision, that doubt exists as to whether any future benefits will be received, and that even if benefits are expected they cannot be measured. As a result of the ruling, research and development costs no longer appear as intangible assets on the balance sheet.

SUMMARY

This chapter dealt with the disposition of plant assets, with natural resources, and with intangible assets. When an asset is sold, the balances in the asset and related accumulated depreciation accounts must be eliminated. The difference between the book value and the amount received represents the gain or loss. If an asset is retired without sale, the asset and the related depreciation must be removed from the accounts. The loss from any asset destroyed is reduced by any insurance proceeds received. When dissimilar assets are exchanged, both gains and losses may be recognized. But when similar assets are exchanged, only material losses are recognized. No gains are recognized. The Internal Revenue Code does not allow, for tax purposes, recognition of either gains or losses on exchanges of similar assets. Subsidiary plant asset records are often maintained to increase control over assets.

Natural resources include mines, quarries, oil reserves, gas deposits, and timber stands. Natural resources should be recorded at acquisition costs plus development costs, less any accumulated depletion. The amount of depletion recognized in a period is an estimate of the cost of the portion of the resource that was removed during the period. Intangible assets are nonphysical and noncurrent assets, including goodwill, patents, copyrights, franchises, trademarks, and leaseholds. Only purchased intangibles are recorded in the accounting records. Intangible assets should be amortized over the shortest of their economic useful life, their legal life, or 40 years. Leasehold improvements should be written off over the life of the lease or the life of the improvements, whichever is shorter.

QUESTIONS

1. When depreciable plant assets are sold for cash, how is the gain or loss measured?

2. A plant asset that cost $15,000 and has a related accumulated depreciation account balance of $15,000 is still being used in business operations. Would it be appropriate to continue recording depreciation on this asset? Explain. When should the asset's cost and accumulated depreciation be removed from the accounting records?

3. Factory equipment and $10,000 cash are exchanged for a delivery truck. How should the cost basis (cash price) of the delivery truck be measured?

4. A plant asset is disposed of by exchanging it for a new asset of a similar type. How should the cost basis of the new asset be measured under generally accepted accounting principles?

5. A plant asset is exchanged for an asset of a similar type. What is the cost basis of the new asset for tax purposes?

6. What advantages can accrue to a company that maintains subsidiary plant asset records?

7. **a.** Distinguish between depreciation, depletion, and amortization. Name two assets that are subject to depreciation; to depletion; to amortization.

   b. Distinguish between tangible and intangible assets, and classify the above-named assets accordingly.

8. A building with an estimated physical life of 40 years was constructed at the site of a coal mine. The coal mine is expected to be completely exhausted within 20 years. Over what length of time should the building be depreciated, assuming that it will be abandoned after all the coal has been extracted? Why?

9. What are the characteristics of intangible assets? Give an example of an asset that has no physical existence but is not classified as an intangible asset.

10. Over what length of time should intangible assets be amortized?

11. You note that a certain store seems to have a steady stream of regular customers, a favorable location, courteous employees, high-quality mer-

chandise, and a reputation for fairness in dealing with customers, employees, and suppliers. Does it follow automatically that this business has goodwill?

12. What is the difference between a leasehold (under an operating lease contract) and a leasehold improvement? Is there any difference in the accounting procedures applicable to each?

13. Benson Company leased a tract of land for 40 years at an agreed annual rental of $10,000. The effective date of the lease was July 1, 1985. During the last six months of 1985, Benson constructed a building on the land at a cost of $250,000. The building was placed in operation on January 2, 1986, at which time it was estimated to have a physical life of 50 years. Over what period of time should the building be depreciated? Why?

14. What reasons justify the immediate expensing of most research and development costs?

EXERCISES

1. Plant equipment originally costing $72,000, on which $48,000 of depreciation has been accumulated, is sold for $18,000. Prepare the journal entry to record the sale.

2. A machine costing $8,000, on which $6,000 of depreciation has been accumulated, is completely destroyed by fire. What journal entry should be made to record the machine's destruction and the resulting fire loss under each of the following unrelated assumptions:

   a. The machine is *not* insured.
   b. The machine *is* insured, and it is estimated that $1,500 will be recovered from the insurance company.

3. Spinks Company owns an automobile acquired on July 1, 1984, at a cash cost of $10,400. At that time, it was estimated to have a life of four years and a $800 salvage value. Depreciation has been recorded through June 30, 1987, on a straight-line basis. On July 1, 1987, the auto is traded in for a new auto. The old auto has a cash value of $2,000. Cash of $9,200 is paid. Prepare the journal entry to record the trade-in under generally accepted accounting principles.

4. Equipment costing $22,000 which had been depreciated $15,000 was disposed of on January 2, 1986. What journal entries are required to record the equipment's disposition under each of the following unrelated assumptions?

   a. The equipment was sold for $9,000 cash.
   b. The equipment was sold for $5,800 cash.
   c. The equipment was retired from service and hauled to the junk yard. No material was salvaged.
   d. The equipment was exchanged for similar equipment having a cash price of $30,000. A trade-in allowance of $10,000 was received, and the balance was paid in cash.
   e. The equipment was exchanged for similar equipment having a cash

price of $30,000. A trade-in allowance of $5,000 was received, and the balance was paid in cash. (Record this transaction twice: first, for tax purposes, and second, for financial reporting purposes.)

5. Spikes Company paid $1 million for the right to extract all of the mineral-bearing ore, estimated at 5 million tons, from a certain tract of land. During the first year, Spikes Company extracted 500,000 tons of the ore and sold 400,000 tons. What part of the $1 million should be charged to expense during the first year?

6. The Walter Company purchased a patent on January 1, 1970, at a total cost of $136,000. In January 1980 the company successfully defended a suit alleging infringement of another's patent rights. The legal fees amounted to $30,000. What will be the amount of patent cost amortized in 1986? (The useful life of the patent is the same as its legal life—17 years.)

7. Alvin Company leased a building under an operating lease for a 20-year period beginning January 1, 1986. The company paid $80,000 in cash and agreed to make annual payments equal to 1 percent of the first $500,000 of sales and one half of 1 percent of all sales over $500,000. Sales for 1986 amounted to $1,500,000. Payment of the annual amount will be made on January 12, 1987. Prepare journal entries to record the cash payment of January 1, 1986, and the proper expense to be recognized for the use of the leased building in 1986.

PROBLEMS

7-1. The Arthur Company began operations in January 1983. The following transactions related to plant asset accounts occurred between 1983 and 1986.

1983
Jan. 2 Purchased the following:
  (1) A machine for $32,000 cash.
  (2) Office equipment for $18,000 cash.
  (3) A delivery truck for $13,000 cash.
Dec. 31 Recorded one year's depreciation on the plant assets purchased on January 2. The following information was used to determine depreciation for the year:

Asset	Estimated Useful Life	Estimated Salvage Value	Depreciation Method
Machine	10 years	$1,000	Double-declining-balance
Office equipment .	8 years	–0–	Straight-line
Delivery truck . .	5 years	500	Sum-of-the-years'-digits

1984
Oct. 1 The delivery truck (uninsured) was completely destroyed in an accident.
Dec. 31 Recorded depreciation for 1984 on the machine and the office equipment.

1985
Sept. 1 The office equipment was sold for $10,000 cash.
Dec. 31 Recorded depreciation for 1985 on the machine.

1986
Oct. 1 Exchanged the machine and $30,000 cash for a similar new machine, which has a cash price of $40,000.
Dec. 31 Recorded depreciation on the new machine, which has an estimated useful life of 10 years and no salvage value. The double-declining-balance method was used.

Required:

Prepare journal entries to record the above transactions.

7-2. On January 2, 1983, the Spengler Company purchased a delivery truck for $42,000 cash. The truck has an estimated useful life of six years and an estimated salvage value of $2,000. The double-declining-balance method of depreciation is being used.

Required:

a. Prepare a schedule which shows how the truck's book value on January 1, 1986, would be computed.

b. Assume that the truck is to be disposed of on July 1, 1986. What journal entry is required to record depreciation for the six months ended June 30, 1986?

c. Prepare the journal entries to record the disposition of the truck on July 1, 1986, under each of the following unrelated assumptions:

(1) The truck is sold for $6,000 cash.

(2) The truck is sold for $14,000 cash.

(3) The truck is retired from service, and it is expected that $3,000 will be received from the sale of salvaged materials.

(4) The truck and $40,000 cash are exchanged for office equipment having a cash price of $56,000.

(5) The truck and $44,000 cash are exchanged for a new delivery truck which has a cash price of $60,000.

(6) The truck is completely destroyed in an accident. Cash of $5,600 is expected to be recovered from the insurance company.

7-3. Ringold Company purchased a new 1986 model automobile on September 1, 1986. The cash price of the new car was $5,200, and the company received a trade-in allowance of $1,000 for a 1984 model. The 1984 model had been acquired on September 1, 1984, at a cost of $4,800. Depreciation had been recorded through December 31, 1985, on a double-declining-balance basis, with four years of useful life expected. At the time of the trade-in, the 1984 automobile had a cash value (fair value) of $1,000.

Required:

Prepare journal entries to record the exchange of the automobiles under (a) the tax method and (b) the theoretically correct accounting method.

7-4. Shelton Company acquired a mine for $9 million. The mine contained an estimated 9 million tons of ore. It was also estimated that the land would have a value of $800,000 when the mine was exhausted and that only 8 million tons of ore could be economically extracted. A building was erected on the property at a cost of $1,200,000. The building has an estimated useful life of 35 years and no scrap value. Specialized mining equipment was installed at a cost of $1,650,000. This equipment has an estimated useful life of seven years and an estimated $42,000 salvage value. The company began operating on July 1, 1985. During the fiscal year ended June 30, 1986, 800,000 tons of ore were extracted. The company decided to use the units-of-production basis to record depreciation on the building and the sum-of-the-years'-digits method to record depreciation on the equipment.

Required:

Prepare journal entries to record the depletion and depreciation charges for the fiscal year ended June 30, 1986. Show calculations.

7–5. The Kirby Mining Company, on January 2, 1986, acquired ore deposits at a cash cost of $1,785,000. The ore deposit contains an estimated 3 million tons. Present technology will allow the economic extraction of only 85 percent of the total deposit. Machinery, equpiment, and temporary sheds are acquired at a cost of $306,000. These assets will have no further value to the company when the ore body is exhausted; they have a physical life of 12 years. In 1986, 350,000 tons of ore are extracted. The company expects the mine to be exhausted in 10 years, with sharp variations in annual production.

Required:

a. Compute the depletion charge for 1986.

b. Compute the depreciation charge for 1986 under each of the following methods: (1) straight-line, (2) sum-of-the-years'-digits, (3) double-declining-balance, and (4) units-of-production.

c. Which depreciation method do you believe to be most appropriate in the circumstances cited?

7–6. The Ken Company purchased a patent for $120,000 on January 2, 1986. The patent was estimated to have a useful life of 10 years. The $120,000 cost was properly charged to an asset account and amortized in 1986. On July 1, 1987, the company incurred legal and court costs of $36,000 in a successful defense of the patent in an infringement suit.

Required:

Compute the patent amortization cost for 1987.

7–7. The Boston Company spent $41,650 to purchase a patent on January 2, 1985. It was assumed that the patent will be useful during its full legal life which began on January 2, 1985. In January 1986 the company successfully defended a suit alleging infringement of another's patent rights at a cost of $8,000. Also in January 1986, the company paid $12,000 to obtain patents that could, if used by competitors, make the earlier Boston patent useful. The purchased patents, which will never be used, have an effective date of January 2, 1986.

Required:

Give the entries to record the information relative to the patents in 1985 and 1986.

7–8. On July 1, 1985, the Danish Company had the following balances in its Plant Asset and Accumulated Depreciation accounts:

	Asset	Accumulated Depreciation
Land	$ 200,000	
Leasehold	150,000	
Buildings	1,876,000	$258,500
Equipment . . .	816,000	260,000
Trucks	142,000	42,650

Additional information:

(1) The leasehold covers a plot of ground leased on July 1, 1980, for a period of 25 years.

(2) The office building is on the leased land and was completed on July 1, 1981, at a cost of $576,000. Its physical life is set at 40 years. The factory building is on the owned land and was completed on July 1, 1980, at a cost of $1,300,000. Its life is also set at 40 years. Neither building has any expected salvage value.

(3) Equipment is depreciated at $6\frac{2}{3}$ percent per year on its cost.

(4) The company owns three trucks—A, B, and C. Truck A, purchased on July 1, 1983, at a cost of $32,000, has a life of three years and a scrap value of $2,000. Truck B, purchased on January 2, 1984, at a cost of $50,000, has a life of four years and a scrap value of $4,000. Truck C, purchased on January 2, 1985, at a cost of $60,000, has a life of five years and a scrap value of $6,000.

The following events occurred in the fiscal year ended June 30, 1986:

1985

July 1   Rent for July 1, 1985–June 30, 1986, on leased land is paid, $19,000.

Oct. 1   Truck A is traded in on Truck D. Cash price of the new truck is $64,000. Cash of $54,000 is paid. Truck D has a life of four years and a scrap value of $3,500.

1986

Feb. 2   Truck B is sold for $28,000 cash.

June 1   Truck C (uninsured) is completely demolished in an accident.

Required:

Prepare journal entries to record the above transactions and the necessary June 30, 1986, adjusting entries. Use the straight-line depreciation method.

7–9. On January 1, 1986, the Turner Company had the following balances in its plant asset and accumulated depreciation accounts:

	Asset	Accumulated Depreciation
Land	$ 40,000	
Leasehold . . .	50,000	
Buildings . . .	219,600	$18,375
Equipment . . .	192,000	89,100
Trucks	28,800	14,025

Additional information:

(1) The leasehold covers a plot of ground leased on January 1, 1982, for a period of 20 years.

(2) Building 1 is on the owned land and was completed on July 1, 1985, at a cost of $126,000. Its life is set at 40 years. Building 2 is on leased land and was completed on July 1, 1982, at a cost of $93,600. Its life is also set at 40 years on its cost. Neither building has an estimated salvage value.

(3) Equipment is depreciated at 12.5 percent per year.

(4) Truck A, purchased on January 1, 1984, at a cost of $9,600, was given a life of 2½ years and a scrap value of $600. Truck B, purchased on July 1, 1984, at a cost of $8,400, was given a life of two years and a scrap value of $1,400. Truck C, purchased on July 1, 1985, at a cost of $10,800, was given a life of three years and a scrap value of $1,350.

The following events occurred in 1986:

Jan. 2 Rent for 1986 on leased land is paid, $5,600.

Apr. 1 Truck B is traded in on Truck D. Cash price of the new truck is $9,600. A trade-in allowance of $1,800 is granted ($1,800 is also the cash value of Truck B). the balance is paid in cash. Truck D is given a life of 2½ years and a scrap value of $600. (Do not use tax method.)

1 Truck A is sold for $1,800 cash.

Required:

Prepare journal entries to record the 1986 transactions and the necessary December 31, 1986, adjusting entries, assuming a calendar-year accounting period. Use the straight-line depreciation method.

8　STOCKHOLDERS' EQUITY

The corporation is the major form of business enterprise in terms of economic power. One of the reasons for this is that a corporation can raise huge amounts of capital by selling shares of its stock to the public. Thus, the owners' interest in a corporation is usually called stockholders' or shareholders' equity. Other advantages of the corporation include the stockholders' limited liability and the ease of transferring ownership by selling the shares of stock owned. Limited liability means that a stockholder is not personally responsible (liable) for the debts of the corporation. The stockholder can lose only the amount invested.

The goals of accounting for stockholders' equity are to show the **sources** of **equity** capital and the **rights** of the various capital investors in the corporation. In addition to capital invested by owners, equity capital may be obtained by the retention of earnings in the corporation. The corporation may also obtain capital by issuing bonds or short-term debt. Accounting for this type of capital is discussed in another chapter, but it should be noted that the rights of equity capital holders rank below those of debt holders. This means that in times of economic hardship, all legal liabilities must be met before equity holders can share in the assets of the business. Thus, the major risks and rewards of a business lie with those who provide equity capital.

This chapter deals with accounting for various types of paid-in capital (including capital stock) and retained earnings. The chapter appendix discusses accounting for investments in the capital stock of other companies.

Capital Stock Authorized, Issued, and Outstanding

The corporate charter states the maximum number of shares and the par value, if any, per share of each class of stock that the corporation is authorized to issue—thus the term **authorized shares.** The total ownership interest in a corporation rests with the holders of its **outstanding shares** of stock—that is, the shares authorized and **issued** and currently held by stockholders. If, for example, a corporation is authorized to issue 30,000 shares of common stock but has issued only 14,000 shares, the holders of the 14,000 shares are the sole owners of the corporation.

Each outstanding share of stock of a given class has identical rights and privileges with every other outstanding share of that class. Shares authorized but not yet issued are referred to as **unissued shares.** These shares possess no rights.

CLASSES OF CAPITAL STOCK

Common Stock

Every corporation will have common stock outstanding. The primary rights of the **common** stockholder include the right to (1) share in earnings when they are declared as dividends; (2) subscribe to additional offerings of the same stock in proportion to the amount currently held; (3) share in assets upon liquidation; and (4) share in management through the election of a board of directors which guides the broad policy decisions of the business. The equity of the common stockholders is often referred to as the residual equity in a corporation, meaning that all other claims rank ahead of the claims of the common stockholders. The primary risks and rewards of ownership accrue to the common stockholder.

Preferred Stock

A corporation may need more equity capital than that provided by the common stockholders. Usually, the corporation will need to attract a different type of investor—one that is more interested in stable earnings on an investment. To do this, a class of stock granting certain preferences and called **preferred stock** may be issued. Usually, preferred stock is **preferred as to dividends,** although it can also be **preferred as to assets** in case of liquidation.

If stock is *preferred as to dividends,* its holders are entitled to a specified dividend per share before the payment of any dividend on the common stock. A stock preferred as to dividends is **cumulative** if all **dividends in arrears** (required dividends not paid in prior years) on this stock and the current dividend must be paid before dividends can be paid on the common stock. For example, assume that a company has $100,000 par value of 9 percent cumulative preferred stock outstanding, $100,000 par value of common stock outstanding, and $30,000 of retained earnings. No dividends have been paid for two years, including the current year. The preferred stockholders are entitled to dividends of $18,000 ($100,000 × .09 × 2 years) before any dividend can be paid to the common stockholders. If a preferred stock is **noncumulative,** a dividend that is not paid in any one year does not need to be paid in any future year. Because omitted dividends are lost forever, noncumulative preferred stocks hold little attraction for investors and are seldom issued.

Dividends in arrears are never shown as a liability of the corporation since dividends are not a legal liability until they have been declared by the board of directors. Because the amount of dividends in arrears may influence the decisions of users of a corporation's financial statements, such dividends should be and usually are disclosed in a footnote.

If stock is preferred as to assets in case of liquidation, its holders are entitled to receive par value or a larger specified amount per share (called liquidation value) before the common stockholders receive any distribution of assets. To illustrate the preference as to assets feature, assume that a corporation has $100,000 par value of preferred stock outstanding, $200,000 par value of common stock outstanding, and, after paying its liabilities, cash of $240,000 to distribute to its stockholders. If the preferred stock is preferred as to assets at par value and there are no dividends in arrears, the preferred stockholders will receive $100,000, with $140,000 being paid to common stockholders. If the preferred stock is not preferred as to assets, the $240,000 is prorated between the preferred and common stockholders in the ratio of the dollar total of the classes: $80,000 [($100,000/$300,000) × $240,000] to the preferred stockholders and $160,000 to the common stockholders.

The issuance of preferred stock may have other advantages for the corporation: (1) since preferred stocks usually have no voting rights, their issuance will not weaken the control of the common stockholders; and (2) the return (dividend) is usually fixed, thus giving **financial leverage** to the common stockholders.

Financial leverage. Financial leverage is the use of debt or preferred stock to increase (or perhaps decrease) earnings per share to common stockholders. Favorable financial leverage results when earnings per share (EPS) increase because of the issuance of preferred stock or debt. As an example of financial leverage, assume that the organizers of a corporation have two possible ways of getting capital: (1) issue 40,000 shares of $10 par value common stock for $400,000; or (2) issue 20,000 shares of $10 par value common stock for $200,000 and 2,000 shares of $100 par, 8 percent preferred stock for $200,000. Assume that net income of $80,000 per year is expected. The earnings to the common stockholders on a per share basis (net income, less preferred dividends, divided by number of common shares outstanding) and as a percentage of the original investment are shown in Illustration 8.1. Favorable leverage results when debt or preferred stock is used to increase the earnings per share of the common shareholders. In Illustration 8.1 the earnings per share of common stock are greater with preferred stock outstanding, and therefore, at that level of earnings there is favorable financial leverage. The result is earnings of $3.20 per share with the preferred stock and $2.00 per share without the preferred stock.

Financial leverage works in both directions. If net income in the above example should drop to $20,000, the corresponding earnings per common share would be $0.20 for the corporation with preferred stockholders and $0.50 for the all-common-stock corporation. Thus, in certain cases, the risks of financial leverage may offset the advantages. This is also true for long-term debt, which is another means of obtaining leverage.

Illustration 8.1
ILLUSTRATION OF SUCCESSFUL FINANCIAL LEVERAGE

	With Preferred	Without Preferred
Net income	$80,000	$80,000
Preferred dividends	16,000	0
Net income to common stock	$64,000	$80,000
Number of common shares outstanding	20,000	40,000
Earnings per share of common stock	$ 3.20	$ 2.00

Convertible preferred stock. In recent years, large amounts of new preferred stock have been issued in corporate mergers or acquisitions. The preferred stock issued was often convertible; that is, the holder of the stock could exchange it when desired for shares of common stock of the same corporation at a conversion ratio stated in the preferred stock contract.

Convertible preferred stock is attractive to the investor because of (1) the stability of dividends and (2) the opportunity to participate in the growth of the corporation through the conversion privilege. Issuing preferred stock is also attractive to a corporation because it avoids the use of debt that will have to be repaid and that bears interest which must be paid regardless of the level of net income.

To illustrate this latter attraction, assume that the Olsen Company issued 2,000 shares of 8 percent, $100 par value convertible preferred stock at $100 per share. The stock can be converted at any time into four shares of Olsen common stock which has a current market value of $25 per share. Assume further that in the next several years the company's net income increases sharply and that it increases the dividend of the common stock from $1.50 to $3.00

per share. The common stock now sells at $50 per share. The holder of one share of preferred stock could convert the stock into four shares of common stock and increase the annual dividend from $8 (from the preferred) to $12 (from the common). Or if one so desired, one could sell the preferred share at a substantial gain since the preferred stock would sell in the market for about $200—the market value of the four shares of common into which it is convertible. Or one may continue to hold the preferred stock in the expectation of realizing an even larger gain at a later date.

Virtually all preferred stocks, whether convertible or not, are callable by the issuing corporation. If a stock is callable, the issuing corporation may force the owners to surrender the stock for redemption. Holders of convertible preferred have the choice of either surrendering the stock or converting it into common shares. Preferred shares are usually callable at a small premium of 3 or 4 percent of the par value of the stock. If the stock is surrendered, the holder of record receives the par value, the call premium, any dividends in arrears, and a prorated portion of the current period's dividend. Assuming that there are no cumulative dividends in arrears and no current dividends to be prorated, the entry to record the call (and retirement) by the payment of $103 cash for a share of $100 par value preferred stock that was originally issued at par value, is:

Preferred Stock	100	
Retained Earnings	3	
Cash		103
To record the call and retirement of a share of preferred stock.		

Balance Sheet Presentation

As previously noted, the balance sheet should show the sources of capital and the rights of the various holders. It should also indicate the status of issued and unissued shares. To illustrate, assume that a corporation is authorized to issue (1) 20,000 shares of $100 par value, 8 percent, cumulative, convertible preferred stock, all of which have been issued and are outstanding; and (2) 400,000 shares of $10 par value common stock, of which 160,000 shares have been issued at par and are outstanding. The stockholders' equity section of the balance sheet (assuming $600,000 of retained earnings) would be:

Stockholders' equity:		
Preferred stock—$100 par value, 8% cumulative, convertible; authorized, issued, and outstanding, 20,000 shares	$2,000,000	
Common stock—$10 par value; authorized, 400,000 shares; issued and outstanding, 160,000 shares	1,600,000	$3,600,000
Retained earnings		600,000
Total stockholders' equity		$4,200,000

A footnote to the balance sheet would state the rate at which the preferred stock is convertible into common stock.

Shares with par value. Each share of capital stock—common or preferred—will, according to the terms of the charter of the issuing corporation, be of **par value** or of **no par value.** The par value, if any, will be stated in the corporate charter and will be printed on the stock certificates. Par value may be of any amount.

Par value serves two purposes. First, it is the amount per share that is recorded in the capital stock account for each share outstanding. Second, the par value of the outstanding shares is often the legal or stated capital of the corporation. A corporation is forbidden by law to declare dividends or to acquire its own stock if such action will reduce stockholders' equity below the legal capital of the corporation. If stock is issued at a discount from par, the stockholders may be liable to the creditors up to the total discount from par value.

Par value is not an indication of the amount of stockholders' equity per share (book value per share, as it is called) that is recorded in the accounting records of the corporation. The stockholders' equity consists of **paid-in** or **contributed capital** and **retained earnings,** and the latter may be either positive or negative. Nor does par value give any clue to the market value of the stock, because market value is based largely upon investors' expectations concerning future net income and dividends and general market prospects.

Shares without par value. It is possible to have common stock without par value. Quite often, though, such stock will have a **stated value.** This stated value, like par value, may be set at any amount by the board of directors. The accounting treatment for par value stock and stated value stock is the same. The shares are carried in the capital account at either the par value or the stated value. Any proceeds in excess of par or stated value should be recorded in a separate paid-in capital account.

As an illustration, assume that the DeWitt Corporation, which is authorized to issue 20,000 shares of capital stock without par value, assigned a stated value of $15 per share to its stock. The 20,000 authorized shares were issued for cash at $20 per share. The entry would appear as follows:

Cash	400,000	
Common Stock		300,000
Paid-in Capital in Excess of Stated Value (20,000		
shares × $5)		100,000
To record the issuance of 20,000 shares of stock		
with a stated value of $15 at $20 per share.		

The stockholders' equity section of the balance sheet would be as follows:

Stockholders' equity:
Common stock—no par value, stated value, $15; 20,000 shares
 authorized, issued, and outstanding $300,000
Paid-in capital in excess of stated value 100,000
Total stockholders' equity $400,000

The $100,000 received over and above the stated value of $300,000 should be carried permanently as paid-in capital because it is a part of the capital originally contributed by the stockholders. But the stated capital of the DeWitt Corporation is $300,000—the stated value of the shares issued.

Shares without par or stated value. If a corporation issues shares **without par value** to which **no stated value** is assigned or required by state law, the entire amount received is credited to the capital stock account. The entire amount received for such shares is the amount of stated capital.

In the above illustration of the DeWitt Corporation, if no stated value had been assigned to the shares, the entry would have been:

Cash 400,000
  Common Stock 400,000
  To record the issuance of 20,000 shares of stock at
  $20 per share.

The stockholders' equity section of the company's balance sheet would be:

Stockholders' equity:
Common stock—no par or stated value; 20,000 shares
 authorized, issued, and outstanding $400,000
Total stockholders' equity $400,000

Recording Capital Stock Issued

Stock is often issued through underwriters who guarantee the corporation a fixed price per share and make a commission by selling the stock to the public at a slightly higher price. To illustrate, assume that an underwriter guaranteed the sale of 300,000 shares at $20 per share net to the company and that its selling price to the public was $21. Assume further that shares are authorized and that their par value is $10 per share. The entry to record the receipt of the net proceeds would be:

Cash 6,000,000
  Common Stock 3,000,000
  Paid-in Capital in Excess of Par
   Value 3,000,000
  To record the issuance of 300,000 shares of $10
  par value common stock at $20 per share.

After completion of the transaction, the stockholders' equity section of the balance sheet would be:

```
Stockholders' equity:
Common stock—$10 par value; authorized, 500,000
      shares; issued and outstanding, 300,000 shares   . . . .   $3,000,000
Paid-in capital in excess of par value   . . . . . . . . .      3,000,000
Total stockholders' equity   . . . . . . . . . . . . .         $6,000,000
```

The computation is as follows:

```
Gross proceeds, 300,000 × $21   . . . . . . . . . . .      $6,300,000
Underwriter's charge   . . . . . . . . . . . . . . . .        300,000
   Proceeds to company   . . . . . . . . . . . . . . .     $6,000,000
Par value, 300,000 × $10   . . . . . . . . . . . . . .      3,000,000
Capital in excess of par   . . . . . . . . . . . . . .     $3,000,000
```

Typically only $6 million is recorded as the capital received, since it represents the net proceeds to the company.

Sometimes capital stock is issued in exchange for noncash assets. In these situations, the transaction should be recorded at the fair market value of the stock or of the assets, whichever is more clearly determinable.

Values Associated with Capital Stock

Book value. The book value of a corporation is the total of its recorded net asset values, or simply total stockholders' equity. When only common stock is outstanding, **book value per share** is computed by dividing the stockholders' equity by the number of shares outstanding. For example, if a corporation has stockholders' equity consisting of capital stock of $100,000 and retained earnings of $50,000 and has 10,000 shares outstanding, the book value per share is $15 ($150,000 ÷ 10,000 shares).

When two or more classes of capital stock are outstanding, the computation of book value per share is more complex. The usual approach is to assume that the assets and liabilities are liquidated at book value. Preferred shareholders are typically entitled to at least par value plus cumulative dividends in arrears. The provision in the preferred stock contract will govern, and it may, for example, state specifically the amount that the holder of the preferred stock is entitled to receive in *liquidation* (the liquidation value) in addition to cumulative dividends, if any.

As an illustration, assume that the Celoron Company's stockholders' equity is as follows:

```
Stockholders' equity:
Preferred stock—$50 par value, 8%, cumulative, 8,000
      shares   . . . . . . . . . . . . . . . . . . . . . . .   $  400,000
Common stock—$10 par value, 400,000 shares   . . . . . . .     4,000,000
Paid-in capital in excess of par value—preferred   . . . . . .     40,000
Retained earnings   . . . . . . . . . . . . . . . . . . . .       600,000
Total stockholders' equity   . . . . . . . . . . . . . . . .   $5,040,000
```

Illustration 8.2
BOOK VALUE COMPUTATIONS

		Total	Per Share
Total stockholders' equity		$5,040,000	
Book value of preferred stock (8,000 shares):			
Liquidation value ($52 × 8,000) . . .	$416,000		
Dividends (1 year at $32,000)	32,000	448,000	$56.00
Book value of common (400,000			
shares)		$4,592,000	11.48

Assume that the preferred stock has a liquidation value of $52 and that dividends on the preferred stock have not been paid this year. The book values for each class of stock are shown in Illustration 8.2.

Relationship of book value, par value, and market value. Par value and book value are related only to the extent that the par value of the stock is one element of the stockholders' equity—on which book value is computed. Book value and market value are related only to the extent that the market forces consider book value important. But market value is less dependent on book value than on (1) the company's future earning power and possible dividend payments, (2) the present financial position of the company, and (3) the current state of the economy and other general stock market influences. Thus, a share of common or preferred stock may sell in a market for much more or much less than its book value or for more or less than its par value.

OTHER SOURCES OF PAID-IN (OR CONTRIBUTED CAPITAL)

The goal of paid-in capital accounts is to **show the sources of capital.** An account is usually established for each source of capital, for example, preferred stock, common stock, and capital in excess of par value from common stock issuances. The major source of capital is investment by stockholders. But sometimes a company may receive **donated capital.** This often happens when a city donates land and a building to a corporation to encourage it to locate there. Proper recording would show the source as Paid-in Capital—Donations. For example, assume that the Chamber of Commerce gave a building worth $300,000 and land worth $120,000 to a corporation. The entry required is:

Land	120,000	
Building	300,000	
Paid-in Capital—Donations		420,000
To record receipt of donated land and building.		

Other changes in the capital accounts might include: (1) capitalization of retained earnings through issuance of a stock dividend and

217

(2) gains on treasury stock transactions (both of which are discussed later in this chapter).

The following stockholders' equity section of a balance sheet illustrates the reporting of capital:

Paid-in capital:		
Preferred stock—$100 par value; authorized, issued, and outstanding, 4,000 shares	$ 400,000	
Common stock—no par value; stated value, $5 per share; authorized, issued, and outstanding, 200,000 shares	1,000,000	$1,400,000
Paid-in capital in excess of par or stated value:		
From preferred stock issuances	$ 40,000	
From stock dividends	1,000,000	
From donations	10,000	1,050,000
Total paid-in capital		$2,450,000
Retained earnings		500,000
Total stockholders' equity		$2,950,000

RETAINED EARNINGS

In general, the stockholders' equity in a corporation is made up of two elements: (1) **paid-in (or contributed capital** and (2) **retained earnings.** Retained earnings is the term used to describe the increase in stockholders' equity resulting from profitable operation of the corporation. As such, it shows the source of assets received but not distributed to stockholders as dividends. Thus, both categories indicate the source of assets received by the corporation—actual investment by the stockholders and investment by the stockholders in the sense of dividends forgone. For now, the balance in the Retained Earnings account will be viewed as the difference between (1) the net income of the corporation during its existence to date and (2) the sum of dividends declared during the same period.

When the Retained Earnings account has a negative (or debit) balance, a *deficit* exists. It is shown under that title as a negative amount in the stockholders' equity section of the balance sheet.

Dividends

Dividends are *distributions of earnings by a corporation to its stockholders.* The normal dividend is a cash dividend, but additional shares of the corporation's own capital stock may also be distributed as dividends.

Since dividends are the means whereby the owners of a corporation share in the earnings of the corporation, they usually are charged against retained earnings. They must be declared by the board of directors and recorded in the minutes book. The significant dates concerning dividends are the date of *declaration,* the date of *record,* and the date of *payment*. For example, the board of directors of the Clayton Corporation may declare on May 5, 1986, a cash dividend of $1.25 per share to stockholders of record on July 1, 1986, payable on July 10. The **date of declaration** is the date the board takes action·in the form of a motion that dividends be paid. This action creates the liability for dividends payable. The **date of record** is the date established by the board to determine who will receive the dividends. The stockholders on the date of record are determined from the corporation's records (a subsidiary stockholders' ledger). The **date of payment** is the date of actual payment of the dividend. Since a financial transaction occurs on the date of declaration (a liability is incurred) and on the date of payment (cash is paid), journal entries will be required on these dates. No journal entry is required on the date of record.

Cash dividends. **Cash dividends** are a cash distribution of earnings by a corporation to its stockholders. To illustrate the entries for cash dividends, consider the following example. On Jaunary 21, 1986, a corporation's board of directors declares a 2 percent (or $2,000) quarterly cash dividend on $100,000 of outstanding preferred stock (one fourth of the annual dividend on 1,000 shares of $100 par value, 8 percent preferred stock). The dividend will be paid on March 1, 1986, to stockholders of record on February 5, 1986. The entries at the declaration and payment dates are as follows:

```
1986
Jan. 21  Retained Earnings (or Dividends)    . .    2,000
            Dividends Payable  . . . . . . .                2,000
         Dividends declared: 2 percent on
         $100,000 of outstanding preferred stock,
         payable March 1, 1986, to stockholders
         of record on February 5, 1986.

Mar. 1   Dividends Payable  . . . . . . . .    2,000
            Cash   . . . . . . . . . . . .               2,000
         Paid the dividend declared on January 21,
         1986.
```

No entry is made on the date of record.

When a cash dividend is declared, some companies debit the Dividends account instead of Retained Earnings. The Dividends account is closed to Retained Earnings at the end of the year. A legally declared cash dividend is a current liability of the corporation, so Dividends Payable will be presented as a current liability on the balance sheet.

Stock dividends. A corporation may declare a **stock dividend,** which is a dividend that is payable in additional shares of the declaring corporation's capital stock. Stock dividend declarations usually provide that the distribution of additional shares be of the same class of stock as that held by the stockholders—for example, additional common stock to common stockholders. The usual accounting for a stock dividend distribution is to transfer a sum from retained earnings to permanent paid-in capital. The amount transferred per share for a stock dividend depends on the size of the stock dividend.

Stock dividends have no effect on the total amount of stockholders' equity. They merely decrease retained earnings and increase paid-in capital by an equal amount. Immediately after the declaration and distribution of a stock dividend, each share of similar stock has a lower book value per share. This is because more shares are outstanding with no increase in total stockholders' equity.

Stock dividends do not affect the individual stockholder's percentage of ownership in the corporation. For example, if a stockholder owns 1,000 shares in a corporation having 100,000 shares of stock outstanding, that stockholder owns 1 percent of the outstanding shares. After a 10 percent stock dividend, the stockholder will still own 1 percent of the outstanding shares—1,100 of 110,000 outstanding.

Reasons for declaring a stock dividend include:

1. Retained earnings may have become large relative to total stockholders' equity, or the corporation may simply desire a larger permanent capitalization.
2. The market price of the stock may have risen above a desirable trading range. A large stock dividend will generally reduce the per share market value of the company's stock.
3. The corporation may wish to have more stockholders and expects to increase their number by increasing the number of shares outstanding.
4. Stock dividends may be used to silence stockholders' demands for dividends from a corporation that does not have sufficient cash to pay cash dividends.

Recording small stock dividends. A stock dividend of less than 20 to 25 percent of the previously outstanding shares is assumed to have little effect on the market value of the shares. Thus, *the dividend should be accounted for at the present market value of the outstanding shares.*

Assume a corporation is authorized to issue 20,000 shares of $100 par value common stock, of which 8,000 shares are outstanding. Its board of directors now declares a 10 percent stock dividend (800 shares). The market price of the stock is $125 per share immediately before the stock dividend is announced. Since distributions of less than 20 to 25 percent of the previously outstanding shares are to be accounted for at market value, the entry for the declaration of the dividend is as follows (assuming the dividend was declared on August 10, 1986):

```
Aug. 10   Retained Earnings (or Stock
                Dividends)  .  .  .  .  .  .  .  .  .  .   100,000
                   Stock Dividend Distributable—
                   Common    .  .  .  .  .  .  .  .                      80,000
                   Paid-in Capital—Stock Dividend  .  .                 20,000
                To record the declaration of a 10 percent
                stock dividend; shares to be distributed
                on September 20, 1986, to stockholders
                of record on August 31, 1986.
```

The entry to record the issuance of the shares is as follows:

```
Sept. 20   Stock Dividend Distributable—
                   Common    .  .  .  .  .  .  .  .  .    80,000
                   Common Stock    .  .  .  .  .  .                      80,000
                To record distribution of 800 shares of
                common stock as authorized in stock divi-
                dend declared on August 10, 1986.
```

The **Stock Dividend Distributable—Common account** is a stockholders' equity account that is credited for the par or stated value of the shares distributable when recording the declaration of a stock dividend. Since a stock dividend distributable (payable) is not payable with assets, it is not a liability. If a balance sheet is prepared between the date of declaration of the 10 percent dividend and the date of issuance of the shares, the proper statement presentation of the effects of the stock dividend is as follows:

```
Stockholders' equity:
  Paid-in capital:
    Common stock, $100 par value; authorized, 20,000
      shares; issued and outstanding, 8,000
      shares  .  .  .  .  .  .  .  .  .  .  .  .  .  .  .   $800,000
    Stock dividend distributable on September 20, 1986,
      800 shares at par value  .  .  .  .  .  .  .  .  .      80,000
    Total par value of shares issued and to be
      issued  .  .  .  .  .  .  .  .  .  .  .  .  .  .  .   $880,000
    From capitalization of retained earnings through
      declaration of stock dividend  .  .  .  .  .  .  .      20,000
         Total paid-in capital  .  .  .  .  .  .  .  .  .            $ 900,000
  Retained earnings  .  .  .  .  .  .  .  .  .  .  .  .                 150,000
Total stockholders' equity  .  .  .  .  .  .  .  .  .  .             $1,050,000
```

Recording large stock dividends. Stock dividends of over 20 to 25 percent of the previously outstanding shares are considered to be large stock dividends. One purpose of a large stock dividend is to reduce the market value of the stock; therefore, the old market value of the stock should not be used in the entry. *Such dividends are accounted for at their par or stated value rather than at their market value.* Stocks without par or stated value are accounted for at the amounts established by the laws of the state of incorporation or by the board of directors.

To illustrate the treatment of a stock dividend of over 20 to

25 percent, assume X Corporation has authorized capital of 10,000 shares of $10 par value common stock and has 5,000 shares issued and outstanding. X Corporation declares a 30 percent stock dividend (1,500 shares) on September 20, 1986, to be issued on October 15, 1986. The required entries are:

Sept. 20	Retained Earnings (or Stock Dividends)	15,000	
	Stock Dividend Distributable . . .		15,000
	To record the declaration of a 30 percent stock dividend		
Oct. 15	Stock Dividend Distributable	15,000	
	Common Stock		15,000
	To record the issuance of the 30 percent stock dividend.		

Note that, in contrast to the small stock dividend that was accounted for at market value, the 30 percent stock dividend was accounted for at par value (1,500 shares × $10 = $15,000). Because of the differences in accounting for large and small stock dividends, the relative size of the stock dividend must be determined before making any journal entries.

Stock splits. A **stock split,** as used in *Accounting Research Bulletin No. 43,* is a distribution of additional shares of the issuing corporation's stock for which the corporation receives no assets and for the purpose of causing a large reduction in the market price per share of the outstanding stock. The usual stock split is one in which the old shares are replaced by an increased number of new shares, with a corresponding reduction in the par value per share. A two-for-one split doubles the shares outstanding, a three-for-one split triples the shares, and so on. The par value per share is usually reduced at the time of the split so that the total dollar amount credited to the Common Stock account remains the same. For instance, in a two-for-one split, the par value per share is usually halved.

The entry to record a stock split depends on the particular circumstances. Usually, only the number of shares outstanding and the par or stated value need to be changed in the records. Thus, a two-for-one stock split in which the par value of the shares decreased from $20 to $10 and the number of shares originally outstanding was 5,000 would be recorded as follows:

Common Stock—$20 par value	100,000	
Common Stock—$10 par value		100,000
To record a two-for-one stock split, 5,000 shares of $20 par value common stock were replaced by 10,000 shares of $10 par value common stock.		

TREASURY STOCK

Nature of Treasury Stock

Treasury stock is capital stock, either preferred or common, that has been issued and reacquired by the issuing corporation. It has not been canceled, and it is legally available for reissuance. Treasury stock and unissued capital stock differ in that treasury stock has been issued at some time in the past, while unissued capital stock never has been issued.

Treasury stock may be acquired by purchase or in settlement of a debt. The corporation laws of most states consider treasury stock as **issued** but **not outstanding.** Treasury shares cannot be voted, and dividends are not paid on them.

Generally, as a matter of law, when a corporation acquires treasury stock at a cost (not as a gift), an equal amount of retained earnings is not available for dividends until the treasury stock is reissued or formally retired. As a result, the cost of treasury stock typically will not exceed the amount of retained earnings at the date of its acquisition. Thus, dividends plus treasury stock purchases must not impair the legal (or stated) capital of the corporation. if a corporation is subject to such a law, the retained earnings available for dividends are limited to the amount of retained earnings in excess of the cost of the treasury shares.

Treasury Stock in the Balance Sheet

The acquisition of treasury stock is normally recorded by a debit to a Teasury Stock account and a credit to Cash for its cost, as follows:

Treasury Stock	75,000	
Cash		75,000
To record acquisition of shares of the company's own stock.		

The treasury stock should not be reported as an asset on the balance sheet. Rather, it is reported as a deduction from the sum of the paid-in capital and retained earnings, as follows:

Stockholders' equity:
Common stock—authorized and issued, 40,000 shares; par value $10 per share, of which 5,000 shares are in the treasury	$400,000
Retained earnings (including $75,000 restricted by acquisition of treasury stock)	500,000
Total	$900,000
Less: Treasury stock at cost, 5,000 shares	75,000
Total stockholders' equity	$825,000

Treasury Stock Transactions

To illustrate the accounting for treasury stock, assume that the Hillside Corporation, with stockholders' equity consisting solely of capital stock and retained earnings, acquired 2,000 shares of its capital stock for $70,000. Two months later, when the market price of the stock was $40 per share, it issued 800 shares to officers and employees as bonuses. A year later, when it needed cash, it sold the rest of the shares at $30 each. The entries required are:

(1) Treasury Stock (2,000 shares × $35)   70,000
         Cash   70,000
      To record acquisition of 2,000 shares of the
      company's own stock.

(2) Salaries and Bonuses Expense (800 shares
         × $40)   32,000
         Treasury Stock (800 shares × $35)   28,000
         Paid-in Capital—Treasury Stock Transactions   4,000
      To record issuance of 800 shares of treasury stock
      as bonuses.

(3) Cash (1,200 shares × $30)   36,000
      Paid-in Capital—Treasury Stock
         Transactions   4,000
      Retained Earnings   2,000
         Treasury Stock (1,200 shares
            × $35)   42,000
      To record sale of 1,200 shares of treasury stock
      for cash.

In T-account format these entries would appear as follows:

Cash				Treasury Stock				Paid-in Capital—Treasury Stock Transactions			
Bal.	xxx	(1)	70,000	(1)	70,000	(2)	28,000	(3)	4,000	(2)	4,000
(3)	36,000					(3)	42,000				

Salaries and Bonuses Expense				Retained Earnings			
Bal.	xxx			(3)	2,000	Bal.	xxx
(2)	32,000						

The acquisition of the shares is recorded at cost ($70,000). The issuance of the 800 shares as bonuses requires a debit to the Salaries and Bonuses Expense account for the market value of the shares, a credit to Treasury Stock for the cost of the shares, and a credit to a paid-in capital account for the excess of the fair value of the shares over their cost. When the remaining shares are issued, the deficiency of issue price from cost is charged against Paid-in Capital—Treasury Stock Transactions *until the credit balance in the account is exhausted.* The remaining deficiency is then charged to Retained Earnings.

If at the end of the fiscal year the Paid-in Capital—Treasury Stock Transactions account contained a positive (credit) balance, it would be reported in the balance sheet below capital stock as Paid-in Capital in Excess of Par (or Stated) Value. The gain on the transaction represents an increase in invested capital.

EXTRAORDINARY ITEMS, CHANGES IN ACCOUNTING PRINCIPLES, AND PRIOR PERIOD ADJUSTMENTS

In the determination of net income, more useful information is provided if revenues generated and expenses incurred in the normal operations of a business are reported separately from unusual, nonrecurring gains and losses. In addition, a more useful presentation results if certain corrections of accounting errors are reported in the retained earnings statement rather than the income statement.

Extraordinary Items

Abuses in the financial reporting of gains and losses as **extraordinary items** led to the issuance of *APB Opinion No. 30* (September 1973). In the *Opinion*, **extraordinary items** are defined as those events that are unusual in nature *and* that occur frequently. Note that both conditions must be met—unusual nature and infrequent occurrence. Whether an item is unusual and infrequent is to be determined in the light of the environment in which the firm operates. Examples include gains or losses that are the direct result of a major casualty (a flood), a confiscation of property by a foreign government, or a prohibition under a newly enacted law. Such items are to be included in the determination of periodic net income, but disclosed separately (net of their tax effects, if any) in the income statement. **Net-of-tax effect** is used for extraordinary items, changes in accounting principles, and prior period adjustments whereby items are shown at the dollar amounts remaining after deducting the effects on such items of the income taxes (federal and state, if any) payable currently. *FASB Statement No. 4* further directs that gains and losses from the early extinguishment of debt are extraordinary items. Income before extraordinary items must be reported and then income after extraordinary items must be reported as shown in Illustration 8.3. **Income before extraordinary items** is income from operations less applicable income taxes.

Gains or losses related to ordinary business activities are not extraordinary items regardless of their size. For example, material write-downs of uncollectible receivables, obsolete inventories, and intangible assets are not extraordinary items. But such items may be separately disclosed as part of net income from continuing activites.

Changes in Accounting Principles

A company's reported net income and financial position can be altered materially by changes in accounting principles. **Changes in accounting principles** (accounting changes) are changes in accounting data caused by changes in accounting principles such as a change in inventory valuation method (for example, from Fifo to Lifo) or a change in depreciation method (for example, from accelerated to straight-line). According to *APB Opinion No. 20,* a company should consistently apply the same accounting methods from one period to another. But a change may be made if the newly adopted method is preferable and if the change is adequately disclosed in the financial

Illustration 8.3
INCOME STATEMENT
Showing Extraordinary Item and a Change in Accounting Principles

ANSON COMPANY
Income Statement
For the Year Ended December 31, 1986

Net sales		$41,000,000
Other revenues		2,250,000
Total revenue		$43,250,000
Cost of goods sold	$22,000,000	
Administrative, selling, and general expenses	12,000,000	34,000,000
Net income before income taxes		$ 9,250,000
Federal income taxes (50%)		4,625,000
Net income before extraordinary item and the cumu-cumulative effect of an accounting change		$ 4,625,000
Extraordinary item:		
Loss from flood damage	$ 40,000	
Less: tax effect	20,000	(20,000)
		$ 4,605,000
Change in accounting principles:		
Cumulative effect on prior years' income of changing to a different depreciation method	$ 6,000	
Less: tax effect	3,000	3,000
Net income		$ 4,608,000
Earnings per share of common stock (1,000,000 shares outstanding):		
Net income before extraordinary item and the cumulative effect of an accounting change		$ 4,625
Extraordinary item		(0.020)
Cumulative effect on prior years' income of changing to a different depreciation method		0.003
Net income		$ 4.608

statements. In the period in which an accounting change is made, the nature of the change, its justification, and its effect on net income must be disclosed in the financial statements. Also, the cumulative effect of the change on prior years' income (net of tax) must be shown in the income statement for the year of change (see Illustration 8.3).

As an example of an accounting change, assume that Anson Company purchased a machine on January 2, 1984, for $30,000. The machine has a useful life of five years with no scrap value expected. Anson Company decided to depreciate the machine for financial reporting purposes using the sum-of-the-years'-digits method. At the beginning of 1986, the company decided to change to the straight-line method of depreciation. The cumulative effect of the change in accounting method is computed as follows:

Under SYD depreciation:
Depreciation for 1984:   5/15($30,000) = $10,000
Depreciation for 1985:   4/15($30,000) =   8,000
Balance in accumulated depreciation
    at the beginning of 1986   . . . . $18,000

Under S-L depreciation (if it had been used):
Depreciation for 1984: $30,000/5 = $ 6,000   Difference
Depreciation for 1985: $30,000/5 =   6,000 $6,000
Balance that would have been in
    accumulated depreciation at
    the beginning of 1986   . . . . $12,000

The accumulated depreciation account balance would have been
$6,000 less under the straight-line method. Also, depreciation ex-
pense over the two years would have been $6,000 less. Therefore,
Anson Company corrects the appropriate account balances by reducing the accumulated depreciation account balance by $6,000 and
creating an account entitled Cumulative Effect of Change in Accounting Method, which will be closed to Retained Earnings during
the normal closing process and thereby correct the previous years'
misstated amounts of depreciation. The journal entry would be:

Accumulated Depreciation—Machinery   6,000
    Cumulative Effect of Change in Accounting
        Method   6,000
    To record the effect of changing from sum-of-the-
    years'-digits depreciation to straight-line
    depreciation on machinery.

The cumulative effect of changing to the straight-line depreciation
method is reported in Illustration 8.3 at $3,000 since the assumed
tax effect is 50 percent, ($6,000 × .5 = $3,000). (Income tax allocation
procedures are covered in Chapter 19.)

**Prior Period
Adjustments**

According to *FASB Statement No. 16,* **prior period adjustments** consist
almost entirely of corrections of errors in previously published financial statements. Corrections of abnormal, nonrecurring errors that
may have been caused by the improper use of an accounting principle
or by mathematical mistakes are prior period adjustments.

To illustrate a prior period adjustment, assume that land costing
$200,000 was expensed rather than capitalized. This caused a
$100,000 underpayment of income taxes. The mistake subsequently
was discovered and the following entry was made:

Land   200,000
    Federal Income Taxes Payable   100,000
    Prior Period Adjustment—Correction of Error in
        Expensing Cost of Land   100,000
    To correct an accounting error involving land.

In the statement of retained earnings (see Illustration 8.4), prior period adjustments are treated as adjustments of the opening balance of retained earnings.

Illustration 8.4
STATEMENT OF RETAINED EARNINGS

ANSON COMPANY
Statement of Retained Earnings
For the Year Ended December 31, 1986

Retained earnings, January 1, 1986	$5,000,000
Prior period adjustment	
Correction of error of expensing land (net of tax effect of $100,000)	100,000
Adjusted retained earnings, January 1, 1986	$5,100,000
Add: Net income	4,608,000
	$9,708,000
Less: Dividends	500,000
Retained earnings, December 31, 1986	$9,208,000

Accounting for Tax Effects

Most extraordinary items, accounting changes, and prior period adjustments will affect the amount of income taxes payable, with the result that questions arise as to proper reporting procedure. To prevent distortions, *APB Opinion No. 9* recommends that extraordinary items and prior period adjustments be reported *net of their tax effects,* as shown in Illustrations 8.3 and 8.4. Changes in accounting principles are also reported net of their tax effects. The tax effect of an item may be shown separately (as for the flood loss and change in accounting principles in Illustration 8.3) or may be mentioned parenthetically with only the net amount shown (as for the correction of error in Illustration 8.4).

EARNINGS PER SHARE

One final item needs to be discussed regarding corporations and income statement presentations, and that is earnings per share. A major item of interest to investors and potential investors is how much a company earned during the current year, both in total and for each share of stock outstanding. Earnings per share is calculated only for the residual or common shares of ownership. **Earnings per share** is computed as net income minus preferred stock dividends divided by the number of common shares outstanding. Income available to common stockholders is net income less any dividends on preferred stock.

Earnings per share (EPS) is usually calculated and presented for each major category on the face of the income statement. In other words, an EPS calculation is made for ordinary income after taxes, extraordinary items, and accounting changes. Notice in Illustration 8.3 the earnings per share amounts are reported at the bottom of the illustration.

Stockholders can compare the earnings per share of two companies more easily than total dollars of income. EPS is very useful in making decisions about the price to pay for stock and the return on that investment. Also, earnings per share is related to market price per share of stock in that, if EPS increases, generally market price per share also increases.

SUMMARY

The goal in accounting for stockholders' equity is to show the sources of capital contributed to the corporation and to show the relevant claims held by the capital contributors. The corporation obtains equity capital (as opposed to debt capital) from three main sources: (1) common stockholders, (2) preferred stockholders, and (3) earnings retained in the business. Most of the risks and rewards of ownership lie with the holders of common stock. Preferred stock is often issued to attract potential investors who are more interested in stability of return. Recent preferred stock issues have been convertible into common stock in an attempt to make them more attractive.

Most stock issued will have either a par value or a stated value. If so, this amount is credited to a capital stock account. All proceeds in excess of par or stated value are recorded in separate capital in excess of par (or stated) value accounts.

Book value can be computed for common and preferred stock. Book value per share amounts usually differ from either the par value or the market value of the shares.

Dividends are distributions of assets (usually cash) and are charged to retained earnings. But is quite common for companies to declare stock dividends in which additional shares are issued to the current holders. The issuance of small stock dividends (less than 20 to 25 percent) results in capitalizing a portion of retained earnings equal to the current market value of the shares issued. The issuance of a large stock dividend (more than 20 to 25 percent) often results in capitalizing retained earnings equal to the par value of the shares issued.

A stock split increases the number of shares outstanding and decreases the par or stated value of each share. It has no effect upon the stockholders' equity account balances.

Treasury stock is stock acquired by the issuing company. It is generally held for possible issuance to employees or for other reasons. The cost of the stock, if any, is considered a reduction of total equity and is shown as a deduction from total stockholders' equity—not as an asset.

The APB and the FASB have distinguished between extraordinary items (to be shown in the income statement) and prior period adjustments (which are in a sense corrections of the beginning retained earnings balance). Prior period adjustments consist almost solely of corrections of accounting errors. Such adjustments should be quite rare. Either a prior period adjustment or an extraordinary item should be shown net of its tax effect, if any.

When an accounting change is made, the cumulative effect of the change on prior years' earnings must be shown on the income statement for the year of change, net of its tax effects.

APPENDIX

STOCK INVESTMENTS Sometimes companies invest in the stocks of other companies. Such investments may actually consist of marketable securities in that the stocks may be readily marketable. But stocks are rarely purchased as temporary investments of idle cash. They are usually acquired either for long-term investment or in an attempt to speculate in the stock market.

The reasons for investing on a long-term basis in the securities of other companies include the desire to (1) establish an affiliation with another business, (2) acquire control over another business, or (3) secure a continuing stream of revenue from the investment over a period of years.

Reporting Securities in the Balance Sheet Determining how securities should be classified in the balance sheet depends on management's intent and may be summarized as follows:

1. If the securities held are readily marketable, they should be shown as current assets if they *will* be converted into cash in the normal operating cycle of the business. If they will not be converted, they should be considered noncurrent assets and reported in the investments section of the balance sheet.
2. If the securities are not readily marketable, they may not be classified as current assets unless they mature in the coming operating cycle and there is no doubt as to their redemption.

Valuation of equity securities. The FASB, in *Statement No. 12,* describes the method of accounting for marketable equity securities.[1] It requires the use of the lower-of-cost-or-market method for marketable **equity** securities (with certain limited exceptions). Marketable equity securities are to be carried at the lower of total cost or

---

[1] "Accounting for Certain Marketable Securities," *Statement of Financial Accounting Standards No. 12* (Stamford, Conn., 1975), p. 31.

total market for all securities classified as **current, taken as a group,** and for securities classified as **noncurrent, taken as a group.**

Current marketable equity securities. For the securities classified as current, any excess of total cost over total market is debited to an account such as Net Unrealized Loss on Current Marketable Equity Securities, which is shown in the income statement. The credit is to a current asset valuation allowance account such as Allowance for Market Decline of Current Marketable Equity Securities. The entry would appear as follows (assuming that the cost is $16,000 and the market is $15,500):

```
Net Unrealized Loss on Current Marketable Equity
   Securities  . . . . . . . . . . . . . . . . .  500
      Allowance for Market Decline of Current Marketable
         Equity Securities  . . . . . . . . . . . .          500
   To record write-down of current marketable equity securities
   to total market value.
```

The balance sheet presentation would be as follows:

```
Current assets:
   Current marketable equity securities  . . .  $16,000
   Less: Allowance for market decline    . . .      500  $15,500
```

Any later recovery in the total market price (up to the amount of the original cost) would be debited to the asset valuation allowance and would be credited to an account such as Net Unrealized Gain on Current Marketable Equity Secutiries that would be shown in the income statement. The entry would appear as follows (assuming that the market recovered by $400):

```
Allowance for Market Decline of Current Marketable
   Equity Securities  . . . . . . . . . . . . . .  400
      Net Unrealized Gain on Current Marketable Equity
         Securities  . . . . . . . . . . . . . .            400
   To record the $400 recovery of total market value of
   current marketable equity securities.
```

The balance sheet presentation would now be:

```
Current assets:
   Current marketable equity securities  . . .  $16,000
   Less: Allowance for market decline    . . .      100  $15,900
```

Noncurrent marketable equity securities. Any "temporary" losses on noncurrent equity securities (long-term investments) are debited to a stockholders' equity account (but not deducted from net income) and credited to an asset valuation allowance account. The account debited might be entitled, Net Unrealized Loss on Noncurrent Marketable Equity Securities. Thus, the entry might be as follows (assuming that the cost is $32,000 and the market price $31,000):

```
Net Unrealized Loss on Noncurrent Marketable Equity
    Securities  .  .  .  .  .  .  .  .  .  .  .  .  .  .  .   1,000
        Allowance for Market Decline of Noncurrent
            Marketable Equity Securities  .  .  .  .  .  .  .              1,000
    To record write-down of noncurrent marketable equity
    securities to total market value.
```

The balance sheet presentation would be:

```
Investments:
    Noncurrent marketable equity securities  .  .  .   $32,000
    Less: Allowance for market decline  .  .  .  .      1,000    $31,000
```

The Net Unrealized Loss on Noncurrent Marketable Equity Securities could be reported in the stockholders' equity section of the balance sheet as a deduction from the total of the par value of the stock outstanding plus any paid-in capital in excess of par value, or a deduction from total stockholders' equity.

Later recoveries in market value up to cost, but not above cost, would be debited to the allowance account and credited to the unrealized loss account as follows (assume that the market increases by $1,700):

```
Allowance for Market Decline of Noncurrent Marketable
    Equity Securities  .  .  .  .  .  .  .  .  .  .  .  .  .   1,000
        Net Unrealized Loss on Noncurrent Marketable Equity
            Securities  .  .  .  .  .  .  .  .  .  .  .  .  .              1,000
    To write the noncurrent marketable equity securities back
    up to original cost.
```

Thus, the entry would increase stockholders' equity by $1,000 (not $1,700) but would not increase reported income. If a loss on an individual noncurrent security is determined to be "permanent," it is recorded as a realized loss and deducted in measuring income. The entry would be (assuming a permanent loss of $1,400):

```
Realized Loss on Noncurrent Marketable Equity
    Securities  .  .  .  .  .  .  .  .  .  .  .  .  .  .  .   1,400
        Investment in Noncurrent Marketable Equity
            Securities  .  .  .  .  .  .  .  .  .  .  .  .  .              1,400
    To record the permanent loss of $1,400 on noncurrent
    marketable equity securities.
```

Any subsequent recovery in market value would be ignored until the security is sold.

The equity method. The equity method should be used for an investment in common stock that gives an investor the ability to exercise significant influence over a company's operating and financial policies (even though the investor holds less than 50 percent of the voting stock). In the absence of evidence to the contrary, holding 20 percent or more of the common stock indicates the ability to exercise significant influence, and holding less than 20 percent does not. In situations where there is the ability to exert significant influence, the investor is required to use the equity method of accounting for its investment.[2] Under the equity method, the investor initially records the investment at cost and then adjusts the carrying amount to recognize its share of the other company's earnings or losses after the date of acquisition. Dividends received are deducted from the investment. We shall not deal with this method further. In this appendix, we shall assume that investments in the common stock of other companies represent less than 20 percent of the outstanding shares.

Entry to record acquisition. When the common or preferred stocks of other corporations are acquired, they should be recorded at cost, which is the cash outlay or the fair value of the asset given in exchange. Since the stock acquired will usually be purchased from another investor through a broker, the cost will normally consist of the price paid for the stock plus a commission to the broker. For example, assume that Brewer Corporation purchased as a temporary investment 1,000 shares of Cowen Corporation common stock at $15 per share through a broker who charged $100 for services rendered in acquiring the stock. Brewer would record the transaction as follows:

```
Current Marketable Equity Securities  . . . . . .  15,100
    Cash   . . . . . . . . . . . . . . . . .         15,100
    To record purchase of 1,000 shares of Cowen common
    at $15 plus $100 broker's commission.
```

Cash dividends on investments. The usual accounting for the receipt of dividends on stock investments is to debit Cash and credit Dividend Revenue when the cash dividend check is actually received. This accounting for dividends is acceptable for tax purposes and is widely followed by investors.

An alternative will be required when a dividend is declared in one accounting period which will not be paid until the following period. Assume that the Cowen Corporation declared a cash dividend of 20 cents per share on December 1, 1985, to stockholders of record as of December 20, 1981, payable on January 15, 1986. Under these circumstances an entry should be made either on December 20 or as an adjusting entry on December 31, as follows:

```
Dividends Receivable   . . . . . . . . . . .  200
    Dividend Revenue   . . . . . . . . . . . .       200
    To record dividend of 20 cents per share on Cowen
    common stock due January 15, 1986.
```

When the dividend is collected on January 15, the entry would be a debit to Cash and a credit to the Dividends Receivable account.

---

[2] APB, "The Equity Method of Accounting for Investments in Common Stock," *APB Opinion No. 18* (New York: AICPA, 1971).

In this manner the dividend is recorded as revenue in the period in which it is earned.

Stock dividends and stock splits. A stock dividend consists of the distribution by a corporation of additional shares of its stock to its stockholders. Usually the distribution consists of additional common stock to common stockholders. Such a distribution is not considered to be a revenue-producing transaction to the holders of the stock. A stock dividend is viewed simply as having the effect of dividing the stockholders' equity into a larger number of smaller pieces. It simply increases the number of shares a stockholder holds, but it does not change his or her percentage of ownership of the outstanding shares.

Thus, the accounting for stock dividends consists only of a notation in the accounts of the number of shares received and a change in the average per share cost of the shares held. For example, if 100 shares of Company A common stock are held, which cost $22 per share, and Company A distributes a 10 percent stock dividend, the number of shares held is increased to 110 and the cost per share is now $20 ($2,200 ÷ 110 shares = $20 per share).

Similarly, when a corporation splits its stock, the only accounting entry required is a notation indicating the receipt of the additonal shares. If Smith Company owned 1,000 shares of Jones Company common stock and Jones Company split its stock on a two-for-one basis, Smith would own 2,000 shares after the split, and the cost per share would be halved.

Sales of stock investments. When stock holdings are sold, the gain or loss on the sale is the difference between the net proceeds received and the carrying value of the shares sold. Assume, for example, that 100 shares of Thacker Company common stock are sold for $75 per share. The broker deducted his or her commission and other taxes and charges of $62 prior to making the remittance to the seller. If the seller's cost was $5,000, the required entry is:

Cash	7,438	
Current marketable Equity Securities		5,000
Gain on Sale of Investments		2,438
To record gain on sale of investments.		

The realized gain on the sale of investments is shown in the income statement, regardless of whether the securities were classified as current or noncurrent equity securities.

QUESTIONS

1. What are the basic rights associated with a share of capital stock, assuming that only one class of stock is outstanding?

2. A corporation has outstanding 5,000 shares of 8 percent, $50 par value, cumulative preferred stock. Dividends on this stock have not been declared for two years. Is the corporation liable to its preferred stockholders for these dividends? How should the dividends be shown in the balance sheet, if at all?

3. What is a similarity and what are some differences between a 20-year bond and a cumulative preferred stock? Why might an investor desire preferred stock? Why might a corporation issue a preferred stock that is both convertible and callable?

4. Assuming that no preferred stock is outstanding, how can the book value per share of common stock be determined? Of what significance is it? What is its relationship to market value per share?

5. What are the two parts of stockholders' equity in a corporation? Explain the difference between them. What does the balance in retained earnings mean to an investor? Why might a company with a $4 million credit balance in retained earnings need to raise additional capital to finance a $1 million plant?

6. The following dates are associated with a cash dividend of $100,000: July 15, July 31, and August 15. Identify each of the three dates. What is the accounting impact of each date?

7. What is the effect of each of the following on the total stockholders' equity of a corporation: (a) declaration of a cash dividend, (b) payment of a cash dividend, (c) declaration of a stock dividend, and (d) issuance of a stock dividend?

8. Distinguish between a small stock dividend and a large stock dividend. How is each accounted for?

9. What is treasury stock? Where does it appear on the balance sheet?

10. Distinguish between extraordinary items and prior period adjustments. Explain why it is important that the two be carefully distinguished.

11. (Based on the chapter appendix) Explain briefly the accounting for stock dividends and stock splits from the investor's point of view.

12. (Based on the chapter appendix) Carefully explain the main problem encountered in classifying marketable securities in the balance sheet.

EXERCISES

1. Smith Corporation's stockholders' equity consists of 2,000 authorized, issued, and outstanding shares of 5 percent preferred stock with a $50 par value and 100,000 authorized shares of $10 par value common stock, of which 80,000 shares are outstanding. Both classes of stock were issued at par. The retained earnings balance was $1,260,000 on January 1, 1985. During 1985, Smith had net income of $9,000. The preferred stock is preferred as to dividends. On December 24, 1985, Smith declared the annual preferred dividend and a 3 percent dividend on its common shares. All dividends were paid in cash on February 18, 1986. Give all necessary journal entries to record the dividend declaration and payment.

2. Pearlie Corporation has outstanding 1,000 shares of $100 par value convertible preferred stock that were issued at par value. Each share is convertible into four shares of $20 stated value common stock. Give the entry to record conversion of all 1,000 preferred shares.

3. Vancouver, Inc. called in all of its outstanding 400 shares of $200 par value preferred stock. The stock was cumulative, entitled to $200 per share plus cumulative dividends in liquidation, and callable at $210. Given the entry to record the calling of the preferred stock, assuming that it was originally issued at par. Give the entry that would have been required if the stock had originally been issued at $206. In both cases, assume that no unpaid cumulative dividends are in arrears and that there are no current dividends to be prorated.

4. Tramel Corporation has received $1 million in cash by issuing 10,000 shares of stock. Give the journal entry to record the issuance, assuming that:

   a. The stock had a par value of $50 per share.

   b. The stock had a stated value of $60 per share.

   c. The stock had no par or stated value.

5. One hundred shares of $100 par value common stock are issued to promoters of a corporation in exchange for land needed by the corporation for a plant site. Experienced appraisers have recently estimated the value of the land to be $17,000. At what amount should the land be recorded on the books?

6. Randall Company has outstanding 2,000 shares of cumulative preferred stock with a $5 annual dividend per share and 10,000 shares of common stock without par or stated value. No dividends were paid in 1984 or 1985. At the beginning of 1986, the retained earnings account had a debit balance of $6,000. During 1986, Randall had net income of $92,500. If a dividend of $3 per share is declared on the common stock on December 31, 1986, what is the ending balance in retained earnings?

7. Legrant Company has outstanding 200,000 shares of common stock, $10 par value, that were issued at an average price of $20 per share. Retained earnings total $1,800,000. The current market price of the common stock is $40 per share. The total authorized stock consists of 500,000 shares.

   a. Give the required journal entry to record the declaration of a 10 percent stock dividend.

   b. Give the required journal entry to record a 30 percent stock dividend.

8. Elene Corporation's balance sheet shows total assets of $800,000, liabilities of $300,000, and retained earnings of $300,000. Jim Ellis owns 400 shares of Elene's 20,000 outstanding shares of capital stock. Elene now declares and issues a 10 percent stock dividend. Compute the book value per share and in total of Steve's investment in Elene Corporation:

   a. Before the stock dividend.

   b. After the stock dividend.

9. Nelson Company's stockholders' equity consists of 25,000 authorized

shares of $20 par value common stock, 10,000 of which have been issued at par, and retained earnings of $400,000. The company now splits its stock, two for one by calling in the old shares and issuing new $10 par value shares.

    a. Give the required journal entry.

    b. Suppose instead that the company declared and later issued a 10 percent stock dividend. Give the required journal entries, assuming that the market value on the date of declaration was $25.00 per share.

10. Fran Company has outstanding 100,000 shares of $5 stated value common stock, all issued at $6 per share, and retained earnings of $200,000. The company acquired 1,000 shares of its stock from the widow of a deceased stockholder for cash at book value.

    a. Give the entry to record acquisition of the stock.

    b. Give the entry to record the subsequent reissuance of this stock at $10 per share.

    c. Give the entry to record the reissuance of the stock at $7 per share instead of at $10 per share as in **b.**

11. The stockholders' equity section of the balance sheet of Lakewood Corporation on December 31, 1985, shows 100,000 shares of authorized and issued $20 stated value common stock, of which 8,000 shares are held in the treasury. On this date, the board of directors declared a cash dividend of $2 per share to stockholders of record on January 10, payable January 21, 1986. Give the required dated journal entries.

12. (Based on the chapter appendix.) Black Company purchased as a temporary investment on July 1, 1986, 100 shares of Percy Company common stock at $28 per share plus a total commission of $75. Black received a cash dividend of $1 per share on August 12, 1986. On November 1, Black sold all of the above shares for $35 per share, less total commissions and taxes of $80. Record all of the above in Black Company's T-accounts.

PROBLEMS

8–1. Pall Company has outstanding 2,000 shares of cumulative preferred stock with a $4 annual dividend per share and 10,000 shares of no par value common stock. No dividends were paid in 1986 or 1987. At the beginning of 1988, the company had a deficit of $10,000. During 1988, it had net income of $70,000.

Required:

    Assuming that a dividend of $2 per share was declared on the common stock, compute the December 31, 1988, balance in retained earnings.

8–2. The Jennie Company issued all of its 5,000 shares of authorized preferred stock on July 1, 1985, at $210 per share. The preferred stock has a par value and a liquidation value of $200 per share and is entitled to a cumulative basic preference dividend of $16 per share. On July 1, 1985, Jennie also issued its 20,000 authorized shares of $30 stated value common stock at $80 per share.

On June 30, 1987, the end of the company's second fiscal year of operations, its retained earnings amounted to $190,000. No dividends have been declared or paid on either class of stock since the date of issue.

Required:

    a. Prepare the stockholders's equity section of the Jennie Company's June 30, 1987, balance sheet.

    b. Compute the book value per share of each class of stock.

8-3. Zeller Brothers, Inc., is a corportion in which all of the outstanding preferred and common stock is held by the four Zeller brothers. The brothers have an agreement stating that upon the death of one brother, the remaining brothers will purchase from his estate his holdings of stock in the company at book value. The agreement also stipulates that the land owned by the company be valued at fair market value, that inventory be valued at its current replacement cost, and that whatever other adjustments are needed to place the accounts on a sound accounting basis be made prior to computing book value.

The stockholders' equity accounts of the company on June 30, 1986, the date of James Zeller's death, show:

Stockholders' equity:

Preferred stock—6 percent, $100 par value; $100 liquidation value; 4,000 shares authorized, issued, and outstanding	$ 400,000
Paid-in capital in excess of par—preferred	20,000
Common stock—no par value; stated value, $5; 60,000 shares authorized, issued, and outstanding	300,000
Paid-in capital from recapitalization	300,000
Retained earnings	40,000
Total stockholders' equity	$1,060,000

The fair market value of the land held by the company and carried in its accounts at $40,000 is $100,000, and the current replacement cost of the inventory is $32,000 more than the amount at which it is carried in the accounts, although no improper accounting is involved. It is also agreed by the three remaining brothers and the accountant representing Mrs. James Zeller that the accounts fail to include a proper accrual of $20,000 for pensions payable to employees. No dividends have been paid on the cumulative preferred stock in the last one-half year.

At the time of his death James Zeller held 2,000 shares of preferred stock and 10,000 shares of common stock.

Required:

Compute the amount which the remaining brothers must pay to the estate of James Zeller for the preferred and common stock which he held at the time of his death.

8-4. The following information relates to the Ricardo Corporation for the year 1986 or on the dates indicated:

Net income for the year	$320,000
Dividends declared on common stock	40,000
Dividends paid on common stock during 1986	50,000
Dividends declared on preferred stock	16,000
Dividends received on investments	4,000
Retained earnings, January 1	810,000
Amount over par value received from preferred stock issued during the year	8,000

Required:

Prepare a statement of retained earnings for the year ended December 31, 1986.

8-5. The stockholders' equity section of the Alden Company's June 30, 1986, balance sheet is

Capital stock—common, $50 par value; 5,000 shares authored; 4,000 shares issued and outstanding	$200,000
Retained earnings	115,000
	$315,000

On June 30, 1986, the board of directors declared a $5 per share cash dividend to stockholders of record as of July 15, payable July 31.

Required:

a. Assuming no change in the amount of retained earnings except that caused by the dividend and no change in the number of shares outstanding between June 30 and July 31, compute the book value per share of common stock:
(1) Just prior to the declaration of the dividend.
(2) Just after the declaration of the dividend.
(3) Just after the payment of the cash dividend.

b. Assume that, instead of a cash dividend, a 5 percent stock dividend is issued on August 15 and is to be recorded at $70 per share (the market price on the declaration date). Show how this would affect the book value per share, assuming no change in retained earnings except that caused by the dividend.

c. Assume that Jimmy Brown owned 100 shares of stock in the Alden Company before the stock dividend. Compute the book value of his investment before the stock dividend and after the stock dividend.

8–6. On January 1, 1986, the Lorenzo Corporation's stockholders' equity section appeared as follows:

Stockholders' equity:

Paid-in capital:		
Preferred stock—$200 par value; authorized, issued, and outstanding, 5,000 shares	$1,000,000	
Common stock—$20 par value; authorized, 50,000 shares; issued and outstanding, 20,000 shares	400,000	$1,400,000
Retained earnings		600,000
Total stockholders' equity		$2,000,000

Required:

a. Prepare the stockholders' equity section on July 1, 1986, after the issuance of a 10 percent stock dividend to common stockholders. Market value per share at date of declaration was $130.

b. Ignore *a,* and prepare the stockholders' equity section on July 1, 1986, after a two-for-one common stock split. Market value per share before the split was $130.

8–7. The stockholders' equity of the Colorado Company as of December 31, 1986, consisted of 20,000 shares of authorized and outstanding $10 par value common stock, paid-in capital in excess of par of $100,000, and retained earnings of $200,000.

Following are selected transactions for 1987:

May 1 Acquired 4,000 shares of its own common stock at $25.
June 1 Reissued 1,000 shares of $28.
Oct. 1 Declared a cash dividend of $1 per share payable to stockholders as of October 14.
Nov. 14 Reissued 2,000 shares at $23.
Dec. 1 Paid the cash dividend declared on October 1.

Net income for the year was $30,400. No other transactions affecting retained earnings occurred during the year.

Required:

a. Prepare journal entries to record the treasury stock and dividend transactions.

b. Prepare the stockholders' equity section of the December 31, 1987, balance sheet.

c. Compute the book value per share as of December 31, 1987.

8–8. Selected account balances of the Atwood Company at December 31, 1986, are:

Bonds payable, 7 percent, due May 1, 1987	$1,200,000
Common stock—no par value; 100,000 shares authorized, issued, and outstanding; stated value of $20 per share	2,000,000
Retained earnings	570,000
Dividends payable (in cash, declared December 15 on preferred stock)	16,000
Accrued lawsuit damages	320,000

Preferred stock—8 percent, par value $200; 1,000 shares
   authorized, issued, and outstanding 200,000
Paid-in capital from donation of plant site 100,000
Paid-in capital in excess of par value—preferred 8,000

Required:

Present in good form the stockholders' equity section of the balance sheet.

8–9. Selected accounts of the Claude Company for the year ended December 31, 1987, are:

Sales, net	$1,560,000
Interest expense	80,000
Cash dividends on common stock	160,000
Selling and administrative expense	240,000
Cash dividends on preferred stock	80,000
Rent revenue	440,000
Cost of goods sold	640,000
Flood loss (has never occurred before)	240,000
Interest revenue	80,000
Other revenue	120,000
Depreciation and maintenance on rental equipment	160,000
Stock dividend on common stock	400,000
Litigation loss	480,000
Cumulative effect on prior years' income of changing to a different depreciation method (credit)	40,000

The applicable federal income tax rate is 50 percent. All of the above items of expense, revenue, and loss are includable in the computation of taxable income. The litigation loss resulted from a court award of damages for patent infringement on a product that the company produced and sold in 1983 and 1984 and discontinued in 1984. Retained earnings as of January 1, 1987, were $5.6 million.

Required:

Prepare an income statement and a statement of retained earnings for 1987.

8–10. Selected accounts of the Glenn Corporation for the year ended December 31, 1986, are:

Sales, net	$16,600,000
Interest expense	800,000
Cash dividends on preferred stock	760,000
Stock dividends on common stock	2,800,000
Selling and administrative expense	840,000
Cost of goods sold	9,000,000
Loss from earthquake (extraordinary item)	1,800,000
Service revenue	1,320,000
Depreciation on equipment	1,400,000
Additional federal income taxes for 1983	200,000
Litigation loss	2,000,000

The applicable federal income tax rate is 50 percent. All of the above items of expense, revenue, and loss are includable in the computation of income taxes payable. The litigation loss resulted from a court award for damages due to patent infringement on a product that Glenn produced in 1980 and 1981 and discontinued in 1982. Retained earnings as of December 31, 1986, were reported as 44 million.

Required:

Prepare:

a. The income statement for 1986.

b. The statement of retained earnings for 1986.

8–11. (Based on the chapter appendix.) The Jenkins Company acquired as a temporary investment on July 15, 1986, 500 shares of Peyton Company $100 par value common stock at 98 plus a broker's commission of $175. On August 1, 1986, Jenkins Company received a cash dividend of 75 cents per share. On November 3, 1986, it sold 250 of these shares at 106, less a broker's commission of $135. On December 1, 1986, the Peyton Company issued the shares comprising a 100 percent stock dividend declared on its common stock on November 18.

Required:

a. Present entries in T-account format to record all of the above data.

b. If management now decides that the remaining shares are to be held for affiliation purposes—Peyton Company has become a major customer—indicate how they should be shown in the balance sheet. Assume that the market value is $22,500.

9

DEBT FINANCING AND BOND INVESTMENTS

In chapter 8, stockholders' equity was discussed as a source of capital. Now the other source of capital is discussed—short- and long-term debt. Also discussed is the topic of investments in bonds of other companies, since the discussion is quite similar to the discussion of bonds payable.

SHORT-TERM FINANCING

Why would a business need short-term financing; that is, why would it need to use the bank's or some other creditor's money for short periods of time? A business usually expects the cash inflow from the sale of goods or services to exceed the cash outflow for the purchase of goods for resale or for the purchase of supplies, labor services, utilities, and so on. Also, some expenses, such as depreciation expense, do not involve an outflow of cash in the current period. But at certain times in the life of a business the inflow of cash may not be greater than the outflow of cash from operations. This can be caused by: (1) the delay in the receipt of cash due to giving customers credit terms on amounts due (though the business at least partly offsets this by the use of credit on its own purchases in order to delay the payment of cash); (2) the seasonal buildup of inventory, such as that which occurs in department stores just before the Christmas holiday; or (3) an expansion in operations caused by an expected future increase in sales. Some of the ways in which a business can obtain short-term financing are discussed below.

Short-Term Commercial Bank Loans

When a business needs additional financing it may go to a commercial bank to borrow on a short-term basis. When the loan is granted, the bank normally asks the borrower to sign a promissory note. A **promissory note** is an unconditional promise in writing made and signed by the borrower (the maker) obligating the borrower to pay the lender (the payee) or someone else who legally acquired the note a certain sum of money on demand or at a definite time. Normally, only the maker and the payee are parties to the instrument, but sometimes others who legally acquire the note or guarantee payment also become parties.

Nature of interest. Most notes bear an explicit (or stated) charge for interest. **Interest** is the fee charged for the use of money through time. It is an expense to the maker of the note and a revenue to the payee of the note. In commercial transactions interest is commonly figured on the basis of 360 days per year. The elapsed time in a fraction of a year between two stated days is computed by counting the exact number of days—omitting the day the money is borrowed but counting the day it is paid back. A note falling due on a Sunday or a holiday is due on the following business day.

Assume that we desire to calculate the interest on a $1,000 note with an interest rate of 6 percent and a life of 60 days. It can be done thus:

$$\text{Principal} \times \text{Rate of interest} \times \text{Time} = \text{Interest}$$

$$\$1,000 \times \frac{6}{100} \times \frac{60}{360} = \$10$$

Giving your own note to the bank. In instances in which a borrower presents his or her own non-interest-bearing note to a bank with a request for a loan, the bank computes the amount of interest on the face value of the note, deducts the amount computed from the face value, and gives the balance, the proceeds, to the borrower. The amount deducted is often called the bank discount, and the process of computing the amount is referred to as discounting. To illustrate this process, assume that a bank discounts a customer's $20,000, 90-day, non-interest-bearing note at 12 percent. The calculation of interest is:

$$\$20,000 \times \frac{12}{100} \times \frac{90}{360} = \$600$$

The $600 interest is deducted from the $20,000, and the borrower receives $19,400. Assuming the above transaction occurred on December 1, 1986, it would be recorded by the borrower as follows:

Cash		Notes Payable—Discount		Notes Payable	
12/1 19,400		12/1 600			12/1 20,000

Note that the borrower does not receive $20,000, but $19,400. Since the borrower will pay $600 for the use of this sum for a period of 90 days, the rate of interest is actually higher than 12 percent. (If $600 is the interest on $20,000 at 12 percent for 90 days, then $600 is more than 12 percent on $19,400 for 90 days.) Note also that the bank must discount this note in order to introduce interest into the transaction. If the bank advanced $20,000 on this non-interest-bearing note, it would not earn any interest from this loan because at maturity it will receive only $20,000.

The Notes Payable—Discount account used above is a contra account to Notes Payable. Assuming that December 31, 1986, is the end of the borrower's accounting period, it would be necessary to record interest expense for the month of December as follows (the debit and credit are dated 12/31, and the debit balance of $600 shown in Notes Payable—Discount is the balance in the account **before** making the latest entry):

Interest Expense		Notes Payable—Discount	
12/31 200		Bal. 600	12/31 200

In the current liability section of the December 31, 1986, balance sheet, the note and the discount would appear as follows:

Notes payable	. . . . .	$20,000
Less: Discount	. . . . .	400 $19,600

When the note is paid at maturity the accounts would be affected as follows (maturity date is March 1, 1987):

Cash		Notes Payable—Discount		Notes Payable	
Bal. xxx	3/1 20,000	Bal. after 12/31 adjust- ment 400	3/1 400	3/1 20,000	Bal. 20,000

Interest Expense	
3/1 400	

In journal entry form this transaction would appear as follows:

Notes Payable	20,000	
Interest Expense	400	
Cash		20,000
Notes Payable—Discount		400
To record payment of the note.		

The above changes reduce the Notes Payable—Discount and Notes Payable accounts to zero balances. Notice that the difference in the cash paid out ($20,000) and that originally received ($19,400) is equal to the total interest expense ($600). The interest relates to a 90-day period, 30 days of which fall in the year ending December 31, 1986, and 60 days of which fall in the following year. Thus, the amount charged to interest expense should be $200 in 1986 and $400 in 1987.

An alternative approach the borrower may use in the loan arrangement with the bank is to compute interest on the amount requested, add this to the amount requested, and draw a note for the total of the two. Thus, the borrower would sign a 90-day, non-interest-bearing note for $20,600 and would receive $20,000. At the date of borrowing the entry would be:

Cash		Notes Payable—Discount		Notes Payable	
(a) 20,000		(a) 600			(a) 20,600

The borrower could use a second alternative loan arrangement by giving a $20,000, 90-day, 12 percent interest-bearing note. At the date of borrowing the required entry is:

Cash		Notes Payable	
(a) 20,000			(a) 20,000

At maturity the borrower pays both the face amount of the note and interest at the rate stated in the note on that face amount (a total of $20,600). The $600 paid over and above the $20,000 face of the note represents interest expense to the borrower.

Notes Arising from Business Transactions

A company may have notes receivable and/or notes payable arising from transactions with customers or suppliers. When a company is the maker of a note with a supplier as the payee, the company has **received** short-term financing from that supplier. When a company is the payee of a note and a customer is the maker, the company has **supplied** short-term financing to that customer. A note may result from the conversion of an overdue open account or directly from merchandise transactions. To illustrate, assume that on October 6, 1986, Fox Company, the payee, receives from Kent Company, the maker, a 60-day, $18,000 note. The interest rate is 12 percent, and the note results from the previous sale (on October 4) of merchandise by Fox Company to Kent Company. The interest will be earned over the life of the note and will not be paid until maturity. December 5, 1986. The entries for both the payee and the maker are:

FOX COMPANY, PAYEE

To record sale:

Accounts Receivable					Sales		
10 /4	18,000					10/4	18,000

To record receipt of note:

Notes Receivable				Accounts Receivable			
10/6	18,000			Bal	18,000	10/6	18,000

To record receipt of principal and interest:

Cash				Notes Receivable			
12/5	18,360			Bal.	18,000	12/5	18,000

Interest Revenue			
		12/5	360

KENT COMPANY, MAKER

To record purchase:

Purchases					Accounts Payable		
10/4	18,000					10/4	18,000

To record giving of note:

Accounts Payable				Notes Payable			
10/6	18,000	Bal.	18,000			10/6	18,000

To record payment of principal and interest:

Notes Payable				Cash			
12/5	18,000	Bal	18,000	Bal	xxx	12/5	18,360

Interest Expense			
12/5	360		

A note is **dishonored** if the maker fails to pay it at maturity. The payee of the note may debit either Accounts Receivable or Dishonored Notes Receivable and credit Notes Receivable for the face of the note. If interest is due, it should be debited to the same account to which the dishonored note is debited and credited to Interest Revenue. The maker should merely debit the amount of interest incurred to Interest Expense and credit Interest Payable. When a note cannot be paid at maturity, the maker sometimes either pays the interest on the original note or includes it in the face of a new note given to take the place of the old note.

Discounting Notes Receivable

When a company issues its own note payable to a bank, it is directly liable to the bank at the maturity date of the loan. Such notes payable are shown in the balance sheet as liabilities.

Instead of borrowing directly, a company may use another method of obtaining short-term financing from a bank. A note receivable held by the company may be endorsed and then sold to a bank. The bank discounts the note and gives the company cash in exchange for it. Thus, a note receivable discounted arises. The company which sells the note receivable is contingently, instead of directly, liable to the lending bank; that is, the company must pay the bank the amount due at maturity only if the maker of the note fails to pay the obligation.

The cash proceeds from notes receivable discounted are computed as follows:

1. Determine the maturity value of the note (face value plus interest). This is the amount the bank will collect at maturity. For a non-interest-bearing note, the face of the note equals the maturity value. For an interest-bearing note, the face of the note plus interest for the life of the note equals the maturity value.

2. Determine the discount period; that is, count the exact number of days from the date of sale of the note to the date of maturity. Exclude the date of sale but include the date of maturity in the count. The discount period, of course, can never be longer than the life of the note.

3. Using the rate of discount charged by the bank, compute the discount on the maturity value (principal plus interest) for the discount period.

4. Deduct the bank discount from the maturity value to find the cash proceeds.

The contingent liability for the notes receivable discounted is usually shown in the accounts by recording the face value of the note in a Notes Receivable Discounted account. This is done even though the contingent liability includes the interest. If the original maker does not pay the bank at the maturity date, the company that sold the note to the bank will be held liable.

Example. Assume that on May 4, 1986, Carlson Company received a $10,000 note from Thomas (the maker). The note bears interest at 12 percent and matures in 60 days from May 4. On May 14, 1986, Carlson Company (the endorser) sold the note to the Michigan National Bank, which discounted the note at 14 percent. The discount and the cash proceeds are determined as follows:

Face value of note	$10,000.00
Add: Interest at 12% for 60 days	200.00
Maturity value	$10,200.00
Less: Bank discount on $10,200 at 14% for 50 days . . .	198.33
Cash proceeds	$10,001.67

The entry would be as follows:

	Cash		Interest Revenue	
5/14	10,001.67		5/14	1.67

Notes Receivable Discounted	
	5/14 10,000.00

If the book value of the note had exceeded the proceeds, the difference would have been debited to an Interest Expense account.

Balance sheet presentation of notes receivable discounted. In the above illustration a balance sheet prepared for Carlson Company as of December 31, 1986, should show a contingent liability in the amount of $10,000 for notes receivable discounted. Assume that the total of all notes receivable is $70,000. One acceptable method of presenting this information in the balance sheet is:

Assets

Current assets:

Cash	$xx,xxx
Accounts receivable	xx,xxx
Notes receivable (Note 1)	60,000

> Note 1: At December 31, 1986, the company is contingently liable for $10,000 of customers' notes receivable which it has endorsed and discounted at the local bank. These notes are not included in the $60,000 of notes shown.

Although the contingent liability is actually for the note plus the accrued interest to maturity ($10,200), for convenience it is customarily shown only for the face of the note ($10,000).

Discounted notes receivable paid by maker. When a note receivable has been sold, it is usually the duty of the endorsee (the holder) to present the note to the maker for payment at maturity. Sometimes the note designates the place of payment. If the maker pays the endorsee (the bank in the above illustrations) at maturity, the endorser is thereby relieved of contingent liability. If the note is not paid at maturity, the endorsee can collect from the endorser, who, in turn, can try to collect from the maker.

Assume that Thomas (above) pays his $10,000 note plus interest of $200 to the Michigan National Bank on July 3, 1986—the note's maturity date. Carlson Company, which sold the note to the bank, has been relieved of the possibility of being held liable on the note and, therefore, will show the following changes in its accounts.

Notes Receivable				Notes Receivable Discounted			
5/4	10,000	7/3	10,000	7/3	10,000	5/14	10,000

These changes reduce Thomas' Notes Receivable account and the related Notes Receivable Discounted account on Carlson's books to zero balances.

If Thomas dishonors the note at maturity instead of paying it, the Michigan National Bank will collect the principal ($10,000), interest ($200), and any protest fee (assume it is $5) from Carlson Company. Besides removing the note from the Notes Receivable and Notes Receivable Discounted accounts as shown above, Carlson Company will also show the following changes in its accounts:

Cash		Accounts Receivable	
xxx	10,205	10,205	

Carlson Company will then try to collect $10,205 from Thomas. If this cannot be done, the $10,205 should be removed from the Accounts Receivable account and treated as a loss from bad debts.

LONGER TERM FINANCING

Although it is conceivable that once a company begins operations it can finance the acquisition of additional long-term or plant assets out of operating cash flows, this is often not possible. It is quite common for companies to use long-term sources of financing to acquire such assets. Chapter 8 discussed the use of capital stock to acquire long-term funds. This chapter discusses some of the more common forms of long-term debt financing.

Notes Payable

Notes payable may be either short term or long term, but they are usually short term. Since these have been discussed earlier, we will not deal with them again in this section except to say that when payables (or receivables) have maturities **exceeding** approximately one year they are to be recorded at their present cash value.[1] The procedure is similar to that used in calculating the proceeds of a discounted bank loan. To illustrate, assume that we are the

---

[1] "Interest on Receivables and Payables," *APB Opinion No. 21* (New York: AICPA, 1971).

maker of a $1,000 face value note bearing no explicit rate of interest that is due one year from its date. (Even though this does not exceed "approximately one year" and technically would not have to be recorded at its present value, we will assume that the company chooses to do so). Assume also that the rate of interest to be used in reducing this note to its present value is 16 percent. To solve for the present value, we have to ask the question, "What amount, if invested at 16 percent, would grow to $1,000 one year from now?" If we let x equal that amount, our formula would be:

$$x + 0.16x = \$1{,}000$$
$$1.16x = \$1{,}000$$
$$x = \frac{\$1{,}000}{1.16}$$
$$x = \$862.07$$

Assuming that the note payable resulted from the purchase of a machine, it would be recorded as follows:

Machinery		Notes Payable—Discount		Notes Payable	
(a) 862.07		(a) 137.93			(a) 1,000

At the due date, $1,000 would be paid to the payee and $137.93 would be (or would have been) recorded as interest expense. The accounting for the interest in this type of transaction is quite similar to that used when a company discounts its own note at the bank.

Mortgage Notes Payable

Another form of long-term financing is a mortgage note payable. This is a note payable that is secured by a mortgage, that is, an obligation to give up certain property that has been pledged to the payee in case the maker defaults on the payments. Most of us become familiar with this form of financing when we purchase a home. Business firms also sometimes use this method of financing when they acquire assets such as buildings.

This form of financing will be illustrated by assuming that a company acquires a small building. The company makes a constant lump-sum payment each month (exclusive of real estate taxes) which at first pays mostly interest and very little prinicipal. Assume that the mortgage on the building (acquired in 1977) is $35,000, that the interest rate is 8 percent, and that the life of the note is 25 years. There are mortgage payment schedule books which indicate that the monthly payment for principal and interest is $271. Here is how the first two months' and the last month's payments are applied:

	Monthly Payment	Interest at 8 Percent on Principal Balance	Payment on Principal ($271 Less Interest)	Principal Balance
Date of purchase				$35,000.00
1st month	$271	$233.33	$ 37.67	34,962.33
2nd month	271	233.08	37.92	34,924.41
300th month	271	2.00	269.00	0

Notice that interest is calculated on the latest principal balance. For instance, when the first $271 payment is made, interest is calculated as follows:

$$\frac{\$35,000 \times 0.08}{12} = \$233.33$$

It is necessary to divide by 12 because the interest rate is 8 percent per **year** and we are calculating the amount for one **month.** The excess of the payment over the interest is applied against the principal ($37.67 in the first payment above). Thus, the principal balance decreases slowly (but more rapidly each month) so that the last $271 payment at the end of 25 years pays interest (approximately $2) on the remaining principal balance (approximately $269) and then reduces the principal balance to zero.

Since the building is pledged (or mortgaged) as security for the loan, if the company does not keep up the payments, the party to which payment is due can foreclose on the mortgage and take over the building. As a practical matter, many lending institutions are quite lenient in allowing a few back payments to be made up rather than take this drastic step.

Bonds Payable

A **bond** is a long-term debt owed by its issuer. Physical evidence of the debt lies in a negotiable **bond certificate.** Long-term notes usually mature in 10 years or less, while bond maturities often run for 20 years or more. A bond derives its value primarily from two promises made by the borrower to the lender, or bondholder. The borrower promises to pay (1) the **face value** or **principal amount** of the bond on a specific maturity date in the future; and (2) periodic interest at a specified rate on face value at stated dates, usually semiannually, until maturity date.

A bond issue generally consists of numerous $1,000 bonds, rather than one very large bond. For example, a company seeking to borrow $100,000 would issue one hundred $1,000 bonds, rather than one $100,000 bond. Investers with smaller amounts of cash to invest are able to purchase the bonds.

Accounting for Bonds When a company issues bonds, it incurs a long-term liability on which periodic interest payments must be made, usually twice a year. If interest dates fall on other than balance sheet dates, interest will need to be accrued in the proper periods. The following example illustrates the accounting for bonds issued at face value.

On December 31, 1986, Smith Company, with an accounting year ending on December 31, issued $100,000 face value of 10-year, 12 percent bonds for cash of $100,000. The bonds are dated December 31, 1986, call for semiannual interest payments on June 30 and December 31, and mature on December 31, 1996. Smith Company made all required cash payments when due. The entries for the 10 years are summarized below.

On December 31, 1986, the date of issuance

```
1986
Dec 31   Cash  . . . . . . . . . . .   100,000
             Bonds Payable  . . . . . . .           100,000
         To record bonds issued at face value.
```

On each June 30 and December 31 for 10 years, beginning June 30, 1986:

```
June 30
and
Dec. 31  Bond Interest Expense
             ($100,000 × 0.12 × ½)  . . . . .   6,000
             Cash  . . . . . . . . . . .           6,000
         To record periodic interest payment.
```

On December 31, 1996, the maturity date:

```
1986
Dec. 31  Bonds Payable  . . . . . . . .   100,000
             Cash  . . . . . . . . . . .           100,000
         To record bond redemption.
```

Note that no adjusting entries are needed when an interest payment date falls on the last day of the accounting period. The income statement for each of the 10 years 1987 to 96 would show Bond Interest Expense of $12,000; the balance sheet at the end of each of the years 1986 to 94 would report Bonds Payable of $100,000 in long-term liabilities. At the end of 1995, the bonds would be reclassified as a current liability because they will be paid within the next year.

But the real world is seldom so uncomplicated. For example, Smith's fiscal year may end on October 31. If so, the June 30 entry remains unchanged, but an adjusting entry is needed on October 31 to accrue interest for the four months, July through October. That entry would read:

```
1986
Oct. 31   Bond Interest Expense
            ($100,000 × 0.12 × 4/12)    . . . . .    4,000
              Accrued Bond Interest Payable   . .              4,000
          To accrue four months' interest expense.
```

The December 31 entry would then read:

```
1986
Dec. 31   Bond Interest Expense
            ($100,000 × 0.12 × 2/12)    . . . . .    2,000
          Accrued Bond Interest Payable   . . . .    4,000
            Cash   . . . . . . . . . . .                       6,000
          To record semiannual interest payment.
```

Each year similar entries would be made for the semiannual payments and the fiscal year-end accrual. The $4,000 Accrued Bond Interest Payable would be reported as a current liability on the October 31 balance sheet for each year.

Bonds issued at face value between interest dates. Bonds are not always issued on the date they start to bear interest. An issue might be delayed several weeks or months for many reasons, such as expected changes in economic conditions. When bonds are issued between interest dates, the purchaser is required to pay for the interest accrued since the preceding interest date (or the date of the bonds if issued during the first interest period). This accrued interest payment is necessary because the issuer of outstanding bonds is required to pay investors a full six months' interest at each interest date. The bonds are reported to be selling at a stated price "plus accrued interest."

Suppose Smith Company issued its bonds on April 30, 1987, instead of on December 31, 1986. The entry required is:

```
1987
Apr. 30   Cash   . . . . . . . . . . . . .   104,000
            Bonds Payable   . . . . . . . .             100,000
            Accrued Bond Interest Payable
              ($100,000 × 0.12 × 4/12)   . . . .          4,000
          To record bonds issued at face value plus
          accrued interest.
```

This entry records the cash received for the accrued interest as a liability. The entry required on June 30, 1987, when the full six months' interest is paid is:

```
1987
June 30   Bond Interest Expense   . . . . . . .   2,000
          Accrued Bond Interest Payable   . . . .   4,000
            Cash   . . . . . . . . . . .                      6,000
          To record bond interest payment.
```

This entry records $2,000 interest expense on the $100,000 of bonds that were outstanding for two months. The $4,000 is the amount previously collected from the bondholders on April 30 as accrued interest and is now being returned to them.

Bond Prices and Interest Rates

The price of a bond issue sold to investors often differs from its face value. A difference between face value and price will exist whenever the market rate of interest differs from the contract rate of interest on the bonds. The **contract rate of interest** is stated in the bond indenture and printed on the face of each bond and is also called the **stated, coupon,** or **nominal rate.** The contract rate is used to determine the actual amount of cash that will be paid each interest period. The **market interest rate,** also called the **effective interest** or **yield rate,** is the minimum rate of interest investors are willing to accept on bonds of a particular risk category. The market rate fluctuates from day to day, responding to the supply and demand for money.

Contract and market rates of interest are likely to differ. The contract rate must be set before the bonds are actually sold to allow time for such things as printing the bonds. By the time the bonds are sold and the market rate becomes known, the established contract rate could be higher or lower than the fluctuating market rate. *If the contract rate is higher than the market rate, the bonds will sell for more than face value.* Investors will be attracted to bonds offering a contract rate greater than the market rate for such bonds and will bid up their price. *If the contract rate is lower than the market rate, the bonds will sell for less than face value.* Investors will not be interested in bonds bearing a contract rate less than the market rate unless the bonds' price falls. The amount a bond sells for above face value is called a **premium:** if sold for less than face value, the reduction is called a **discount.**

The effect of selling a bond at a premium or discount is to adjust the contract rate of interest on the bond to the market rate. To illustrate using a short-term note: Assume that you paid the Nance Company $9,800 for its $10,000, 10 percent note that matures in one year. The contract interest rate is 10 percent. But, if Nance pays the note at maturity, the effective rate of interest in the transaction is about 12.2 percent. Your actual interest earned is $1,200—the difference between the amount collected at the end of one year, $11,000 (principal plus interest), and the amount invested, $9,800. The effective rate of interest is 12.2 percent ($1,200/$9,800) per annum, simple interest.

Computing Bond Prices

Computing long-term bond prices is a more complex process than finding the effective rate of interest on a one-year note at simple interest. The process involves finding present values by using compound interest. The concept of present value is explained in the Appendix to this chapter. If you do not understand the present value concept, you should read the Appendix before continuing.

To compute the price investors will pay for a given bond issue, compute the present value of the bonds. Present value is computed by discounting promised cash flows in the bonds—principal and interest—using the market or effective interest rate. Market rate is used because the bonds must yield at least this rate or investors will invest in alternative investments that do. The life of the bonds is stated in terms of interest periods, which indicate how frequently interest is compounded. The interest rate used is the effective rate **per interest period,** which often is found by dividing the annual rate by the number of times interest is paid per year.

Bonds issued at face value. Specific steps involved in computing the price of a bond are illustrated by an example. Assume $100,000 face value of 12 percent bonds are issued by Rex Company to yield 12 percent. The bonds are dated and issued on July 1, 1986; call for semiannual interest payments; and mature on July 1, 1989. The bonds will sell at face value because they offer 12 percent and investors seek 12 percent. There is no reason to offer a premium or demand a discount. One way to prove the bonds would be sold at face value is by showing that their present value is $100,000:

	Present Value Factor	Present Value
Principal of $100,000 due in six periods multiplied by present value factor for 6% from Table II, Appendix C (end of text)	$100,000 × 0.70496 =	$ 70,496
Interestof $6,000 due at end of each of six periods multiplied by present value factor for 6% from Table III, Appendix C (end of text)	$6,000 × 4.91732 =	29,504
Total price (present value)		$100,000

The schedule shows that if investors seek an effective rate of 6 percent per six-month period, they should pay $100,000 for these bonds. When the bonds are sold on July 1, 1986, the entry required debits Cash and credits Bonds Payable for $100,000.

Bonds issued at a discount. Assume the Rex Company bonds are sold to yield the market rate of 14 percent—actually 7 percent per semiannual period. The present value and selling price of the bonds is computed as follows:

	Present Value Factor	Present Value
Principal of $100,000 due in six periods multiplied by present value factor for 7% from Table II Appendix C (end of text)	$100,000 × 0.66634 =	$66,634
Interest of $6,000 due at end of each six periods multiplied by present value factor for 7% from Table III, Appendix C (end of text)	$6,000 × 4.76654 =	28,599
Total price (present value)		$95,233

Note that in computing present value of the bonds, the actual cash interest payments that will be made were used. The amount of cash flow does not change with changes in the market interest rate. Also, the market rate per semiannual period—7 percent—was used in finding interest factors in the tables. The journal entry to record issuance of the bonds is:

```
1986
July 1   Cash  . . . . . . . . . . . . . . .   95,233
         Discount on Bonds Payable  . . . . . .   4,767
            Bonds Payable  . . . . . . . . .            100,000
            To record bonds issued at a discount.
```

Note in recording the bond issue, Bonds Payable is credited for the face value of the debt. The difference between face value and price received is debited to a contra account to Bonds Payable. Bonds Payable and the Discount on Bonds Payable are reported in the balance sheet as follows:

```
Long-term liabilities:
   Bonds payable, 12%, due July 1, 1988  . . .  $100,000
   Less: Discount on bonds payable  . . . . . .     4,767   $95,233
```

The **$95,233** is called the **carrying value** or **net liability** of the bonds.

Bonds issued at a premium. Assume that Rex Company issued the $100,000 face value of 12 percent bonds to yield 10 percent. The bonds would sell at a premium calculated as follows:

	Present Value Factor	Present Value
Principal of $100,000 due in six periods multiplied by present value factor for 5% from Table II, Appendix C (end of text)	$100,000 × 0.74622 =	$ 74,622
Interest of $6,000 due at end of each of six periods multiplied by present value factor for 5% from Table III, Appendix C (end of text) .	$6,000 × 5.07569 =	30,454
Total price (present value)		$105,076

The journal entry to record the issuance of the bonds is:

```
1986
July 1   Cash  . . . . . . . . . . . . . . .   105,076
            Bonds Payable  . . . . . . . . . .           100,000
            Premium on Bonds Payable  . . . .             5,076
            To record bonds issued at a premium.
```

Carrying value of these bonds at issuance is $105,076 consisting of face value of $100,000 and premium of $5,076. Premium is shown on the balance sheet as an addition to face value.

Discount/Premium Amortization

When bonds are issued at a discount or premium, total actual interest expense on the bonds differs from total interest paid periodically in cash. A discount increases and a premium decreases the cash interest to actual interest. For example, if $100,000 face value of Rex Company bonds were issued for $95,233, the total interest cost of borrowing would be $40,767: $36,000 (six payments of $6,000) plus the discount of $4,767. The $4,767 discount must be allocated (amortized) to the six periods that benefit from the use of borrowed money. *APB Opinion No. 21* recommends an amortization procedure called the **effective interest rate method,** or, simply, the **interest method.**

Under the interest method, *interest expense for any interest period is equal to the effective (market) rate of interest at date of issuance times the carrying value of the bonds at the beginning of that interest period.* Using the Rex Company example of $100,000 face value of 12 percent bonds sold to yield 14 percent, the carrying value at the beginning of the first interest period is the selling price of $95,233. The interest expense for the first semiannual period would be recorded in this way:

```
1986
Dec. 31   Bond Interest Expense
              ($95,233 × 0.14 × ½)    . . . . . .    6,666
                  Cash ($100,000 × 0.12 × ½)  . . .              6,000
                  Discount on Bonds Payable    . . .              666
              To record discount amortization and in-
              terest payment.
```

Note that interest expense is calculated using the effective interest rate. The cash payment is calculated using the contract rate. The discount amortized for the period is the difference between the two amounts.

After the above entry, the carrying value of the bonds is $95,899. The balance in the discount account was reduced by $666 to $4,101. Assuming a fiscal year ending on June 30, the entry to accrue six months' interest at year-end is:

```
1987
June 30   Bond Interest Expense
              ($95,899 × 0.14 × ½)    . . . . . .    6,713
                  Accrued Bond Interest Payable   . .              6,000
                  Discount on Bonds Payable    . . .              713
              To accrue six months' interest and dis-
              count amortization.
```

If the Rex Company bonds had been issued to yield 10 percent, the premium would be $5,076. But interest expense would be calculated in the same manner as for bonds sold at a discount, that is, as carrying value times effective interest rates. The entry would differ somewhat, showing a debit to the premium account. The entries for the first two interest periods are:

```
1986
Dec. 31   Bond Interest Expense
            ($105,076 × 0.10 × ½)    . . . . .    5,254
          Premium on Bonds Payable   . . . . .      746
            Cash   . . . . . . . . . . .                    6,000
          To record interest payment and premium
          amortization.

1987
June 30   Bond Interest Expense
            ($104,330 × 0.10 × ½)    . . . . .    5,216
          Premium on Bonds Payable   . . . . .      784
            Accrued Bond Interest Payable   . .            6,000
          To accrue six months' interest expense
          and premium amortization.
```

Discount and premium amortization schedules. A discount amortization schedule (Illustration 9.1) and a premium amortization schedule (Illustration 9.2) can be prepared to aid in preparing entries for interest expense. Companies usually prepare such schedules when bonds are first issued, often using standard computer programs. The schedules are then referred to whenever journal entries for interest are to be made. The schedules show the amount of the entries as if no adjusting entries were prepared the day before the interest date. The amounts may still be used in preparing the necessary adjusting entries. Note that, in each period, the amount of interest expense changes; expense gets larger when a discount is involved and smaller when a premium is involved. The reason is the carrying value to which a constant interest rate is applied changes each interest payment date. With a discount, carrying value increases; with a premium, it decreases. But cash is always a constant amount determined by multiplying face value by the contract rate per interest period.

Note that interest expense in Illustration 9.1 of $40,767 agrees with the earlier computation of total interest expense. In Illustration

Illustration 9.1
DISCOUNT AMORTIZATION SCHEDULE

(A) Interest Payment Date	(B) Interest Expense Debit (E × 0.14 × ½)	(C) Cash Credit ($100,000 × 0.12 × ½)	(D) Discount on Bonds Payable Credit (B − C)	(E) Carrying Value of Bonds Payable (E + D)
Issue price, 7/1/86 . . .				$ 95,233
1/1/87	$ 6,666	$ 6,000	$ 666	95,899
7/1/87	6,713	6,000	713	96,612
1/1/88	6,763	6,000	763	97,375
7/1/88	6,816	6,000	816	98,191
1/1/89	6,873	6,000	873	99,064
7/1/89	6,936*	6,000	936	100,000
	$40,767	$36,000	$4,767	

* Includes rounding difference.

Illustration 9.2
PREMIUM AMORTIZATION SCHEDULE

(A) Interest Payment Date	(B) Interest Expense Debit ($E \times 0.10 \times \frac{1}{2}$)	(C) Cash Credit ($\$100,000 \times 0.12 \times \frac{1}{2}$)	(D) Premium on Bonds Payable Debit ($C - B$)	(E) Carrying Value of Bonds Payable ($E - D$)
Issue price, 7/1/86				$105,076
1/1/87	$ 5,254	$ 6,000	$ 746	104,330
7/1/87	5,216	6,000	784	103,546
1/1/88	5,177	6,000	823	102,723
7/1/88	5,136	6,000	864	101,859
1/1/89	5,093	6,000	907	100,952
7/1/89	5,048	6,000	952	100,000
	$30,924	$36,000	$5,076	

9.2, total interest expense is shown as $30,924, which is equal to $36,000 (six $6,000 payments) **less** the $5,076 premium. In both illustrations, the carrying value of the bonds at the maturity date is face value.

Adjusting entry for partial period. Illustration 9.2 can be used to obtain amounts needed if interest must be accrued for a partial period. Assume the fiscal year of the bond issuer ends on August 31. The adjusting entry needed on August 31, 1986, is:

```
1986
Aug. 31  Bond Interest Expense ($5,254 × 2/6)  . . . .  1,751
            Premium on Bonds Payable ($746 × 2/6)  . .    249
               Accrued Bond Interest Payable
                  ($6,000 × 2/6)  . . . . . . . . .             2,000
         To record two months' accrued interest.
```

The entry records interest for two months, July and August, of the six-month interest period ending on January 1, 1987. The first line of Illustration 9.2 shows the interest expense and premium amortization for the six months. The above entry thus records two sixths (or one third) of the amounts for this six-month period. The remaining four months' interest is recorded when the first payment is made on January 1, 1987. That entry reads:

```
1987
Jan. 1  Accrued Bond Interest Payable  . . . . . .  2,000
        Bond Interest Expense ($5,254 × 4/6)  . . . .  3,503
        Premium on Bonds Payable ($746 × 4/6)  . . .    497
           Cash  . . . . . . . . . . . . . . . .            6,000
        To record interest expense and interest payment.
```

Similar entries for August 31 and January 1 will be made in the remaining years of the life of the bonds. The amounts will differ from those in the above entry because the interest method of accounting for bond interest is being used.

The straight-line method. When applied to bond discount or premium, **the straight-line method of amortization** is a procedure that allocates an equal amount of discount or premium to each month the bonds are outstanding. The amount is calculated by dividing the discount or premium by the total number of months from date of issuance to maturity date. For example, if the $100,000 face value of Rex Company bonds were sold for $95,233, the $4,767 discount would be charged to interest expense at a rate of $132.42 ($4,767/36) per month. Interest expense for each six-month period then would be $6,795, [$6,000 + ($132.42 × 6)]. The entry to record the expense would have the same form as under the interest method.

The $5,076 premium on the $100,000 face value of bonds sold for $105,076 would be amortized at a rate of $141 ($5,076/36) per month. The entry for the first period's expense on bonds sold at a premium reads:

```
1987
Jan. 1   Bond Interest Expense  . . . . . . . . . .   5,154
         Premium on Bonds Payable ($141 × 6)   . . .     846
             Cash   . . . . . . . . . . . . . .                 6,000
             To record interest payment and premium amorti-
             zation.
```

Interest expense is recorded at a **constant amount** under the straight-line method and at a **constant rate** under the interest method. Since the interest method is theoretically correct, *APB Opinion No. 21* states that the straight-line method may be used only when it does not differ materially from the interest method. In many cases, differences will not be material. In the premium example above, the difference in the first period's interest expense is only $100 ($5,254 − $5,154), and may not be material.

Redeeming Bonds Payable

Bonds may be paid at maturity, purchased in the market and retired, or called. Each of these actions is referred to as redemption of bonds or extinguishment of debt. If bonds are paid at maturity, any related discount or premium would have been amortized. The only entry required would debit Bonds Payable and credit Cash. More typical redemptions are discussed below.

An issuer may redeem some or all of its outstanding bonds before maturity date by calling them. Or bonds may be purchased in the market and retired. In either case, the accounting is the same. Assume that on January 1, 1988, $10,000 face value of the bonds in Illustration 9.2 are called or purchased in the market at 103. Bond prices usually are quoted as percentages—the 103 means 103 percent of face value. For a $1,000 bond, the price is $1,030. A quote of 99.5 means a price of $995 for a $1,000 bond. In both cases, accrued interest, if any, will be added to the price. Assume that coupons for the interest due on this date have been detached so there is no accrued interest. A look at the last column on the line dated 1/1/88 in Illustration 9.2 reveals that the carrying value of the bonds is $102,723, which consists of Bonds Payable of $100,000 and Premium on Bonds Payable of $2,723. Since 10 percent of the bond issue is redeemed, 10 percent must be removed from each of these two accounts. A loss is incurred for the excess of the price paid for the bonds, $10,300, over their carrying value, $10,272. The required entry reads:

Bonds Payable	10,000	
Premium on Bonds Payable	272	
Loss on Bond Redemption	28	
Cash		10,300
To record bonds redeemed.		

According to *FASB Statement No. 4,* gains and losses from **voluntary early** retirement of bonds are extraordinary items, if material. Such gains and losses are reported in the income statement, net of their tax effects, as described in Chapter 8.

LONG-TERM BOND INVESTMENTS

Bonds may be purchased as either short-term or long-term investments. The main short-term reason is to earn at least a nominal rate of return on cash that would otherwise be temporarily idle. This section deals with the accounting treatment for long-term investment in bonds. Long-term investments in bonds usually are made for reasons other than a return on idle cash. A company may invest on a long-term basis in another company to guarantee needed raw materials. Or one company could be a dealer or distributor of the other company's products. In any event, the most common reason is establishment of a long-term relationship between two companies. Long-term bond investments are reported in the Investments section in the balance sheet below the current assets section, whether such bonds are marketable or not.

Accounting for Bond Investments

Long-term investments in bonds are recorded in a single account at cost that includes any discount or premium on the purchase. Although not set up in a separate account as it is for the issuing company, a discount or premium on long-term bond investments is amortized.

Bonds purchased at a discount. For example, assume that on July 1, 1986, Fenn Company purchased $100,000 face value of 12 percent bonds for $95,233, a price that yields 14 percent. These bonds were described in Illustration 9.1. The entry to record the purchase is:

Bond investments	95,233	
Cash		95,233
To record bonds purchased at a discount.		

If a broker's commission was paid to acquire the bonds, it would be added to the Bond Investments account.

Since Fenn intends to hold the bonds to maturity, the discount is amortized over the remaining life of the bonds, using the interest method. Interest revenue and discount amortization on the bonds purchased by Fenn are computed the same way the issuer's expense and amortization are computed: multiply the bond price by the effective rate per period. The first period's interest revenue is $6,666 ($95,233 × 0.14 × ½). Discount amortized is $666 ($6,666 − $6,000). If Fenn has a calendar accounting year, the required adjusting entry is:

Dec. 31	Accrued Bond Interest Receivable	6,000	
	Bond Investments	666	
	Interest Revenue		6,666
	To record accrued interest revenue.		

Note in the entry, the amount added to the Bond Investments account is equal to the discount amortized on the issuer's books. The discount is amortized even though it is not set up in a separate account on the investor's books. The original discount is $4,767, and this amount must be included in interest revenue on Fenn's books during the life of the bonds. Illustration 9.3 shows how the $4,767 is added to periodic interest revenue and to Bond Investments. The debits gradually increase the Bond Investments account balance to face value at the maturity date.

Fenn's December 31, 1986, balance sheet would show Accrued Bond Interest Receivable of $6,000, and Bond Investments of $95,899. If Fenn's Fiscal year ended on November 30, the adjusting entry on that date would be the same as the December 31 entry, except all amounts would be five sixths of the December 31 amounts.

If the straight-line method is used, discount amortization would

Illustration 9.3
DISCOUNT AMORTIZATION SCHEDULE

(A)	(B)	(C)	(D)	(E)
				Carrying Value
	Cash Debit	Interest Rev-	Bond Invest-	of Bond
Interest	($100,000 ×	enue Credit	ments Debit	Investments
Date	0.12 × ½)	(E × 0.14 × ½)	(C − B)	(E + D)
Purchase price, 7/1/86				$ 95,233
1/1/87	$ 6,000	$ 6,666	$ 666	95,899
7/1/87	6,000	6,713	713	96,612
1/1/88	6,000	6,763	763	97,375
7/1/88	6,000	6,816	816	98,191
1/1/89	6,000	6,873	873	99,064
7/1/89	6,000	6,936*	936	100,000
	$36,000	$40,767	$4,767	

* Includes rounding difference.

be $795 ($4,767/6) per period and interest revenue would be $6,795 ($6,000 + $795).

Bonds purchased at a premium. To illustrate accounting for bonds purchased at a premium, assume Ace Company paid $105,076 for $100,000 face value of 12 percent bonds, a price that yields 10 percent. These are the bonds in Illustration 9.2. The entry to record the purchase would debit Bond Investments and Credit Cash for $105,076.

Here again, interest revenue for the first interest period can be computed by multiplying the purchase price by the effective interest rate: $105,076 \times 0.10 \times \frac{1}{2} = \$5,254$. The entry to record the $5,254 is:

Cash	6,000	
Bond Investments		746
Interest Revenue		5,254
To record interest revenue collected.		

The premium is amortized by crediting the Bond Investments account. If bonds are held to maturity, the balance in the Bond Investments account would be gradually decreased to the maturity value of $100,000 (Illustration 9.4). Interest revenue for the second six months can be read from Illustration 9.4. Or it can be computed: ($105,076 − $746) × 0.10 × ½ = $5,216. If the straight-line method were used, the periodic amortization of the premium would be $846 ($5,076/6). Interest revenue would be a constant amount each semi-annual period of $5,154 ($6,000 − $846).

Sale of Bond Investments

When bond investments are sold, a gain or loss usually must be recorded. Gain or loss is computed as the difference between the price received and the carrying value of the bonds on the date sold. Suppose that on July 1, 1988, when their carrying value was $101,859

Illustration 9.4
PREMIUM AMORTIZATION SCHEDULE

(A) Interest Date	(B) Cash Debit ($100,000 × 0.12 × ½)	(C) Interest Revenue Credit (E × 0.10 × ½)	(D) Bond Investments Credit (B − C)	(E) Carrying Value of Bond Investments (E − D)
Purchase price, 7/1/86				$105,076
1/1/87	$ 6,000	$ 5,254	$ 746	104,330
7/1/87	6,000	5,216	784	103,546
1/1/88	6,000	5,177	823	102,723
7/1/88	6,000	5,136	864	101,859
1/1/89	6,000	5,093	907	100,952
7/1/89	6,000	5,048	952	100,000
	$36,000	$30,924	$5,076	

(Illustration 9.4), the Ace Company sold all of its bonds for $102,500, less a $500 broker's commission. The required entry is:

```
Cash  . . . . . . . . . . . . . . . .   102,000
   Bond investments  . . . . . . . . . . .          101,859
   Gain on Sale of Bond Investments   . . . .           141
   To record sale of bond investments.
```

There was no accrued interest because the sale occurred on an interest payment date. If it had not been an interest payment date, an additional entry would have been needed to record interest earned and discount or premium amortized to date of sale. The gain or loss on the sale of the investment is reported in the income statement.

Valuation of Bond Investments

Long-term bond investments are carried and reported at amortized cost. Amortized cost is equal to acquisition cost plus discount amortized or less premium amortized. An exception exists when a substantial, permanent decline in value occurs. Bond investments are then written down by debiting an account called Loss on Market Decline of Bond Investments and crediting Bond Investments.

Once bond investments have been written down, traditional accounting conservatism dictates they may not be written up, not even to their original cost, if market price recovers. The written down amount serves as the basis for computing gain or loss when the bonds are sold.

SUMMARY

This chapter has been concerned with financing activities and investments in the financial obligations of other companies; it includes both short-term and long-term items.

When a company finds itself in a position in which cash outflows temporarily exceed cash inflows, it may have to seek short-term financing. It may decide to borrow from a commercial bank by giving its own note payable. The company may seek to borrow from suppliers by delaying the time of payment for goods purchased. (This often results in notes payable to those suppliers.) Or, the company may decide to sell to a bank notes receivable which it obtained from customers. In the last instance, the company is contingently liable for the note; that is, if the maker of the note does not pay the bank at maturity, the company will have to pay the note.

Longer-term financing is sometimes necessary to acquire additional long-term assets such as property, plant, and equipment. Notes payable are sometimes used for this purpose. Long-term notes must be recorded at their present value (while short-term notes are usually recorded at their face value). Quite often these notes are secured by a mortgage on certain property. A mortgage is a conditional transfer of property which is actually transferred to the payee if the maker does not meet its obligations under the terms of the note.

A common form of mortgage notes payable is that arising from the purchase of a home. Businesses sometimes use this same form of long-term financing. Bonds are one of the longest-term debt issues commonly used. Bonds may or may not be secured by a mortgage against specific property.

A bond is a long-term liability that derives its value from two promises made to the purchaser: the company will repay the principal at a specified later time and pay periodic interest charges until that time.

Interest is generally paid in semiannual amounts. If interest payment dates and balance sheet dates do not coincide, interest must be accrued into the proper periods. When bonds are issued between interest payment dates investors will pay for the accrued interest since the preceding interest date. This accrued interest is refunded to them on the next interest date.

A bond may be issued at face value, at a discount, or at a premium. Discounts and premiums exist because of differences between the stated interest rate on a bond and the market rate of interest. If the market rate is greater than the stated rate, the bonds will be issued at a discount. If the market rate is less than the stated rate, the bond will be issued at a premium. The issue price of a bond is equal to the present value of the principal plus the present value of the interest payments. The rate of interest used in discounting to find the present value is the market rate.

If a bond is issued at a discount or premium, total interest expense differs from the amount of cash interest paid each period. The discount or premium is amortized over the life of the bond through a procedure called the interest method. Interest expense is computed as the market rate of interest times the carrying value of the bonds at the beginning of the interest period. Cash interest to be paid is the contract rate of interest times the face (principal) of the bonds. The difference between these two amounts is the discount or premium to be amortized.

Bonds may be purchased as long-term investments. Long-term investments in bonds are recorded at cost that would include any discount or premium. Discount or premium is amortized using the interest method. When bond investments are sold, a gain or loss is recorded as the difference between selling price and carrying value of the investment.

APPENDIX

FUTURE VALUE AND PRESENT VALUE

The concepts of interest, future value, and present value are widely applied in business decision making. Accountants may be better able to account properly for business activity if they understand how the concepts of interest, future value, and present value influence this activity.

Interest

As a general definition, interest is the **time value of money.** More specifically, it is the cost incurred from borrowing money or the revenue earned from lending money. The cost or revenue typically is measured by comparing the amount loaned with the amount repaid. Thus, if $100 is borrowed and $110 is repaid one year later, the interest cost (revenue) is $10 and the interest rate is 10 percent per annum ($10/$100). But there is more to the concept of interest than the amount that is recorded as interest revenue or interest expense. The foregone opportunity to earn interest must be considered. If you have money and earn no interest on it, you have a cost in the sense of a revenue foregone.

The concept of the time value of money stems from the logical preference for a dollar today rather than a dollar at any future date. Most individuals would prefer having a dollar today rather than at some future date because: (1) the risk exists that the future dollar will never be received; and (2) if the dollar is on hand now, it can be invested resulting in an increase in total dollars possessed at that future date.

Most business decisions involve a comparison of cash flows in and out of the firm. To be useful in decision making, such comparisons must be in terms of dollars of the same point in time. That is, the dollars held now must be accumulated or rolled forward or future dollars must be discounted or brought back to today before comparisons are valid. Such comparisons involve future and present value concepts.

Future Value

The **future value** or **worth** of any investment is the amount to which a sum of money invested today will grow in a stated time period at a specified interest rate. The interest involved may be simple interest or compound interest. **Simple interest** is interest on principal only. For example, $1,000 invested today for two years at 12 percent simple interest will grow to $1,240 since interest is $120 per year. The principal of $1,000, plus 2 × $120, is equal to $1,240. **Compound interest** is interest on principal and on interest of prior periods. For example, $1,000 invested for two years at 12 percent compounded annually will grow to $1,254.40. Interest for the first year is $120, ($1,000 × 0.12). For the second year, interest is earned on the principal plus the interest of the previous year, $120. Thus, the interest for the second year is $134.40, ($1,120 × 0.12). Future value at the end of year two is $1,254.40. The $1,254.40 is found by adding the second year's interest ($134.40) to the value at the beginning of the second year $1,120. These computations of future value may be portrayed graphically (see Illustration 9.5).

Illustration 9.5 shows the growth of $1,000 to $1,254.40 when the interest rate is 12 percent compounded annually. The effect of compounding is $14.40—the interest in the second year that was based on the interest computed for the first year, or $120 × 0.12 = $14.40.

The task of computing the future value to which any invested amount will grow at a given rate for a stated period is aided by the use of interest tables. An example is Table I in Appendix C at the end of this text. To use the Appendix C tables, first determine the number of compounding periods involved. The compounding period tells how frequently interest is computed and added to the base upon which future interest calculations will be based. A compounding period may be any length of time, such as a day, a month, a quarter, a half-year, or a year, but normally not more than a year. The number of compounding periods is equal to the number of years in the life of the investment times the number of the compoundings in a year. Five years compounded annually is five periods, five years compounded quarterly is 20 periods, and so on.

Next, determine the interest rate per compounding period. Interest rates are usually quoted in annual terms. In fact, federal law requires statement of the interest rate in annual terms in certain situations. Divide the annual rate by the number of compounding periods per year to get the proper rate per period. Only with an annual compounding will the annual rate be the rate per period.

Illustration 9.5
GRAPHIC ILLUSTRATION OF FUTURE VALUE

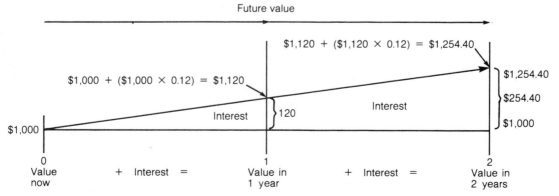

All other cases involve a lower rate. For example, the rate per period will be 1 percent if the annual rate is 12 percent, compounded monthly.

To use the table in a given situation, find the number of periods involved in the Period column. Move across the table to the right, stopping in the column headed by the interest rate per period, which yields a number called a factor. The factor shows the amount to which an investment of $1 will grow for the periods and the rate involved. To compute future value of the investment, multiply the number of dollars in the given situation by this factor. For example, suppose your parents tell you that they will invest $8,000 at 12 percent for four years and give you the amount to which this investment will grow if you graduate from college in four years. How much will you receive at the end of four years if the interest rate is 12 percent compounded annually? How much will you receive if the interest rate is 12 percent compounded quarterly?

In Appendix C, Table I, in the 4 period row in the 12 percent column, you find the factor 1.57352. Multiply the factor by $8,000 to get $12,588.16 as the answer to the first question. Then look for 16 in the Period column and under 3 percent for the needed factor to answer the second question. The factor is 1.60471, and the value of your investment is $12,837.68. The more frequent compounding would add $249.52 ($12,837.68 − $12,588.16) to the value of your investment. The reason for this difference in amounts is that 12 percent compounded quarterly is a higher rate than 12 percent compounded annually.

Present Value

Present value is the current worth of a future cash receipt and is essentially the reverse of future value. In future value, a sum of money is possessed now and its future worth must be calculated. In present value, rights to future cash receipts are possessed now and their current worth is to be calculated. Future cash receipts are discounted to find their present value. To discount future receipts is to deduct interest from them. If the proper interest rate is used, it should not matter to you whether you have cash in an amount equal to present value or have the rights to the larger amount of future receipts.

Assume that you have the right to receive $1,000 in one year. If the appropriate interest rate is 12 percent compounded annually, what is the present value of this $1,000 future cash receipt? You know that the present value is less than $1,000 because $1,000 due in one year is not worth $1,000 today. You also know that the $1,000 due in one year is equal to some amount, P, plus interest on P at 12 percent for one year. In other words, $P + 0.12P = \$1,000$, and $1.12P = \$1,000$. Dividing $1,000 by 1.12, you get $892.86. If the $1,000 was due in two years, you would find its present value

269

QUESTIONS

1. Why might a business have need for short-term financing even when cash inflows are expected to exceed cash outflows?

2. How is interest calculated on a note?

3. How is interest introduced into a situation where a note is non-interest-bearing?

4. What does it mean for a note to be dishonored?

5. Describe the process of discounting a note receivable. What happens if the maker fails to pay the bank at maturity?

6. How are the cash proceeds determined when a note receivable is discounted?

7. What effect does the maturity date have on the carrying value of notes payable?

8. On a mortgage note payable does the interest expense per period increase or decrease over time? Why?

9. What two promises are made by the issuer of a bond to the lender, or bondholder?

10. When bonds are issued between interest dates, why is it appropriate that the issuing corporation receive cash equal to the amount of accrued interest in addition to the issue price of the bonds?

11. Why would anyone be willing to pay more than face value for bonds?

12. Conceptually, how is the price at which a bond will sell computed?

13. What method(s) is (are) used to amortize discounts and premiums on bonds?

14. How are losses or gains from the early extinguishment of debt to be reported?

15. Describe the accounting for bonds purchased at a discount when they are to be held to maturity.

16. For long-term bond investments, in which account(s) is (are) premiums and discounts carried?

17. When bond investments are sold, what must be done regarding interest before recording the gain or loss?

18. (Based on the chapter appendix) Why isn't Table II used for finding the present value of an annuity?

EXERCISES

1. John Swift goes to the bank and asks to borrow $4,000 at 10½ percent for a 60-day period. Using T-accounts, show how to record the proceeds received for each of the following alternatives:

   a. He signs a note for $4,000. Interest is deducted from the face amount in determining the proceeds.

   b. He received $4,000, and signs a note for the interest plus the amount borrowed.

c. He receives $4,000 and signs an interest-bearing note for that amount. The interest is to be paid at the maturity date.

2. Using T-accounts, give the entries at the maturity date for each of the alternatives given in 1, assuming that the loan is repaid. Also assume that repayment is made before the end of the accounting period.

3. Hale gives his 90-day, $40,000, 12 percent note to Floyd in exchange for merchandise. Using T-accounts, give the entries each will make on the maturity date, assuming that payment is made.

4. Referring to 3 above and using T-accounts, give the entries for each at the maturity date assuming that Hale defaults.

5. Norris Company gave a 120-day, $10,000, 12 percent note to Forest Company on July 6, 1986. Forest Company sold the note to the bank on August 20, 1986. The rate of discount was 12 percent. Determine the entries each company would make on the date of discounting.

6. In Exercise 5, if Norris Company fails to make payment on the maturity date, what entry or entries are required on the books of each company?

7. On December 31, 1986, Apple Company issued $100,000 face value of 10-year, 8 percent bonds for cash of $82,075, a price to yield 11 percent. The bonds pay interest semiannually and mature December 31, 1996.

   a. State which was higher: the effective rate of interest or the nominal rate.

   b. Compute the bond interest expense for the first six months of 1987 using the interest method.

8. Alex Company purchased $20,000 of the bonds issued by Apple Company (Exercise 7) as a long-term investment. Prepare a journal entry to record the investment. Prepare the entry to record the interest revenue earned on the bonds in the first six months of 1987 using the interest method.

9. Compute the annual interest expense on the bonds in Exercise 7 and the interest revenue on the bonds in Exercise 8 assuming the bond discount is amortized under the straight-line method.

10. After recording the payment of the interest coupon due on July 1, 1986, the accounts of the Brook Company showed Bonds Payable of $200,000 and Premium on Bonds Payable of $7,048. The $200,000 face value, five-year, 12 percent bonds, (interest payable semiannually on January 1 and July 1), were originally issued to yield 10 percent. Prepare the entry to accrue interest on December 31, 1986. Use the interest method.

11. On April 30, 1986, the end of its fiscal year, Roxa Company prepared an adjusting entry to record $2,222 of accrued interest revenue earned on $50,000 face value of 12 percent bonds that were purchased on January 1, 1986, to yield 14 percent. The bonds are dated January 1, 1986, and call for semiannual interest payments on July 1 and January

1. Prepare the entry to record the interest revenue, the discount amortization, and the collection of interest on July 1, 1986.

12. On June 30, 1986 (a semiannual interest payment date), Paul Company redeemed all of its $200,000 face value of 10 percent bonds outstanding by calling them at 105. The bonds were originally issued on June 30, 1982, at 100. Prepare entries to record the payment of the interest and the redemption of the bonds on June 30, 1986.

13. (Based on the Appendix) Conceptually, what is the present worth of a lump-sum payment of $100,000 due in five years? If the going market rate of interest on investments of this type is 10 percent per year and the present value of $1 due in five years at 10 percent is 0.62092, what is its specific worth?

14. (Based on the Appendix) Conceptually, what is the present worth of a series of semiannual payments of $10,000 due at the end of each six months of the next five years? If the going market rate of interest on investments of this type is 10 percent per year and the present value of an annuity of $1 for 10 periods at 5 percent is 7.72173, what is its specific worth?

PROBLEMS

9–1. On November 1, 1986, the Chapman Company presented its own $48,000 120-day non-interest-bearing note to the B&D National Bank, which discounted it at 11 percent.

Required:

Using T-accounts, give the entries required on Chapman's books as of November 1, December 31 (the company's closing date), and the maturity date.

9–2. Following are selected transactions of the Cranwood Company:

Oct. 31 Presented its own 30-day, $30,000, non-interest-bearing note to the First State Bank, which discounted it at 11 percent.

Nov. 8 Received a $20,000, 30-day, 12 percent note from the Lively Company in settlement of an account receivable. The note is dated November 8.

15 Purchased merchandise by issuing its own 60-day note for $12,000. The note is dated November 15 and bears interest at 12 percent.

20 Sold the Lively Company note to the First State Bank, which discounted the note at 13 percent.

30 The First State Bank notified the Cranwood Company that it had charged the note of October 31 against the company's checking account.

Required:

Assume that all notes falling due after November 30 were paid in full on their due dates by their respective makers. Give the journal entries required on Cranwood's books for each of the above transactions and each of the necessary adjustments assuming a fiscal year accounting period ending on November 30. Also give the journal entries required on Cranwood's books for payment of the notes due after November 30.

9–3. Hunter Company is seeking to issue $200,000 face value of 10 percent, 15-year bonds. The bonds are dated June 30, 1986; call for semiannual interest payments; and mature on June 30, 2000.

Required:

a. Compute the price investors should offer if they seek a yield of 8 percent on these bonds. Also, compute the first six months' interest assuming the bonds are issued at this price. Use the interest method.

b. Repeat part *(a)* assuming investors seek a yield of 12 percent.

9–4. On July 1, 1986, Green Corporation issued $100,000 face value of 10 percent, 10-year bonds. The bonds call for semiannual interest payments and mature on July 1, 1986. Green received cash of $88,530, a price that yields 12 percent.

On September 30, 1986, Green also borrowed $50,000 on a 10-year mortgage note that called for 40 equal quarterly payments of $2,261. The note bears interest at 12 percent per year.

Required:

Assume that Green's fiscal year ended on March 31. Prepare entries to record the bond interest expense on January 1, 1987, and the adjustment needed on March 31, 1987, using the interest method. Also, prepare entries to record the first two quarterly payments on the mortgage note.

9–5. Allied Company issued $100,000 face value of 15 percent, 20-year bonds on October 1, 1986. The bonds are dated October 1, 1986, call for semiannual interest payments on April 1 and October 1, and are issued to yield 16 percent (8 percent per period).

Required:

a. Compute the amount received for the bonds.

b. Prepare an amortization schedule similar to that shown in Illustration 9.1. Enter data in the schedule for only the first two interest periods. Use the interest method.

c. Prepare journal entries to record issuance of the bonds, the first six months' interest expense on the bonds, and the adjustment needed on May 31, 1987, assuming Allied's fiscal year ends on that date.

9–6. Bowen Company purchased $10,000 face value of the Allied Company bonds (Problem 9–5) when they were issued on October 1, 1986, as a long-term investment.

Required:

   a. Prepare entries to record purchase of the bonds, receipt of the first six months' interest, and the adjustment needed on June 30, 1987, assuming a fiscal year ended on that date. Use the interest method.

   b. Assume that the Bowen Company sold all of these bonds on October 1, 1995, for cash of $9,950, after detaching the interest coupon due on this date. The bonds have a carrying value, properly adjusted to date, of $9,514. Prepare the journal entry to record the sale.

9–7. Cook Company issued $100,000 face value of 18 percent, 20-year bonds on October 1, 1986. The bonds are dated October 1, 1986, call for semiannual interest payments on April 1 and October 1, and are issued to yield 16 percent (8 percent per period).

Required:

   a. Compute the amount received for the bonds.

   b. Prepare an amortization schedule similar to that shown in Illustration 9.2. Enter data in the schedule for only the first two interest periods. Use the interest method.

   c. Prepare entries to record the issuance of the bonds, the first six months' interest on the bonds, and the adjustment needed on June 30, 1987, assuming Cook's fiscal year ends on that date.

9–8. Kent Corporation purchased $30,000 face value of the Cook bonds (Problem 9–7) when they were issued on October 1, 1986, as a long-term investment.

Required:

   a. Prepare journal entries to record the purchase of the bonds, the receipt of the first six months' interest, and the adjustment needed on September 30, 1987, assuming a fiscal year ending on that date. Use the interest method.

   b. Assume that on October 1, 1996, Cook called all of the bonds at 105. Kent received a check for $34,200, including $2,700 as payment of the semiannual interest due on this date. Prepare the entry to record the receipt of the $34,200. The properly adjusted carrying value of the bonds on this date was $32,959.

10 STATEMENT OF CHANGES IN FINANCIAL POSITION

A firm's income statement and balance sheet often do not provide answers to all the questions raised by users of financial statements. Questions such as the following are not answered by reviewing either or both the income statement or the balance sheet. How much working capital or cash was generated by operations? Why is such a profitable firm only able to pay such meager dividends? How much was spent for new plant and equipment, and where did the company get the funds for the expenditures? How was the company able to pay a dividend when it incurred a net loss for the year?

The statement that provides information to answer these types of questions is called the **statement of changes in financial position.** This statement reports the flows of funds into and out of a business in an accounting period and often is called a **funds statement.** The APB requires that a statement of changes in financial position be presented for each period for which an income statement and a balance sheet are presented.[1] This chapter defines several concepts of funds and illustrates the procedures used to prepare a statement of changes in financial position.

---

[1] APB, "Reporting Changes in Financial Position, *APB Opinion No. 19* (New York: AICPA, 1971), par. 7.

USES OF THE STATEMENT OF CHANGES IN FINANCIAL POSITION

The statement of changes in financial position summarizes the financing and investing activities of a firm for a period. It reports upon past management decisions regarding such matters as issuance of capital stock or sale of long-term bonds. The statement directly reports information that is otherwise obtainable only in bits and pieces from the balance sheets and statements of income and retained earnings. Included in the statement is information on cash or working capital flows which are vital to a firm's financial health. Such information is useful to management and all other interested parties, especially creditors and investors.

Management Uses

Management can use the statement of changes to determine why there are cash or working capital shortages if the company has been experiencing problems in these areas. Management may, after study of the information, change its dividend policy to conserve funds. Or the statement may show a flow of funds from operations large enough to finance all projected capital needs internally rather than through borrowings or stock issues. Since the statement presents all significant financing and investing activities, management can see the effects of its past major policy decisions in quantitative form by reviewing the statement of changes.

Creditor and Investor Uses

Information on the statement of changes in financial position may provide creditors and investors with valuable clues to:

1. The extent to which internally generated funds cover projected capital needs.
2. The likelihood of the company paying or increasing future dividends.
3. Management's preferences toward financing and investing.
4. The firm's ability to make principal and interest payments on its debt.
5. Whether, in the light of available resources, a planned expansion is feasible.

THE CONCEPT OF FUNDS

The term **funds** needs to be defined before changes in financial position can be measured. Funds are usually defined as either working capital or cash. Both definitions are included among the acceptable bases on which to prepare a statement of changes in financial position.

Funds Defined as Working Capital

Funds have typically been defined as working capital. **Working capital** is equal to current assets minus current liabilities. *Using the working capital definition of funds, any transaction that increases or decreases working* *capital is included in the statement of changes.* The borrowing of cash by the use of long-term bonds would be included because the transaction increases total current assets, thus increasing working capital. The purchase of a plant asset on a short-term credit basis would be included because it reduces working capital by increasing total current liabilities. Defining funds as working capital also permits exclusion of many routine transactions. Examples are collections of an account receivable or payments of an account payable. The first transaction merely substitutes one current asset (cash) for another (accounts receivable). The second transaction reduces a current asset (cash) and reduces a current liability (accounts payable). Both transactions change the **composition** of working capital, but not its **amount.**

Funds Defined as Cash

When funds are defined as cash, any transaction that increases or decreases cash is included in the statement of changes in financial position. Many examples can be given, including transactions involving cash received from collections of accounts receivable and from sale of plant assets, as well as cash payments to retire long-term or short-term debt. When the cash basis of funds is strictly applied, only transactions that affect cash are reported.

  Other significant financing and investing activities. Strict adherence to the cash or the working capital concept of funds could lead to the omission of significant transactions from the statement of changes in financial position. For example, a firm might double its assets by issuing common stock for some land and buildings. Since this transaction did not change the amount of working capital (no current asset or current liability was affected) nor did it change the amount of cash, it would not appear on the statement of changes if either of the above concepts of funds was strictly applied. But in developing the principles underlying the presentation of changes, *APB Opinion No. 19* requires a firm to report all significant financing and investing activities, regardless of whether cash or working capital is used to measure basic fund flows. Because the above transaction is a significant investing and financing event, it would be reported on the statement of changes.

Major Sources and Uses of Funds

No matter how the term *funds* is defined, there are some basic sources and uses of funds in a business. A source of funds is a transaction that brings cash or working capital into the business, while a use of funds is a transaction that removes cash or working capital from the business. The major source of funds in a firm is operations. Sales creates inflows of funds while expenses cause outflows. In general, then, net income produces a positive flow of funds while a net loss drains funds out of a firm in a negative flow. The major

Illustration 10.1
SOURCES AND USES OF FUNDS

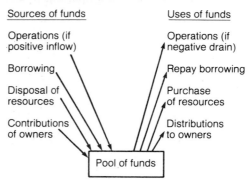

sources and uses of funds are portrayed graphically in Illustration 10.1.

Funds from Operations

The amount of funds provided by operations differs from net income because certain items that are included in determining net income do not affect either cash or working capital. The most common example is depreciation expense. The journal entry to record depreciation requires a debit to an expense account and a credit to an accumulated depreciation account. Neither account is a cash or working capital account, which suggests that the transaction has no effect on funds. But depreciation was deducted in arriving at net income. As a result, net income understates funds from operations. If net income is used as a starting point in measuring funds from operations, depreciation expense must be added back to net income.

Consider the following example. Company A had net income for the year of $20,000 after deducting depreciation of $10,000. Company B had a net loss for the year of $4,000 after deducting $10,000 of depreciation. Although A earned income and B experienced a loss, both companies have a positive funds flow from operations as shown below:

	Company A	*Company B*
Net income (loss)	$20,000	$(4,000)
Add depreciation expense (which did not require use of funds)	10,000	10,000
Positive funds flow from operations	$30,000	$ 6,000

Only if B's loss had exceeded $10,000 would there have been a negative flow of funds from operations for the company.

There are other expenses and losses which are added back to

net income because they do not reduce the amount of funds which flow into the company. These items include depletion expense, amortization of intangible assets such as patents and goodwill, amortization of discount on bonds payable, and losses from disposals of noncurrent assets. These addbacks are often called **nonworking capital (nonfund) charges or expenses.**

To illustrate why bond discount amortization is added back to net income, consider the following journal entry that would be recorded to amortize that discount:

```
Interest Expense  . . . . . . . . . . . . .    400
     Interest Payable . . . . . . . . . . .            370
     Discount on Bonds Payable . . . . . . .             30
   To record interest expense and amortize bond dis-
   count.
```

The debit to interest expense reduces net income by $400, but the effect on working capital or funds is only $370, the amount credited to the current liability account, Interest Payable. Therefore, the deduction from net income for interest expense was $30 larger than the actual effect on working capital. The $30 is the amount of bond discount amortization that must be added back to net income.

To illustrate the addback of the losses from disposals of noncurrent assets, assume that Quick Company sold a piece of equipment for $6,000. The equipment had cost $10,000 and had accumulated depreciation of $3,000. The journal entry to record the sale is:

```
Cash  . . . . . . . . . . . . . . . . . .   6,000
Accumulated Depreciation  . . . . . . . . . 3,000
Loss on Sale of Equipment . . . . . . . . . 1,000
     Equipment  . . . . . . . . . . . . . .          10,000
   To record disposal of equipment at a loss.
```

The only funds account in the above journal entry is Cash. The $6,000 inflow from the sale of the equipment will be shown on the funds statement as a source of funds. The loss amount does not reduce working capital and is added back in converting net income to funds from operations.

There are also items called **nonworking capital (nonfund) credits or revenues** that must be deducted from net income in order to compute funds provided by operations. Such items include amortization of bond premiums, gains from disposals of noncurrent assets, earnings from investments carried under the equity method, and amortization of discounts on bond investments. In regard to the latter, the journal entry to record interest earned on bond investments purchased at a discount is as follows:

```
Cash (Interest Receivable)  . . . . . . . . .   780
Bond Investments  . . . . . . . . . . . . .      20
     Interest Revenue  . . . . . . . . . . .            800
   To record interest earned on bond investments and
   amortize the bond discount.
```

The funds effect is the $780, but $800 was included in net income. So the $20 investment discount needs to be deducted from net income to show the actual funds effect. The $20 is a nonfund producing revenue item.

The next section of the chapter covers the various procedures used to prepare the statement of changes in financial position on a working capital basis. Then, the statement of changes in financial position focusing on cash flows is presented.

STATEMENT OF CHANGES IN FINANCIAL POSITION—WORKING CAPITAL BASIS

The financial statements and additional data for the Welby Company, Illustration 10.2, will be used to prepare the company's statement of changes in financial position on a working capital basis. To prepare the statement, the change in working capital is first determined, and then all of the noncurrent accounts are analyzed for changes that affected working capital.

Determining the Change in Working Capital

Opinion No. 19 states that a separate **statement of changes in working capital** should accompany the statement of changes in financial position. Such a statement is presented in Illustration 10.3. Alternatively, a **schedule of changes in working capital components** may be presented immediately under the statement of changes in financial position, as in Illustration 10.4. This form will be used in the problems at the end of the chapter.

In Illustration 10.3, note that changes in current assets cause working capital to change in the same direction, while changes in current liabilities cause working capital to change in the opposite direction. Thus, both the $10,000 increase in accounts receivable and the $5,000 decrease in accounts payable increased working capital. The $4,000 decrease in inventory and the $2,000 increase in accured liabilities decreased working capital. The schedule shows that Welby's working capital increased $20,000 during the year. The $20,000 increase in working capital is what must be explained by analyzing the noncurrent accounts. The statement of changes in financial position reports the causes of the change in working capital.

Analyzing the Noncurrent Accounts

At first, it may seem quite unusual to seek causes of the change in working capital by looking at the noncurrent (nonworking capital) accounts. But bear in mind that a transaction which is recorded **solely** in two working capital accounts can never increase or decrease working capital. Consider the effects upon working capital of collections of receivables, purchases of merchandise, and payment of accounts payable. These transactions change the **composition** of working capital, but not its **amount**. The noncurrent accounts must be analyzed for transactions affecting the amount of working capital.

Illustration 10.2
FINANCIAL STATEMENTS AND OTHER DATA

WELBY COMPANY
Balance Sheet

	December 31	
	1986	*1985*
Assets		
Cash	$ 21,000	$ 10,000
Accounts receivable	30,000	20,000
Inventory	26,000	30,000
Plant assets	70,000	50,000
Accumulated depreciation	(10,000)	(5,000)
Total assets	$137,000	$105,000
Liabilities and Stockholders' Equity		
Accounts payable	$ 10,000	$ 15,000
Accrued liabilities	2,000	0
Common stock ($10 par value)	90,000	60,000
Retained earnings	35,000	30,000
Total liabilities and stockholders' equity	$137,000	$105,000

WELBY COMPANY
Income Statement
For the Year Ended December 31, 1986

Sales		$140,000
Cost of goods sold		100,000
Gross margin		$ 40,000
Operating expenses and taxes	$ 25,000	
Depreciation	5,000	30,000
Net income		$ 10,000

Additional data:

1. Plant assets purchased for cash during 1986, $20,000.
2. Common stock with a par value of $30,000 was issued at par for cash.
3. Cash dividends declared in 1984, $5,000.

In this case, there are four noncurrent accounts to analyze: Plant Assets, Accumulated Depreciation, Common Stock, and Retained Earnings.

1. Because of the importance of working capital provided by operations, the analysis of the noncurrent accounts begins by reviewing the Retained Earnings account. Retained Earnings is the account to which net income or loss for the period was closed. The $5,000 increase in this account consists of $10,000 of net income less $5,000 of dividends. The net income amount can be found in the income statement. Both net income and dividends must be entered on the statement of changes in financial position in Illustration 10.4. The $5,000 of dividends reduced working capital

Illustration 10.3
STATEMENT OF CHANGES IN WORKING CAPITAL

WELBY COMPANY
Statement of Changes in Working Capital
For the Year Ended December 31, 1986

	December 31		Working Capital	
	1986	1985	Increase	Decrease
Current assets:				
Cash	$21,000	$10,000	$11,000	
Accounts receivable	30,000	20,000	10,000	
Inventory	26,000	30,000		$ 4,000
Total current assets	$77,000	$60,000		
Current liabilities:				
Accounts payable	$10,000	$15,000	5,000	
Accrued liabilities	2,000	–0–		2,000
Total current liabilities	$12,000	$15,000		
Working capital	$65,000	$45,000		
Increase in working capital				20,000
			$26,000	$26,000

when they were declared and paid. The declaration of dividends is a **use of working capital,** and is shown under **financial resources applied.** The $10,000 net income is used as the starting figure in determining working capital from operations. Net income of $10,000 is entered on the statement in the financial resources provided section under **working capital from operations.**

2. The plant assets account increased by $20,000 during the year. The additional data indicate that $20,000 of plant assets were purchased during the period. A purchase of plant assets is a use of funds and is entered under **financial resources applied.**

3. The $5,000 increase in the accumulated depreciation account equals the amount of depreciation expense for the period. Because depreciation does not affect or use up working capital, it must be added back to net income to convert net income to working capital from operations. **Working capital from operations** could be measured **directly** by deducting only those expenses that affect working capital from sales. For the Welby Company, the computation would be: $140,000 — $100,000 — $25,000 = $15,000. But, in actual practice, the indirect or addback method is used almost exclusively. The **indirect or addback method** is a way of determining working capital from operations that starts with net income and adjusts for expenses and revenues that do not affect working capital. Two reasons for this preference are: (a) the details of the income statement need not be repeated, and (b) the addback

Illustration 10.4
STATEMENT OF CHANGES IN FINANCIAL POSITION—WORKING CAPITAL BASIS

WELBY COMPANY
Statement of Changes in Financial Position—Working Capital Basis
For the Year Ended December 31, 1986

Financial resources provided:

Working capital from operations:		
Net income		$10,000
Add nonworking capital expenses:		
Depreciation		5,000
Working capital from operations		$15,000
Issuance of common stock		30,000
Total financial resources provided		$45,000
Financial resources applied:		
Purchase plant assets	$20,000	
Dividends	5,000	
Total financial resources applied		25,000
Increase in working capital		$20,000

Schedule of changes in working capital
  components

Increase (decrease) in current assets:		
Cash		$11,000
Accounts receivable		10,000
Inventory		(4,000)
		$17,000
Increase (decrease) in current liabilities:		
Accounts payable	$ (5,000)	
Accrued liabilities	2,000	3,000
Increase in working capital		$20,000

method's use of net income ties in directly to the income statement.

4. The $30,000 increase in common stock resulted from the issuance of stock at par as disclosed in the additional data. The $30,000 is entered as a source of working capital under **financial resources provided.**

The analysis of the noncurrent accounts is now complete. Note that the current accounts were not dealt with except to find the net change in working capital which is reported as the final item in the statement of changes in financial position.

The completed statement of changes in financial position and schedule of changes in working capital components are shown in Illustration 10.4. The headings **Sources of working capital** and **Uses of working capital** could have been used instead of the all-inclusive headings of **Financial resources provided** and **Financial resources applied.** The latter headings seem appropriate because of the APB requirement of reporting all significant investing and financing activities.

STATEMENT OF CHANGES IN FINANCIAL POSITION—CASH BASIS

Having presented a simple illustration showing the preparation of a statement of changes in financial position that focused on working capital, a statement of changes on a cash basis will be illustrated. Such a statement deals primarily with reporting the sources and uses of cash and is often referred to simply as a **cash flow statement.**

A cash basis statement of changes in financial position differs from one focusing on working capital primarily in the funds from operations section. A cash basis statement reports both cash and working capital from operations. **Cash flow from operations** is the net amount of cash received or disbursed on items which normally appear on the income statement and is obtained by converting accrual basis net income to a cash basis amount.

Cash Provided by Operations

There are two steps in converting net income to cash basis income. First, convert net income to working capital from operations by adding back or deducting from net income those items that did not use up or provide working capital. Second, convert working capital from operations to cash from operations by including the changes that occurred in current accounts other than cash. Applying these two steps to the Welby Company financial statements and other data in Illustration 10.2 yields the following schedule:

Net income		$10,000
Add expenses not reducing working capital—depreciation		5,000
Working capital from operations		$15,000
Effects of changes in components of operating working capital on cash:		
Increase in accounts receivable	$(10,000)	
Decrease in inventory	4,000	
Decrease in accounts payable	(5,000)	
Increase in accured liabilities	2,000	(9,000)
Cash provided by operations		$ 6,000

The $10,000 increase in accounts receivable is deducted from accrual basis net income to convert it to cash basis income. If accounts receivable increased in a period, sales to customers exceeded collections from customers. Accrual basis sales revenue is greater than cash basis sales revenue, and net income needs to be reduced by $10,000.

To clarify the effect of the inventory change upon the conversion, assume that all purchases are for cash. Cost of goods sold on a cash basis is the amount paid for merchandise during the period. Purchases would be $96,000, computed as follows:

Ending inventory	$ 26,000
+ Cost of goods sold	100,000
Cost of goods available for sale . . .	$126,000
− Beginning inventory	30,000
Purchases	$ 96,000

If all purchases are for cash, cost of goods sold under the cash basis is $96,000, which is $4,000 less than the $100,000 accrual basis amount. Thus, $4,000 must be added to accrual basis net income to convert it to the cash basis.

But, because accounts payable changed, purchases were on account. Accounts payable decreased during the year, so suppliers were paid more in cash during the year than was purchased from them. Thus, expenses on a cash basis were $5,000 greater than on an accrual basis. So, $5,000 is deducted from accrual basis net income to convert it to cash basis.

Alternatively, since cost of goods sold on a cash basis is the amount of cash paid for goods during the period, the following calculation could have been made rather than the two preceding computations:

Accounts payable, January 1	$ 15,000
Purchases (from prior schedule)	96,000
Total	$111,000
Accounts payable, December 31	10,000
Cash paid to suppliers during the year . .	$101,000

Cash basis cost of goods sold is $101,000, or $1,000 more than the accrual basis amount. Net income on a cash basis is, then, $1,000 less than the accrual basis amount. The $1,000 deduction agrees with the net amount of the individual analyses: $5,000 deducted for the decrease in accounts payable, and $4,000 added for the decrease in inventory nets out to a $1,000 deduction.

Accrued liabilities would be handled in a manner similar to accounts payable. Prepaid expenses would be treated the same as accounts receivable or inventory. These conversion procedures can be summarized as follows:

For changes in these working capital items:	Make these adjustments to convert accrual basis net income to cash basis net income:	
	Add a(n)	*Deduct a(n)*
Accounts receivable	Decrease	Increase
Inventory	Decrease	Increase
Prepaid expenses	Decrease	Increase
Accounts payable	Increase	Decrease
Accrued liabilities	Increase	Decrease

Notice in this summary that in converting from the accrual to cash basis, all changes in current assets accounts are handled in a similar manner. All changes in current liability accounts are also handled in a similar manner, but that manner is exactly the opposite from the handling of the current asset changes.

The complete adjustment or conversion procedure used in the following comprehensive example is summarized below:

Accrual basis net income
+ Expenses and losses not reducing working capital
− Revenues and gains not producing working capital
= Working capital from operations
+ or − Changes in working capital accounts related to operations
= Cash from operations

Cash Basis Statement Preparation

The complete statement of changes in financial position on a cash basis is presented in Illustration 10.5. A comparison of this statement with the one in Illustration 10.4 shows that the two statements are virtually identical, except for the section **Effects of changes in components of operating working capital on cash** in the cash basis

Illustration 10.5
STATEMENT OF CHANGES IN FINANCIAL POSITION—CASH BASIS

WELBY COMPANY
Statement of Changes in Financial Position—Cash Basis
For the Year Ended December 31, 1986

Financial resources provided:		
Cash from operations:		
Net income		$10,000
Add nonworking capital expenses:		
Depreciation		5,000
Working capital from operations		$15,000
Effects of changes in components of operating working capital on cash:		
Increase in accounts receivable	$(10,000)	
Decrease in inventory	4,000	
Decrease in accounts payable	(5,000)	
Increase in accrued liabilities	2,000)	(9,000)
Cash provided by operations		$ 6,000
Issuance of common stock		30,000
Total financial resources provided		$36,000
Financial resources applied:		
Purchase plant assets	$ 20,000	
Dividends	5,000	
Total financial resources applied		25,000
Increase in Cash		$11,000
Cash, December 31, 1985		10,000
Cash, December 31, 1986		$21,000

statement in Illustration 10.5. There are two reasons for this similarity:

1. Most sources and uses of funds involve cash receipts and disbursements and would be reported in the same way whether cash or working capital is the focus of attention.
2. The cash basis statement was prepared by focusing on working capital first and then making the adjustments necessary to convert working capital from operations to cash from operations.

A COMPREHENSIVE ILLUSTRATION

Presented and discussed below is a more complete example of the procedures followed to prepare a cash basis statement of changes in financial position. A working paper (shown later in Illustration 10.8) is used to aid in preparing the statement. The working paper in Illustration 10.8 could, with only minor revision (described later), be adapted to a working capital focus.

The basic data for the example are found in Illustration 10.6 and Illustration 10.7, which present the income statement and comparative balance sheets of The United States Corporation. Assume the following information about the noncurrent accounts is available:

1. There were no purchases of investments during the year. Investments with an $8,000 cost were sold for $9,700.
2. Land and buildings valued at $65,000 ($45,000 for the buildings and $20,000 for the land) were acquired, subject to a mortgage note of $35,000.
3. During the year, the corporation disposed of equipment which had an original cost of $20,000 and accumulated depreciation of $16,500. The equipment was sold for $2,600.
4. The common stock was sold for cash.

The working paper in Illustration 10.8 for The United States Corporation is used to analyze the transactions and prepare the statement of changes in financial position. The discussion which follows will describe the items and trace their effects in the entries made on the working paper.

The steps in preparing the working paper are as follow:

1. Enter the account balances of all balance sheet accounts at the beginning of the period in the first column and at the end of the period in the fourth column. Notice the debit items are listed first, followed by the credit items.
2. Total the debits and the credits in the first and fourth columns to determine that debits equal credits in each column.
3. Write **financial resources provided** immediately below the total

Illustration 10.6
STATEMENT OF INCOME AND RETAINED EARNINGS

THE UNITED STATES CORPORATION
Statement of Income and Retained Earnings
For the Year Ended December 31, 1986

Net sales		$1,464,200
Cost of goods sold		871,150
Gross margin		$ 593,050
Operating expenses:		
Salaries	$215,000	
Depreciation expense ($3,250, buildings; $31,050, equipment)	34,300	
Supplies	7,320	
Advertising	90,000	
Taxes, payroll and other	26,000	
General administrative expenses	123,780	
Total operating expenses		496,400
Net income from operations		$ 96,650
Other revenue:		
Interest earned	$ 1,950	
Gain on sale of long-term investments	1,700	3,650
		$ 100,300
Other expenses:		
Interest expense	$ 3,800	
Loss on sale of equipment	900	4,700
Net income before federal income taxes		$ 95,600
Deduct: Federal income taxes		45,250
Net income to retained earnings		$ 50,350
Retained earnings, January 1		84,100
		$ 134,450
Deduct: Dividends declared		18,000
Retained earnings, December 31		$ 116,450

of the credit items. Skip sufficient lines on which to record all sources of funds. Then write **financial resources applied.**

4. Analyzing entries are entered in the second and third columns. The entries, which may be made in any order, serve two functions: *(a)* they explain the change in each account and *(b)* they record the sources and uses of funds. These entries will be discussed individually.

5. Total the debits and credits in the second and third columns. There will be one pair of totals for the balance sheet items and another pair for the sources and uses of funds. The bottom portion of the working paper is used to prepare the formal statement of changes in financial position.

Completing the Working Paper

The working paper in Illustration 10.8 is completed by analyzing the change in each noncash balance sheet account. Changes in cash

Illustration 10.7
COMPARATIVE BALANCE SHEET

THE UNITED STATES CORPORATION
Comparative Balance Sheets
December 31, 1985, and 1986

	1986	1985	*Increase Decrease**
Assets			
Current assets:			
Cash	$ 46,300	$ 40,900	$ 5,400
Accounts receivable (net)	112,160	101,000	11,160
Inventories	130,600	115,300	15,300
Prepaid expenses	3,100	4,700	1,600*
Total current assets	$292,160	$261,900	$30,260
Investments	$ 17,000	$ 25,000	$ 8,000*
Property, plant, and equipment:			
Land	$100,000	$ 80,000	$20,000
Buildings	175,000	130,000	45,000
Accumulated depreciation—buildings	(29,750)	(26,500)	(3,250)
Equipment	198,000	175,000	23,000
Accumulated depreciation—equipment	(57,650)	(43,100)	(14,550)
Total property, plant, and equipment	$385,600	$315,400	$70,200
Total assets	$694,760	$602,300	$92,460
Liabilities and Stockholders' Equity			
Current liabilities:			
Accounts payable	$ 91,420	$ 86,870	$ 4,550
Accrued liabilities	9,890	12,230	2,340*
Estimated federal income tax liability	12,000	14,100	2,100*
Total current liabilities	$113,310	$113,200	$ 110
Long-term liabilities:			
Mortgage note payable, 10% (on land and buildings)	$ 35,000	$ –0–	$35,000
Bonds payable, 8%, due 1986	40,000	40,000	–0–
Total long-term liabilities	$ 75,000	$ 40,000	$35,000
Total liabilities	$188,310	$153,200	$35,110
Stockholders' equity:			
Common stock, stated value, $50 per share	$390,000	$365,000	$25,000
Retained earnings	116,450	84,100	32,350
Total stockholders' equity	$506,450	$449,100	$57,350
Total liabilities and stockholders' equity	$694,760	$602,300	$92,460

Illustration 10.8

UNITED STATES CORPORATION
Working Paper for Statement of Changes in Financial Position—Cash Basis
For the Year Ended December 31, 1986

	Account Balances 12/31/85	Analysis of Transactions for 1986		Account Balances 12/31/86
		Debit	Credit	
Debits				
Cash	40,900	(1) 5,400		46,300
Accounts receivable	101,000	(10) 11,160		112,160
Inventories	115,300	(11) 15,300		130,600
Prepaid expenses	4,700		(12) 1,600	3,100
Investments	25,000		(2) 8,000	17,000
Land	80,000	(3) 20,000		100,000
Buildings	130,000	(3) 45,000		175,000
Equipment	175,000	(5) 43,000	(4) 20,000	198,000
Totals	671,900			782,160
Credits				
Accumulated depreciation— buildings	26,500		(6) 3,250	29,750
Accumulated depreciation— equipment	43,100	(4) 16,500	(6) 31,050	57,650
Accounts payable	86,870		(13) 4,550	91,420
Accrued liabilities	12,230	(14) 2,340		9,890
Federal income tax liability	14,100	(15) 2,100		12,000
Mortgage note payable	–0–		(3) 35,000	35,000
Bonds payable	40,000			40,000
Common stock	365,000		(7) 25,000	390,000
Retained earnings	84,100	(9) 18,000	(8) 50,350	116,450
Totals	671,900	178,800	178,800	782,160

can be explained by changes in the noncash balance sheet accounts because every change in cash was accompanied by a change in a noncash balance sheet account. After entries have been properly made to analyze all changes in noncash balance sheet accounts, the working paper will show all sources and uses of cash. The explana-

Illustration 10.8 *(concluded)*

	Account Balances 12/31/85	Analysis of Transactions for 1986		Account Balances 12/13/86
		Debit	Credit	
Financial resources provided:				
By operations:				
Net income		(8) 50,350		
Depreciation—buildings		(6) 3,250		
Depreciation—equipment		(6) 31,050		
Loss on sale of equipment		(4) 900		
Gain on sale of investments			(2) 1,700	
Increase in accounts receivable			(10) 11,160	
Increase in inventories			(11) 15,300	
Decrease in prepaid expenses		(12) 1,600		
Increase in accounts payable		(13) 4,550		
Decrease in accrued liabilities			(14) 2,340	
Decrease in federal income tax				
liability			(15) 2,100	
Other sources:				
Sale of investments		(2) 9,700		
Assumption of mortgage note		(3) 35,000		
Sale of equipment		(4) 2,600		
Issuance of common stock		(7) 25,000		
Financial resources applied:				
Acquisition of land and buildings			(3) 65,000	
Acquisition of equipment			(5) 43,000	
Payment of cash dividends			(9) 18,000	
Increase in cash for year			(1) 5,400	
Totals		164,000	164,000	

tions below are keyed to the entries on the working paper by numbers.

Entry 1. The beginning and ending cash balances are compared to determine the change for the year, which is a $5,400 increase.

An entry is made on the working paper debiting Cash for $5,400 and crediting Increase in Cash for the Year under financial resources applied. This entry indicates that of the cash flowing into the company during the year, $5,400 was used to increase the Cash balance. The entry also sets out the change in cash that the statement seeks to explain. No further attention need be paid to cash in completing the working paper.

Attention is now directed toward changes in other balance sheet accounts. These accounts can be dealt with in any order. But, in order to group certain items, the noncurrent accounts are analyzed first.

Entry 2. Investments is the first noncurrent account. The additional information discloses that investments were sold at a gain which was recorded in the following manner:

Cash	9,700	
Investments		8,000
Gain on Sale of Investments		1,700

Since cash changes and their causes are the focus of the working paper, the following entry is made on the working paper to show the source of cash.

Sale of Investments	9,700	
Investments		8,000
Gain on Sale of Investments		1,700

The working paper now shows $9,700 cash provided by sale of investments and a $1,700 reduction in cash provided by operations. The gain on sale of investments is removed from cash provided by operations and included as part of the cash provided by sale of investments. If the $9,700 cash received from the sale is reported and the gain is not removed from cash provided by operations, the $1,700 gain is shown or counted twice. Note that the working paper entry is identical to the original journal entry for the sale, except for the $9,700 debit. Instead of debiting Cash, a properly described source of cash is debited. The sources and uses of cash are shown in the lower section of the working paper. The $8,000 credit accounts fully for the decrease in the Investments account.

Entry 3. The changes in the Land and Buildings accounts resulted from the following entry:

Land	20,000	
Buildings	45,000	
Cash		30,000
Mortgage Note Payable		35,000

The transaction requires two entries on the working paper. First, Land and Buildings are debited for $20,000 and $45,000, respectively, and a cash applied item described as **Acquisition of land and buildings** is credited for $65,000. Second, a source of cash called **Assump-**

tion of Mortgage Note is debited and **Mortgage Note Payable** is credited for $35,000. In other words, the transaction is treated as if the mortgage note was issued for cash and then $65,000 cash had been spent to acquire land and buildings. This transaction is an example of a significant financing and investing activity that must be included on the statement even though it did not affect funds.

Entry 4. The Equipment account shows a net increase of $23,000 resulting from two transactions: a $43,000 purchase and a $20,000 retirement. The net change in the account must be analyzed to show both cash applied and cash provided. The amount shown under **Other sources** from sale of equipment is the amount received for the equipment. These data were included in the additional information given. The computation can be summarized as follows:

Cost of equipment sold	$20,000
Less: Accumulated depreciation	16,500
Book value of equipment sold	$ 3,500
Less: Loss on sale	900
Cash received	$ 2,600

The complete working paper entry for sale of equipment is:

Sale of Equipment	2,600	
Accumulated Depreciation—Equipment	16,500	
Loss on Sale of Equipment	900	
Equipment		20,000

This entry records cash provided by sale of equipment and explains part of the changes in Equipment and Accumulated Depreciation—Equipment. The loss is added back to net income as a noncash deduction in arriving at net income. The loss has exactly the same effect as depreciation, or the write-off of any noncash asset.

Entry 5. This entry debits the Equipment account and credits Acquisition of equipment for the $43,000 cash spent to acquire new equipment.

Entry 6. This entry adds $3,250 building depreciation and $31,050 equipment depreciation back to net income and credits the respective accumulated depreciation accounts. The $31,050 credit to the accumulated depreciation account for equipment less the $16,500 debit to this account in Entry 4 explain fully the increase in this account from $43,100 to $57,650.

Entry 7. This entry shows the $25,000 cash received from sale of common stock as an Other source of cash. The entry also explains completely the change in the Common Stock account. If stock had been sold for more than its stated value of $50 per share, the excess would be recorded in a separate Paid-In Capital in Excess of Stated Value account. But only the total amount of cash received from the issuance would have been reported on the statement of changes in financial position as a single figure because only the total amount received is significant.

Entry 8. The statement of retained earnings and the income statement reveal that net income for 1984 was $50,350. Entry 8 records the $50,350 as the starting point in measuring cash from operations and credits Retained Earnings as a partial explanation of the change in that account.

Entry 9. This entry debits Retained Earnings and credits Payment of Cash Dividends for the $18,000 of dividends declared and paid. The entry also completes the explanation of the change in Retained Earnings ($84,100 + $50,350 − $18,000 = $116,450).

If Retained Earnings had changed for reasons other than net income or cash dividends, the causes of the changes must be determined in order to decide whether they should be reported in the statement of changes in financial position. Transactions such as stock dividends and stock splits would not be reported because they lack significance from an analytical viewpoint and because these items never affect cash or working capital. But an entry must be made on the working paper to explain the changes caused by a stock dividend or split, even if cash was not affected. All changes in all noncash accounts must be explained to show that a change affecting cash was not overlooked.

The next task is to analyze changes in current accounts other than Cash. Most of these accounts are closely related to operations, and their changes are included in converting net income to cash from operations. The changes in the current accounts are analyzed in the manner previously discussed (see pages 286–88).

Entry 10. The $11,160 increase in accounts receivable must be deducted from net income when converting it to cash from operations. If accounts receivable increased, sales to customers exceeded cash received from customers. Accrual basis revenue and net income are larger than revenue (receipts) and net income on a cash basis. To convert net income to cash basis, the $11,160 must be deducted.

The working paper technique used makes the recording of these effects almost mechanical. Accounts Receivable must be debited for $11,160 to increase it from $101,000 to $112,160. If Accounts Receivable is debited, a credit must be entered for an item that can be entitled "Increase in Accounts Receivable." The increase is a deduction from net income in converting it to cash from operations.

Entry 11 is virtually a duplicate of entry 10, except that it involves inventories rather than receivables.

Entry 12 is similar to the above two entries, except that it is reversed because prepaid expenses decreased.

Entry 13 records the effect of an increase in accounts payable on net income in converting it to cash from operations.

Entries 14 and *15* record the effects of decreases in two other current liability accounts in converting net income to cash from operations.

The analysis of the noncash accounts is now complete. To be sure that a change has not been overlooked, the debits and credits in the middle two columns opposite the 1985 balances are added to or subtracted from those balances, line by line. If the working paper has been properly prepared, the results will be the 1986 balances listed in the fourth column. For example, the $43,000 debit is added to the beginning balance for Equipment, and the $20,000 credit deducted to get an ending balance of $198,000. Next, the debits and credits for the balance sheet account entries and for the funds statement items are added to make sure that they are equal in both sections. Note that entries made in the working paper are used only to derive cash flows into and out of the firm. These entries are not entered in the firm's accounting system because the transactions which caused the fund flows have already been recorded.

The Formal Statement

The data in the lower section of the working paper are now used to prepare the formal statement of changes in financial position shown in Illustration 10.9. A standard format has not been prescribed for this statement. Both the APB and FASB have recommended experimentation using alternative forms.

Several features of Illustration 10.9 should be noted. Its two sections are headed "Financial resources provided" and "Financial resources applied" reflecting the reporting of all significant financing and investing activities as required by *Opinion No. 19*. The headings are appropriate since an exchange involving assumption of liability on a mortgage note for land and buildings is reported. Note that the statement reports both working capital and cash provided by operations.

Losses on the Working Paper

If a firm incurs a net loss for a period, the entry on the working paper debits Retained Earnings and credits Net Loss under Financial Resources Provided by Operations. Then the net loss is adjusted for the nonfund items. After these adjustments, the firm may have funds provided by or applied to operations. If funds were applied to operations, all data relative to the net loss and its adjustments will be shown in the "Resources applied" section of the formal statement of changes in financial position.

Working Paper for Statement of Changes on a Working Capital Basis

Entries 2 through 9 shown above for a statement of changes prepared under the cash basis analyze noncurrent account changes which had a cash effect. Since cash is an element of working capital, the same entries would be made in preparing a statement of changes focusing on working capital.

Illustration 10.9
STATEMENT OF CHANGES IN FINANCIAL POSITION—CASH BASIS

THE UNITED STATES CORPORATION
Statement of Changes in Financial Position—Cash Basis
For the Year Ended December 31, 1986

Financial resources provided:

By operations:

Net income				$ 50,350
Add:	Charges not requiring outlay of funds:			
	Depreciation—building	$ 3,250		
	Depreciation—equipment	31,050		
	Loss on sale of equipment	900	35,200	
				$ 85,550
Deduct:	Credits not providing funds:			
	Gain on sale of investments		1,700	
Working capital provided by operations				$ 83,850
Effect of change in components of operating working capital on cash:				
	Increase in accounts receivable	$(11,160)		
	Increase in inventories	(15,300)		
	Decrease in prepaid expenses	1,600		
	Increase in accounts payable	4,550		
	Decrease in accrued liabilities	(2,340)		
	Decrease in federal income tax liability	(2,100)	(24,750)	
Cash provided from operations				$ 59,100
Other resources provided:				
	Sale of investments	$ 9,700		
	Sale of equipment	2,600		
	Issuance of common stock	25,000		
	Assumption of mortgage note	35,000	72,300	
	Total financial resources provided			$131,400

Financial resources applied:

Acquisition of land and building		$ 65,000	
Acquisition of equipment		43,000	
Payment of cash dividends		18,000	
Total financial resources applied			126,000
Increase in cash for the year			$ 5,400
Cash: Beginning of year			40,900
Cash: End of year			$ 46,300

The first line of a working paper for a statement of changes focusing on working capital for The United States Corporation would show $148,700 of working capital at the end of 1985 and $178,850 at the end of 1986. Entry 1 would debit Working Capital for $30,150 and credit Increase in Working Capital on the last line of the working paper. This single working capital amount would be substituted for the nine current asset and current liability accounts listed on the working paper for a cash basis statement of changes.

Also, note in The United States Corporation illustration that entries for net income and nonworking capital charges and credits are grouped to make it easy to compute working capital from operations. This amount is $83,850 which was computed by totaling the first five items in the lower section of the working paper in Illustration 10.8.

WORKING CAPITAL OR CASH FLOWS

In the past, statements of changes in financial position have generally focused on working capital flows. Such statements were prepared for several reasons. Information was needed about the flows of liquid assets (working capital) through a firm; such flows are the life-blood of a business. Constant changes in accounting principles yielded net income amounts that often were not good measures of such liquid asset flows from operations. Attention focused on working capital rather than cash because little significance was attached to the composition of working capital. Working capital turned over quickly enough so that if not now in cash form, it would be shortly.

The Shift toward Cash Flows

Recent events suggest that in the coming years statements of changes in financial position will focus increasingly upon cash flows. In the recent periods of high rates of inflation and depressed economic conditions, many firms experienced severe cash flow, not working capital, problems. The FASB noted the importance of cash flows in the Conceptual Framework Project, and made the statement "that the reporting of meaningful components of cash flows is generally more useful than reporting changes in working capital."[2] Shortly after publication of this statement, the Financial Executives Institute recommended that its members adopt the cash basis in preparing a statement of changes in financial position.[3] Approximately 95 percent of the companies with securities traded on the New York Stock Exchange and the American Stock Exchange are represented in the Financial Executives Institute.

The shifting of attention from working capital flows to cash flows also is supported by developments in modern finance. The investment decision is seen more clearly as one in which cash outlays are compared with expected cash returns, appropriately discounted for time and risk. Management, investors, and creditors are all alike in that each invests cash to get future cash returns. Thus, information is needed to enable users to make predictions of the amounts, timing, and uncertainty surrounding expected cash receipts. Information also is needed to provide feedback on prior assessments of cash flow.

Information on prior cash flows provides a better basis for making predictions of cash flows than does information on past working

---

[2] FASB, "Reporting Income, Cash Flows, and Financial Position of Business Enterprises," *Proposed Statement of Financial Accounting Concepts,* Exposure Draft (Stamford, Conn., 1981), p. xi.

[3] Financial Executives Institute, *Alert,* December 14, 1981.

capital flows. This statement is true because it has been shown that past cash flows often differed sharply from working capital flows. For example, a rapidly expanding business will most likely find that it is increasing its working capital by expanding inventories and accounts receivable, yet never seeming to have enough cash to meet current bills. Cash flow analysis is required to reveal such problems.

SUMMARY

The statement of changes in financial position is one of the four major statements prepared by business firms. The purpose of the statement is analytical in that it attempts to explain how financial resources were acquired during a period, how financial resources were used, and what the net effect was on the company's working capital or cash position. Being an analytical tool, the statement of changes in financial position is an excellent means for assessing the quality of an organization's management.

In preparing the statement of changes in financial position, the first step is to prepare a schedule of changes in working capital. Then, each noncurrent balance sheet account is analyzed to see what effect changes in it had on working capital during the period. These changes in noncurrent account balances are organized in terms of representing either financial resources provided or financial resources applied during the period.

Some firms prefer to prepare the statement of changes in financial position on a cash basis instead of a working capital basis. This statement focuses on cash flows into and out of an organization. A key element in the preparation of the cash basis statement is to adjust the income statement from an accrual to a cash basis. Once this adjustment has been made, changes in noncurrent balance sheet accounts are analyzed for their effects on the Cash account, and the resulting cash inflows and cash outflows are organized into a formal cash basis statement of changes in financial position.

QUESTIONS

1. The term **funds** is used in many different ways in accounting. Indicate several of these uses other than those given in this chapter. What are the concepts of funds as the term is used in a statement of changes in financial position?

2. If the net income for a given period is $25,000, does this mean that there is an increase of cash of the same amount? Why or why not?

3. Explain the difference between the direct and indirect methods for computing working capital from operations.

4. What are the major sources of funds in a business? What are the major uses of funds?

5. Does the declaration or the payment of dividends affect working capital? Why?

6. Why might a company have a positive inflow of cash from operations even though operating at a net loss?

7. What are nonfund (nonworking capital or noncash) expenses? Of what significance are they?

8. Describe the treatment of a gain on the sale of equipment in preparing a statement of changes in financial position.

9. Why might an analysis of working capital flow be unsuitable for short-run planning?

10. Why is it unlikely that cash flow from operations will be equal to net income for the same period?

11. In what respects does cash flow analysis differ from working capital flow analysis?

12. In the preparation of a funds statement under the working capital basis, why are the noncurrent accounts analyzed rather than the current accounts?

13. Depreciation is often referred to as a source of funds. Is depreciation a source of funds? Explain.

14. Give two reasons why analysts seem to prefer cash flow statements to statements that report working capital flows.

EXERCISES

1. Indicate how the following data should be reported in a statement of changes in financial position. A company purchased land valued at $60,000 and a building valued at $120,000 by payment of $30,000 by check, signing a $45,000 interest-bearing note due in six months, and by assuming a $105,000 mortgage on the property.

2. A company sold for $5,000 equipment having an original cost of $7,000 and on which $4,000 of depreciation had been recorded. The gain was included in net income. How should these data be shown in the statement of changes in financial position and why?

3. The following data are from the Automobile and the Accumulated Depreciation—Automobile accounts of a certain company:

Automobile

Date			Debit	Credit	Balance
Jan.	1	Balance brought forward			$8,000
July	1	Traded for new auto		$8,000	–0–
	1	New auto	$8,800		8,800

Accumulated Depreciation—Automobile

Jan.	1	Balance brought forward			$6,000
July	1	One-half year's depreciation . . .		$1,000	7,000
	1	Auto traded	$7,000		–0–
Dec. 31		One-half year's depreciation . . .		1,100	1,100

The old auto was traded for a new one with the difference in values paid in cash. The income statement for the year shows a loss on the exchange of autos of $600.

301

Indicate the dollar amounts, the descriptions of these amounts, and their exact locations in a statement of changes in financial position.

4. Following are balance sheet data for the Stevens Corporation.

	December 31, 1987	December 31, 1986
Cash	$ 47,000	$ 26,000
Accounts receivable	141,000	134,000
Inventories	83,000	102,000
Prepaid expenses	9,000	11,000
Plant assets (net of accumulated deprecia-tion)	235,000	230,000
Accounts payable	122,000	127,000
Accrued expenses payable	40,000	41,000
Capital stock	300,000	300,000
Retained earnings	53,000	35,000

Calculate the change in working capital for the year 1987.

5. Refer to the information in Exercise 4. Assume that the depreciation recorded in 1987 was $15,000. Compute the cash applied to purchase of plant assets assuming no assets were sold or scrappped in 1987.

6. Use the data in Exercise 4. Assume the net income for 1987 was $24,000, that depreciation was $15,000, and that dividends declared and paid were $6,000. Prepare a statement of changes in financial position using the working capital basis.

7. Refer to the data in Exercises 4 and 6. Prepare a statement of changes in financial position under the cash basis.

8. Given that net income for the year was $60,000, patent amortization was $1,500, loss on sale of patents was $3,000, depreciation was $6,000, gain on sale of equipment was $1,800, and accumulated depreciation on equipment was $30,000. Compute working capital from operations.

9. A company's financial statements for a given year show sales of $1,500,000, net income of $150,000, and accounts receivable on January 1 of $132,000 and $141,000 on December 31. Compute the effect of the above information on net income as a measure of cash from operations.

10. The income statement of a company shows cost of goods sold of $1,050,000 and net income of $150,000; inventory on January 1 was $153,000 and on December 31 was $189,000; accounts payable for merchandise purchases were $114,000 on January 1 and $126,000 on December 31. Compute the effects of the above information on net income as a measure of cash from operations.

11. The operating expenses and taxes (including $30,000 of depreciation) of a company for a given year were $300,000. Net income was $150,000. Prepaid insurance decreased from $9,000 to $6,000 during the year, while accrued wages increased from $12,000 to $18,000 during the year. Compute the effects of the above on net income as a measure of cash from operations.

12. Assume that the data in Exercises 9, 10 and 11 above are for the same company. Prepare the section of the statement of changes in financial position showing conversion of net income to cash from operations. Show both working capital and cash from operations.

13. Dividends payable increased by $3,000 during the year in which total dividends declared were $60,000. What amount of dividends appears in the statement of changes in financial position under the working capital basis? What amount appears in the same statement prepared under the cash basis?

14. Fill in the following chart showing how increases and decreases in these accounts affect the conversion of accrual basis income to cash basis income.

	Add a(n)	Deduct a(n)
Accounts receivable		
Inventories		
Prepaid expenses		
Accounts payable		
Accrued liabilities		

PROBLEMS

10–1. The information given below is related to the Packer Corporation.

PACKER CORPORATION
Comparative Balance Sheets
December 31, 1985, and 1986

	December 31	
	1986	1985
Assets		
Cash	$ 30,000	$ 40,000
Accounts receivable, net	112,000	80,000
Inventories	200,000	160,000
Equipment	550,000	420,000
Accumulated depreciation	(160,000)	(140,000)
Investments	100,000	20,000
Total assets	$832,000	$580,000
Liabilities and Stockholders' Equity		
Accounts payable	$ 29,000	$ 25,000
Accrued liabilities	3,000	5,000
Capital stock—common—$10 par	500,000	400,000
Paid-in capital in excess of par	200,000	100,000
Retained earnings	100,000	50,000
Total liabilities and stockholders' equity	$832,000	$580,000

Additional data:

1. Net income was $90,000 for the year.
2. Fully depreciated equipment costing $20,000 was sold for $5,000 and equipment costing $150,000 was purchased for cash.
3. Depreciation expense for the year was $40,000.
4. Investments were purchased, $80,000.

5. An additional 5,000 shares of common stock were issued for cash at $40 per share.

6. Cash dividends of $40,000 were declared and paid.

Required:

Prepare a statement of changes in financial position (working capital basis) including a schedule of changes in components.

10–2. Using the information in Problem 10–1, prepare a statement of changes in financial position using the cash basis.

10–3. The income statement for the Taylor Company for the year ended December 31, 1986, shows:

Net sales		$640,000
Cost of goods sold	$375,000	
Operating expenses	100,000	
Major repairs	50,000	
Interest expense	15,000	
Loss on sale of equipment	8,000	548,000
Net income before taxes		$ 92,000
Federal income taxes		48,000
Net income		$ 44,000

Comparative balance sheets for the company show:

TAYLOR COMPANY
Comparative Balance Sheets
December 31, 1985, and 1986

	December 31	
	1986	*1985*
Assets		
Current assets:		
Cash	$ 48,000	$ 40,000
Accounts receivable, net	97,000	76,000
Inventories	210,000	180,000
Prepaid expenses	16,000	6,000
Total current assets	$371,000	$302,000
Property, plant, and equipment:		
Buildings	$100,000	$100,000
Accumulated depreciation—buildings	(55,000)	(50,000)
Equipment	185,000	130,000
Accumulated depreciation—equipment	(63,000)	(60,000)
Total property, plant, and equipment	$167,000	$120,000
Total assets	$538,000	$422,000

Liabilities and Stockholders' Equity

Current liabilities:

Accounts payable	$ 56,500	$ 82,500
Accrued expenses payable	16,500	14,500
Federal income taxes payable	48,000	45,000
Total current liabilities	$121,000	$142,000

Long-term liabilities:

Bonds payable, 15%	100,000	100,000
Total liabilities	$221,000	$242,000

Stockholders' equity:

Capital stock—$100 par	$250,000	$150,000
Paid-in capital in excess of par	25,000	–0–
Retained earnings	42,000	30,000
Total stockholders' equity	$317,000	$180,000
Total liabilities and stockholders' equity	$538,000	$422,000

Additional data:

1. Capital stock was issued for cash.

2. Accrued expenses payable relate solely to operating expenses.

3. Depreciation on equipment for the year amounted to $15,000. Equipment sold had an original cost of $30,000.

4. Dividends declared and paid during the year totaled $32,000.

5. Accounts payable arose solely from purchases of merchandise.

Required:

    a. Prepare a working paper for a statement of changes in financial position under the working capital basis (see description on page 297).

    b. Prepare a formal statement of changes in financial position under the working capital basis.

10–4. a. Use the data in Problem 10–3 and prepare a working paper for a statement of changes in financial position under the cash basis.

    b. Prepare a formal statement of changes in financial position under the cash basis for Taylor Company for the year ended December 31, 1986.

10–5. Given below are comparative balance sheets and other data of the David Corporation.

DAVID CORPORATION
Comparative Balance Sheets
June 30, 1985, and 1986

June 30

Assets

Cash	$ 372,000	$ 204,000
Accounts receivable	1,155,000	666,000
Inventories	1,260,000	1,308,000
Prepaid insurance	6,000	9,000
Land	480,000	540,000
Buildings	3,360,000	1,860,000
Machinery and tools	1,320,000	720,000
Accumulated depreciation	(1,245,000)	(786,000)
Total assets	$6,708,000	$4,521,000

Liabilities and Stockholders' Equity

Accounts payable	$ 195,000	$ 270,000
Accrued liabilities	132,000	18,000
Bank loans (due in 90 days)	87,000	102,000
Mortgage bonds payable	600,000	300,000
Discount on bonds payable	(12,000)	(15,000)
Common stock—$100 par	2,700,000	900,000
Paid-in capital in excess of par	90,000	–0–
Retained earnings	2,916,000	2,946,000
Total liabilities and stockholders' equity . .	$6,708,000	$4,521,000

Additional data:

1. Net income for the year was $120,000.

2. Discount on bonds payable amortized was $3,000.

3. Depreciation for the year was $549,000.

4. Dividends declared and paid were $150,000.

5. Additional common stock was issued at $105 per share.

6. The mortgage bonds were issued at face value as partial payment for a building valued at $1,500,000. Machinery and tools were purchased for $690,000.

7. There was a gain of $12,000 on the sale of land.

8. Fully depreciated machinery with a cost of $90,000 was scrapped and written off.

Required:

  a. Prepare a working paper for a statement of changes in financial position under the working capital basis (see description on page 297).

  b. Prepare the formal statement of changes in financial position under the working capital basis.

10–6. The Rivers Corporation comparative balance sheets at December 31, 1985 and 1986, and the statements of income and retained earnings for 1986 are presented below. Assume that the accounts payable are for merchandise purchases only and that the accrued expenses payable are for accrued expenses included in the Other expenses in the income statement.

RIVERS CORPORATION
Comparative Balance Sheets
December 31, 1985, and 1986

	December 31	
	1986	*1985*
Assets		
Current assets:		
Cash	$ 15,000	$ 20,000
Accounts receivable	127,000	98,000
Inventories	122,000	112,000
Prepaid insurance	3,000	4,000
Total current assets	$267,000	$234,000
Property, plant, and equipment:		
Land	$ 50,000	$ 30,000
Buildings	200,000	100,000
Accumulated depreciation—buildings	(25,000)	(20,000)
Equipment	230,000	215,000
Accumulated depreciation—equipment	(125,000)	(100,000)
Total property, plant, and equipment	$330,000	$225,000
Total assets	$597,000	$459,000
Liabilities and Stockholders' Equity		
Current liabilities:		
Accounts payable	$ 94,000	$ 90,000
Federal income taxes payable	36,000	30,000
Accrued salaries and wages payable	4,000	3,000
Accrued expenses payable	6,000	4,000
Total current liabilities	$140,000	$127,000
Long-term liabilities:		
Bonds payable, 9%	100,000	100,000
Total liabilities	$240,000	$227,000
Stockholders' equity:		
Capital stock—common	$300,000	$200,000
Paid-in capital in excess of par	15,000	–0–
Retained earnings	42,000	32,000
Total stockholders' equity	$357,000	$232,000
Total liabilities and stockholders' equity	$597,000	$459,000

RIVERS CORPORATION
Income Statement and Statement of Retained Earnings
For the Year Ended December 31, 1986

Sales (net)		$900,000
Cost of goods sold		600,000
Gross margin		$300,000
Salaries and wages	$150,000	
Depreciation	37,000	
Insurance	2,000	
Other expenses (including interest)	50,000	
Loss on sales of equipment	1,000	240,000
Net income before federal income taxes		$ 60,000
Federal income taxes		26,000
Net income		$ 34,000
Retained earnings, December 31, 1985		32,000
		$ 66,000
Less: Dividends		24,000
Retained earnings, December 31, 1986		$ 42,000

Additional data:

1. Equipment having an original cost of $10,000 and on which $7,000 of depreciation was recorded was sold at a loss of $1,000. Equipment additions were for cash.

2. $5,000 of cash and all of the additional capital stock issued during the year were exchanged for land and a building.

Required:

a. Prepare a working paper for a statement of changes in financial position using the cash basis.

b. Prepare the formal statement of changes in financial position using the cash basis.

11 FINANCIAL STATEMENT ANALYSIS

Financial statements are issued to communicate useful information to interested parties. If this objective is not met, the statements serve no useful purpose. Careful analyses and interpretations made by the user will often clarify an underlying message and bring out relationships, thus adding to the statement's ability to communicate. To make such analyses, however, the statement user must become skilled in methods of financial statement analysis. The purpose of financial statement analysis is to establish and present the relationships and trends found in financial statement data. Based upon this analysis, the users will draw their own conclusions and act accordingly.

Managers, employees, investors, creditors, business counselors, and executives of trade associations are among those who at one time or another will be interested in the financial statements of a specific firm. For example, a commercial bank loan officer will decide whether or not to grant a loan to a firm after the firm's financial statements have been analyzed. In making a decision, the loan officer will pay close attention to the firm's ability to pay its debt. A current stockholder may decide to sell his or her stock in the company after analyzing the company's financial statements and comparing its earnings history with that of another firm.

FINANCIAL STATEMENT ANALYSIS

Several types of analysis may be performed on a company's financial statements. Comparisons or relationships are almost always helpful since they enhance the utility of accounting information. For example, little useful information is conveyed by a statement that a firm's net income was $100,000 last year. Some utility is added if it is known that the prior year's net income was $25,000. Even more information is available if the amounts of sales and assets of a firm are known. Such comparisons or relationships may be expressed as:

1. Absolute increases and decreases for an item from one period to the next.
2. Percentage increases and decreases for an item from one period to the next.
3. Trend percentages.
4. Percentages of single items to an aggregate total.
5. Ratios.

Items 1 and 2 make use of comparative financial statements. **Comparative financial statements** present the same firm's financial statements for two or more successive periods in side-by-side columns. The calculation of dollar or percentage changes in the statement items or totals is known as **horizontal analysis.** This type of review helps detect changes in a firm's performance and highlights trends.

Trend percentages (item 3) are very similar to horizontal analysis except that a base year is selected and comparisons are made to the base year. Trend percentages are useful for comparing financial statements over several years because they disclose changes and trends occurring through time.

Information may also be gained by analyzing a financial statement of a firm for a single year to understand its composition. **Vertical analysis** (item 4) consists of the study of a single financial statement by expressing each item on the statement as a percentage of a significant total. Vertical analysis is especially useful in analyzing income statement data such as the percentage of cost of goods sold to sales or the gross margin on sales. When financial statements are presented showing only percentages and no absolute amounts, they are called **common-size statements.**

Ratios (item 5) are expressions of logical relationships between certain items in the financial statements. As with vertical analysis, a single period's financial statements are used. Thus, many ratios can be computed from the same set of financial statements. The choice of ratios that should be prepared is limited only by the requirement that the items used to construct a ratio have a logical relationship to one another.

HORIZONTAL AND VERTICAL ANALYSIS: AN ILLUSTRATION

Illustrations 11.1 and 11.2 show comparative financial statements of The Martin Corporation for the years ended December 31, 1986, and 1987. These statements will serve as a basis for an illustration of horizontal and vertical analysis. The comparative statements can

Illustration 11.1
COMPARATIVE BALANCE SHEETS

THE MARTIN CORPORATION
Comparative Balance Sheets
December 31, 1986, and 1987

	December 31		Increase or Decrease* 1987 over 1986		Percentage of Total Assets December 31	
	(1)	(2)	(3)	(4)	(5)	(6)
				Per-		
	1987	1986	Dollars	centage	1987	1986
Assets						
Current assets:						
Cash	$ 80,200	$ 55,000	$25,200	45.8	12.6	10.0
Accounts receivable, net	124,200	132,600	8,400*	6.3*	19.6	24.1
Notes receivable	55,000	50,000	5,000	10.0	8.7	9.1
Inventories	110,800	94,500	16,300	17.2	17.4	17.1
Prepaid expenses	3,600	4,700	1,100*	23.4*	0.6	0.9
Total current assets	$373,800	$336,800	$37,000	11.0	58.8R	61.1R
Property, plant, and equipment:						
Land	$ 21,000	$ 21,000	$ –0–	–0–	3.3	3.8
Building	205,000	160,000	45,000	28.1	32.3	29.0
Less: Accumulated depreciation	(27,000)	(22,400)	(4,600)	21.0	(4.3)	(4.1)
Furniture and fixtures	83,200	69,800	13,400	19.2	13.1	12.7
Less: Accumulated depreciation	(20,800)	(14,100)	(6,700)	47.5	(3.3)	(2.6)
Total property, plant, and equipment	$261,400	$214,300	$47,100	22.0	41.2R	38.9R
Total assets	$635,200	$551,100	$84,100	15.3	100.0	100.0
Liabilities and Stockholders' Equity						
Current liabilities:						
Accounts payable	$ 70,300	$ 64,600	$ 5,700	8.8	11.1	11.7
Notes payable	20,000	15,100	4,900	32.5	3.1	2.8R
Taxes accrued	36,800	30,200	6,600	21.9	5.8	5.5
Total current liabilities	$127,100	$109,900	$17,200	15.7	20.0	20.0R
Long-term liabilities:						
Mortgage notes payable, land and building, 12%, 1990	43,600	60,800	17,200*	28.3*	6.9	11.0
Total liabilities	$170,700	$170,700	$ –0–	0.0	26.9	31.0
Stockholders' equity:						
Common stock, par value $10 per share	$240,000	$200,000	$40,000	20.0	37.8	36.3
Retained earnings	224,500	180,400	44,100	24.4	35.3	32.7
Total stockholders' equity	$464,500	$380,400	$84,100	22.1	73.1	69.0
Total liabilities and stockholders' equity	$635,200	$551,100	$84,100	15.3	100.0	100.0

R Rounding difference.

311

Illustration 11.2
COMPARATIVE STATEMENTS OF INCOME AND RETAINED EARNINGS

THE MARTIN CORPORATION
Comparative Statements of Income and Retained Earnings
For the Years Ended December 31, 1986, and 1987

	Year Ended December 31		Increase or Decrease* 1987 over 1986		Percentage of Net Sales	
	(7)	(8)	(9)	(10) Per-centage	(11)	(12)
	1987	1986	Dollars		1987	1986
Net sales	$986,400	$765,500	$220,900	28.9	100.0	100.0
Cost of goods sold	623,200	500,900	122,300	24.4	63.2	65.4
Gross margin	$363,200	$264,600	$ 98,600	37.3	36.8	34.6
Operating expenses:						
Selling	$132,500	$ 84,900	$ 47,600	56.1	13.4	11.1
Administrative	120,300	98,600	21,700	22.0	12.2	12.9
Total operating expenses	$252,800	$183,500	$ 69,300	37.8	25.6	24.0
Net operating income	$110,400	$ 81,100	$ 29,300	36.0	11.2	10.6
Other expenses	3,000	2,800	200	7.1	0.3	0.4
Net income before federal income taxes	$107,400	$ 78,300	$ 29,100	37.2	10.9	10.2
Federal income taxes	48,300	31,700	16,600	52.4	4.9	4.1
Net income	$ 59,100	$ 46,600	$ 12,500	26.8	6.0	6.1[R]
Retained earnings	180,400	146,300	34,100	23.3		
	$239,500	$192,900	$ 46,600	24.2		
Dividends declared	15,000	12,500	2,500	20.0		
Retained earnings	$224,500	$180,400	$ 44,100	24.4		

[R] Rounding difference.

be analyzed to disclose certain relationships among the various items included in those statements. Management may use these relationships in making business decisions; investors and creditors also may use them when deciding whether to invest in or loan money to the firm.

Analysis of Balance Sheet

Examination of the comparative balance sheet reveals (among other items) the following:

Columns 1, 2, and 3 in Illustration 11.1 show the absolute dollar amounts for each item for December 31, 1986, and December 31, 1987, and the change for the year. If the change between the two dates is an increase from 1986 to 1987, the change is shown as a positive figure. If the change is a decrease, it is so indicated by an asterisk (*).

Examples of the items highlighted by the first three columns are:

1. Current assets have increased $37,000, consisting largely of a $25,200 increase in cash, while current liabilities have increased only $17,200.
2. Total assets have increased $84,100, while liabilities have remained unchanged.
3. The increase in total assets has been financed by the sale of common stock, $40,000, and by the retention of earnings, $44,100.

Column 4 in Illustration 11.1 expresses the dollar change in column 3 as a percentage of column 2. Frequently, percentage increases and decreases are more informative than absolute amounts, as illustrated by the current asset and current liability changes. Although the absolute amount of current assets has increased more than twice the amount of current liabilities, the percentages reveal that current assets increased 11 percent, while current liabilities increased 15.7 percent. Thus, current liabilities are increasing at a rate faster than the current assets that will be used to pay them. But, in view of the substantial amount of cash possessed, the company is not likely to fail to pay its debts as they come due. The 28.3 percent decrease in mortgage notes payable will lead the analyst to conclude that interest charges will be lower in the coming years. The 20 percent increase in common shares outstanding will tend to reduce earnings per share.

Columns 5 and 6 express the dollar amounts of each item in columns 1 and 2 as percentages of total assets (equities). Vertical analysis of The Martin Corporation's balance sheet is used to disclose an account's relative significance to total assets (equities) which aids in assessing the importance of changes in that account. For example, although prepaid expenses declined $1,100 in 1987, a decrease of 23.4 percent, the account represents less than 1 percent of total assets and, therefore, probably would not be investigated further. The vertical analysis also shows that long-term debt financing decreased from 11.0 percent of total assets to 6.9 percent in 1987, a minus 4.1 percent. The percentage of stockholder financing to total assets of the company increased from 69.0 to 73.1, a plus 4.1 percent.

Analysis of Income Statement

The amounts in columns 7 and 8 in Illustration 11.2 are the dollar amounts for the years 1986 and 1987. The amounts and percentages in columns 9 through 12 are computed in the same manner as the balance sheet amounts in Illustration 11.1 except that the items in columns 11 and 12 are percentages of net sales. Examination of the comparative statements of net income and retained earnings shows the following:

1. Sales increased 28.9 percent in 1987.
2. Gross margin increased 37.3 percent in 1987.

3. Selling expenses increased 56.1 percent in 1987.
4. Federal income taxes rose by 52.4 percent in 1987.
5. Net income increased 26.8 percent, while dividends increased 20.0 percent.
6. Net income per dollar of sales remained virtually constant over the two years.

Considering both horizontal and vertical analysis information, the analyst would conclude that an increase in the gross margin rate from 34.6 percent to 36.8 percent, coupled with a 28.9 percent increase in sales, resulted in a 37.3 percent increase in gross margin in 1987. The increase in net income was held to 26.8 percent because selling expenses increased 56.1 percent and income taxes increased 52.4 percent. Predicting net income for 1988 would be aided if the analyst knew whether this increase in selling expenses is expected to recur. Other expenses remained basically the same on a percentage-of-sales basis over the two years.

Proper analysis does not stop with the calculation of increases and decreases in amounts or percentages over several years. Such changes generally indicate areas worthy of further investigation. They are merely clues that may lead to significant findings. Accurate predictions depend on a host of factors including economic and political conditions; management's plans regarding new products, plant expansion, and promotional outlays; and the expected activities of competitors.

TREND PERCENTAGES

Trend percentages are also referred to as index numbers and are used for comparison of financial information over time to a base year. Trend percentages are calculated by:

1. Selecting a base year.
2. Assigning a weight of 100 percent to the amounts appearing in the base year financial statements.
3. Expressing the amounts shown on the other years' financial statements as a percentage of base year amounts. The percentages are computed by dividing nonbase amounts by the base year amounts and then multiplying the result by 100.

As an example, the following information is given:

	1986	1987	1988	1989
Sales	$350,000	$367,500	$441,000	$485,000
Cost of goods sold	200,000	196,000	230,000	285,000
Gross margin	$150,000	$171,500	$211,000	$200,000
Operating expenses	145,000	169,000	200,000	192,000
Net income before taxes	$ 5,000	$ 2,500	$ 11,000	$ 8,000

Letting 1986 be the base year, trend percentages would be calculated for each year by dividing sales by $350,000; cost of goods sold by $200,000; gross margin by $150,000; operating expenses by $145,000; and net income before income taxes by $5,000. After all divisions have been made, each result would be multiplied by 100, and the resulting trends would appear as follows:

	1986	1987	1988	1989
Sales	100	105	126	139
Cost of goods sold	100	98	115	143
Gross margin	100	114	141	133
Operating expenses	100	117	138	132
Net income before taxes	100	50	220	160

Trend percentages indicate changes that are taking place in an organization and highlight the direction of the changes. The percentages can provide clues as to which items need further investigation or analysis. In reviewing trend percentages, a manager or investor should pay close attention to the trends in related items, such as the cost of goods sold in relation to sales. Trend analysis that shows a constantly declining gross margin rate may be a signal that trouble lies ahead in diminished income or actual losses. The nature and direction of changes in trend analysis data may be seen more clearly when such data are presented graphically.

Expressing changes as percentages is usually straightforward as long as the amount in the base year is positive—that is, not zero or negative. A $30,000 increase in notes receivable cannot be expressed in percentages if the increase is from zero last year to $30,000 this year. Also, an increase in net income from a loss last year of $10,000 to income this year of $20,000 cannot be expressed in percentage terms.

RATIO ANALYSIS

Logical relationships exist between certain accounts or items in a firm's financial statements. These accounts may appear on the same statement or they may appear on two different statements. The dollar amounts of the related accounts or items are usually set up in fraction form and called ratios. Even though rates rather than ratios are sometimes calculated, general practice is to refer to all of these calculations as ratios. These ratios can be broadly classified as (1) liquidity ratios, (2) equity or solvency ratios, (3) profitability ratios, and (4) market ratios.

Liquidity Ratios

Liquidity ratios are used to indicate a firm's debt-paying ability, especially its short-term debt-paying ability. Thus, these ratios are designed to show the firm's general capacity to meet maturing current liabilities and its ability to generate cash to pay these liabilities.

Current or working capital ratio. Working capital is the excess of current assets over current liabilities. The ratio that relates these two categories is known as the **current** or **working capital ratio.** The current ratio indicates the ability of a company to pay its current liabilities from current assets and, in this way, shows the strength of the company's working capital position.

The current ratio is computed by dividing total current assets by total current liabilities:

$$\text{Current ratio} = \frac{\text{Current assets}}{\text{Current liabilities}}$$

The ratio usually is stated in terms of the number of dollars of current assets to each dollar of current liabilities (although the dollar signs usually are omitted). Thus, if current assets total $75,000 and current liabilities total $50,000, the ratio is expressed as 1.5 to 1, or the firm has $1.50 of current assets for each $1 of current liabilities.

The current ratio provides a better index of a firm's ability to pay current debts than does the absolute amount of working capital. To illustrate, assume that Company A and Company B have current assets and current liabilities on December 31, 1986, as follows:

	Company A	Company B
Current assets . . .	$11,000,000	$200,000
Current liabilities . .	10,000,000	100,000
Working capital . . .	$ 1,000,000	$100,000
Current ratio	1.1:1	2:1

Company A has 10 times as much working capital as Company B. But Company B has superior debt-paying ability since it has two dollars of current assets for each dollar of current liabilities. Company A has only $1.10 of current assets for each $1 of current liabilities.

Short-term creditors are particularly interested in the current ratio. They expect to receive payment from conversion of inventories and accounts receivable into cash. Long-term creditors are also interested in the current ratio because a firm that is unable to pay short-term debts may be forced into bankruptcy. For this reason, many bond indentures contain a provision requiring the borrower to maintain at least a certain minimum current ratio. A firm can increase its current ratio by issuing long-term debt or capital stock or by selling noncurrent assets.

A firm must also guard against a current ratio that is too high, especially if caused by idle cash, slow-paying customers, and slow-moving inventory. Decreased net income and rates of return on assets and stockholders' equity follow when too much capital that could be used profitably elsewhere is tied up in current assets.

Referring back to The Martin Corporation data in Illustration 11.1, the current ratios for the two years are as follows:

	December 31		Amount of Increase
	1987	*1986*	
Current assets *(a)*	$373,800	$336,800	$37,000
Current liabilities *(b)*	127,100	109,900	17,200
Working capital *(a − b)* . .	$246,700	$226,900	$19,800
Current ratio *(a ÷ b)*	2.94:1	3.06:1	

Thus, although Martin's working capital increased by $19,800, or 8.7 percent, its current ratio fell from 3.06 to 1 to 2.94 to 1, reflecting the fact that its current liabilities increased faster than its current assets.

Acid-test or quick ratio. The current ratio is not the only measure of a firm's short-term debt-paying ability. Another measure is the **acid-test (quick) ratio,** which is the ratio of quick assets (cash, marketable securities, and net receivables) to current liabilities. The formula for the acid-test ratio is:

$$\text{Acid-test ratio} = \frac{\text{Quick assets}}{\text{Current liabilities}}$$

Inventories and prepaid expenses are excluded from this computation because they might not be readily convertible into cash. Short-term creditors are interested particularly in this ratio since it relates the "pool" of cash and immediate cash inflows to immediate cash outflows.

The acid-test ratios for 1986 and 1987 for the Martin Corporation are:

	December 31		Amount of Increase
	1987	*1986*	
Quick assets *(a)*	$259,400	$237,600	$21,800
Current liabilities *(b)*	127,100	109,900	17,200
Net quick assets *(a − b)* . .	$132,300	$127,700	$ 4,600
Acid-test ratio *(a ÷ b)*	2.04:1	2.16:1	

In deciding whether the acid test ratio is satisfactory, a good starting point is to consider the quality of the marketable securities and receivables. An accumulation of poor quality temporary investments or receivables, or both, could cause an acid-test ratio to appear deceptively favorable. Poor quality when referring to marketable securities means securities that are likely to generate losses upon disposition; poor quality receivables are those that may be uncollectible or not collectible until long past due. The quality of receivables depends primarily upon their age, which can be assessed by preparation of an aging schedule or by calculating accounts receivable turnover.

Accounts receivable turnover. **Turnover** is the relationship between the amount of an asset and some measure of its use. **Accounts receivable turnover** is the number of times per year that the average amount of receivables is collected. The ratio (rate) is calculated by dividing net credit sales by average net accounts receivable, that is, accounts receivable after deducting the allowance for doubtful accounts. The formula is:

$$\text{Accounts receivable turnover} = \frac{\text{Net credit sales}}{\text{Average net accounts receivable}}$$

When a ratio or rate is based on an income statement item and a balance sheet item, the balance sheet item usually should be an average. Ideally, the divisor in the accounts receivable turnover should be computed by averaging the end-of-month balances or end-of-week balances of net accounts receivable outstanding during the period. The greater the number of observations used, the more accurate the resulting average is. Often though, only the beginning-of-year and end-of-year balances are averaged because this information is easily obtainable from comparative financial statements. Sometimes a formula calls for the use of an average balance, but only the year-end amount is available. Then the analyst must use the year-end amount.[1]

The numerator should only contain sales on account because those are the only sales that appear in accounts receivable. But if cash sales are relatively small, or if their proportion to total sales remains fairly constant, reliable results can be obtained by using total net sales. In most cases, the analyst may have no choice in the matter because the amounts of cash and credit sales are not reported.

Accounts receivable turnover rates for The Martin Corporation are shown below. Assume net accounts receivable on January 1, 1986, were $121,200.

---

[1] These general comments about the balance sheet item in a ratio apply to the other ratios involving balance sheet items discussed in this chapter.

	1987	1986	Amount of Increase or Decrease*
Net sales *(a)*	$986,400	$765,500	$220,900
Accounts receivable:			
January 1	$132,600	$121,200	$ 11,400
December 31	124,200	132,600	8,400*
Total	$256,800	$253,800	$ 3,000
Average accounts receivable *(b)*	$128,400	$126,900	
Turnover of accounts receivable *(a ÷ b)*	7.68	6.03	

The turnover rate provides an indication of how quickly the receivables are being collected and is valuable for comparison purposes. For The Martin Corporation in 1987, the turnover rate indicates that accounts receivable are collected or turned over slightly more than seven times per year. This rate may be better understood and more easily compared with a firm's credit terms if it is converted into days.

Number of days' sales in accounts receivable. The **number of days' sales in accounts receivable,** which also is called the **average collection period for accounts receivable,** is calculated as follows:

$$\text{Number of days' sales in accounts receivable (average collection period of accounts receivable)} = \frac{\text{Number of days in year (365)}}{\text{Accounts receivable turnover}}$$

Using the turnover rates for The Martin Corporation, the number of days' sales in accounts receivable decreased from about 61 days (365/6.03) in 1986 to 48 days (365/7.68) in 1987. The change means the average collection period of the corporation's accounts receivable decreased from 61 to 48 days. Thus, the calculation measures the average liquidity of accounts receivable and gives an indication of their quality. Quality is defined as the probability of collection in full. The quality of an account receivable decreases with age. A comparison of the average collection period with the credit terms extended customers by the firm will provide further insight into the quality of the accounts receivable. For example, receivables arising under terms of 2/10, n/30 that have an average collection period of 75 days need to be investigated further.

Inventory turnover. A firm's inventory turnover rate shows the number of times its average inventory is sold during a period. **Inventory turnover** is calculated as follows:

$$\text{Inventory turnover} = \frac{\text{Cost of goods sold}}{\text{Average inventory}}$$

Inventory turnover relates a measure of sales volume to the average amount of goods on hand to produce this sales volume.

Assume the inventory on January 1, 1986, was $85,100. Then the following schedule shows that the inventory turnover rate for The Martin Corporation increased slightly to 6.07 times per year in 1987 from 5.58 times per year in 1986. These turnover rates also mean that the company sold its average inventory in about 60 days (365/6.07) in 1987 as contrasted to about 65 days (365/5.58) in 1986.

	1987	1986	Amount of Increase
Cost of goods sold (a)	$623,200	$500,900	$122,300
Inventories:			
January 1	$ 94,500	$ 85,100	$ 9,400
December 31	110,800	94,500	16,300
Total	$205,300	$179,600	$ 25,700
Average inventory (b)	$102,650	$ 89,800	
Inventory turnover (a ÷ b)	6.07	5.58	

In attempting to earn a satisfactory income, the costs of storage, obsolescence, and implicit interest in owning inventory must be balanced against the possible loss of sales from not having inventory to sell. Other things being equal, the management that is able to maintain the higher inventory turnover rate is considered more efficient. Yet, other things are not always equal. For example, a firm that achieves a high inventory turnover rate by keeping extremely small inventories on hand may incur larger ordering costs, may lose quantity discounts, and may be losing sales due to lack of stock.

Total assets turnover. Total assets turnover shows the relationship between dollar volume of sales and average total assets used in the business and is calculated as follows:

$$\text{Total assets turnover} = \frac{\text{Net sales}}{\text{Average total assets}}$$

This rate measures the efficiency of the use of capital invested in assets, assuming a constant margin of income on each dollar of sales. The larger the dollar volume of sales made per dollar of invested capital, the larger will be the income on each dollar invested in the assets of the business. For The Martin Corporation, the total assets turnover rates for 1987 and 1986 are shown below. Assume total assets as of January 1, 1986, were $510,200.

	1987	1986	Amount of Increase
Net sales *(a)*	$ 986,400	$ 765,500	$220,900
Total assets:			
January 1	$ 551,100	$ 510,200	$ 40,900
December 31	635,200	551,100	84,100
Total	$1,186,300	$1,061,300	$125,000
Average total assets *(b)*	$ 593,150	$ 530,650	
Total assets turnover *(a ÷ b)* . .	1.66:1	1.44:1	

In 1986, each dollar of total assets produced $1.44 of sales; and in 1987, each dollar of total assets produced $1.66 of sales, or an increase of $0.22 of sales per dollar of investment in the assets.

Equity or Solvency Ratios

Equity (solvency) ratios indicate the financial structure of the firm. Equity ratios show the relationship of debt and equity financing.

Equity (or owners' equity) ratio. The two basic sources of assets are owners (stockholders) and creditors, and the interests of both groups are referred to as total equities. But in ratio analysis, the term **equity** generally refers only to owners' equity. Thus, the **equity (solvency) ratio** indicates the proportion of total assets (or equities) that is provided by owners (stockholders) on any given date. The formula for the equity ratio is:

$$\text{Equity ratio} = \frac{\text{Owners' equity}}{\text{Total assets (equities)}}$$

The Martin Corporation's liabilities and stockholders' equity, taken from Illustration 11.1, are shown below. The schedule shows that the company's stockholders increased their proportionate equity in the firm's assets by additional investment in the company's common stock and by retention of income earned during the year.

	December 31, 1987		December 31, 1986	
	Amount	Percent	Amount	Percent
Current liabilities	$127,100	20.0	$109,900	20.0
Long-term liabilities	43,600	6.9	60,800	11.0
Total liabilities	$170,700	26.9	$170,700	31.0
Common stock	$240,000	37.8	$200,000	36.3
Retained earnings	224,500	35.3	180,400	32.7
Total stockholders' equity . .	$464,500	73.1	$380,400	69.0
Total equity (equal to total assets)	$635,200	100.0	$551,100	100.0

The Martin Corporation's equity ratio increased from 69.0 percent (or .69 to 1) in 1986 to 73.1 (or .731 to 1) percent in 1987. The equity ratio must be interpreted carefully. From a creditor's point of view, a high proportion of owners' equity is desirable. A high percentage indicates the existence of a large protective buffer for creditors in the event the company suffers a loss. But from an owner's point of view, a high proportion of owners' equity may or may not be desirable. If borrowed funds can be used by the business to generate income in excess of the net after-tax cost of the interest on such borrowed funds, a lower percentage of owners' equity may be desirable.

Following is a brief illustration of the effect on The Martin Corporation if it were more highly leveraged (i.e., had a larger proportion of debt). Assume that Martin Corporation could have financed its present operations with $40,000 of 12 percent bonds instead of 4,000 shares of common stock. The effect on income for 1987 would be as follows assuming a marginal federal income tax rate of 50 percent:

Net income as presently stated (Illustration 11.2)	$59,100
Deduct additional interest on debt (0.12 × $40,000)	4,800
	$54,300
Add reduced tax due to interest deduction (0.5 × $4,800) . .	2,400
Adjusted net income	$56,700

As shown, net income would be less. But there would be 4,000 fewer shares outstanding. As a result, earnings per share would be increased to $2.84 ($56,700/20,000) from $2.46 ($59,100/24,000). Since investors place heavy emphasis upon earnings per share amounts, many companies in recent years have introduced larger portions of debt into their capital structures to increase earnings per share. This practice is not without its dangers because financial leverage magnifies losses as well as earnings per share since there are fewer shares of stock over which to spread the loss.

It should also be pointed out that too low a percentage of owners' equity (too much debt) may be hazardous from the owners' standpoint. A period of business recession may result in operating losses and shrinkages in the value of assets (such as receivables and inventories) leading to an inability to meet fixed payments for interest and principal on debt. This in turn may cause stockholders to lose control of the company because the company may be forced into liquidation.

Owners' equity/debt ratio. The relative equities of owners and creditors may be expressed in several ways. To say that creditors hold a 26.9 percent interest in the assets of The Martin Corporation on December 31, 1987, is equivalent to saying stockholders hold a

73.1 percent interest. In many cases, the relationship is expressed as a ratio—**owner's equity/debt ratio.** Such a ratio for The Martin Corporation would be 2.23 to 1 ($380,400/$170,700) on December 31, 1986, and 2.72 to 1 ($464,500/$170,700) on December 31, 1987. This ratio is sometimes inverted and called the debt/equity ratio. Some analysts use only long-term debt rather than total debt in calculating these ratios.

Profitability Ratios

Profitability is an extremely important measure of a firm's operating success. Profitability ratios reveal (1) income statement relationships showing the ability of a firm to cover its expenses or (2) relationships of income statement and balance sheet items showing the rate of earnings on assets employed by the firm.

Rate of return on operating assets. The best measure of income performance without regard to sources of assets is the relationship of net operating income to operating assets, which is known as the **rate of return on operating assets** (earning power percentage). There are two elements in the determination of this rate: **operating margin** and **turnover of operating assets.**

Operating margin reflects the percentage of each dollar of net sales that becomes net operating income. Net operating income excludes extraordinary items, nonoperating revenues, such as interest revenue, and nonoperating expenses, such as interest expense and income taxes. The formula for operating margin is:

$$\text{Operating margin} = \frac{\text{Net operating income}}{\text{Net sales}}$$

Turnover of operating assets shows the dollars of sales for each dollar invested in operating assets. Operating assets are all assets actively used in producing operating revenues. Year-end operating assets typically are used even though an average would be better in theory. Examples of nonoperating assets are land held for future use, a factory building rented to another company, and long-term bond investments. Total assets should not be used in evaluating earnings performance due to the inclusion of nonoperating assets that do not contribute to the generation of sales. The formula for the turnover of operating assets is:

$$\text{Turnover of operating assets} = \frac{\text{Net Sales}}{\text{Operating Assets}}$$

The rate of return on operating assets of a firm then is equal to operating margin multiplied by turnover of operating assets. The more a company earns per dollar of sales and the more sales it makes per dollar invested in operating assets, the higher will be the return per dollar invested. Rate of return on operating assets may be expressed by the following formulas:

$$\text{Rate of return on operating assets} = \text{Operating margin} \times \text{Turnover of operating assets}$$

or

$$\text{Rate of return on operating assets} = \frac{\text{Net operating income}}{\text{Net sales}} \times \frac{\text{Net sales}}{\text{Operating assets}}$$

Since net sales appears as both a numerator and a denominator, it can be canceled out, and the formula for rate of return on operating assets becomes:

$$\text{Rate of return on operating assets} = \frac{\text{Net operating income}}{\text{Operating assets}}$$

But it is more useful for analytical purposes to leave the formula in the form which shows margin and turnover separately.

Securing desired rate of return on operating assets. Companies that are to survive in the economy must attain some minimum rate of return on operating assets. This minimum can be obtained in many different ways. To illustrate, consider a grocery store and a jewelry store each with a rate of return of 8 percent on operating assets. The grocery store normally would have a low margin and a high turnover, while the jewelry store would have a high margin and a low turnover.

	Margin $\times$	Turnover $=$	Rate of Return on Operating Assets
Grocery store . . .	1% $\times$	8.0 times $=$	8%
Jewelry store . . .	20% $\times$	0.4 times $=$	8%

The rates of return on operating assets for The Martin Corporation for 1986 and 1985 are calculated below.

	1987	1986	Amount of Increase
Net operating income *(a)*	$110,400	$ 81,100	$ 29,300
Net sales *(b)*	$986,400	$765,500	$220,900
Operating margin *(a ÷ b = c)*	11.19%	10.59%	
Net sales *(d)*	$986,400	$765,500	$220,900
Total assets (all operating assets) *(e)* . .	$635,200	$551,100	$ 84,100
Turnover of operating assets *(d ÷ e = f)*	1.55:1	1.39:1	
Rate of return on operating assets *(c × f)*	17.34%	14.72%	

Rate of return on operating assets is designed to show the earning power of the company as a bundle of assets. By disregarding both nonoperating assets and nonoperating income, rate of return on operating assets measures the profitability of the firm in carrying out its primary business functions.

Net income to net sales. Net income as a percentage of net sales **(net income to net sales)** is obtained by dividing net income for the period by net sales of the period:

$$\text{Net income to net sales} = \frac{\text{Net income}}{\text{Net sales}}$$

This ratio measures the proportion of the sales dollar that remains after deduction of all expenses. The computations for The Martin Company are:

	1987	1986	Amount of Increase
Net income *(a)*	$ 59,100	$ 46,600	$ 12,500
Net sales *(b)*	$986,400	$765,500	$220,900
Ratio of net income to net sales *(a ÷ b)* . .	5.99%	6.09%	

Although the ratio of net income to net sales indicates the net amount of profit on each sales dollar, a great deal of care must be exercised in the use and interpretation of this ratio. The amount of net income includes all types of nonoperating items that may occur in a particular period; therefore, net income includes the effects of such things as extraordinary items and interest charges. Thus, a period that contains the effects of an extraordinary item will not be comparable to a period that contains no extraordinary items. Also, since interest expense is deductible in the determination of income while dividends are not, net income is affected by the methods used to finance the firm's assets.

Net income to average stockholders' equity. From the stockholders' point of view, an important measure of the income-producing ability of a company is the relationship of **net income to average stockholders' equity** or the **rate of return on average stockholders' equity.** The ratio also is often referred to simply as **return on equity (ROE).** Stockholders are interested in the ratio of operating income to operating assets as a measure of the efficient use of assets by management. But stockholders are even more interested in knowing what return was earned by the company on each dollar of owners' equity invested. The formula for net income to average stockholders' equity is:

$$\text{Net income to average stockholders' equity} = \frac{\text{Net income}}{\text{Average stockholders' equity}}$$

The ratios for The Martin Company are shown below. Assume that total stockholders' equity on January 1, 1986, was $321,500.

	1987	1986	Amount of Increase
Net income *(a)*	$ 59,100	$ 46,600	$ 12,500
Total stockholders' equity:			
January 1	$380,400	$321,500	$ 58,900
December 31	464,500	380,400	84,100
Total	$844,900	$701,900	$143,000
Average total stockholders' equity *(b)*	$422,450	$350,950	
Ratio of net income to stockholders' equity *(a ÷ b)*	13.99%	13.28%	

The increase in the ratio from 13.28 percent to 13.99 percent would be regarded favorably by stockholders. This ratio indicates that for each average dollar of capital invested by a stockholder, the company earned 14 cents in 1987.

Earnings per share. Probably the measure used most widely to appraise a firm's operating ability is **earnings per share** of common stock (hereafter simply **EPS**). An EPS amount is usually computed for common stock and is equal to income available to common stockholders divided by weighted-average number of shares of common stock outstanding. The financial press regularly publishes actual and forecasted EPS amounts for many corporations, together with period-to-period comparisons. The Accounting Principles Board noted the significance attached to EPS by requiring that such amounts be reported on the face of the income statement.[2]

Calculation of EPS may be a fairly simple or a highly complex problem, depending upon the corporation's capital structure. A firm has a simple capital structure if it has no outstanding securities that can be exchanged for common stock such as convertible bonds or convertible preferred stocks. If a firm has such securities outstanding, it has a complex capital structure. A firm with a simple capital structure reports a single EPS amount calculated as follows:

$$\text{EPS of common stock} = \frac{\text{Income available to common stockholders}}{\text{Weighted-average number of common shares outstanding}}$$

---

[2] AICPA, *APB Opinion No. 15.* "Earnings per Share" (New York, 1969), par. 12.

The numerator in the EPS fraction is equal to net income less the current year's preferred stock dividends, whether declared or not.

Weighted-average number of shares. The denominator in the EPS fraction is the weighted-average number of common shares outstanding for the period. If the number of shares outstanding changed during the period, the change in shares must be weighted for the fractional period. For example, assume that 80,000 shares were outstanding at the beginning of the year and that 14,000 shares were issued on June 30. The 14,000 shares are weighted by one half for the half year they were outstanding. The weighted-average number of shares outstanding for the year is 87,000: 80,000 shares outstanding all year, plus 14,000 shares outstanding for a half year, which is the equivalent of 7,000 shares outstanding all year. Another way of describing this situation is to say that 80,000 shares were outstanding for one-half year and 94,000 shares for one-half year, for an average of 87,000 shares for the year. If the company had purchased 1,000 shares of treasury stock on September 30, the calculation would read:

80,000 shares × ½ year (January–June)	= 40,000
94,000 shares × ¼ year (July–September)	= 23,500
93,000 shares × ¼ year (October–December)	= 23,250
Weighted-average number of common shares outstanding . .	86,750

A weighted average for the common shares outstanding should be computed whenever shares are issued or acquired during a period. Such changes increase or decrease the capital invested in the company, which should affect income available to stockholders. Shares should be considered outstanding only during those periods that the related capital investment was available to help produce income.

For The Martin Corporation, which had no preferred stock outstanding in either 1987 or 1986, earnings per share of common stock are computed as follows:

	1987	1986	Amount of Increase
Net income *(a)*	$59,100	$46,600	$12,500
Average number of shares of common stock outstanding *(b)*	22,000	20,000	2,000
Earnings per share of common stock *(a ÷ b)*	$2.69	$2.33	

Martin's average number of shares outstanding for 1986 was 20,000. This amount was calculated by dividing the December 31, 1986, common stock balance ($200,000) by the par value ($10) per share and making the assumption that no shares were issued in 1986. During 1987, however, 4,000 shares of common stock were issued. Assuming this transaction took place on July 1, the following calculation is made:

$$
\begin{array}{lr}
\text{20,000 shares} \times \text{½ year} = & \text{10,000} \\
\text{24,000 shares} \times \text{½ year} = & \underline{\text{12,000}} \\
\text{Weighted-average} & \\
\quad \text{shares for 1987} & \underline{\text{22,000}}
\end{array}
$$

EPS and stock dividends or splits. When additional shares are issued during the period as a result of a stock dividend or stock split, no attempt is made to average the number of shares outstanding at different times during the year as is done when additional shares are issued for cash or other property. The reason for not calculating a weighted-average number of shares is that the stock split or the stock dividend is not viewed as being a change in substance; it is simply a division of the stockholders' interest into more pieces.

When comparing earnings per share before and after a stock split or stock dividend, the earnings per share for all years should be adjusted to the same basis. Assume a company reports earnings per share as follows: 1985, $1 ($1,000,000/1,000,000 shares); 1986, $1.25 ($1,250,000/1,000,000 shares); and 1987, $0.75 ($1,500,000/2,000,000 shares). But a two for one stock split occurred in 1986. The first two years' figures should be adjusted for the stock split in order to be comparable to the 1987 figure. The number of shares in the divisor should be doubled for 1985 and 1986, so as to be the same as in 1987. Thus, earnings per share would be $0.50 ($1,000,000/2,000,000 shares) for 1985, and $0.625 ($1,250,000/2,000,000 shares) for 1986. Then the proper trend can be seen:

Year	Earnings per Share
1985	$0.500
1986	0.625
1987	0.750

Primary EPS and fully diluted EPS. In the merger wave of the 1960s, corporations often issued securities to finance their acquisitions of other companies. Many of the securities issued were **calls on common** or possessed **equity kickers.** These terms mean that the securities were convertible into, or exchangeable for, shares of their issuers' common stock. As a result, many complex problems arose in computing EPS. *APB Opinion No. 15* provided guidelines for solving these problems. A company with a complex capital structure must present primary EPS and fully diluted EPS data. But, because of the complexities faced, further discussion and illustration of these two EPS amounts must be reserved for an intermediate accounting text.

Times interest earned ratio. Another relationship that focuses attention upon the position of a particular class of investor—in this case, the long-term creditor—is the ratio of income available for interest charges to the amount of such charges. For example, if the amount of income before interest and income taxes is $100,000 and the interest expense for the period is $10,000, the ratio is 10 to 1. In such a case the interest is said to have been earned 10 times.

Long-term creditors are interested in knowing whether the company is earning enough so that even if a drop in income should occur, it could continue to earn enough to meet its interest payments. It is true that interest must usually be paid regardless of whether income is sufficient to cover it. But it is also true that a company probably could not continue to pay interest in excess of income for a long period of time. Thus, the long-term creditors are interested in knowing the likelihood that they will continue to receive interest payments as they become due.

The number of times that the present interest is earned is one measure of a company's ability to meet interest payments. And, of course, since interest is deductible for income tax purposes, net income before interest and income taxes is used since there would be no tax if interest were equal to or greater than net income before interest and taxes. In formula form, the **times interest earned ratio** is:

$$\text{Times interest earned ratio} = \frac{\text{Net income before interest and taxes}}{\text{Interest expense}}$$

Times preferred dividends earned ratio. Preferred stockholders, like bondholders must usually be satisfied with a fixed dollar return on their investments. They are interested in the company's ability to make preferred dividend payments each year. This can be measured by computing the number of times preferred dividends are earned. The **times preferred dividends earned ratio** can be computed as follows:

$$\frac{\text{Times preferred dividends}}{\text{earned ratio}} = \frac{\text{Net income after income taxes}}{\text{Preferred dividends}}$$

Suppose a company has net income after income taxes of $48,000 and has $100,000 (par value) of 8 percent preferred stock outstanding. The number of times the preferred dividends are earned would be:

$$\frac{\$48,000}{\$8,000} = 6 \text{ times}$$

The higher this rate, the higher the probability that the preferred stockholders will receive their dividends each year. A preferred stockholder would be much more likely to expect to continue to receive dividends from a company that is earning eight times the dividend payment than one that is earning only twice the payment.

Market Ratios

Market ratios are computed using information from a company's financial statements and information about the market price of the company's stock. These ratios are used for comparing various stocks being traded in the marketplace; they help investors assess relative risks or benefits of different stocks.

Yield on common stock and price-earnings ratio. The **earnings yield** on a stock investment is the annual earnings per share as a percentage of the current market price per share. Thus, a firm's earnings yield per share of common stock is calculated as follows:

$$\text{Earnings yield on common stock} = \frac{\text{Earnings per share}}{\text{Current market price per share}}$$

Suppose, for example, that a company had earnings per share of common stock of $2 and that the quoted market price of the stock on the New York Stock Exchange was $30. The earnings yield on common stock would be:

$$\frac{\$2}{\$30} = 6\frac{2}{3} \text{ percent}$$

This ratio when inverted is called the **price-earnings ratio.** In the case just cited the price-earnings ratio is:

$$\text{Price-earnings ratio} = \frac{\text{Current market price per share}}{\text{Earnings per share}} = \frac{\$30}{\$2} = 15:1$$

Investors would say that this stock is selling at 15 times earnings or at a multiple of 15. These investors might have a multiple in mind as being the proper one that should be used to judge whether the stock is underpriced or overpriced. Different investors will have different estimates of the proper price-earnings ratio for a given stock and also different estimates of the future earnings prospects of the firm. These different estimates are two of the factors which cause one investor to sell stock at a particular price and another investor to buy at that price.

Dividend yield and payout ratios. The dividend paid per share of common stock is also of much interest to common stockholders. When the dividend is divided by the current market price per share, the result is called the **dividend yield.**

If the company referred to immediately above paid a $1.50 per share dividend, the dividend yield would be:

$$\text{Dividend yield on common stock} = \frac{\text{Dividend per share}}{\text{Current market price per share}}$$

$$= \frac{\$1.50}{\$30.00} = 5 \text{ percent}$$

One additional step is to divide the dividend per share by the earnings available per share to determine the **payout ratio on common stock** as follows:

$$\text{Payout ratio} = \frac{\text{Dividend per share}}{\text{Earnings per share}} = \frac{\$1.50}{\$2.00} = 75 \text{ percent}$$

A payout ratio of 75 percent means that the company paid out 75 percent of the earnings per share in the form of dividends. Some investors are attracted by the stock of companies that pay out a large percentage of their income. Other investors are attracted by the stock of companies that retain and reinvest a large percentage of their income. The tax status of the investor has a great deal to do with this. Investors in very high tax brackets often prefer to have the company reinvest the income with the expectation that this will result in share price appreciation that would be taxed at capital gains rates when the shares are sold. Dividends are taxed at ordinary income rates, which may be much higher than capital gains rates.

Yield on preferred stock.   Preferred stockholders compute dividend yield in a manner similar to the computation of dividend yield for common stockholders. Suppose a company has 2,000 shares of $100 par value, 8 percent preferred stock outstanding which has a current market price of $110 per share. The dividend yield is computed as follows:

$$\text{Dividend yield on preferred stock} = \frac{\text{Dividend per share}}{\text{Current market price per share}}$$

$$= \frac{\$8}{\$110} = 7.27 \text{ percent}$$

Through the use of dividend yield rates, different preferred stocks having different annual dividends and different market prices can be compared.

Many of the ratios presented in this chapter are summarized conveniently in Illustration 11.3.

Illustration 11.3 SUMMARY OF RATIOS

Ratio	Formula	Significance
Current ratio	Current assets ÷ Current liabilities	Test of debt-paying ability
Acid-test (quick) ratio	(Cash + Net receivables + Marketable securities) ÷ Current liabilities	Test of immediate debt-paying ability
Accounts receivable turnover	Net credit sales ÷ Average net accounts receivable	Test of quality of accounts receivable
Average collection period of accounts receivable (number of days' sales in accounts receivable)	Number of days in year ÷ Accounts receivable turnover rate	Test of quality of accounts receivable
Inventory turnover	Cost of goods sold ÷ Average inventory	Test of whether or not a sufficient volume of business is being generated relative to inventory
Total assets turnover	Net sales ÷ Average total assets	Test of whether or not volume of business generated is adequate relative to amount of capital invested in business
Equity ratio	Owners' (Stockholders') equity ÷ Total equities	Index of long-run solvency and safety
Rate of return on operating assets	Net operating income ÷ Operating assets	Measure of managerial effectiveness
Net income to stockholders' equity	Net income ÷ Average stockholders' equity	Measure of what a given company earned for its stockholders from all sources as a percentage of the stockholders' investment
EPS (of common stock)	Net income available to common stockholders ÷ Average number of shares of common stock outstanding	Tends to have an effect on the market price per share
Times interest earned ratio	Income before interest and taxes ÷ Interest expense	Indicates likelihood that long-term creditors will continue to receive their interest payments
Times preferred dividends earned ratio	Net income ÷ Preferred dividends	Indicates the probability that preferred stockholders will receive their dividend each year
Earnings yield on common stock	EPS ÷ Current market price per share	Useful for comparison with other stocks
Price-earnings ratio	Current market price per share ÷ EPS	Index of whether a stock is relatively cheap or expensive
Dividend yield	Dividend per share ÷ Current market price per share	Useful for comparison with other stocks
Payout ratio on common stock	Dividend per share ÷ EPS	Index of whether company pays out a large percentage of income as dividends or reinvests most of its income

FINAL CONSIDERATIONS IN FINANCIAL STATEMENT ANALYSIS

Comparative financial statements facilitate analysis of changes and possible trends. Generally, three to five years are necessary for evaluation. There is no substitute for informed judgment in financial analysis. Percentages and ratios are useful **guides** to aid comparisons. The financial analyst uses these tools to uncover potential strengths and weaknesses. The analyst should try to discover the **basic causes** behind changes and trends. For example, declining income may be due to poor management, declining product demand, poor cost control, an inefficient sales force, and so on. By examining key items on financial statements, the analyst can make informed judgments as to the chances for continued profitability.

Companies do not operate in an economic vacuum. It is important to place financial statement analysis within an industry and economic environment context. Acceptable current ratios, gross margin percentages, debt to equity ratios, and so on, vary widely depending upon environmental conditions and the industry in which the company operates. Even within an industry, legitimate variations may exist. For example, a retail discount store may operate at a relatively low gross margin percentage; this does not necessarily mean that its operating philosophy is inferior to that of its higher margin competitors. Additionally, within the same company over time, small percentage declines may indicate potential trouble. For example, a small percentage decline in gross margin percentage may be a danger signal because large dollar amounts may be involved.

The potential investor should realize that acquiring the ability to make informed judgments is a long process and is not acquired overnight. Using ratios and percentages mechanically is a sure road to wrong conclusions.

Need for Comparable Data

Analysts must be sure that their comparisons are valid—whether the comparisons be of items for different periods or dates or for items of different companies in the same period. Consistent accounting practices must be followed from period to period if interperiod comparisons are to be made. It is the accountant's responsibility to disclose any material changes in method or departures from consistent practice.

Influence of External Factors

Facts and conditions not disclosed by the financial statements may affect their interpretation. A single important event may have been largely responsible for a given relationship. For example, a new product may have been unexpectedly put on the market by competitors, making it necessary for the company under study to sacrifice its inventory of a product suddenly rendered obsolete. Such an event would affect the percentage of gross margin to net sales severely.

General business conditions within the business or industry of the company under study must be considered. A downward trend in income, for example, is less alarming if the trend in the industry or in business in general is also downward rather than limited to a single corporation.

Consideration should be given to the possible seasonal nature of the businesses under study. If the balance sheet date represents the seasonal peak in the volume of business, for example, the ratio of current assets to current liabilities may acceptably be much lower than if the balance sheet date is in a season of low activity.

Need for Comparative Standards

Relationships between financial statement items become more meaningful when standards are available for comparison. Comparison with standards provides a starting point for the analyst's thinking and leads to further investigation and, ultimately, to conclusions and business decisions. Such standards consist of (1) those that the analyst has in his or her own mind as a result of experience and observation; (2) those provided by the records of past performance and position of the business under study; and (3) those provided about other enterprises—for example, data available through trade associations, universities, research organizations, and governmental units.

Impact of Inflation

The utility of conventional financial statements has been questioned in recent years more than ever before. There is one primary reason for this—the statements fail to reveal the impact of inflation upon the reporting entity. One of the primary rules to be followed in making comparisons is to be sure that the items being compared are comparable. The old adage is that one should not add apples and oranges and call the total either apples or oranges. Yet, the accountant does exactly this when dollars of different real worth are added or subtracted as if they were the same. The worth of a dollar has been steadily declining as inflation surges strongly through our economy.

Considerable debate has existed over the proper response by accounting to inflation. Some argue that we should change our unit of measure from the nominal, unadjusted dollar to a dollar of constant purchasing power. Others maintain that only by adopting current values or current costs as the attribute measured will the real effects of inflation upon an entity be revealed. How each of these alternative approaches could be implemented and what they are likely to reveal is discussed in Chapter 12.

SUMMARY

The data contained in financial statements represents a quantitative summary of a firm's operations and activities. If a manager, investor, or creditor is skillful at using these statements much can be learned about a company's strengths, weaknesses, developing problems, operating efficiency, and profitability.

Many analytical techniques are available to assist managers and others in using financial statements and to assist them in assessing the direction and importance of trends and changes that are taking place in a company. We have discussed three such techniques—dollar and percentage changes in statements, trends analysis, and ratio analysis. In regard to ratio analysis, we have discussed (1) liquidity ratios, (2) solvency ratios, (3) profitability ratios, and (4) market ratios. We have noted that ratios and other analytical techniques are not ends in themselves, but rather represent a starting point in evaluating an organization. Once ratios are computed, the analyst should look for *basic causes* behind changes and trends which are observed. You may want to examine Appendix B at the end of the text and determine how you would go about analyzing the 1983 Financial Statements of the General Motors Corporation using some of the techniques you have learned in this and preceding chapters.

QUESTIONS

1. The higher the accounts receivable turnover rate, the better off the company is. Do you agree? Why?

2. Can you think of a situation where the current ratio is very misleading as an indicator of short-term debt-paying ability? Does the acid-test ratio offer a remedy to the situation you have described? Describe a situation where the acid-test ratio will not suffice either.

3. Before the Mitchell Company issued $10,000 of long-term notes (due more than a year from the date of issue) in exchange for a like amount of accounts payable, its acid-test ratio was 2 to 1. Will this transaction increase, decrease, or have no effect on the current ratio? The equity ratio?

4. Through the use of turnover rates, explain why a firm might seek to increase the volume of its sales even though such an increase can be secured only at reduced prices.

5. Indicate which of the relationships illustrated in the chapter would be best to judge:
   a. The short-term debt-paying ability of the firm.
   b. The overall efficiency of the firm without regard to the sources of assets.
   c. The return to owners of a corporation.
   d. The safety of long-term creditors interest.
   e. The safety of preferred stockholders' dividends.

6. Indicate how each of the following ratios or measures is calculated:
   a. Payout ratio.
   b. Earnings per share of common stock.

c. Price-earnings ratio.

d. Yield on common stock.

e. Yield on preferred stock.

f. Times interest earned.

g. Times preferred dividends earned.

h. Return on stockholders' equity.

7. How is the rate of return on operating assets determined? Is it possible for two companies with "operating margins" of 5 percent and 1 percent, respectively, to both have a rate of return of 20 percent on operating assets? How?

8. Cite some of the possible deficiencies in accounting information, especially regarding its use in analyzing a particular company over a 10-year period.

EXERCISES

1. Income statement data for Brown Company for 1986 and 1987 are:

	1987	1986
Net sales	$1,450,000	$1,076,000
Cost of goods sold	1,016,000	698,000
Operating expenses	220,000	194,000
Administrative expenses	130,000	110,000
Income taxes	32,000	30,000

Prepare a horizontal and vertical analysis of the above income data in a form similar to that in Illustration 1.2. Comment on the results of this analysis.

2. Under each of the three conditions listed below, compute the current ratio after each of the transactions described. Current assets are now $200,000. (Consider each transaction independently of the others.) The current ratio before the transactions is:

a. 1 to 1.

b. 2 to 1.

c. 1 to 2.

Transactions:
1. Purchased $200,000 of merchandise on account.
2. Purchased $100,000 of machinery for cash.
3. Issued stock for $100,000 cash.

3. A company has sales of $1,825,000 per year. Its average accounts receivable balance $365,000.

a. What is the average number of days an account receivable is outstanding?

b. Assuming released funds can be invested at 10 percent, how much could the company earn by reducing the collection period of the accounts receivable to 40 days?

c. What assumption must you make in order for this income calculation to be correct?

4. From the following partial income statement calculate the inventory turnover for the period.

Net sales		$1,042,900
Cost of goods sold:		
Beginning inventory	$100,000	
Purchases	740,000	
Cost of goods available for sale . .	$840,000	
Less: Ending inventory	116,000	
Cost of goods sold		$724,000
Gross margin		$318,900
Operating expenses		150,000
Net operating income		$168,900

5. The Small Company had 80,000 shares of common stock outstanding on January 1, 1986. On April 1, 1986, it issued 20,000 additional shares for cash. The income available for common stockholders for 1986 was $400,000. What amount of earnings per share of common stock should the company report?

6. A company paid interest of $8,000, incurred federal income taxes of $22,000 and had net income (after taxes) of $42,000. How many times was the interest earned?

7. The Silver Company had 8,000 shares of $100 par value, 5 percent, preferred stock outstanding. Net income after taxes was $240,000. The market price per share was $160.

   a. How many times were the preferred dividends earned?

   b. What was the yield on the preferred stock assuming the regular preferred dividends were declared and paid?

8. A company had 18,000 shares of $25 par value common stock outstanding. Net income was $60,000. Current market price per share is $80. Compute the price-earnings ratio.

9. Factory, Inc., had net sales of $1,320,000, gross margin of $560,000, and operating expenses of $340,000. Total assets (all operating) were $1,100,000. Compute Factory's rate of return on operating assets.

10. Markus Company started 1986 with 100,000 shares of common stock outstanding. On March 31, it issued 16,000 shares for cash; and on September 30, it purchased 8,000 treasury shares for cash. Compute the weighted-average number of common shares outstanding for the year.

11. Chad Company started 1987 with total stockholders' equity of $900,000. Its net income for 1987 was $240,000, and $40,000 of dividends were declared. Compute the rate of return on average stockholders' equity for 1986.

12. A company reported EPS of $2 ($200,000/100,000 shares) for 1986, ending the year with 100,000 shares outstanding. In 1987, the company earned net income of $330,000, issued 40,000 shares of common stock for cash on September 30, and distributed a 100 percent stock dividend on December 31, 1987. Compute EPS for 1986 and compute the adjusted EPS for 1986 that would be shown in the 1986 annual report.

PROBLEMS

11–1. Presented below are Hopkins Company's comparative balance sheets at the end of 1986 and 1987. The comparative statements of income and retained earnings for the years ended December 31, 1986, and 1987, are also given.

HOPKINS COMPANY
Comparative Balance Sheets
December 31, 1986, and 1987

	1987	1986
Assets		
Current assets:		
Cash	$ 20,400	$ 11,100
Accounts receivable, net	58,100	56,500
Inventory	144,500	150,100
Total current assets	$223,000	$217,700
Plant assets, net	188,000	179,000
Total assets	$411,000	$396,700
Liabilities and Stockholders' Equity		
Current liabilities:		
Accounts payable and accruals	$ 57,000	$121,700
Notes payable	40,000	100,000
Total current liabilities	$ 97,000	$221,700
Long-term liabilities		
Bonds payable	120,000	–0–
Total liabilities	$217,000	$221,700
Stockholders' equity:		
Common stock	$100,000	$100,000
Retained earnings	94,000	75,000
Total stockholders' equity	$194,000	$175,000
Total liabilities and stockholders' equity	$411,000	$396,700

HOPKINS COMPANY
Comparative Statements of Income and Retained Earnings
For the Years Ended December 31, 1986, and 1987

	1987	1986
Net sales	$824,500	$785,700
Cost of goods sold	523,100	501,100
Gross margin	$301,400	$284,600
Operating expenses:		
Selling	$121,100	$128,500
Administrative	112,200	103,900
Total operating expenses	$233,300	$232,400
Net operating income	$ 68,100	$ 52,200
Interest expense	18,400	12,000
Income before income taxes	$ 49,700	$ 40,200
Income taxes	20,000	16,000
Net income	$ 29,700	$ 24,200
Retained earnings, January 1	75,000	60,800
	$104,700	$ 85,000
Dividends	10,700	10,000
Retained earnings, December 31	$ 94,000	$ 75,000

Required:

a. Perform horizontal and vertical analysis of the above financial statements in a manner similar to that shown in Illustrations 11.1 and 11.2.

b. Comment on the results obtained.

11-2. You are given the following data for a company:

	1986	1987	1988	1989
Sales	$900,000	$1,030,000	$1,200,000	$1,700,000
Cost of goods sold . .	600,000	650,000	900,000	1,300,000
Gross margin	$300,000	$ 380,000	$ 300,000	$ 400,000
Operating expenses . .	240,000	256,000	294,000	352,000
Net operating income .	$ 60,000	$ 124,000	$ 6,000	$ 48,000

Required:

a. Prepare a statement showing the trend percentages for each of the above items, using 1986 as the base year.

b. Comment on the trends noted.

11-3. From the following data for the Harvey Company compute the *(a)* working capital; *(b)* current ratio; and *(c)* acid-test ratio, all as of both dates; and *(d)* comment briefly on the company's short-term financial position.

	December 31, 1987	December 31, 1986
Notes payable (due in 90 days) . . .	$188,000	$154,000
Merchandise inventory	800,000	704,800
Cash	253,240	313,400
Marketable securities	124,000	75,000
Accrued liabilities	48,000	55,200
Accounts receivable	470,000	460,000
Accounts payable	277,600	181,200
Allowance for doubtful accounts . . .	59,200	38,400
Bonds payable, due 1998	370,000	392,000
Prepaid expenses	16,200	18,600

11-4. On December 31, 1986, the Block Company's current ratio was 3 to 1. Assume that the following transactions were completed on that date and indicate *(a)* whether the amount of working capital would have been increased, decreased, or unaffected by each of the transactions; and *(b)* whether the current ratio would have been increased, decreased, or unaffected by each of the transactions. (Consider each transaction independently of all the others.)

Transactions:

1. Purchased merchandise on account.
2. Paid a cash dividend declared on November 15, 1987.
3. Sold equipment for cash.
4. Temporarily invested cash in marketable securities.
5. Sold obsolete merchandise for cash (at a loss).
6. Issued 10-year bonds for cash.
7. Amortized goodwill.
8. Paid cash for inventory.

9. Purchased land for cash.
10. Returned merchandise which had not been paid for.
11. Wrote off an account receivable as uncollectible.
12. Accepted a 90-day note from a customer in settlement of customer's account receivable
13. Declared a stock dividend on common stock.

11–5. The following are comparative balance sheets of the Simmons Corporation on December 31, 1986, and 1987:

SIMMONS CORPORATION
Comparative Balance Sheets
December 31, 1986, and 1987

	December 31, 1987	December 31, 1986
Assets		
Cash	$ 300,000	$ 340,000
Accounts receivable, net	260,000	300,000
Merchandise inventory	180,000	220,000
Plant assets, net	400,000	180,000
Total assets	$1,140,000	$1,040,000
Liabilities and Stockholders' Equity		
Accounts payable	$ 160,000	$ 100,000
Notes payable	140,000	172,000
Common stock	440,000	440,000
Retained earnings	400,000	328,000
Total liabilities and stockholders' equity .	$1,140,000	$1,040,000
Other data:		
Sales	$1,840,000	$1,600,000
Gross margin	760,000	680,000
Selling and administrative expenses . .	480,000	440,000
Interest expense	16,000	8,000
Cash dividends	152,000	60,000

During 1987, a note in the amount of $100,000 was given for equipment purchased at that price. Unlike the company's other notes, which are short term, the $100,000 note matures in 1998.

Required:

a. Prepare comparative income statements that show percentage of net sales for each item.

b. Prepare comparative balance sheets that show percentage of total assets for each item.

c. Prepare a schedule that shows the percentage of each current asset to the total of current assets as of both year-end dates.

d. Compute the current ratios as of both dates.

e. Compute the acid-test ratios as of both dates.

f. Compute the percentage of stockholders' equity to total equity (or total assets) as of both dates.

11–6. The following balance sheet and supplementary data are for the Baldwin Corporation for 1987:

BALDWIN CORPORATION
Balance Sheet
December 31,1987
Assets

Current assets:

Cash	$ 300,000	
Marketable securities	160,000	
Accounts receivable, net	260,000	
Inventory	220,000	$ 940,000

Property, plant, and equipment:

Plant assets	$3,400,000	
Less: Accumulated depreciation . . .	250,000	3,150,000
Total assets		$4,090,000

Liabilities and Stockholders' Equity

Current liabilities:

Accounts payable	$ 170,000	
Bank loans payable	70,000	$ 240,000

Long-term liabilities:

Mortgage notes payable, due in 1998 . .	$ 90,000	
Bonds payable 6%, due December 31, 1998	430,000	520,000
Total liabilities		$ 760,000

Stockholders' equity:

Common stock par value $50 per share . .	$2,200,000	
Appropriation for bond sinking fund . . .	80,000	
Retained earnings	1,050,000	3,330,000
Total liabilities and stockholders' equity . . .		$4,090,000

Supplementary data:

1. 1987 net income after taxes amounted to $300,000.

2. 1987 income before interest and taxes, $600,000.

3. 1987 cost of goods sold was $800,000.

4. 1987 net sales amounted to $1,500,000.

5. Inventory on December 31, 1986 was $150,000.

6. Interest expense for the year was $30,000. (Some long-term liabilities were paid during the year.)

Required:

Calculate the following ratios. Where you would normally use the average amount for an item in a ratio but the information is not available to do so, use the year-end balance. Show computations.

a. Current ratio.

b. Percentage of net income to stockholders' equity.

c. Turnover of inventory.

d. Average collection period of accounts receivable (there are 365 days in 1987).

e. Earnings per share of common stock.

f. Number of times interest was earned.

g. Stockholders' equity ratio.

h. Percentage of net income to total assets.

i. Turnover of total assets.

j. Acid-test ratio.

11–7. The following information is available about three companies:

	Operating Assets	Net Operating Income	Net Sales
Company A . . .	$ 300,000	$ 40,000	$ 440,000
Company B . . .	1,800,000	130,000	4,000,000
Company C . . .	8,000,000	1,050,000	7,500,000

Required:

a. Determine the operating margin, turnover of operating assets, and rate of return on operating assets for each company.

b. In the subsequent year the following changes took place (no other changes occurred):

Company A bought some new machinery at a cost of $50,000. Net operating income increased by $4,000 as a result of an increase in sales of $80,000.

Company B sold some equipment it was using that was relatively unproductive. The book value of the equipment sold was $200,000. As a result of the sale of the equipment, sales declined by $100,000 and operating income declined by $2,000.

Company C purchased some new retail outlets at a cost of $2,000,000. As a result, sales increased by $3,000,000 and operating income increased by $160,000.

1. Which company has the largest absolute change in:

  a. Operating margin?

  b. Turnover of operating assets?

  c. Rate of return on operating assets?

2. Which one realized the largest dollar change in operating income? Explain this in view of the rate of return on operating asset changes.

11–8. The following information is available for the Roberts Company:

	1987	1986
Net sales	$840,000	$520,000
Net income before interest and taxes	220,000	170,000
Net income after taxes	111,000	126,000
Interest expense	18,000	16,000
Stockholders' equity, December 31 (on December 31, 1985, $400,000)	610,000	470,000
Common stock, par value $100, December 31 .	520,000	460,000

Additional shares of common stock were issued on January 1, 1987.

Required:

Compute the following for both 1986 and 1987.

a. Earnings per share of common stock.

b. Percentage of net income to net sales.

c. Rate of return on average stockholders' equity.

d. Number of times interest was earned.

Compare and comment.

12 ACCOUNTING THEORY; INFLATION ACCOUNTING

ACCOUNTING THEORY

Accounting theory is a "set of basic concepts and assumptions and related principles that explain and guide the accountant's actions in identifying measuring, and communicating economic information."[1] First, the underlying assumptions or concepts are discussed.

UNDERLYING ASSUMPTIONS OR CONCEPTS

The underlying assumptions or basic concepts of accounting mentioned in Chapter 1 are discussed more fully in this chapter. Other concepts are also introduced, discussed, and illustrated.

Entity

An **entity** is a specific unit, such as a business, for which accounting information is gathered. An entity has an existence apart from its owners, creditors, employees, and other interested parties. For a single proprietorship, the business, not the individual, is the accounting entity. Financial statements must identify the entity for which they are prepared; and their content must be limited to reporting the activities, resources, and obligations of that entity.

---

[1] American Accounting Association, *A Statement of Basic Accounting Theory* (Sarasota Fla., 1966), pp. 1–2.

Going Concern (Continuity)

The **going-concern (continuity)** assumption states that an entity will continue to operate indefinitely unless there is evidence that the entity will terminate. An entity is terminated by ceasing business operations and selling the assets. The process of termination is called **liquidation.** If liquidation appears likely, the going-concern assumption can no longer be used.

The going-concern assumption often is used to justify the use of costs, rather than market values, in measuring assets. Market values are thought to be of little or no significance to an entity that intends to use rather than sell its assets. On the other hand, if an entity is to be liquidated, market values should be used to report assets.

The going-concern assumption permits the accountant to record certain items as assets. For example, printed advertising matter may be on hand to be used to promote a special sale next month and may have little, if any, value to anyone but its owner. Prepaid advertising is recorded as an asset because its owner is expected to continue operating long enough to benefit from it.

Money Measurement

Accounting measurements normally will be expressed in money terms. **Money measurement** means quantification in terms of a monetary unit of measurement, such as the dollar, instead of quantification in terms of physical or other units of measurement—feet, inches, grams, and so on. The unit of measure (the dollar in the United States) is identified in the financial statements.

The monetary unit, the dollar, also provides accountants with a common unit of measure in reporting upon economic activity. Without using the monetary unit, it would be impossible to add buildings, equipment, and inventory on a balance sheet. Even if prepared, such a statement would probably be of little value to anyone.

Stable dollar. The **stable dollar** assumption is that fluctuations in the value of the dollar are insignificant and may, therefore, be ignored. Use of the stable dollar assumption means that a portion of the cost of a building acquired in 1974 is deducted as depreciation, without adjustment for change in the value of the dollar, from revenues earned in 1986 in arriving at the net income for 1986. The 1974 and 1986 dollars are treated as equal units of measure, even though substantial price inflation has occurred over the 12-year period. The inflation rate experienced in the middle to late 1970's has created interest in the problem of adjusting financial statements for changes in the general price level. Inflation accounting will be discussed in more detail later in this chapter.

Periodicity (Time Periods)

The **periodicity (time periods)** assumption is that an entity's life can be subdivided into time periods for purposes of reporting on its economic activities. Accountants subdivide the life of an entity into periods and prepare reports on the activities of those periods to provide useful and timely financial information to investors and creditors. The reports cover relatively short periods of time. The time periods usually are of equal length so that valid comparisons can be made of a company's performance from period to period. The length of the period must be stated in the financial statements.

Accrual basis. Financial statements better reflect the financial status and operations of a firm when prepared under the accrual basis of accounting. Under the accrual basis, revenues are recorded when services are rendered or products are sold and delivered. Expenses are recorded as incurred.

Approximation and judgment. Many accounting measurements are estimates. To provide periodic financial information, estimates must often be made of such things as expected uncollectible accounts and useful lives of depreciable assets. Uncertainty about future events prevents precise measurement and makes estimates necessary. Accounting estimates are often reasonably accurate because they are made by an informed accountant. The need to exercise judgment prevents accountants from stating a set of inflexible rules such as depreciate all trucks over three years regardless of their useful lives. (While inflexible rules may be used for tax purposes, such as ACRS depreciation, they are not normally used for financial reporting.)

General Purpose Financial Statements

Results of the financial accounting process are presented in general purpose financial statements. General purpose financial statements are presented to external parties and top-level internal managers. The statements try to meet the common needs of these and other users. Special purpose financial information can be developed from accounting records. For example, some information needed by management to decide whether to purchase a new computer may be obtained from the accounting records rather than directly from the financial statements.

Substance over Form

In some instances, the economic substance of a transaction may conflict with its legal form. A contract that is legally a lease may, in fact, be equivalent to a purchase. For example, a company may have a three-year contract to lease (rent) an auto at a stated monthly rental fee. At the end of the lease period, upon the payment of a nominal sum (say, $1), the company will receive title to the auto. The economic substance of this transaction is to purchase rather than lease the auto. The accountant should always record the economic substance of a transaction rather than be guided by the legal form of the transaction.

Consistency

Consistency generally requires a company to use the same accounting principles and reporting practices through time; this concept bars indiscriminate switching of principles and methods, such as changing depreciation methods every year. Consistency does not bar a change in principles if the information needs of users are better served by the change. When a change in principles is made, disclosure of the change, reasons for the change, and its effect on net income, if significant, are required.

Other Assumptions or Concepts

The **transactions approach** is used in financial accounting. Under the transactions approach, every transaction has a **dual** effect upon each party engaging in it. This assumption gives rise to the double-entry form of accounting.

Also, financial statements are **fundamentally related** and articulate (interact) with each other. For example, the amount of net income is carried from the income statement to complete the statement of retained earnings (or owner's equity). The ending balance on the statement of retained earnings is carried to the balance sheet to bring total assets and total equities into balance.

MEASUREMENT IN ACCOUNTING

Accounting is often defined as a measurement process. The accountant seeks to measure the assets, liabilities, and stockholders' (owners') equity of an accounting entity. Changes that occur in assets, liabilities, and stockholders' equity are also measured, and the effects of these changes are assigned to particular time periods to find net income of the accounting entity.

Measuring Assets

Cash is measured at its specified amount. Claims to cash, such as notes and accounts receivable, are measured at their expected cash inflows, taking into consideration possible uncollectibles. Inventories, prepaid expenses, plant assets, and intangibles are originally measured at their costs at time of acquisition.

Measuring Liabilities

Liabilities are measured in terms of the cash that will be paid or the value of services that will be performed to satisfy the liabilities.

Measuring Changes in Assets and Liabilities

Some changes in assets and liabilities are easily measured by the accountant. Such changes include the exchange of one asset for another of equal value, acquisition of an asset on credit, and payment of a liability. Other changes in assets and liabilities are more difficult to measure because they affect net income and stockholders' equity. The accountant must determine when a change has taken place and the amount of the change. These decisions involve matching revenues and expenses and are guided by the principles discussed below.

**THE MAJOR
PRINCIPLES**

Generally accepted accounting principles are presented in the discussion that follows. The effects of these principles have been mentioned previously; the purpose here is to expand the coverage.

**The Exchange Price
(or Cost) Principle**

The **exchange price (or cost) principle** means that transfers of resources are recorded at prices agreed upon by the parties to the exchange at the time of exchange. Thus, for any firm, this exchange price principle determines (1) what goes into the accounting system—transaction data; (2) when it is recorded—at the time of exchange; and (3) the amounts—exchange prices—at which assets, liabilities, stockholders' equity, revenues, and expenses are recorded. As applied to certain assets, this principle is often called the *cost principle,* meaning that, initially, assets are recorded at historical cost. **Historical cost** is the amount paid or fair value of liability incurred or other resource surrendered to acquire an asset. The term **exchange price principle** is preferable to the term **cost principle** because it seems inappropriate to use cost principle when referring to liabilities, stockholders' equity, and assets such as cash and accounts receivable.

The Matching Principle

Using the **matching principle,** net income of a period is determined by associating or relating revenues earned in a period with expenses incurred to generate the revenues. The logic underlying this principle is that whenever economic resources are used, someone will want to know what was accomplished and at what cost. Every evaluation of economic activity will involve matching benefit with sacrifice. The application of the matching principle is discussed and illustrated below.

Revenue Recognition

Revenue is the inflow of assets from the sale of goods and services to customers; it is measured by the amount of cash expected to be received from the customer. A question arises as to when this revenue should be recorded (credited to a revenue account). The general answer given by the **revenue recognition principle** is that the revenue should be *earned* and *realized* before it is recognized (recorded).

  The earning of revenue. All activities undertaken by a firm to create revenues are part of the earnings process. The actual receipt of cash from a customer may have been preceded by many activities including (1) placing advertisements, (2) calling on the customer several times, (3) submitting samples, (4) acquiring or manufacturing goods, and (5) delivering goods. Costs were incurred for these activities. Revenue actually was being earned by these activities, even though in most instances accountants do not recognize revenue until time of sale because of the requirement that revenue be substantially earned before it is recognized (recorded). This requirement is referred to as the **earnings principle.**

The realization of revenue. Under the **realization principle,** revenue is recognized only after the seller acquires the right to receive payment from the buyer. The seller acquires the right to receive payment from the buyer at the time of sale for merchandise transactions and when services have been performed in service transactions. Legally, a sale of merchandise occurs when title to the goods passes to the buyer. As a practical matter, accountants generally record revenue when goods are delivered.

The advantages of recognizing revenue at the time of sale are that (1) delivery of goods is an observable event; (2) revenue is measurable; (3) risk of loss due to price decline or destruction of goods has passed to the buyer; (4) revenue has been earned, or substantially so; and (5) because the revenue has been earned, expenses and net income can be determined. As discussed below, the disadvantage of recognizing revenue at the time of sale is that the revenue might not be recorded in the period in which most of the activity creating it occurred.

Exceptions to the Realization Principle

The following examples illustrate instances in which practical considerations may cause accountants to vary the point of revenue recognition from point of sale. These examples illustrate the effect that the business environment has on the development of accounting principles and standards.

Cash basis of revenue recognition. Some small firms record revenues and expenses at the time of cash collection and payment. This procedure is known as the **cash basis** of accounting. The cash basis is acceptable primarily in service enterprises that do not have substantial credit transactions or inventories.

Installment basis of revenue recognition. When the selling price of goods sold is to be collected in installments (such as monthly or annually) and considerable doubt exists as to collectibility, the installment basis of accounting may be used. Such sales are made in spite of the doubtful collectibility because the margin of profit is high and the goods can be repossessed if the payments are not received. The **installment basis** is a revenue recognition procedure in which the gross margin on an installment sale is recognized in proportion to the cash collected on the receivable. In other words, under the installment basis, gross margin on a sale (selling price of a good minus its cost) is recognized as cash is collected from customers. For example, assume the following facts concerning a stereo set:

Date of Sale	Selling Price	Cost	Gross Margin (Selling price − Cost)	Gross Margin Percentage (Gross margin ÷ Selling price)
October 1, 1986	$1,000	$600	($1,000 − $600 = $400)	($400 ÷ $1,000) = 40 percent

Ten equal monthly installment payments of $100 each are required to pay for the set (10 × $100 = $1,000). If three monthly payments are received in 1986, the total amount of cash received in 1986 is $300 (3 × $100). The total gross margin to recognize or record in 1986 is computed as cash received times gross margin percentage, or $300 × 0.40 = $120.

The other installments are collected when due so that a total of $700 is received in 1987. The total gross margin to recognize in 1987 is $280 ($700 × 0.40). In summary, the total receipts and gross margin recognized in the two years are as follows:

	Total Amount of Cash Received	Gross Margin Recognized
1986	$ 300	$120
1987	700	280
Total	$1,000	$400

The installment basis of revenue recognition is accepted for tax purposes. But for accounting purposes, since the installment basis delays revenue recognition beyond the time of sale, it is acceptable only when considerable doubt exists as to collectibility of the installments.

Revenue recognition on long-term construction projects. Revenue from a long-term construction project can be recognized under two different methods: (1) the completed-contract method or (2) the percentage-of-completion method. The **completed-contract method** is a method of recognizing revenue on long-term projects in which no revenue is recognized until the period in which the project is completed. At that point, all revenue is recognized even though the contract may have required three years to complete. Thus, the *completed-contract method recognizes revenues at the point of sale.* Costs incurred on the project are carried forward in an inventory account (Construction in Process) and are charged to expense in the period in which the revenue is recognized.

Some accountants argue that it is unreasonable to wait so long to recognize any revenue. Revenue-producing activities have been performed during each year of construction, and revenue should be recognized even if estimates are needed. The **percentage-of-completion method** is a method of recognizing revenue based on the estimated stage of completion of a long-term project. The stage of completion is measured by comparing actual costs incurred in a period with the total estimated costs to be incurred on the project. To illustrate, assume that a firm has a contract to build a dam for

$22 million that has an estimated construction cost of $20 million, as shown:

Sales Price of Dam	Estimated Costs to Construct Dam	Estimated Gross Margin (Sales price − Estimated Costs)
$22 million	$20 million	$22 million − $20 million = $2 million

By the end of the first year (1986), the company had incurred **actual** construction costs of $15 million. The $15 million of construction costs are 75 percent of total estimated construction costs ($15 million ÷ $20 million = 75 percent). Under the percentage-of-completion method, the 75 percent figure would be used to **assign** revenue to the first year. In 1987, another $2 million of construction costs are incurred. The dam will be completed in 1988. The amount of revenue to assign to 1986 and 1987 is determined as follows:

Year	Ratio of Actual Construction Costs to Total Estimated Construction Costs	× Agreed Price of Dam =	Amount of Revenue to Recognize
1986 . . .	($15 million ÷ $20 million) = 75 percent	× $22 million =	16.5 million
1987 . . .	($2 million ÷ $20 million) = 10 percent	× $22 million	$2.2 million

The amount of gross margin in 1986 is equal to revenue of $16.5 million minus construction costs of $15 million. Thus, $1.5 million of gross margin is recognized in 1986. Gross margin in 1987 would be $0.2 million or $200,000, computed as $2.2 million of revenues minus construction costs of $2 million. Period costs, such as general and administrative expenses, would be deducted from gross margin to determine net income. For instance, assuming general and administrative expenses were $50,000 in 1987, net income would be $150,000 ($200,000 − $50,000).

Revenue recognition at completion of production. Recognizing revenue at the time of completion of production or extraction is called the **production basis.** The production basis is considered acceptable procedure for many farm products such as wheat, corn, and soybeans and for certain precious metals (gold). The reasons advanced to justify recognizing revenue prior to sale for these products include the homogeneous nature of the products, the fact that the products can usually be sold at stated market prices, and the difficulties sometimes encountered in determining unit production costs.

Recognizing revenue upon completion of production or extraction is accomplished by debiting inventory (an asset) and crediting a revenue account for the expected selling price of the goods. All costs incurred in the period can then be treated as expenses. For example, assume that 2,000 ounces of gold are mined at a time its market price is $400 per ounce. The entry to record the extraction of 2,000 ounces of gold would be:

```
Inventory of Gold (2,000 ounces × $400)  . . . .  800,000
     Revenue from Extraction of Gold   . . . . .            800,000
     To record extraction of 2,000 ounces of gold. Selling
     price is $400 per ounce.
```

If expenses in producing the gold were $600,000, net income on the gold mined would be $200,000.

Expense and Loss Recognition

An **expense** is the outflow or using up of assets in the generation of revenue. An expense is incurred **voluntarily** to produce revenue. For instance, the cost of a television set delivered by a dealer to a customer in exchange for cash can readily be thought of as an asset expiration to produce revenue. Similarly, the cost of services such as labor can be thought of as expiring in the production of revenue.

Losses are also asset expirations, but they are **involuntary** and do not produce revenue. Fire losses are an example. The cost of an uninsured building that was destroyed in a fire is a loss suffered involuntarily with no revenue being generated.

The measurement of expense. Most assets used in operating a business are measured in terms of historical costs. Therefore, expenses resulting from expired assets are measured in terms of the historical costs of those assets. Other expenses are paid for currently and are measured in terms of their current costs.

The timing of expense recognition. The matching principle implies that a relationship exists between expenses and revenues. For certain expenses, the relationship is easily seen as in the case of goods delivered to customers. When a direct relationship cannot be seen, the costs of assets with limited lives may be charged to expense in the periods benefited on a systematic and rational allocation basis. Depreciation of plant assets is an example. In other instances, the relationship between expense and revenue can only be assumed to exist, as in the case of a contribution to the local community fund. Consequently, the timing of expense recognition is guided by the concepts of product costs and period costs.

Product costs are costs incurred in the acquisition or manufacture of goods. Included as product costs for purchased goods are invoice, freight, and insurance-in-transit costs. For manufacturing firms, product costs include all costs of materials, labor, and factory operations necessary to produce goods. Product costs are assumed to attach to the goods purchased or produced and are carried in inventory accounts as long as the goods are on hand. Product costs are charged to expense when the goods are sold. The result is a precise matching of cost of goods sold expense and its related revenue.

Period costs are costs that cannot be traced to specific revenues and that are, as a result, expensed in the period in which incurred. Selling and administrative costs are examples of period costs.

MODIFYING CONVENTIONS

In certain instances, accounting principles might not be strictly applied because of modifying conventions. **Modifying conventions** are customs emerging from accounting practice that alter results that would be obtained from a strict application of accounting principles. Two such modifying conventions are materiality and conservatism.

Materiality. **Materiality** is a modifying convention that allows the accountant to deal with immaterial (unimportant) items in a theoretically incorrect, expedient manner. Small dollar amount items often do not make a difference in a decision and are considered to be *immaterial* to the decision. Large dollar amount items usually do make a difference in a decision and are considered to be *material* (important) to the decision. The accountant records all material items in a theoretically correct way. *Immaterial items may be recorded in a theoretically incorrect way simply because it is more convenient and less expensive to do so.* For example, the purchase of a wastebasket may be debited to an expense account rather than an asset account even though the wastebasket has an expected useful life of 10 years. It simply is not worth the expense of recording depreciation expense on such a small item over its life.

There is more to materiality than relative size of dollar amounts. The very nature of the item may make it material. For example, it may be quite significant to know that a firm is paying bribes or making illegal political contributions even if the dollar amounts of such items are relatively small.

Conservatism. **Conservatism** means being cautious or prudent and making sure that any errors in estimates tend to understate rather than overstate net assets and net income. Conservatism is the accountant's response to the uncertainty faced in the environment in which accounting is practiced. Many accounting measurements are estimates and involve the exercise of judgment. In such cases, conservatism tells the accountant "to play it safe." Playing it safe usually involves trying to avoid overstating net assets or net income.

Conservatism may be applied differently in various firms, causing decreased comparability among their financial statements. Conservative reporting may cause investors to act in a manner not in their best interest. Investors may, for example, dispose of their interest in a firm because income of the firm did not meet investors' expectations. Yet this failure of income to reach expectations may have been due solely to a conservative measurement of inventories. Thus, a fine line exists between conservative and incorrect accounting.

The Conceptual Framework Project

The Appendix to this chapter discusses the Conceptual Framework Project of the Financial Accounting Standards Board. The Conceptual Framework Project is designed to resolve some disagreements as to the proper theoretical foundation for accounting. The project is underway as of this writing. The initial results of the project that pertain to the content of this text are presented in the chapter Appendix.

International Accounting

Appendix A at the end of the text discusses international accounting. Methods to harmonize accounting principles and standards throughout the world are continuing to develop. You may wish to read Appendix A now or after you have covered some or all of the other chapters.

INFLATION—A SERIOUS REPORTING PROBLEM

Many users have questioned the adequacy of financial statement information. This questioning has arisen largely from the fact that in the past, no attempt was made to include the impact of inflation upon the results of operations and financial position of the reporting company. One of the most serious problems ever faced by accountants—how to account for and report financial data in periods of inflation—is now discussed.

In response to some criticisms of historical cost accounting, accountants have recently used various alternatives to deal with the problem of inflation. A **period of inflation** is a time during which prices in general are rising, while a **period of deflation** is when prices in general are falling. Only in periods of high inflation has the historical cost approach to recording accounting data been severely criticized. During times of inflation, the historical cost approach often reports income when the economic value of the owner's investment has not even been maintained.

There are two widely recommended accounting approaches to the problem of inflation. One is general price-level adjusted accounting, also known as constant dollar accounting. This approach shows financial statement historical cost figures as adjusted for changes in the general price level. The other approach is current cost accounting. The current cost approach shows the current cost or value of items in the financial statements.

THE NATURE AND MEASUREMENT OF INFLATION

In a period of inflation, the "real value" of the dollar—its ability to purchase goods and services—is falling. In a period of deflation, the real value of the dollar is rising.

Changes in the general level of prices are measured by means of a general price index such as the consumer price index (CPI). A **price index** is a weighted average of prices for various goods and services. A base year is chosen and assigned a value of 100 for comparative purposes. If the index stands at 108 a year later, this means that prices in general rose 8 percent during the year. An index of 200 would mean that prices on the average have doubled. Prices of individual types of items may change at different rates and may, in some cases, actually decline. For example, the CPI shows that prices for a "basket" of selected consumer goods doubled in the decade of the 1970s. But during that same decade, gasoline prices quadrupled, while the price of electronic handheld calculators declined very sharply.

The real value or purchasing power of the dollar relative to that of the base year is shown by the reciprocal of the price index. The ratio is merely inverted. For example, if the index for 1986 is 200 and for 1976 is 100, the price index is 200/100, meaning that prices have doubled since 1976. Alternatively, the reciprocal of the price index is 100/200, meaning that the value of the dollar in 1986 has dropped to one half or 50 percent of its purchasing power in 1976.

It is said that financial reports are inadequate in periods of inflation because accounting measurements consist largely of dollars of historical cost. **Historical cost accounting** measures accounting transactions in terms of the actual dollars expended or received. Such a measurement system has worked well in periods of stable prices. But the system does not work well when the dollar, in terms of its purchasing power, is a sharply changing unit of measure.

To illustrate, assume that a tract of land was purchased for $4,000 and held several years before being sold for $5,000. While the land was held, a general price index rose from 100 to 140. Historical cost accounting would report recovery of the $4,000 cost and income from gain on sale of land of $1,000. Measured in terms of dollars of constant purchasing power, a far different result is obtained. To get back the purchasing power originally invested in the land, the land would have to be sold for $5,600 ($4,000 × 140/100). Since only $5,000 was received, no income has been earned because the cost has not been recovered. In fact, a loss of $600 of current purchasing power was incurred.

CONSEQUENCES OF IGNORING EFFECTS OF INFLATION

As shown in the example above, transactions and, therefore, financial statements that have not been adjusted for the effects of inflation may yield misleading information. Such information may make comparisons of firms difficult. Suppose Company A acquired a tract of land for $200,000 several years ago. Now Company B acquired a virtually identical tract of land for $300,000, paying the higher price because prices in general have risen 50 percent since Company A bought its land. Immediately, both companies sold their land for $300,000 each. Company A would appear to have the more efficient management because it was able to earn $100,000 on the sale of the land, while Company B earned $0. In reality, the two companies are in the same position relative to the sale of the land because they have the same number of dollars of current purchasing power. The financial statement difference is caused by recording the land at its historical cost.

As another example, assume that the asset acquired was a depreciable asset instead of land. Company A and Company B earn exactly the same number of dollars of revenues and incur, except for depreciation, exactly the same number of dollars of expenses. If both companies had assumed a 10-year useful life on the asset and apply straight-line depreciation, Company A will have a larger net income than Company B simply due to the fact that the historical cost of its depreciable asset and, therefore, its recorded depreciation expense is lower than for Company B.

Failure to adjust for the impact of inflation may lead to conclusions that are not valid. A five-year summary of sales may show that sales dollars have increased 50 percent over the period. If sales prices have increased 60 percent over the five years, physical sales volume has actually declined.

There are many other consequences that flow from a failure to adjust financial reports for the effects of inflation. Companies are paying taxes on "income" when in reality, costs may not have been covered. Also, financial reports that fail to reflect the impact of inflation may be misleading to individual decision makers causing them to make decisions that are not in their best interests.

ACCOUNTING RESPONSES TO INFLATION

There are two basic types of price changes: general and specific. **General price changes** relate to the changing value of the dollar in relation to the economy as a whole. **Specific price changes** relate to changes in prices of specific items in the economy. Specific price changes may move in the same direction as, or a different direction from, changes in the value of a dollar. They may also move at a different rate. Specific price changes generally reflect the availability or supply of a particular item. For example, although there has been a great deal of inflation in the past few years, the cost of a personal computer has declined dramatically. This is due to improved technology and, therefore, increased availability of the computer. The general price change was in one direction, and the specific price change was in the other.

Two Alternatives

Because of these two types of price changes, two widely recommended approaches to accounting for changing prices have developed. These are:

1. Change the unit of measure from the nominal dollar to a dollar of constant purchasing power; this approach is referred to as **constant dollar accounting.**

2. Change the unit of measure from historical cost to current cost or value; this approach is called **current cost accounting.**

An example of these two approaches is necessary before turning to a more detailed illustration. Assume the following facts regarding the purchase and resale of 1,000 units of product:

Date	Transaction		Amount	Price-Level Index
January 1, 1986	Purchased 1,000 units		$ 6,000	100
December 31, 1986	Sold	1,000 units	10,000	120

The current cost of the units on December 31, 1986, was $7,800. The company incurred $1,600 of expenses to sell the units.

Under conventional (historical cost) accounting, net income from continuing operations for 1986 would be:

Sales		$10,000
Cost of goods sold	$6,000	
Other expenses	1,600	7,600
Net income from continuing operations		$ 2,400

The $2,400 of income results from deducting the historical cost of the goods sold as well as the other expenses from sales revenue. The company appears to be better off after the transactions because it has not only recovered the original dollar investment in the goods, together with the expenses incurred, but has an additional $2,400. No attention is paid to the fact that the dollars recovered do not have the same purchasing power as those originally invested. The fact that current replacement cost of the goods sold exceeds their historical cost by $1,800 ($7,800 − $6,000) also is ignored.

What would a statement reporting on the company's net income from continuing operations for 1986 contain under the alternative approaches given above? The possible reports are shown in Illustration 12.1.

Illustration 12.1
ALTERNATIVE REPORTING APPROACHES—STATEMENT OF NET INCOME FROM CONTINUING OPERATIONS

	Statement of Net Income from Continuing Operations					
	Historical Cost Accounting		Constant Dollar Accounting		Current Cost Accounting	
Sales		$10,000		$10,000		$10,000
Cost of goods sold	$6,000		$7,200		$7,800	
Other expenses	1,600		1,600		1,600	
Total expenses		7,600		8,800		9,400
Net income from continuing operations		$ 2,400		$ 1,200		$ 600

Constant dollar accounting. In the column headed "Constant Dollar Accounting," in Illustration 12.1, cost of goods sold is restated into end-of-1986 dollars by the use of a ratio of the current price index to the old price index: $6,000 × 120/100 = $7,200. The $7,200 is the amount of purchasing power invested in the goods expressed in the end-of-1986 dollars. Thus, the $7,200 is restated into the same dollars in which the sales revenue is expressed. The $1,600 of other expenses are assumed to be selling expenses incurred at point of sale (such as sales commissions) and are already stated in end-of-1986 dollars. All dollar amounts are now expressed in comparable terms—end-of-1986 dollars. The company is better off because it has increased its purchasing power by $1,200. Under constant dollar accounting, income means an increased ability to acquire goods and services.

Current cost accounting. The **current cost** of an asset is the amount that would have to be paid currently to acquire the asset. In the column headed "Current Cost Accounting," net income from continuing operations is computed by deducting the current cost of replacing the goods sold, together with other expenses, from current revenues. No adjustments are made for general price-level changes. Rather, this method focuses on specific price-level changes. Calculating net income from continuing operations in this manner is supported on the grounds that the sale of an inventory item leads directly to a further action—replenishment of the inventory—if the firm is to remain a going concern. A better picture of a firm's ability to compete in its markets may also be provided by comparing current revenues with current costs rather than with outdated historical costs. An argument can be made that the $600 represents "disposable" income. Only $600 or less can be distributed to owners without reducing the scale of operations.

Choosing the correct method. With two different methods of adjusting for inflation available, the question of which is the correct method arises. There is no direct answer possible. Each method is correct if one accepts the definitions of cost and income implicit in the method. A much more important question is: Which method is more useful to users of the financial reports? The answer to this question is of considerable concern to many people, including members of the FASB and the staff of the SEC. But, as of this writing, the question remains unanswered.

CONSTANT DOLLAR ACCOUNTING

As already discussed briefly, historical dollar amounts in financial statements may be converted or restated into a number of constant dollars that have an equivalent amount of purchasing power. When adjusted for inflation, conventional financial statements are called constant dollar or general price-level adjusted financial statements.

In the past, inflation adjusted statements generally have been recommended, not required, as supplementary information to conventional financial statements. In 1979, the FASB issued a standard that **requires** certain large, publicly-held corporations to present certain supplementary information about the effects of inflation.[2]

Converting the Income Statement

Presented below is an example of how the income statement can be adjusted for changes in the general price level. Knowing how this is done will lead to a better understanding of the FASB requirements. To serve as a basis for illustration, the income statement of the Foster Company is presented in Illustration 12.2.

To convert historical dollars into constant end-of-year dollars, the formula is:

$$\text{Historical dollars} \times \frac{\text{Price index at end of current period}}{\text{Price index at date of historical transaction}} = \text{Constant dollars}$$

In order to convert the income statement of the Foster Company, certain assumptions must be made or information provided. These data are as follows:

---

[2] FASB, *Statement of Financial Accounting Standards No. 33*, "Financial Reporting and Changing Prices" (Stamford, Conn., 1979).

1. The general price-level index stood at 100 on December 31, 1985, and at 108 on December 31, 1986.

2. Sales, purchases, other expenses, and taxes were incurred uniformly throughout the year. This means that, on the average, these items were incurred when the price index was 104.

3. Inventories are costed on a FIFO basis. The beginning inventory was acquired when the price index was 98, and the ending inventory was acquired when the index stood at 106.

4. The price index was 54 when the plant assets were acquired.

The following procedures were applied in the conversion of the Foster Company income statement. First, all items incurred uniformly throughout the year are converted by multiplying their historical amounts by a ratio of 108/104. Beginning inventory is converted using a ratio of 108/98, while ending inventory is converted to constant dollars by multiplying by 108/106. Since depreciation is calculated on the historical costs of the related assets that were acquired when the index stood at 54, depreciation expense is converted using a ratio of 108/54. Illustration 12.3 shows the restated income statement for the Foster Company.

In Illustration 12.3, note the inclusion of an item called purchasing power gain on monetary items. After converting amounts in the income statement to constant dollars, one must determine the amount of gain or loss in purchasing power experienced during the period.

Purchasing power gains and losses. Purchasing power gains and losses result from holding monetary assets and liabilities during inflation or deflation. **Monetary items** are cash and other assets and liabilities that represent fixed claims to cash such as accounts and notes receivable and payable. **Nonmonetary items** include all items on the balance sheet other than monetary items. A **purchasing**

Illustration 12.2
INCOME STATEMENT—HISTORICAL COST BASIS

FOSTER COMPANY
Income Statement
For the Year Ended December 31, 1986

Sales			$200,000
Cost of goods sold:			
Inventory, December 31, 1985		$ 20,000	
Purchases		160,000	
Goods available for sale		$180,000	
Inventory, December 31, 1986		40,000	140,000
Gross margin			$ 60,000
Depreciation		$ 4,000	
Other expenses		46,000	50,000
Net income			$ 10,000

Illustration 12.3
INCOME STATEMENT—CONSTANT DOLLAR BASIS
(End-of-Year Dollars)

FOSTER COMPANY
Restated Income
For the Year Ended December 31, 1986
(in constant end-of-year 1986 dollars)

	Historical Dollars		Conversion Ratio		Constant Dollars
Sales	$200,000	×	108/104	=	$207,692
Cost of goods sold:					
Inventory, December 31, 1985	$ 20,000	×	108/98	=	$ 22,041
Purchases	160,000	×	108/104	=	166,154
Goods available for sale	$180,000				$188,195
Inventory, December 31, 1986	40,000	×	108/106	=	40,755
Cost of goods sold	$140,000				$147,440
Gross margin	$ 60,000				$ 60,252
Expenses:					
Depreciation	$ 4,000	×	108/54	=	$ 8,000
Other expenses	46,000	×	108/104	=	47,769
Total expenses	$ 50,000				$ 55,769
Net income from continuing operations	$ 10,000				$ 4,483
Purchasing power gain on monetary items					2,625
Net income	$ 10,000				$ 7,108

power gain results from holding monetary liabilities during inflation or monetary assets during deflation. A **purchasing power loss** results from holding monetary assets during inflation or monetary liabilities during deflation.

Assume that Don Baker holds $1,000 of cash during a year in which prices in general rose 25 percent. Even though Don still has his $1,000 at year-end, he has less purchasing power than he did at the beginning of the year. Don needs to have $1,250 ($1,000 × 125/100) at year-end to be as well off as he was at the start of the year. Therefore, during the year, Don has sustained a purchasing power loss of $250.

Conversely, a gain results from being in debt during inflation. Assume that Karen Ross owes $600 during a year in which prices rise 40 percent. The original debt has a year-end purchasing power equivalent of $840 ($600 × 140/100). Karen can satisfy the debt by paying $600 currently. Thus, she has experienced a purchasing power gain of $240.

If Foster Company, in Illustration 12.2, experienced a purchasing power gain of $2,625 during 1986, this amount would be added to net income from continuing operations on the restated income statement. This gives a net income on a constant dollar basis of

$7,108, which is nearly 30 percent less than the net income shown on the conventional (historical cost) income statement.

Converting the Balance Sheet

Illustration 12.4 presents the balance sheet of Foster Company as of December 31, 1986, on the historical cost basis.

Illustration 12.4
BALANCE SHEET—HISTORICAL COST BASIS

FOSTER COMPANY
Balance Sheet
December 31, 1986

Assets

Cash	$ 10,000
Inventory	40,000
Plant assets, net	60,000
Land	48,000
Total assets	$158,000

Liabilities and Stockholders' Equity

Accounts payable	$ 8,000
Bonds payable	40,000
Capital stock	100,000
Retained earnings	10,000
Total liabilities and stockholders' equity	$158,000

In converting the balance sheet from conventional historical accounting to constant dollar accounting, one must apply a ratio to most items on the balance sheet. The ratio relates the price-level index at the end of the period to the index that existed when the item was acquired. This enables us to see the number of dollars in today's purchasing power it would have taken to acquire items that were, in reality, acquired at other points in time. In converting the balance sheet, a distinction is drawn between monetary and nonmonetary items. Since monetary items are expressed in fixed amounts of cash, there is no need to convert these in preparing a constant dollar balance sheet. The fact that the purchasing power of the dollar has declined, for example, will not cause customers to pay more than the stated amount of their accounts receivable balance even though the dollars received by the company are worth less than when the customer bought the goods.

Illustration 12.5 is the converted balance sheet for 1986 for Foster Company. Notice that the monetary items are the same as they appeared in the conventional balance sheet. This is because the monetary items are fixed in amount.

The values of nomonetary items, however, fluctuate with chang-

Illustration 12.5
BALANCE SHEET—CONSTANT DOLLAR BASIS

FOSTER COMPANY
Restated Balance Sheet
December 31, 1986

	Historical Dollars	Conversion Ratio	Constant Dollars
Cash	$ 10,000		$ 10,000
Inventory	40,000	108/106	40,755
Plant assets, net . . .	60,000	108/54	120,000
Land	48,000	108/54	96,000
Total	$158,000		$266,755
Accounts payable . . .	$ 8,000		$ 8,000
Bonds payable	40,000		40,000
Capital stock	100,000	108/54	200,000
Retained earnings . . .	10,000		18,755
Total	$158,000		$266,755

ing price levels. To adjust their recorded (historical) dollar amounts into current price levels, multiply the historical cost by a ratio whose numerator is the current price index and whose denominator is the index at the acquisition or issuance date. We will make the following assumptions: (1) Land and plant assets were acquired on January 1, 1975, when the company was formed and all the stock was issued. The price level index at that time was 54. (2) Ending inventory for 1986 was acquired on October 31, 1986, when the price-level index was 106.

Using the above assumptions and the price indexes given, the ending 1986 inventory is adjusted by the ratio 108/106. The equivalent purchasing power invested in the land in terms of December 31, 1986, dollars is $96,000 ($48,000 × 108/54). This $96,000 **is the cost of the land** in terms of December 31, 1986, purchasing power, **not its current value,** which may be more or less than $96,000. The capital stock is adjusted in the same manner as land. The retained earnings amount in the converted balance sheet is simply the amount needed to bring the equity side of the balance sheet into balance with the total of the assets. This step completes the conversion of the balance sheet from historical dollars into constant dollars.

Constant Dollar Accounting—Pro and Con

The advantages of constant dollar accounting include the following:

1. Measurement of the impact of inflation upon a company is objective because adjustments are based on historical cost.
2. Comparability of the financial statements between firms is im-

proved because of the use of the same procedures and the same index numbers.

3. There is greater comparability of the financial statements of a single company through time since effects of price-level changes are removed.

The disadvantages of constant dollar accounting include:

1. Benefits resulting from the use of such statements have not been shown to be in excess of the cost of preparing these statements.
2. The assumption that the impact of inflation affects all firms equally is not true.
3. Only one deficiency—the changing value of the measuring unit— is corrected, the effects of specific price changes are ignored. This is undoubtedly the most significant limitation to constant dollar accounting.

CURRENT COST ACCOUNTING

An income statement for Foster Company on a current cost basis will now be discussed. Management has determined that the current cost (value) of the cost of goods sold was $146,000 and current cost of the plant assets was $160,000 on December 31, 1985, and $180,000 on December 31, 1986. There were no additions or retirements of plant assets in 1986. Foster Company depreciates its plant assets over a 20-year life or an annual rate of 5 percent on a straight-line basis.

Current cost depreciation for 1986 can be computed by multiplying the average current cost of the plant assets for the year times the annual depreciation rate of 5 percent. The amount is:

$$\frac{\$160,000 + \$180,000}{2} \times 5 \text{ percent} = \$8,500$$

The $146,000 current cost of goods sold and $8,500 current cost depreciation are shown in an income statement prepared under current cost accounting. There is no need to adjust sales or other expenses since they are already expressed at current cost for the year.

Illustration 12.6 contains the amounts that would be reported in the two income statements shown for the Foster Company thus far, plus the amounts that would be shown under the current cost basis.

Current Cost Accounting—Pro and Con

The advantages of current cost accounting include:

1. Specific current costs incurred by a firm are shown instead of costs adjusted for general price-level changes.
2. Current costs, rather than costs based on historical costs, are deducted from current revenue to calculate net income.

Illustration 12.6
INFLATION IMPACT DISCLOSURES

FOSTER COMPANY
Statement of Income from Continuing Operations Adjusted for Changing Prices
For the Year Ended December 31, 1986

	Historical Cost	Constant Dollar (end-of-year dollars)	Current Cost
Sales	$200,000	$207,692	$200,000
Cost of goods sold	$140,000	$147,440	$146,000
Depreciation expense	4,000	8,000	8,500
Other expenses	46,000	47,769	46,000
Total	$190,000	$203,209	$200,500
Net income (loss) from continuing operations	$ 10,000	$ 4,483	$ (500)
Purchasing power gain on monetary items		$ 2,625	

3. If dividends (owner's withdrawals) are limited to an amount equal to or less than current cost income from continuing operations, the economic capital of the firm is maintained.

The disadvantages of current cost include:

1. Current costs are subjective.
2. Current costs may be difficult and costly to determine.

THE FASB REQUIREMENTS

FASB Statement No. 33 calls for disclosure by companies in their annual reports of the impact of general inflation and of specific price changes upon income and other selected items. The Statement does not require full, completely adjusted financial statements, nor does it affect the way in which the basic (primary) financial statements are prepared, since all required disclosures are to be reported only as supplementary information. The Statement applies only to publicly-held companies with total assets in excess of $1 billion (after deducting accumulated depreciation) or to those having $125 million (before deducting accumulated depreciation) of inventories and property, plant, and equipment. Thus, about 1,200 to 1,400 large, publicly-held companies are directly affected. The FASB also encourages all companies to report the effects of inflation by applying the methods described in *FASB Statement No. 33.*

For fiscal years ended on or after December 25, 1979, affected companies are to report as supplementary information:

1. Net income on a constant dollar basis (historical cost adjusted for the effects of general inflation).

2. Net income on a current cost basis.

3. Purchasing power gain or loss on monetary items.[3]

Other disclosure requirements including a five-year summary of selected financial data are discussed in more advanced texts on accounting. An example of how an actual company reports inflation data can be seen in Appendix B at the end of the text.

Uncertainty over whether constant dollar information or current cost information is preferable initially caused the FASB to require both types. In 1984 the FASB decided that constant dollar information should not be required for companies reporting current cost information. The FASB concluded that constant dollar disclosures are less useful than current cost information. As of this writing a revised standard changing the *FASB Statement No. 33* requirements was expected to become effective in 1985.

SUMMARY

Accounting theory is a set of basic assumptions and concepts and related principles. This theory explains and guides the accountant's actions in identifying, measuring, and communicating economic information. The underlying assumptions or concepts include entity, going concern, money measurement, periodicity, general purpose financial statements, substance over form, consistency, and others.

The accountant seeks to measure the assets, liabilities, and stockholders' (owners') equity of an accounting entity. Changes in these items are also measured and assigned to particular time periods to find net income.

The major principles used in accounting include the exchange price (cost) principle, matching, revenue recognition, and expense and loss recognition. Exceptions are sometimes made in following these principles. For instance, in revenue recognition sometimes the cash basis, installment basis, percentage-of-completion basis, or completion of production basis are used.

Modifying conventions are customs emerging from accounting practice which alter results that would be obtained from a strict application of accounting principles. Two such modifying conventions are materiality and conservation.

Inflation represents a serious reporting problem. In periods of high inflation, the use of historical cost in financial statements has been criticized. Accountants have developed two approaches to report the effects of inflation. One approach is general price-level adjusted accounting, also called constant dollar accounting. This ap-

---

[3] Ibid., pars. 29–35.

proach shows historical cost amounts adjusted for changes in the general price level. The other approach is the current cost approach, which shows the current cost or value of items in the financial statements. In 1979, the FASB issued *FASB Statement No. 33* that requires certain large, publicly-held corporations to present certain supplementary information about the effects of inflation. It appears that the requirements will change as of 1985.

APPENDIX

THE CONCEPTUAL FRAMEWORK PROJECT

The exact nature of the basic concepts and related principles comprising accounting theory has been debated for years. The debate continues today even though numerous references can be found to generally accepted accounting principles (GAAP). To date, all attempts to present a concise statement of GAAP have received only limited acceptance.

This limited success has led many accountants to suggest that the starting point is to seek agreement on the objectives of financial accounting and reporting. The belief is that if one (1) carefully studies the environment, (2) knows what objectives are sought, (3) can identify certain qualitative traits of accounting information, and (4) can define the basic elements of financial statements, one can discover the principles and standards that will lead to the attainment of the stated objectives. The FASB has taken the first three steps in the above approach in "Objectives of Financial Reporting by Business Enterprises" and in "Qualitative Characteristics of Accounting Information."[4] The fourth step is represented by "Elements of Financial Statements of Business Enterprises."[5]

Objectives of Financial Reporting

Financial reporting objectives are the broad overriding goals sought by engaging in financial reporting. Objectives provide informed investors and creditors with information useful in making rational

---

[4] FASB, *Statement of Financial Accounting Concepts No. 1*, "Objectives of Financial Reporting by Business Enterprises" (Stamford, Conn., 1978). FASB, *Statement of Financial Accounting Concepts No. 2*, "Qualitative Characteristics of Accounting Information" (Stamford, Conn., 1980). Copyright © by the Financial Accounting Standards Board, High Ridge Park, Stamford, Connecticut 06905, U.S.A. Quoted (or excerpted) with permission. Copies of the complete document are available from the FASB.

[5] FASB, *Statement of Financial Accounting Concepts No. 3*, "Elements of Financial Statements of Business Enterprises (Stamford, Conn., 1980). Copyright © by the Financial Accounting Standards Board, High Ridge Park, Stamford, Connecticut 06905, U.S.A. Quoted (or excerpted) with permission. Copies of the complete document are available from the FASB.

investment and credit decisions. According to the FASB, the first objective of financial reporting is to

> provide information that is useful to present and potential investors and creditors and other users in making rational investment, credit, and similar decisions. The information should be comprehensible to those who have a reasonable understanding of business and economic activities and are willing to study the information with reasonable diligence.[6]

The term **other users** is interpreted broadly and includes employees, security analysts, brokers, and lawyers. Financial reporting should provide information to all who are willing to learn to use it properly. Although the Board's objectives are stated in terms of the corporate form of business organization, they apply equally well to single proprietorships and partnerships.

The second objective of financial reporting is to

> provide information to help present and potential investors and creditors and other users in assessing the amounts, timing, and uncertainty of prospective cash receipts from dividends [owner withdrawals] or interest and the proceeds from the sale, redemption, or maturity of securities or loans. Since investors' and creditors' cash flows are related to enterprise cash flows, financial reporting should provide information to help investors, creditors, and others assess the amounts, timing, and uncertainty of prospective net cash inflows to the related enterprise.[7]

This objective ties the cash flows of investors (owners) and creditors to the cash flows of the enterprise, a tie-in that appears entirely logical. Enterprise cash inflows are the source of cash for dividends (owner withdrawals), interest, and redemption of maturing debt.

Third, financial reporting should

> provide information about the economic resources of an enterprise, the claims to those resources (obligations of the enterprise to transfer resources to other entities and owners' equity), and the effects of transactions, events, and circumstances that change its resources and claims to those resources.[8]

A number of conclusions can be drawn from these three objectives and from a study of the environment in which financial reporting is carried out. Financial reporting should provide information about an enterprise's past performance because such information is used as a basis for prediction of future enterprise performance. Financial reporting should focus on income and its components, despite the emphasis in the objectives upon cash flows. Income computed under the accrual basis provides a better indicator of ability

---

[6] FASB, *Statement of Financial Accounting Concepts No. 1,* pp. viii.

[7] Ibid.

[8] Ibid.

to generate favorable cash flows than do statements prepared under the cash basis. Functional reporting does not seek to measure the value of a business, but to provide information that may be useful for doing so. Financial reporting does not seek to evaluate management's performance, predict income, assess risk, or estimate earning power, but should provide information to persons who wish to do so.

These conclusions are some of those reached in *Statement of Financial Accounting Concepts No. 1.* As the Board says, these statements "are intended to establish the objectives and concepts that the Financial Accounting Standards Board will use in developing standards of financial accounting and reporting."[9] How successful the Board will be in the approach adopted remains to be seen. But it appears likely that the obstacle of conflicting objectives barring success in previous efforts to specify accounting principles has been removed.

Qualitative Characteristics

Qualitative characteristics are those characteristics that accounting information should possess to be useful in decision making. This is a difficult criterion to apply. The usefulness of accounting information in a given instance depends not only on information characteristics but also on the capabilities of the decision makers and their professional advisers, if any. Accountants cannot specify who the decision makers are, their characteristics, the decisions to be made, or the methods chosen to make the decisions; therefore attention is directed to characteristics of accounting information. The FASB's graphic summarization of the problems faced is presented in Illustration 12.7.[10]

Relevance

For information to have **relevance,** it must be pertinent to or bear upon a decision. The information must "make a difference" to someone who does not already have the information. Relevant information is capable of making a difference in a decision either by affecting user predictions of outcomes of past, present, or future events or by confirming or correcting expectations. Note that information need not be a prediction to be useful in developing, confirming, or altering expectations. Expectations are commonly based on the present or past. For example, any attempt to predict future income of a firm would quite likely start with a review of present and past income. Also, information that merely confirms prior expectations may be less useful, but is still relevant since it reduces uncertainty.

Some types of accounting information are under attack today because of an alleged lack of relevance. For example, it is argued that the fact that a tract of land cost its owner $1 million over 40

---

[9] Ibid., p. i.

[10] FASB, *Statement of Financial Accounting Concepts No. 2,* p. 15.

Illustration 12.7
A HIERARCHY OF ACCOUNTING QUALITIES

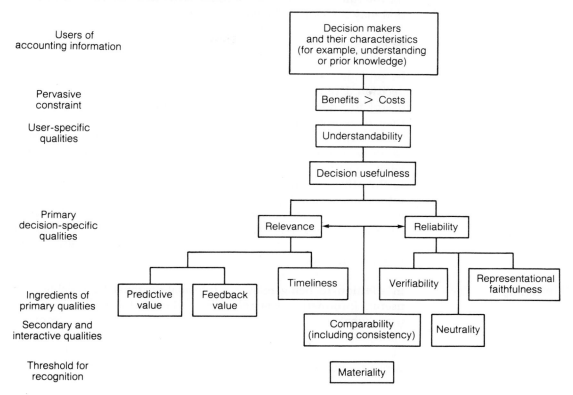

years ago and is reported in the current balance sheet at that amount is irrelevant (except for possible tax implications) to users for decision making today. Such attacks have encouraged research into the types of information that are relevant to users. The attacks have also brought forth suggestions that a different valuation basis, such as current cost, be used in reporting such assets.

Predictive value and feedback value. Because actions taken now can affect only future events, information is obviously relevant when it possesses **predictive value** or improves users' abilities to predict outcomes of events. Information that reveals the relative success of users in predicting outcomes possess **feedback value.** Because feedback reports on past activities, it can make a difference in decision making by (1) reducing uncertainty in a situation, (2) refuting or confirming prior expectations, and (3) providing a basis for further predictions. For example, a report on the first quarter's income of a firm reduces the uncertainty surrounding the amount of such income, confirms or refutes the predicted amount of such income, and provides a possible basis for one to predict income for the full year. With regard to the latter item, accounting information may possess predictive value, but it does not consist of predictions. Making predictions is a function performed by the decision maker, not the accountant.

Timeliness. **Timeliness** requires that accounting information be provided at a time when it may be considered in reaching a decision. Utility of information decreases with age. It is much more useful to know what the net income for 1985 was in early 1986 than to receive this information a year later. If information is to be of any value in decision making, it must be available before the decision is made; if not, the information is useless. In determining what constitutes timely information, consideration must be given to the other qualitative characteristics and to the cost of gathering information. For example, a timely estimated amount for uncollectible accounts may be more valuable than a later, verified actual amount. Timeliness alone cannot make information relevant, but otherwise relevant information might be rendered irrelevant by a lack of timeliness.

Reliability

In addition to being relevant, information must be reliable to be useful. Information has **reliability** when it faithfully depicts for users what it purports to represent. Thus, accounting information is reliable if users can depend upon it to reflect the underlying economic activities of the organization. The reliability of information depends upon its representational faithfulness, verifiability, and neutrality.

Representational faithfulness. Insight into this quality may be gained by considering a map. A map possesses representational faithfulness when it shows roads and bridges (among other things) where roads and bridges actually exist. There is correspondence between what is shown on the map and what is present physically. Similarly, there is **representational faithfulness** when accounting statements on economic activity correspond to the actual underlying activity. An accounting measurement may show what it is designed to show and still not be useful if what it measures is irrelevant. Recall the example of the tract of land acquired over 40 years ago. The historical cost information may be irrelevant to the informed, but to uninformed persons who believe that accounting statements show values or the current worth of a business, there exists representational failure. The reasonably informed user, for whom accounting reports are designed, understands that assets typically are reported at historical cost and that accounting information is based upon numerous estimates, approximations, allocations, and the application of judgment.

Effects of bias. Accounting measurements are biased if they are consistently too high or too low. Bias in accounting measurements may exist due to the choice of measurement method or to bias introduced either deliberately or through lack of skill by the measurer. These two types of bias are discussed below.

Completeness. To be free from bias, information must be sufficiently complete to ensure that it validly represents the underlying events and conditions. **Completeness** means that it must fully disclose all significant information in a way that aids understanding and does not mislead. Relevance of information also may be reduced if information that would make a difference to a user is omitted. Currently, full disclosure generally requires presentation of a balance sheet, an income statement, a statement of changes in financial position, and necessary footnotes and supporting schedules. Such statements are to be complete, with items properly classified and segregated (such as reporting sales revenue separately from other revenues). Required disclosures may be made in (1) the body of the financial statements, (2) in the notes to such statements, (3) in special communications, and (4) in the president's letter or in other management reports in the annual report.

Another aspect of completeness is that full disclosure must be made of all changes in accounting principles and their effects.[11] Also disclosure should be made of unusual activities (loans to officers), changes in expectations (losses on inventory), depreciation expense for the period, long-term obligations entered into that are not recorded by the accountant (a 20-year operating lease on a building), new arrangements with certain groups (pension and profit-sharing plans for employees), significant events that occur after the date of the statements (loss of a major customer), and accounting policies (major principles and their manner of application) followed in preparing the financial statements.[12] Because of its emphasis upon disclosure, this aspect of reliability is often called the full-disclosure principle.

Verifiability. Financial information has **verifiability** when it can be substantially duplicated by independent measurers using the same measurement methods. Verifiability is directed toward eliminating measurer bias rather than measurement method bias. The requirement that financial information be based upon objective evidence is based upon demonstrated needs of users for reliable, unbiased financial information. Unbiased information is needed especially when parties with opposing interests (credit seekers and credit grantors) rely upon the same information. Reliability of information is enhanced if it is verifiable.

---

[11] APB, *APB Opinion No. 20,* "Accounting Changes" (New York: AICPA, July 1971).

[12] APB, *APB Opinion No. 22,* "Disclosure of Accounting Policies" (New York: AICPA, April 1971).

Financial information will never be free of subjective opinion and judgment; it will always possess varying degrees of verifiability. Some measurements can be supported by canceled checks and invoices. Others, such as periodic depreciation charges, can never be verified because of their very nature. Thus, financial information in many instances is verifiable only in that it represents a consensus as to what would be reported if the same procedures had been followed by other accountants.

Neutrality. **Neutrality** in accounting information means that the information should be free of measurement method bias. The primary concern should be the relevance and reliability of the information that result from application of the principle, not the effect that the principle may have on a particular interest. "To be neutral, accounting information must report economic activity as faithfully as possible, without coloring the image it communicates for the purpose of influencing behavior in *some particular direction.*"[13] Accounting standards should not be developed and used like certain tax regulations that seek deliberately to foster or restrain certain types of activity. Verification seeks to eliminate measurer bias; neutrality seeks to eliminate measurement method bias.

Comparability (and Consistency)

When **comparability** in financial information exists, reported differences and similarities in information are real and not the result of differing accounting treatments. Comparable information will reveal relative strengths and weaknesses in a single company through time and between two or more companies at the same point in time.

Consistency leads to comparability of financial information for a single company through time. Comparability between companies is more difficult to achieve because the same activities may be accounted for in different ways. For example, B may use one method of depreciation, while C accounts for an identical asset in similar circumstances using another method. A high degree of intercompany comparability in accounting information will not exist unless the same activities are required to be accounted for in the same manner across companies and through time.

Pervasive Constraints

As Illustration 12.7 shows, there are two pervasive constraints faced in providing useful information. First, benefits secured from the information must be greater than the cost of providing that information. Second, only material items need be disclosed and accounted for strictly in accordance with generally accepted accounting principles (GAAP).

Cost/benefit analysis. Accounting information is a commodity and, like all commodities, is desired only if it provides benefits

---

[13] FASB, *Statement of Accounting Concepts No. 2.* par. 100.

greater than its cost. But, unlike most commodities, accounting information has no direct cost to users, since all costs are borne by the provider of the information. This fact has led users and authoritative organizations to demand ever greater amounts of financial information. These demands have often been answered with claims that the information desired costs more than it is worth. Such a contention was encountered frequently when the FASB proposed requiring disclosure of the impact of inflation upon financial statements. Complicating the issue is the fact that there is no agreed-upon method of measuring benefits of information and that even measurement of cost cannot be carried out without some disagreement. Yet, in the development of accounting standards, an attempt must be made to ensure that the benefits of required disclosures exceed the cost of providing the disclosures.

Materiality. As discussed earlier in the chapter, the basic idea inherent in materiality is simply that one need be concerned only with significant items; insignificant ones can be ignored. Materiality has been defined by the FASB as "the magnitude of an omission or misstatement of accounting information that, in the light of surrounding circumstances, makes it probable that the judgment of a reasonable person relying on the information would have been changed or influenced by the omission or misstatement."[14] The term **magnitude** in this definition suggests that the materiality of an item may be assessed by looking at its **relative size.** A $10,000 error in an expense in a firm with earnings of $30,000 would seem to be material. The same error in a firm earning $30 million may not be material.

The Basic Elements of Financial Statements

Having discussed objectives of financial reporting and qualitative characteristics of accounting information, basic elements of financial statements will be considered. A most important task in developing a conceptual framework for any discipline is that of identifying and defining its basic elements. The following definitions by the FASB are likely to have a major impact on financial accounting. Most of the terms were defined earlier in this text in a less precise way to convey a general understanding of the terms. The more technical definitions are as follows (these items are not repeated in the glossary):

> **Assets** are probable future economic benefits obtained or controlled by a particular entity as a result of past transactions or events affecting the enterprise.
> **Liabilities** are probable future sacrifices of economic benefits arising from present obligations of a particular entity to transfer assets

---

[14] Ibid., p. xv.

or provide services to other entities in the future as a result of past transactions or events.

Equity is the residual interest in the assets of an entity that remains after deducting its liabilities. In a business enterprise, the equity is the ownership interest.

Comprehensive income is the change in equity (net assets) of an entity during a period from transactions and other events and circumstances from nonowner sources. It includes all changes in equity during a period except those resulting from investments by owners and distributions to owners.

Revenues are inflows or other enhancements of assets of an entity or settlements of its liabilities (or a combination of both) during a period from delivering or producing goods, rendering services, or other activities that constitute the entity's ongoing major or central operations.

Expenses are outflows or other using up of assets or incurrences of liabilities (or a combination of both) during a period from delivering or producing goods, rendering services, or carrying out other activities that constitute the entity's ongoing major or central operations.

Gains are increases in equity (net assets) from peripheral or incidental transactions of an entity and from all other transactions and other events and circumstances affecting the entity during a period except those that result from revenues or investments by owners.

Losses are decreases in equity (net assets) from peripheral or incidental transactions of an entity and from all other transactions and other events and circumstances affecting the entity during a period except those that result from expenses or distributions to owners.

Investments by owners in the entity are increases in net assets of a particular enterprise resulting from transfers to it from other entities of something of value to obtain or increase ownership interests (or equity) in it. Assets are most commonly received as investments by owners, but that which is received may also include services or satisfaction or conversion of liabilities of the enterprise.

Distributions by the entity to owners are decreases in net assets of a particular enterprise resulting from transferring assets, rendering services, or incurring liabilities by the enterprise to owners. Distributions to owners decrease ownership interests (or equity) in an enterprise.[15]

Note that the requirement that assets and liabilities be based on past transactions normally rules out the recording of contracts that are mutual promises to do something, such as entering into an employment contract with an officer. On a similar basis, the accountant does not record an asset and a liability when a contract is signed whereby the entity agrees to purchase a certain number of units of a product over a coming period of time.

---

[15] FASB, *Statement of Financial Accounting Concepts No. 3*, p. 26.

QUESTIONS

1. Name the assumptions underlying generally accepted accounting principles. Comment on the validity in recent years of the stable unit of measurement assumption.

2. Why does the accountant assume the existence of an entity?

3. When is the going-concern assumption not to be used?

4. What is meant by the term **accrual basis of accounting?** What is its alternative?

5. What does it mean to say that accountants record substance rather than form?

6. If a company changes an accounting principle because the change better meets the information needs of users, what disclosures must be made?

7. What is the exchange price (or cost) principle? What is the significance of adhering to this principle?

8. What two requirements generally must be met before revenue will be recognized in a period?

9. Under what circumstances, if any, is the receipt of cash an acceptable time to recognize revenue?

10. What two methods may be used in recognizing revenues on long-term construction contracts?

11. Define expense. What principles guide the recognition of expense?

12. How does an expense differ from a loss?

13. What is meant by the accounting term **conservatism?** How does it affect the amounts reported in the financial statements?

14. Does materiality relate only to relative size of dollar amounts?

15. How might it be argued that a tax supposedly upon income is really a tax upon capital?

16. What are the two basic approaches that might be used to reveal the impact of inflation upon financial statements?

17. Explain what the significance is of the dollar amount attached to an asset under constant dollar accounting.

18. If an index of the general level of prices rose 15 percent in a period, what is the effect upon the value or real worth of the dollar?

19. How is the dollar amount shown for land adjusted under constant dollar accounting?

20. Explain the typical adjustment of sales and most expenses under constant dollar accounting.

21. Identify whether each of the following items is a monetary or nonmonetary item.
    a. Cash.
    b. Equipment.

c. Notes receivable.

d. Merchandise inventory.

e. Accounts receivable.

f. Patents.

g. Common stock.

h. Land.

i. Accounts payable.

j. Buildings.

22. What are purchasing power gains and losses? When do purchasing power gains occur? When do purchasing power losses occur?

23. In the supplementary disclosures required by *FASB Statement No. 33,* what basis of accounting measurement is to be applied?

24. What is the major deficiency in constant dollar accounting?

25. (Based on the Appendix) Identify the three major parts of the conceptual framework project that are included in the text.

26. (Based on the Appendix) In general, what are the qualitative characteristics? Which are the primary qualitative characteristics?

EXERCISES

1. Match the items in Group A with the proper descriptions in Group B.

Group A

1. Going concern (continuity). 6. Stable dollar.

2. Consistency. 7. Matching.

3. Disclosure. 8. Materiality.

4. Periodicity. 9. Exchange prices.

5. Conservatism. 10. Entity.

Group B

a. An assumption relied on in the preparation of the primary financial statements that would be unreasonable when the inflation rate is high.

b. Concerned with relative dollar amounts.

c. The usual basis for the recording of assets.

d. Required if the accounting treatment differs from that previously accorded a particular item.

e. An assumption that would be unreasonable to use in reporting on a firm that had become insolvent.

f. None of these.

g. Requires a company to use the same accounting procedures and practices through time.

h. An assumption that the life of an entity can be subdivided into time periods for purposes of reporting.

i. Discourages undue optimism in measuring and reporting net assets and net income.

j. Requires separation of personal activity from business activity in the recording and reporting processes.

2. Smith Company sells its products on an installment sales basis. Data for 1985 and 1986 are as follows:

	1985	1986
Installment sales	$50,000	$60,000
Cost of goods sold on installment . . .	35,000	45,000
Other expenses	7,500	10,000
Cash collected from 1985 sales . . .	30,000	15,000
Cash collected from 1986 sales . . .		40,000

a. Compute the net income for 1986 assuming use of the accrual (sales) basis of revenue recognition.

b. Compute the net income for 1986 assuming use of the installment method of recognizing gross margin.

3. A firm has a contract to build a ship at a price of $200 million and an estimated cost of $160 million. In 1985, costs of $40 million were incurred. Under the percentage-of-completion method how much revenue would be recognized in 1986?

4. A company follows a practice of expensing the premium on its fire insurance policy when it is paid. In 1986, it charged to expense the $720 premium paid on a three-year policy covering the period July 1, 1986, to June 30, 1989. In 1983, a premium of $660 was charged to expense on the same policy for the period July 1, 1983, to June 30, 1986.

a. State the principle of accounting that was violated by this practice.

b. Compute the effects of this violation on the financial statements for the calendar year 1986.

c. State the basis upon which the company's practice might be justified.

5. Bates Company produces a product at a cost of $20 per unit that it sells for $30. The company has been very successful and is able to sell all of the units that it can produce. During 1986, the company manufactured 50,000 units, but because of a transportation strike, it was able to sell and deliver only 40,000 units.

a. Compute the gross margin for 1986 following generally accepted accounting principles. The cost of the units sold should be entitled Cost of goods sold and treated as an expense.

b. Compute the gross margin for 1986 assuming that the realization principle is ignored and that revenue is recognized as production is completed.

6. Assume the following facts regarding the purchase and sale of 100 units of a product:

Date	Transaction	Amount	Price-level Index
January 1, 1986	Purchased 100 units	$ 6,000	100
December 31, 1986 . . .	Sold 100 units	10,000	110

The company incurred $1,200 of expenses to sell the units. The replacement cost of the units on December 31, 1986, was $7,000. Prepare a schedule showing net income from continuing operations under historical cost accounting, constant dollar accounting, and current cost accounting.

7. The cost of goods sold section of the conventional (historical cost) income statement for the Hillard Company was:

Cost of goods sold:
Inventory, December 31, 1985 . . .	$20,000
Purchases	60,000
Goods available for sale	$80,000
Inventory, December 31, 1986 . . .	10,000
Cost of goods sold	$70,000

The general price-level index was 100 on December 31, 1985, and 110 on December 31, 1986. The FIFO inventories were acquired when the index stood at 96 for the beginning inventory and 108 for the ending inventory. Purchases were incurred uniformly throughout the year. Convert the cost of goods sold section of the income statement to end-of-year constant dollar amounts.

8. C Company's plant assets at December 31, 1985, had a historical cost of $100,000 and accumulated depreciation of $40,000 (10 percent annual depreciation rate). There were no additions or retirements in 1986. The current cost of the plant assets on December 31, 1985, was $140,000 and on December 31, 1986, was $160,000. Compute the current cost depreciation for 1986.

9. In each of the situations given, determine the amount of purchasing power gain or loss.

a. You hold cash of $60,000 during a year in which prices in general rose 10 percent.

b. You are in debt $30,000 during a year in which prices in general rose 8 percent.

10. A building was acquired for $200,000 on January 1, 1971, when the price index was 50. At what amount would it be shown in a restated constant dollar balance sheet prepared as of December 31, 1986, assuming the price index then is 150?

11. The $50,000 ending inventory was acquired on September 30, 1986, when the price index was 140. What amount would be shown for this item in a restated constant dollar balance sheet prepared as of December 31, 1986, assuming the price level then is 150?

12. ABC Company was organized on January 1, 1986. It immediately issued all of its stock for $160,000 and borrowed $40,000 on a long-term note (interest expense on the note is to be ignored). The $200,000 was then paid for a tract of land. There were no further transactions in 1986. An index of the general level of prices rose from 120 to 126 during 1986. The land had a market value of $230,000 on December 31, 1986. Prepare the balance sheet for December 31, 1986, in end-of-1986 dollars.

PROBLEMS

12–1. The Square-Deal Real Estate Sales Company sells lots in its development in Flash Flood Canyon under terms calling for small cash down payments with monthly installment payments spread over a few years. Following are data on the company's operations for its first three years:

	1984	1985	1986
Gross margin rate	45%	48%	50%
Cash collected in 1985 from			
sales of lots made in	$40,000	$50,000	$60,000

The total selling price of the lots sold in 1986 was $200,000, while general and administrative expenses (which are not included in the costs used to determine gross margin) were $50,000.

Required:

    a. Compute the net income for 1986 assuming revenue is recognized upon the sale of a lot.

    b. Compute net income for 1986 assuming use of the installment method of accounting for sales and gross margin.

12–2. Given below are the contract prices and construction costs relating to all of the Grady Company's long-term construction contracts (in millions of dollars):

		Costs Incurred		
	Contract Price	Prior to 1986	In 1986	Cost Yet to Be Incurred
On contracts completed				
in 1985	$ 8.0	–0–	$7.0	–0–
On incomplete contracts . . .	24.0	$4.0	8.0	$8.0

General and administrative expenses for 1986 amounted to $300.000.

Required:

    a. Compute net income for 1986 using the completed-contract method.

    b. Compute net income for 1986 using the percentage-of-completion method. Assume that the general and administrative expenses are not to be treated as a part of the construction cost of the contracts.

12–3. In each of the circumstances described below, the accounting practices followed may be questioned. You are to indicate whether you agree or disagree with the accounting employed and to state the assumptions, concepts, or principles on which you would rely to justify your position.

    1. The cost of certain improvements to leased property having a life of five years was charged to expense because the improvements would revert to the lessor when the lease expires in three years.

    2. The salaries paid to the top officers of the company were charged to expense in the period in which they were incurred, even though

381

the officers spent over half of their time planning next year's activities.

3. A company spent over $8 million in developing a new product and then spent an additional $9 million promoting it. All of these costs were incurred and charged to expense this year even though future years would also benefit.

4. No entry was made to record the belief that the market value of the land owned (carried in the accounts at $58,000) increased.

5. No entry was made to record the fact that costs of $100,000 were expected to be incurred in fulfilling warranty provisions on products sold this year. The revenue from products sold was recognized this year.

6. The acquisition of a tract of land was recorded at the price paid for it of $108,000, even though the company would have been willing to pay $125,000.

7. A truck acquired at the beginning of the year was reported at year-end at 80 percent of its acquisition price, even though its market value then was only 65 percent of its original acquisition price.

12–4. A partial income statement for the Stillwagon Company for the year ended December 31, 1986, in terms of historical dollars is given below:

STILLWAGON COMPANY
Partial Income Statement
For the Year Ended December 31, 1986

Sales		$105,000
Cost of goods sold	$67,600	
Depreciation	4,000	
Other expenses	21,000	92,600
Net income from continuing operations		$ 12,400

The sales were made rather uniformly throughout the year. Other expenses were also incurred rather uniformly throughout the year and largely on a cash basis. Thus, their historical cost is substantially equal to their current cost. The depreciation reported relates to a machine acquired at a cost of $40,000 which is being depreciated over a 10-year life on a straight-line basis.

The current cost of the goods sold was $75,000 at the time of their sale. The current cost (gross) of the machine was $65,000 at the beginning of 1986 and $75,000 at the end of the year. An index of the general level of prices stood at 80 when the machine was acquired, at 100 at the beginning of 1986, averaged 105 for 1986, and ended the year at 110. This same index stood at 104 when the goods sold were acquired.

Required:

a. Prepare a statement showing constant dollar net income from continuing operations in constant end-of-year 1986 dollars for the year ended on that date.

b. Prepare a statement showing current cost net income from continuing operations for the year ended December 31, 1986.

12–5. North Springs Company was organized on December 31, 1985. It immediately paid a year's rent of $24,000 on a building in advance, purchased $12,000 of supplies, and purchased $40,000 of cleaning equipment. It began operations on January 1, 1986.

During 1986, services were rendered for customers and other expenses were incurred uniformly throughout the year. An index of the general level of prices stood at 80 at the beginning of the year, averaged 100 for the year, and ended the year at 120. The income statement for the year is as follows:

NORTH SPRINGS COMPANY
Income Statement
For the Year Ended December 31, 1986

Service revenue		$100,000
Supplies expense	$ 8,000	
Rent expense	24,000	
Depreciation expense . . .	10,000	
Other expenses	40,000	82,000
Net income		$ 18,000

Required:

Prepare a schedule converting the income statement for 1986 into constant end-of-year 1986 dollars. The purchasing power loss on net monetary items was $14,000.

12–6. The following is a partial income statement for the Jeffries Corporation for the year ended June 30, 1987.

JEFFRIES CORPORATION
Partial Income Statement
For the Year Ended June 30, 1987

Sales		$110,000
Cost of goods sold . . .	$63,000	
Depreciation	6,000	
Other expenses	12,100	81,100
Net income		$ 28,900

Sales were made uniformly throughout the year, while cost of goods sold consisted of goods acquired when the general price index stood at 105. This index was 120 on June 30, 1987, and had averaged 110 for the preceding 12 months. The current cost of the goods sold was $72,500.

The depreciation reported is on a machine which cost $30,000 when the general price index stood at 90. The machine had a current cost of $50,000 on June 30, 1986, and on June 30, 1987, the current cost was $60,000. All other expenses were incurred uniformly throughout the year, were paid in cash, and were basically equal to their current cost at time of incurrence.

Required:

a. Prepare a statement showing constant dollar net income from continuing operations in end-of-year dollars for the year ended June 30, 1987.

b. Prepare a current cost statement of net income from continuing operations for the year ended June 30, 1987.

12–7. Beverly Company began business on January 2, 1986, when an index of the general level of prices stood at 100. This index rose uniformly throughout the year, averaging 125 for the year, and ending at 150. Beverly's conventional balance sheet for December 31, 1986, was as follows:

BEVERLY COMPANY
Balance Sheet
December 31, 1986

Assets

Cash	$100,000
Inventory	60,000
Equipment, net of accumulated depreciation	100,000
Total assets	$260,000

Liabilities and Stockholders' Equity

Current liabilities	$ 20,000
Capital stock	220,000
Retained earnings	20,000
Total liabilities and stockholders' equity	$260,000

The inventory and equipment were acquired when Beverly went into business. No additional stock was issued during 1986.

Required:

Prepare a schedule showing the conversion of the conventional balance sheet on December 31, 1986, into constant dollars as of that date.

12–8. Larson Company was organized on December 31, 1985. It immediately paid a year's rent of $54,000 on a building in advance, purchased $27,000 of supplies, and purchased $90,000 of delivery equipment. It began operations on January 1, 1986.

Revenues were earned and expenses were incurred evenly throughout 1986. An index of the general level of prices was 95 at the beginning of the year, averaged 110 for the year, and rose to 125 at year-end. The conventional income statement for the year is as follows:

LARSON COMPANY
Income Statement
For the Year Ended December 31, 1986

Services revenue		$225,000
Supplies expense	$18,000	
Rent expense	54,000	
Depreciation expense	22,500	
Other expenses	90,000	184,500
Net income		$ 40,500

Required:

a. Prepare a schedule converting the income statement into constant December 31, 1986, dollars. The purchasing power loss on net monetary items was $21,251.

b. Assuming you are evaluating this company, what would you conclude about its income performance?

13 ACCOUNTING IN MANUFACTURING COMPANIES

The accounting concepts and procedures discussed thus far in this text have been limited to companies providing services and to those buying goods in finished form and reselling the goods. A retailing company that buys goods in finished form for resale has only one type of inventory—merchandise available for sale. The next few chapters deal with companies that *manufacture* a product that is then sold to other firms or to final customers. Manufacturing firms have three inventories—materials, work in process, and finished goods.

The objective of a manufacturer is to convert raw materials into a product that can be sold at a profit. For example, a furniture manufacturer converts lumber, cloth, foam rubber, and other raw materials into chairs, tables, and sofas to be sold to customers. All of these actions are taken to make a profit.

While the goods are being manufactured, the materials, labor, and other manufacturing costs are part of work in process inventory. When products are completed, their costs become part of the finished goods inventory until they are sold.

A manufacturer needs to know the cost per unit of goods manufactured. Such information is needed to determine the cost of goods sold; to determine the cost of inventories; and for decisions regarding product pricing, planning, and performance evaluation.

COST CLASSIFICATIONS IN MANUFACTURING FIRMS

Because they involve the manufacture as well as the sale of a product, a manufacturing firm's activities are usually more extensive and complex than those of a merchandising firm. A manufacturer's activities can be classified broadly as (1) manufacturing or production, (2) marketing or selling, and (3) general or administrative. Since the accumulation of marketing and administrative costs under the accrual basis of accounting was dealt with in earlier chapters, only brief attention will be paid to these costs in the discussion below. Attention will be focused on manufacturing costs.

Manufacturing Costs

The cost of manufacturing a product includes the costs of (1) direct materials, (2) direct labor, and (3) manufacturing overhead.

Direct materials. **The basic materials that are included in the finished product, that are clearly traceable to the product whose manufacture caused their use, are called direct materials.** Thus, iron ore is a direct material to a steel company, while steel is a direct material to an auto manufacturer. But some minor direct materials are often not accounted for as direct materials. For example, glue and thread used in manufacturing furniture may not be accounted for as direct materials, although they could be, simply because it is not practical to trace these items to the finished product. They would be described as *supplies* or *indirect materials* and accounted for as manufacturing overhead.

Direct materials costs include the cost of the actual quantity of the materials used, priced at net invoice price, plus delivery costs. Some firms also include storage and handling costs. Direct materials inventory may be accounted for using specific identification, Fifo, Lifo, or average cost.

Direct labor. **The services of employees who actually work on the materials to turn them into finished products are called direct labor.** The direct labor costs of a product include those labor costs that are clearly traceable to or readily identifiable with the product or are caused by its manufacture. Evidence that a labor cost is directly related to a product can be established by showing that the amount of labor cost incurred varies with the number of units produced. Thus, the services of the machinist, the assembler, the cutter, and the painter are classified as direct labor. But some labor services may not be accounted for as direct labor, even though they tend to vary directly with the number of units produced, because they are costly or difficult to trace to the finished product. These services are broadly described as *indirect labor* and are accounted for as manufacturing overhead. Materials handling costs may be an example.

Direct labor cost is usually measured by multiplying the number of hours of direct labor services received by the hourly wage rate. The actual cost of direct labor is considerably higher than this amount because of other costs, such as employer's payroll taxes, pension costs, paid vacations, paid sick leaves, and other "fringe benefits." These other costs may amount to as much as 25 to 50 percent of the hourly wage paid. Although sometimes accounted for as part of direct labor cost, these other costs are commonly included in manufacturing overhead.

Manufacturing overhead. There are many alternative names for manufacturing overhead, including factory indirect costs, factory burden, and manufacturing expense. However named, **this cost category includes all costs incurred in making a product, except those costs accounted for as direct materials and direct labor costs.** Manufacturing overhead serves as a repository for all manufacturing costs that are not included as direct materials or direct labor costs. As already noted, manufacturing overhead may include certain direct materials and direct labor costs because it is not practical to trace them to the units produced.

Some of the more common types of manufacturing overhead costs incurred include indirect materials, indirect labor, repairs and maintenance, depreciation of factory buildings and machinery, pensions, payroll taxes and other fringe benefits, utilities, insurance and taxes on factory property, and overtime wage premiums paid direct laborers. Indirect labor includes the salaries and wages earned by factory employees who do not work directly on the products produced but serve indirectly in their manufacture. This includes the services of timekeepers, inspectors, janitors, engineers, supervisors, materials handlers, and toolroom personnel. Overtime wage premiums are usually included in manufacturing overhead rather than being included as direct labor costs traced directly to the products worked on. The reason for this is that the need to work overtime can usually be traced to all production, not the manufacture of a given product that, by chance, happened to be the one worked on during the overtime period.

Manufacturing cost terminology. The sum of the direct materials costs and the direct labor costs incurred to manufacture a product is called **prime cost.** The sum of the direct labor costs and the manufacturing overhead costs related to a product is often referred to as **conversion cost.** The sum of all manufacturing costs is called **product cost, inventory cost, or factory cost.** Product cost (1) represents the factory costs incurred to manufacture the product which are "attached" to the product, (2) is the amount at which completed goods are carried in inventory until sold, and (3) is the amount used to measure the cost of goods sold expense when the products are actually sold. These cost relationships are shown in Illustration 13.1.

The product cost concept will be discussed further below. Classifying a cost as a product cost means that it will be recognized as

Illustration 13.1
COST RELATIONSHIPS

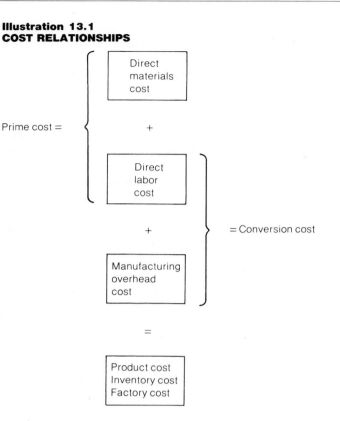

an expense only when the product is sold, not when the cost is recorded. Thus, the purchase of direct materials is an acquisition of an asset; the use of the direct materials creates another asset—the product; the direct materials used are recognized as an expense only when the finished product is sold.

Selling and Administrative Costs

Selling and administrative costs differ from manufacturing costs. Selling and administrative costs are incurred in the general administration of the organization and to **dispose** of the product, not to produce it.

Selling (marketing) costs. Selling or marketing costs are generally classified as order-getting and order-filling costs. These terms are virtually self-explaining. Order-getting costs are costs incurred in seeking orders for products or services. They include the cost of advertising, market research, selecting and training personnel, and maintaining sales offices, as well as sales salaries and commissions. Order-filling costs are the costs incurred from the time a product has been completed until the time it is delivered to a customer and the resulting account receivable is collected. Thus, order-filling costs include the costs of warehousing, delivery, installation, and servicing as well as the costs of billing a customer, processing payments received, and bad debts.

Administrative (general) costs. All costs not classified as manufacturing or selling costs are classified as administrative or general costs. This category includes the costs of the various staff departments—accounting, finance, personnel, legal, and so on. It also includes executives' salaries and executive office expenses, donations, litigation costs, and research and development costs. How these costs are classified will differ among firms.

Costs classified as selling and administrative costs are often called **period costs,** as contrasted to product costs. Period costs are not attached to products and are not carried in inventory accounts, but are recorded as expenses of the period in which they are incurred. Thus, a sales manager's salary will be recorded as an expense in the period in which it is incurred. This is true even though the manager may be working on projects that will benefit future periods. The salary will be treated as a period cost and charged to expense because the amount to be carried forward is not material in amount or is difficult to measure, or both.

Variable and Fixed Costs

Another of the most useful ways in which to classify the above costs is by their behavior—that is, according to how a cost changes as activity (output) changes. A cost may increase or decrease in total amount as activity increases or decreases, or it may remain constant despite changes in the level of activity.

Variable costs. **Variable costs are those costs that vary in total amount directly with changes in the level of activity or output.** The best examples are found in the direct materials used in making a product. Every electric washing machine produced has one electric motor. If each motor costs $5, then the motor cost of one machine is $5, of two machines is $10, of 100 machines is $500, and so on. If the profit plans call for the production of 10,000 washing machines, then the planned cost of the motors is $50,000. Similarly, the labor cost of installing the motors is a variable cost. In merchandising firms, the best examples of variable costs are the cost of goods sold and sales commissions. Both will vary with the dollar volume of sales.

Fixed costs. **Fixed costs are costs that remain constant in total amount over wide variations in the level of activity.** For example, the annual license for an automobile may cost $50, whether the auto is driven 1,000 miles or 100,000 miles or some other number of miles during the year. The same is true for the annual premium on an insurance policy on the auto. Property taxes, depreciation, rent, executives' salaries, and advertising are further examples of fixed costs. Fixed costs are often called time-related costs to distinguish them from volume-related costs.

Fixed costs present a special type of problem in determining the unit cost of producing a certain product. Since the total cost is fixed, cost **per unit** may vary widely if output varies. If the site on which a factory building is located is rented at an annual rent of $100,000, then the rental cost per ton of output is $1.00 if 100,000 tons are produced, $0.50 if 200,000 tons are produced, and only $0.10 if 1,000,000 tons are produced. Thus, fixed cost per unit decreases with increases in output and increases with decreases in output. This situation will be dealt with in some detail in a later chapter.

THE GENERAL COST ACCUMULATION MODEL

In manufacturing companies a primary cost objective is to measure the cost per unit to manufacture a product. Unit product costs are measured under the principle that such costs consist of (1) direct materials and direct labor plus (2) a fair share of the indirect factory costs incurred. This cost information is needed for financial reporting and pricing and is required for income tax purposes.

Product and Cost Flows

The accounting systems of manufacturing firms tend to have a similar general framework because the products manufactured flow through each firm in a similar order. Raw or basic materials are acquired; direct labor services and other factory services are used to process the materials into completed products ready for sale. The accounting records are set up in such a way as to show a flow of costs through the records that matches the physical flow of products through the firm. These relationships are shown graphically in Illustration 13.2.

Physically, the products move from the raw materials warehouse to the production department. During production they become partially-completed manufactured products and are called **work in process inventory.** Eventually they are completed manufactured products and are called **finished goods inventory.** The completed products are then moved to the finished goods warehouse, from which they are delivered to customers. The accounting records show the flow of costs from the Materials Inventory into the Work in Process Inventory, where the costs of direct labor and other factory services are added. When the products are completed, their costs are moved to the Finished Goods Inventory account, and, upon sale, these costs are transferred to the Cost of Goods Sold account.

Because the manufacturer has products in various stages of completion, its accounts and financial statements will typically show three types of inventories: Materials Inventory, Work in Process Inventory, and Finished Goods Inventory. At any given time the

Illustration 13.2
PRODUCT AND COST FLOWS

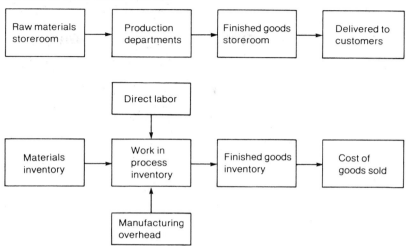

amount or balance in each of these accounts will depend on many factors, including the availability of materials and the level of customer demand.

Accounting for Cost and Revenue Flows

Knowledge of the general flow of costs and revenues through a manufacturing firm is of value in understanding a cost system. For this reason, an example using dollar amounts is presented below and summarized graphically in Illustration 13.3. The lines running between accounts show the transfer or flow of costs from one account to the next.

To begin the illustration, it is assumed that the inventories of the Braxton Company as of July 1, 1986, were:

Materials inventory	$10,000
Work in process inventory . .	20,000
Finished goods inventory . . .	40,000

The company's activities for July are summarized below, together with further explanation.

The Flow of Direct Materials Costs

During July, $40,000 of materials were purchased on account and $30,000 were issued to production from the storeroom. The entries required (numbered to key to the entries in the T-accounts in Illustration 13.3) are:

1. Materials Inventory	40,000	
Accounts Payable		40,000

To record purchases of raw materials on account.

393

Illustration 13.3
COST AND REVENUE FLOWCHART

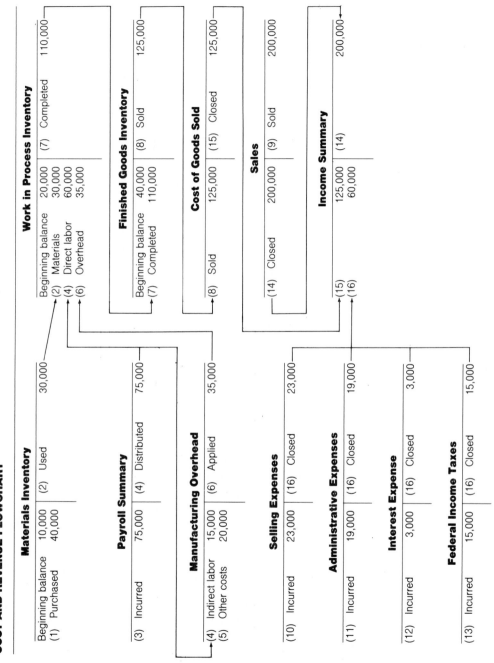

Materials Inventory

Beginning balance	10,000	(2) Used	30,000	
(1) Purchased	40,000			

Payroll Summary

(3) Incurred	75,000	(4) Distributed 75,000

Manufacturing Overhead

(4) Indirect labor	15,000	(6) Applied 35,000
(5) Other costs	20,000	

Selling Expenses

(10) Incurred	23,000	(16) Closed 23,000

Administrative Expenses

(11) Incurred	19,000	(16) Closed 19,000

Interest Expense

(12) Incurred	3,000	(16) Closed 3,000

Federal Income Taxes

(13) Incurred	15,000	(16) Closed 15,000

Work in Process Inventory

Beginning balance	20,000	(7) Completed	110,000
(2) Materials	30,000		
(4) Direct labor	60,000		
(6) Overhead	35,000		

Finished Goods Inventory

Beginning balance	40,000	(8) Sold	125,000
(7) Completed	110,000		

Cost of Goods Sold

(8) Sold	125,000	(15) Closed	125,000

Sales

(14) Closed	200,000	(9) Sold	200,000

Income Summary

(15)	125,000	(14)	200,000
(16)	60,000		

(Note: In order to focus attention upon cost and revenue flows, the credit to Accounts Payable is not included in Illustration 13.3.)

2. Work in Process Inventory 30,000
   Materials Inventory 30,000
   To record direct materials issued to production.

The Flow of Labor Costs

Two groups of employees are likely to be involved in the accounting for labor costs. One group is concerned with **payroll accounting**— that is, determining the total wages earned, the various deductions, and the net pay of each employee. The second group engages in **labor cost accounting**—that is, determining which accounts are to be charged with what amount of labor costs. Under such a procedure, an account common to both groups is needed to tie together the separate accounting activities. In Illustration 13.3, this account is called Payroll Summary. The account is a temporarily established account called a clearing account; it is debited when payrolls are prepared by the payroll department and credited when labor costs are distributed by the factory accounting department. Normally, the Payroll Summary account will have a zero balance at the end of any accounting period. During the period, the account will have a balance only because of the time lag between the preparation and the distribution of the payroll.

The factory payrolls for July amounted to $75,000—$60,000 of direct labor and $15,000 of indirect labor. Payroll withholdings amounted to $3,500 of social security taxes, $8,000 of federal income taxes, and $500 of union dues. the entries required (keyed 3 and 4 in Illustration 13.3) are:

3. Payroll Summary 75,000
   Social Security Taxes Payable 3,500
   Federal Income Taxes Withheld 8,000
   Union Dues Withheld 500
   Accrued Payroll 63,000
   To record factory payroll and various withholdings.

4. Work in Process Inventory 60,000
   Manufacturing Overhead 15,000
   Payroll Summary 75,000
   To distribute labor costs for the month.

The accrued payroll will be paid in cash to the employees, while the amounts withheld will be paid on their behalf to the federal government and the union at a later date. Entries showing such payments are omitted here as not being relevant to our purposes, as are the various credits in entry 3. Entry 3 records the various liabilities incurred upon receipt of factory employee services. Entry 4 adds to Work in Process Inventory the cost of the labor traceable to the products being manufactured and transfers those labor costs not traceable to products to Manufacturing Overhead.

The Flow of Overhead Costs

The indirect costs of operating the factory during the period included repairs of $1,000, property taxes of $1,500, equipment rent of $2,500, payroll taxes of $3,500, utilities of $4,000, insurance of $2,000, and building depreciation of $5,500. Entry 5 shows the recording of these costs:

5. Manufacturing Overhead	20,000	
Cash		1,000
Accounts Payable		4,000
Accrued Property Taxes Payable		1,500
Unexpired Insurance		2,000
Prepaid Rent		2,500
Accumulated Depreciation		5,500
Accrued Payroll Taxes Payable		3,500
To record factory indirect costs for the period.		

Entries would also be made in supporting accounts or records maintained for each type of manufacturing overhead cost incurred. The credits assumed to accompany the $20,000 debit to manufacturing overhead are omitted from Illustration 13.3 as not being relevant to the showing of cost flows.

The manufacturing overhead costs are as much a part of the cost of the period's production as are the costs of direct materials and direct labor. These costs must, therefore, be added to the costs already in the Work in Process Inventory account, and this is done in entry 6:

6. Work in Process Inventory	35,000	
Manufacturing Overhead		35,000
To assign overhead to work in process.		

The assignment of overhead to work in process is a problem that is dealt with later. For purposes of Illustration 13.3, it is assumed that the overhead incurred during a period is to be assigned to the production of the period.

The Flow of Finished Goods

As shown in Illustration 13.3, for product costing purposes, Work in Process Inventory is charged with the materials, labor, and overhead costs of producing goods. When the goods are completed and transferred out of production, an entry is made to transfer their cost from Work in Process Inventory to Finished Goods Inventory. Assuming that goods costing $110,000 were completed and transferred, the entry needed is:

7. Finished Goods Inventory	110,000	
Work in Process Inventory		110,000
To record transfer of completed goods.		

Now assume that goods costing $125,000 were sold on account for $200,000. Entries are required to record the sale of the goods and to record the transfer out of the Finished Goods Inventory account of the cost of the goods sold. The required entries are:

8. Cost of Goods Sold 125,000
       Finished Goods Inventory 125,000
     To record cost of goods sold.

9. Accounts Receivable 200,000
       Sales 200,000
     To record sales on account.

Once again, since we are concerned with costs and revenues, the debit to Accounts Receivable in entry 9 is omitted from Illustration 13.3.

To complete the explanation of the entries in the accounts in Illustration 13.3, assume that selling expenses of $23,000, administrative expenses of $19,000, interest expense of $3,000, and federal income taxes of $15,000 were incurred in July. The required entries are:

10. Selling Expenses 23,000
        Various asset and liability accounts . . 23,000
      To record selling expenses incurred in July.

11. Administrative Expenses 19,000
        Various asset and liability accounts . . 19,000
      To record administrative expenses incurred in
      July.

12. Interest Expense 3,000
        Accrued Interest Payable 3,000
      To record interest expense incurred in July.

13. Federal Income Taxes 15,000
        Federal Income Taxes Payable 15,000
      To record estimated income taxes for July.

Subsidiary records or accounts would be kept for the various types of selling and administrative expenses incurred, but, for brevity, they are omitted here. The credits in entries 10 and 11 would be to such accounts as Cash, Accounts Payable, Salaries Payable, and Accumulated Depreciation. They are omitted from Illustration 13.3, as are the credits in entries 12 and 13, to keep attention directed toward manufacturing costs and income statement items.

Although the accounts are usually formally closed only at the end of the accounting year, entry 14 records the closing of the Sales revenue account for the month of July as an illustration of the annual entry:

14. Sales 200,000
        Income Summary 200,000
      To close Sales revenue account.

Entries 15 and 16 are required to close the expense accounts:

15. Income Summary 125,000
        Cost of Goods Sold 125,000
      To close Cost of Goods Sold account.

16. Income Summary	60,000	
Selling Expenses		23,000
Administrative Expenses		19,000
Interest Expense		3,000
Federal Income Taxes		15,000
To close other expense accounts.		

The closing process would, of course, be completed by debiting the Income Summary account and crediting the Retained Earnings account for $15,000. Here again, this entry is omitted for brevity.

As a technical matter, accounting for the costs of manufacturing operations ends with entry 7. The other entries are included to provide a complete set of illustrative entries for a manufacturing company.

FINANCIAL REPORTING BY MANUFACTURING COMPANIES

Typically, it is easy to determine from a balance sheet or an income statement whether the issuing company is a merchandiser or a manufacturer.

The Balance Sheet

The balance sheet (or the notes thereto) will typically disclose separately the manufacturer's inventories of materials, work in process, and finished goods. In contrast, a merchandiser will report a single merchandise inventory amount. The manufacturer's statement may also show, as intangible assets, patents and trademarks relating to the products manufactured and sold. The statement may also contain greater detail in the property, plant, and equipment section because of the ownership of assets used in manufacturing.

The Income Statement

The preparation of an income statement is considerably more complex for a manufacturer than for a merchandiser. The manufacturer incurs many additional costs in producing goods than does a merchandiser which buys them ready for sale. Because of this greater detail, a question arises as to how detailed an income statement should be. To a large extent, the answer depends upon who will use the statement.

If the income statement is to be published in an annual report, it is usually in a very condensed form, differing little from a merchandiser's income statement. Such a statement is shown in Illustration 13.4, which reports on the activities of the Braxton Company that are summarized in Illustration 13.3. Although it is common practice to include comparative data (the income statement for July 1985) when financial statements are released to the public, such data are omitted here.

The same type of income statement could be used in reporting to top management and to the board of directors. When so used, it is likely to be in comparative form, containing data for the same

Illustration 13.4

BRAXTON COMPANY
Income Statement
For the Month Ended July 31, 1986

Sales		$200,000
Cost of goods sold	$125,000	
Selling expenses	23,000	
Administrative expenses . .	19,000	
Interest expense	3,000	
Federal income taxes . . .	15,000	185,000
Net income		$ 15,000

period last year, and to include budgeted data. It is also likely to be supported by a statement of the cost of goods manufactured and sold and with schedules showing the details of the selling and administrative expenses, complete with comparative and budgeted data.

The Statement of Cost of Goods Manufactured and Sold

Illustration 13.5 contains the statement of cost of goods manufactured and sold for the Braxton Company for the month of July 1986. Note how the statement shows the costs incurred during the month for materials, labor, and overhead and describes this total as **Cost to manufacture.** By adding to this amount the July 1 inven-

Illustration 13.5

BRAXTON COMPANY
Statement of Cost of Goods Manufactured and Sold
For the Month Ended July 31, 1986

Direct materials		$ 30,000
Direct labor		60,000
Manufacturing overhead:		
Indirect labor	$15,000	
Building depreciation	5,500	
Utilities	4,000	
Payroll taxes	3,500	
Equipment rent	2,500	
Insurance	2,000	
Property taxes	1,500	
Repairs	1,000	35,000
Cost to manufacture		$125,000
Add: Work in process, July 1, 1986		20,000
		$145,000
Deduct: Work in process, July 31, 1986 . .		35,000
Cost of goods manufactured		$110,000
Add: Finished goods, July 1, 1986		40,000
Cost of goods available for sale		$150,000
Deduct: Finished goods, July 31, 1986 . . .		25,000
Cost of goods sold		$125,000

tory of work in process and subtracting the July 31 inventory of work in process, the **Cost of goods manufactured** (completed) during the period is shown. When the July 1 finished goods inventory is added to this amount, the **Cost of goods available for sale** is obtained. This amount less the July 31 finished goods inventory yields the **Cost of goods sold.** At this stage, note the following similarity:

Merchandiser: Beginning merchandise inventory + Purchases
                        − Ending merchandise inventory = Cost of goods sold

Manufacturer: Beginning finished goods inventory + Cost of goods manufactured
                        − Ending finished goods inventory = Cost of goods sold

Careful attention should be paid to the terminology used in the statement of cost of goods manufactured and sold. Note the similarity between Cost to manufacture and Cost of goods manufac-

Illustration 13.6
A MANUFACTURING COMPANY'S TOTAL OPERATIONS

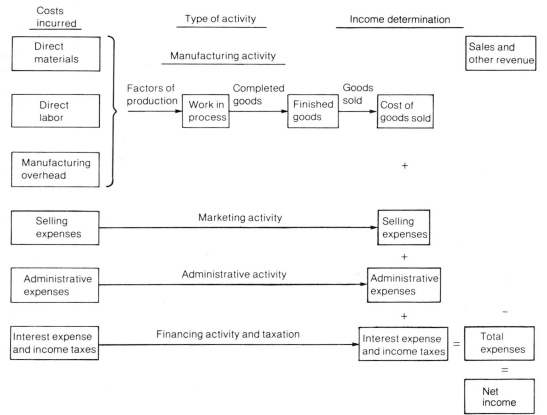

tured. The former consists of the costs of all of the resources put into production in the period. The latter consists of the cost of goods completed and includes cost to manufacture and the change in the Work in Process inventory from the beginning to the end of the period.

A Graphic Summary
The discussion of a manufacturer's activities that lead to the recognition of net income is summarized graphically in Illustration 13.6. Several implications of the accounting for such activities are worth stressing again.

First, accounting for the costs of manufacturing operations is an integral part of the overall accounting system of the manufacturer. No separate system is used to accumulate manufacturing cost information.

Second, as Illustration 13.6 shows, manufacturing costs are considered product costs, are attached to the products manufactured, and are run through work in process and finished goods inventories. They are recognized as expenses when the products to which they attach are sold. Selling and administrative costs are treated as period costs and expensed in the period in which they are incurred. They are not "inventoriable" costs.

MANUFACTURING OVERHEAD RATES
To focus on the general pattern of cost flows shown in Illustration 13.3, certain aspects in accounting for manufacturing overhead were not discussed. These aspects arise primarily because the costs of a wide variety of factory services having no common physical basis of measurement must be allocated to many different products. By their nature and for practical reasons, such costs are not traceable to, or identifiable with, any given unit of product.

Before attention is directed to these aspects, the terms **cost center, production center,** and **service center** need to be introduced and defined. A cost center is an accounting unit of activity for accumulating costs having a common objective. That is, the items of cost recorded as having been incurred by a given cost center all seek to accomplish the same objective or purpose. Thus, the costs incurred in the assembly department of a furniture manufacturer seek to bring about the assembly of furniture and can, therefore, be allocated to the products assembled. A cost center in which work is performed on units of product is called a production center. A service center is a cost center in which work indirectly related to the goods produced is performed. A toolroom, maintenance department, power plant, and even a company cafeteria are examples of service centers. In some manufacturing entities, the costs incurred in the service centers are allocated to the production centers quarterly or even monthly. These allocated costs then enter into the development of the overhead rate used to charge indirect costs to the products.

Predetermined Overhead Rates

In the above discussion, overhead rates were determined at the end of a period (say, a month). But, although some companies follow such a procedure, it is far more common to use a **predetermined** overhead rate to allocate overhead to production. The rate is usually set at the beginning of the year. The reasons for this more common practice include the following:

1. Overhead costs are seldom incurred uniformly throughout the year; for example, heating costs will be larger in winter. No useful purpose is served in allocating less cost to a unit produced in the summer than to one produced in the winter.

2. The volume of goods produced may vary from month to month, with accompanying sharp fluctuations in average unit cost if some overhead costs are fixed.

3. Unit costs of production are known sooner. Using a predetermined rate, overhead costs can be assigned to production when direct materials costs and direct labor costs are assigned. Without a predetermined rate, unit costs would not be known until the end of the month, or even much later if bills for overhead costs are late.

4. Some overhead costs may be better viewed as losses due to inefficiencies rather than costs properly assigned to units of product.

Computing predetermined overhead rates. The mechanics of computing predetermined overhead rates are the same as those used for actual rates except for the use of budgeted, rather than actual, levels of costs and levels of activity. Budgeted overhead costs are first estimated and charged to the various cost centers. Budgeted service center costs are then reassigned to production centers. Budgeted production center costs are then divided by the estimate of the level of activity to compute the predetermined rates. The computation of the predetermined overhead rate would be as follows:

$$\text{MOH rate} = \frac{\text{Budgeted (estimated) manufacturing overhead costs}}{\text{Budgeted (estimated) level of activity}}$$

The activity base used to calculate the predetermined overhead rate can be a variety of things such as machine hours, direct labor hours, direct labor cost, or production amounts. For example, assume that budgeted overhead was estimated to be $950,000 for the next accounting period and the following estimated levels of activity were available: estimated production is 750,000 units, estimated direct labor hours are 50,000 hours, estimated direct labor costs are

$500,000, and the estimated machine hours are 45,000 hours. The various overhead rates that could be computed are illustrated:

Estimated Overhead Costs	÷	Activity Levels	=	Overhead Rate
$950,000	÷	750,000 units of production	=	$ 1.27 per unit produced
950,000	÷	50,000 direct labor hours	=	19.00 per direct labor hour
950,000	÷	$500,000 direct labor costs	=	1.90 per dollar of direct labor
950,000	÷	45,000 machine hours	=	21.11 per machine hour

It should be noted that each of these rates must be applied to the kind of activity upon which the rate is calculated. The general format for applying (charging to the product costs) overhead is:

$$\text{MOH applied} = \text{MOH rate} \times \text{Actual activity level}$$

Choosing the level of activity to be used in setting predetermined overhead rates is a special problem that will now be discussed.

Levels of activity. Setting overhead rates, especially when large amounts of fixed overhead costs are incurred, involves the difficult problem of choosing the level of activity to be used. It would be possible to wait until the end of the period and then use actual rates to apply overhead to production. Thus, if $100,000 of fixed overhead costs were incurred and 10 units were produced, the overhead cost per unit would be $10,000. If 1,000 units were produced, it would be $100. And the wide fluctuation in unit cost would be due solely to the differing number of units produced.

But suppose that the plant was designed to produce 100,000 units per period. Now, might it not be logical to argue that the overhead to be absorbed by each unit is $1 ($100,000 ÷ 100,000) and that any underabsorbed overhead from producing less than 100,000 units is a loss from idle capacity? Many accountants say yes. Thus, the issue is: What level of activity should be used in setting overhead rates?

Among the different levels of activity that might be used, the three most commonly found in practice today are:

1. Practical capacity—the maximum attainable output of a plant. This is the theoretical capacity less allowance for the fact that individuals can seldom achieve perfection. Its use results in charging to production only the costs of the facilities actually used. If a plant operated at 60 percent of capacity, 60 percent of its fixed costs would be charged to production, and the remaining 40 percent would be treated as a period cost (loss).

2. Normal capacity or activity—the level of activity expected

to prevail over the long run, say, three to five years. Its use is based on the belief that over the long run all manufacturing costs are to be absorbed in production and recovered through sale of the goods.

3. Expected activity—the estimated level of activity for the coming period. This level of activity has the objective of absorbing all fixed overhead for a period in the production of that period.

The level of activity problem illustrated. To illustrate, consider the data in the following schedule. Assume that fixed overhead costs are $480,000 per period and that variable overhead costs amount to $1.50 per direct labor hour.

	Direct Labor Hours for the Year	Budgeted Overhead for the Year		
		Variable	Fixed	Total
Practical capacity . . .	100,000	$150,000	$480,000	$630,000
Normal capacity . . .	80,000	120,000	480,000	600,000
Expected activity . . .	60,000	90,000	480,000	570,000

From these data, three predetermined overhead rates could be computed as follows:

1. Practical capacity rate: $630,000 ÷ 100,000 = $6.30 per direct labor hour.
2. Normal capacity rate: $600,000 ÷ 80,000 = $7.50 per direct labor hour.
3. Expected activity rate: $570,000 ÷ 60,000 = $9.50 per direct labor hour.

Note that in each of these rates variable overhead accounts for $1.50 of the total rate. Thus, it is the fixed overhead rate that varies. If the actual overhead costs incurred during the year amounted to $480,000 fixed and $75,000 variable and the actual direct labor hours of services received amounted to 50,000 hours, the actual overhead rate would be $11.10 ($555,000 ÷ 50,000).

Note further the differing amounts of overhead that would be applied to work in process, depending upon the level of activity used in setting the rate when 50,000 hours of direct labor services were received:

Practical capacity-based rate: 50,000 × $6.30 = $315,000
Normal capacity-based rate: 50,000 × $7.50 = $375,000
Expected activity-based rate: 50,000 × $9.50 = $475,000

Underapplied or overapplied overhead. When overhead is applied to production using predetermined rates, the manufacturing overhead account is credited with **estimated** amounts applied to work in process inventory because the rate is based on estimates when it is established. Under these circumstances, it is highly unlikely that the actual costs debited to the account will exactly equal the overhead applied. A **debit balance** will remain if actual overhead exceeds applied overhead, and overhead will be **underapplied** or **underabsorbed.** A **credit balance** will remain if applied overhead exceeds actual overhead, and overhead will be **overapplied** or **overabsorbed.**

Refer to Illustration 13.3. If overhead is allocated to production using a predetermined rate of 50 percent of direct labor cost, entry 6 on page 396 would read:

```
Work in Process Inventory  . . . . . . . . .  30,000
    Manufacturing Overhead  . . . . . . . .          30,000
    To assign overhead to work in process.
```

Since $35,000 of actual overhead costs were charged to Manufacturing Overhead, the account would have a $5,000 debit balance representing underapplied overhead for the period.

Reasons for underapplied or overapplied overhead. Underapplied or overapplied overhead may be a result of unexpected events such as price changes, a severe winter, or excessive repairs; it may also be the result of inefficiency. But underapplied overhead is more likely to be caused by incurring costs at a higher level than that set in the typical "tight" budget. On the other hand, overapplied overhead is likely to be the result of operating at a higher actual level than that used in setting the overhead rate and to the existence of fixed overhead costs.

Disposition of underapplied or overapplied overhead. Any under- or overapplied overhead balance can be carried forward in interim balance sheets if the probability exists that it will be reduced or offset by future operations. At year-end, any remaining balance could be allocated to Work in Process Inventory, Finished Goods Inventory, or Cost of Goods Sold by recomputing the cost of production for the year, using actual overhead rates.

As an alternative, charging underapplied overhead off as a loss of the period has particular merit if it results from idle capacity or from unusual circumstances. But, as a practical matter, underapplied or overapplied overhead is frequently transferred to Cost of Goods Sold. Little distortion of net income or of assets results from this treatment if the amount transferred is small or if most of the goods produced during the year were sold. Thus, the entry to dispose of the $5,000 of underapplied overhead in the example would read:

```
Cost of Goods Sold  . . . . . . . . . . . . .  5,000
    Manufacturing Overhead  . . . . . . . . .          5,000
    To dispose of underapplied overhead.
```

The next two chapters continue the discussion of accounting for a manufacturing company. The discussion will include job order and process costing as well as an explanation of standard costs.

SUMMARY

The costs incurred by a manufacturing firm are usually classified broadly as manufacturing (production), selling (marketing), and administrative (general). Manufacturing costs are incurred to manufacture a product and are often referred to as product costs. Product costs include the cost of direct materials and direct labor and an allocated share of the manufacturing overhead costs (indirect factory costs). Selling costs are further classified as order getting and order filling. Most of the remaining costs incurred by a manufacturer are called administrative or general costs. This category usually excludes interest expense and federal and state income taxes. All costs that are not considered product costs are called period costs. Product costs attach to the product, and when the product is sold they are charged to expense as part of the cost of goods sold expense. Period costs are treated as expenses of the period in which they are incurred.

Another way of classifying costs is by their behavior when activity changes. Variable costs are those costs that vary in total amount directly with changes in the level of activity or output. Fixed costs are costs that remain constant in total amount over wide variations in the level of activity.

The cost accumulation system of a manufacturer is part of its accounting system. Generally, costs flow through this system in a manner that matches the physical flow of products from materials storeroom to production department to finished goods warehouse to customers.

In contrast to a merchandiser's single inventory account, a manufacturer's balance sheet will often show three inventory accounts: Materials Inventory, Work in Process Inventory, and Finished Goods Inventory. The financial reporting by a manufacturer will also include the preparation of a statement of cost of goods manufactured and sold.

Manufacturing overhead is allocated to products by use of predetermined overhead rates. These rates are set initially by assigning all overhead to production or service centers. Service center costs are then reassigned to production centers. Production center costs (including assigned service center costs) are then allocated to products, using the overhead rates obtained by dividing the costs by estimates of the level of activity, such as direct labor hours.

Three levels of activity which may be used when setting overhead rates are practical capacity, normal capacity or activity, and expected activity. The use of these will result in differing amounts of under- or overapplied overhead in a given situation.

The use of rates determined in advance to assign overhead to production usually results in underapplied or overapplied overhead. As a practical matter, such balances are closed to Cost of Goods Sold at the end of the year.

1. Identify the three broad classifications of costs incurred by manufacturing firms. Indicate why it is important that costs not be incorrectly classified.

2. Identify the three elements of cost incurred in manufacturing a product, and indicate the distinguishing characteristics of each.

3. Why might a firm claim that the total cost of employing a person is $10.30 per hour even though the employee's wage rate is $6.50 per hour? How should this difference be classified, and why?

4. In general, what is the relationship between cost flows in the accounts and the flow of physical products through a factory?

5. What is meant by the term *product cost?* State the general principle under which product costs are accumulated.

6. What is the general content of a statement of cost of goods manufactured and sold? What is its relationship to the income statement?

7. What is the typical accounting for the overtime wage premium paid a direct laborer? Why? Under what circumstances might an alternative accounting be considered preferable?

8. Why are certain costs referred to as period costs? What are the major types of period costs incurred by a manufacturer?

9. What deficiencies do you see in an accounting system that assigns the actual overhead incurred in a month to the production of that month?

10. Why is the manufacturing overhead rate determined prior to the year in which it is used?

11. What is a manufacturing overhead rate? Why is the application of overhead to production through the use of such a rate almost an absolute necessity?

12. What is the reason, other than errors in estimating costs, for overapplied overhead?

13. When overhead is applied to production via a predetermined overhead rate, is it correct to speak of the per unit product costs computed as actual costs?

14. Indicate the possible dispositions of a balance in the Manufacturing Overhead account and the reasoning or circumstances in which each would seem preferable.

15. What is a service center or department? How does it differ from a production center?

16. Explain the usual accounting for service center costs in setting overhead rates.

17. What levels of capacity or activity could be used in setting overhead rates? What is the main objective sought in the use of each level?

EXERCISES

1. During a given week, $120,000 of direct materials and $10,000 of indirect materials were issued by the storeroom to the production department. Give the required journal entry or entries.

2. As prepared by the payroll department, the week's factory labor payroll amounted to $232,000, from which the following were withheld: social security taxes, $11,200; union dues, $4,000; and federal income taxes, $24,000. The payroll is to be paid next Friday. Analysis of the payroll shows that it consists of $196,000 of direct labor and the following wages and salaries: inspectors, $7,600; supervisors, $4,400; electricians, $6,400; timekeepers, $4,800; janitors, $7,200; and warehousemen, $5,600. Give the entry to record the incurrence of the above labor costs and their distribution to proper accounts.

3. Given below are some costs incurred by an automobile manufacturer. Classify these costs as direct materials, direct labor, manufacturing overhead, selling, or administrative.

a. Salary of the cost accountant.

b. Cost of automobile radios installed in autos.

c. Cost of stationery used in president's office.

d. Supplies used in cost accountant's office.

e. Wages of a factory inspector.

f. Payroll taxes on assembly-line worker's wages.

g. Repair parts used to repair factory machine.

h. Cost of labor services to install radios in autos.

i. Depreciation on automobiles driven by company's top executives.

j. Cost of magazines purchased for the engineering department.

4. Review the list of costs in Exercise 3, and indicate which of the costs listed are likely to vary directly with the number of autos produced.

5. The following data pertain to the B Company for the year ended June 30, 1986:

Direct materials used	$ 400,000
Direct labor	800,000
Work in process, 7/1/85	80,000
Work in process, 6/30/86	120,000
Finished goods, 7/1/85	200,000
Finished goods, 6/30/86	280,000
Manufacturing overhead	1,200,000

Compute the cost of goods manufactured and sold. Also, prepare one entry to summarize the transfer of completed goods for the year.

6. Larry Thomas was paid for 48 hours of work as a carpenter for Home Constructors, Inc., for last week. His total wages amounted to $624— 40 hours at $12 per hour plus 8 hours of Saturday work at $18 per hour (time and a half). He worked 32 hours of regular time on House 124 and 8 hours of regular time and 7 hours of overtime on House 125. He was idle one hour on Saturday, waiting for materials to be delivered. Saturday work is common in the construction industry during good weather.

How much of the wages paid Larry Thomas should be considered a cost of House 124? Of House 125? As manufacturing overhead? Explain.

7. Lennox Company sells 25-inch television sets which it assembles from purchased parts. In 1986 it purchased 10,000 picture tubes at $30 each. Of these 10,000 tubes, 25 were used by Lennox in testing their product life, 5 were used to replace burned-out tubes in display models, and 9,000 were issued to production. Of the 9,000 placed in production, 7,000 were in units completed, of which 6,000 were sold.

As of December 31, 1986, how much of the $300,000 cost of purchased picture tubes should appear in each of the following accounts?

a. Materials Inventory.

b. Work in Process Inventory.

c. Finished Goods Inventory.

d. Manufacturing Overhead.

e. Selling Expense.

f. Cost of Goods Sold.

8. Ohio Company applies overhead to production by use of a predetermined overhead rate of $6 per direct labor hour. During the week ended July 17, Ohio received 2,100 hours of direct labor services from its employees that were chargeable to specific units of product. Give the journal entry to record the application of overhead to production.

9. Grey Company estimated its overhead for 1986 at $800,000 ($200,000 fixed and $600,000 variable) based on a normal activity of 400,000 direct labor hours. At the end of 1986, manufacturing overhead was overapplied by $6,000, while actual direct labor hours amounted to 404,000. Analyze the $6,000 as to the reasons for its existence.

10. Give the journal entry required in Exercise 9 to reflect a practical disposition of the overhead balance.

11. Assume that at the end of 1986, in Exercise 9, the costs of the 404,000 actual direct labor hours were lodged in the following accounts: Work in Process, 40,400 hours; Finished Goods, 101,000 hours; and Cost of Goods Sold, 262,600. Give the journal entry to allocate the overhead balances to these accounts.

12. For each of the following cases (*a* through *e*), fill in the missing data as indicated by the blank spaces. Assume that overhead rates are based on estimated fixed overhead and normalized production.

Case	Fixed Over-head Rate	Estimated Fixed Overhead	Normalized Production (units)	Actual Production (units)	Fixed Over-head Applied
a	$10	$ _____	25,000		$260,000
b	—	180,000		27,000	162,000
c	—	420,000	30,000	31,000	
d	12	_____	40,000	35,000	
e	16	320,000	_____	_____	288,000

PROBLEMS

13–1. A number of costs that would affect business decisions in the factory operations of different companies are listed below. These costs may be fixed or variable with respect to some measure of volume or output, and they may be classified as direct materials (DM), direct labor (DL), or manufacturing overhead (MO).

(1) Glue used to attach labels to bottles containing a patented medicine.
(2) Compressed air used in operating machines turning our products.
(3) Insurance on factory building and equipment.
(4) A production department supervisor's salary.
(5) Rent on factory machinery.
(6) Iron ore and coke in a steel mill.
(7) Oil, gasoline, and grease for forklift trucks.
(8) Services of painters in building construction.
(9) Cutting oils used in machining operations.
(10) Cost of food served in a factory employees' cafeteria.
(11) Payroll taxes and fringe benefits related to direct labor.
(12) The plant electricians' salaries.
(13) Sand for a glass manufacturer.
(14) Copy editor's salary for a book publisher.

Required:

a. List the numbers 1 through 14 down the left side of a sheet of paper. After each number, write the letters *V* (for variable) or *F* (for fixed) and either DM (for direct materials), DL (for direct labor), or MO (for manufacturing overhead) to show how you would classify the similarly numbered cost item given above.

b. With which of your own answers given for part **a** could you take issue? Discuss.

13–2. Selected data for Gregory Company for the month of July are as follows:

Materials issued (including $10,000 of indirect materials)	$ 370,000
Factory payrolls (all direct labor except $20,000)	420,000
Finished goods inventory, July 1	140,000
Finished goods inventory, July 31	160,000
Total costs charged to Work in Process in July	1,160,000
Work in process inventory, July 1	120,000
Work in process inventory, July 31	140,000

Required:

    a. Compute the amount of manufacturing overhead costs assigned to production in July.

    b. Give journal entries to record the cost of the goods completed in July and the cost of the goods sold in July.

13–3. The following data relate to the Joy Company for the month of August.

    (1) Purchased materials on account, $140,000.

    (2) Materials issued, $160,000, including $4,000 of indirect materials.

    (3) Factory payroll for the month, $184,000.

    (4) Payroll costs distributed: direct labor, $160,000; and indirect labor, $24,000.

    (5) Other overhead costs incurred: factory depreciation, $140,000; property taxes, $32,000; repairs, $20,000; utilities, $16,000; and other, $12,000.

    (6) Selling expenses incurred, $120,000; and administrative expenses incurred, $110,000.

    (7) Actual overhead is assigned to production.

    (8) Cost of goods completed and transferred, $520,000.

    (9) Sales on account, $800,000.

  (10) Cost of goods sold, $500,000.

August 1 inventory balances were:

Materials	$36,000
Work in process	44,000
Finished goods	84,000

Required:

    Enter the above data in T-accounts, thus preparing a cost and revenue flowchart similar to the one illustrated in the chapter. You need not prepare or enter closing entries.

13–4. The production and revenue-producing activities of the Murphy Company for the year ended December 31, 1986, are summarized below:

Sales	$800,000	Sales commissions	$ 70,000
Factory maintenance	14,000	Interest expense	10,000
Factory depreciation	32,000	Direct labor cost	180,000
Factory insurance and taxes	16,000	Indirect materials	13,000
Indirect labor	30,000	Advertising expense	50,000
Payroll-related costs—factory	48,000	Administrative salaries	96,000
Other administrative expenses	24,000	Other selling expenses	30,000
Factory utilities	11,000	Work in process, 1/1	40,000
Work in process, 12/31	42,000	Finished goods, 1/1	30,000
Finished goods, 12/31	80,000	Direct materials	128,000

Federal income taxes are estimated at 60 percent of net income before such taxes. A total of 40,000 units was manufactured in 1986.

Required:

a. Prepare a statement of cost of goods manufactured and sold for 1986.

b. Prepare a condensed income statement for the year 1986.

c. Compute the company's direct labor cost per unit in 1986. Also, assuming that fixed overhead consists of factory depreciation, insurance, and taxes, compute the fixed overhead cost per unit for 1986.

d. Assume use of the straight-line method of computing depreciation and that tax rates, wages, and prices are expected to remain fairly stable in 1987. If the company expects to produce 50,000 units in 1987, what is its expected per unit direct labor cost? Its total direct labor cost? How much fixed factory overhead should it expect to incur? What is its expected fixed overhead cost per unit?

e. Give the reasons for the differences and the similarities noted in the total and unit costs computed in **c** and **d**.

13–5. Morelli Company operates a number of machines that process a single product. Study of past records and engineering studies indicates that 30 units of product should be processed per machine-hour at a variable overhead cost of $12 per hour. Fixed overhead costs should amount to $72,000 per month.

Actual production and actual overhead costs for June and July were:

Month	Units Processed	Overhead Cost
June . . .	100,000	$111,500
July	90,000	109,800

Required:

a. Compute the amount of overhead cost in total and per unit that should have been incurred in June and in July.

b. Compute the per unit actual overhead cost, the per unit actual fixed overhead cost, and the per unit actual variable overhead cost for June and July. Actual fixed overhead costs were $72,000 per month.

c. Comment on the reasons for the differences noted in the amounts computed in **b**.

13–6. Selected budgeted (based on normal activity) and actual data on productive activities and on overhead costs for Chen Company for 1986 are given below:

	Budgeted	Actual
Total manufacturing overhead . .	$1,600,000	$1,630,000
Direct labor cost	$1,000,000	$1,030,000
Direct labor hours	200,000	202,000
Machine-hours	160,000	162,000

Required:

a. Compute three different overhead rates that might be used to apply overhead to production.

b. For each of the rates computed in **a,** compute the amount of overhead applied to production and the amount of underapplied or overapplied overhead for 1986.

c. Assume that one unit of product manufactured in 1986 had an actual materials cost of $80 and an actual direct labor cost of $42. Also assume that the unit required eight direct labor hours and six machine-hours. Compute the unit's total cost under each of the different overhead rates computed in **a.**

13–7. Lawrence Company applies overhead to production using a predetermined overhead rate based on machine-hours. Budgeted data for 1986 are:

Level of Activity		Budgeted Machine-Hours	Budgeted Overhead
Practical capacity	. . .	150,000	$780,000
Normal activity	. . . .	100,000	580,000
Expected activity	. . . .	120,000	660,000

Two hours of machine time are needed to complete a unit of product.

Required:

a. Without making any calculations, would you expect overhead to be underapplied or overapplied in 1986, if normal activity is used to set the rate? Why?

b. Compute the predetermined overhead rates that Lawrence might use.

c. Compute the variable and fixed portions of these rates.

d. Assume that the overhead rate used was based on normal activity, that actual overhead amounted to $665,000, and that 122,000 machine-hours were used to process 60,500 units of product in 1986. Compute the underapplied or overapplied overhead for that year.

13–8. Fox Company's controller, after reviewing the new production processes and recently installed machines, has suggested that the old plantwide, single predetermined overhead rate based on direct labor hours be replaced by separate rates and that the rate in Production Center X be based on direct labor hours and in Production Center Y on machine-hours. In the company's operations, a unit of product is worked on in both A and B. Budget estimates, based on normal activity, for 1986 are:

		Total	Production Center X	Production Center Y
Manufacturing overhead	. .	$432,000	$192,000	$240,000
Direct labor hours	. . . .	144,000	48,000	96,000
Machine-hours	. . . . .	36,000	12,000	24,000

Cost records show the following per unit costs and hours for a unit of product completed in 1986:

	Production Center X	Production Center Y
Direct materials used	$100	$56
Direct labor cost	$ 64	$80
Direct labor hours used . . .	24	40
Machine-hours used	16	20

Required:

a. Compute the single, plantwide overhead rate that the company would have used prior to the change to separate rates for production centers.

b. Compute the per unit cost of the product, using this single rate.

c. Compute the separate production center rates suggested by the controller.

d. Compute the per unit cost of the product, using separate production center rates to apply overhead. Compare this per unit cost with the per unit cost computed in **b,** and comment on any difference.

e. Assume that in 1986 the actual overhead incurred in Center X was $206,000, with 50,040 direct labor hours received. In Center Y, actual overhead was $242,000, with 24,008 machine-hours received. Compute the underapplied or overapplied overhead for each center.

13–9. The income statement for Kirk, Inc., for 1986 was as follows:

KIRK, INC.
Income Statement
For the Year Ended December 31, 1986

Sales (20,000 units)		$400,000
Cost of goods sold	$360,000	
Other expenses (all fixed) . .	100,000	460,000
Net loss		$ (60,000)

The $60,000 loss for 1986 continued a pattern of losses of this size occurring over the past few years. Selling prices and sales volume have remained unchanged over these years. Production volume has amounted to 20,000 units annually at a variable cost of $3 per unit, while fixed manufacturing overhead totals $300,000 annually. There were no inventories at the start or end of 1986.

Despite the fact that the costs incurred in 1987 were at the same levels as those incurred in 1986, the company's new president proudly presented the following income statement to the board of directors:

KIRK, INC.
Income Statement
For the Year Ended December 31, 1987

Sales (20,000 units)		$400,000
Cost of goods sold	$210,000	
Other expenses (all fixed) . .	100,000	310,000
Net income		$ 90,000

The board was so delighted with the company's "turnaround" from losses to net income that it voted the president a bonus of $20,000. A week later, after collecting the bonus, the president resigned "to pursue other challenges."

Required:

a. Explain carefully, through use of a schedule showing units and dollar amounts, how the president was able to effect the "turnaround" from losses to earnings.

b. How might the above misleading portrayal of $90,000 of net income have been prevented, or at least brought to the attention of the board?

14 COST ACCUMULATION SYSTEMS—JOB ORDER AND PROCESS; VARIABLE COSTING

The preceding chapter dealt with (1) manufacturing costs and their flow through the accounts, (2) the application of overhead to production, and (3) reporting net income of a manufacturing company. Little attention was paid to the procedures and accounting records used in accumulating costs or to the determination of unit costs for units of product.[1] How these costs are determined depends upon the type of cost system employed—a job order cost or a process cost system.

Attention in this chapter is directed to the two major types of cost accumulation systems found in practice—the **job order cost** system and the **process cost** system. In each system the goal is to determine the unit costs of the products manufactured. As already noted, unit costs are needed in determining the cost of the goods sold and the cost of the ending inventories of work in process and finished goods. Unit costs may also be used in determining payments to be received under contracts based on "full" cost and in setting selling prices.

---

[1] It is a mistake to assume that *the* unit cost can be found with any precision. All we have are different techniques for finding *a* cost figure. *Assumptions* must be made regarding the use of Fifo, Lifo, or weighted-average inventory cost; how much depreciation to charge against a given period and a unit of product; and similar considerations. *Reasonable* (but arbitrary) allocations must be made. Also, for decision-making purposes future costs rather than past costs must often be used.

JOB ORDER COST SYSTEMS

Timely and Useful Information

When a job order cost system is used, costs are accumulated by individual jobs or batches of output. A job may consist of 1,000 chairs, 10 sofas, 5 miles of highway, a single machine, a dam, or a building. A job cost system is generally used when the products being manufactured can be separately identified or when goods are produced to meet a customer's particular needs, such as constructing a house. Job costing is also used in other types of construction, in motion pictures, in job printing, and more.

Under job order costing, an up-to-date record of the costs incurred on a job is kept in order to provide management with cost data on a timely basis. For example, management may want to know the cost of producing 100 desks when the desks are completed. Managers can also receive reports as often as desired, even daily, on such matters as materials used, labor costs incurred, goods completed, total and detailed production costs, and whether production costs are in line with expectations.

Basic Records in Job Costing

Illustration 14.1 shows the basic records or source documents used in a job order cost system. These include:

1. The **job order sheet,** on which all of the costs—direct materials, direct labor, and applied overhead—of producing a given job or batch of products are summarized. The job order sheet is the key document in the system, and is used to control production costs by comparing actual costs with budgeted costs. One sheet is maintained for each job, and the file of job order sheets for unfinished jobs is the subsidiary ledger for the Work in Process Inventory account. When the goods are completed and transferred, the job order sheets are transferred to a completed jobs file and the number of units and their unit costs are recorded on inventory cards supporting the Finished Goods Inventory account.

2. The **stores** (or **materials**) **card,** one of which is kept for each type of direct and indirect materials maintained in inventory. The stores card shows the quantities (and costs) of each type of material received, issued, and on hand for which the storekeeper is responsible. When a job is started, direct materials are ordered from the storeroom on a **materials requisition,** which shows the types, costs, and quantities of the materials ordered.

3. The **work** (or **time**) ticket, which shows who worked on what job for how many hours and at what wage rate. All of each employee's daily hours must be accounted for on one or more work tickets.

4. The **manufacturing overhead cost sheet,** which summarizes the

Illustration 14.1
BASIC RECORDS IN A JOB ORDER COST SYSTEM

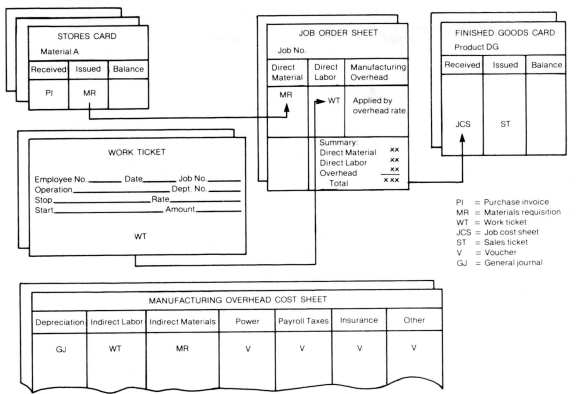

various factory indirect costs incurred. One sheet is maintained for each production center and each service center.

5. The **finished goods card** or **record,** one of which is maintained for each type of product manufactured and sold. Each card contains a running record of units and costs of products received, sold, and on hand.

The general flow of costs through the accounting system of a firm using a job order cost system is shown in Illustration 14.2. This illustration should be studied carefully and related to the documents used to record costs that are shown in Illustration 14.1 in order to gain a full understanding of a job order cost system.

Job Order Costing— An Example

To illustrate a job order cost system, especially the tie-in between the general ledger accounts and the subsidiary records, an example

Illustration 14.2
JOB ORDER SYSTEM COST FLOWS

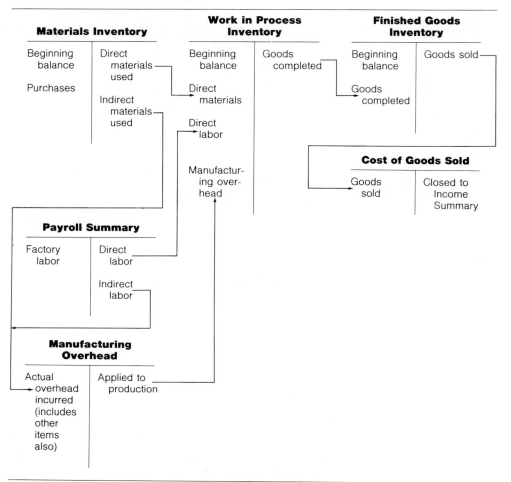

is presented below. The example covers the month of July, for which the beginning inventories were:

Materials inventory (Material A, $10,000; Material B, $6,000; various indirect materials, $4,000)	$20,000
Work in process inventory (Job No. 106; direct materials, $4,200; direct labor, $5,000; and overhead, $4,000)	13,200
Finished goods inventory (500 units of Product AB at a cost of $11 per unit)	5,500

The example further assumes that Job No. 106 was completed in July, and that, of the two jobs started in July (Nos. 107 and 108), only Job No. 108 is incomplete at the end of July. The transactions, and the journal entries to record them, are given below:

1. Purchased $10,000 of Material A and $15,000 of Material B on account.

```
Materials Inventory  . . . . . . . . . .  25,000
    Accounts Payable  . . . . . . . . . .            25,000
    To record purchase of direct materials.
```

2. Issued direct materials: Material A to Job No. 106, $1,000, to Job No. 107, $8,000, and to Job No. 108, $2,000; Material B to Job No. 106, $2,000, to Job No. 107, $6,000, and to Job No. 108, $4,000. Indirect materials issued to all jobs, $1,000.

```
Work in Process Inventory  . . . . . . . .  23,000
Manufacturing Overhead  . . . . . . . . . .   1,000
    Materials Inventory  . . . . . . . . .            24,000
    To record direct and indirect materials issued.
```

3. Factory payroll for the month, $25,000; social security and income taxes withheld, $4,000.

```
Payroll Summary  . . . . . . . . . . . .  25,000
    Various liability accounts for taxes withheld  . .      4,000
    Accrued Wages Payable  . . . . . . . . .           21,000
    To record factory payroll for July.
```

4. Factory payroll paid, $19,000.

```
Accrued Wages Payable  . . . . . . . . . .  19,000
    Cash  . . . . . . . . . . . . . . .               19,000
    To record cash paid to factory employees in July.
```

5. Payroll costs distributed: direct labor, $20,000 (Job No. 106, $5,000; Job No. 107, $12,000; and Job No. 108, $3,000); and indirect labor, $5,000.

```
Work in Process Inventory  . . . . . . . .  20,000
Manufacturing Overhead  . . . . . . . . . .   5,000
    Payroll Summary  . . . . . . . . . . .            25,000
    To distribute factory labor costs incurred.
```

6. Other manufacturing overhead costs incurred:

```
Payroll taxes accrued  . . . . . . . . . . .  $ 3,000
Repairs (on account)  . . . . . . . . . . .     1,000
Property taxes accrued  . . . . . . . . . .     4,000
Heat, light, and power (on account)  . . . . .     2,000
Depreciation  . . . . . . . . . . . . . .       5,000
                                              $15,000

Manufacturing Overhead  . . . . . . . . . .  15,000
    Accounts Payable  . . . . . . . . . . .             3,000
    Accrued Payroll Taxes  . . . . . . . . .             3,000
    Accrued Property Taxes Payable  . . . . .             4,000
    Accumulated Depreciation  . . . . . . . .             5,000
    To record manufacturing overhead costs incurred.
```

7. Manufacturing overhead applied to production (at rate of 80 percent of direct labor cost):

Job No. 106, Product DG (0.80 × $5,000)		$ 4,000
Job No. 107, Product XY (0.80 × $12,000) . . .		9,600
Job No. 108, Product OR (0.80 × $3,000)		2,400
		$16,000

Work in Process Inventory	16,000	
Manufacturing Overhead		16,000
To record application of overhead to production.		

8. Jobs completed and transferred to finish goods storeroom (see page 424 for details):

Job No. 106 (4,000 units of Product DG @ $6.30)		$25,200
Job No. 107 (10,000 units of Product XY @ $3.56)		35,600
		$60,800

Finished Goods Inventory	60,800	
Work in Process Inventory		60,800
To record completed production for July.		

9. Sales on account for the month: 500 units of Product AB for $8,000, cost, $5,500; and 10,000 units of Product XY for $62,000, cost, $35,600 (Job No. 107).

Accounts Receivable	70,000	
Sales		70,000
To record sales on account for July.		
Cost of Goods Sold	41,100	
Finished Goods Inventory		41,100
To record cost of goods sold in July.		

After the above entries have been posted to the accounts of the company, the Work in Process Inventory and Finished Goods Inventory accounts would appear (in T-account form) as follows:

Work in Process Inventory

July 1 balance	13,200	Completed	60,800
Direct materials used	23,000		
Direct labor cost incurred	20,000		
Overhead applied	16,000		

Finished Goods Inventory

July 1 balance	5,500	Sold	41,100
Completed	60,800		

The Work in Process Inventory account has a balance at July 31 of $11,400, which agrees with the total costs charged thus far to Job No. 108, as is shown in Illustration 14.3. These costs consist of direct materials, $6,000; direct labor, $3,000; and manufacturing overhead, $2,400. The Finished Goods Inventory account has a balance at July 31 of $25,200. The finished goods inventory card for Product DG supports this amount (see Illustration 14.3), showing that there are indeed units of Product DG on hand having a total cost of $25,200.

Note that the entries in the ledger accounts given above are often made from summaries of costs and are thus entered only at the end of the month. On the other hand, in order to keep management informed as to costs incurred, the details of the various costs incurred may be recorded more frequently, often daily.

The above example should be studied until the real advantages of using overhead rates (including predetermined rates) are clear. Three jobs were worked on during the month. Job No. 106 was started last month and completed in July. Job No. 107 was started and completed in July. And Job No. 108 was started but not finished in July. Each required different amounts of direct materials and direct labor (and, perhaps, different types of direct labor). Under these conditions, there is simply no way to apply overhead to products without the use of a rate based on some level of activity. Note also that the use of a predetermined overhead rate permits the computation of unit costs of Job Nos. 106 and 107 at the time of their completion rather than waiting until the end of the month. But this advantage is secured only at the cost of keeping more detailed records of the costs incurred. As we shall see below, the other major cost system—process costing—requires far less record keeping, but the computation of unit costs is more complex.

PROCESS COST SYSTEMS

Many business firms manufacture huge quantities of a single product or similar products (paint, paper, chemicals, gasoline, rubber, and plastics) on a continuous basis over long periods of time. There is no separate job or specific batch of units; rather, production is continuous over the year or several years. Since there is no separate job, job costs cannot be accumulated. Rather, costs must be accumulated for each process that a product undergoes on its way to completion. This situation calls for another type of cost system, one that yields unit costs by **processes** or by departments for a stated period of **time** rather than by jobs without regard to time periods. Under this system the processes or departments serve as cost centers for which costs are accumulated for the entire period (month, quarter, or year). These costs are divided by the number of units (tons, pounds, gallons, or feet) produced in order to get a broad, average unit cost. Such a system is known as a **process cost system.**

Illustration 14.3
SUPPORTING INVENTORY CARDS AND JOB ORDER SHEETS

STORES CARD *Material A*		
Received	Issued	Balance
$10,000		$10,000 20,000
	$1,000	19,000
	8,000	11,000
	2,000	9,000

STORES CARD *Material B*		
Received	Issued	Balance
$15,000		$ 6,000 21,000
	$2,000	19,000
	6,000	13,000
	4,000	9,000

JOB ORDER SHEET (Product DG)   Job No. 106

Date	Direct Materials	Direct Labor	Manufacturing Overhead
July 1 July	$4,200 A: 1,000 B: 2,000 $7,200	$ 5,000 5,000 $10,000	$4,000 4,000 $8,000

Job completed (4,000 units of Product DG @ $6.30). Total cost, $25,200.

JOB ORDER SHEET (Product XY)   Job No. 107

Date	Direct Materials	Direct Labor	Manufacturing Overhead
July	A: $ 8,000 B: 6,000 $14,000	$12,000	$9,600

Job completed (10,000 units of Product XY @ $3.56). Total cost, $35,600.

JOB ORDER SHEET (Product OR)   Job No. 108

Date	Direct Materials	Direct Labor	Manufacturing Overhead
July	A: $2,000 B: 4,000	$3,000	$2,400

Job incomplete (1,000 units of Product OR). Cost to date, $11,400.

FINISHED GOODS CARD *Product AB*		
Received	Issued	Balance
	$5,500	$5,500 –0–

FINISHED GOODS CARD *Product DG*		
Received	Issued	Balance
$25,200		$25,200

FINISHED GOODS CARD *Product XY*		
Received	Issued	Balance
$35,600	$35,600	$35,600 –0–

Basic System Design   Process cost systems have the same general design as that shown in Illustration 14.2. Costs of the factors of production are first recorded in separate accounts for materials inventory, labor, and overhead. These costs are then transferred to work in process inventory. A process cost system usually has more than one work in process inventory account. Such an account is kept for each processing center in order to determine the unit cost of each process. All products manufactured may be subjected to the same processing in a specified **sequential** order, as depicted in Illustration 14.4. The products are

Illustration 14.4
COST FLOWS IN A PROCESS COST SYSTEM

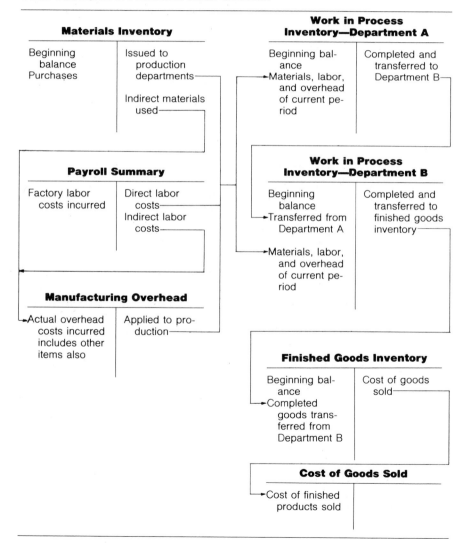

started in Department A, processed, transferred to Department B, processed further, and then transferred to finished goods inventory.

Or the products manufactured may require **parallel** processing. In parallel processing, all products do not undergo the same processing and do not pass through the same departments. For example, a basic material may be entered into Department 1 that yields two products for further processing. One product may be transferred to Department 2 and then to Department 4 for further processing before being transferred to finished goods inventory. The second product is processed in Departments 3 and 5 before being transferred to finished goods inventory. Graphically, the processing is:

Under the above processing pattern, the accounting system would contain five work in process inventory accounts and unit costs would be determined for the five processes.

Accounting for overhead. In process costing, manufacturing overhead will be initially recorded in supporting records or accounts for the various producing and service centers. Service center costs will then be allocated to the producing centers. Then, either the actual overhead incurred for the period (usually a month) will be applied to work in process inventory, or overhead will be applied through the use of a predetermined rate. If the quantity of units produced and the amounts of overhead costs incurred are roughly equal through time, applying actual overhead to production will yield reasonable product costs. But, if production and the amounts of overhead costs incurred are not fairly stable, the use of a predetermined rate will prevent the reporting of sharp differences in monthly unit costs. For example, if all production employees took their two-week paid vacations in July, unit costs may be considerably higher in July than in June.

Process Costing Illustrated

Assume that a company sells a chemical product which it processes in two departments. In Department A the basic materials are crushed, powdered, and blended. In Department B the product is tested, packaged and labeled, and transferred to finished goods inventory. The production and cost data for the month of June are:

	Department A	Department B
Units started, completed, and transferred	11,000	9,000
Units on hand at June 30, partially completed . .	–0–	2,000
Beginning inventory	–0–	–0–
Direct materials	$16,500	$1,100
Direct labor	5,500	5,900
Actual manufacturing overhead	4,500	5,600
Applied manufacturing overhead	4,400	5,900

From the above data, the Work in Process Inventory—Department A account can be constructed and, summarized, it will appear as follows:

Work in Process Inventory—Department A

Direct materials	16,500	Transferred to Department B—	
Direct labor	5,500	11,000 units @ $2.40	26,400
Overhead (80 percent of direct labor cost)	4,400		

Since all of the units started were completed and transferred, it follows that all of the costs assigned to Department A should be transferred to Department B. The unit cost in Department A is computed simply by dividing the total costs of $26,400 by the 11,000 units completed and transferred to get an average unit cost for the month of $2.40.

But the computations are seldom this simple. One complication is faced whenever partially completed beginning and ending inventories are present. Assume that Department B's Work in Process Inventory account for June, before recording the cost of the units transferred out, is as follows:

Work in Process Inventory—Department B

Transferred from Department A	26,400	
Direct material	1,100	
Direct labor	5,900	
Overhead (100 percent of direct labor)	5,900	

The task now faced is to divide the total costs charged to the department in June, $39,300, between the units transferred out and those remaining in the department. The $39,300 cannot be divided by 11,000 to get an average unit cost because the 11,000 units are not alike; 9,000 are finished, but 2;000 are only partially finished.

The problem is solved through use of the concept of equivalent units of production.

Equivalent units. Essentially, the concept of equivalent units involves expressing a given number of partially completed units as a smaller number of fully completed units. For example, 1,000 units brought to a 50 percent state of completion are the equivalent of 500 units that are 100 percent complete. We assume that the same amount of costs must be incurred to bring 1,000 units to a 50 percent level of completion as would be required to complete 500 units.

The first step in computing the equivalent units produced in Department B is to determine the stage of completion of the unfinished units. These units are 100 percent complete as to transferred-in costs, or they would not have been transferred out of Department A. But the units may have different stages of completion as to the materials, labor, and overhead costs added in Department B. (It is usually assumed that the units are at the same stage of completion as to conversion costs—labor and overhead.) All direct materials are added at the start of processing in Department B. Thus, the ending inventory is 100 percent complete as to materials. Since the units transferred out must be complete, equivalent production for materials is 11,000 units—9,000 transferred out and 2,000 on hand, 100 percent complete. Next, assume that the 2,000 units are, on the average, 50 percent complete as to conversion. Equivalent production, then, for labor and overhead is 10,000 units—9,000 units transferred and 2,000 brought to a 50 percent completion state, which is the equivalent of 1,000 fully complete units.

Let us return to our original example of Department B. With equivalent units of production known, the unit costs of the processing in Department B and the total per unit cost can now be computed:

	Transferred In	Materials	Conversion	Total
Costs to be accounted for:				
Charged to Department B . .	$26,400	$ 1,100	$11,800	$39,300
Equivalent units	11,000	11,000	10,000	
Unit costs	$2.40	$0.10	$1.18	$3.68

The conversion cost in the above schedule consists of $5,900 of direct labor and an equal amount of overhead, since the latter is applied at a rate of 100 percent of labor cost.

With unit costs computed, the $39,300 of costs charged to Department B in June can now be divided between costs transferred out and costs remaining as the cost of the department's ending inventory:

		Transferred In	Materials	Conversion	Total
Cost accounted for:					
Costs transferred out	. .	$21,600	$ 900	$10,620	$33,120
Costs of inventory	. . .	4,800	200	1,180	6,180
Costs accounted for	. .	$26,400	$1,100	$11,800	$39,300

The total costs transferred out of $33,120 consist of $21,600 of Department A's cost (9,000 × $2.40), $900 of materials costs (9,000 × $0.10), and $10,620 of conversion costs (9,000 × $1.18). The cost of the ending inventory in Department B of 2,000 units, complete as to materials and 50 percent complete as to conversion, consists of the following:

Costs from Department A (2,000 × $2.40)		$4,800
Costs added by Department B:		
Materials (2,000 × $0.10)	$ 200	
Conversion (2,000 × 0.5 × $1.18)	1,180	1,380
Total cost of ending inventory		$6,180

The completed units transferred out of Department B will be carried in finished goods inventory at a cost of $3.68 each ($2.40 + $1.28) until sold, at which time they would be charged to the Cost of Goods Sold expense account. The unit costs of production—$2.40 in Department A and $1.28 ($0.10 + $1.18) in Department B—are watched closely by management, with explanations sought for unexpected variations.

The journal entries for the above for the month of June are as follows:

```
1. Work in Process Inventory—Department A    . . .  16,500
     Work in Process Inventory—Department B   . . .   1,100
        Materials Inventory   . . . . . . . . .              17,600
     To record materials placed in production in June.

2. Payroll Summary  . . . . . . . . . . . . .  11,400
        (Various withholding accounts and accrued
           wages payable)  . . . . . . . . . .               11,400
     To record factory payroll for June.

3. Work in Process Inventory—Department A    . . .   5,500
   Work in Process Inventory—Department B    . . .   5,900
     Payroll Summary   . . . . . . . . . . .               11,400
     To distribute factory labor costs (assumed that all
     such costs are chargeable directly to production de-
     partments).

4. Manufacturing Overhead  . . . . . . . . . .  10,100
        (Various accounts—cash, accounts payable, ac-
        cruals, and accumulated depreciation)   . . .        10,100
     To record actual overhead costs incurred in June.
```

429

5. Work in Process Inventory—Department A . . .   4,400
   Work in Process Inventory—Department B   . . .   5,900
      Manufacturing Overhead   10,300
   To apply overhead to production using predetermined rates based on direct labor cost: Department A, 80 percent; and Department B, 100 percent.

6. Work in Process Inventory—Department B   . . .   26,400
   Work in Process Inventory—Department A   .   26,400
   To record transfer of goods from Department A to Department B.

7. Finished Goods Inventory   33,120
   Work in Process Inventory—Department B   .   33,120
   To record transfer of completed goods from Department B to finished goods.

Assuming that 6,000 units were sold in June at a price of $10 per unit, the following entries would be required:

8. Accounts Receivable   60,000
   Sales   60,000
   To record sales on account.

9. Cost of Goods Sold   22,080
   Finished Goods Inventory   22,080
   To record cost of goods sold in June, 6,000 units @ $3.68.

The Cost of Production Report

The computation of unit costs is even more complex when there are both beginning and ending inventories in a processing center. This problem, and the key report in process costing, is discussed in this section.

The following data are for Department 3 of the A Company for the month of June 1986:

Units

Units in beginning inventory, complete as to materials, 60% complete as to conversion	6,000
Units transferred in from Department 2	18,000
Units completed and transferred out	16,000
Units in ending inventory, complete as to materials, 50% complete as to conversion	8,000

Costs

Cost of beginning inventory:		
Cost transferred in from preceding department in May	$12,000	
Materials added in May in Department 3	6,000	
Conversion costs (equal amounts of labor and overhead)	3,000	$21,000
Costs transferred in from preceding department in June		37,200
Costs added in Department 3 in June:		
Materials	$18,480	
Conversion (equal amounts of labor and overhead	18,000	36,480
Total costs in beginning inventory and placed in production in Department 3 in June		$94,680

How the total of $94,680 of costs charged to Department 3 in June is divided between the cost of the units transferred out and the cost of the units remaining on hand in inventory is shown in Illustration 14.5. This report is discussed by explaining the four steps usually undertaken to prepare it.

1. Trace the physical flow of the actual units into and out of the department. The section labeled "Units" in Illustration 14.5 shows that 6,000 units were on hand at the beginning of June and that 18,000 units were transferred in, making a total of 24,000 units that must be accounted for. Of these 24,000 units, 16,000 units were completed and transferred out, and 8,000 partially completed units were retained in the department.

2. Convert the actual units to equivalent units. Illustration 14.5 shows the procedures followed to compute **average** unit costs. (Other procedures would be used if unit costs on a Fifo or Lifo basis were desired. Discussion of these methods will be left to a more advanced text.) Equivalent units, under the average method, consist of units completed and transferred plus the equivalent units in the ending inventory, or 24,000 equivalent units for transferred in and for materials, and 20,000 equivalent units for conversion. The observant reader will note that these amounts include units fully or partially completed last month and on hand in Department 3's beginning inventory. The reason for this is explained in Step 3.

3. Compute unit costs for each element of cost, using the equivalent units computed above and the total costs charged to the department. Under the average method, this involves dividing the equivalent units of production for the period, **including all units in the beginning inventory,** into the costs charged to the department, **including the costs of the beginning inventory. Thus, the costs of the beginning inventory are treated as if they were incurred in the current period. And all units in the beginning inventory are treated as if they were produced in the current period.** The unit costs computed are, as a result, averages across the current period and a portion of the prior period, rather than being strictly those of the current period. Despite this lack of exactness, the average method is widely used; it avoids many fine details of little practical value that emerge under Fifo or Lifo. As shown in Illustration 14.5, average unit costs for June are: costs transferred in, $2.05; materials costs, $1.02; and conversion costs, $1.05. As already noted, management watches these costs closely.

4. The equivalent units transferred out and those remaining in inventory can now be multiplied by the unit costs computed in Step 3 above. Completion of this step divides the total costs charged to the department into costs to be transferred out and costs that remain in the department's work in process inventory account. Thus, the cost of the ending inventory would be computed as follows:

costs of the products produced. **All fixed costs are assumed to be costs of the period and are charged to expense.** The only difference between full costing and variable costing is in the treatment of fixed manufacturing costs. Under full costing they are treated as product costs, and under variable costing they are treated as period costs. The cost flows under variable costing and under absorption costing are shown graphically in Illustration 14.6. Note that the major difference involves the flow of fixed overhead costs.

Variable and Absorption Costing Compared

The differences between variable and full costing can be seen from an example comparing the income statement that would result from applying each technique to the same data. Assume the following data:

8,000 equivalent units transferred in @ $2.05	$16,400
8,000 equivalent units of materials costs @ $1.02	8,160
4,000 equivalent units of conversion costs @ $1.05	4,200
Total cost of ending inventory	$28,760

The total cost of the units completed and transferred out can be computed by multiplying 16,000 units by the total unit cost ($4.12) and, as shown, amounts to $65,920. The sum of the cost of the ending inventory and the cost of the units transferred out must equal the total of the costs charged to the department, which was

Beginning inventory . . .	–0–	Variable costs (per unit):		
Production (units)	10,000	Direct materials		$2.00
Sales (units)	9,000	Direct labor		1.00
Fixed costs:		Manufacturing overhead . .		0.30
Manufacturing overhead .	$ 6,000	Total		$3.30
Selling expenses . . .	15,000	Variable selling expenses		
Administrative expenses .	12,000	(per unit)		$0.20
Total	$33,000	Selling price (per unit) . . .		$8.00

Income statement under variable costing. Under variable costing the income statement for the year would be as shown in Illustration 14.7. Note that all of the fixed manufacturing costs are considered costs of the period and are not included in inventories.

Income statement under conventional costing. Illustration 14.8 contains the income statement that would be prepared under full costing. Note that the fixed manufacturing costs are included as part of the product cost and that some of these costs are included in the ending inventory.

The ending inventory is priced at so-called full cost; that is, the cost of ending inventory includes fixed manufacturing overhead. Since the total cost of producing 10,000 units is $39,000, then the unit cost is $3.90 and the 1,000 units in inventory are carried at $3,900. Also, under the conventional income statement approach, no distinction is drawn between fixed and variable selling expenses, and no attempt is made to compute the amount by which sales revenue exceeds the variable costs of the period. Thus, the total selling expenses for the period, consisting of $15,000 of fixed expenses and variable expenses of $1,800 (9,000 units at $0.20), are shown as one lump-sum amount.

Different valuations for inventory. In comparing the two income statements, note that net income computed by using conventional (absorption) costing is greater than net income computed by using variable costing ($8,100 − $7,500 = $600). This difference will always result if production exceeds sales in an accounting period; that is, the finished goods ending inventory increases. The reason for this is that the fixed manufacturing overhead costs are held in inventory and thus decrease cost of goods sold under absorption costing. Under variable costing, the entire amount of fixed manufacturing overhead costs is considered a period cost and charged to expense in the period incurred; this explains the $600 difference between the net income in Illustration 14.8 and Illustration 14.7. In Illustration 14.7, the fixed manufacturing overhead charged as a period cost was $6,000. In Illustration 14.8, the fixed manufacturing overhead charged to cost of goods sold was $5,400 [($6,000 (Fixed MOH) ÷ 10,000 units produced) × 9000 units sold]. The difference

Illustration 14.6
COST FLOWS UNDER VARIABLE COSTING

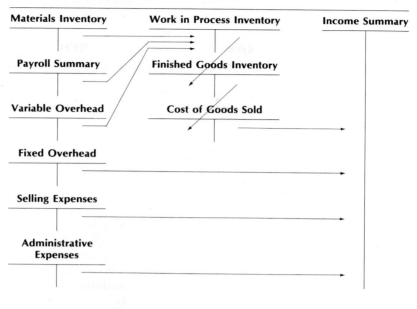

COST FLOWS UNDER ABSORPTION COSTING

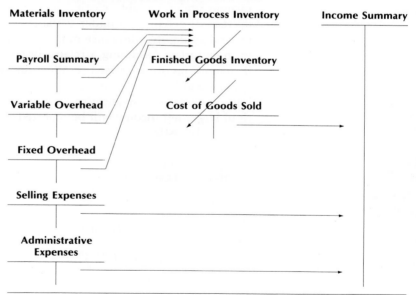

Illustration 14.7
INCOME STATEMENT UNDER VARIABLE COSTING

Sales (9,000 units at $8)		$72,000
Cost of goods sold:		
Variable production costs incurred		
(10,000 units at $3.30)	$33,000	
Less: Inventory (1,000 units at $3.30)	3,300	29,700
Manufacturing margin		$42,300
Variable selling expenses (9,000 units at $0.20)		1,800
Marginal income		$40,500
Period costs:		
Manufacturing overhead	$ 6,000	
Selling expenses	15,000	
Administrative expenses	12,000	33,000
Net income		$ 7,500

between the expenses is $600 ($6,000 — $5,400) which is held in ending inventory under absorption costing.

The analysis is more complicated when both beginning and ending inventories are involved. But the difference in net income can be determined by ascertaining whether the amount of fixed overhead in inventory under full costing increased or decreased from the beginning to the end of the year. If fixed overhead increased, net income under variable costing will be smaller. If fixed overhead decreased, net income under variable costing will be greater. As a general guide, the difference in income can be related to the **change** in inventories. Assuming a relatively constant level of production, if inventories are increased (production exceeded sales) smaller net income will be reported under variable costing than under full costing. Conversely, if inventories are decreased (sales exceeded production) larger net income will be reported under variable costing than under full costing.

Illustration 14.8
INCOME STATEMENT UNDER CONVENTIONAL COSTING

Sales (9,000 units at $8)		$72,000
Cost of goods sold:		
Variable costs of production (10,000 units at $3.30) . .	$33,000	
Fixed overhead costs	6,000	
Total costs of producing 10,000 units	$39,000	
Less: Inventory (1,000 units at $3.90)	3,900	35,100
Gross margin on sales		$36,900
Operating expenses:		
Selling ($15,000 fixed plus 9,000 at $0.20 each) . . .	$16,800	
Administrative	12,000	28,800
Net income		$ 8,100

Variable Costing—Pro and Con

Variable costing is not at present considered an acceptable method of costing for income measurement and inventory valuation, nor is it allowed for tax purposes. Variable costing is considered unacceptable because it does not include in inventory all the costs of producing the goods and because it misstates the period's charges against revenues. Currently accepted practice requires that all of the costs of producing a given product be attached to that product and treated as an expense only when the product is sold.

Advocates of variable costing prefer to treat fixed manufacturing costs as part of the costs of being ready to produce. Such costs, they contend, should be charged to the period and not to the production of the period; that is, they believe the relationship between such costs and production to be so remote that the costs should be expensed in the period in which they are incurred. In this way, variable costing avoids the reporting of fluctuations in net income found under full costing when **production** varies from period to period. Net income should be a function of sales, not of production—or so the advocates of variable costing maintain.

The type of information accumulated under variable costing, especially the classification of costs as fixed and variable, undoubtedly helps management to gain a thorough understanding of the relationships between cost, volume, and income. And certainly the responsibility for and the control of costs are more readily determined and secured through a proper classification of costs. Variable costing is a useful management tool; and for this reason its use is likely to increase.

SUMMARY

The job order cost system and the process cost system are the two major types of cost accumulation systems used by manufacturing companies.

In a job order system, costs are accumulated by jobs, regardless of the time period in which the jobs were worked on and completed. The costs of completing a job—direct materials, direct labor, and manufacturing overhead—are recorded in some detail on a subsidiary work in process record known as a job order sheet. The costs of direct materials and direct labor can be traced to specific jobs through use of materials requisitions and work tickets. Manufacturing overhead is applied using a predetermined rate. In this way, unit costs can be computed for a job as soon as it is completed, even though a number of different jobs may have been worked on at the same time in the same period.

Process cost systems are used to gather the costs of manufacturing large quantities of similar products on a continuous basis. Costs are accumulated for each of the processes that a product undergoes on its way to completion. As a result, a process cost system is likely to have a number of Work in Process accounts, with one account kept for each processing center. Manufacturing overhead may be applied to production through use of a predetermined rate or on an actual basis.

Unit costs are computed for each department for materials, labor, and overhead. Unit costs are computed by using equivalent units of production in a department for a period. Under the average (rather than the FIFO or LIFO) method, equivalent production consists of the number of units completed and transferred plus the equivalent units of work done on the ending inventory. Average unit costs are then computed by dividing the total costs charged to a department for a period (including the cost of the beginning inventory) by the department's equivalent production for the period (including the equivalent units in the beginning inventory). The unit costs and the equivalent units produced are then used to divide the total costs charged to a department between the costs that are to be transferred out and the costs that remain in the department as the cost of the ending inventory.

The cost of production report summarizes both the units and the costs charged to a department; it shows how these units and costs were accounted for either by being transferred to the next department or by remaining in the department. The cost of production report also shows the department's current unit costs for materials, labor, and overhead and the total unit cost. Variations in period-to-period unit costs are closely watched by management. Explanations may be required for unexpected differences.

Under full costing, some part of all the costs incurred to produce a product, including fixed manufacturing overhead, is attached to each unit produced. Under an alternative, called variable costing, fixed overhead costs are not applied to production but are treated as period costs, that is, as expenses when incurred. The two cost concepts, when applied to the same data, will generally yield different net income amounts because they use different amounts for beginning and ending work in process and finished goods inventories.

Variable costing, by stressing the distinction between fixed and variable costs, provides information that is useful in discerning the relationship between costs, volume, and income. But the measurements it generates for inventories and net income are not yet considered generally acceptable for external reporting or for tax purposes.

QUESTIONS

1. What is the basic purpose of any costing system?

2. In what respects does a process cost system differ from a job order cost system? What factors should be taken into consideration in determining which type of system should be employed?

3. What is a job order sheet? Explain how it is used.

4. What questions might be raised regarding an assertion that a given product has a unit manufacturing cost of $10?

5. What is meant by the term **equivalent production?** Of what use is the computation of the number of units of equivalent production?

6. Distinguish between the number of units completed and transferred during a period and the equivalent production for that same period.

7. What is the basic information reported in a cost of production report?

8. Under what circumstances would the equivalent units for materials differ from those for labor and overhead in the same department in the same period? Under what circumstances would they be the same?

9. Should the overtime premium paid on direct labor in a job cost system be charged to the specific jobs worked on? Can you give examples supporting both an affirmative and a negative answer?

10. Under what circumstances in a process cost system is the assignment of overhead to production through use of a predetermined rate definitely preferable to assigning the actual overhead incurred?

11. It requires less effort to operate a job cost system than a process cost system. Do you agree or disagree? Explain.

12. What essential feature distinguishes variable costing from absorption costing?

13. Under what circumstances would you expect the net income under variable costing to be larger than under full costing? What is the reason for this difference?

EXERCISES

1. Job No. 506 has, at the end of the second week in March, an accumulated total cost of $8,400. In the third week, $2,000 of direct materials was used on the job, 200 hours of direct labor were charged to the job at $10 per hour; and manufacturing overhead was applied on the basis of $5.00 per direct labor hour for fixed overhead and $4 per hour for variable overhead. Job No. 506 was the only job completed in the third week. Compute the cost of Job No. 506, and give the journal entry required to record its completion.

2. Sanchez Company applies overhead to jobs at a rate of 120 percent of direct labor cost. When completed, Job No. 814 was charged with $3,600 of overhead. Compute the direct labor cost charged to the job.

3. Terri Company's Work in Process Inventory account contained the following for June:

Work in Process Inventory

Direct materials	1,000,000	Goods completed	1,400,000
Direct labor	400,000		
Manufacturing overhead	1,000,000		

Job No. 972 is the only incomplete job at the end of June, and it has been charged with $300,000 of direct materials. Terri applies overhead to its jobs using a rate based on direct labor cost. Compute the direct labor cost and the manufacturing overhead charge to Job No. 972.

4. Compute the equivalent production in each case given below:

   a. Units started in production during the month, 30,000; units completed and transferred, 22,000; and units in process at the end of the month (60 percent complete), 8,000.

   b. Units in process at beginning of month (30 percent complete), 5,000; units started during month, 20,000; and units in process at end of month (40 percent complete), 10,000.

5. Assume that the data in **4a** relate to labor for May in Department A. If the total labor cost for the department consisted of 2,010 hours at $12 per hour, compute:

   a. The labor cost per equivalent unit of production for the month.

   b. The labor cost of the ending inventory in the department.

6. The Bronze Company, which uses a job order cost system, has just completed a job for State Bank—a special order for 200 gold-plated mechanical pencils. Direct material cost was $1,000; direct labor cost— 200 hours at $10 per hour. Budgeted direct labor for this year was $800,000, while overhead was budgeted at $2,000,000. If the overhead rate is expressed as a percentage of direct labor cost, what is the total cost and the unit cost of the bank's order?

7. In Department A, materials are added uniformly throughout processing. The beginning inventory was considered 50 percent complete, as was the ending inventory. Assume that there were 1,000 units in the beginning inventory and 3,000 in the ending inventory, and that 16,000 units were completed and transferred. If average unit costs are to be computed, what is the equivalent production for the period?

8. If in Exercise 7 the total costs charged to the department amounted to $140,000, including the $4,020 cost of the beginning inventory, what is the cost of the units completed and transferred?

9. Barnes Company processes the single product that it manufactures through Process A and Process B sequentially. Records show the following with respect to units processed in October:

	Process A		Process B	
	Units	Percent Complete	Units	Percent Complete
Inventory October 1	8,000	60	5,000	80
Inventory October 31	4,000	75	6,000	50
Units started in production . .	20,000		24,000	
Units transferred out	24,000		23,000	

Compute the equivalent production for both processes for October.

10. The following data relate to Department A, in which all material is added at the start of processing and in which the weight of the finished product is equal to the weight of the direct materials used:

Inventory, June 1:

Materials cost (400 pounds)	$ 780
Conversion cost (20% complete)	110
Direct materials used (2,000 pounds at $2.01)	4,020
Direct labor (300 hours at $4.40)	1,320
Overhead (at 150% of direct labor cost)	1,980

Inventory, June 30:

Materials cost (600 pounds, 100% complete)	?
Conversion cost (600 pounds, ⅔ complete)	?

Using the above data, compute:

a. The number of pounds transferred out of the department in June.

b. The unit cost per equivalent unit for materials and conversion (use the average method).

c. The cost of the product transferred out.

d. The cost of the ending inventory.

e. The change in the conversion cost per unit from May to June.

11. The following data are for a certain company for the year 1986:

Sales (40,000 units)	$400,000
Raw materials used (48,000 units at $3)	144,000
Direct labor cost incurred	48,000
Manufacturing overhead incurred:	
Variable	14,400
Fixed	19,200
Selling and administrative expenses:	
Variable	24,000
Fixed	80,000

Assume that one unit of raw materials goes into each unit of finished goods, that there is an ending inventory of finished goods of 8,000 units, that there are no other beginning or ending inventories, and that the variable and fixed overhead rates (based on normal activity of 48,000 units) were $0.30 and $0.40, respectively. Compute the earnings before income taxes under **(a)** full costing and **(b)** variable costing.

12. Given below are the costs of the finished goods inventories of the Z Company:

Cost Element	Beginning Inventory	Ending Inventory
Direct materials	$ 60,000	$ 6,000
Direct labor	100,000	10,400
Overhead:		
Variable	40,000	4,000
Fixed	30,000	4,000

Assume that the Z Company employs an absorption costing technique in costing its products and that there were no work in process inventories at the beginning or end of the year. State how much the company's net income before income taxes for the year would have differed if it could have used a variable costing technique for tax purposes.

PROBLEMS

14-1. Walker Company employs a job order cost system. As of January 1, 1986, its records showed:

Raw materials and supplies	$160,000
Work in process	344,000
Finished goods (50,000 units at $8) . . .	400,000

The work in process inventory consists of two jobs:

No.	Materials	Labor	Manufacturing Overhead	Total
110	$ 60,000	$ 80,000	$40,000	$180,000
111	68,000	64,000	32,000	164,000
	$128,000	$144,000	$72,000	$344,000

Summarized below are manufacturing data for the company for 1986:

(1) Raw materials and supplies purchased on account, $660,000.

(2) Factory payrolls accrued, $1,360,000; social security taxes withheld, $68,000; and federal income taxes withheld, $120,000.

(3) Manufacturing overhead costs incurred: depreciation, $40,000; heat, light, and power, $16,000; and miscellaneous, $24,000.

(4) Direct materials and supplies requisitioned: for Job No. 110, $104,000; for Job No. 111, $192,000; for Job No. 112, $320,000; and supplies requisitioned, $16,000.

(5) Payrolls distributed: direct labor—$160,000 for Job No. 110, $320,000 for Job No. 111, and $480,000 for Job No. 112; factory supervision, $160,000; and indirect labor, $240,000.

(6) Overhead is assigned to work in process at the same rate per dollar of direct labor cost as in 1985.

(7) Job Nos. 110 and 111 were completed.

(8) The cost of goods sold for the year was $1,376,000.

Required:

Prepared general journal entries to record the above summarized data, as well as all closing entries for which you have sufficient information.

14-2. Garrett, Inc., uses a process cost system to accumulate the costs it incurs in producing aluminum awning stabilizers. The costs incurred in the finishing department are shown for the month of May. The May 1 inventory consisted of 30,000 units which were fully complete as to materials, 80 percent complete as to conversion. The inventory's total cost of $480,000 consisted of $360,000 of costs transferred in from the molding department, $50,000 of finishing department material costs, and $70,000 of conversion costs.

Costs from molding department (excluding costs in beginning inventory)		$1,200,000
Costs added in finishing department in May (excluding costs in beginning inventory):		
Materials	$106,000	
Conversion	218,960	324,960
Total		$1,524,960

The finishing department received 100,000 units from the molding department; 106,000 units were completed and transferred; and 24,000 units complete as to materials and 60 percent complete as to conversion, were left in the May 31 inventory.

Required:

  a. Prepare a cost of production report for the finishing department for the month of May.

  b. Compute the average unit cost for conversion for April in the finishing department.

14–3. Casual Corporation employs a job order cost system. The company's manufacturing activities in July 1986, its first month of operation, are summarized as follows:

	Job Number			
	501	502	503	504
Direct materials . . .	$8,000	$5,800	$12,600	$6,000
Direct labor cost . . .	$6,600	$6,000	$ 8,400	$2,400
Direct labor hours . .	1,100	1,000	1,400	400
Units produced . . .	200	100	1,000	300

Manufacturing overhead is applied at a rate of $2 per direct labor hour for variable overhead, $3 per hour for fixed overhead.

Job Nos. 501, 502, and 503 were completed in July.

Required:

  a. Compute the amount of overhead charged to each job.

  b. Compute the total and unit cost of each completed job.

  c. Prepare the entry, in general journal form, to record the transfer of completed jobs to Finished Goods.

  d. Compute the balance in the July 31, 1986, Work in Process account, and provide a schedule of the costs charged to each incomplete job to support this balance.

14–4. The Carson, Inc., general ledger on June 1, 1986, shows the following balances:

Sales	$8,000,000
Raw materials inventory	400,000
Work in process inventory . . .	180,000
Finished goods inventory	500,000
Manufacturing overhead	2,000 Cr.
Accrued salaries and wages . .	8,000
Cost of goods sold	6,000,000
Selling expenses	600,000
Administrative expenses	800,000

The work in process inventory consists of the following:

Job No. 2734:

Material	. . .	$132,000
Labor	. . . .	16,000
Overhead	. . .	32,000
		$180,000

Summarized, the transactions occurring in June 1986 were:

(1) Raw materials purchased on account, $520,000.

(2) Payroll for the month, $89,500; social security taxes withheld, $4,800; and federal income taxes withheld, $8,000.

(3) Materials issued during the month: direct, $220,000; and indirect, $32,000. Of the direct materials, $10,000 is assignable to Job No. 2734, the balance of Job No. 2735.

(4) The payroll for the month consisted of direct labor, $60,000 (Job No. 2734, $12,000; Job No. 2735, $48,000); factory supervision, $1,600; factory maintenance, $2,400; sales salaries, $9,500; and office and officers' salaries, $16,000.

(5) The manufacturing overhead rate is 200 percent of the direct labor cost.

(6) Other costs incurred in June (on account or accrued except for depreciation and amortization):

Rent (60% factory, 40% administrative) . .	$40,000
Factory heat, light, and power	22,000
Factory machinery repairs	7,600
Amortization of patents	14,800
Depreciation on factory machinery . . .	18,000
Taxes on factory machinery	3,600
Various selling expenses	40,000

(7) Job No. 2734 was completed during the month.

(8) Sales for June, $1,200,000; the cost of these sales was $620,000.

Required:

a. Prepare journal entries to record the above summarized data.

b. Prepare any necessary adjusting and closing entries.

c. Prepare a condensed income statement for the year ended June 30, 1986.

14–5. The following data are for the initial processing center of the Danforth Company for the month of July. All material is added at the beginning of the processing operation.

Work in process inventory, July 1 (10,000 pounds, 40% complete as to conversion):	
Direct materials	$10,000
Direct labor	1,600
Manufacturing overhead (200% of direct labor cost) . . .	3,200
	$14,800

Added in July:

Direct materials (90,000 pounds)	$91,800
Direct labor (2,000 hours at $16)	32,000
Manufacturing overhead	64,000
	$187,800

The work in process inventory at July 31 consisted of 30,000 units (pounds), one third complete as to processing.

Required:

Compute the following:

a. Number of pounds completed and transferred out of the processing center.

b. The equivalent units of production for materials, labor, and overhead for July (assuming average unit costs are to be computed).

c. The average unit costs for July for materials, labor, and overhead.

d. The cost of the pounds transferred out in July.

e. The cost of the July 31 work in process inventory.

f. The average unit labor cost last month (June).

14–6. Jervey Company manufactures a product called a Savem. The company uses a process cost system to determine product costs. Following are cost and production data for the Handle Department for the month of June:

	Units	Materials Costs	Conversion Costs
Inventory, June 1	20,000	$1,790	$2,200
Placed in production in June . .	60,000	5,410	9,560
Inventory, June 30	30,000	?	?

The June 1 inventory was complete as to materials and 50 percent complete as to conversion. The June 30 inventory was complete as to materials and 20 percent complete as to conversion.

Required:

Prepare a cost of production report.

14–7. Lane Drug Company manufactures Sure-Stop, a cold remedy, in a blending department from which the remedy is transferred to the bottling department. Production and cost data for the bottling department for June are as follows:

Work in process, June 1 (40,000 pints):

Transferred-in costs (100% complete)	$ 40,000
Bottling materials (100% complete)	16,000
Conversion costs (50% complete)	8,000
	$ 64,000

Added in June:

Transferred-in (120,000 pints)	123,200
Bottling materials for 120,000 units	51,200
Conversion costs	49,000
	$223,400

All materials in the bottling department are added at the beginning of processing, and their amounts are determined by the number of pints of Sure-Stop transferred in. The ending inventory for June was 20,000 units, 100 percent complete as to materials and 50 percent complete as to conversion.

Required:

a. Prepare a cost of production report for the bottling department for the month of June.

b. Compute the per unit conversion cost in the department for the prior month (May).

c. Give the journal entry needed to record the transfer of the units completed in the bottling department in June.

14–8. Potter Company employs a full-cost system in accounting for the single product it manufactures. The following are selected data for the year 1986:

Sales (10,000 units)	$400,000
Direct materials used (12,000 units at $6)	144,000
Direct labor cost incurred	48,000
Variable manufacturing overhead	14,400
Fixed manufacturing overhead	19,200
Variable selling and administrative expenses	24,000
Fixed selling and administrative expenses	80,000

One unit of direct materials goes into each unit of finished goods. Overhead rates are based on a practical capacity of 12,000 units and are $1.20 and $1.60 per unit for variable and fixed overhead. The only beginning or ending inventory is the 2,000 units of finished goods on hand at the end of 1986.

Required:

a. Prepare an income statement for 1986 under variable costing.

b. Prepare an income statement for 1986 under full costing.

c. Explain the reason for the different net income as between **a** and **b.**

14–9. The Denver Division of the Kinston Company produces a single product which it sells for $18 each. Its production costs are variable costs of $4 per unit and $960,000 per year of fixed overhead costs. Normal activity for fixed overhead absorption is 160,000 units per year.

On December 31, 1984, the division's finished goods inventory consisted of 20,000 units with a total cost of $200,000 ($80,000 variable; $120,000 fixed). Sales and production data for the years 1985, 1986, and 1987 are:

Year	Sales in Units	Dollars of Sales	Production in Units	Variable Production Costs
1985 . . .	100,000	$1,800,000	110,000	$440,000
1986 . . .	100,000	1,800,000	80,000	320,000
1987 . . .	100,000	1,800,000	180,000	720,000

Required:

    a. Prepare income statements for the division for each of the years 1985, 1986 and 1987 under full costing.

    b. Repeat part **a** under variable costing.

    c. Comment briefly on the differences noted and the reasons therefor. Specifically, consider the following questions: Under which method does income vary with sales volume? Under which method does the volume of production affect income? Why might the production for 1987 have been increased to 180,000 units? What are the implications of increasing production for 1987 to 180,000 units on future income as shown in the Kinston Company's external financial statements?

15 STANDARD COSTS FOR CONTROL

STANDARD COSTS

The job order and process cost systems were discussed in Chapter 14. These systems are used to gather actual historical cost data. But because such data say little about how efficiently operations were conducted, many firms find it helpful to develop standard costs for such purposes and introduce them into their job order or process cost systems. Thus, standard costs can be used in both job order cost and process cost systems as is shown in the appendix to this chapter.

The Nature of Standard Costs

A standard cost is a carefully predetermined measure of what a cost **should be under stated conditions;** it is a goal to be sought rather than an estimate of what a cost will be. If a standard is properly set, achieving the standard represents a reasonable level of performance. Standards are often derived from the budgets that have been prepared. Budgets are a comprehensive guideline of what is anticipated will occur in the future.

Standards are set from either an ideal perspective or a practical perspective. **Ideal standards** are set under the assumption that all the conditions used for setting the standards are ideal. For example, it is assumed that the production process will operate at full capacity; materials, labor costs, and overhead costs will be minimized; and materials, labor, and overhead will be utilized at the maximum level of efficiency. This approach establishes standards that are virtually impossible to achieve.

The practical approach establishes achievable standards that are based on past experience and information. However, to be of any real value the standards must be more than mere estimates derived from extending historical trends into the future. Usually engineering and time and motion studies are undertaken to determine the material, labor, and other requirements for producing a unit of product. Knowledge of the actual working conditions in a plant is needed, and general economic conditions must be studied because they will affect the costs of the materials and services that must be purchased. Thus, **practical standards** are achievable.

The goal is to set a standard cost for each unit of product to be manufactured by determining the standard costs of the direct materials, direct labor, and factory overhead needed to produce it. The **standard direct materials cost** is made up of a standard number of units of each material required, multiplied by a standard price for each. Similarly, the **standard direct labor cost** consists of the standard number of hours of direct labor needed, multiplied by the standard labor or wage rate. The **standard overhead cost** of a unit is usually based on a predetermined rate which is computed from standard (budgeted) overhead costs and standard production, although it may be expressed as a rate per unit of some measure of activity, such as direct labor hours. Thus, in both a standard cost system and an actual cost system, overhead is assigned to production through use of a predetermined rate. The **two systems differ** in that an actual cost system collects actual costs for materials and labor, whereas a standard cost system gathers standard costs and transfers those costs through the system into finished goods.

Advantages of Using Standard Costs

A number of benefits result from the use of a standard cost system. These benefits include (1) cost control, (2) the provision of information useful in managerial planning and decision making, (3) more reasonable inventory measurements, (4) cost savings in record keeping, and (5) possibly some reductions in the costs incurred.

Cost control is secured largely by setting standards for each type of cost incurred—materials, labor, and overhead. The amounts by which actual costs differ from standard costs are recorded in **variance** accounts. These variances provide a starting point for judging the effectiveness of managers in controlling the costs for which they are held responsible. For example, it is far more useful to know that actual direct materials costs of $52,015 in a certain center exceeded standard by $6,015 than merely to know that actual materials costs amounted to $52,015. Thus, a standard cost system highlights **exceptions,** that is, instances in which things are not going as planned. Further investigation will show whether or not an exception is caused by factors under management's control. For example, the exception (the variance) may be caused by inefficient use of materials, or it may be the result of inflation. In either case, the standard cost system has served as an early warning system by highlighting a potential problem for management. On the other hand, little attention is usually paid to actual costs when such costs differ only slightly from standard.

If management develops appropriate standards and succeeds in controlling costs, future actual costs should be fairly close to standard. When actual and standard costs are close, standard costs can be used in preparing budgets and in estimating costs for bidding on jobs.

In a standard cost system, all units of a given product are carried in inventory at the same unit cost. It seems logical that physically identical units should have the same cost. But under an actual cost system, unit costs for batches of identical products may differ because more labor and overhead were assigned to one batch simply because a machine was out of adjustment when the batch was produced. Under a standard cost system, such costs would not be included in inventory. Instead, they would be charged to variance accounts. These accounts are discussed below.

Although standard cost systems may appear to require more detailed record keeping than an actual cost system, the reverse is actually true. In a job order system, for example, detailed accounts or records must be kept of the various types of materials used on each job as well as the various types and quantities of labor services received. But, in a standard cost system, standard cost sheets may be printed in advance showing quantities, unit costs, and total costs for the materials, labor, and overhead needed to produce a given amount of a certain product. Thus, when a job is started, the job order sheet shows all of the various costs that apply to it. There is no need to post individual materials requisitions to individual job order sheets. One entry can be made at the end of the month for the total materials used. Also, since inventories are carried at standard cost, the problems of assumed cost flows—LIFO, FIFO, and so forth—disappear.

The use of standard costs may cause employees to become quite cost conscious and to seek improved methods of completing their tasks. This may result in cost savings.

COMPUTING VARIANCES

As noted above, a **variance exists when standard prices and/or quantities differ from actual prices and/or quantities.** It is logical to look upon a variance as favorable when the actual cost is less than the standard cost, and to view the variance as **unfavorable** when the actual cost exceeds standard. But it does not follow automatically that these terms should be equated with good and bad. Such an appraisal should be made only after the **causes** of the variance are known.

Variances cannot serve as essential elements in cost control until they have been isolated. Thus, attention is directed first to the computation of the dollar amount of a variance. The discussion and illustrations that follow are based on the activities of the Alpha Company, which manufactures and sells a single product having the following standard costs:

```
Materials—5 sheets @ $6          . . . . . . . . . .  $30
Direct labor—2 hours @ $10       . . . . . . . . . .   20
Manufacturing overhead—2 direct labor hours @ $5  . . .   10
Total standard cost per unit     . . . . . . . . . .  $60
```

Additional data regarding the productive activities of the Alpha Company will be presented as needed.

Materials Variances

The standard materials cost of any product is simply the standard **quantity** of materials that should be used, multiplied by the standard **price** that should be paid for those materials. Actual costs may differ from standard costs for materials because of the actual quantity of the materials used or because of the actual price paid for the materials. This fact suggests the need to isolate two variances for materials—a **price variance** and a **usage variance.** But there are other reasons for so doing. First, different individuals may be responsible for each variance—a purchasing agent for the price variance and a production manager for the usage variance. Second, the materials may not be purchased and used in the same period. The variance associated with the purchase should be isolated in the period of purchase; the variance associated with usage should be isolated in the period of use. As a general rule, the sooner a variance can be isolated, the greater is its value in cost control. And, finally, it is unlikely that a single materials variance—the difference between the standard cost and the actual cost of the materials used—would be of any real value to management.

Materials price variance. The standard price for material meeting certain engineering specifications is usually set by the purchasing and accounting departments. Consideration will, of course, be given to market conditions, vendors' quoted prices, the optimum size of a purchase order, and other factors. Purchasing materials at a price other than standard gives rise to a materials price variance.

The materials price variance (MPV) is the difference between the actual price (AP) and the standard price (SP) multiplied by the actual quantity (AQ) of the materials purchased. In equation form, the materials price variance is:

$$MPV = (AP - SP) \times AQ \text{ purchased}$$

To illustrate, assume that the Alpha Company was able, because of the entry into the market of a new foreign supplier, to purchase 60,000 sheets of material at a price of $5.90 each, for a total cost of $354,000. Since the standard price is $6 per sheet, the materials price variance, using the above formula, is:

$$MPV = (AP - SP) \times AQ \text{ purchased}$$
$$MPV = (\$5.90 - \$6.00) \times 60,000$$
$$MPV = -\$0.10 \times 60,000$$
$$MPV = -\$6,000 \text{ (favorable)}$$

The materials price variance of $6,000 is considered favorable since the materials were acquired for a price less than standard. (Why it is expressed as a negative amount will be explained later.) If the actual price had exceeded the standard price, the variance would be considered unfavorable because more costs were incurred than were allowed by the standard. In T-account form the entry to record the purchase of the materials is:

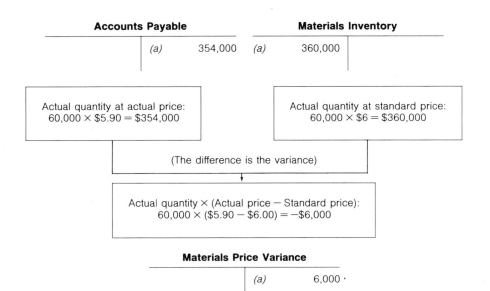

453

The general journal entry to record the purchase of the materials is:

a. Materials Inventory 360,000
     Materials Price Variance   6,000
     Accounts Payable   354,000
  To record the purchase of materials
  at less than standard cost.

Note that the Accounts Payable account shows the actual debt owed to suppliers and the Materials Inventory account shows the *standard price* of the actual quantity of materials purchased, while the Materials Price Variance account shows the difference between the actual price and the standard price multiplied by the actual quantity purchased.

Materials usage variance (materials quantity variance). Since it is largely a matter of physical aspects or product specifications, the standard quantity of materials to be used in making a product is usually set by the engineering department. But if the quality of materials used varies with price, the accounting and purchasing departments may take part in special studies to find the "right" quality.

The materials usage variance shows whether the amount of materials used was more or less than the standard amount allowed. This variance shows only differences from standard caused by the quantity of materials used; it does not include price variances. Thus, the materials usage variance (MUV) is equal to the actual quantity used (AQ) minus the standard quantity allowed (SQ) multiplied by the standard price (SP). The equation for the materials usage variance is:

$$MUV = (AQ - SQ) \times SP$$

To illustrate, assume that the Alpha Company used 55,500 sheets of materials to produce 11,000 units of a product for which the standard quantity allowed is 55,000 sheets (5 × 11,000). Since the standard price of the material is $6 per sheet, the materials usage variance of $3,000 would be computed as follows:

$$MUV = (AQ - SQ) \times SP$$
$$MUV = (55,500 - 55,000) \times \$6$$
$$MUV = 500 \times \$6$$
$$MUV = \$3,000 \text{ (unfavorable)}$$

The variance is unfavorable because more materials were used than the standard amount allowed to complete the job. If the standard quantity allowed had exceeded the quantity actually used, the materials usage variance would have been favorable. The recording in T-accounts of the use of materials is as follows:

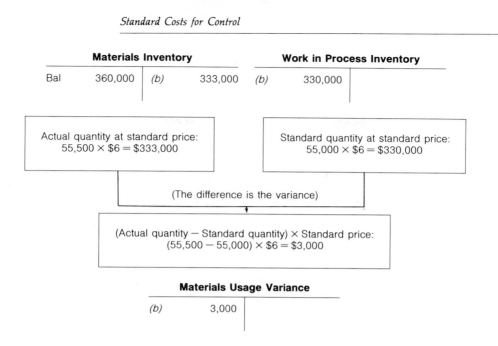

Materials Inventory

| Bal | 360,000 | *(b)* | 333,000 |

Work in Process Inventory

| *(b)* | 330,000 |

Actual quantity at standard price:
55,500 × $6 = $333,000

Standard quantity at standard price:
55,000 × $6 = $330,000

(The difference is the variance)

(Actual quantity − Standard quantity) × Standard price:
(55,500 − 55,000) × $6 = $3,000

Materials Usage Variance

| *(b)* | 3,000 |

The general journal entry to record the use of materials is:

b. Work in Process Inventory 330,000
   Materials Usage Variance 3,000
      Materials Inventory 333,000
   To record the use of materials and to
   establish the materials usage variance.

The Materials Usage Variance shows the standard cost of the excess materials used. Note also that the Work in Process Inventory account contains standard quantities at standard prices.

The equations for both of the above materials variances were expressed so that positive amounts were unfavorable variances and negative amounts were favorable variances. Unfavorable variances are debits in variance accounts because they add to the costs incurred, which, of course, are recorded as debits. Similarly, favorable variances are shown as negative amounts because they are reductions in costs. Favorable variances are recorded in variance accounts as credits. This format will be used in this text. But a word of caution is in order. Far greater understanding is achieved if reason or logic is relied upon to determine whether a variance is favorable or unfavorable. If more materials than standard are used, or if a price greater than standard is paid, the variance is unfavorable. If the reverse is true, the variance is favorable.

Labor Variances

The standard labor cost of any product is equal to the standard quantity of labor time allowed, multiplied by the standard wage rate that should be paid for this time. The actual labor cost may differ from the standard labor cost because of the **quantity** of labor used or the **wages** paid for labor, or both. Both of the labor variances relate to the same period because labor services cannot be purchased in one period, stored, and then used in the next period.

Labor rate variance.   The labor rate variance shows how much the actual labor cost of a product differed from its standard cost because the actual pay rates differed from the standard rates. In this respect, the labor rate variance is similar to the materials price variance. Typically, actual wage rates are set in contract bargaining between a firm and the employees' union.

The labor rate variance (LRV) is computed by taking the difference between the actual rate (AR) paid and the standard rate (SR) allowed and multiplying it by the actual hours (AH) of labor services received. The labor rate variance formula is:

$$LRV = (AR - SR) \times AH$$

To continue our Alpha Company example, assume that the direct labor payroll of the company consisted of 22,200 hours and a total cost of $233,100 (an average actual hourly rate of $10.50). With a standard labor rate of $10 per hour, the labor rate variance is:

$$LRV = (AR - SR) \times AH$$
$$LRV = (\$10.50 - \$10.00) \times 22,200$$
$$LRV = \$0.50 \times 22,200$$
$$LRV = \$11,100 \text{ (unfavorable)}$$

The variance is positive and unfavorable, since the actual rate paid exceeded the standard rate allowed. If the reverse were true, the variance would be favorable. The recording of the variance will be presented after the labor efficiency variance has been illustrated and discussed.

Labor efficiency variance.   The labor efficiency variance is, in effect, a quantity variance. The labor efficiency variance shows whether the actual labor time required to complete a period's output or a given job was more or less than the standard amount allowed. The standard amount of labor time needed to complete a product is usually set by the firm's engineering department; it may be based on time and motion studies, and it may be the subject of contract bargaining with the employees' union.

The labor efficiency variance (LEV) is computed by taking the difference between the actual hours (AH) required and the standard hours (SH) allowed and multiplying it by the standard rate (SR) per hour as follows:

$$LEV = (AH - SH) \times SR$$

To illustrate, assume that the 22,200 hours of labor time received from its employees by the Alpha Company resulted in production with a standard labor time of 22,000 hours. Since the standard labor rate is $10 per hour, the labor time variance is $2,000 (unfavorable), computed as follows:

$$LEV = (AH - SH) \times SR$$
$$LEV = (22,200 - 22,000) \times \$10$$
$$LEV = 200 \times \$10$$
$$LEV = \$2,000 \text{ (unfavorable)}$$

The variance is unfavorable since more hours than standard were required to complete the period's production. If the reverse had been true, the variance would be favorable.

A graphic illustration may aid in understanding the relationship between standard and actual labor cost and the computation of the labor variances. Illustration 15.1, which is deliberately not drawn to scale, is based upon the following data relating to the Alpha Company:

Standard labor time per unit	2 hours
Equivalent units produced in period	11,000 units
Standard labor rate per direct labor hour	$10
Total direct labor wages paid (at average rate of $10.50 per hour)	$233,100
Actual direct labor received	22,200 hours

The standard labor time allowed for the period's output was 22,000 hours (11,000 units at 2 hours per unit). The standard labor cost of the output, then, is $220,000 (22,000 hours at $10 per hour,

Illustration 15.1
STANDARD LABOR COST AND LABOR VARIANCES

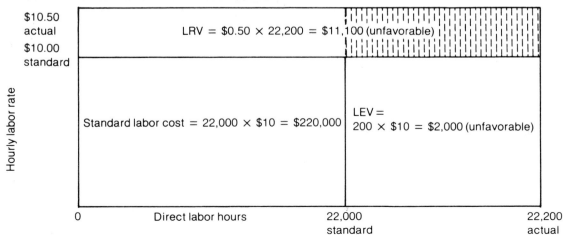

457

the standard labor rate). The labor time or efficiency variance is the standard cost of the extra hours of labor required [(22,200 − 22,000) × $10], or $2,000. The actual labor rate is $10.50 per hour. The labor rate variance, then, is the 50 cents per hour ($10.50 − $10.00) of above-standard wages paid multiplied by the standard hours allowed (22,000) and, by convention, the above-standard wages paid per hour on the extra hours required (200)—the shaded area in the upper right-hand corner of the rectangle. The variation from standard shown by this shaded area is actually caused by both extra hours and above-standard wages per hour. But, as shown, the shaded area is included in the labor rate variance, since this variance is based on actual hours worked.

The T-account entry to charge Work in Process Inventory with direct labor cost and to set up the two labor variances for the Alpha Company would be as follows:

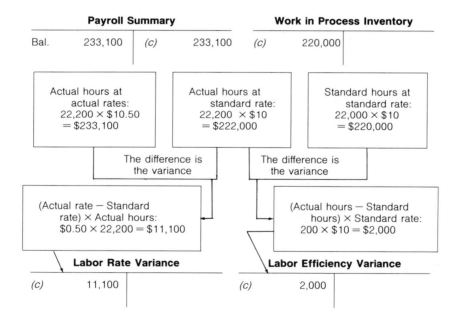

The general journal entry to charge the direct labor cost to Work in Process Inventory is:

c. Work in Process Inventory 220,000
   Labor Rate Variance 11,100
   Labor Efficiency Variance 2,000
      Payroll Summary 233,100
   To charge work in process with direct labor and
   to establish the two labor variances.

With the above entry, the gross wages earned by direct production employees ($233,100) are distributed: $220,000 (the standard labor cost of the production) to Work in Process Inventory and the balance to the two labor variance accounts. Note that the labor rate variance is not caused by paying employees more wages than they are entitled to receive. The more likely reason is that employees with different pay rates can complete the same task and that too much higher hourly rated employee time was used on a given job. Also, if some overtime premium pay is expected in setting standards, then variation from expected amounts can cause a labor rate variance. But, typically, the hours of labor employed are more likely to be under the control of management, and for this reason the labor efficiency variance is watched more closely.

Summary of labor variances. The accuracy of the computation of the two labor variances can be readily checked by comparing their sum with the difference between actual and standard labor cost for a period. In the Alpha Company illustration, this difference was:

Actual labor cost incurred	$233,100
Standard labor cost allowed	220,000
Total labor variance (unfavorable) . . .	$ 13,100

This $13,100 is made up of two labor variances, both unfavorable:

Labor efficiency variance (200 × $10)	$ 2,000
Labor rate variance (22,200 × $0.50)	11,100
Total labor variance (unfavorable)	$13,100

Overhead Variances

In a cost system using standard costs, overhead is applied to the goods produced by means of a standard overhead rate. This rate is set prior to the start of the period through use of a flexible overhead budget. This budget is called a flexible (or variable) budget because it shows the budgeted amount of overhead for various levels of output or volume. Total budgeted overhead will vary as output varies because some overhead costs are variable. But the fixed nature of some overhead costs means that total overhead will not vary in proportion with output.

The flexible budget for the Alpha Company for the period is shown in Illustration 15.2. Note that the illustration shows the overhead costs expected to be incurred at three levels of activity: 90 percent, 100 percent, and 110 percent of capacity. For product costing purposes, the expected level of activity must be estimated and a rate set based on that level. *The level chosen is called the* **standard volume**

Illustration 15.2

ALPHA COMPANY
Flexible Manufacturing Overhead Budget

	90%	100%	110%
Percent of capacity	90%	100%	110%
Direct labor hours	18,000	20,000	22,000
Units of output	9,000	10,000	11,000
Variable overhead:			
Indirect materials	$ 7,200	$ 8,000	$ 8,800
Power	9,000	10,000	11,000
Royalties	1,800	2,000	2,200
Other	18,000	20,000	22,000
Total variable overhead	$36,000	$ 40,000	$ 44,000
Fixed overhead:			
Insurance	$ 4,000	$ 4,000	$ 4,000
Property taxes	6,000	6,000	6,000
Depreciation	20,000	20,000	20,000
Other	30,000	30,000	30,000
Total fixed overhead	$60,000	$ 60,000	$ 60,000
Total manufacturing overhead	$96,000	$100,000	$104,000

Standard overhead rate ($100,000 ÷ 20,000 hours) $5

of output. This standard volume of output may be expressed in terms of percent of capacity, units of output, and/or direct labor-hours. In our example it is assumed to be at 100 percent of capacity, at which level 10,000 units are expected to be produced and 20,000 direct labor hours of services are expected to be used. The standard total overhead rate is $5 ($100,000 ÷ 20,000 hours) per direct labor hour. The $5 per hour overhead rate is used in applying overhead to production. Knowing the separate rates for variable and fixed overhead is sometimes useful for analysis purposes. The variable overhead rate is $2 ($40,000 ÷ 20,000 hours) per hour, and the fixed overhead rate is $3 ($60,000 ÷ 20,000 hours) per hour. If the expected volume had been 18,000 direct labor-hours (90 percent of capacity), the standard overhead rate would have been $5.33 ($96,000 ÷ 18,000 hours). If the standard volume had been 22,000 direct labor-hours (110 percent of capacity), the standard overhead would have been $4.73 ($104,000 ÷ 22,000 hours).

To continue the illustration, assume that Alpha Company incurred $108,000 of actual manufacturing overhead costs in the period in which 11,000 units of product were produced. The standard number of direct labor hours allowed for this production is 22,000 hours. The company had only expected to produce 10,000 units (standard production) and had used that level to determine the total overhead rate of $5 per direct labor hour. The actual costs would be debited to Manufacturing Overhead and credited to a variety of accounts such as Accounts Payable, Accumulated Depreciation, Unexpired

Insurance, Accrued Property Taxes Payable, and so on. The entry, in T-account form, to record the application of $110,000 of overhead to production (22,000 hours at $5 per hour) would be:

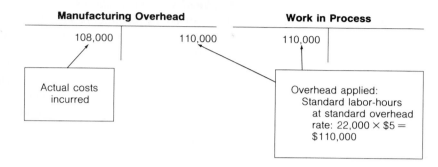

Manufacturing Overhead		**Work in Process**

The general journal entry to apply manufacturing overhead to production would be:

```
Work in Process     . . . . . . . . .     110,000
      Manufacturing Overhead   . . . . . . . .           110,000
      To apply manufacturing overhead to production
      (22,000 hours at $5 per hour).
```

The above accounts show that manufacturing overhead has been overapplied to production by the $2,000 credit balance in the Manufacturing Overhead account. Such overapplication of overhead will occur whenever actual production is greater than standard production. Although various complex computations can be made for overhead variances, a simple approach will be used. This approach consists of the calculation of an overhead volume variance and an overhead budget variance. This approach is known as the two-variance approach to overhead variances.

The overhead budget variance. The **overhead budget variance (OBV)** (also called the spending or controllable variance) shows in one amount how efficiency operations were conducted in the sense of the prices paid for and the amounts of the overhead services used. This overhead variance is similar to a combined price and usage variance for materials or labor. The overhead budget variance (OBV) is equal to the difference between total actual overhead costs (Actual OH) and total budgeted overhead costs (BOH) for the **actual** output attained. Since the total actual overhead was $108,000 and the total budgeted overhead was $104,000 (from Illustration 15.2) for 11,000 units (22,000 standard direct labor-hours), the overhead budget variance is computed as follows:

$$OBV = Actual\ OH - BOH$$
$$OBV = \$108,000 - \$104,000$$
$$OBV = \$4,000\ (unfavorable)$$

The variance is unfavorable because actual overhead costs were $108,000 while, according to the flexible budget, they should have been $104,000.

Overhead volume variance. The **overhead volume variance (OVV)** is caused by producing at a level other than that used in setting the standard overhead application rate. Because fixed overhead does not change over a wide range of activity, any deviation from planned production will cause the application rate to be incorrect. The overhead volume variance shows whether plant assets produced more or fewer goods than expected. The overhead volume variance is the difference between the budgeted amount of overhead (BOH) for the **actual volume achieved** and the applied overhead (applied OH). The overhead volume variance equation is:

$$OVV = BOH - \text{Applied OH}$$

In the Alpha Company illustration, the 11,000 units produced in the period have a standard labor allowance of 22,000 hours. The flexible budget in Illustration 15.2 shows that the budgeted overhead for 22,000 direct labor hours is $104,000. Overhead is applied to work in process on the basis of standard hours allowed for a particular amount of production, in this case 11,000 units or 22,000 hours at $5 per hour. The overhead volume variance then is:

$$OVV = BOH - \text{Applied OH}$$
$$OVV = \$104,000 - \$110,000$$
$$OVV = -\$6,000 \text{ (favorable)}$$

Notice that the amount of the overhead volume variance is related solely to fixed overhead. In Illustration 15.2, fixed overhead at all levels of activity is $60,000. Since Alpha Company computed its overhead application rate on the basis of 20,000 direct labor hours, the fixed overhead rate was $3 per direct labor-hour. Alpha worked 2,000 (22,000 − 20,000) more standard hours than was expected. The overhead volume variance can also be calculated as follows:

$$\left(\begin{array}{c} \text{Number of hours used in setting predetermined overhead rates} \end{array} - \begin{array}{c} \text{Number of standard hours allowed for production level achieved} \end{array}\right) \times \begin{array}{c} \text{Fixed overhead rate per hour} \end{array}$$

$$(20,000 - 22,000) \times \$3 = -\$6,000 \text{ (favorable)}$$

The variance is favorable since the company achieved a higher level of production than was expected.

Recording overhead variances. If desired, a formal entry can be made in the accounts showing the two parts of the $2,000 net overhead variance. The T-account entry for the Alpha Company would be as follows—the debits and credits are keyed with the letter (*f*):

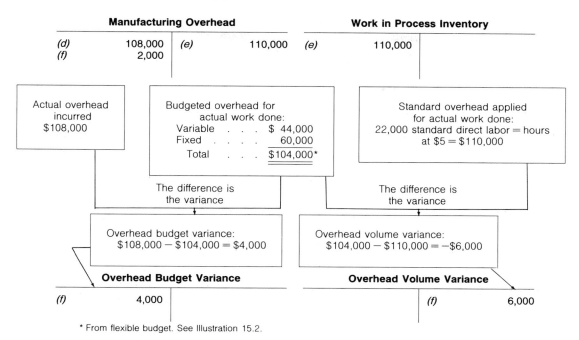

* From flexible budget. See Illustration 15.2.

The general journal entries related to overhead are as follows:

d. Manufacturing Overhead 108,000
       Various Accounts 108,000
       To record actual overhead.

e. Work in Process 110,000
       Manufacturing Overhead 110,000
       To record the application of overhead to work
       in process.

f. Manufacturing Overhead 2,000
    Overhead Budget Variance 4,000
       Overhead Volume Variance 6,000
       To record the variances related to overhead and
       close the manufacturing overhead account.

The first entry records the actual overhead costs incurred during the period by Alpha Company. The second entry applies overhead to Work in Process at the rate of $5 per standard direct labor-hour (22,000). The final entry reduces the Manufacturing Overhead account balance to zero and recognizes the two variances calculated for overhead; these two variance accounts analyze the causes of the overapplied overhead for the period.

Summary of overhead variances. The accuracy of the two overhead variances can be easily determined by comparing the sum of the volume and budget variances with the difference between the costs of actual and standard overhead. For the Alpha Company example, the difference between actual and standard overhead was:

Actual overhead incurred	$108,000
Standard overhead allowed (22,000 direct	
labor-hours × $5 per hour)	110,000
Total overhead variance (favorable)	−$ 2,000

This difference is made up of the two overhead variances:

Overhead budget variance—Unfavorable	
($108,000 − $104,000)	$ 4,000
Overhead volume variance—Favorable	
[$104,000 − (22,000 × $5)]	−6,000
Total overhead variance	−$ 2,000

GOODS COMPLETED AND SOLD

To complete our Alpha Company example, assume that 11,000 units were completed and transferred to finished goods, 10,000 units were sold on account at a price equal to 160 percent of standard cost, there was no beginning or ending work in process inventory, and there was no beginning finished goods inventory. In the T-accounts below, entry *(g)* shows the transfer of the standard cost of the units completed, $660,000 (11,000 × $60), from Work in Process Inventory to Finished Goods Inventory. Entry *(h)* records the sales for the period, $960,000, while entry *(i)* records the cost of goods sold, $600,000 (10,000 × $60).

Work in Process Inventory

(b) Materials	330,000	*(g)* Completed	660,000
(c) Labor	220,000		
(e) Overhead	110,000		

Finished Goods Inventory

(g) Completed	660,000	*(i)* Sold	600,000

Accounts Receivable

(h)	960,000

Cost of Goods Sold

(i) Sold	600,000

Sales

(h)	960,000

In journal entry form, entries *(g)*, *(h)*, and *(i)* are:

g. Finished Goods Inventory 660,000
    Work in Process Inventory 660,000
    To transfer the standard cost of units
    completed (11,000 × $60).

h. Accounts Receivable 960,000
    Sales 960,000
    To record sales for the period.

i. Cost of Goods Sold 600,000
    Merchandise Inventory 600,000
    To record cost of goods sold for
    the period.

Work in Process Inventory has been debited with the standard cost of materials, labor, and overhead put into production. Therefore, the entry recording the transfer of the standard cost of the completed units, $660,000 (11,000 at $60), reduces the Work in Process Inventory account to a zero balance. Note that the Finished Goods Inventory account is charged with the standard cost of goods completed and credited with the standard cost of the goods sold. Thus, the ending inventory consists of the units actually on hand (1,000) at their standard cost of $60 each, or $60,000. Sales for the period amount to 10,000 units at $96 each (160 percent of $60). It is fairly common practice to base selling prices on standard costs (at least partially).

INVESTIGATING VARIANCES FROM STANDARD

Once variances have been isolated, management must decide which ones should be investigated further. Since so many variances occur, they cannot all be investigated. Management needs some selection guides. Possible guides include (1) the absolute size of the variance, (2) the size of the variance relative to the cost incurred, and (3) whether the cost incurred is considered controllable or noncontrollable. The opinions of knowledgeable operating personnel should be sought.

Statistical analysis may also be used in deciding which variances to investigate. For instance, the mean (average) value of actual costs could be determined for a period of time. Management might decide that only future variances which deviate from the mean by more than a certain amount or percentage would be investigated.

Any analysis of variances is likely to disclose some variances that are controllable within the company and others that are not. Prices paid for materials purchased may be largely beyond the control of the buyer. But the amounts used may be controllable internally. Also, although separate variances are isolated, they are not always as independent as they may appear to be. An unfavorable labor rate variance may result from using higher paid employees in a certain task; but this may result in a favorable labor efficiency variance resulting from greater productivity and possibly in a favorable materials usage variance that occurred because the more skilled employees caused less spoilage. Variances should be investigated carefully before being used to appraise the performance of a given individual or department.

DISPOSING OF VARIANCES FROM STANDARD

At the end of the year, variances from standard may be (1) viewed as losses due to inefficiency and closed to the Income Summary account; (2) allocated as adjustments of the recorded cost of Work in Process Inventory, Finished Goods Inventory, and Cost of Goods Sold; or (3) closed to Cost of Goods Sold. Theoretically, the alternative chosen should depend upon whether the standards set were reasonably attainable standards and upon whether the variance was controllable by company employees. An unfavorable materials price variance caused by an unexpected price change may be considered an added cost since it is likely to be uncontrollable. On the other hand, there is little merit in treating the fixed costs of idle plant capacity as anything but a loss. As a practical matter, and especially if they are small, the variances are usually closed to the Cost of Goods Sold account rather than allocated. They are typically unfavorable (due to the common practice of setting "tight" standards). This practice tends to reduce reported net income below the amounts that would be reported if the variances were treated as cost elements and allocated to the inventory accounts and Cost of Goods Sold.

Entry *(j)* in the T-accounts below reflects this practical disposition of the variances in our continuing example of the Alpha Company:

Materials Price Variance				Materials Usage Variance				Labor Rate Variance			
(j)	6,000	*(a)*	6,000	*(b)*	3,000	*(j)*	3,000	*(c)*	11,100	*(j)*	11,100

Labor Efficiency Variance				Overhead Budget Variance				Overhead Volume Variance			
(c)	2,000	*(j)*	2,000	*(f)*	4,000	*(j)*	4,000	*(j)*	6,000	*(f)*	6,000

Cost of Goods Sold	
(i)	600,000
(j)	8,100

In journal entry form, entry *(j)* would read as follows:

Materials Price Variance	6,000	
Overhead Volume Variance	6,000	
Cost of Goods Sold	8,100	
Materials Usage Variance		3,000
Labor Efficiency Variance		2,000
Overhead Budget Variance		4,000
Labor Rate Variance		11,100

    To close variance accounts.

Variances are not reported separately in statements released to the public; they are simply included in the amount reported for cost of goods sold. In statements prepared for internal use, the variances may be listed separately at the standard cost amount after the listing for the cost of goods sold.

SUMMARY

Standard costs may be introduced on either a full-cost or a variable-cost basis into either job cost or process cost systems as one means of attempting to appraise the efficiency with which operations are conducted. Standard costs are not merely estimates but carefully predetermined measures of what costs should be. The setting of standards will often involve engineering and time and motion studies and knowledge of both working conditions within a plant and of general economic conditions.

The advantages secured from using standard costs include cost control, the provision of information useful in managerial planning, more rational inventory values, cost savings in record keeping, and, possibly, a general reduction in the costs incurred.

Typically, at least six variances from standard costs will be computed. These six variances are:

1. Materials usage variance = (Actual quantity − Standard quantity) × Standard price.
2. Materials price variance = (Actual price − Standard price) × Actual quantity.
3. Labor rate variance = (Actual rate − Standard rate) × Actual quantity.
4. Labor efficiency variance = (Actual hours − Standard hours) × Standard rate.
5. Overhead budget variance = Actual overhead − Budgeted overhead for actual volume.
6. Overhead volume variance = Budgeted overhead − Applied overhead.

Variances may be isolated at different steps in the accounting process. As a general rule, the sooner a variance can be isolated, the better it serves as a means of cost control. Although variances may be allocated to Work in Process Inventory, Finished Goods

Inventory, and Cost of Goods Sold at the end of a period, as a practical matter they are usually closed to the Cost of Goods Sold account.

In deciding which variances to investigate, one might consider (1) the absolute size of the variance, (2) the size of the variance relative to the cost incurred, and (3) whether the cost incurred is considered controllable or uncontrollable.

APPENDIX

APPLYING STANDARD COSTS IN JOB ORDER AND PROCESS COST SYSTEMS

Standard Costs in a Job Cost System

In a job cost system, production quantities are known in advance, and this permits a much earlier isolation of some variances than in a process cost system, in which equivalent production is known only at the end of a period. This early isolation of variances is illustrated in the following example.

Assume that the A Company accounts for the manufacture of its products in a job cost system in which standard costs are recorded. Its flexible budget monthly amounts (at a standard activity of 8,000 direct labor hours) are variable overhead, $24,000, and fixed overhead, $16,000, yielding a standard variable overhead rate of $3 and a standard fixed overhead rate of $2 per direct labor hour.

There was no inventory of work in process as of June 1. During June two jobs were started, for which the standard specifications were:

	Job 101	Job 102
Direct materials	$20,000	$50,000
Direct labor:		
2,000 hours at $4	8,000	
5,000 hours at $4		20,000
Overhead:		
2,000 hours at $5	10,000	
5,000 hours at $5		25,000
Total standard cost	$38,000	$95,000

The A Company's activities for June 1986 are summarized as follows:

a. Raw materials with a standard cost of $79,500 were purchased on account at an actual price of $80,150.

b. Standard direct materials were issued for both jobs. In addition, excess materials were requisitioned: Job No. 101, $400; and Job No. 102, $700.

c. Analysis of the factory payrolls debited to Payroll Summary shows that they consisted of $10,000 of indirect labor ($4,000 variable and $6,000 fixed) and direct labor of 6,000 hours (Job No. 101, 1,980 hours; and Job No. 102, 4,020 hours) at a total cost of $24,600. Job No. 101 was completed.

d. Various overhead costs incurred: variable, $14,500; and fixed, $10,200.

e. Standard overhead assigned to production: Job No. 101, $10,000; and Job No. 102, 4,020 hours at $5 per hour, $20,100. (Note: Standard overhead is assigned to Job No. 101 since it was completed; Job No. 102 is incomplete, but within standard.)

f. Job No. 101 was completed and transferred to the finished goods storeroom.

g. Sales for the month—all units in Job No. 101 at a total price of $60,000.

The entries to isolate the variances are as follows:

a. Materials Inventory 79,500
   Materials Price Variance 650
      Accounts Payable 80,150
   To record purchase of materials and to isolate materials price variance.

b. Work in Process 70,000
   Materials Usage Variance 1,100
      Materials Inventory 71,100
   To charge standard materials to production and to charge excess materials requisitioned to a variance account.

c. Work in Process 24,080
   Manufacturing Overhead 10,000
   Labor Rate Variance 600
      Labor Efficiency Variance 80
      Payroll Summary 34,600
   To distribute labor costs and to isolate labor variances:

Job No. 101 (2,000 hours at $4) .	$ 8,000
Job No. 102 (4,020 hours at $4) .	16,080
Total labor to work in process	$24,080

   Labor efficiency variance on Job No. 101: (1,980 actual hours − 2,000 standard hours) × $4 = −$80 (favorable).
   Labor rate variance: ($4.10 actual wage rate − $4.00 standard rate) × 6,000 hours = $600 (unfavorable).

d. Manufacturing Overhead 24,700
      Accounts Payable (and various other accounts) 24,700
   To record incurrence of overhead costs.

e. Work in Process 30,100
      Manufacturing Overhead   30,100
      To apply standard overhead to production: Job No.
      101—$10,000 (standard amount, job com-
      pleted); Job No. 102—4,020 hours at
      $5 = $20,100 (based on standard labor, job in-
      complete).

f. Finished Goods 38,000
      Work in Process   38,000
      To record transfer of completed Job No. 101 at
      standard.

g. Accounts Receivable 60,000
      Sales   60,000
      To record sales for the month.

      Cost of Goods Sold 38,000
      Finished Goods   38,000
      To record cost of goods sold (Job No. 101,
      $38,000).

Note that in the above entries the materials and labor variances are isolated rather routinely in the recording process. But the overhead variances must be computed separately at the end of the period, unless the standard production for the period is known before then. For the A Company, the overhead variances are:

Overhead budget variance:
  Actual costs incurred (entries *c* and *d* above) $34,700
  Standard costs allowed (from flexible budget:
    $16,000 + 6,020 standard hours at $3) 34,060
    Unfavorable overhead budget variance . . . . . . $ 640

Overhead volume variance:
  Budgeted fixed overhead $16,000
  Standard fixed overhead applied to production
    (6,020* hours at $2) 12,040
    Unfavorable overhead volume variance   3,960
    Total unfavorable overhead variance $4,600

* 6,020 hours are used in the calculations because standard hours allowed for Job No. 101 are 2,000, and standard hours allowed thus far on Job No. 202 are 4,020, for a total of 6,020 hours.

The following entry isolates the two overhead variances in the accounts:

Overhead Budget Variance 640
Overhead Volume Variance 3,960
    Manufacturing Overhead   4,600
    To set up separate overhead variance accounts.

Note that the credit to Manufacturing Overhead of $4,600 reduces that account to a zero balance (for previous entries to account, see entries *c, d,* and *e* above), thus proving the accuracy of the computations.

Typically, the overhead variances and the materials and labor variances will be summarized in a report prepared periodically for internal management. Such a report could be called a "Summary of Variances from Standard."

Standard Costs in a Process Cost System

To provide a brief illustration of how standard costs might be incorporated into a process cost system, the following example is presented.

Assume that the P Company manufactures a product for which the standard specifications are:

Materials—2 pounds at $2 per pound	$4.00
Direct labor—0.5 hours at $4 per hour	2.00
Overhead—0.5 hours at $3 per hour	1.50
Total standard cost	$7.50

The fixed overhead included in the standard cost is based upon a monthly flexible budget which (at the standard activity level of 60,000 standard labor hours) shows budgeted variable overhead of $120,000 and budgeted fixed overhead of $60,000.

P Company charges Work in Process Inventory with actual quantities and actual costs. (An alternative would be to charge Work in Process Inventory with actual quantities at standard costs. This practice would isolate some variances sooner.) Entries made to its Work in Process Inventory account for the month of May 1986 were:

Direct materials (180,500 pounds at $2.02)	$364,610
Direct labor (40,100 hours at $3.95)	158,395
Actual fixed overhead	58,700
Actual variable overhead	80,500
Total cost put into production	$662,205
Standard cost of units completed and transferred	
(70,000 at $7.50)	525,000
Balance, May 31, 1986	$137,205

Production records show that 70,000 units were completed and transferred and that 20,000 units of product remain in process at the end of the month. These units are complete as to materials and 50 percent complete as to processing.

From the above information, the equivalent production for the period in terms of standard units of product can be computed as follows:

	Materials	Labor and Overhead
Units started and finished	70,000	70,000
Equivalent units in ending inventory	20,000	10,000
Equivalent production	90,000	80,000

Now enough information is available to permit the calculation of all of the variances which are summarized in the "Summary of Variances from Standard" shown in Illustration 15.3.

Illustration 15.3

P COMPANY
Summary of Variances from Standard
Month Ended May 31, 1986

Materials:
Price variance (180,500 pounds at $0.02)	$ 3,610	
Usage variance (500 pounds at $2)	1,000	
Total unfavorable materials variance		$ 4,610

Labor:
Rate variance (40,100 hours at $0.05)	− $2,005	
Efficiency variance (100 hours at $4)	400	
Net favorable labor variance		− 1,605

Overhead:
Budget variance—fixed ($58,700 − $60,000) + variable ($80,500 − $80,000)	− $800	
Volume variance ($60,000 − $40,000)	20,000	
Net unfavorable overhead variance		19,200
Total variance from standard for the month		$22,205

Since the actual price paid for materials was $0.02 per pound above standard, the materials price variance is the actual use of 180,500 pounds multiplied by $0.02. Since the standard materials allowed for 90,000 equivalent units is 180,000 pounds (90,000 × 2) there is a materials usage variance of 500 pounds times $2. Both variances are unfavorable.

The average wage rate paid employees was $0.05 less than standard; thus, a favorable rate variance of this amount multiplied by actual hours of 40,100 emerges. The standard labor allowed for the production of the period (80,000 × 0.5 hours) is 100 hours less than the actual. Hence, an unfavorable labor efficiency variance was experienced.

Fixed overhead costs were $1,300 less than the budgeted amount, while variable overhead costs exceeded their budgeted amount for the actual production in May by $500. Together they yield a net favorable variance of $800. Because the standard fixed overhead applied to production of $40,000 is less than the budgeted fixed overhead for the month of $60,000, there is an unfavorable volume variance of $20,000. These variances amount to $19,200 for overhead and to $22,205 as the total variance (unfavorable) from standard for the month.

The variances shown in Illustration 15.3 can be formally recorded in the accounts and the Work in Process Inventory relieved of the month's variances by the following entry:

Materials Price Variance	3,610	
Materials Usage Variance	1,000	
Labor Efficiency Variance	400	
Overhead Volume Variance	20,000	
Labor Rate Variance		2,005
Overhead Budget Variance		800
Work in Process		22,205
To set up variances from standard for the month.		

Subtracting the $22,205 from the previously given balance of $137,205 in the Work in Process account leaves a balance of $115,000, which is equal to the standard cost of the ending inventory. The standard cost of the ending inventory can be separately computed as follows:

Direct materials (20,000 units, 2 pounds per unit, 100% complete, unit cost $4)	$ 80,000
Direct labor (20,000 units, 50% complete, unit cost $2)	20,000
Overhead (20,000 units, 50% complete, unit cost $1.50)	15,000
Total standard cost of ending inventory	$115,000

QUESTIONS

1. Is a standard cost an estimated cost? What is the primary objective of employing standard costs in a cost system? What are some of the other advantages of using standard costs?

2. How can it be maintained that the use of standard costs permits the application of the principle of management by exception?

3. What are some of the problems surrounding the interpretation of variances in a standard cost system?

4. Compute the materials price and usage variances from the following data:

> Standard—1,000 units at $20 per unit.
> Purchased—1,200 units at $20.25; used—995 units.

5. What might be a plausible explanation for a given company having a substantial favorable materials price variance and a substantial unfavorable materials usage variance?

6. What is the usual cause of a favorable or unfavorable labor rate variance? What other labor variance is isolated in a standard cost system?

Of the two variances, which is more likely to be under the control of management? Explain.

7. Identify the type of variance indicated by each situation below and whether it is a favorable or unfavorable variance.

   a. The cutting department of a company during the week ending July 15 cut 12 size S cogged wheels out of three sheets of 12-inch high-tempered steel. Usually three wheels of such size are cut out of each sheet.

   b. A company purchased and installed a new expensive cutting machine to handle expanding orders. This purchase and the related depreciation had not been anticipated when the overhead rate was set.

   c. Edwards, a band saw operator, was on vacation last week. Lands took his place for the normal 40-hour week. Edwards' wage rate is $5.40 per hour, while Lands' is $5.20 per hour. Production was at capacity last week and the week before.

8. Is the overhead budget variance essentially a "price" or a "usage" variance? Explain.

9. Theoretically, how should variances from standard be disposed of? What is typically their practical disposition?

10. Would you expect the normal overhead volume variance to be favorable or unfavorable? Explain.

11. How do standard costs control?

EXERCISES

1. During the month of July a department completed 2,000 units of a product which had a standard material cost of 4,000 square feet at $0.80 per square foot. The actual material used consisted of 4,050 square feet at a cost of $3,321. Compute the materials usage and materials price variances, and indicate clearly whether each is favorable or unfavorable.

2. Compute the labor variances in the following circumstances:

Actual direct labor payroll (19,800 hours)	$162,360
Standard labor allowed per unit, 4 hours at $8 . . .	32
Equivalent production for the month (in units) . . .	5,000

3. During March, 100 units of a given product were produced. These units have a standard labor cost of one hour at $8 per hour in Process X and of two hours at $7.00 per hour in Process Y. Assume that James worked 95 hours on Process X during the month, for which he earned $836, and that Brown worked 205 hours on Process Y, for which he earned $1,394. Compute the labor cost variances for each process.

4. The following relate to the manufacturing activities of the Towers Company for the month of May 1986:

Standard activity (units)	50,000
Actual production (units)	40,000
Budgeted fixed overhead	$ 60,000
Variable overhead rate (per unit) . .	$ 4.00
Actual fixed overhead	$ 60,800
Actual variable overhead	$156,600

Compute the overhead budget variance and the overhead volume variance.

5. In Exercise 4, if the actual production had been 65,000 units, what would the overhead volume variance have been?

6. The standard cost variance accounts of the Tory Company at the end of its fiscal year had the following balances:

Materials price variance (unfavorable)	$10,000
Materials usage variance (unfavorable) . . .	8,000
Labor rate variance (favorable)	−6,000
Labor efficiency variance (unfavorable) . . .	22,000
Overhead budget variance (favorable) . . .	−2,000
Overhead volume variance (unfavorable) . .	12,000

Set up T-accounts for the above variances; enter the above balances in these accounts; then prepare one journal entry to record the closing of these variance accounts in the manner in which they are usually disposed of in practice.

PROBLEMS

15–1. Tom Harman, the president of the Barthey Company, has a problem. It does not involve substantial dollar amounts, but it does involve the important question of responsibility for variances from standard costs. He has just received the following report:

Total materials costs for the month of May (6,900 lbs. @ $4.80 per lb.)	$33,120
Unfavorable materials price variance [($4.80 − $4.00) × 6,900 lbs.]	(5,520)
Unfavorable materials usage variance [(6,900 lbs. − 6,000 lbs.) × $4.00]	(3,600)
Standard materials at standard price for the actual production in May	$24,000

Tom has discussed the unfavorable price variance with Jill Sanders, the purchasing officer. She agrees that, under the circumstances, she should be held responsible for most of the materials price variance. But she objects to the inclusion of $720 (900 lbs. of excess materials used @ $0.80 per lb.). This, she argues, is the responsibility of the production department. If it had not been so inefficient in the use of materials, she would not have had to purchase the extra 900 pounds. On the other hand, Don Wolf, the production manager, who agrees that he is basically responsible for the excess quantity of materials used, does not agree that the above materials usage variance should be revised to include the $720 of unfavorable price variance on the excess materials used. "That's Jill's responsibility," he says.

Tom now turns to you for help. Specifically, he wants you to tell him:

1. Who is responsible for the $720 in dispute?

2. If responsibility cannot be clearly assigned, in which price variance should the accounting department include the variance? Why?

3. Are there likely to be other circumstances in which materials variances cannot be considered the responsibility of the person who is most likely to be considered responsible for them? Explain.

Required:

Prepare written answers to the three questions asked by Tom Harman.

15–2. During the month of March a department completed 5,000 units of a product which had a standard material cost of 6,000 square feet at $0.30 per square foot. The actual material used consisted of 6,100 square feet at an actual cost of $1,708. The actual purchase of this material amounted to 9,000 square feet at a total cost of $2,520.

Required:

a. Using T-accounts, prepare entries for (1) the purchase of the materials and (2) the issuance of materials to production.

b. Make the necessary journal entries for 1 and 2 from part **a.**

15–3. The welding department of the Republic Company produced 40,000 units during the month of November. The standard direct labor per unit is two hours. The standard rate per hour is $18. During the month, 82,000 direct labor hours were worked at a cost of $1,508,800.

Required:

a. Draw a diagram similar to Illustration 15.1 showing the determination of the two labor variances.

b. Record the labor data in a journal entry and post the entry to T-accounts.

15–4. The monthly budgeted fixed overhead of the Houston plant of the RLA Company is absorbed into production, using a rate based upon a standard volume of output of 100,000 units per month. The flexible overhead budget for the month allows $150,000 for fixed overhead and $2 per unit of output for variable overhead. The actual overhead for the month consisted of $151,200 of fixed overhead and the actual variable overhead given below.

Required:

Compute the overhead budget variance and the overhead volume variance, assuming that the actual production in units and the actual variable overhead in dollars were:

a. 75,000 units and $152,000.

b. 110,000 units and $225,400.

15–5. The Robinson Company manufactures and sells two rather similar table lamps, each of which is assembled and packaged in Department III. The expected volume of activity for this department is 100,000 direct labor hours, at which level budgeted fixed overhead is $140,000, while variable overhead is budgeted at $2.40 per direct labor hour.

In May, a total of 81,300 direct labor hours was worked in the department, 1,300 of which were in excess of the standard labor allowed for the month's production. The actual overhead for the month consisted of $139,400 of fixed overhead and $196,600 of variable overhead.

Required:

Compute the two overhead variances for the month of May, showing your computations.

15–6. Based on a standard volume of output of 80,000 units per month, the standard cost of the product manufactured by the Dexter Company is:

Direct materials (0.25 pounds) . . .	$ 2.00
Direct labor (0.5 hours)	4.00
Variable overhead	3.50
Fixed overhead	1.50
	$11.00

During the month of May, 82,000 units were produced and the following costs were incurred:

Direct materials (20,650 pounds at $8.20) . . .	$169,330
Direct labor (41,080 hours at $7.80)	320,424
Variable overhead	289,400
Fixed overhead	121,040

Required:

Compute the materials price and usage variances, the labor rate and efficiency variances, and the overhead budget and volume variances.

15–7. The Jeffers Company, Inc. has determined the standard production volume to be 75,000 units per month. The standard costs associated with this level of output were determined to be:

Direct materials (10 units) . .	$ 6.00
Direct labor (1.25 hours) . . .	10.00
Variable overhead	4.50 per unit produced
Fixed overhead	2.00 per unit produced
	$22.50

During February, 73,000 units were produced and the following costs were incurred.

Direct materials (750,000 units at $0.58) . .	$435,000
Direct labor (90,000 hours at $8.10)	729,000
Variable overhead	306,600
Fixed overhead	153,300

Required:

a. Compute the materials price and usage variances, the labor rate and efficiency variances, and the overhead budget and volume variances. Indicate whether each variance is favorable or unfavorable.

b. Prepare journal entries to record the variances and an entry to close out the variances assuming that they are not material.

15–8. (Based on the chapter appendix.) The Baker Manufacturing Company employs a job order standard cost accounting system. The standard cost of the material used is $1.60 per square foot, while the standard labor cost is $8 per hour. Overhead is assigned to jobs at the rate of $6 per standard direct labor hour. Based upon a standard volume of activity of 60,000 direct labor hours, the flexible budget allows $120,000 of fixed overhead and $4 of variable overhead per direct labor hour for the month of June 1986.

Work in process is charged with standard quantities and standard prices. On June 1, 1986, one job (No. 301) was in process, to which the following standard costs have already been assigned:

Material (2,500 square feet)	$4,000
Labor (400 direct labor hours)	3,200
Manufacturing overhead ($6 per standard direct labor hour)	2,400
Total	$9,600

When completed, the standard quantities for Job No. 301 are 4,000 square feet of material and 500 hours of direct labor.

During the month of June 1986, the following transactions and events occurred:

(1) Purchased 600,000 square feet of material at $1.56 per square foot.

(2) Materials issued:

Job No.	Actual Quantity	Standard Quantity
301	1,600 sq. ft.	1,500 sq. ft.
All others	420,000 sq. ft.	421,200 sq. ft.
	421,600 sq. ft.	422,700 sq. ft.

(3) The direct labor costs and hours for the month were:

Incurred on:	Actual Hours	Standard Hours	Actual Cost
Job No. 301	104	100	$ 868
All other jobs	51,096	51,000	413,932
	51,200	51,100	$414,800

(4) The appropriate amount of overhead was assigned to the jobs.

(5) The actual overhead incurred during the month was $310,000.

(6) Job No. 301 was completed during the month. Other production also completed during the month has a standard cost of $1,040,000.

Required:

a. Prepare general journal entries for each of the numbered transactions given above.

b. Compute and prepare general journal entries to record the overhead budget variance and the overhead volume for the month.

15–9. (Based on the chapter appendix.) The Markov Company employs a process cost system with standard costs to account for the product it manufactures in a two-step process through Departments A and B. The standard cost of this product in Department A is:

Direct materials (10 units at $16) . . .	$160
Direct labor (5 hours at $12)	60
Variable overhead (5 hours at $8) . .	40
Fixed overhead (5 hours at $4) . . .	20
	$280

The flexible overhead budget, based on 60,000 direct labor hours as a standard volume of activity, allows $240,000 of fixed overhead plus $8 per direct labor hour. Materials price variances are isolated at the time of purchase, labor rate variances when payrolls are distributed. Materials usage and labor efficiency variances are isolated at the end of the month, when production is known. Standard overhead is assigned to production and overhead variances isolated at the end of the month, when production and actual costs are known.

There was no work in process inventory as of July 1, 1986, in Department A. Selected, summarized data for the month are:

(1) Purchased 121,000 units of raw material for $1,926,320.

(2) Direct materials requisitioned by Department A, 110,580 units.

(3) Of the payroll costs for the month, 49,900 hours with a total cost of $599,520 are chargeable to Department A.

(4) Total overhead costs incurred by the department for the month consist of $241,800 of fixed overhead and $402,200 of variable overhead.

(5) A total of 9,000 units was completed during the month, and 2,000 units remain in process, 100 percent complete as to materials and 50 percent complete as to labor and overhead.

(6) Overhead is assigned to production on the basis of standard labor hours.

Required:

a. Prepare journal entries to record the above summarized data. (In the illustration in the chapter appendix, all variances were isolated at the end of the period. Use logic to isolate them as required in this problem.)

b. Compute the materials usage variance and the labor efficiency variance, and prepare journal entries to remove them from Work in Process Inventory.

c. Compute and prepare journal entries to record the overhead budget variance and the overhead volume variance.

d. Assuming the variances isolated are for the year ending July 31, 1986, prepare an entry that represents a practical disposition of these variances.

16

RESPONSIBILITY ACCOUNTING AND SEGMENT ANALYSIS

In a responsibility accounting system, **each accounting report contains only (or at least clearly segregates) those items which are controllable by the responsible manager;** this is the fundamental principle of responsibility accounting. Thus, responsibility accounting refers to an accounting system that collects, summarizes, and reports accounting data according to the **responsibility** of individual managers. A responsibility accounting system seeks to provide information to evaluate each manager on the revenue and expense items over which that manager has primary **control** (the authority to influence). The business entity must be well organized so that responsibility is assignable to individual managers.

Clear lines of authority and responsibility must exist throughout the organization. The various managers of the company, their responsibility levels, and the lines of authority existing within the entity should be as clearly defined as those shown in the organization chart in Illustration 16.1. If clear areas of authority cannot be determined, it is very doubtful that responsibility accounting can be implemented. Lines of authority should follow a specified path. For example, a plant supervisor may report to a plant manager, who reports to a vice president of manufacturing, who is responsible to the president. The president is ultimately responsible to the stockholders or their elected representatives, the board of directors. In a sense, the president is responsible for all revenue and expense

Illustration 16.1
FUNCTIONAL CORPORATE ORGANIZATION CHART
INCLUDING FOUR LEVELS OF MANAGEMENT

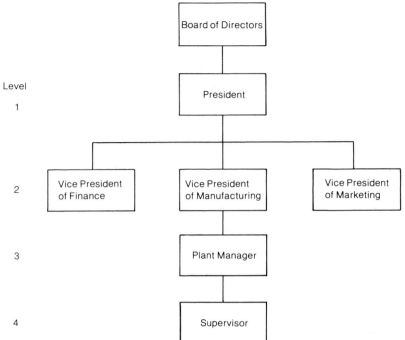

items of the firm, since at the presidential level all items are controllable. But the president will usually delegate authority to various managers, since the president cannot keep fully apprised of the day-to-day operating details of each of the firm's segments.

Reference is often made to levels of management. The president is usually considered the first-level manager. All the managers who report directly to the president are second-level managers. Notice on the organization chart (in Illustration 16.1) that the individuals within a given level are on a horizontal line across the chart. But not all managers within a certain level have equal authority and responsibility. The relative authority of certain types of managers will vary from firm to firm.

While the president may delegate much decision-making power, some revenue and expense items may be exclusively under the president's control. For example, large capital (plant and equipment) expenditures may be approved only by the president. Hence, depreciation, property taxes, and other related expenses should not be designated as the plant manager's responsibility, since these costs are not primarily under the plant manager's control. The controllability criterion is crucial in determining the content of the reports for each manager. For example, at the supervisor level, perhaps only direct materials and direct labor are appropriate for the task of measuring performance. But at the plant manager level many other costs, not controllable at a lower level, are controllable and are therefore included in the performance evaluation of the plant manager.

The Concept of Control

A manager must be able to exercise primary control over an item before being held responsible for it. Unfortunately, controllability is rarely absolute. Quite frequently, some factors which change the amount of a budgeted item are beyond the control of a manager. For example, the imposition of a 10 percent excise tax by a governmental authority may decrease the sales of certain items in a particular segment. Even though the manager is given authority to control the sales revenue, in this case external factors beyond the manager's control have altered the actual results. Internal factors may also be beyond a manager's control. For example, raw materials usage may be excessive because, in an effort to save money, the purchasing department bought low-quality materials. Most revenue or expense items have some elements of noncontrollability in them.

The theoretical requirement that a manager have absolute control over items for which that manager is held responsible must often be compromised. The manager is usually responsible for items in which *relative* control is present. **Relative control means that the manager has the predominant control over most of the factors which influence the given budget item.** The use of relative control may lead to some motivational problems, since the manager is evaluated on results that may not reflect that manager's efforts. Nevertheless, most budget plans assign control on a relative control basis in order to develop and use segmental budgets.

Responsibility Reports—How They Relate to Each Other

A unique feature of a responsibility accounting system is the amount of detail in the various reports issued to the different levels of management. For example, a performance report to a particular supervisor would include the dollar amounts, actual and budgeted, of all the revenue and expense items under that supervisor's control. But the report issued to the plant manager would show only the totals from all the supervisors' reports and any additional items subject to the plant manager's control, such as the plant administrative expense. The report to the vice president of manufacturing would contain only the totals of all the plants. Because a responsibility accounting system selectively condenses data, the report to the president does not consist of stapling together the reports of all the plant supervisors. Only the summary totals of the subordinate levels are reported (see Illustration 16.4). This lack of detail, which seems a hindrance to performance analysis, actually results in the practice of "management by exception." Since modern business enterprises are becoming increasingly complex, it has become necessary to filter and condense accounting data so that they may be analyzed quickly. Most executives do not have the time to study detailed accounting reports, searching for problem areas. Reporting only summary totals highlights those areas that need attention, so that the executive can make more efficient use of available time.

The reports issued under the responsibility accounting system are interrelated since the totals from one level are carried forward in the report to the next higher management level. The control reports submitted to the president include all revenue and expense items (in summary form) since the president is responsible for controlling the profitability of the entire firm.

The condensation which occurs at successive levels of management is justified on the basis that the appropriate manager will take the necessary corrective action. Hence, performance details need not be reported except to the particular manager. The manager should be able to describe to the immediate supervisor the action that was taken to correct an undesirable situation. For example, if direct labor cost has been excessively high in a particular department, the supervisor should seek to correct the cause of this variance. The plant manager, upon noticing the unfavorable total budget variance of the department, will investigate. The supervisor should be able to respond that the appropriate corrective action was taken. Hence, it is not necessary to report to the vice president of manufacturing that a particular department within one of the plants is not operating satisfactorily, since the plant manager has already attended to the matter. If the plant as a whole under a plant manager has been performing poorly, then the summary totals which have been reported to the vice president of manufacturing will disclose this situation and an investigation of the plant manager's problems might be indicated.

Responsibility Reports— Noncontrollable Items

In preparing responsibility accounting reports, there are two basic ways of handling revenue or expense items which are noncontrollable at the manager's level. First, they may be omitted entirely from the reports and then included in the reports at the management levels at which they become controllable. As a result, each level of reports contains only those items which are controllable at that level. The second method includes all revenue and expense items which can be traced directly or allocated indirectly to a particular manager. This method represents a full-costing approach. When used, care must be taken to separate controllable from noncontrollable items in such reports.

Timeliness of reports. In order for accounting reports to be of maximum benefit, they must be timely; that is, reports should be prepared as soon as possible after the end of the performance measurement period. Timely reports allow prompt corrective action to be taken. Reports that are excessively delayed lose their effectiveness as control devices. For example, a report on the previous month's operations that is not received until the end of the current month is virtually useless for analyzing poor performance areas and taking corrective action. Reports should be issued regularly. Regular reports are desirable since they enable trends to be spotted. The appropriate management action can then be initiated before major problems occur. Regularity is also important because it leads managers to rely on the reports and to become familiar with their contents.

Simplicity of reports. Reports should be relatively simple. Care should be taken to avoid confusing terminology. Particularly at lower levels of management, aggregate dollar amounts may not be sufficient. Results should also be expressed in physical units when appropriate. It is desirable to report budgeted amounts as well as actual amounts. Often a year-to-date analysis is included in addition to an analysis of the current period. The inclusion of variances from budgeted amounts permits relative performance to be ascertained. Carefully analyzing budget variances highlights the significant deviations from the budgeted plan, allowing management to spot problem areas quickly. Thus, the use of variances is helpful in applying the management-by-exception principle.

Responsibility Reports—Illustration

The following illustration is designed to show how responsibility accounting reports in an organization are interrelated.

We will assume an organization with four management levels, of which the president, vice president (manufacturing), plant manager, and supervisor are representative (see Illustration 16.2). The fourth level is considered to be the supervisor and so on up to the first level, the president (as shown in Illustration 16.3).

The reports shown in Illustration 16.4 contain only controllable expenses. Notice that only the totals from the supervisor's responsibility report are included in the plant manager's report. In turn, only the totals on the plant manager's report are included in the report for the vice president, and so on. The detailed data from the lower level reports are summarized and carried onto the report for the next higher level. Also, new controllable costs are introduced into the reports for levels 3, 2, and 1 which were not included in a lower level report. For instance, the president's office expense, included as the first item in the president's report, and the vice presidents' salaries were not reported at a lower level (because they were not controllable at a lower level).

The reports also show variation from the budgeted amounts for the month and for the year to date.

On the basis of the reports (see Illustration 16.4), it is probable

Illustration 16.2
ORGANIZATION CHART

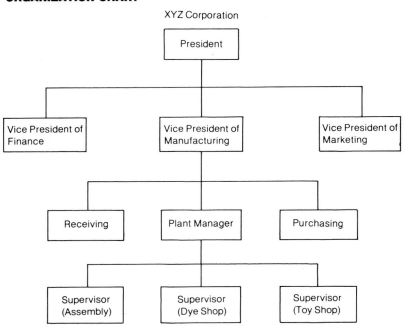

Illustration 16.3
RESPONSIBILITY REPORTS

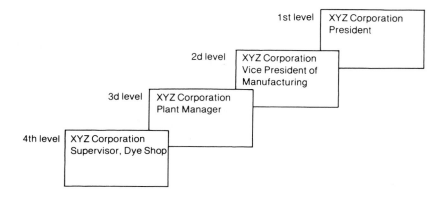

Illustration 16.4
RESPONSIBILITY REPORT

XYZ CORPORATION

Fourth level:
  Supervisor, dye shop

Controllable Expenses	Amount		Over or (Under) Budget	
	This Month	Year to Date	This Month	Year to Date
Repairs and maintenance	$ 200	$ 1,000	$ 10	$ 40
Supplies	180	850	80	95
Tools	100	300	(10)	81
Overtime	200	450	80	14
Total (include in report for next higher level) . .	$ 680	$ 2,600	$ 160	$ 230

Third level:
  Plant manager

Controllable Expenses	Amount		Over or (Under) Budget	
	This Month	Year to Date	This Month	Year to Date
Plant manager's office expense	$ 800	$ 9,100	$ (50)	$ (100)
Dye shop costs	680	2,600	160	230
Toy shop costs	1,000	5,000	80	130
Assembly	400	1,300	60	240
Salaries of supervisors	5,000	25,000	–0–	–0–
Total (include in report for next higher level) . .	$ 7,880	$ 43,000	$ 250	$ 500

Second level:
  Vice president of manufacturing

Controllable Expenses	Amount		Over or (Under) Budget	
	This Month	Year to Date	This Month	Year to Date
Vice president's office expense	$ 2,840	$ 9,500	$ (50)	$ (800)
Plant departmental costs	7,880	43,000	250	500
Purchasing	380	2,500	100	200
Receiving	700	3,000	300	900
Salaries of plant manager and heads of purchasing and receiving	7,000	35,000	–0–	–0–
Total (include in report for next higher level) . .	$18,800	$ 93,000	$ 600	$ 800

First level:
  President

Controllable Expenses	Amount		Over or (Under) Budget	
	This Month	Year to Date	This Month	Year to Date
President's office expense	$ 1,000	$ 5,000	$ 100	$ 200
Vice president of manufacturing	18,800	93,000	600	800
Vice president of marketing	8,700	19,000	400	800
Vice president of finance	4,000	15,000	800	900
Vice presidents' salaries	9,000	45,000	–0–	–0–
Total	$41,500	$177,000	$1,900	$2,700

is given later in the chapter.

Investment centers. Closely related to the profit center concept is the concept of an investment center. Each segment is considered an investment center which is evaluated on the basis of the rate of return that it can earn on a specified investment base. Rate of return is computed by dividing segmental earnings by the appropriate investment base. For example, a segment that earns $100,000 on an investment base of $1,000,000 is said to have a rate of return on investment of 10 percent. Of course, there is a question as to the appropriate investment base that should be utilized in calculating return on investment.

The logic for using investment centers as bases for performance evaluation is that segments with larger amounts of resources should produce more earnings than segments with smaller amounts of re-that the supervisor would take immediate action to see why supplies and overtime were significantly over the budget this·month. The plant manager might ask the supervisor what the problems were and whether they are now under control. The vice president might ask the same question of the plant manager (and of the head of receiving). And the president might ask each of the vice presidents why the budget was exceeded this month.

Responsibility Centers Various references have been made to the **segments** of a business enterprise. Examples of segments are divisions, departments, product lines, and service centers. The organization of appropriate business segments is crucial to successful budgeting. The segments of a business enterprise must be defined according to function or product line. For example, companies have traditionally been organized along

sources. By calculating rates of return for performance evaluation, the relative effectiveness of a segment is measured. Thus, the segment with the highest percentage return is presumably the most effective in utilizing its resources. When the absolute amount of earnings is used to measure performance, larger segments will have a distinct advantage over smaller segments.

Normally the assets available to the division make up the base. But there are differences of opinion among accountants as to whether depreciable assets should be shown at cost less accumulated depreciation, at cost, or at current replacement cost. The use of these bases is discussed later in the chapter.

After the appropriate investment base has been selected and valued to the satisfaction of the manager, problem areas can remain since most segment managers have limited control over certain items. For instance, capital expenditure decisions are often made by the top-level management of the company. Another problem area may exist if the firm has a centralized credit and collection segment. Thus, the manager may have little control over the amount of accounts receivable shown as segment assets. It is usually argued that all segments are given the same treatment and that the inclusion of noncontrollable items in the investment base is therefore appropriate. But in order to avoid adverse reactions it is important that the segment managers agree to this proposition.

SEGMENTAL ANALYSIS The fundamentals of responsibility accounting have been described. Now we will expand the discussion of the investment center concept. Some other aspects of segmental analysis will also be discussed.

The concept of decentralization is relevant to the discussion. Decentralization refers to the extent to which management decision making is dispersed to lower echelons of the organization. In other words, the extent of decentralization refers to the degree of control which segment managers have over the revenues, expenses, and assets of their segments. When a segment manager has control over all three of these, the investment center concept can be used. Thus, the more decentralized the decision making in an organization, the more applicable is the investment center concept to the segments of the organization. The more centralized the decision making, the more likely is one to find responsibility centers established as expense centers.

Typical investment centers are large, autonomous segments of very large companies. These segments are often separated from one another by location, types of products, functions, and/or necessary management skills. Segments such as these often seem like separate companies to an outside observer. But the investment center concept can be applied wherever the manager has control over revenues, expenses, and assets—even in relatively small companies.

The advantages of decentralized decision making include the following:

1. Increased control over their segments gives managers experiences which train them for high-level positions in the company. The added responsibility and authority also represent "job enlargement" and often result in increased job satisfaction and motivation.

2. Top management can be more removed from day-to-day decision making at the lower echelons of the company and can manage by the exception principle. Removing top management from everyday problem solving enables it to concentrate on long-range planning and on control of the most significant problem areas.

3. Decisions can be made at the point where problems arise. It is often difficult for members of top management to make appropriate decisions when they are not intimately involved with the problem that has to be solved.

4. Since decentralization enables the investment center concept to be applied, performance evaluation criteria such as return on investment and residual earnings can be used. These concepts will be explained later in the chapter.

Concepts Used in Segmental Analysis

The concepts of variable cost, fixed cost, direct cost, indirect cost, net income of a segment, and contribution to indirect expenses need to be understood before the investment center analysis can begin. Variable cost and fixed cost were treated in Chapter 13. The other concepts will now be discussed.

Direct cost and indirect cost. As stated earlier in the chapter, costs may be either directly or indirectly related to a particular cost objective (a segment, a product, and so on). In other words, a cost is not "direct" or "indirect" in and of itself. It is only "direct" or "indirect" in relation to a given cost objective.

A cost is a direct cost of a cost objective if it is traceable to that cost objective. A cost is an indirect cost of a cost objective if it is not traceable to that objective but has been allocated to that objective. A particular cost may be direct for one cost objective and indirect for another cost objective. For instance, the salary of the manager of a company segment may be a direct cost of that segment but an indirect cost of one of the products manufactured by that segment.

Since a direct cost is traceable to a cost objective, it is likely that the cost will be eliminated if the cost objective is eliminated. For instance, if the plastics segment of a business is eliminated, the salary of the manager of that segment is likely to be eliminated. In any particular case, one may be able to think of a direct cost which would not be eliminated if the cost objective were eliminated, but this is the exception rather than the rule.

An indirect cost is not traceable to a cost objective. Therefore, an indirect cost only becomes an expense of the cost objective through allocation. An example is a situation in which the depreciation expense on the company headquarters building is allocated as an expense to each segment of the company. If a particular segment is eliminated, it is not likely that the expense will disappear; instead, that expense will be allocated to the remaining segments. Again, it may be possible in a given situation to identify an indirect cost which would be eliminated if the cost objective were eliminated, but this would be an exception to the general rule.

Since the direct costs of a unit are clearly identified with that unit, there is a **tendency** for such items to be **controllable** by the manager of that unit. And since the indirect costs of a unit become costs of a unit only through allocation, there is a **tendency** for such items to be **noncontrollable** by the manager of that unit. Indirect costs are controllable at some higher level, as is true for all costs. But care must be taken not to equate direct and controllable costs. A cost such as the salary of the supervisor of a unit may be direct to that unit and noncontrollable by that supervisor. But many costs are direct to a given unit and controllable by its manager.

Net income of a segment. To measure the contribution which a segment makes to overall company income, the income statement shown in Illustration 16.5 may be used. The **contribution margin** is equal to sales less variable expenses. The same concept can be expressed on a per unit basis, and it is used that way in Chapter 18.

Notice in the illustration that all variable expenses are direct expenses. Some fixed expenses are direct, while others are indirect.

An alternative format which could be used in reporting for a

Illustration 16.5
SEGMENTAL NET INCOME

	Segment		
	A	B	Total
Sales	$1,000,000	$700,000	$1,700,000
Less: Variable expenses (all direct expenses)	500,000	410,000	910,000
Contribution margin	$ 500,000	$290,000	$ 790,000
Less: Direct fixed expenses	120,000	170,000	290,000
Contribution to indirect expenses . . .	$ 380,000	$120,000	$ 500,000
Less: Indirect fixed expenses	90,000	160,000	250,000
Net income	$ 290,000	$ (40,000)	$ 250,000

segment is one which shows gross margin but does not show the contribution margin. That format would be as follows:

Sales	$XX
Less: Cost of goods sold	XX
Gross margin	$XX
Less: Other direct expenses	XX
Total*	$XX
Less: Indirect fixed expenses . . .	XX
Net Income	$XX

* This total may be labeled "contribution to indirect expenses" only if no indirect fixed manufacturing costs are included in the cost of goods sold.

This format moves the fixed direct manufacturing expenses into the category of cost of goods sold. Since some fixed costs are being deducted from sales immediately, the contribution margin figure cannot be shown. Also, some of the variable costs (selling and administrative) move down with the other direct expenses.

To illustrate, assume that detailed data for Segment A of Illustration 16.5 are as shown in the center column in Illustration 16.6. These data can be grouped into a "Contribution margin format," as shown on the left-hand side of Illustration 16.6 or into a "Gross margin format," as shown on the right-hand side. Using either format, indirect fixed expenses could be deducted to arrive at net income.

In determining the contribution which a segment makes to company profits, it is tempting to use the net income of the segment, since this figure is used in evaluating the performance of the entire company. But there is a problem with using this means of evaluation for segments within a company. Certain indirect fixed expenses are allocated to the segment, and the bases of allocation are often very arbitrary.

Arbitrary allocations of indirect fixed expenses. As stated above, indirect fixed expenses, such as depreciation on the home office administrative building or on the computer facility maintained at the home office, can be allocated to segments only on some arbitrary basis. An attempt is often made to allocate such expenses on the basis of benefit received, but this is not always possible. For instance, how does one determine the benefit which a given segment receives if the company makes a charitable contribution to a worthy cause? Yet costs such as these must be allocated to the segments on some basis if a net income approach is used.

For certain indirect expenses, allocations can be made on the basis of benefit received. For instance, if Segment A utilized 4,000 hours of the total of 10,000 hours of computer time, it could be charged with 40 percent of the total cost of the computer facility

Illustration 16.6
ALTERNATIVE FORMATS FOR ARRIVING AT CONTRIBUTION TO INDIRECT EXPENSES

Contribution Margin Format

Sales	$1,000,000
Less: Variable expenses	500,000
Contribution margin	$ 500,000
Less: Direct fixed expenses	120,000
Contribution to indirect expenses	$ 380,000

Given

Sales	$1,000,000
Variable manufacturing expenses	450,000
Fixed direct manufacturing expenses	20,000
Variable selling and administrative expenses	50,000
Fixed direct selling and administrative expenses	100,000

Gross Margin Format

Sales	$1,000,000
Less: Cost of goods sold	470,000
Gross margin	$ 530,000
Less: Other direct expenses	150,000
Contribution to indirect expenses*	$ 380,000

* In situations where indirect fixed manufacturing costs are included in the cost of goods sold, this title should not be used. Instead, the title "Total" should be used.

since this is proportional to the benefit received. (Where the benefit received is very clear-cut, one might even argue that the expense should be treated as a direct expense.)

For certain other expenses, allocations are made on the basis of responsibility for incurrence. For instance, assume that Segment A contracts with a magazine to run an advertisement which will benefit it and various other segments of the company. Often the entire cost of the advertisement will be allocated to Segment A since it was responsible for incurring that portion of the total advertising expense.

When neither "benefit" nor "responsibility" can be used to allocate indirect fixed expenses, some other basis which seems reasonable in the circumstances must be found. Often, such expenses are allocated on the basis of net sales for lack of a better basis for allocation. For instance, if Segment A's net sales are 60 percent of total company sales, then 60 percent of a certain indirect expense would be allocated to Segment A.

Due to the arbitrary nature of allocations of indirect fixed expenses, many companies do not allocate these expenses to their segments. Instead, these companies calculate the contribution to indirect fixed expenses and use this figure to determine the earnings contribution of each segment.

Contribution to indirect expenses. The net income figure for a segment does not show the amount by which company earnings would decrease if the segment were discontinued.

If management relied on the net income figure for a segment to judge the segment's contribution to income, it might conclude that Segment B in Illustration 16.5 should be eliminated. But what would have been the effect on earnings if Segment B had been eliminated? This action would have had the following effect:

Reduction in revenues		$700,000
Reduction in expenses:		
Variable expenses	$410,000	
Direct fixed expenses	170,000	580,000
Reduction in earnings of the company		$120,000

Notice that the reduction in earnings of $120,000 which would have resulted from eliminating Segment B is shown by its contribution to indirect expenses in Illustration 16.5.

The contribution to indirect expenses is a useful figure for determining whether or not a segment should be retained. For this reason and because the allocation of indirect fixed expenses are so arbitrary, many companies utilize an income statement (for internal use) which employs the format shown in Illustration 16.7.

495

Illustration 16.7
SEGMENTAL CONTRIBUTION TO INDIRECT EXPENSES

	Segment		
	A	B	Total
Sales	$1,000,000	$700,000	$1,700,000
Less: Variable expenses	500,000	410,000	910,000
Contribution margin	$ 500,000	$290,000	$ 790,000
Less: Direct fixed expenses	120,000	170,000	290,000
Contribution to indirect expenses . . .	$ 380,000	$120,000	$ 500,000
Less: Indirect fixed expenses			250,000
Net income			$ 250,000

Here the contribution margin format was utilized, although the gross margin format could have been used. Notice that no attempt is made to allocate indirect fixed expenses to the segments. This format focuses attention on the number of dollars which a segment contributes toward covering indirect expenses. If all indirect expenses are covered, then, of course, there is net income for the period.

Neither the net income of a segment approach nor the contribution to indirect expenses approach has utilized the investment center concept. The "investment base" has not yet been introduced into the analysis.

Investment Center Analysis

Consideration of the investment base transforms the performance criteria into an investment center analysis. You will recall that for a responsibility center to be treated as an investment center, the manager of that center must have control over revenues, expenses, and assets (investment). The following two criteria include the concept of investment base in the analysis. They are ROI (return on investment) and RE (residual earnings).

Return on investment (ROI). It seems reasonable that a segment which has a large amount of assets should earn more (in an absolute sense) than a segment which has a small amount of assets. Return on investment gives consideration to this by calculating the return (earnings) as a percentage of the assets employed (investment). The return on investment formula is:

$$\text{ROI} = \frac{\text{Earnings}}{\text{Investment}}$$

To illustrate, assume the facts shown in Illustration 16.8 for a company with three segments. Using ROI as a criterion for evaluating the segments, Segment 3 is performing the best (25 percent), Segment 2 is next (20 percent), and Segment 1 is performing the worst (10 percent).

Illustration 16.8
COMPUTATION OF RETURN ON INVESTMENT

	Segment			
	(1)	*(2)*	*(3)*	*Total*
a. Earnings	$ 100,000	$ 250,000	$ 500,000	$ 850,000
b. Investment	1,000,000	1,250,000	2,000,000	4,250,000
Return on investment:				
a ÷ b	10%	20%	25%	20%

Definitions of earnings and investment. Although this concept appears to be quite simple and forthright, its use presents several difficulties. These difficulties center on what is considered to be "earnings" and what is considered to be "investment." Illustration 16.9 shows the possible combinations of definitions of these terms which may be used and the situations in which they are appropriate.

The first set of definitions could conceivably be used for segmental evaluation, but we do not recommend its use. The indirect fixed expenses which are allocated to a segment prevent the use of this set of definitions for evaluating the earnings contribution of the segment. The presence of expenses which are not under the control of the manager prevents its use for evaluating the performance of the manager. Only if an evaluation of the earning power of an entire company is being made should the first set of definitions be

Illustration 16.9
POSSIBLE DEFINITIONS OF "EARNINGS" AND "INVESTMENT"

Possible Definitions of "Earnings"	Possible Definitions of "Investment"	When to Use the Definitions
1. Net income of the segment*	Total assets† directly or indirectly related to the segment (including those related to indirect fixed expenses allocated to the segment)	To evaluate the earning power of an entire company
2. Contribution to indirect expenses	Assets directly used by and identified with the segment	To evaluate the **rate** of earnings contribution of a segment
3. "Controllable" earnings—this would start with contribution to indirect expenses and would eliminate any revenues and direct expenses which were not under the segment manager's control (for example, the segment manager's own salary)	Assets under the "control" of the segment manager	To evaluate the earnings **performance** of the **manager** of the segment

* Often net *operating* earnings are used. This is defined as earnings before interest and taxes (EBIT).
† *Operating* assets are often used in the calculation. Assets not used in normal operations, such as land held for future use, are excluded.

used. Even then it may be preferable to use an ROI calculation which measures earning power without regard to the sources of assets; this can be done by dividing net operating income by operating assets, as was shown in Chapter 11. For definitions of these terms, see the notes to Illustration 16.9.

The second set of definitions is useful in evaluating the **rate** of earnings contribution of a segment. Indirect fixed expenses which are allocated to the segment are eliminated from the computation. Also, assets which are not directly used by the segment are eliminated from the investment base. The second set of definitions is not useful in evaluating the performance of the **manager** since items not under the control of the manager would be included.

The third set of definitions is useful in evaluating the earnings performance of a segment manager since all items not under the control of the manager have been eliminated. A fundamental principle of responsibility accounting is to evaluate responsibility center managers only on items under their control.

Valuation base. Another problem with the denominator is to determine what *valuation base* to use for plant assets. Some possibilities include original cost less accumulated depreciation, original cost, and current replacement cost. Each of these bases shall now be considered.

Original cost less accumulated depreciation is probably the most widely used valuation base. Original cost is the price paid to acquire an asset. One advantage of this method is that the amount can be readily determined. There are several disadvantages. The first is that many different methods of depreciation exist (straight line, sum-of-the-years' digits, double-declining balance, and so on). These different depreciation methods lead to different income amounts and to different asset amounts for two segments which would otherwise be identical. Thus, meaningful interfirm comparisons and intrafirm comparisons with other segments are hampered. Also, with this method, the older the plant assets, the higher the ROI tends to be. This results from the fact that the book value of the plant assets decreases as accumulated depreciation increases and earnings remain about the same or increase as a result of inflation. Also, when a segment with old plant assets is compared to a segment with new plant assets, the former will have a further advantage in that the original cost of the assets was lower.

The use of **original cost** gets rid of the problem of decreasing book values resulting from the growth in accumulated depreciation; but it does not solve the price-level problem. The ROI may still increase over time because earnings tend to increase due to inflation. Also, the earnings on old assets need to be much less than the earnings on new assets in order to achieve the same *rate* of return.

When **current replacement cost** is used, the problem of differing depreciation methods and the price-level problem disappear. Current replacement cost is the cost of replacing the present assets with similar assets which are in the same condition as those now in use. The one disadvantage of this method is that current replacement costs are often difficult to determine. But with the emphasis that is now being focused on this concept by the Financial Accounting Standards Board, these data may be more readily available in the future.

Expanded form of ROI computation. It is useful at times to break the ROI formula into two parts, as follows:

$$\text{ROI} = \frac{\text{Earnings}}{\text{Sales}} \times \frac{\text{Sales}}{\text{Investment}}$$

The first term, Earnings/Sales, is called **margin.** It is the percentage relationship of earnings to sales. This percentage also shows the number of cents of earnings that attach to each dollar of sales.

The second term, Sales/Investment, is called **turnover.** It is the number of times by which sales per year exceed the investment in assets.

Breaking the ROI formula into these two components is useful in determining a strategy for increasing the margin or the turnover or the net effect of the two in a particular case. For instance, assume that the manager of a segment is faced with the following return on investment for the past year:

$$\text{ROI} = \text{Margin} \times \text{Turnover}$$

$$\text{ROI} = \frac{\text{Earnings}}{\text{Sales}} \times \frac{\text{Sales}}{\text{Investment}}$$

$$\text{ROI} = \frac{\$100,000}{\$2,000,000} \times \frac{\$2,000,000}{\$1,000,000}$$

$$\text{ROI} = 5 \text{ percent} \times 2 \text{ times}$$

$$\text{ROI} = 10 \text{ percent}$$

The manager desires to increase ROI for the coming year. The following are illustrative of the strategies which might be used (each strategy is independent of the others).

1. Concentrate on increasing the margin while holding turnover constant. Pursuing this strategy would involve leaving selling prices as they are and making every effort to increase efficiency so as to reduce expenses. By doing so, expenses might be reduced by $40,000 without affecting sales and investment; if so, the new ROI would be:

$$\text{ROI} = \frac{\text{Earnings}}{\text{Sales}} \times \frac{\text{Sales}}{\text{Investment}}$$

$$\text{ROI} = \frac{\$140,000}{\$2,000,000} \times \frac{\$2,000,000}{\$1,000,000}$$

$$\text{ROI} = 7 \text{ percent} \times 2 \text{ times}$$

$$\text{ROI} = 14 \text{ percent}$$

2. Concentrate on increasing the turnover by reducing the investment in assets while holding income and sales constant. Working capital might be reduced or some land might be sold, reducing investment in assets by $200,000 without affecting sales and earnings; if so, the new ROI would be:

$$\text{ROI} = \frac{\text{Earnings}}{\text{Sales}} \times \frac{\text{Sales}}{\text{Investment}}$$

$$\text{ROI} = \frac{\$100,000}{\$2,000,000} \times \frac{\$2,000,000}{\$800,000}$$

$$\text{ROI} = 5 \text{ percent} \times 2.5 \text{ times}$$

$$\text{ROI} = 12.5 \text{ percent}$$

3. Perhaps actions could be taken which would affect both margin and turnover. An advertising campaign would probably increase sales and earnings. (Getting rid of nonproductive depreciable assets would decrease investment while increasing earnings.) Assume that an advertising campaign increased sales by $500,000 and earnings by $50,000. ROI would then be:

$$\text{ROI} = \frac{\text{Earnings}}{\text{Sales}} \times \frac{\text{Sales}}{\text{Investment}}$$

$$\text{ROI} = \frac{\$150,000}{\$2,500,000} \times \frac{\$2,500,000}{\$1,000,000}$$

$$\text{ROI} = 6 \text{ percent} \times 2.5 \text{ times}$$

$$\text{ROI} = 15 \text{ percent}$$

In the above example, both margin and turnover were increased as a result of the advertising campaign. But sometimes an increase in one is accompanied by a decrease in the other. For instance, assume that the advertising campaign increased sales by $500,000 but only increased earnings by $12,500. The resulting ROI would be:

$$\text{ROI} = \frac{\text{Earnings}}{\text{Sales}} \times \frac{\text{Sales}}{\text{Investment}}$$

$$ROI = \frac{\$112,500}{\$2,500,000} \times \frac{\$2,500,000}{\$1,000,000}$$

$$ROI = 4.5 \text{ percent} \times 2.5 \text{ times}$$

$$ROI = 11.25 \text{ percent}$$

In this illustration, the margin decreased from 5 percent to 4.5 percent, but turnover increased from 2 times to 2.5 times. The net result was an increase in ROI from 10 percent to 11.25 percent.

Residual earnings. The use of return on investment (ROI) can result in what is called "suboptimization." This term is defined as the situation in which segment managers take an action that is in their own (their segment's) interest but not in the best interests of the company as a whole.

To illustrate, assume that the manager of Segment 3 in Illustration 16.8 has an opportunity to take on a project involving an investment of $100,000 which will return 22 percent (or $22,000). Since the segment is already realizing a return on investment of 25 percent, the manager may decide to reject the project. But the overall company rate of return is only 20 percent, and this would be increased if the manager accepted the project.

To prevent suboptimization, the **residual earnings** concept is sometimes applied. Residual earnings are defined as the amount of earnings of a segment in excess of the desired minimum rate of return. This desired minimum rate is always equal to or greater than the cost of capital (the cost of raising capital—which is explained more fully in Chapter 20). In formula form, residual earnings are:

$$\frac{\text{Residual}}{\text{earnings}} = \text{Earnings} - (\text{Investment} \times \text{Desired minimum ROI})$$

When the earnings contribution of a segment is evaluated, "earnings" would be "contribution to indirect expenses" and "investment" would be "assets directly used by and identified with the segment." When the earnings performance of a segment manager is evaluated, "earnings" would be "controllable earnings" and "investment" would be "assets under the control of the segment manager." The residual earnings concept is generally not used for evaluating an entire company, since the problem of suboptimization for the company as a whole does not exist (by definition).

Using the data from Illustration 16.8 residual earnings would be found as shown in Illustration 16.10 (assuming a desired minimum ROI of 10 percent).

If the manager of Segment 3 were to accept the proposal mentioned above (a 22 percent return on an investment of $100,000),

Illustration 16.10
COMPUTATION OF RESIDUAL EARNINGS

	Segment			
	(1)	*(2)*	*(3)*	*Total**
a. Earnings	$ 100,000	$ 250,000	$ 500,000	850,000
b. Investment	1,000,000	1,250,000	2,000,000	4,250,000
c. Desired minimum ROI:				
$b \times 10\%$	100,000	125,000	200,000	425,000
d. Residual earnings:				
$a - c$	–0–	125,000	300,000	425,000

* Depending on the set of definitions used for earnings and investment, the total column may include amounts which do not equal the total when adding across. This is because some expenses will not be allocated and some assets will not be assigned to the segments if definition sets 2 or 3 in Illustration 16.9 are used.

the last two columns of Illustration 16.10 would be changed as follows:

	Segment 3	Total
a. Earnings	$ 522,000	$ 872,000
b. Investment	2,100,000	4,350,000
c. Desired minimum ROI:		
$b < t3x10\%$	210,000	435,000
d. Residual earnings:		
$a - c$	312,000	437,000

This example shows that the use of the residual earnings concept will prevent suboptimization in situations like this. The segment rated as the best is the one with the greatest amount of residual earnings rather than the one with the highest ROI rate. Segment managers will take those actions which will increase their residual earnings.

In evaluating the performance of a segment manager, comparisons should be made not only with the current budget and with other segments within the company but also with past performance in that segment and with similar segments in other companies. Consideration must be given to general economic conditions, to market conditions for the product being produced, and so on. A superior manager in Company A may be earning a return of 12 percent, which is above the return for similar segments in other companies but below the return for other segments in Company A. The other segments in Company A may be more profitable because of market conditions and the nature of the products rather than the performance of the segment manager. Careful judgment must be used whenever the performance of a responsibility center manager is being evaluated.

Transfer prices in segmental reporting. An introductory discussion of transfer prices was presented earlier in the chapter. The topic needs to be covered in greater depth here.

In many companies, segments sell goods or services to other segments within the company. Since no actual revenues accrue to the selling segment from these transactions, artificial revenues need to be created in order to use the profit or investment center concepts. As indicated earlier, there are various means for setting the transfer price. The transfer price will be used as revenue for the selling segment and as expense for the buying segment. Therefore, both segments have a keen interest in what price is set, and conflict may arise.

There does not seem to be a consensus in the literature regarding the procedure for establishing a transfer price in a given situation. Some of the possibilities for setting the transfer price include using:

1. Actual variable cost.
2. Actual full cost.
3. Standard variable cost.
4. Standard full cost.
5. Any of the four above plus a profit margin.
6. Market price.
7. Negotiated price.
8. Arbitrated price.

We discourage the use of actual cost since this allows the selling segment to pass on its inefficiencies to the buying segment. Thus, standard costs are preferable to actual costs. Also, the use of costs (with no profit margin) would severely hamper the use of the earnings center or investment center concepts. (There could be a "return" only in the sense that a positive contribution to indirect expenses might exist if the full cost was used as a transfer price.) It seems preferable to include some profit margin in the transfer price.

Ideally, an outside market exists for the item, and the outside price can be used in setting the transfer price. Where no such price exists, the transfer price may have to be negotiated between the two segments involved. If an agreement cannot be reached, an arbitration process may be necessary or the segment may have to be treated as an expense center.

In view of the above discussion, a procedure which seems reasonable in establishing a transfer price in a given situation is as follows:

1. If an outside market for the part exists, the best price of a reputable supplier might be used as the transfer price. Use of this price treats the segments involved as though they are actually separate

companies engaging in an "arm's-length" transaction. Occasionally, a price somewhat below the market price can be justified, based on savings in shipping costs, administrative costs, and so on, from selling internally. Or, the selling segment may have excess productive capacity which would otherwise lie idle. If the selling segment can obtain a transfer price of anything in excess of its variable costs of supplying the good or service, it will increase its earnings. Thus, the selling segment may be willing to accept a price below the market price. Use of an impartial arbitration board might be called for in making such adjustments to market price unless they can be negotiated by the two segments involved.

After the price has been established, the two segments must decide whether to "do business" with each other. The general rules are as follows:

a. The buying segment should be required to buy internally as long as the transfer price is not **above** some bona fide available outside price. This approach assumes that the selling segment can sell its output in the external market. Chapter 19 covers the situation where the decision is to make or buy a part, which is relevant if the selling segment cannot sell its output externally.

b. The selling segment should be required to sell internally as long as the transfer price allows the selling segment to earn as much on internal "sales" as on external sales.

2. If there is no outside market price, have the managers of the two segments involved negotiate a price.

3. Where there is no outside market price and negotiation fails, use arbitration.

a. Each segment could select one member of the arbitration board and then those two members could select the third member. The two segments could commit themselves to accepting and using the transfer price set by the arbitration board for a given period of time.

b. A floor price of the standard variable cost of supplying the good or service plus a profit margin, and a ceiling price of the full cost of supplying the good or service plus a profit margin, might be used by the board. The use of standard variable cost plus a profit margin could be justified for short-run use, since fixed costs do not change in the short run. Standard full costs plus a profit margin should be used in the long run, since all costs must be covered in the long run.

c. If arbitration would create too much hard feeling among representatives of the two segments, the good or service should be transferred at the standard full cost of supplying it (or the actual full cost if no standard cost system is in use) and the supplying segment should be treated as an expense center rather than an earnings or investment center.

In every case, top management should determine whether setting a transfer price at a particular level will cause segment managers to take actions which result in suboptimization. Top management must also decide whether to permit some suboptimization in order to promote the autonomy of segments or to discourage suboptimization so as to maximize overall company profits.

Segmental Reporting in External Financial Statements

Formerly, segmental information was reported only to management for internal decision-making puproses. In December 1976, the Financial Accounting Standards Board issued *Statement of Financial Accounting Standards No. 14*, entitled "Financial Reporting for Segments of a Business Enterprise." This statement requires publicly held companies to publish certain segmental information in their annual financial statements the information is not required in interim financial statements). Thus, external users of financial statements will have segmental information to aid them in their decision regarding such companies.

SUMMARY

A feature of the reports prepared under a responsibility accounting system is that the details in each report vary according to the level of management addressed. Higher levels of management need not be informed of the details of lower level activities since corrective action, if needed, has already taken place. The reports are related with summary totals (actual and budgeted) for the current period and the year to date being carried forward from one report to the next higher level report. All expenses and revenues (actual and per master budget) are summarized in the report to the president who is responsible for the profitability of the firm.

Responsibility reports should normally contain only items controllable at the reporting manager level. But, if a report contains noncontrollable items, they should be clearly separated from controllable items. Since timeliness enhances their utility, reports should be prompt and issued on a regular basis. Reports should be easy to understand—avoiding confusing accounting terminology—and should, when possible, show both dollars and units. The reports should permit the causes of variances to be analyzed.

For segmental analysis, costs are classified as direct and indirect. The direct costs of a segment can be traced to the segment and are the costs that would disappear if the segment were eliminated. The indirect costs would not disappear, and such costs cannot be traced to a segment and are associated with a segment only by allocation. Because they involve arbitrary allocations, indirect fixed expenses often are not allocated to the segments. Rather, a segmental contribution to indirect expenses is computed, which shows the amount by which the earnings of the company would decline if the segment were eliminated.

When a manager has control over the revenues, expenses, and assets (investment) of a segment, the investment center concept can be used to analyze the segment's activities. Such analyses typically involve calculation of the return on investment (ROI) or residual earnings (RE). Several alternative bases of valuation for plant assets may be used when calculating ROI, including original cost less depreciation, original cost, and current cost. The latter basis seems preferable although the first is widely used. Residual earnings may be used in segmental analysis in order to avoid the problem of suboptimization.

A transfer price must be used when a segment provides goods and services to another segment of the company in order for the selling segment to have a revenue amount for segmental analysis. The transfer price may be based on an external market price, if one exists. If an external price does not exist, the transfer price will have to be based on cost—actual or standard, full or variable, with or without a profit margin—or otherwise negotiated or arbitrated.

QUESTIONS

1. What is the fundamental principle of responsibility accounting?

2. Name three possible reporting bases for evaluating business segments.

3. What is the logic of using an investment center as a basis for performance evaluation?

4. How soon after the end of the performance measurement period should accounting reports be prepared? Explain.

5. Compare and contrast an expense center and an investment center.

6. Which categories of items must a segment manager have control over for the investment center concept to be applicable?

7. What connection is there between the extent of decentralization and the investment center concept?

8. Give some of the advantages of decentralized decision making.

9. Differentiate between a direct cost and an indirect cost of a segment. What happens to each category if the segment to which it is related is eliminated?

10. It is possible for a cost to be "direct" to one cost objective and "indirect" to another cost objective? Explain.

11. Indicate how each of the following is calculated for a segment:
    a. Gross margin.

b. Contribution margin.

c. Contribution to indirect expenses (under the two different formats).

d. Net income.

12. Describe some of the methods by which indirect expenses are usually allocated to a segment.

13. Give the general formula for return on investment (ROI). How may this formula be split into two components?

14. Give the three sets of definitions for "earnings" and "investment" which may be used in ROI calculations, and state when each set is applicable.

15. Give the various valuation bases that could be used for plant assets in investment center calculations. Discuss some of the advantages and disadvantages of these bases.

16. In what way is the use of the residual earnings (RE) concept superior to the use of return on investment (ROI)?

17. How are residual earnings determined?

18. If the residual earnings for Segment Manager A are $50,000, while the residual earnings for Segment Manager B are $100,000, does this necessarily mean that B is a better manager than A?

19. What purpose is served by setting transfer prices?

20. Assuming that an outside market exists for a part "sold" by Segment 1 to Segment 2, what procedure would you recommend for setting the transfer price? What rules would you have regarding whether the two segments must do business with each other after the transfer price has been set?

21. If there is no external market for the part referred to in Question 20, how should the transfer price be set? What if agreement cannot be reached?

EXERCISES

1. Describe a segment of a business enterprise that is best treated as an expense center. List four indirect expenses that may be allocated to such an expense center.

2. Douglas Company manufactures refrigerators. Below are listed several costs that occur. Indicate whether or not the shop supervisor can control each of the listed items.

a. Depreciation.

b. Repairs.

c. Small tools.

d. Supplies.

e. Bond interest.

3. List five important factors that should be considered in designing reports for a responsibility accounting system.

4. Given the following data, prepare a schedule which shows contribution margin, contribution to indirect costs, and net income of the segment:

Direct fixed expenses	$ 30,000
Indirect fixed expenses	25,000
Sales	250,000
Variable expenses	170,000

What would be the effect on company earnings if the segment was eliminated?

5. Three segments (A, B, and C) of the Hawker Company have net sales of $600,000, $400,000, and $200,000, respectively. A decision is made to allocate the pool of $60,000 of administrative overhead expenses of the home office to the segments, based on net sales.

   a. How much should be allocated to each of the segments?

   b. If Segment C is eliminated, how much would be allocated to A and B?

6. Two segments (tires and batteries) showed the following data for the most recent year:

	Tires	Batteries
Contribution to indirect expenses	$ 50,000	$ 144,000
Assets directly used by and identified with the segment	250,000	600,000
Sales	1,000,000	1,800,000

   a. Calculate return on investment (ROI) for each segment in the most direct manner.

   b. Calculate return on investment (ROI) utilizing the margin and turnover components.

7. Determine the effect of each of the following on the margin, turnover, and ROI of the tire segment in Exericse 6. Consider each change independently of the others.

   a. Direct variable expenses were reduced by $5,000, and indirect expenses were reduced by $7,500. Sales and assets were unaffected.

   b. Assets used by the segment were reduced by $50,000, while earnings and sales were unaffected.

   c. An advertising campaign increased sales by $100,000 and earnings by $16,000. Assets directly used by the segment remained unaffected.

8. The Young Company has three segments: red, white, and blue. Data concerning "earnings" and "investment" are as follows:

	Red	White	Blue
Contribution to indirect expenses	$ 20,000	$ 45,000	$ 70,000
Assets directly used by and identified with the segment	100,000	300,000	800,000

Assuming that the minimum desired return on investment is 10 percent, calculate the residual earnings of each of the segments. Do the results indicate that any of the segments should be eliminated?

9. Assume that for the red segment in Exercise 8, $5,000 of the direct

expenses and $20,000 of the segmental assets are not under the control of the segment manager. Top management wishes to evaluate the segment manager's earnings performance. Calculate the manager's return on investment and residual earnings. (Because certain expenses and assets are not controllable by the segment manager, the minimum desired ROI is 15 percent.)

PROBLEMS

16–1. You were given the following information for the Fletcher Company for the year ended December 31, 1986:

Controllable Expenses	Plant Manager Budget	Plant Manager Actual	Vice President of Manufacturing Budget	Vice President of Manufacturing Actual	President Budget	President Actual
Office expense	$ 4,500	$ 6,000	$ 7,500	$10,500	$ 15,000	$ 10,500
Printing shop	3,000	3,000				
Iron shop	1,500	1,350				
Toaster shop	12,000	12,000				
Purchasing			15,000	16,500		
Receiving			7,500	9,000		
Inspection			12,000	10,500		
Sales manager					120,000	105,000
Controller					90,000	75,000
Treasurer					60,000	45,000
Personnel manager					30,000	45,000

Required:

Prepare the responsibility accounting reports for three levels of management—plant manager, vice president of manufacturing, and president.

16–2. The Roland Corporation has three production plants, X, Y, and Z. These plants are treated as responsibility centers. The following summarizes the results for the month of March 1986:

Plant	Revenue	Expenses	Investment Base (gross assets)
X	$ 750,000	$375,000	$ 7,500,000
Y	1,500,000	600,000	11,250,000
Z	2,250,000	825,000	24,000,000

Required:

a. If the plants are treated as profit centers, which plant manager appears to have done the best job?

b. If the plants are treated as investment centers, which plant manager appears to have done the best job? (Assume that plant managers are evaluated in terms of ROI on gross assets.)

c. Do the results of profit center analysis and investment center analysis give different findings? If so, why?

16–3. Burns, Inc., allocates expenses and revenues to the two segments, R and S, that it operates. It extends credit to customers under a revolving charge plan whereby all account balances not paid within 30 days are charged interest at the rate of 1½ percent per month.

Given below are selected revenue and expense accounts and some additional data needed to complete the allocation of the one revenue amount and the expenses.

Revenue and Expenses (allocation bases)

Revolving charge service revenue (net sales)	$20,000
Home office building occupancy expense (net sales)	15,000
Buying expenses (net purchases)	50,000
General administrative expenses (number of employees in department)	25,000
Insurance expense (relative average inventory plus cost of equipment and fixtures in each department)	6,000
Depreciation expense on home office equipment (net sales) . .	10,000

Additional data:

	Segment R	Segment S	Total
Number of employees	3	7	10
Sales (net)	$100,000	$200,000	$300,000
Purchases (net)	80,000	120,000	200,000
Average inventory	20,000	40,000	60,000
Cost of equipment and fixtures .	30,000	60,000	90,000

Required:

a. Prepare a schedule showing allocation of the above items to segments R and S.

b. Present criticisms of some of these allocation bases.

16–4. Rose, Inc., is a company with two segments, 1 and 2. Its revenues and expenses for 1986 are as follows:

	Segment 1	Segment 2	Total
Sales (net)	160,000	$240,000	$400,000
Direct expenses:*			
Cost of goods sold	75,000	165,000	240,000
Selling	22,800	12,000	34,800
Administrative:			
Bad debts	5,000	3,000	8,000
Insurance	4,000	2,000	6,000
Interest	800	400	1,200
Indirect expenses (all fixed):			
Selling			30,000
Administrative			42,000

* All the direct expenses are variable except insurance and interest, which are fixed.

Required:

a. Prepare a schedule showing the contribution margin, the contribution to indirect expenses of each segment, and net income for the company as a whole. Do not allocate indirect expenses to the segments.

b. Assume that indirect selling expenses are to be allocated on the basis of net sales and that indirect administrative expenses are to be allocated on the basis of direct administrative expenses.

Prepare a statement (starting with the contribution to indirect expenses) which shows the net income of each segment.

c. Comment on the appropriateness of the "earnings" amounts shown in parts *(a)* and *(b)* for determining the earnings contribution of the segments.

16–5. The Russell Corporation has three segments. Results of operations for 1986 were as follows:

	Segment 1	Segment 2	Segment 3	Total
Sales	$25,000,000	$15,000,000	$10,000,000	$50,000,000
Variable expenses .	18,000,000	8,500,000	6,750,000	33,250,000
Fixed expenses:				
Direct	3,500,000	1,250,000	500,000	5,250,000
Indirect				2,500,000

The following direct fixed expenses were not under the control of the segment manager: segment 1, $250,000; segment 2, $175,000; and segment 3, $200,000.

For the company's total operating assets of $70,000,000, the following facts exist:

	Segment 1	Segment 2	Segment 3
Assets directly used by and identified with the segment	$35,000,000	$20,000,000	$10,000,000
Assets under the "control" of the segment manager	30,000,000	16,000,000	8,000,000

Required:

a. Prepare a statement showing the contribution margin and the contribution to indirect expenses for each segment and the total income of the Smith Corporation.

b. Determine the ROI for evaluating (1) the earning power of the entire company, (2) the rate of income contribution of each segment, and (3) the earnings performance of each segment manager.

c. Comment on the results of part *(b)*.

16–6. The Hollis Company operates with three segments, K, L, and M. Data regarding these segments are as follows:

	Segment K	Segment L	Segment M
Contribution to indirect expenses	$ 90,000	$ 50,000	$ 40,000
Earnings controllable by the manager	125,000	75,000	64,000
Assets directly used by and identified with the segment . .	500,000	400,000	200,000
Assets under the "control" of the segment manager . . .	440,000	355,000	180,000

Required:

a. Calculate the ROI for each segment and each segment manager. Rank them from highest to lowest.

b. Assume that the minimum desired rates of return are 12 percent for a segment and 20 percent for a segment manager. Calculate the RE for each segment and each manager. Rank them from highest to lowest.

c. Repeat *(b)*, but now assume the desired minimum rates of return are 17 percent for a segment and 25 percent for a segment manager. Rank them from highest to lowest.

b. Comment on the rankings achieved.

16–7. The Orange segment of the Beverage Corporation reported the following data for 1986:

Contribution to indirect expenses	$ 2,100,000
Assets directly used by and identified with the segment . .	16,800,000
Sales	33,600,000

Required:

a. Determine the margin, turnover, and ROI for the segment in 1986.

b. Determine the effect on margin, turnover, and ROI of the segment in 1987 if each of the following changes were to occur. Consider each one separately, and assume that any items not specifically mentioned remain the same as in 1986.

1. A new labor contract with the union increased expenses by $600,000 for 1987.
2. A strike in early 1987 shut down operations for two months. Sales decreased by $9,000,000, cost of goods sold by $6,000,000, and other direct expenses by $1,800,000.
3. Introduction of a new product caused sales to increase by $12,000,000, cost of goods sold by $8,400,000, and other direct expenses by $900,000. Assets increased by $1,800,000.
4. An advertising campaign was launched. As a result, sales increased by $3,000,000, cost of goods sold by $2,100,000, and other direct expenses by $900,000.

17

THE BUDGET—FOR PLANNING AND CONTROL

Effective utilization of the scarce resources of time and wealth requires planning. But planning alone is insufficient. Control must also be exercised to see that if a plan is feasible, it is actually carried out. A budget is a tool widely used in planning and controlling the use of scarce resources.

There are various types of budgets. **Responsibility budgets** were covered in the preceding chapter. Responsibility budgets are designed to evaluate the performance of individual managers. **Capital budgets** will be covered in Chapter 20. Capital budgets are prepared in order to evaluate particular long-term projects, such as the addition of equipment or the relocation of a plant. Another type of budget, the **master budget,** is the topic of this chapter. The master budget consists of two parts, the **operating budget** and the **financial budget.** The operating budget is a projected income statement. The financial budget is a projected balance sheet.

Before discussing the master budget, we will take up some considerations regarding budgeting in general.

Purposes of Budgets   In business, a budget is simply a plan showing how management intends to acquire and use resources and to control the acquisition and use of resources during a coming time period. The budget has often been referred to as a formal quantitative expression of management's plans. Yet a budget is much more than that; it forces all levels of management to think ahead, anticipate results, and take action to remedy possible poor results.

Budgets may be used to motivate individuals, causing them to strive vigorously to achieve stated goals; they may also be used to appraise the performance of individuals. For instance, the standard variable cost of producing a given part at a given cost center is a budget figure against which actual performance can be compared in order to evaluate the performance of that cost center.

Many other benefits result from the preparation and use of budgets. The activities of the business are better coordinated; individual members of its management become aware of the problems of other management members; employees may become cost-conscious and seek to conserve resources; the organizational plans of the enterprise may be reviewed more often and changed where needed; and a breadth of vision, which might not otherwise be developed, is fostered.

Considerations in Preparing Budgets

Uncertainty with regard to future developments is a poor excuse for failure to budget; in fact, the less stable the conditions, the more necessary and desirable is budgeting. Obviously, stable operating conditions permit greater reliance on past experience as a basis for budgeting. But it must be emphasized that budgets are based on more than past results. Future plans must also be considered.

A budget plan should explicitly spell out management's assumptions relating to (1) the state of the economy over the planning horizon; (2) plans for adding, deleting, or changing product lines; (3) the nature of the industry's competition; and (4) the effect of existing or possible government regulations. If the assumptions change during the budget period, an analysis of the effects of those changes should be made and consideration should be given to that analysis in the evaluation of the company's performance.

In the preparation of a budget, accounting data play an important part. The details of the budget must be in agreement with the accounts maintained in the company's ledgers. The accounts, in turn, must be designed to facilitate the preparation of the budget and the usual financial statements as well as the numerous reports—cost and financial—that are prepared quarterly, monthly, weekly, or even daily to help exercise operational control.

During the budget period, repeated comparisons of accounting data and budgeted projections should be made and the differences investigated. But it should be noted that budgeting is not a substitute for management and that a budget is not self-operating. Instead, the budget is designed merely as a tool—but an important one—of managerial control.

Budget periods vary in length, but they usually coincide with the accounting period. Normally, the budget period is broken into months or quarters, and the greater the uncertainty faced, the more likely is the budget period to be broken into short periods.

Some General Principles of Budgeting

Budgeting involves the coordination of financial and nonfinancial planning to satisfy the goals and objectives of the organization. Although there is no foolproof way to prepare an effective budget, the following points should be considered carefully when preparing a budget:

A. Top-management support.

  All levels of management must be aware of the importance of the budget to the firm. Plans must be stated explicitly, and overemphasis on pure mechanics avoided. Overall broad objectives of the company must be decided upon and communicated throughout the organization.

B. Participation in goal setting.

  It is generally believed that an employee is more likely to strive to achieve organizational goals if the employee participates in setting those goals.

C. Responsibility accounting.

  People should know their own performance goals. Only those costs over which an individual has predominant control should be used in the evaluation of the individual's performance.

D. Communication of results.

  People should be informed of their own progress in a timely and meaningful manner. Effective communication implies (1) timeliness, (2) reasonable accuracy, and (3) understandability. Results should be communicated in such a manner that adjustments can be made, if needed.

E. Flexibility.

  As the basic assumptions underlying the preparation of the budget are altered during the year, the budget should be restated so that the efficiency of the actual level of operations can be analyzed.

Behavioral Implications of Budgeting

Too often the term **budget** has very negative connotations to personnel who feel that they are **subjected to** a budget. Often in the past, a budget has been imposed by management without giving consideration to the opinions and feelings of the personnel affected. Such imposed budgets may bring on both overt and subtle resistance. Such resistance may be encountered for a number of reasons. These might include a lack of understanding about the program, concern about status, an expectation of increased pressure, a feeling that the method of performance evaluation is unfair, a feeling that the goals are unrealistic and unattainable, lack of confidence in the manner in which accounting figures are generated, and a preference for

515

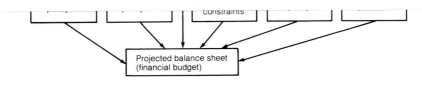

517

more informal communication and evaluation. Often these objections are completely unfounded, but the important thing is that the employees may not believe they are, and this may make it very difficult to accomplish the aims of budgeting. The problems encoun-

get will often require the preparation of work sheets. These analyses include items such as planned accounts receivable collections and balances, planned materials purchases and inventories, changes in all accounts affected by operating costs, and the amount of federal income taxes payable. Dividend policy, financing policy and constraints, credit policy, and any planned capital expenditures also affect the amounts shown in the financial budget.

We will now illustrate the preparation of a master budget for the Randal Company. If you follow the example closely, you should be able to prepare a master budget for an actual company.

THE MASTER BUDGET ILLUSTRATED

Preparing the Planned Operating Budget in Units

The planned operating budget at the expected level of operations is first developed in terms of units rather than dollars in the illustration. Since revenues and the bulk of the costs to be incurred will vary with volume, forecasts of revenues and costs can be derived more easily after quantities have been established. After analyzing various factors affecting sales, assume that sales for the year are forecast at 100,000 units. Quarterly sales are expected to be 20,000, 35,000, 20,000, and 25,000 units. In line with the company policy of stabilizing production, the 100,000 units will be produced uniformly throughout the year at the rate of 25,000 units per quarter. A simplifying assumption made at this time is to assume away the existence of any beginning or ending work in process inventories. A more realistic assumption would be that work in process inventories will remain stable throughout the year.

From the above data, a schedule of budgeted sales and production in terms of units is prepared, as shown in Illustration 17.2. Note the fluctuation in the ending inventory which must be accepted if sales vary and the management policy of stable production is to

Illustration 17.2

RANDAL COMPANY
Planned Sales and Production
(in units of product)

	Quarter Ending	
	March 31, 1986	*June 30, 1986*
Sales forecast in units	20,000	35,000
Production planned	25,000	25,000
Increase (decrease) in finished goods inventory	5,000	(10,000)
Planned beginning finished goods inventory	10,000*	15,000
Planned ending finished goods inventory	15,000	5,000

* Actual on January 1.

be implemented. Thus, the finished goods inventory serves the function of absorbing the difference between production and sales. A management decision has been made that it is less costly to deal with fluctuating inventories than with fluctuating production.

Preparing the Planned Operating Budget in Dollars

The operating budget is now converted from units into dollars. A forecast of expected selling prices must be made. In addition, an analysis of costs must be made along the lines previously outlined. The forecast selling prices and costs are as shown in Illustration 17.3. Note that the costs are classified according to whether they are variable or fixed in nature and are budgeted accordingly. **Variable costs** are those which vary in total directly with production or sales. **Fixed costs** are those which are unaffected in total by the relative level of production or sales. Thus, variable costs are budgeted as a constant amount **per unit,** while fixed costs are budgeted only in total. Individual budgets could be prepared for each of the identifiable units of the entity and accumulated to form the overall budget; this is true for each budget area to be discussed in the remainder of the chapter.

Illustration 17.3

RANDAL COMPANY
Budget Estimates of Selling Price and Costs
For the Quarters Ending March 31 and June 30, 1986

Forecast selling price per unit . . . . . . $	20
Manufacturing costs:	
Variable (per unit manufactured)	
Raw materials	2
Direct labor	6
Overhead	1
Fixed overhead (total each quarter) . . .	75,000
Selling and administrative expenses:	
Variable (per unit sold)	2
Fixed (total each quarter)	100,000

A schedule showing the development of the forecast for cost of goods manufactured and sold is now prepared, as shown in Illustration 17.4. Separate schedules are then prepared for all of the selling and administrative expenses and their totals entered for each of the first two quarters, as shown in Illustration 17.5. Except for the income tax accrual, all of the items appearing in the operating budget (Illustration 17.5) have been explained previously. Income taxes are budgeted at an assumed level of 50 percent of net income before taxes.

Illustration 17.5 shows the resulting operating budgets. As noted

Illustration 17.4

RANDAL COMPANY
Planned Cost of Goods Manufactured and Sold

	Quarter Ending	
	March 31, 1986	June 30, 1986
Beginning finished goods inventory	$130,000*	$180,000
Cost of goods manufactured:		
Raw materials (25,000 × $2)	$ 50,000	$ 50,000
Direct labor (25,000 × $6)	150,000	150,000
Variable overhead (25,000 × $1)	25,000	25,000
Fixed overhead (per Illustration 17.3) . . .	75,000	75,000
Cost of goods manufactured (25,000 units at $12)	$300,000	$300,000
Goods available for sale	$430,000	$480,000
Ending finished goods inventory:		
15,000 at $12†	180,000	
5,000 at $12		60,000
Cost of goods sold	$250,000	$420,000

* Actual on January 1.
† First-in, first-out procedure assumed.

previously, if the above operating budget does not reveal the desired net income, new plans will have to be formulated and new budgets developed. But the purpose of preparing such an operating budget is to gain some knowledge of what the outcome of a period's activities will be prior to their actual occurrence.

Illustration 17.5

RANDAL COMPANY
Planned Operating Budget
For Quarters Ending March 31, and June 30, 1986

	Quarter Ending	
	March 31, 1986	June 30, 1986
Forecast sales (20,000 and 35,000 at $20) . . .	$400,000	$700,000
Cost of goods sold (per Illustration 17.4)	250,000	420,000
Gross margin	$150,000	$280,000
Selling and administrative expenses:		
Variable (20,000 and 35,000 at $2)	$ 40,000	$ 70,000
Fixed (per Illustration 17.3)	100,000	100,000
Total expenses	$140,000	$170,000
Net income before income taxes	$ 10,000	$110,000
Estimated federal income taxes (50%)	5,000	55,000
Net income	$ 5,000	$ 55,000

THE FLEXIBLE OPERATING BUDGET

One of the basic principles of budgeting is to adjust the budget for changes in assumptions, or changes in the level of operations. To cope with such changes, a technique known as flexible budgeting has been developed. The preparation of a flexible operating budget will include detailed estimates of expenses at various levels of output. For example, a flexible budget of manufacturing overhead costs at varying levels of output would be as shown in Illustration 17.6.

Illustration 17.6
FLEXIBLE OPERATING BUDGET

Element of Overhead	Volume (percentage of capacity)			
	70 Percent	80 Percent	90 Percent	100 Percent
Supplies	$ 4,200	$ 4,800	$ 5,400	$ 6,000
Power	11,500	13,000	14,500	16,000
Insurance	4,500	4,500	5,000	5,000
Maintenance	12,000	13,000	14,000	14,800
Depreciation	20,000	20,000	20,000	20,000
Supervision	28,000	28,000	28,000	28,000
	$80,200	$83,300	$86,900	$89,800

In Illustration 17.6, supplies are considered a strictly variable cost, although there are probably few costs that vary in an exact linear relationship with output. Power is a mixed (or semivariable) cost, since a fixed lumped sum must be paid at low levels of usage and above that level the cost varies directly with output. Depreciation and supervision are fixed costs. Insurance and maintenance are step variable costs since they increase in steps as volume increases.[1] When a flexible budget is prepared, the amount of costs considered to be the budgeted amount in appraising performance is read from the flexible budget for the actual level of output experienced.

BUDGET VARIANCES

A budget variance is defined as the difference between an actual cost experienced at a certain level of operations and the budgeted amount for that same level of operations. Budget variances may be viewed as indicators or indices of efficiency, since they emerge from a comparison of "what was" with "what was planned or expected." To compute a budget variance, a flexible budget must be used. As an illustration of a way in which a flexible budget may be used, assume that the departmental budget in Illustration 17.6 is prepared based on the expectation of producing 100,000 units of product—the 100 percent of capacity level. Under that expecta-

---

[1] See pages 543–47 for a more complete description of the various types of cost behavior.

tion, the budgeted amount for supplies would be $6,000, or $0.06 per unit. If at the end of the period, the actual amount of supplies consumed amounted to $5,600, the first impression is that there was a favorable variance of $400. But if the production of the period was only 90,000 units, there was actually an unfavorable variance of $200. The flexible budget shows that at 90 percent of capacity, the supplies that should have been consumed amount to only $5,400. Consequently, there appears to have been some inefficiency involved in the use of supplies, and an unfavorable budget variance of $200 ($5,600 − $5,400) is said to exist.

In another situation, maintenance may have been budgeted at $13,000 for a given period in the expectation that 80,000 units of product would be produced; this is at the 80 percent of capacity level. If actual maintenance costs total $13,900 for the period, this does not mean that an unfavorable variance of $900 has been incurred. Production volume must be known; assume it to be 90,000 units. At this level, maintenance costs are budgeted at $14,000, and, therefore, a favorable variance of $100 was actually experienced.

The main advantage of the use of a flexible operating budget along with the planned operating budget is that they allow for appraisal of performance on two levels. First, comparison of actual results with the planned operating budget permits the deviation from expected output to be analyzed. Then, given the actual level of operations, the actual costs can be compared with the expected costs for that level of output shown in the flexible operating budget.

The existence of flexible or formula budgets makes it unnecessary to prepare new budget estimates when the actual volume differs from the expected volume. In the case of directly variable costs, the expected cost at any level can be computed easily. In the case of certain mixed (or semivariable) costs which are partially fixed and partially variable, the budget amount for any level of operations other than that presented can be computed from the following formula: Budget amount = Fixed costs + (Variable costs per unit × Units of output). More complicated formulas are needed if the relationship between costs and volume above a minimum level of costs is not linear, that is, if the costs do not vary proportionately with production.

Step variable costs change only when a sufficiently large increase in production occurs, as, for example, when one additional inspector must be added for each 20 percent of capacity utilized. Such step variable costs can usually be read directly from the flexible budget.

The preparation of budgets for selling expenses and for general administrative expenses is similar to the preparation of the manufacturing overhead budget. Several supporting budgets may be involved, such as budgets for advertising expenses, office expenses, and payroll department expenses. In each case the supporting budget may show the fixed, variable, mixed and step variable expenses at various levels of sales volume.

THE FLEXIBLE OPERATING BUDGET AND BUDGET VARIANCES ILLUSTRATED

The Randal Company has prepared a planned operating budget and a detailed flexible operating budget for the quarter ending March 31, 1986. The planned operating budget is based on the data in Illustration 17.3. The planned operating budget, based on expected sales of 20,000 units and expected production of 25,000 units, and the actual results for the year are shown in Illustration 17.7.

Illustration 17.7

RANDAL COMPANY
Comparison of Planned Operating Budget and Actual Results

	Planned Operating Budget	Actual	Budget Variance (Unfavorable)
Sales	$400,000	$380,000	$(20,000)
Cost of goods sold:			
Beginning finished goods inventory	$130,000	$130,000	$ –0–
Cost of goods manufactured:			
Raw materials	$ 50,000	$ 62,500	$(12,500)
Direct labor	150,000	143,750	6,250
Variable overhead	25,000	31,250	(6,250)
Fixed overhead	75,000	75,000	–0–
Cost of goods manufactured	$300,000	$312,500	$(12,500)
Goods available for sale	$430,000	$442,500	$(12,500)
Ending finished goods inventory	180,000	200,000	20,000
Cost of goods sold	$250,000	$242,500	$ 7,500
Gross margin	$150,000	$137,500	$(12,500)
Selling and administrative expenses:			
Variable	$ 40,000	$ 28,500	$ 11,500
Fixed	100,000	95,000	5,000
Total expenses	$140,000	$123,500	$ 16,500
Net income before income taxes	$ 10,000	$ 14,000	$ 4,000
Estimated federal income taxes (50%)	5,000	7,000	(2,000)
Net income	$ 5,000	$ 7,000	$ 2,000

Assume that (1) the actual selling price of all units was $20 per unit, (2) actual production was 25,000 units, and (3) actual sales were 19,000 units. The comparison of the original planned operating budget with the actual results yields some useful information; it shows where actual performance deviated from planned performance. Sales were 1,000 units lower than expected; gross margin was $12,500 less than expected; and net income was $2,000 more than expected. But the comparison does not show the expected expenditures for the actual level of output attained. This latter comparison is useful for expense control purposes.

Since the company expected to sell 20,000 units, but only sold

19,000, an analysis of operations for purposes of controlling expenses can best be made by using a flexible operating budget for the production of 25,000 units and sale of 19,000 units. Such an analysis is presented in Illustration 17.8. In instances in which the number of units produced equals the number of units sold, the beginning and ending inventory amounts may be excluded from the analysis, since they are equal in amount.

Illustration 17.8

RANDAL COMPANY
Comparison of Flexible Operating Budget and Actual Results
For Quarter Ended March 31, 1986

	Flexible Operating Budget	Actual	Budget Variance (Unfavorable)
Sales (19,000 units)	$380,000	$380,000	–0–
Cost of goods sold:			
Beginning finished goods inventory	$130,000	$130,000	$ –0–
Cost of goods manufactured:			
Raw materials (25,000 units)	$ 50,000	$ 62,500	$(12,500)
Direct labor (25,000 units)	150,000	143,750	6,250
Variable overhead (25,000 units)	25,000	31,250	(6,250)
Fixed overhead	75,000	75,000	–0–
Cost of goods manufactured	$300,000	$312,500	$(12,500)
Goods available for sale	$430,000	$442,500	$(12,500)
Ending finished goods inventory	192,000	200,000	8,000
Cost of goods sold	$238,000	$242,500	$ (4,500)
Gross margin	$142,000	$137,500	$ (4,500)
Selling and administrative expenses:			
Variable	$ 38,000	$ 28,500	$ 9,500
Fixed	100,000	95,000	5,000
Total expenses	$138,000	$123,500	$ 14,500
Net income before income taxes	$ 4,000	$ 14,000	$ 10,000
Estimated federal income taxes (50%)	2,000	7,000	(5,000)
Net income	$ 2,000	$ 7,000	$ 5,000

A number of items become readily apparent when a comparison is made between the actual expenses incurred and the expected expenses for the actual level of output. The flexible operating budget (Illustration 17.8) reveals some inefficiencies. For instance, the cost of goods sold was $4,500 unfavorable rather than $7,500 favorable, and the variable selling and administrative expenses were only $9,500 favorable rather than $11,500 favorable. In an actual situation the individual expenses making up the variable selling and administrative expenses would be listed separately so that tighter control could be exercised over each one.

Net income was $5,000 more than expected at a sales level of 19,000 units. The main reason for the increase in net income was the lower than expected amounts of selling and administrative expenses. Variable selling and administrative expenses were only $1.50 ($28,500/19,000) per unit instead of the $2.00 expected; fixed selling and administrative expenses were only $95,000 instead of the $100,000 expected.

PREPARING THE FINANCIAL BUDGET FOR THE RANDAL COMPANY

The starting point in preparing the financial budget is to examine the balance sheet which existed as of the beginning of the budget period. The balance sheet as of December 31, 1985, is shown in Illustration 17.9.

Illustration 17.9

RANDAL COMPANY
Balance Sheet
December 31, 1985
Assets

Current assets:		
Cash		$ 130,000
Accounts receivable		200,000
Inventories:		
Raw materials	$ 40,000	
Finished goods	130,000	170,000
Prepaid expenses		20,000
Total current assets		$ 520,000
Property, plant, and equipment:		
Land		$ 60,000
Buildings	$1,000,000	
Less: accumulated depreciation	400,000	600,000
Equipment	$ 600,000	
Less: accumulated depreciation	180,000	420,000
Total property, plant, and equipment		$1,080,000
Total assets		$1,600,000

Liabilities and Stockholders' Equity

Current liabilities:		
Accounts payable		$ 80,000
Accrued liabilities		160,000
Federal income taxes payable		100,000
Total current liabilities		$ 340,000
Stockholders' Equity:		
Capital stock (100,000 shares of $10 par value)		$1,000,000
Retained earnings		260,000
Total stockholders' equity		$1,260,000
Total liabilities and stockholders' equity		$1,600,000

The planned operating budget, shown in Illustration 17.5, as well as the other illustrations previously shown, will also be helpful in preparing the financial budget. We will identify where the numbers contained in the illustrations which follow came from so that you will better understand how to prepare the financial budget.

Accounts Receivable

To prepare a financial budget, schedules other than the ones which have already been prepared in connection with the operating budget are needed. The first of these schedules is shown in Illustration 17.10. This schedule is prepared under the assumption that 60 percent of the current quarter's sales plus all of the uncollected sales of the prior quarter are collected in that quarter. Several other simplifying assumptions are made, namely, that there are no sales returns or allowances, no discounts, and no uncollectible accounts. Obviously, in an actual planning situation, allowance may have to be made for these items. It is also assumed that all sales are made on a credit basis.

Illustration 17.10

RANDAL COMPANY
Planned Accounts Receivable
Collections and Balances

	Quarter Ending	
	March 31, 1986	*June 30, 1986*
Planned balance at beginning of quarter . .	$200,000*	$160,000
Planned sales for period	400,000	700,000
Total	$600,000	$860,000
Projected collections during quarter	440,000	580,000
Planned balance at end of quarter	$160,000	$280,000

* Actual on January 1.

Inventories

A schedule of inventories should be prepared, starting with the planned purchases and inventory of raw materials. The planned

Illustration 17.11

RANDAL COMPANY
Planned Material Purchases and Inventories

	Quarter ending	
	March 31, 1986	*June 30, 1986*
Planned usage (25,000 × $2)	$50,000	$50,000
Planned ending inventory (½ × 25,000 × $2) . . .	25,000	25,000
Planned raw materials available for use	$75,000	$75,000
Inventory at beginning of quarter	40,000	25,000
Planned purchases for quarter	$35,000	$50,000

* Actual on January 1.

usage and cost per unit are calculated from the production schedules. Assuming no work in process inventories, the inventories will consist of raw materials and finished goods.

Illustration 17.11 shows the planned purchases and inventories of raw materials. The raw materials inventory had been built up above the normal level of one half of next quarter's planned usage because of a strike threat in the supplier company. This threat has now passed, and the inventory will be reduced in the first quarter to the normal planned level.

The calculation of planned ending finished goods inventories was included in Illustration 17.4.

Accounts Affected by Operating Costs

Although individual schedules could be prepared for each of the accounts affected by operating costs, for illustrative purposes a schedule combining the analyses of all the accounts affected by material purchases or operating costs will be prepared.

The following assumptions are made:

1. All purchases of raw materials are made on account.
2. Direct labor incurred is credited to accrued liabilities.
3. Manufacturing overhead incurred was credited to the following accounts:

	Quarter Ending	
	March 31	June 30
Accounts Payable	$ 16,000	$ 13,000
Accrued Liabilities	60,000	64,000
Prepaid Expenses	6,000	5,000
Accumulated Depreciation—Building	5,000	5,000
Accumulated Depreciation—Equipment	13,000	13,000
Total	$100,000	$100,000

4. Selling and administrative expenses incurred were credited to the following accounts:

	Quarter Ending	
	March 31	June 30
Accounts Payable	$ 5,000	$ 10,000
Accrued Liabilities	130,000	154,000
Prepaid Expenses	2,000	3,000
Accumulated Depreciation—Building	1,000	1,000
Accumulated Depreciation—Equipment	2,000	2,000
Total	$140,000	$170,000

5. Planned cash payments are as follows:

	Quarter Ending	
	March 31	June 30
Accounts Payable	$ 80,000	$ 56,000
Accrued Liabilities	330,000	354,000
Prepared Expenses	–0–	10,000
Total	$410,000	$420,000

Illustration 17.12 shows the analyses of accounts credited as a result of the above data. The illustration provides a considerable amount of information needed in constructing financial budgets for the quarters ended March 31, 1986, and June 30, 1986. The balances for both dates for Accounts Payable, Accrued Liabilities, Prepaid Expenses (the only debit balanced account shown), Accumulated Depreciation—Building, and Accumulated Depreciation—Equipment are computed in the schedule.

Federal Income Taxes Payable

A separate schedule could be prepared showing the changes in the Federal Income Taxes Payable account; it will be omitted here. The balances reported in the financial budgets are derived under the assumption that one half of the $100,000 liability shown in the December 31, 1985, balance sheet is paid in each of the first two quarters of 1986 (see Illustration 17.13). The accrual for the current quarter is added (see Illustration 17.5). Thus, the balance at March 31, 1986, is $100,000 − $50,000 + $5,000 = $55,000. The balance at June 30, 1986, is $55,000 − $50,000 + $55,000 = $60,000. At June 30, the balance is equal to the accrual for the current year of $5,000 for the first quarter and $55,000 for the second quarter.

Cash Budget

After the above analyses have been prepared, the cash budget can be prepared and the balance of the cash account at both dates can be determined. Since cash flow was dealt with in Chapter 10, only a limited discussion will be undertaken here. Reference is made in Illustration 17.13 as to where the information came from, with the exception of payment of federal income tax liability and payment of dividends. As stated earlier, it is assumed that the company pays one half of the $100,000 income tax liability shown in the December 31, 1985, balance sheet in each of the first two quarters ($50,000 in each quarter). It is also assumed that $20,000 of dividends will be paid in the first quarter and $40,000 in the second quarter. For the Randal Company, the cash budget would be as shown in Illustration 17.13.

The Financial Budgets

The financial budgets for the quarters ended March 31, 1986, and June 30, 1986, are now prepared and are as shown in Illustration 17.14.

Illustration 17.12

RANDAL COMPANY
Analyses of Accounts Credited for Material Purchases and Operating Costs

	Total Debits	Accounts Payable	Accrued Liabilities	Prepaid Expenses*	Accumulated Depreciation — Building	Equipment
Purchases or operating costs, quarter ending March 31: (credits made to five accounts shown at right)						
Raw materials (per Illustration 17.11)	$ 35,000	$ 35,000				
Direct labor (per Illustration 17.4)	150,000		$150,000			
Overhead (per Illustration 17.4)	100,000	16,000	60,000	$ 6,000	$ 5,000	$ 13,000
Selling and administrative expense (per Illustration 17.5)	140,000	5,000	130,000	2,000	1,000	2,000
Total	$425,000	$ 56,000	$340,000	$ 8,000	$ 6,000	$ 15,000
Beginning balances (per Illustration 17.9)		$ 80,000	$160,000	$20,000*	$400,000	$180,000
Total		$136,000	$500,000	$12,000	$406,000	$195,000
Planned cash payments (debits made to accounts shown)		80,000	330,000			
Planned balances, March 31		$ 56,000	$170,000	$12,000*	$406,000	$195,000
Purchases or operating costs, quarter ending June 30 (credits made to five accounts shown at right):						
Raw materials (per Illustration 17.11)	$ 50,000	$ 50,000				
Direct labor (per Illustration 17.4)	150,000		$150,000			
Overhead (per Illustration 17.4)	100,000	13,000	64,000	$ 5,000	$ 5,000	$ 13,000
Selling and administrative expense (per Illustration 17.5)	170,000	10,000	154,000	3,000	1,000	2,000
Total	$470,000	$ 73,000	$368,000	$ 8,000	$ 6,000	$ 15,000
Total including March 31 balances		$129,000	$538,000	$ 4,000*	$412,000	$210,000
Planned cash payments (debits made to accounts shown)		56,000	354,000	10,000		
Planned balances, June 30		$ 73,000	$184,000	$14,000*	$412,000	$210,000

* Debit balance.

Illustration 17.13

RANDAL COMPANY
Planned Cash Flows and Cash Balances

	Quarter Ended	
	March 31, 1985	June 30, 1985
Planned balance at beginning of quarter	$130,000*	$ 90,000
Planned cash receipts:		
Collections of accounts receivable (per Illustration 17.10)	440,000	580,000
Total	$570,000	$670,000
Planned cash disbursements:		
Payment of accounts payable (per Illustration 17.12)	$ 80,000	$ 56,000
Payment of accrued liabilities (per Illustration 17.12)	330,000	354,000
Payment of federal income tax liability	50,000	50,000
Payment of dividends	20,000	40,000
Expenses prepaid (per Illustration 17.12)	–0–	10,000
Total disbursements	$480,000	$510,000
Planned balance at end of quarter	$ 90,000	$160,000

* Actual on January 1.

The completion of the financial budgets for the two quarters completes the preparation of the master budget. Management now has on hand information which will assist it in appraising the policies it has instituted before these policies are actually implemented. If the results of these policies, as shown by the master budget, are unsatisfactory, the policies can be changed before serious difficulty is encountered. For example, the Randal Company management decided to stabilize production. The master budget shows that production can be stabilized even though sales fluctuate widely. The planned ending inventory at June 30 may be considered somewhat low in view of the fluctuations in sales, but management does have advance information of this fact.

SUMMARY

A budget is one of management's most useful tools for planning and controlling income, cash flow, and other aspects of a business. A well-prepared budget forces management to think ahead, anticipate results, and take action when the actual results differ from the expected results. Used effectively, a budget can motivate employees. Used ineffectively, a budget can cause employee disenchantment and possible disruption.

A planned operating budget is a projected income statement at the expected level of operations for the next accounting period, usually a year. Before the planned operating budget is prepared,

Illustration 17.14

RANDAL COMPANY
Projected Balance Sheet

	March 31, 1986	June 30, 1986
Assets		
Current assets:		
Cash (per Illustration 17.13)	$ 90,000	$ 160,000
Accounts receivable (per Illustration 17.10)	160,000	280,000
Inventories:		
Raw materials (per Illustration 17.11)	25,000	25,000
Finished goods (per Illustration 17.4)	180,000	60,000
Prepaid expenses (per Illustration 17.12)	12,000	14,000
Total current assets	$ 467,000	$ 539,000
Property plant, and equipment:		
Land (per Illustration 17.9)	$ 60,000	$ 60,000
Buildings ($1,000,000 less accumulated depreciation of $406,000 and $412,000) (per Illustrations 17.9 and 17.12)	594,000	588,000
Equipment ($600,000 less accumulated depreciation of $195,000 and $210,000) (per Illustrations 17.9 and 17.12)	405,000	390,000
Total property plant, and equipment	$1,059,000	$1,038,000
Total assets	$1,526,000	$1,577,000
Liabilities and Stockholders' Equity		
Current liabilities:		
Accounts payable (per Illustration 17.12)	$ 56,000	$ 73,000
Accrued liabilities (per Illustration 17.12)	170,000	184,000
Federal income taxes payable (per discussion on page 530)	55,000	60,000
Total current liabilities	$ 281,000	$ 317,000
Stockholders equity:		
Capital stock (100,000 shares of $10 par value) (per Illustration 17.9)	$1,000,000	$1,000,000
Retained earnings (see below)	245,000*	260,000†
Total stockholders' equity	$1,245,000	$1,260,000
Total liabilities and stockholders' equity	$1,526,000	$1,577,000

* $260,000 (per Illustration 17.9) + income of $5,000 less dividends of $20,000.

† $245,000 + income of $55,000 less dividends of $40,000.

many detailed budgets are prepared for the items included in it. A sales forecast must be made first. Then a sales budget can be prepared. Next a production budget can be prepared based upon the sales prediction and upon company inventory and production policies. Purchases and expense budgets (in flexible format) may also be prepared.

A flexible operating budget is also prepared for the next accounting period. The flexible budget is actually a series of budgets, one of which corresponds to the actual level of performance. Actual results can be compared with expected results for the actual level of activity. Comparison of actual results and expected results at actual output may yield a **budget variance.** The budget variance is defined as the deviation of actual performance from expected performance at the actual level of operations.

The use of a flexible budget in combination with the original planned operating budget allows for performance evaluation at two levels. First, by comparing actual results with the original planned operating budget the reasons for the deviation of the actual level of output from the level of output originally expected can be investigated. Then, given the actual level of output, the efficiency of operations at that level can be appraised by comparing actual results with the amounts shown in the flexible budget for the actual level of operations.

Participation in the preparation of budgets generally improves the motivational aspects of budgeting. Participation gives the persons who have responsibility for performance a voice in setting the goals for the forthcoming period.

The preparation of an effective budget requires top-management support and the timely communication of results. The accountant should strive to design the accounting system to reflect the operations of the business, and at the same time to facilitate responsibility reporting.

The master budget is made up of a projected income statement (the operating budget) and a projected balance sheet (the financial budget). It indicates the overall goals of the enterprise. Use of a master budget allows management to appraise new policies before they are implemented.

To prepare a projected balance sheet, each account in the statement must be analyzed. The statement is derived from the operating budget and from policy decisions about dividends, inventory, credit, capital expenditures, and financing plans. After other accounts have been analyzed, a cash budget is prepared. The cash budget includes planned cash receipts and planned cash disbursements. A cash budget indicates whether or not a company will be able to pay its maturing obligations and expenses.

QUESTIONS

1. What are the three main objectives of budgeting?

2. What is meant by the term **management by exception?** How does the concept relate to budgeting?

3. What are five basic principles which, if followed, should improve the possibilities of preparing a meaningful budget? Why is each important?

4. What is the difference between an "imposed" budget and a "participatory" budget?

5. Define and explain a budget variance. A budget variance implies the use of what kind of budget?

6. What are the two major budgets in the master budget? Which should be prepared first? Why?

7. Distinguish between master and responsibility budgets.

8. What is a flexible budget? What is meant by the term **formula budgeting?**

9. The budget established at the beginning of a given period carried an item for supplies in the amount of $40,000. At the end of the period, the supplies used amounted to $44,000. Can it be concluded from these data that there was inefficient use of supplies or that care was not exercised in purchasing the supplies?

10. Management must make certain assumptions about the business environment when preparing a budget. What areas should be considered?

11. Why is budgeted performance better than past performance as a basis for judging actual results?

EXERCISES

1. The Davis Shoe Company has decided to produce 120,000 pairs of shoes at a uniform rate throughout 1986. The sales department of the Davis Shoe Company has estimated sales for 1986 according to the following schedule.

	Sales in Units
First quarter	32,000
Second quarter	26,000
Third quarter	30,000
Fourth quarter	42,000
Total for 1986	130,000

If the December 31, 1985, inventory is estimated to be 16,000 pairs of shoes, prepare a schedule of planned sales and production in units for the first two quarters of 1986.

2. Labor and materials of Alan Corp. are considered to be variable costs. Expected production for the year is 100,000 units. At that level of production, labor cost is budgeted at $750,000 and materials cost is expected to be $330,000. Prepare a flexible budget for labor and materials for possible production levels of 70,000, 80,000, and 90,000 units or production.

3. Assume that in Exercise 2, actual production was 80,000 units and materials cost was $270,000, while labor cost was $594,000. What is the budget variance?

4. The following data apply to the collection of accounts receivable for the Miles Company.

Current balance—February 28—$200,000 (of which $120,000 relates to February sales).
Planned sales for March—$250,000.

Assumptions: 70 percent of sales are collected in the month of the sales; 20 percent in the following month; and the remaining 10 percent in the second month after the sales. Prepare a schedule of planned collections and ending balance for accounts receivable as of March 31, 1986.

5. The Tenner Company expects to sell 30,000 units of Whisbees during the next quarter at a price of $20 per unit. Production costs (all variable) are $7.00 per unit. Selling and administrative expenses are: variable, $5.00 per unit; fixed, $160,000 in total. What is the budgeted net income? (Do not consider taxes.)

6. Fixed production costs for the Harrison Company are budgeted at $160,000, assuming 40,000 units of production. Actual sales for the period were 35,000 units, while actual production was 40,000 units. Actual fixed costs used in computing the cost of goods sold were $140,000. What is the budget variance?

PROBLEMS

17–1. During January 1986, the Sunset Company plans to sell 20,000 units at a price of $40 per unit. Selling expenses are estimated to be $80,000 plus 2 percent of sales revenue. General and administrative expenses are estimated to be $60,000 plus 1 percent of sales revenue. Income tax expense is estimated to be 40 percent of net operating income.

Sunset plans to produce 25,000 units during January, with estimated variable costs per unit as follows: $4 for materials, $10 for labor, and $6 for variable overhead. The fixed overhead cost is estimated at $40,000 per month. The finished goods inventory at January 1, 1986, is 4,000 units, with a cost per unit of $20. The company uses Fifo inventory procedure.

Required:

Prepare a projected income statement for January 1986.

17–2. The Thomas Company prepares monthly operating and financial budgets. Estimates of sales (in units) are made for each month. Production is scheduled at a level high enough to take care of current needs and to carry into each month one half of that month's unit sales. Raw materials, direct labor, and variable overhead are estimated at $4, $8, and $2 per unit, and fixed overhead is budgeted at $308,000 per month. Sales for April, May, June, and July are estimated at 100,000, 120,000, 160,000 and 120,000 units. The inventory at April 1 consists of 50,000 units with a cost of $16.40 per unit.

Required:

a. Prepare a schedule showing the budgeted production in units for April, May, and June 1986.

b. Prepare a schedule showing the budgeted cost of goods sold for the same three months, assuming that the Fifo method is used for inventories.

17–3. Net operating income for the Baker Company for 1985 was as follows:

Sales		$4,000,000
Costs of goods sold:*		
Raw materials	$800,000	
Direct labor	600,000	
Fixed overhead	400,000	
Variable overhead	240,000	2,040,000
Gross margin		$1,960,000
Selling expenses:		
Variable	$240,000	
Fixed	360,000	600,000
		$1,360,000
General and administrative expenses:		
Variable	$320,000	
Fixed	480,000	800,000
Net operating income		$ 560,000

* Since production was equal to sales, beginning and ending inventories may be ignored.

An operating budget is prepared for 1986, with sales forecast at a 20 percent increase solely from volume. Raw materials, direct labor, and all costs labeled variable above are completely variable. Fixed costs are expected to continue as above, except for a $40,000 increase in fixed general and administrative costs. Assume that production was equal to sales so that beginning and ending inventories may be ignored in parts **a** and **b** below.

The actual operating data for 1986 are:

Sales	$4,600,000
Raw materials	940,000
Direct labor	700,000
Fixed overhead	410,000
Variable overhead	270,000
Variable selling expense	276,000
Fixed selling expense	364,000
Variable general and administrative expense	380,000
Fixed general and administrative expense	540,000

Required:

a. Prepare a budget report comparing the 1986 planned operating budget with the actual 1986 data.

b. Prepare a budget report which would be useful in appraising the performance of the various persons charged with responsibility for providing satisfactory earnings. (Hint: Prepare budget data on a flexible basis.)

c. Comment on the difference revealed by the two reports.

17–4. The following data are presented for the T. K. Anderson Company for use in preparing its 1986 operating budget:

Plant capacity	500,000 units
Expected sales	450,000 units
Expected production	450,000 units
Forecast sales price	$10.00 per unit

Manufacturing costs:
Variable:

Raw material	$4.00
Direct labor	$2.00
Overhead	$1.00
Fixed	$225,000

Selling and administrative expenses:

Variable	$0.50
Fixed	$200,000

Assume no beginning inventory. Taxes are 40 percent of pretax earnings. The actual sales price was $9.50 per unit. The actual production in units was equal to the actual sales in units. Thus, beginning and ending inventories may be ignored.

Required:

a. Prepare a planned operating budget for the year ended December 31, 1986.

b. The actual results for the T. K. Anderson Company for the year ended December 31, 1986, were as follows:

Sales		$4,750,000
Costs of goods sold:		
Materials	$1,900,000	
Direct labor	1,050,000	
Variable overhead	600,000	
Fixed overhead	225,000	3,775,000
		$ 975,000
Selling and administrative expense:		
Variable	$ 250,000	
Fixed	200,000	450,000
Income before taxes		$ 525,000
Income tax at 40%		210,000
Net income		$ 315,000

Using a flexible budget, analyze the efficiency of operations and the company's sales policy. Comment on the results for 1986.

17–5. The Holly Company is in the process of preparing its master budget for the year ended December 31, 1986. Management is interested in the responsibility budget to be prepared for the sales department. The sales manager and the general manager have met with all department heads and have given you the following estimates relating to next year's expectations:

(1) At present, the company employs 40 full-time salesmen with a base salary of $350 per month. In addition, it has eight regional managers with a base salary of $15,000 per year, while the one sales manager draws $30,000 per year.

(2) Sales for the current year are estimated at $9 million. The 40 full-time salesmen are given 5 percent sales commissions on about 70 percent of total sales and 3 percent sales commissions on 20 percent of sales, while the remaining 10 percent of sales are not subject to commission. Approximately one third of the sales are made in the first three months of the year.

(3) Advertising commitments have been made with major magazines. These commitments are for $15,000 per month.

(4) The company is planning a special in-store promotion during January–February–March. Special incentives are given to the retailers in the form of supplies, aids, and advertising assistance up to 2 percent of total gross sales during the month. Past history has shown that the retailers take advantage of about three fourths of these incentives.

(5) A supplementary advertising campaign will also be used during the first quarter of 1986 and will average $30,000 for January and $20,000 during the next two months.

(6) Salesmen's travel allowances average $150 per month for each of the 40 salesmen.

(7) Selling supplies average 1 percent of gross sales.

(8) Sales department clerical salaries are set at $2,500 per month. Rent for sales offices is $6,000 per month.

(9) The sales department will conduct a special market test of a new product during the first quarter. Nonrecurring expenses of $45,000 associated with this test are expected to be incurred.

Required:

Prepare a detailed expense budget for the sales department for the first quarter of 1986.

17–6. The MDA Manufacturing Company is in the process of preparing a schedule of the planned cost of goods sold and the ending inventory for the quarters ended March 31, 1986 and June 30, 1986. The following data relate to expected activity for the two quarters:

(1) Expected sales:

March quarter	$400,000
June quarter	$300,000
September quarter	$600,000

(2) The selling price per unit is $40.

(3) The company policy is to carry a beginning-of-the-period inventory equal to 20 percent of the next period's requirements. The beginning inventory at January 1, 1986, was 2,000 units valued at $25.00 per unit.

(4) Cost of production is estimated as follows:

Materials	$ 6 per unit
Direct labor	$ 14 per unit
Variable overhead	$ 4 per unit
Fixed overhead	$ 38,000 per quarter

(5) There is no work in process inventory at the beginning or end of any period.

(6) Inventory is computed on a FIFO basis.

Required:

Prepare a schedule of Planned Cost of Goods Manufactured and Sold for the quarters ended March 31, and June 30, 1986. (Hint: Prepare the production schedule in units first.)

17–7.

A & K CORPORATION
Post-Closing Trial Balance
December 31, 1986

	Debits	Credits
Cash	$ 20,000	
Accounts receivable	40,000	
Allowance for doubtful accounts		$ 3,000
Inventories	50,000	
Prepaid expenses	6,000	
Land	50,000	
Buildings and equipment	150,000	
Accumulated depreciation—buildings and equipment		20,000
Accounts payable		30,000
Accrued liabilities (including income taxes)		20,000
Capital stock		200,000
Retained earnings		43,000
	$316,000	$316,000

The A & K Corporation, whose post-closing trial balance at December 31, 1986, appears above, is a rapidly expanding company. Sales amounted to $200,000 in the last quarter of 1986 and are projected at $250,000 and $400,000 for the first two quarters of 1987. This expansion has created a very tight cash position. Management is especially concerned about the probable cash balance at March 31, 1987, since payment in the amount of $30,000 for some new equipment must be made upon delivery on April 2. The current cash balance of $20,000 is considered to be the minimum workable balance.

Additional data:

(1) Purchases, all on account, are to be scheduled so that the inventory at the end of any quarter is equal to one third of the goods expected to be sold in the coming quarter. The cost of goods sold averages 60 percent of sales.

(2) Selling expenses are budgeted at $10,000 fixed plus 8 percent of sales; $2,000 is expected to be incurred on account, $24,000 accrued, $2,800 from expired prepayments, and $1,200 from allocated depreciation.

(3) Purchasing expenses are budgeted at $7,000 fixed plus 5 percent of purchases; $1,000 will be incurred on account, $13,000 accrued, $1,100 from expired prepayments, and $900 from allocated depreciation.

(4) Administrative expenses are budgeted at $12,500 fixed plus 3 percent of sales; $2,000 will be incurred on account, $11,000 accrued, $1,100 from expired prepayments, and $900 from allocated depreciation, while bad debts expense is equal to 2 percent of current sales.

(5) Federal income taxes are budgeted at 50 percent of net operating earnings before taxes and are accrued in Accrued Liabilities. Payments on these taxes are included in the payments on Accrued Liabilities discussed below.

(6) All December 31, 1986, Accounts Payable plus 80 percent of current credits to this account will be paid in the current quarter. All of the December 31, 1986, accrued liabilities will be paid in the current quarter except for $6,000. Of the current quarter's accrued liabilities, all but $24,000 will be paid during the quarter.

(7) Cash outlays for various expenses normally prepaid will amount to $8,000 during the quarter.

(8) All sales are made on account, and 80 percent of the sales are collected in the quarter in which they are made, and all of the remaining sales are collected in the following quarter, except for 2 percent which are never collected. The allowance for doubtful accounts shows the estimated amount of accounts receivable at December 31, 1986, arising from 1986 sales which will not be collected.

Required:

a. Prepare a planned operating budget for the quarter ending March 31, 1987. Supporting schedules for planned purchases and operating expenses should be included.

b. Prepare a financial budget for March 31, 1987. Include supporting schedules analyzing accounts credited for purchases and expenses, showing planned cash flows and the planned cash balance, and showing planned collections on and the planned balance of accounts receivable.

c. Will sufficient cash be on hand April 2 to pay for the new equipment?

18

COST-VOLUME-
PROFIT ANALYSIS

Changes in costs and volume will have an effect on a company's net income in the short run. The effect of such changes can be analyzed by using cost-volume-profit analysis. Specifically, cost-volume-profit analysis can be used to answer such questions as: At what level of sales will a company break even (that is, have neither net income nor a net loss)? What volume of sales is required to generate a certain level of net income? What effect will a change in selling prices, sales volume, or costs have on net income?

The relevant income statement format for cost-volume-profit analysis is as follows:

Revenues	$xx
Less: Variable costs	xx
Contribution margin	$xx
Less: Fixed costs	xx
Net income	$xx

Variable costs, fixed costs, and contribution margin all have been discussed previously and will be utilized in this chapter.

THE BEHAVIOR OF COSTS

Knowledge of the behavior and nature of costs is crucial to management for decision making purposes. Two basic categories of costs are generally used—variable and fixed. As stated previously, **variable costs** (see Illustration 18.1, part *a*) are those which vary directly with changes in volume. For example, if volume increases 10 percent, variable costs increase 10 percent. Certain production costs, such as raw materials and the labor used to convert the raw materials into finished products, vary directly with production volume, while other costs, such as sales commissions, vary directly with sales volume.

As stated previously, **fixed costs** (see Illustration 18.1, part *b*) are those which remain constant over the entire range of output. Fixed costs are often described as time-related costs; that is, they will be incurred simply because of the passage of time if the company continues to operate. Depreciation, property insurance, property taxes, and administrative salaries are examples of time-related costs and are therefore fixed costs.

Besides these two basic categories of variable and fixed costs there are two other types of costs which are in part fixed and in part variable. These include mixed (or semivariable) costs (see Illus-

Illustration 18.1
FOUR TYPES OF COST PATTERNS

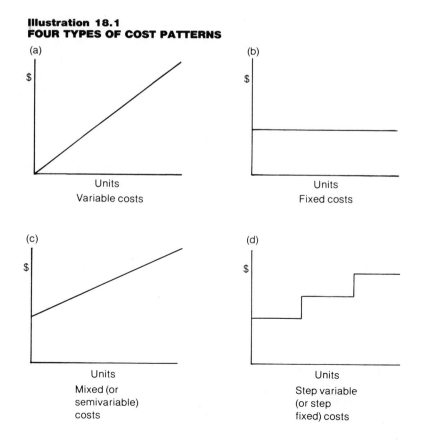

(a)

$ | Units
Variable costs

(b)

$ | Units
Fixed costs

(c)

$ | Units
Mixed (or semivariable) costs

(d)

$ | Units
Step variable (or step fixed) costs

tration 18.1, part *c*) and step variable (or step fixed) costs (see Illustration 18.1, part *d*).

An example of a mixed cost occurs when a given amount of maintenance cost has to be incurred while a plant is completely idle. Once production is under way, additional maintenance costs vary with production volume. These costs may be separated into their fixed and variable components as shown:

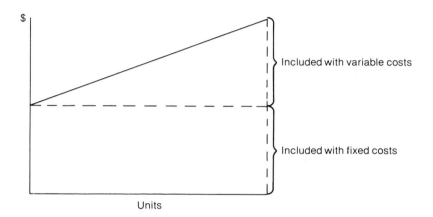

When divided in this way, the top part fits the variable cost pattern as shown in Illustration 18.1, part *a*. The bottom part fits the fixed cost pattern as shown in Illustration 18.1, part *b*.

The other type, step variable costs, is handled in one of two ways. The first is to assume that a straight-line relationship exists, as shown below by the slanted dotted line:

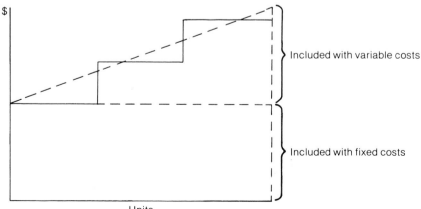

When this method is used, the costs may be separated into their fixed and variable components as was shown for mixed costs.

When step variable costs are present and there are very few steps (one or two usually), it is sometimes useful to treat the costs as "step fixed." To illustrate, assume that between 0 and 40 percent of capacity the cost is $20,000 and that at over 40 percent of capacity it becomes $50,000, as shown:

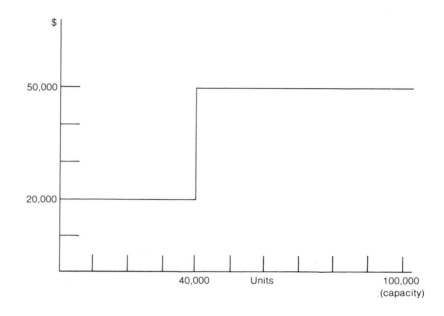

When costs behave in this step fixed manner, the best approach to analyzing operations is to treat the fixed costs as being $20,000 for the 0 to 40 percent level of capacity and as being $50,000 for the 40 to 100 percent level of capacity.

Thus, even though there are four different types of cost patterns, it has been shown that two basic categories—variable and fixed—may be used to include all of them. Before we proceed, one other comment is in order. Some variable costs do not vary in a strictly linear relationship with volume. Rather, they vary in a curvilinear pattern—a 10 percent increase in volume may yield an 8 percent change in costs at lower output levels and an 11 percent change in costs at higher output levels. A curvilinear relationship is diagramed in Illustration 18.2. But, in the remainder of this chapter, variable costs are assumed to vary in a linear relationship with volume. The need for this assumption will become more evident as you proceed through the chapter.

Illustration 18.2
CURVILINEAR COST PATTERN

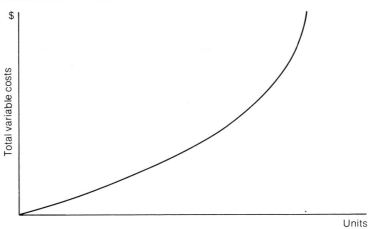

COST-VOLUME-EARNINGS ANALYSIS

In planning future operations, a type of analysis sometimes referred to as cost-volume-profit analysis is undertaken. In such an analysis, the company's break-even point is calculated. A company is said to break even for a given period if the sales revenue and the costs charged to that period are exactly equal. As a result, no element of income or loss remains. Thus, **the break-even point is defined as that level of operations where revenues and costs are equal.**

Undertaking a careful and accurate cost-volume profit analysis requires a knowledge of costs and their behavior as volume changes. Management must be able to distinguish among the different types of costs involved in its operations. Of course, the types and quantities of cost data accumulated will depend on the costs of obtaining more refined data compared to the benefits resulting from doing so. Within this constraint, it is desirable to compute break-even points for each area of decision making within the company. Some important classifications of cost data for break-even analysis are by product, territory, salesperson, class of customer, and method of selling.

Several procedures are available for calculating a break-even point. It may be expressed in (1) dollars of sales revenue, (2) in number of units produced (sold), or (3) as a percentage of capacity.

Assume that a company manufactures a single product which it sells for $20. Fixed costs per period total $40,000, while variable costs are $12 per unit, or 60 percent of the sales price. A linear relationship between variable costs and sales revenue is assumed to exist. Thus, variable costs are, within a given range of sales activity or sales volume, a constant percentage of sales. In this example, variable costs are 60 percent of sales. The sales revenue needed to break even is computed as follows:

$$\text{Sales } (S) = \text{Fixed costs } (FC) + \text{Variable costs } (VC)$$

Fixed costs are known to be $40,000, while variable costs as a percentage of sales are equal to $0.60S$. Substituting, then, the equation becomes:

$$S = \$40,000 + 0.60S$$
$$S - 0.60S = \$40,000$$
$$0.40S = \$40,000$$
$$S = \$40,000 \div 0.40$$
$$S = \$100,000$$

Sales at the break-even point are $100,000, and this can easily be proven. At that level, fixed costs will be $40,000 and variable costs will be $60,000 (0.60 × $100,000). The break-even point in units can be computed by dividing total sales revenue at the break-even point by the selling price per unit ($100,000 ÷ $20 = 5,000 units).

If desired, the break-even point can be expressed in terms of capacity. Newspaper reports often refer to the break-even point of the steel industry, or of a company in that industry, as being a stated percentage of capacity, for example, 65 percent. If in the example presented above the output capacity of the plant was 25,000 units, the break-even point in terms of plant capacity is 20 percent (5,000 ÷ 25,000).

The Break-Even Chart The break-even chart in Illustration 18.3 presents graphically the break-even point for the above company. Each break-even chart (or analysis) is assumed to be valid only for a specified **relevant range** of volumes. For volumes outside these ranges, the incurrence of different costs will alter the assumed relationship. For example, if only a few units were produced, the variable costs per unit would probably be quite high. Also, to produce more than 10,000 units it may be necessary to add to plant capacity, thus incurring additional fixed costs, or to work extra shifts, thus incurring overtime charges and other inefficiencies. In either case, the cost relationships first assumed are no longer valid. The illustration is based on the data presented previously, which are **relevant** for output from 500 to 10,000 units. Different cost and revenue patterns may exist outside these limits.

The chart in Illustration 18.3 shows that the break-even volume of sales is $100,000 (5,000 units at $20). At this level of sales, fixed costs and variable costs are exactly equal to sales revenue, as shown:

Revenues	. . . .	$100,000
Less: Variable costs	. . . .	60,000
Contribution margin	. . . .	$ 40,000
Less: Fixed costs	. . . .	40,000
Net income	. . . .	$ –0–

The break-even (cost-volume-profit) chart shows that a period of complete idleness would produce a loss of $40,000, the amount of fixed costs, while output of 10,000 units would produce net income of $40,000. Other points which can be read show that with sales of 7,500 units total revenue would be $150,000. At that point, total costs would amount to $130,000, leaving net income of $20,000.

The break-even point can be lowered by increasing the selling price per unit, decreasing the total fixed costs, or decreasing the variable cost per unit. This lowering of the break-even point can be seen by studying Illustration 18.3 and visually imagining an increase in the slope of the sales line, a diminished distance between the variable costs and total costs lines, or a decrease in the slope

Illustration 18.3
THE BREAK-EVEN CHART

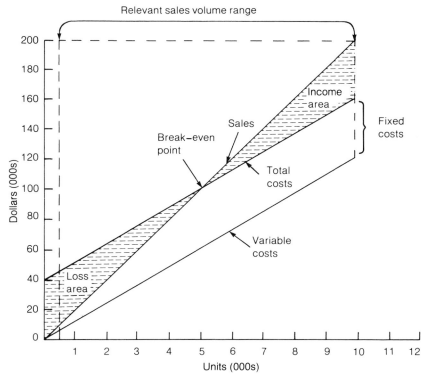

of the variable costs line. Taking opposite actions will raise the break-even point.

For example, assume that a company currently has variable costs of $15 per unit, fixed costs of $27,000, and a selling price of $60 per unit. Thus, its break-even point is $36,000 ($27,000/0.75), or 600 ($36,000/$60) units. If the company can increase its selling price by 5 percent while holding variable costs and fixed costs at the same level, the break-even point will decrease by approximately $562.50, as shown below:

$$S = FC + VC$$
$$S = \$27,000 + \frac{\$15}{\$60 + 0.05(\$60)}S$$
$$S = \$27,000 + \frac{15}{63}S$$
$$48/63\ S = \$27,000$$
$$S = \$35,437.50 \text{ break-even point if the selling price increases by 5\%}$$

Original break-even point	$36,000.00
Break-even point with 5% increase in selling price	35,437.50
Decrease in break-even volume of sales	$ 562.50

Margin of Safety

If a company's current sales are above its break-even point, then the company is said to have a **margin of safety** equal to the difference between current sales and sales at the break-even point. The margin of safety is the amount by which sales can decrease before a loss will be incurred. For example, assume that current sales are $250,000 and that sales at the break-even point are $200,000. The margin of safety is $50,000, or 20 percent of sales, computed as follows:

$$\text{Margin of safety} = \text{Current sales} - \text{Break-even sales}$$
$$= \$250,000 - \$200,000 = \$50,000$$

or

$$\text{Margin of safety} = \frac{\text{Current sales} - \text{Break-even sales}}{\text{Current sales}}$$
$$= \frac{\$250,000 - \$200,000}{\$250,000}$$
$$= 20\%$$

The Contribution Margin Concept

As shown at the beginning of this chapter, contribution margin is defined as the amount by which revenue exceeds the variable costs incurred in securing that revenue. This amount is often referred to as marginal income; it may be computed for a given number of units (or dollars of sales) or per unit or per dollar of sales.

Using the preceding data (selling price per unit of $20 and variable costs per unit of $12, with total fixed costs of $40,000), the contribution margin per unit is $8. The sale of one additional unit will add $20 to total revenues, $12 to total costs, and $8 to net income (ignoring income taxes). From this information, the break-even point in units can be computed. Each unit contributes $8 to the coverage of fixed costs, and fixed costs total $40,000. Thus the sale of 5,000 units will be necessary to cover the fixed costs. The formula is:

Break-even point in units = Fixed costs ÷ Contribution margin per unit

At the break-even point, the total contribution margin will equal the total fixed costs, as shown in Illustration 18.4.

The break-even point in terms of dollars of sales can also be computed by dividing the fixed costs per period by the contribution margin rate. This rate is computed by dividing the contribution margin by the sales price per unit. In the above example the contribution margin rate is 40 percent ($8 ÷ $20); and the break-even point is $100,000 of sales revenue ($40,000 ÷ 0.40).

In addition, the net income at any level of output can be computed as the contribution margin per unit multiplied by the number of units sold, less the total fixed costs. Using the above data, the

Illustration 18.4
BREAK-EVEN CHART SHOWING THAT FIXED COSTS EQUAL CONTRIBUTION MARGIN AT THE BREAK-EVEN POINT

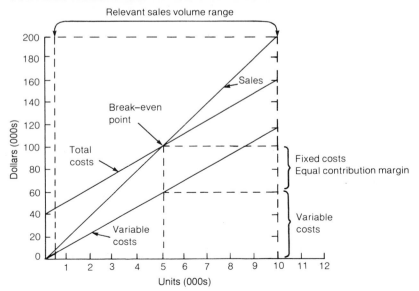

net income at the 80 percent level of capacity can be determined. First, multiply 8,000 units (0.80 × 10,000) by $8, obtaining $64,000; then subtract the fixed costs of $40,000, leaving net income of $24,000. In this case the contribution margin more than covers the total fixed costs. The remainder is net income (ignoring income taxes), as shown in Illustration 18.5.

A simple example may aid in reinforcing the understanding of some of these concepts. As stated earlier, break-even analysis can be used to analyze the cost-volume-profit relationships for a venture or project. Suppose that one of the major airlines wanted to know how many seats would have to be sold on a certain flight for the flight to break even. To solve this problem the costs have to be identified and separated into fixed and variable categories.

The fixed costs are those that do not vary with different levels of seats filled. These include such costs as the fuel required to fly the plane with crew (no passengers) to the destination; depreciation on the plane and facilities utilized on this flight; salaries of the crew members, gate attendants, and maintenance and refueling personnel; and miscellaneous fixed costs.

The variable costs include those costs which vary directly with the number of passengers. These might include such costs as extra fuel consumed per passenger; food and beverages included in the price of the ticket; baggage-handling costs per passenger; and miscellaneous variable costs.

Assume that, after analyzing the various costs and classifying

Illustration 18.5
BREAK-EVEN CHART SHOWING SALES LEVEL FOR DESIRED INCOME

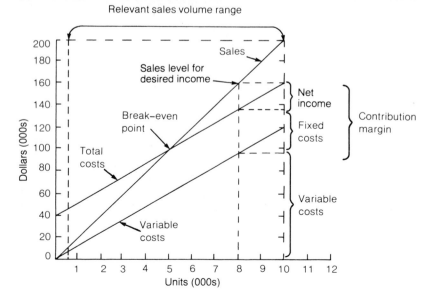

them as fixed or variable, the fixed costs for a given flight are $12,000. The variable costs are $25 per passenger, and tickets are sold at $125. This yields a contribution margin per ticket of $100 ($125 − $25). Assume also that there are 300 seats on the aircraft.

The break-even point can be expressed in dollars, in number of passengers, or in percent of capacity.

The sales revenue needed to break even is:

$$\text{Sales } (S) = \text{Fixed costs } (FC) + \text{Variable costs } (VC)$$
$$S = \$12,000 + 0.2S$$
$$0.8\ S = \$12,000$$
$$S = \$15,000$$

It may also be found by using the contribution margin rate, as follows:

$$\text{BEP (dollars)} = \frac{FC}{\text{Contribution margin rate}} = \frac{\$12,000}{80 \text{ percent}} = \$15,000$$

The break-even point in terms of number of passengers may be found by dividing the break-even point in dollars ($15,000) by the selling price per unit ($125). Thus, $15,000/$125 = 120 passengers. The break-even point in units may also be found as follows:

$$\text{BEP (units)} = \frac{FC}{\text{Contribution margin}}$$
$$\text{BEP} = \frac{\$12,000}{\$125 - \$25}$$
$$\text{BEP} = 120 \text{ passengers}$$

The break-even point in percent of capacity is:

$$\frac{\text{BEP (units)}}{\text{Total capacity (units)}} = \frac{120 \text{ passengers}}{300 \text{ passengers}} = 40 \text{ percent}$$

Using Cost-Volume-Profit Analysis

Although cost-volume-profit analysis alone is insufficient to support managerial decision making, basic cost-volume-profit relationships should be understood by management. Knowledge of cost-volume-profit relationships can be used by management to determine the effect on income of any change in fixed costs, variable costs, or sales price. For instance, such knowledge may help management to determine (1) whether to increase sales promotion costs in an effort to increase sales volume, (2) whether an order at a lower-than-usual price should be accepted, and (3) whether plant facilities should be expanded. Planning in general is facilitated by careful study of break-even charts. Indeed, it has been said that to be successful management must become "break-even minded."

This form of analysis may also be useful in determining the level of sales volume that is needed to generate some desired level of net income. To illustrate using the preceding data, if management wished to generate $24,000 of net income, the chart in Illustration 18.5 shows that sales volume must be 8,000 units, $160,000, or 80(8,000 ÷ 10,000) percent of capacity.

Now assume that management has the opportunity to operate at 100 percent of capacity if it will increase its fixed costs by investing $10,000 in a sales promotion contract. Will it be profitable for management to make such an investment? The chart in Illustration 18.6 shows that income would increase to $30,000, provided the cost and revenue estimates are correct and the objective of management is to maximize net income.

To illustrate further, assume that currently ABC Company's sales are $60,000, its variable costs $25,000, and its fixed costs $30,000. The company's net income is $5,000, as computed below:

$$\text{Net income } (NI) = \text{Sales } (S) - \text{Variable costs } (VC)$$
$$- \text{Fixed costs } (FC)$$
$$= \$60{,}000 - \$25{,}000 - \$30{,}000$$
$$= \$5{,}000$$

Illustration 18.6
BREAK-EVEN CHART SHOWING INCOME RESULTING FROM ACTION TAKEN

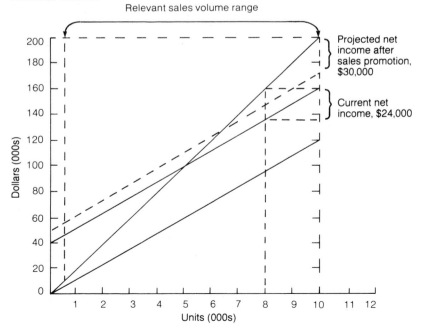

A 5 percent increase in sales price, with variable costs and fixed costs remaining the same, would have the following effect on the income of ABC Company:

$$NI = \$60,000 \ (1.05) - \$25,000 - \$30,000$$
$$= \$63,000 - \$25,000 - \$30,000$$
$$= \$8,000$$

ABC Company's net income will increase by $3,000, or 60 percent ($3,000/$5,000).

Now, suppose that the company's sales prices increase by 5 percent (over $60,000) and that its variable costs increase by 10 percent. Net income would be $5,500, as computed below:

$$NI = \$60,000(1.05) - \$25,000(1.10) - \$30,000$$
$$= \$63,000 - \$27,500 - \$30,000$$
$$= \$5,500$$

The result is an increase in net income of $500, or 10 percent ($500/$5,000).

Some of the practical aspects of cost-volume-profit relationships will be discussed in the remainder of the chapter.

SOME PRACTICAL ASPECTS OF COST-VOLUME-PROFIT ANALYSIS

Cost-Volume-Profit Analysis for the Multiproduct Firm

The previous discussion allowed us to talk of the break-even point in terms of units, sales dollars, or percentage of capacity. When computing the break-even point for a multiproduct firm, we will use sales dollars. Also, the assumption must be made that the product mix—that is, the number of units of each type of product sold— is known in advance.

To illustrate the situation for a multiproduct firm, assume the following historical data:

	Products							
	1		2		3		Total	
	Amount	Per-cent	Amount	Per-cent	Amount	Per-cent	Amount	Per-cent
Sales	$60,000	100	$30,000	100	$10,000	100	$100,000	100
Less: Variable expenses . .	40,000	67	16,000	53	4,000	40	60,000	60
Contribution margin	$20,000	33	$14,000	47	$ 6,000	60	$ 40,000	40

Thus, the sales mix for the products is 60–30–10, respectively. In total, variable costs are 60 percent of total sales. If this sales mix can be expected to hold in the future, the break-even point for a future period can be found as follows (assuming fixed costs are $50,000):

$$S = FC + VC$$
$$S = \$50,000 + 0.6S$$
$$0.4\ S = \$50,000$$
$$S = \$125,000$$

The $125,000 can be broken down into products by multiplying it by 60 percent, 30 percent, and 10 percent, respectively.

If historical patterns are not expected to hold in the future, **projected** sales and variable expenses should be used in determining the total expected percentage of variable expenses to total sales.

Methods for Estimating Mixed Costs

Early in the chapter mixed costs were illustrated (see Illustration 18.1, part *c*). In an actual business situation the accountant might have some difficulty in estimating a particular mixed cost. The fixed portion of a particular mixed cost represents the cost of having a service available for use. The variable portion is the cost associated with various levels of activity (usually defined as production or sales volume).

The scatter diagram. One method for estimating the total amount of a mixed cost at various levels of activity is to prepare a scatter diagram in which the actual costs incurred are plotted.

Assume that Illustration 18.7 is a scatter diagram representing the total actual maintenance costs for a firm's fleet of delivery trucks. The dots on the diagram represent actual costs from the past at various levels of activity. The line is drawn through what appears to be the center of the pattern of these dots. In this example, the fixed element of the mixed cost is $23,000. Since the line (called a regression line) rises from $23,000 to $63,000 over the range of 100,000 units, the slope of the variable cost portion is [($63,000 − $23,000)/100,000 units], or $0.40 per unit. Thus, the variable portion of this cost is equal to $0.40 per unit. The data in the chart suggest that the firm's truck maintenance costs can be estimated at $23,000 plus 40 cents for every mile driven.

A more sophisticated method, called the least squares method, could be used to draw the regression line. This method is more precise since it involves statistical analysis, but it will not be presented in this text.

The high-low method. This is another widely used method for identifying the behavior of mixed costs. This method involves the use of only the highest and lowest plots on a scatter diagram to determine the relationship between volume and variable cost.

To illustrate, assume that in Illustration 18.7 the lowest plot is

Illustration 18.7
SCATTER DIAGRAM

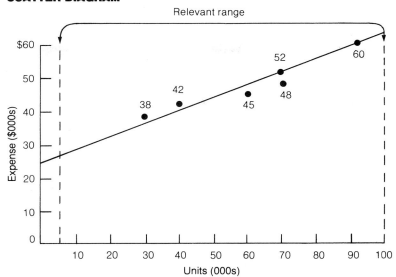

$38,000 of expense at 30,000 units of output and that the highest plot is $60,000 at 80,000 units of output. The amount of variable cost per unit is found as follows:

$$\frac{\text{Change in expense}}{\text{Change in output}} = \frac{\$60,000 - \$38,000}{80,000 \text{ units} - 30,000 \text{ units}} = \frac{\$22,000}{50,000 \text{ units}}$$

$$= \$0.44 \text{ per unit}$$

The fixed cost portion is then found as follows:

Total cost at 80,000 units of output	$60,000
Less: Variable cost at that level of output (80,000 × $0.44)	35,200
Fixed cost at all levels of output within the relevant range	$24,800

The high-low method is less precise than the scatter diagram method since it uses only two data points, either or both of which may not be representative of the data as a whole.

The Meaning of Units as a Measure of Volume

In the various cost-volume-profit charts included throughout this chapter, the horizontal axis has been labeled "units." A practical question is whether this is units of production or units sold. An implicit assumption in this type of analysis is that production is equal to sales. (In other words, it is assumed that inventories do not vary from the beginning to the end of the period.) We know that, in the long run, production must equal sales; but, in the short run, this may not occur.

Some of the costs which a company will incur vary directly with production (e.g., supplies used in manufacturing), and some vary directly with sales (e.g., sales commissions). One should realize the nature of this problem, but it is best to assume that production is equal to sales for this type of analysis. Therefore, whether "units" is labeled units of output or units of sales is irrelevant.

The Nature of Fixed Costs

Until now in this discussion, fixed costs have been treated as if they were all alike. But there are two types of fixed costs which should be identified. They are **committed fixed costs** and **discretionary fixed costs**.

Committed fixed costs. These costs relate to the basic facilities and organization structure which a company must have to continue operations. Changing such costs in the short run would seriously disrupt operations. Examples of committed costs are depreciation on buildings and equipment and the salaries of key executives. In the short run, costs such as these are viewed as not being subject to the discretion or control of management. They result from past decisions which "committed" the company for a period of several years. For instance, once a company constructs a building to house production operations, it is committed to the use of the building for many years. The depreciation on that building is less subject to control by management than some other types of fixed cost.

Discretionary fixed costs. In contrast to committed fixed costs, discretionary fixed costs are related to fixed cost areas which are subject to management control from year to year. Each year management decides how much to spend on advertising, research and development, and employee training and development programs. Since these decisions are made each year they are said to be under the "discretion" of management. Management is not locked in or committed to a certain level of expense for any more than one budget period. The next period it may change the level of expense or eliminate the expense completely.

The philosophy of management can affect to some extent which fixed costs are committed and which are discretionary. For instance, during the recession of the mid-1970s some companies terminated persons in the upper levels of management, while other companies kept their "management team" intact. Thus, in some firms the salaries of top-level managers are discretionary, while in others they are committed.

The discussion of committed fixed costs and discretionary fixed costs is relevant to cost-volume-profit analysis. If a company's fixed costs are almost all committed fixed costs, the company is going to have a more difficult time in reducing its break-even point for the next budget period than if most of its fixed costs are discretionary in nature. A company with a large proportion of discretionary fixed costs may be able to reduce fixed costs dramatically in a recessionary period. By doing this, it may be able to "run lean" and show some income even when economic conditions are difficult. Thus its chances of long-run survival may be enhanced.

Assumptions Made in Cost-Volume-Profit Analysis

The assumptions which must be made in cost-volume-profit analysis are as follows:

1. Selling price and variable costs per unit remain constant throughout the relevant range. This means that more units can be sold at the same price and that there is no change in technical efficiency as volume increases.
2. The number of units produced equals the number of units sold.
3. In multiproduct situations, the product mix is known in advance.
4. Costs can be accurately classified into their fixed and variable portions.

These assumptions have been described as being unrealistic in many situations. But even where there is some truth to this criticism, cost-volume-profit analysis can serve as a useful planning tool. Although cost-volume-profit analysis may lack precision, its use is preferable to pure intuition.

SUMMARY

For purposes of cost-volume-profit analysis, costs must be divided into their fixed and variable portions. The four types of cost patterns are variable, fixed, mixed, and step variable. The mixed costs are separated into their fixed and variable portions through use of the scatter diagram (possibly combined with the least squares method) or the high-low method. The step variable costs can either be converted to a straight-line function and treated as a mixed cost or can be treated as an element of fixed costs (the level of fixed costs will then change in a "step" fashion). Curvilinear costs can be assumed to be straight-line functions.

Computation of the break-even point is an important aspect of cost-volume-profit analysis. The break-even point may be computed in several ways; it may be expressed in terms of dollars of sales revenue, units of product, or percentage of capacity. The break-even point also may be presented graphically in a break-even chart.

One of the important concepts in this type of analysis is the contribution margin (sales price minus variable costs). The contribution margin may be expressed in total or per unit. The contribution margin per unit may be divided into fixed costs to find the break-even point in units. Alternatively, contribution margin may be divided into fixed costs plus desired income to find the number of units which must be sold to achieve the income goal.

Knowledge of cost-volume-profit relationships can be used by management in determining the effect on income of changes in fixed costs, variable costs, or selling prices.

Cost-volume-profit analysis can be applied to multiproduct situations. In such situations it is necessary to assume that the product mix is known in advance. If historical data involving product mix are not expected to hold for a future period, projected data should be used.

Fixed costs may be divided into two categories—committed fixed costs and discretionary fixed costs. Committed fixed costs are those related to the basic facilities and organization structure and thus are less subject to change from year to year than discretionary fixed costs. Committed fixed costs include such items as depreciation expense and executive salaries. Discretionary fixed costs are subject to change from year to year; they include such expenses as advertising, research and development, and management development.

Certain assumptions which must be made regarding cost-volume-profit analysis are said by some to limit its usefulness. But this form of analysis is a valuable planning tool for management.

QUESTIONS

1. What format of the income statement is used in this chapter?

2. Name and describe the four types of cost patterns.

3. What is meant by the term **break-even point?** What factors must be taken into consideration in determining the break-even point?

4. What are the different ways in which the break-even point may be expressed?

5. How is relevant range related to break-even analysis?

6. Why is break-even analysis considered appropriate only for short-run decisions?

7. What is the formula for calculating the break-even point in sales revenue?

8. What formula is used to solve for the break-even point in units? How can this formula be altered to calculate the number of units which must be sold to achieve a desired level of income?

9. Why might a business wish to lower its break-even point? How would it go about lowering the break-even point? What effect would you expect the mechanization and automation of production processes to have upon the break-even point?

10. How is the break-even point calculated for a multiproduct firm?

11. What are the various ways in which the cost line for a mixed cost can be determined? Describe each method.

12. What does the label "units" on the horizontal axis of the break-even chart mean?

13. What is a committed fixed cost? Give some examples.

14. What is a discretionary fixed cost? Give some examples.

15. Give an example of a fixed cost which might be considered committed for one firm and discretionary for another.

16. What assumptions are made in cost-volume profit analysis?

EXERCISES

1. Compute the break-even point for a company in which fixed costs amount to $350,000 and variable costs are 65 percent of sales.

2. Redford Company is currently producing and selling 20,000 units of a given product at $10 per unit. Its average cost of production and sale is $7. It is contemplating an attempt to sell 50,000 units at $8. At this level, the average cost per unit will be $6.50. At which level should it seek to operate?

3. If a given company has fixed costs of $100,000 and variable costs of production of $13.50 per unit, how many units would the company have to sell at a price of $18.50 each in order to break-even? How many units would it have to sell in order to earn $50,000? If 100,000 units represents 100 percent of capacity, what percentage of capacity does this latter level of operations represent?

4. Using the data in Exercise 3, what would be the effect on the break-even point if (consider each part separately):

   a. The price per unit were increased to $19.50?

   b. Fixed costs were lowered by $20,000?

   c. Variable costs were reduced to $12 per unit?

5. Company P sells two products. The sales of Product 1 and Product 2 in the most recent year were $80,000 and $60,000, respectively. The variable costs of the products were $50,000 and $34,000, respectively. The company had fixed costs of $40,000. The sales mix for the next period is estimated to be the same as it was in the most recent year. What is the break-even point in terms of sales revenue?

6. The Parkinson Company uses the high-low method in determining the cost line for a mixed cost. Assume that the low and high plots are as follows:

Volume		Cost
4,000	. . . .	$5,000
10,000	. . . .	8,000

Determine the variable cost per unit and the amount of total fixed costs.

PROBLEMS

18–1. The Earl Company is operating at almost 100 percent of capacity. The company expects the demand for its product to increase by 25

561

percent next year (1987). In order to satisfy the demand for its product, the company is considering two alternatives. The first alternative involves a capital outlay which will increase fixed costs by 15 percent but will have no effect on variable costs. The second alternative will not affect fixed costs but will cause variable costs to increase to 60 percent of the selling price of the company's product.

The Earl Company's condensed income statement for 1986 is shown below:

Sales		$6,000,000
Costs:		
Variable	$2,700,000	
Fixed	1,100,000	3,800,000
Net income before taxes		$2,200,000

Required:

    a. Determine the break-even point for 1987 under each of the alternatives.

    b. Determine the projected net income before taxes for 1987 under each of the alternatives.

    c. Which alternative would you recommend? Why?

18–2. The Maxwell Corporation has a plant capacity of 100,000 units. The variable costs amount to $400,000 at 100 percent capacity. The fixed costs amount to $300,000, but management thinks that this is probably only true between 20,000 and 80,000 units.

Required:

    a. Prepare a break-even chart for the Maxwell Corporation, assuming that its product sells for $10 per unit. Be sure to indicate the **relevant range,** contribution margin, and net income on the chart.

    b. Compute the break-even point by using the equation to verify your chart.

    c. How many units must be sold to have net income (ignoring taxes) of $30,000?

18–3. Following is a summary of operations in 1986 for two companies:

	Company A		Company B	
Sales		$250,000		$250,000
Expenses:				
Fixed	$ 50,000		$175,000	
Variable	150,000		25,000	
Total expenses		200,000		200,000
Net operating income		$ 50,000		$ 50,000

Required:

    a. Compute the break-even point for each company.

    b. Assume that without changes in selling prices the sales of each company decreased by 25 percent. Prepare condensed operating statements, similar to the ones above, which show the effect of the decrease in sales on the operating income of each company.

18–4. The productive capacity of the plant of the Kimball Corporation is 200,000 units, at which level of operations its variable costs amount to $400,000. When the plant is completely idle, the company's fixed costs amount to $100,000. At 60 percent of capacity and below, its fixed costs are $170,000, and at levels above 60 percent of capacity, its fixed costs are $250,000.

Required:

    a. Determine the company's break-even point, assuming that its product sells at $6.25 per unit.

    b. Using only the data given, at what level of operations would it be more economical to close the factory than to operate? In other words, at what level will the operating losses approximate the losses if the factory is completely closed down?

    c. Assume that when the Kimball Corporation is operating at 60 percent of capacity, a decision is made to reduce the selling price from $6.25 per unit to $5 per unit in order to increase sales. At what percentage of capacity must the company operate in order to be profitable at the reduced sales price?

18–5. **a.** In 1986 the Benson Company's sales were $375,000 and its variable costs amounted to $93,750. The company's break-even point is at a sales volume of $400,000. Determine the amount of its fixed costs. What was the net income for 1986?

    b. What would have been the net income of the Benson Company in part *a* above if the 1986 sales volume had been 10 percent higher but selling prices had remained unchanged?

    c. What would have been the net income of the Benson Company in part *a* above if the 1986 variable costs had been 10 percent lower?

    d. What would have been the net income of the Benson Company in part *a* above if the fixed costs in 1986 had been 10 percent lower?

    e. Determine the break-even point for the Benson Company on the basis of the data given in both part *c* above and in part *d* above.

18–6. The Monson Company has fixed costs of $80,000. It sells four products. Its sales and variable costs during 1986 were as follows:

	Products			
	A	*B*	*C*	*D*
Sales	$60,000	$30,000	$70,000	$40,000
Variable costs	40,000	25,000	35,000	15,000

Required:

a. Determine the break-even point for 1987, assuming that the sales mix will remain the same as it was in 1986.

b. Determine the break-even point for 1987 assuming that the sales mix is expected to be in the ratio of 10–30–15–45.

18–7. The Perry Company has identified the variable and fixed costs in its operations. There is a mixed cost which needs to be divided into its fixed and variable portions. The actual data pertaining to this cost are as follows:

Year	Units	Cost
1977	5,200	$6,400
1978	5,000	6,000
1979	5,500	6,700
1980	6,400	6,400
1981	7,100	6,500
1982	7,500	6,900
1983	8,200	7,100
1984	8,900	7,600
1985	9,400	8,000
1986	10,000	8,600

Required:

a. Using the high-low method, determine the total amount of fixed costs and the amount of variable cost per unit. Draw the cost line.

b. Prepare a scatter diagram, plot the actual costs, and visually fit a linear cost line to the points. Estimate the amount of the total fixed costs and the amount of the variable cost per unit.

19

SHORT-TERM DECISIONS; TAX CONSIDERATIONS

SHORT-TERM DECISION MAKING

The short-term decisions which managers must make are based on incremental or differential analysis. These decisions involve operations and include such decisions as whether to change the price of a product, manufacture a part rather than buy it externally, add or drop a product line or department, further process a joint product, and so on. The effects of such decisions are relatively immediate and short run. The decisions can be modified or reversed if things do not proceed as planned. (Long-run decisions, such as building a new plant or investing in additional machinery, are covered in Chapter 20.)

Cost and Revenue Concepts Used in Differential Analysis

The costs which are **relevant** in a given situation are **future** costs which **differ** among alternatives. The difference between the future costs for two alternatives is called the **differential cost.**[1] Past costs are called **sunk costs.** These costs are not relevant in decision making because they have already been incurred, and there is nothing management can do to change history. Also, future costs which do not differ between two alternatives may be ignored since they will affect both alternatives similarly.

Assume that you had invested $100 in some new clothes, think-

---

[1] Some authors equate relevant cost and differential cost. But we use the term *relevant* to identify which costs should be considered in a situation and the term *differential* to identify the amount by which these costs differ.

ing that you would attend a concert on Saturday afternoon. A friend comes by and invites you to go to an amusement park instead. You believe that you will receive equal enjoyment from either alternative. (In some instances, nonquantifiable benefits may differ and they will have to be considered in the final decision.) The cost of admission to attend the concert is $11, while the cost of admission to get into the amusement park is $8. The transportation cost to attend either is $2. In this illustration, the $100 cost of the new clothes is a sunk cost which should be excluded from the decision process. The $2 transportation cost does not differ between the alternatives, so it may be ignored (though the decision will not be affected if it is left in the analysis). Thus, the relevant costs are the future costs of admission, $11 to attend the concert and $8 to get into the amusement park. The differential cost between the two alternatives is $3, as shown below:

RELEVANT REVENUES AND EXPENSES (COSTS) OF ALTERNATIVES

	(1) Concert	(2) Amusement Park	Differential
Revenues	$ 0	$0	$0
Costs	11	8	3
Net benefit in favor of choosing amusement park			$3

This framework can be used in many of the decision situations illustrated in this chapter.

The example above did not have any relevant revenues. The revenues which are relevant are those future revenues which differ among alternatives. The difference in revenues between two alternatives is called **differential revenue.** For certain decisions the revenues do not differ among alternatives. Then the alternative with the least cost should be selected. In other situations the costs do not differ among alternatives. Then the alternative which results in the greatest revenue should be selected. In many decision situations, both future costs and future revenues differ among alternatives. In such situations, the alternative resulting in the greatest positive difference between future revenues and future expenses (costs) should be selected.

As stated above, **differential revenue and cost** are the amounts by which future revenues and future costs differ among alternative courses of action. In many situations the total variable costs differ among alternatives while the total fixed costs do not. This is true where the alternatives being considered are different levels of output and no step variable costs are present. If step variable costs are present, then the differential cost between operating at, say, the

40 percent and the 60 percent level of capacity might include the increase in the total variable costs plus an increment in the "fixed" costs. Thus, differential cost is not synonymous with the difference in variable costs in every instance.

Marginal cost and **marginal revenue** are terms used in economics to describe the increase in total cost and in total revenue resulting from the production and sale of one more unit. But business decisions are more apt to involve choosing between operating levels separated by hundreds or thousands of units, such as seeking to sell 100,000 or 120,000 units in a period. Accountants describe the differences in total revenue and total costs between the two levels as **differential** or **incremental** revenue and costs.

An **opportunity cost** is the potential benefit that is forgone from not following the best alternative course of action. For instance, assume that the two best uses of a plot of land are as a trailer park (annual earnings of $100,000) and as a golf driving range (annual earnings of $60,000). The opportunity cost of utilizing it as a trailer park is $60,000 (the amount which could have been earned in its best alternative use). The opportunity cost of utilizing it as a golf driving range is $100,000, since that is the amount which could have been earned in its best alternative use. These costs are not recorded in the accounting records since they are the costs of **not** doing a certain thing. Opportunity costs come from the discipline of economics.

All of the concepts described so far will be used in this chapter to illustrate the decision process in various types of decisions.

Special Cost Studies for Decision Making

Accounting records are usually designed to provide full cost and revenue data. Such data are suitable for such general purposes as the determination of net income, the control of costs, and managerial planning in general. Yet there are occasions when management faces problems which require the consideration of only selected cost and revenue data. Differential analysis is such an occasion. Several types of short-term decision making involving the use of selected cost and revenue data will now be considered.

Product pricing. Each of the various prices which could be set for a given product represents an alternative course of action. The relevant amounts are the future total sales revenues and the relevant costs (usually only the future variable costs). These relevant amounts are both future amounts which vary among alternatives. Total fixed costs usually remain the same among alternatives and, if so, may be ignored. The goal in selecting a price for a product is to select that price at which total future revenues will exceed total future variable costs by the greatest amount. In other words, select that price which will result in the greatest **total** contribution margin.

A high price is not necessarily the price which will maximize income. There may be some good substitutes for the product. If a high price is set, customers may switch to competing products, so that the quantity which the company sells would decline substantially. Thus, in the maximization of income, the expected volume of sales is as important as the contribution margin per unit of product sold. As stated above, in making any decision regarding the establishment of selling price, management should seek that combination of price and volume which will produce the largest total contribution margin. This is often difficult to do in an actual situation, since management may not know how many units can be sold at each price.

Assume that a company has fixed costs of $10,000 and that its variable cost of production per unit is $5. Estimates of the demand for its product are as follows:

> 20,000 units at $4 per unit
> 15,000 units at $6 per unit
> 10,000 units at $8 per unit
> 5,000 units at $10 per unit

What price should the company set for its product? As shown in the calculation below, it should select a price of $8 per unit, since this will result in the greatest total contribution margin ($30,000).

Choice	Contribution Margin per Unit*	×	Number of Units	=	Total Contribution Margin
1	−$1		20,000		−$20,000
2	1		15,000		15,000
3	3		10,000		30,000
4	5		5,000		25,000

* Sales price — Variable cost per unit.

Special orders. Not infrequently, management is faced with the opportunity to sell its product in two or more different markets at two or more different prices. Price discrimination is unlawful under the Robinson-Patman Act unless it is justified by differences in costs of delivery or selling. But since such cost differences often exist, a single product may be marketed at more than one selling price.

The desirability of keeping physical facilities and personnel working at capacity is obvious. Good business management requires keeping the cost of idleness at a minimum. When operations are at a level less than full capacity, additional business should be sought. Such additional business may be accepted at prices lower than average unit costs because only the future additional costs are relevant. These future additional costs should be matched against the additional future revenues provided. Such costs will be, for the most part, variable costs such as materials and labor. But the possibility exists that certain fixed costs will also be increased. Regardless of the classification of the costs affected by the increased volume, one point is clear. It is the comparison of differential revenue with differential cost—**not** the average costs—that is the important consideration.

Obviously the effect on regular sales of accepting a special order at a lower-than-usual price must be considered. If regular sales are to be unharmed by the acceptance of such a special order, it is essential that separate markets exist, such as in the case of a foreign market and a domestic market.

To illustrate, assume that a given company produces and sells a single product at a variable cost of $8 per unit. The company's annual capacity is 10,000 units, and its annual fixed costs total $48,000. The selling price is $20 per unit, and production and sales are budgeted at 5,000 units. Thus, budgeted net income is $12,000, computed as follows:

Sales (5,000 units at $20)		$100,000
Costs:		
Fixed	$48,000	
Variable (5,000 at $8)	40,000	88,000
Net income		$ 12,000

An order for 3,000 units is received from a foreign distributor at a price of $10 per unit. This $10 price is only half of the regular selling price per unit, and it is also less than the average cost per unit of $17.60 ($88,000 ÷ 5,000 units). But the $10 price offered exceeds the variable cost per unit by $2. If the order is accepted, net income will be $18,000, computed as follows:

Sales (5,000 units at $20; 3,000 units at $10)		$130,000
Costs:		
Fixed	$48,000	
Variable (8,000 at $8)	64,000	112,000
Net income		$ 18,000

To continue to operate at 50 percent of capacity would produce net income of only $12,000. Thus, a contribution margin of $2 per unit on the new asset will result from acceptance of the order, and net income will be increased by $6,000. Because the regular market is unlikely to be affected by the export of the product at a sharply reduced price, the order should be accepted.

Using the decision format illustrated earlier, the analysis would be as follows:

RELEVANT REVENUES AND EXPENSES (COSTS) OF ALTERNATIVES

	(1) Accept Order	(2) Reject Order	Differential
Revenues	$130,000	$100,000	$30,000
Expenses	64,000	40,000	24,000
Net benefit in favor of accepting order			$ 6,000

As a practical matter, "dumping" is the practice of selling excess goods in foreign markets at a price less than the full costs. This is usually prohibited by trade agreements. We will assume that no such agreement exists with the foreign country involved in the example.

In summary, variable costs set a floor for the selling price in marginal or incremental analyses such as those described above. Even if price exceeds variable costs only slightly, the additional business will make a contribution to income. But such "contribution pricing" of marginal business often brings only short-term increases in income. Such pricing should be appraised in the light of long-range effects on the entire price structure of the company and the industry. In the long run, full costs must be covered.

Elimination of Products

Periodically management faces the question of eliminating or retaining given products. To assist in the solution of such a problem, a special study of costs and revenues may be called for. Since the income statement does not automatically associate costs with given products, costs must be reclassified into those which would be changed by the elimination and those which would remain unaffected. In effect, one must simply assume elimination and compare the reduction in revenues (differential revenue) with the eliminated costs (differential cost). Usually such costs as materials and labor and other variable costs will be eliminated and therefore become part of differential cost. The fixed costs will usually remain unaffected and, if so, are not relevant to the decision; but sometimes certain fixed costs are reduced or eliminated when a product is dropped. If revenues resulting from the sale of a product exceed the incremental costs resulting from its sale, a product is making a positive contribution to income. The product should be retained unless an even more profitable alternative exists.

To illustrate, assume that the elimination of Product K is being considered. Product K provides revenue of only $100,000 annually, while the costs with which it is charged by accepted accounting methods amount to $110,000, producing a loss of $10,000. Assume that a careful analysis of the costs reveals that if Product K were dropped, the reduction in costs would be $80,000; the other $30,000 of the costs would continue to be incurred. The latter costs would increase the burden on the remaining products of the company by $30,000 if Product K is dropped. The analysis is as follows:

RELEVANT REVENUES AND EXPENSES (COSTS) OF ALTERNATIVES

	(1) Retain Product K	(2) Drop Product K	Differential
Revenues	$100,000	$0	$100,000
Expenses	80,000	0	80,000
Net benefit of retaining Product K			$ 20,000

It is easily seen that Product K, even though producing no net income, has been contributing $20,000 ($100,000 − $80,000) annually to the net income of the business. Its elimination could be a costly mistake unless there is a more profitable use of the resources that would be released from not producing Product K. For instance, it is possible that the released facilities could be used to produce an alternative product which would make a contribution to income of more than $20,000 per year. If so, Product K should be eliminated and production of the alternative product should proceed. The income from the alternative product is an opportunity cost of retaining Product K, and vice versa.

There may be nonquantifiable reasons for retaining a product even though the quantitative factors indicate that it should be eliminated. Management must consider the effect of elimination or retention on the sales of other products. An unprofitable product may be retained to provide a full line for customers. For example, even if flashbulbs were known to be sold at a loss in a retail drugstore, their sales would probably be continued in order to draw customers into the store and to be able to offer a complete line of photographic products. Likewise, certain services may be retained because of the adverse effect of their elimination on sales of other products. An example is unprofitable warranty work done by a retail automobile dealer. Buyers of new automobiles like to be assured that warranty services are available at their dealer's place of business for the cars they purchase. Even if the services are provided at a loss, it may be wise to retain them.

Eliminating a Department

Before a proper decision can be made about the closing of a department, a detailed analysis of all of the expenses and revenues must be made to determine which expenses and revenues will be eliminated if the department is eliminated. For example, the schedule in Illustration 19.1 shows the assumed amounts of expenses and revenues that would be eliminated if the furnishings department of the Leon Company is eliminated. Obviously, if the furnishings department is eliminated, all of its sales revenue would disappear. It should also be quite obvious that the cost of goods sold would be eliminated if the department is closed.

Operating expenses are then analyzed and classified into those which would be eliminated and those which would not be eliminated if the department is closed. If the total expenses which would be eliminated exceed the total revenue which would be eliminated, the department should be eliminated (unless qualitative factors indicate otherwise). If eliminated revenues exceed eliminated expenses, the department should not be eliminated unless a better alternative use of the space and resources is available. Had the furnishings department been eliminated, net income would have declined by $31,200 (the difference in the reduction of the incremental revenues and expenses, $120,000 − $88,800).

Using the form of analysis that is employed for other decisions, the analysis would appear as follows:

RELEVANT REVENUES AND EXPENSES (COSTS) OF ALTERNATIVES

	(1) Keep Department	(2) Eliminate Department	Differential
Revenues	$120,000	0	$120,000
Expenses	88,800	0	88,800
Net advantage of retaining department			$ 31,200

Possibly the space and facilities now used by the furnishings department could be used to generate future revenues that would exceed future expenses by more than $31,200 per year. If so, that alternative use should be selected.

Illustration 19.1

LEON COMPANY
Estimated Effect on Income of
Discontinuing the Furnishings Department

	Current Amounts	If Department Is Discontinued	
		Eliminated	Not Eliminated
Revenues:			
Net sales	$120,000	$120,000	
Total	$120,000	$120,000	
Expenses:			
Cost of goods sold	$ 74,800	$ 74,800	
Building occupancy	16,000		$16,000
Promotion	6,000	3,000	3,000
Salespeople	11,000	11,000	
Buying	8,600		8,600
Administrative	7,000		7,000
Total	$123,400	$ 88,800	$34,600

Expenses which would be eliminated if a department is eliminated are usually the variable expenses and the direct fixed expenses. Normally the allocated fixed expenses would continue. But there could be exceptions to these generalizations in any given instance.

Discontinuing Sales to a Certain Type of Customer

Retention of a given segment of business is usually advisable if its differential revenues exceed its differential costs (usually variable costs). This form of decision rule has already been illustrated with products and departments. But, as with products or departments, elimination may be in order if there is a more profitable alternative use of resources. This is another way of saying that when the opportunity cost of selling to customers whose purchases are small is considered, an analysis may show that these sales should be discontinued. Assume, for example, that the weekly revenues from customers whose orders total less than $20,000 annually exceed the weekly incremental costs involved by substantially less than the excess of weekly revenues over weekly incremental costs on sales to larger customers. Since the larger customers furnish business which provides a higher contribution margin per week of salesperson effort, it may be advisable to apply greater sales effort to larger customers and to discontinue salespersons' visits to the customers whose purchases are small. (Possibly the smaller customers could be contacted by telephone.) Assume also that there is an adequate supply of new large customers which could be approached for business.

To illustrate, assume the following facts:

	(1) Sell to Large Customers	(2) Sell to Small Customers*	Differential
Revenues per week	$10,000	$6,000	$4,000
Variable costs per week (including cost of goods sold) . . .	4,500	3,750	750
Contribution margin per week	$ 5,500	$2,250	$3,250

* Assume that a salesperson can make one successful call to a large customer per week or three successful calls to small customers per week (average of $2,000 sales revenue per small customer).

Selling to large customers maximizes the contribution margin per unit of time. The company is better off by $3,250 (the difference in the contribution margins) per salesperson per week if sales are to large customers.

Further Processing of Joint Products

In some manufacturing situations several products result from a common raw material or manufacturing process. These are called joint products. An example would be the slaughtering and butchering of any livestock, such as cattle. **Joint product costs** are the costs incurred up to the point at which the joint products are split off from one another. These costs are sunk costs in deciding such issues as whether to process a joint product further before selling it or whether to sell it in its condition at split-off.

Assume that Company Z manufactures two products, A and B, from a common manufacturing process. Each of the products could be sold in its present form or could be processed further and sold at a higher price. Assume the following data:

Product	Selling Price at Split-Off Point per Unit	Cost of Further Processing per Unit	Selling Price per Unit after Further Processing
A	$10	$6	$21
B	12	7	18

The differential revenues and costs of further processing of the two products are:

Product	Differential Revenue of Further Processing	Differential Cost of Further Processing	Net Advantage (Disadvantage) of Further Processing
A	$11	$6	$5
B	6	7	(1)

Based on this analysis, Product A should be processed further, since this will increase earnings by $5 per unit sold. Product B should not be processed further, as this will decrease earnings by $1 per unit sold.

This same form of analysis should also be used in deciding whether low-value products (often called by-products) should be discarded or processed further so that they might be salable. If the differential revenue of further processing exceeds the differential cost, then further processing should be done. If not, the waste products should be discarded.

Make-or-Buy Decisions

Differential analysis is also applied in deciding whether to make or buy a part or material used in the manufacture of a product. In such a case a comparison is made between the price which would be paid for the part if it were purchased and the additional costs which would be incurred if the part were manufactured. If almost all of the costs of manufacture are fixed and would exist in any case, it is likely that manufacturing, rather than purchasing, the part or material would be more economical.

To illustrate, assume that a company is manufacturing a part used in its final product at a cost of $6. The cost components are materials, $3.00; labor, $1.50; fixed factory costs, $1.05; and other variable factory costs, $0.45. The part could be purchased for $5.25. Since the fixed overhead would presumably continue even if the part were purchased, the manufacturing of the part should be continued. The added costs of manufacturing amount to only $4.95 ($3.00 + $1.50 + $0.45). This is 30 cents per unit less than the purchase price of the part, as shown in the following analysis:

RELEVANT REVENUES AND EXPENSES (COSTS) OF ALTERNATIVES

	(1) *Make*	*(2)* *Buy*	*Differential*
Revenues	$0	$0	$0
Expenses	4.95	5.25	0.30
Net advantage of making			$0.30

In certain situations it may be possible to avoid some of the fixed costs by buying outside. If so, these fixed costs should be treated in the same way as the variable costs in the analysis, since they would then be relevant costs.

Also, consideration should be given to the opportunity cost of not utilizing for some other purpose the space required to manufacture the part. If the total opportunity cost of not using the space in its best alternative use is more than 30 cents per unit times the number of units produced, then the part should be purchased from outside.

In some cases the relative cost of manufacturing as opposed to purchasing may be only a minor consideration. Among the many other factors to be considered are the competence of existing personnel to undertake manufacture of the part or material, the availability of working capital, and the cost of any borrowing that may be necessary.

Maximizing Utilization of a Scarce Resource

Consider the following data for a company which is operating near capacity producing three products:

	Product A	Product B	Product C	Total
Sales (incremental revenue)	$400,000	$300,000	$300,000	$1,000,000
Variable costs (incremental costs)	250,000	200,000	250,000	700,000
Contribution margin	$150,000	$100,000	$ 50,000	$300,000
Fixed costs (all allocated)	80,000	60,000	60,000	200,000
Income	$ 70,000	$ 40,000	$ (10,000)	$ 100,000
Units produced	20,000	20,000	20,000	
Sales price per unit	$20.00	$15.00	$15.00	
Variable cost per unit	12.50	10.00	12.50	
Contribution margin per unit	7.50	5.00	2.50	

In the preceding chapter, computation of the break-even point for a multiproduct company was covered. A break-even chart for such a company can also be drawn. The break-even chart for the above firm is shown in Illustration 19.2. Assuming a constant product mix, the computed break-even point is $666,667 (total contribution margin, 30 percent, divided into total fixed costs, $200,000).

One might conclude that, to increase income, the company should try to expand sales while retaining the product mix that existed in the past. But this strategy is not likely to increase sales very much. Such a strategy overlooks the fact that manufacturing capacity is a scarce resource, since the company is currently operating near capacity. Thus, a better strategy would be to alter the mix of products within the constraints which exist. Suppose that the company has a total annual manufacturing capacity of 6,000 hours. Assume that, after careful analysis, it is found that 8 units of Product A, or 9 units of Product B, or 20 units of Product C, can be produced per hour. These production rates are based on the assumption that the full resources of the factory are devoted to manufacturing **only** one product. Assume further that due to specialized equipment requirements and limited consumer demand the following constraints apply to production and sales:

Product	Maximum Production	Maximum Demand
A	30,000	24,000
B	40,000	50,000
C	40,000	60,000

If there were no constraints regarding production time, equipment requirements, or consumer demand, one might be tempted to sell only the product with the highest contribution margin per unit. But because production capacity is a scarce resource, the important variable in this situation is maximization of contribution margin per hour of plant capacity rather than per unit. Contribution margin per hour of plant capacity is computed as follows:

Product	Contribution Margin per Unit	Units Produced per Hour	Contribution Margin per Hour
A	$7.50	8	$60
B	5.00	9	45
C	2.50	20	50

Illustration 19.2
MULTIPRODUCT BREAK-EVEN CHART

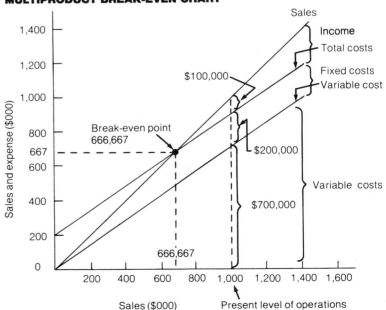

Based on this analysis, Product A still happens to be the most profitable to produce. But assume the maximum production of A is limited by a constraint of estimated consumer demand of 24,000 units as shown below. Product C is the next best alternative; its production is limited by an equipment constraint to 40,000 units. The balance of plant capacity should be devoted to Product B. The results of this analysis are summarized below:

Product	Contribution Margin per Hour	Rank	Maximum Production	Demand	Units to Produce	Time to Produce	Contribution Margin Total†
A . . .	$60	1	30,000	24,000	24,000	3,000	$180,000
B . . .	45	3	40,000	50,000	9,000*	1,000	45,000
C . . .	50	2	40,000	60,000	40,000	2,000	100,000
						6,000	$325,000

* After the number of units of A and C (and the time required to produce them) has been determined, 1,000 hours of productive capacity remains. In that remaining time, 9,000 units of B can be produced.
† Units produced times contribution margin per unit.

Notice that the full amount of plant capacity is utilized. The new earnings are computed as follows:

```
Sales:
    A (24,000 × $20.00)    . . .    $480,000
    B (9,000 × $15.00)     . . . .    135,000
    C (40,000 × $15.00)    . . .      600,000    $1,215,000

Variable costs:
    A (24,000 × $12.50)    . . .    $300,000
    B (9,000 × $10.00)     . . . .     90,000
    C (40,000 × $12.50)    . . .      500,000
                                                     890,000
Contribution margin    . . . .                   $  325,000
Fixed costs    . . . . . . .                        200,000
Earnings    . . . . . . . .                      $  125,000
```

It should be noted that switching to other products may result in a temporary increase in fixed costs. These costs may be due to rearranging production lines, retraining workers, and so forth. Also as pointed out previously, there may be other considerations, such as long-term objectives, that would weigh against increasing or reducing production of a certain product.

The remainder of the chapter is concerned with corporate federal income taxes and their effect on decision making.

THE EFFECT OF CORPORATE INCOME TAXATION ON MANAGEMENT DECISION MAKING

Most corporations organized for profit must file a federal income tax return and pay a corporation income tax. Not-for-profit organizations, specifically exempted by law, do not file an income tax return but must file an annual return of information.

Net Income before Taxes versus Taxable Income

Net income before taxes (as shown on the income statement) and taxable income (as shown in the corporation's tax return) need not necessarily agree; there are various reasons why they might differ. Some of these reasons are:

1. Certain items of revenue and expense included in the computation of business income are excluded from the computation of taxable income. For instance, interest earned on state, county, or municipal bonds is not subject to tax. Only "ordinary" and "necessary" business expenses and "reasonable" amounts of salaries can be deducted for tax purposes. Life insurance premiums are not deductible if the corporation is the beneficiary, and proceeds received from life insurance policies are not taxed. The costs of attempting to influence legislation generally are not deductible. A corporation may deduct from taxable income (1) 85 percent of any dividends received from domestic corporations, (2) charitable contributions only up to 10 percent of taxable income (computed before deducting any contributions), and (3) capital losses only to the extent of capital gains. In some mining industries, depletion deductions (known as percentage depletion) may be deducted in excess of actual cost. Goodwill may not be amortized for tax purposes even though it must be amortized for accounting purposes.

2. The timing of recognition of items of revenue and expense often varies for tax purposes from the timing used in determining business earnings. Interpretations of the tax code have generally held that revenue received in advance is taxable when it is received and that current expenses based on estimates of future costs (such as costs of performance under service contracts) are not deductible until they are actually incurred (an exception is bad debts expense). The installment sales method may be used for tax purposes, but generally cannot be used for accounting purposes. Under the installment sales method, revenue is recognized for tax purposes only when collections are received. Also, different elective methods may be used for tax purposes than are used for financial statements. For instance, the corporation may be using straight-line depreciation for book purposes and a different method for tax purposes. This is a very common practice.

For a given corporation, the reconciliation between income before taxes and taxable income may appear as follows:

Net income before taxes per income statement		$74,000
Add:		
Life insurance premiums paid	$ 700	
Service revenue received in advance	5,000	
Estimated expenses under service contracts	1,000	6,700
		$80,700
Deduct:		
Interest on *New York State* bonds	$3,000	
Difference in depreciation for tax purposes ($8,000) and		
for book purposes ($6,000)	2,000	5,000
Taxable income		$75,700

The investment credit. The Revenue Act of 1971 included two provisions that are of particular importance to business. First, the investment credit of the 1960s was reinstated. This feature permitted taxpayers to deduct seven percent of the cost of acquisition of machinery and equipment (under certain conditions) from their tax liability in the year of purchase. Also included was a provision allowing a 20 percent speedup in allowable depreciation deductions. These two provisions were included in an attempt to stimulate the economy. For the 1975 tax year the investment credit was increased to 10 percent. The Tax Equity and Fiscal Responsibility Act (TEFRA) of 1982 changed the standard 10 percent rate to:

1. Ten percent of the investment if the depreciable base is reduced by one half of the investment credit taken.

2. Eight percent of the investment if there is no reduction in the depreciable base.

Thus, if a business purchases machinery at a cost of $10,000, it may deduct $1,000 from its tax liability and reduce the depreciable base by $500 to $9,500, or it may deduct $800 from its tax liability and leave the depreciable base at $10,000.

To mitigate the alledged abuses of the depreciation deductions and ITC on luxury automobiles, the Tax Reform Act of 1984 placed restrictions on these tax savings. Under the 1984 law, the ACRS deductions are limited to $4,000 per year for each automobile in the first year of service and 6,000 per year thereafter, and the ITC allowed per automobile is $1,000 or $667 if the election is made to reduce ITC in lieu of reducing basis.

Tax rates. The Revenue Act of 1978 set the current corporate income tax rates. These rates are as follows:

Corporate Taxable Income	Tax Rate
$0 to $25,000	15%
$25,000 to $50,000	18
$50,000 to $75,000	30
$75,000 to $100,000	40
Over $100,000	46

With the above rates, corporations could receive a benefit of up to $20,250 in tax savings. The Tax Reform Act of 1984 phased out the benefit for corporations with taxable income in excess of $1 million. The act increased the tax liability on such corporations by the lesser of $20,250 or 5 percent of taxable income in excess of $1 million.

The maximum tax rate on all net long-term capital gains for corporations is 28 percent. Capital gains (or losses) result from the sale of capital assets (and certain other assets) that have been held more than six months. This six month holding period applies to property acquired after June 22, 1984, but before January 1, 1988. The required holding period of property acquired before June 23, 1984, and after December 31, 1987 is more than one year for the gains to receive long-term capital gains treatment. Excluded from capital gains treatment are gains on assets sold in the normal course of business. Thus, a gain on the sale of securities held for investment for the necessary holding period qualifies as a capital gain, while the sale of inventory at a profit does not.

Decisions Affected by Tax Considerations

Management strives to maximize the earnings available for common stockholders per share of common stock outstanding. Management can affect the timing of the recognition of revenues and the incurrence of some expenses and thus affect the timing of taxable income. Since money has "time value," there is an incentive for management to defer the incurrence and payment of income taxes.

Form of business organization. The income of a proprietorship or partnership is considered income to the individual owners whether or not the income is distributed. There is no tax on the business entity itself. Salaries to owners and distributions of income are treated the same under the tax law. In fact, salaries are merely considered a means of distributing income.

The corporate form of organization creates another taxpayer. The corporation itself is taxed on its income. Then when dividends are distributed the stockholders are taxed on the dividends received. This situation is often described as the double taxation of corporate income. Shareholders in high tax brackets often prefer that the corporation retain the income instead of paying dividends (although there are limits, and penalties are imposed for unreasonable accumulations of income). These shareholders may then sell their shares with only 40 percent of the gain being taxed (capital gains income) rather than 100 percent of it (ordinary income).

Under the tax law, certain corporations with a limited number of stockholders may elect to be taxed as partnerships. If this option is exercised, there is no tax levied on the corporation itself. Instead, all taxable income "flows through" to the individual owners and each pays individual income taxes on his or her share. This option tends to negate to some extent the tax implications of the corporate form of organization, though most corporations do not qualify to elect the option.

Size of organization. Instead of organizing as one entity, the owners may use the corporate form to establish more than one taxable entity, each of which is taxed at 15 percent on the first $25,000, 18 percent on the next $25,000, 30 percent on the next $25,000, 40 percent on the next $25,000, and 46 percent on earnings of over $100,000. For instance, one corporation with $200,000 of taxable earnings would be taxed as follows:

15% on the first $25,000	= $ 3,750
18% on the next $25,000	= 4,500
30% on the next $25,000	= 7,500
40% on the next $25,000	= 10,000
46% on the remaining $100,000	= 46,000
	$71,750

If organized and taxed as eight separate corporations, each with $25,000 of taxable income, the tax might be only 15 percent of $200,000, or $30,000. But unless there are good business reasons (other than tax reasons) for multiple corporations, the tax benefit may be reduced or completely disallowed. Certain groups of corporations, controlled by the same five or fewer persons, lost this benefit as of 1975.

Financing arrangements. There are a number of ways of financing business growth. Three external means are by issuing common stock, preferred stock, or bonds; these have been discussed previously, but are included here to emphasize the tax aspects.

Different tax effects result from the use of bonds rather than stock to finance business growth. You should recall that dividends on common and preferred stocks are not deductible in arriving at taxable income. But interest paid on obligations is a deductible business expense in computing taxable income. This tax advantage tends to create a bias toward financing growth by issuing bonds rather than by issuing preferred or common stock. Illustration 19.3 supports this contention.

Assume that the Burgess Company is planning to issue $200,000 (at face value) of securities to finance the construction of a new building. The company is considering issuing either preferred stock with an 8 percent dividend rate on par value or bonds with an 8 percent interest rate. Assume that either obligation can be issued in the market at its face value.

The higher income available for common stockholders if the bonds are issued result from the deductibility of interest, which reduces income taxes by $7,360 ($16,000 × 46 percent).

Of course, there are other considerations in deciding on what method of financing to use. Among them are the supply and demand

Illustration 19.3 TAX EFFECTS OF COMPARATIVE FORMS OF FINANCING

	Preferred Stock		*Bonds*	
Earnings before interest and taxes		$140,000		$140,000
Less: Interest at 8% of $200,000		–0–		16,000
Taxable income		$140,000		$124,000
Taxes:				
15% on first $25,000	$ 3,750		$ 3,750	
18% on next $25,000	4,500		4,500	
30% on next $25,000	7,500		7,500	
40% on next $25,000	10,000		10,000	
46% on remainder	18,400	44,150	11,040	36,790
Income after taxes		$ 95,850		$ 87,210
Less: Preferred dividends				
(8% of $200,000)		16,000		–0–
Income available for common shareholders . . .		$ 79,850		$ 87,210

conditions in the capital market for bonds and for preferred stock (perhaps one could be issued above its face value and the other below its face value), the amounts of debt already employed, and the stability of income. Interest on debt must usually be paid when due if the common stockholders are to retain control of the company, while dividends on preferred stock do not have to be declared and paid. Therefore, the increased risk associated with the issuance of bonds may more than negate the tax advantage.

Mergers. A provision of the tax law permits corporations to carry losses back three years and forward fifteen years. This means that if a company has a loss in a given year it can apply that loss against the taxable income of other years and recover some or all of the taxes it paid during those years. In doing this, it must apply the loss to the oldest year first, then the next oldest, and so on until the loss has been completely "used up" by offsetting it against ordinary taxable income of those years. The corporation recomputes its taxes for these previous years by using the rates then in effect.

An illustration may be helpful. Assume the amounts of taxable income (or loss) below (1984 rates are used to compute taxes paid):

Year		Taxable Income (or loss)	Taxes Paid	Taxes Recovered
1984	. . . . .	$ 15,000	$ 2,250	$2,250
1985	. . . . .	20,000	3,000	3,000
1986	. . . . .	5,000	750	750
1987	. . . . .	(100,000)	–0–	–0–
1988	. . . . .	40,000	–0–	–0–
1989	. . . . .	10,000	–0–	–0–
1990	. . . . .	30,000	3,000	–0–
1991	. . . . .	50,000	8,250	–0–
1992	. . . . .	60,000	11,250	–0–

The loss of $100,000 in 1987 would first be offset against the $15,000 of taxable income in 1984, then the $20,000 in 1985, and next the $5,000 in 1986. The company would recover the taxes previously paid of $6,000. At this point the company would have a carry-forward of $60,000. The company would apply $40,000 of the loss toward taxable income in 1988 and therefore pay no taxes in that year. This leaves $20,000 of the carry-forward remaining. Of this amount, $10,000 would be used to offset taxable income in the next year (1989) and the other $10,000 would be applied against 1990 taxable income.

If the carry-forward had not been used up by the end of the fifteenth year of carry-forward, the remaining portion would have been lost. This provision has encouraged profitable firms to merge with firms having losses. The acquiring firm could then apply those losses against its **own** profits and thereby have some tax-free income. There are certain requirements which have made this practice applicable in fewer situations in recent years.

Accounting Methods Used for Tax Purposes

Cash versus accrual basis. The tax law allows a business to use a modified cash basis of accounting in determining taxable income **unless** inventories are a significant factor in producing income. (The basis is described as "modified" because long-term assets cannot be charged to expense when purchased, nor can all prepaid expenses, such as a three-year insurance premium, be deducted when paid.) Also, revenues must be reported when they are **constructively received** even though the cash is not yet in the possession of the business. For instance, a check received at the end of the year is considered to be revenue even though it has not been cashed. The accrual basis is mandatory for firms having substantial inventories. Since the timing of revenues and expenses differs for these two methods, an executive may determine that either the cash or the accrual basis offers a tax advantage to the company.

Accounting for inventories. There are several ways of accounting for inventories (see Chapter 4). Each of these methods assumes a different flow of costs and thus results in different taxable income if it is used for tax purposes. In recent years many firms have adopted LIFO (last-in, first-out). The last goods purchased are assumed to be the first ones sold. Under this method, during periods of rising prices, the most recent **higher** costs are charged against revenues and the asset, inventory, is shown at lower earlier costs. The result is lower net income and lower taxes. The tax law permits a company to use the LIFO method for tax purposes only if the company uses the method for financial statement purposes.

Depreciation methods. Tax depreciation is substantially different from depreciation used for accounting purposes. In accounting, depreciation methods are designed to match the expense of a capital investment against the revenue the investment produces. Tax depreciation is based on tax law; it does not necessarily have any relationship to the useful life of the asset and makes no attempt to match revenues and expenses.

Prior to 1981, several depreciation methods were available for tax purposes. The Economic Tax Recovery Act of 1981 introduced a depreciation system known as the Accelerated Cost Recovery System (ACRS). This new system is generally mandatory for property placed in service after December 31, 1980.

The primary objective of the ACRS is capital retention through the rapid recovery of capital costs. Capital assets are rapidly depreciated thus allowing high tax deductions early in the life of the asset. Under the ACRS, the concepts of useful life and salvage value are eliminated. Instead, capital assets are grouped into several different classes. Each class has an assigned life over which the assets are depreciated.

Personal property is any movable property such as machinery and automobiles; that is, it is not attached to land. **Real property** is land and any property attached to land such as buildings. For tangible personal property and real property, ACRS provides classes of 3, 5, 10, 15, and 18 years. The composition of these classes is as follows:

Class of Investment	Kind of Assets
3 years	Automobiles, light-duty trucks, machinery, and equipment used in research and development
5 years	All other machinery and equipment such as dies, drills, presses, etc.; petroleum storage facilities, furniture, and fixtures.
10 years	Some public utility property, coal conversion boilers and equipment, and railroad tank cars.
15 years	Public utility property and low income residential real estate.
18 years	All other real property

Once an asset has been classified, the depreciation allowance for each year is determined by applying the ACRS rate to the depreciable basis. A table of the ACRS rates is shown in Illustration 19.4.

The 18 years classification was added by the Tax Reform Act of 1984. Prior to the act's enactment, the 18 years property was part of the 15 years classification established by ERTA.

In using the ACRS table, keep in mind the following three rules:

1. Ignore salvage value. Apply the percentage to the cost of the asset.
2. If an asset is purchased and put into service at any time during the year, it will still receive a full year's depreciation (for tax purposes) for that calendar year.

Illustration 19.4
PERSONAL PROPERTY PLACED IN SERVICE AFTER
DECEMBER 31, 1980*

	Class of Investment			
Ownership Year	3 Years (percent)	5 Years (percent)	10 Years (percent)	15-year (percent)
1 . . .	25	15	8	5
2 . . .	38	22	14	10
3 . . .	37	21	12	9
4 . . .		21	10	8
5 . . .		21	10	7
6 . . .			10	7
7 . . .			9	6
8 . . .			9	6
9 . . .			9	6
10 . . .			9	6
11 . . .				6
12 . . .				6
13 . . .				6
14 . . .				6
15 . . .				6
	100	100	100	100

* The rates for the 18-year service life was not available at this writing.

3. Ignore the estimated useful life of an asset. The number of years that the asset is to be depreciated is determined strictly by its classification, not its useful life.

These depreciation rules apply to both new and used property. Except for depreciable real property (such as a building), the first year percentage allowance is the same regardless of when the property was placed in service during the year.

To illustrate the application of the ACRS, assume that Bigwig Company acquired and placed in service a new machine on July 1, 1984, for $100,000. The machine falls into the five-year class under ACRS. Using the percentages taken from Illustration 19.4, the depreciation allowance for the machine would be as follows:

Year	Cost	× Percent Allowance	= Depreciation Allowance
1984	100,000	0.15	15,000*
1985	100,000	0.22	22,000
1986	100,000	0.21	21,000
1987	100,000	0.21	21,000
1988	100,000	0.21	21,000
1989	100,000	–0–	

* 15 percent × 100,000 = 15,000.

Depreciation is an expense that does not require the outlay of additional capital or cash by the corporation. Therefore, tax depreciation is very desirable since it decreases taxable income and hence the corporation's tax liability. The great advantage of the new ACRS is the early write-off of capital assets for tax purposes. By providing accelerated depreciation for tax purposes, tax savings are provided in the early years of the asset's life. The tax savings in early years can be reinvested and thus increase the earnings per share available for common stockholders for the entire period.

Numerous other examples could be given to show that business decisions are influenced greatly by their tax effects, but this discussion was intended to be illustrative rather than comprehensive. With the advent of relatively high tax rates, tax planning became an essential function of management.

The tax laws are extremely complicated and are changing constantly. Those who desire to stay current with the status of the tax laws, and with the interpretations of these laws made by courts, must specialize in this area.

INTERPERIOD INCOME TAX ALLOCATION

As already mentioned, taxable income and net income before income taxes (for simplicity, pretax income) for a corporation may differ sharply for a number of reasons. In fact, the tax return may show a loss, while the income statement shows positive net income. This raises questions as to what amount of income taxes should be shown in the income statement. The answer lies in the nature of the items causing the difference between taxable income and pretax earnings. Some of the differences are **permanent**—interest earned on municipal bonds is never taxable and is always included in net income. Such differences cause no problem—the estimated actual amount of income taxes payable for the year is shown on the income statement even though this results in reporting only $1,000 of income taxes on $100,000 of pretax income.

The reasons for other differences between taxable income and pretax income are called **timing differences**—that is, differences result from items which are included both in taxable income and in pretax income, but in **different periods.** The items involved will thus have a tax effect. When there are timing differences, generally accepted accounting principles require that **tax allocation** procedures be applied to prevent the presentation of possibly misleading information.

To illustrate, assume (1) that a firm acquires a fleet of automobiles with an estimated life of four years and no expected salvage value for $200,000 (2) that the firm uses the straight-line depreciation method for financial reporting purposes and the ACRS, three-year class method for tax purposes; (3) that for each year of the fleet's life net income before depreciation and income taxes will be $150,000; (4) that no other items cause differences between pretax income and taxable income; and (5) that the tax rate is 40 percent (to simplify the illustration). Under these circumstances, the actual tax liability for each year will be as shown in Illustration 19.5.

Illustration 19.5
CALCULATION OF TAX LIABILITY

	1983	1984	1985	1986	Total
Income before depreciation and income taxes . . .	$150,000	$150,000	$150,000	$150,000	$600,000
Depreciation ACRS basis .	50,000	76,000	74,000	0	200,000
Taxable income	$100,000	$ 74,000	$ 76,000	$150,000	$400,000
Income taxes	$ 40,000	$ 29,600	$ 30,400	$ 60,000	$160,000

If the amounts of income taxes computed above were shown in the income statements for the years 1983–86, net income would be as shown in Illustration 19.6. To report net income as fluctuating this sharply in the circumstances described would, under generally accepted accounting principles, be considered quite misleading. Generally accepted accounting principles indicate that the income taxes should be $40,000 per year since the tax rate is 40 percent and each year has $100,000 of income before taxes. This position is supported by drawing attention to the fact that there is no actual reduction in taxes. Total income taxes for the four years will be $160,000. Any taxes not paid in the early years of the machine's life will be paid later—note the $60,000 of taxes in 1986—when the timing differences reverse. In this case, reversing occurs in 1986 when depreciation is less per tax return than for financial reporting purposes.

Illustration 19.6
NET INCOME WITH NO TAX ALLOCATION

	1983	1984	1985	1986	Total
Earnings before depreciation and income taxes . . .	$150,000	$150,000	$150,000	$150,000	$600,000
Depreciation (straight-line method)	50,000	50,000	50,000	50,000	200,000
Earnings before income taxes	$100,000	$100,000	100,000	100,000	400,000
Income taxes	40,000	29,600	30,400	60,000	160,000
Net income	$ 60,000	$ 70,400	$ 69,600	$ 40,000	$240,000

Consequently, tax allocation procedures should be applied in the above circumstances. Under such procedures, the income statement for each of the four years would be as shown in Illustration 19.7.

Under tax allocation, the reported net income is $60,000 per year. Note especially that the reported income taxes are $40,000 in each year, which seems logical when pretax income is $100,000 and the tax rate is 40 percent.

Illustration 19.7
NET INCOME WITH TAX ALLOCATION

	Each Year	Total for Four Years
Income before depreciation and income taxes . . .	$150,000	$600,000
Depreciation	50,000	200,000
Income before income taxes	$100,000	$400,000
Income taxes	40,000	160,000
Net income	$ 60,000	$240,000

The entries to record the income tax expense, the income taxes payable, the income taxes paid, and the changes in the deferred income taxes payable are summarized in the T-accounts below. The (1) refers to 1983, the (2) to 1984, and so forth.

Federal Income Tax Expense			Federal Income Taxes Payable					Deferred Federal Income Taxes Payable			
(1)	40,000		(1a)	40,000	(1)	40,000	(4)	20,000			
(2)	40,000		(2a)	29,600	(2)	29,600			(2)	10,400
(3)	40,000		(3a)	30,400	(3)	30,400			(3)	9,600
(4)	40,000		(4a)	60,000	(4)	60,000				

The entries keyed with the letter *a* indicate the debits made to record the actual cash paid in settlement of the federal income tax liability. Note that the amount of expense recognized remained constant at $40,000 even though the tax liability varied considerably. The normalizing of the tax expense for each year was accomplished by entries in the Deferred Federal Income Taxes Payable account. As can be seen, the tax expense for the four years is $160,000, and the tax payments for the four years also sum to $160,000. The only difference is that the tax expense is not charged to the year in the same amount as the actual liability for the year. Note also that in our simplified example the Deferred Federal Income Taxes Payable account has a zero balance at the end of four years.

Actual business experience has shown that once a Deferred Federal Income Taxes Payable account is established, it is seldom decreased or reduced to zero. The reason is that most businesses acquire new depreciable assets, at perhaps higher prices. The result is that depreciation for tax purposes continues to be greater than depreciation for financial reporting purposes, and the balance in the Deferred

Federal Income Taxes Payable account also continues to grow. For this reason, many accountants seriously question the validity of tax allocation in circumstances such as those described above. But discussion of this controversial issue must be left to a more advanced text. In the above example, the Deferred Federal Income Taxes Payable account is reported as a long-term liability on the balance sheet because the item causing its existence (the automobiles) is classified as a long-term asset.

In some instances, taxable income will be greater than pretax income because of timing differences, such as when rent collections received in advance are taxed before they are considered earned revenue for accounting purposes. Application of tax allocation procedures in such circumstances will give rise to a balance in an asset account titled Deferred Federal Income Taxes or possibly Prepaid Federal Income Taxes. This account would be reported as a current asset or a noncurrent asset, depending upon whether the item causing it to exist is classified as a current liability or a long-term liability.

SUMMARY

Short-run decisions involve operations and include decisions on pricing, dropping a product or a department, making or buying, further processing a joint product, and so on. The effects of these decisions are rather immediate, and the decisions may be modified if things do not turn out as planned.

The relevant costs in a decision are future costs which differ among alternatives. The amount by which these future costs differ between two alternatives is called the differential cost. Sunk costs should not be included in the analysis. Future costs which do not differ among alternatives may be ignored in the analysis. Relevant revenues are those future revenues which differ among alternatives. The goal is to select the alternative with the greatest positive difference between differential revenue and differential cost.

The goal in selecting a price for a product is to select that price at which total future revenues will exceed total future variable costs by the greatest amount. In other words, management should seek the price that will result in the greatest total contribution margin.

A special order may be accepted if the selling price exceeds the differential cost of accepting the order. The differential cost is usually only the increase in variable costs, but it may include an increment in fixed costs (resulting from the presence of step variable costs). Management must be careful not to violate the Robinson-Patman Act or international antidumping agreements.

In deciding whether to eliminate a product, service to a type of customer, or a department, management must compare the reduction in revenues with the reduction in expenses. If the elimination would reduce revenues more than it would reduce expenses, then the product, customer, or department is making a positive contribution to income and should be retained unless a more profitable alternative use of the released resources is available. There may be nonquantifiable reasons for retaining the product, customer, or department. For instance, the effect on other sales should be considered.

The decision as to whether to further process joint products after the split-off point involves comparing the differential revenue and the differential cost that would result from doing so.

Make-or-buy decisions hinge on whether the price of buying a part outside exceeds the differential cost (usually the variable costs) of making the part. The opportunity cost of the "make" alternative is the amount by which future revenues exceed future expenses for the best alternative use of the space required to make the part.

Where a scarce resource exists in a situation, the goal is to utilize that resource in such a way that the total contribution margin is maximized; this is accomplished by maximizing the contribution margin per unit of the scarce resource.

Net income before taxes as shown on the income statement and taxable income as shown in the corporation's tax return need not agree. Certain items of revenue and expense which are included in the computation of business income are excluded from the computation of taxable income, and vice versa. Also, the timing of the recognition of items of revenue and expense often varies for tax purposes from the timing used in determining business income.

Management decisions regarding the form of an organization, the size of an organization, financing arrangements, capital expenditure decisions, mergers, and methods of accounting for transactions all have an impact on the amount and timing of income tax payments. Since money has "time" value, there is an incentive to defer the incurrence and payment of income taxes.

The estimated amount of income taxes payable for a period as taken from a company's tax return may not be the proper amount of income taxes to report in the income statement. Taxable income and net income before income taxes (pretax income) may differ sharply because of **permanent** and **timing** differences.

Generally accepted accounting principles require that the tax effect of an item be included in income taxes in the year in which the item is included in the income statement—a process called tax allocation.

QUESTIONS

1. Which costs are relevant in deciding between two or more alternative courses of action?

2. What are sunk costs? Why are they not relevant? Give some examples of sunk costs.

3. Define a differential cost and a differential revenue. What other terms are used in place of these terms?

4. How do you calculate the net benefit or advantage of selecting one alternative over another?

5. What is an opportunity cost? How is this cost used in deciding between two or more alternatives?

6. How should management select a selling price for a given product?

7. Why might an American manufacturer sell its product in South America for a price considerably lower than that which it receives in the United States?

8. What is the decision rule for deciding whether to eliminate a product, a department, or sales to a certain type of customer?

9. In the process of manufacturing gasoline, certain tars are produced which have a nominal value of only one cent per gallon. Further processing costs for the tars of three cents per gallon are incurred, and then the tars are sold. The average cost per gallon is six cents, while sales after processing are made at five cents. How would you determine whether this processing of the tars should be discontinued?

10. A company is seeking an additional product to manufacture in now idle space in a building which it owns. The company currently heats and maintains the entire building. One new product under consideration would require the addition of a number of new employees and some equipment. Indicate how you would reach a decision with regard to adding the product.

11. You are the president of a small corporation, and you are currently purchasing a part needed in the product you manufacture and sell. You are considering manufacturing this part yourself. What factors should you consider in reaching your decision?

12. Suppose that the average fixed cost per unit of a given product is $4 and that the product is being sold at a price which covers only $1.60 of the fixed cost. Should the manufacture and sale of the product be discontinued: Why?

13. You overhear three students arguing. Their discussion proceeds as follows:

    Student No. 1: "Management should strive to maximize income after taxes."

    Student No. 2: "Management should strive to maximize the total dollar amount of income available for common stockholders."

    Student No. 3: "Management should strive to maximize earnings per share available for common stockholders."

    Are they all saying essentially the same thing? If not, which one do you most nearly agree with, and why?

14. While the corporate form of organization may have other advantages, it certainly does not offer a tax advantage for the stockholders of a corporation. Comment.

15. A classmate states: "Why all the fuss about deferring revenues and recognizing expenses sooner for tax purposes? All net taxable income is eventually taxed anyway. It is only a matter of putting off the payment. I don't think these manipulations are worth the effort." Comment.

16. What factors might cause the net income on a corporation's income statement to differ from the corporation's taxable income?

17. Name some specific types of management decisions in which tax considerations play an important part.

18. Classified among the long-term liabilities of the A Corporation is an account entitled Deferred Federal Income Taxes Payable. Explain the nature of this account.

EXERCISES

1. Assume that you had invested $480 in a lawn mower to set up a lawn-mowing business for the summer. During the first week you are presented with two opportunities. You can mow the grounds at a housing development (at a fee of $600), or you can help paint a garage (at a fee of $500). The additional costs you will incur are $100 and $40, respectively. These costs include $8 under each alternative for a pair of gloves which will last about one week. Prepare a schedule showing:

  a. The relevant revenues and expenses (costs).

  b. The differential revenue and expense.

  c. The net benefit or advantage of selecting one alternative over the other.

2. The Reed Corporation is operating at 80 percent of capacity and producing 16,000 units. The variable costs amount to $120 per unit. Wholesaler A offers to buy up to 4,000 units at $140 per unit. Wholesaler B proposes to buy 3,000 units at $150 per unit. Which offer, if any, should the Reed Corporation accept?

3. Two companies, Bingham, Inc., and Jones and Company, are competitors. Bingham, Inc., has just installed the latest automated equipment, so that its fixed costs are $60,000. Jones and Company operates in a run-down plant with only $30,000 of fixed costs. Both companies have $100,000 in sales, with gross margins of 20 percent. Compute the gross margins for the two companies assuming a 10 percent drop in sales volume.

4. In the situation described in Exercise 3, which company can bid lower on a special order to regain lost sales? Why?

5. Analysis of Product A reveals that it is losing $2,500 annually. Ten thousand units of Product A are sold at a price of $10 per unit each year. If the variable costs are $8 per unit, what would be the increase (decrease) in company earnings if Product A was eliminated?

6. Department 1 of the Johnson Company has revenues of $100,000, variable expenses of $40,000, direct fixed expenses of $20,000, and allocated, indirect fixed expenses of $50,000. If the department is eliminated, what will be the effect on income?

7. The Hawkins Company manufactures two joint products. At the split-off point they have sales values of:

Product 1   .   .   . $14/unit
Product 2   .   .   . $10/unit

After further processing which costs $8 and $6, respectively, the products can be sold for $30 and $14, respectively. Should further processing be done on both products? Why?

8. The Murphy Corporation is currently manufacturing 20,000 units per year of a part used in its final product. The cost of producing each unit is $21.50. The variable portion of this cost consists of raw materials of $12, direct labor of $6.50, and manufacturing overhead of $1. The company could earn $20,000 per year from the space now used to manufacture this part. Assuming equal quality and availability, what is the maximum price that Murphy Corporation should pay to buy the part rather than make it?

9. Daniels Corporation has taxable income of $10,000, $25,000, and $40,000 in its first three years of operations.
   a. Determine the amount of federal income taxes it will incur each year.
   b. Assume that the fourth year of operations the Daniels Corporation suffered a loss of $40,000. How much could it recover in back taxes?

10. If Corn Corporation has aftertax net income of $120,000, what is the amount of reduction in taxes payable produced by its outstanding 12 percent bonds having a face value of $400,000?

11. The pretax income of the Webster Corporation for a given year amounts to $200,000, while its taxable income is only $160,000. The difference is entirely attributable to additional depreciation taken for tax purposes. If the current income tax rate is assumed to be 40 percent, give the entry to record the income taxes chargeable to the year and the tax liability for the year.

PROBLEMS

19–1. A state government has asked for bids on an order for 200,000 units of Product Z. The Acme Company, which has a productive capacity of 1,000,000 units and is currently operating at 80 percent of capacity, is considering making a bid. The Acme Company's fixed costs amount to $8,000,000, and its variable costs are $80 per unit.

Required:

   a. What is the minimum price that should be bid by the company?
   b. Present two income statements, the first assuming that the bid is unsuccessful and that the price on regular sales is $120 per unit, and the second assuming that the contract is obtained at a bid price of $100 per unit, while regular sales are at $120 per unit.

19–2. The productive capacity of the Johnson Corporation's plant is 400,000 units, at which level of operations the company's variable costs amount to $4,800,000. When the plant is completely idle, the company's fixed costs amount to $500,000. At 60 percent of capacity and below, its fixed costs are $720,000, and at levels above 60 percent of capacity its fixed costs are $1,100,000 (this results from the presence of step variable costs). Assume that when the Johnson Corporation is operating at 60 percent of capacity, an order is received from the Foreign Sales Corporation for 160,000 units at $16 each. If the Johnson Corporation's present market for 240,000 units would not be affected, should the order be accepted? Show your computations in support of your answer.

19–3. Steve Stewart, the president of Stewart's, Inc., is very concerned over the fact that he is unable to generate any net income from Department 3. He has devoted considerable time and a disproportionate part of the expenditures of the business to this department, and it still shows a loss. He has reached the point where he is considering closing Department 3 and expanding his other two departments equally into the space now occupied by it. He believes that this move will neither increase the sales nor lower the costs of the other two departments, but will simply relieve some overcrowding. In condensed form the Stewart's, Inc., income statement for the year ended September 30, 1986, is:

	Dept. 1	Dept. 2	Dept. 3	Total
Net sales	$120,000	$80,000	$40,000	$240,000
Cost of goods sold: . . .	$ 80,000	$50,000	$25,000	$155,000
Advertising expense . .	4,000	3,000	4,000	11,000
Sales salaries	10,000	7,000	3,000	20,000
Delivery expense . .	3,000	2,000	1,000	6,000
Buying expense	6,000	4,000	2,000	12,000
Occupancy expense . .	5,000	2,500	2,500	10,000
Administrative expense .	7,500	5,000	3,500	16,000
Total expenses . . .	$115,500	$73,500	$41,000	$230,000
Net income before income taxes	$ 4,500	$ 6,500	$ (1,000)	$ 10,000
Income taxes (credit) . . .	765	1,105	(170)	1,700
Net income (loss)	$ 3,735	$ 5,395	$ (830)	$ 8,300

All direct departmental expenses would be eliminated if the department was eliminated. Indirect expenses would not be eliminated. Advertising expense is direct to the extent of $3,000 to each of the three departments, while the balance is allocable equally to Departments 1 and 3. All of the sales salaries and related expenses are direct. Delivery expense is all indirect and is allocated on the basis of sales; no reduction is expected if Department 3 is closed. Buying expenses are allocated on the basis of purchases ($90,000, $60,000, and $30,000). If Department 3 is discontinued, these expenses will be reduced by $2,000. Occupancy expenses are all indirect and fixed, and are allocated on the basis of square feet of space occupied (10,000, 5,000, and 5,000). Departments 1 and 2 will each take equal amounts of the space formerly occupied by Department 3 if Department 3 is closed. Administrative expenses are direct to the extent of $4,000, $1,000, and $2,000 to Departments 1, 2, and 3. The indirect expense is allocated on the basis of estimated direct administrative officer time spent on each department, which is in the ratio of $7:8:3$.

Required:

    a. Present an income statement for the year ended September 30, 1986, showing the departmental income that would have resulted if Department 3 had been closed during the year.

    b. Should Department 3 be closed? Explain.

19–4. The Miles Corporation now purchases a certain part for assembly into the company's final product. Because the purchase price has been rising steadily during the past several months, the company is considering using its own facilities to manufacture the part. The company's cost accountant has estimated the manufacturing cost per unit to be as follows:

Direct materials	$10.56
Direct labor	14.45
Overhead, fixed	9.24
Overhead, variable	4.81
	$39.06

For the most part, the fixed overhead consists of depreciation on factory buildings and equipment already owned by the company and used in its manufacturing processes. The price being paid currently to the supplier of the part is $30.65 per unit.

Required:

    a. Assume that the plant of the Miles Corporation is operating at a level substantially below capacity. Would you recommend that the company undertake to manufacture the part rather than continue to buy it? Support your answer with computations.

    b. Assume that the company's plant is now operating profitably at full capacity. How would you determine whether the company should make or buy the part?

19–5. The Ryans Company is planning to manufacture three products (R, S, and T). Ryan's production capacity is limited to 4,000 hours per year, and it is trying to decide what production-sales mix would maximize earnings.

    Relevant data are:

	Products		
	R	S	T
Contribution margin per unit	$8.00	$5.00	$2.50
Number of units which can be produced per hour	8	10	15
Maximum production if only this product is produced (taking into account specialized equipment requirements)	18,000	25,000	35,000
Maximum demand for this product	10,000	35,000	50,000

Required:

Prepare a schedule which includes the:

a. Contribution margin per hour for each product.

b. Ranking of the products in terms of contribution margin per hour.

c. Number of units of each product which should be produced.

d. Time required to produce each product.

e. Total contribution margin (by product and in total).

19–6. The records of the Joiner Corporation show the following for the calendar year just ended:

Sales	$750,000
Interest earned on:	
State of New York Bonds	6,000
City of Detroit Bonds	3,000
Howard County, Ohio, School District No. 1 Bonds	750
Cost of goods sold and other expenses	630,000
Loss on sale of capital asset	6,000
Gain on sale of capital asset acquired two years ago . . .	15,000
Allowable extra depreciation deduction for tax purposes . . .	9,000
Dividends declared	30,000
Revenue received in advance, considered taxable income of this year	6,000
Contribution made to influence legislation (included in the $630,000 listed above)	600

Required:

a. Present a schedule showing the computation of taxable income.

b. Compute the corporation's tax for the current year. (Use the tax rates mentioned in this chapter.)

19–7. The Richards Company had the following amounts of taxable income (loss) in the years indicated:

1980	$30,000
1981	20,000
1982	60,000
1983 . . . (See parts *a*, *b*, and *c* below.)	
1984	40,000
1985	10,000
1986	50,000
1987	70,000
1988	80,000
1989	65,000

Assume that the rates for 1980 are in effect for the entire 10-year period.

Required:

    a. If the loss in 1983 was $110,000, how much would the company recover in back taxes?

    b. If the loss in 1983 was $180,000, how much would the company have to pay in taxes for the period 1984–89?

    c. If the loss in 1983 was $400,000, how much would the company have to pay in taxes for the period 1984–89?

    d. If there is a remaining unused carry-forward at the end of fifteen years, what happens to it?

19–8. On January 1 of Year 1, Ruffer Corporation acquired a fleet of automobiles at a total cost of $100,000, which is expected to have a four-year life and no salvage value. The company uses the ACRS method for tax purposes and the straight-line method for book purposes. There are no other timing differences. Net income before depreciation and income taxes is $100,000 for each of the four years.

Required:

    a. Prepare a schedule showing taxable income and income taxes due for each of the four years (assuming a 40 percent tax rate for the sake of simplicity).

    b. Prepare a schedule showing net income after taxes as this will appear on the income statement, assuming that income tax allocation procedures are followed.

    c. Prepare the year-end adjusting entry required at the end of each of the four years to recognize federal income tax expense.

20 CAPITAL BUDGETING: LONG-RANGE PLANNING

Effective planning for the future is essential to the continuation and success of a company. Decisions about short-run factors such as selling prices, costs, volume, and profits were considered in the preceding chapter. This chapter addresses decisions concerning long-term investments in capital assets, such as buildings and equipment. This part of the planning process is referred to as capital budgeting.

CAPITAL BUDGETING DEFINED

Capital budgeting is the process of considering alternative capital projects and selecting those alternatives that provide the most profitable return on available funds, within the framework of company goals and objectives. A **capital project** includes any long-range endeavor to purchase, build, lease, or renovate buildings, equipment, or other major items of property. Such decisions usually involve very large sums of money and usually bring about a large increase in fixed costs for a number of years in the future.

Once a firm builds a plant or undertakes some other capital expenditure, it becomes less flexible. Poor capital budgeting decisions can be very costly. If a poor capital budgeting decision is implemented, the firm can lose all or part of the funds originally invested. In addition, the capital budgeting decision affects other day-to-day decisions, such as whether to hire and train employees to work with new equipment. If the new equipment is not purchased, the decision to hire and train becomes irrelevant. Other actions taken within the company regarding the project, such as arranging for sources of supply for raw materials, are wasted if the capital budgeting decision is revoked. Poor capital budgeting decisions may also harm the firm's competitive position and image.

For all these reasons, firms must be very careful in their analyses of capital projects. Capital expenditures do not occur as often as ordinary expenditures (such as payroll or inventory purchases) but involve substantial sums of money that are then committed for a long period of time. Therefore, the means by which firms evaluate capital expenditure decisions need to be much more formal and detailed than would be necessary for ordinary purchase decisions.

Investment of funds in a poor alternative can create extensive problems within a company, other than the effect on net income. Workers who were hired for the project might be laid off if the project fails, creating morale and unemployment problems. Many of the fixed costs will still remain, even if the plant is closed or is not producing. Advertising efforts will have been wasted. Stock prices could be affected by the decline in earnings. On the other hand, failure to invest enough funds in a good project can also be costly. Ford's Mustang is an excellent example of this. If, at the time of the original capital budgeting decision, Ford had projected the Mustang's popularity, the company would have expended more funds on the project. Because of undercommitment of funds, Ford found itself short on production capacity which, thereby, caused lost or postponed sales of the automobile.

Finally, the amount of funds available for investment is limited. Thus, once a capital investment decision is made, alternative investment opportunities are lost. The benefits or returns lost by rejecting the best alternative investment are an **opportunity cost.**

PROJECT SELECTION: A GENERAL VIEW

Some techniques will be discussed that are used to evaluate alternative proposals. The techniques include payback, unadjusted rate of return, net present value, profitability index, and time-adjusted rate of return. But first, some concepts used in these techniques need to be discussed.

Time Value of Money

Money received today is worth more than the same amount of money received at a future date such as a month or a year from now. This principle, which involves the use of compound interest, is known as the present value approach. Closely related to present value are the concepts of future worth and the present value of an annuity. These concepts were covered in the Appendix to Chapter 9. If you need to review these concepts, refer back to the Chapter 9 Appendix before continuing with this chapter.

Net Cash Benefits

The **net cash benefit** (as used in capital budgeting) is the net cash inflow expected from a project in a period. The net cash benefit is the difference between the periodic cash inflows and the periodic cash outflows for a proposed project.

Asset addition. Assume, for example, that a firm is considering the purchase of new equipment for $120,000. The equipment is expected to have a useful life of 15 years and no salvage value. The equipment is expected to produce cash inflows (revenue) of $75,000 per year and cash outflows (costs) of $50,000 per year. Ignoring depreciation and taxes, the annual net cash inflow is computed as follows:

Cash inflows	$75,000
Cash outflows . . .	50,000
Net cash inflow . . .	$25,000

Depreciation and taxes. Although depreciation does not involve a cash outflow, it is deductible in arriving at federal taxable income. Thus, depreciation reduces the amount of cash outflow for income taxes. This reduction in cash outflows for income taxes is a tax saving made possible by a depreciation tax shield. A **tax shield** is the amount by which taxable income is reduced due to the deductibility of an item.

Thus, if depreciation is $8,000, the tax shield is $8,000. The tax shield results in a tax saving. The amount of the tax saving can be found by multiplying the tax rate by the amount of the depreciation tax shield. The formula is shown below:

Tax rate $\times$ Depreciation tax shield $=$ Tax saving

Using the data in the previous example and assuming straight-line depreciation (which can be selected even under new tax regulations) of $8,000 per year and a 40 percent tax rate, the amount of the tax saving is $3,200 (40 percent $\times$ $8,000 depreciation tax shield). Now, considering taxes and depreciation, the annual net cash inflow from the $120,000 of equipment is computed as follows:

	To Compute Net Income	To Compute Cash Flow
Cash inflows	$75,000	$75,000
Cash outflows	50,000	50,000
Net cash inflow before taxes . . .	$25,000	$25,000
Depreciation	8,000	
Taxable income	$17,000	
Tax at 40%	6,800	6,800
Net income after taxes	$10,200	
Net cash inflow (after taxes) . . .		$18,200

Considering taxes and depreciation, the net cash inflow is $18,200 instead of the $25,000 computed previously.

Asset replacements. Sometimes a firm has to decide whether to acquire new plant assets to replace existing ones. Such replacement decisions often occur when faster and more efficient machinery and equipment appear on the market.

The computation of net cash benefit is more complex for a replacement decision than for an acquisition decision because cash inflows and outflows for two items (the asset being replaced and the new asset) must be considered. To illustrate, assume that a company operates two machines that were purchased four years ago at a cost of $18,000 each. The estimated useful life of each machine is 12 years (with no salvage value). In order to simplify the illustrations, we assume the use of straight-line depreciation for tax purposes throughout this chapter. Each machine will produce 30,000 units of product each year. The annual cash costs (labor, repairs, etc.) of operating both machines total $14,000.

After the old machines have been used for four years, a new machine becomes available. The new machine can be acquired for $28,000 and has an estimated useful life of eight years (with no salvage value). The new machine will produce 60,000 units annually at a cash cost of $10,000.

There must be a $28,000 cash outflow in the first year to acquire the new machine. The additional annual cash inflow from replacement is computed as follows:

	To Compute Tax	To Compute Cash Flow
Cash operating costs:		
Old machines	$14,000	
New machines	10,000	
Difference—additional taxable income	$ 4,000	$4,000
Depreciation:		
Old machines ($18,000 ÷ 12) × 2	$ 3,000	
New machine ($28,000 ÷ 8)	3,500	
Difference—additional tax deduction	$ (500)	
Additional taxable income	$ 4,000	
Additional tax deduction	(500)	
Net increase in taxable income	$ 3,500	
Additional tax at 40%	$ 1,400	1,400
Additional annual cash inflow		$2,600

Notice that the above figures concentrated only on the differences in costs for each of the two alternatives. Two other items also need to be considered that are relevant to the decision. First, the purchase of the new machine will create a $28,000 cash outflow immediately upon acquisition. Second, the two old machines can probably be sold, and the selling price or salvage value of the old machines will create a cash inflow in the period of disposal. Also, the above example used straight-line depreciation. If an accelerated depreciation method is used, the tax shield is larger in the early years and smaller in the later years of the asset's life.

Out-of-pocket and sunk costs. There is an important distinction between out-of-pocket costs and sunk costs. An **out-of-pocket cost** is one that requires a future outlay of resources, usually cash. Out-of-pocket costs can be avoided or changed in amount. Future labor and repair costs are examples of out-of-pocket costs.

Sunk costs are costs that have already been incurred. Nothing can be done about sunk costs at the present time; they cannot be avoided or changed in amount. The price paid for a machine becomes a sunk cost the minute it is acquired (before that moment it was an out-of-pocket cost). The cost of the machine amount cannot be changed regardless of whether the machine is scrapped or used. Thus, depreciation is a sunk cost. Depletion and amortization of assets such as ore deposits and patents are also sunk costs. A sunk cost is a past cost, while an out-of-pocket cost is a future cost. Only the out-of-pocket costs (the future cash outlays) are relevant to capital budgeting decisions. Sunk costs are not.

Initial cost and salvage value. Any cash outflows necessary to acquire an asset and place it in a position and condition for use are part of the **initial cost of the asset.** If an investment has a salvage value, that value should be treated as a cash inflow in the year of the asset's disposal.

The cost of capital. The cost of capital is important in project selection. Certainly any acceptable proposal should offer a return that exceeds the cost of the funds used to finance it. The cost of capital, usually expressed as a rate, may be computed on an after-tax basis. **Cost of capital** is the cost of all sources of capital (debt and equity) employed by a firm. For convenience, most current liabilities, such as accounts payable and federal income taxes payable, are treated as being without cost. Everything else on the right (equity) side of the balance sheet has a cost. The subject of determining the cost of capital is a controversial topic in the literature of accounting and finance and will not be discussed here. Assumed rates for cost of capital will be used in the rest of the chapter.

PROJECT SELECTION: PAYBACK PERIOD

The payback period of an outlay is often computed to help evaluate an investment proposal. The **payback period** is the period of time during which the net cash savings from an investment must continue in order to recover the initial net cash outlay. In effect, the payback period answers the question: How long will it take the new machine to pay for itself? The formula for the payback period is:

$$\text{Payback period} = \frac{\text{Initial cash outlay}}{\text{Annual net cash inflows (or benefits)}}$$

The payack period for the assets discussed previously can be computed as follows. In regard to the purchase of the $120,000 equipment, which has a net cash inflow of $18,200, the payback period is 6.6 years, computed as follows:

$$\text{Payback period} = \frac{\$120,000}{\$18,200} = 6.6 \text{ years}$$

The payback period for the replacement machine, with a $28,000 cash outflow in the first year and an annual cash inflow of $2,600, is 10.8 years, computed as follows:

$$\text{Payback period} = \frac{\$28,000}{\$2,600} = 10.8 \text{ years}$$

Remember that the payback period indicates how long it will take the machine to pay for itself. The replacement machine has a payback period of 10.8 years, but a useful life of only 8 years. Therefore, since the investment. cannot pay for itself within its useful life, the machine should **not** be purchased to replace the two old machines.

In each of the two examples above, the cash flows per year were uniform. When the annual returns are uneven, a cumulative calculation must be used to determine payback period, as shown in the following situation.

The Neil Company is considering an investment proposal that costs $40,000 and is expected to last 10 years. The projected annual cash inflows are as follows:

Year	Investment	Annual Net Cash Inflows	Cumulative Net Cash Inflows
0	$40,000	—	—
1	—	$8,000	$ 8,000
2	—	6,000	14,000
3	—	7,000	21,000
4	—	5,000	26,000
5	—	8,000	34,000
6	—	6,000	40,000
7	—	3,000	43,000
8	—	2,000	45,000
9	—	3,000	48,000
10	—	1,000	49,000

The payback period in this example is six years—the time it takes to recover the $40,000 original investment.

When payback period analysis is used to evaluate investment proposals, management may use one of the following rules to decide on project selection:

1. Select the investments with the shortest payback periods.
2. Select only those investments that have a payback period of less than a specified number of years.

Both decision rules focus on rapid return of invested capital. If capital can be recovered rapidly, it can be invested in other projects, thereby generating more cash inflows or profits.

Although it is used extensively in capital budgeting due to its simplicity and because cash flow is critical in many businesses, payback period analysis has several important limitations. First, it ignores the periods of time beyond the payback period. For example, the Allen Company is considering two alternative investments that each require an initial outlay of $30,000. Proposal Y will return $6,000 per year for five years, while proposal Z will return $5,000 per year for eight years. The payback period for Y is five years ($30,000/$6,000) and for Z is six years ($30,000/$5,000). But, if the goal is to maximize income, proposal Z should be selected rather than proposal Y, even though Z has a longer payback period. This is because Z will return a total of $40,000 while Y simply recovers investment cost.

Second, payback analysis also ignores the time value of money. For example, consider the following net cash receipts in the first three years expected from two capital proposals:

	Project A	Project B
First year	$15,000	$ 9,000
Second year . . .	12,000	12,000
Third year	9,000	15,000
	$36,000	$36,000

Both projects have the same net cash receipts each year beyond the third year. If the cost of each project is $36,000, then each has a payback period of three years. But common sense indicates that the projects are not equal because money has a time value and can be reinvested to increase income. Since larger amounts of cash are received sooner under project A, it is the preferable project.

PROJECT SELECTION: UNADJUSTED RATE OF RETURN

The unadjusted rate of return is another method of evaluating investment projects. The **unadjusted rate of return** is an approximate calculation of the percentage return on investment of a captial project. It is computed by dividing the average annual income after taxes by the average amount of investment in the project. The average investment is computed as the original outlay divided by 2. The formula for unadjusted rate of return is:

$$\text{Unadjusted rate of return} = \frac{\text{Average annual income after taxes}}{\text{Average amount of investment}}$$

Notice that annual **income** rather than net cash inflows is used in the calculation. Also, some formulas use the initial investment as the denominator instead of the average investment.

As an example, the Thomas Company is considering two proposals that both have useful lives of three years. The firm does not have enough funds to undertake both projects. Information relating to the projects is shown below:

Proposal	Initial Cost	Average Annual Before-Tax Net Cash Inflows	Average Depreciation
1	$72,000	$45,000	$24,000
2	90,000	55,000	30,000

Assuming a 40 percent tax rate, the unadjusted rate of return is determined as follows:

	Proposal 1	Proposal 2
1. Average investment:		
Original outlay ÷ 2	$36,000	$45,000
Annual net cash inflow (before taxes)	$45,000	$55,000
Annual depreciation	24,000	30,000
Annual income (before taxes)	$21,000	$25,000
Income taxes at 40%	8,400	10,000
2. Average net income from investment	$12,600	$15,000
Rate of return (2) ÷ (1)	35%	33⅓%

From these calculations, if Thomas Company makes an investment decision solely on the basis of unadjusted rate of return, proposal 1 would be selected since it has a higher rate.

The unadjusted rate of return can also be computed with the following formula:

$$\text{Rate of return} = \frac{\left(\begin{array}{cc}\text{Average annual before} & \text{Average annual} \\ \text{tax net cash inflow} & \text{depreciation}\end{array}\right)(1 - \text{Tax rate})}{\text{Average investment}}$$

For proposal 1 above, the computation would be as follows:

$$\text{Rate of return} = \frac{(\$45,000 - \$24,000)(1 - 0.4)}{(\$72,000/2)} = \frac{(\$21,000)(0.6)}{\$36,000}$$
$$= \frac{\$12,600}{\$36,000} = 35 \text{ percent}$$

For proposal 2 above, the computation would be as follows:

$$\text{Rate of return} = \frac{(\$55,000 - \$30,000)(1 - 0.4)}{(\$90,000/2)} = \frac{(\$25,000)(0.6)}{\$45,000}$$
$$= \frac{\$15,000}{\$45,000} = 33\tfrac{1}{3} \text{ percent}$$

If the average annual after-tax net cash flow is given, the depreciation can be deducted to arrive at average net income. For instance, for proposal 2:

After-tax net cash inflow ($55,000 − $10,000) . .	$45,000
Deduct depreciation	30,000
Average net income	$15,000

The unadjusted rate of return, like payback period analysis, has several limitations. First, the length of time over which the return will be earned is not considered. Second, the rate allows a sunk cost, depreciation, to enter into the calculation. Since depreciation can be calculated in so many different ways, the rate of return can be manipulated by simply changing the method of depreciation used for the project. Lastly, this method also does not consider the timing of cash flows or the time value of money.

PROJECT SELECTION: NET PRESENT VALUE METHOD AND THE PROFITABILITY INDEX

Net present value method. The **net present value** method uses the concept of the time value of money. Management requires some minimum rate of return on its investments. This required rate of return should be the firm's cost of capital. Since it is difficult to determine the cost of capital, management often selects a target rate of return that it believes to be at or above the cost of capital.

Under the **net present value** method, the minimum rate of return is used to discount to the present all expected cash flows (after tax effects) from a proposed investment. The total present value of the expected cash flows is then compared with the investment amount. If the present value of the expected cash flows equals or exceeds the investment amount, the investment proposal is given further consideration. On the other hand, if the present value of the expected cash flows is less than the investment amount, the proposal is rejected.

To illustrate, the Morris Company is considering an investment that will cost $25,000. Net cash inflows after taxes for the next four years are expected to be $8,000, $7,500, $8,000, and $7,500, respectively. Management requires a minimum rate of return of 14 percent and wants to know if the project is acceptable. The following analysis is developed, using the tables in Appendix C at the end of the text.

	Net Cash Inflow (after taxes)	Present Value of $1 at 14 Percent (from Table II)	Total Present Value
First year	$ 8,000	0.87719	$ 7,018
Second year	7,500	0.76947	5,771
Third Year	8,000	0.67497	5,400
Fourth year	7,500	0.59208	4,441
Total	$31,000		$22,630
Cost of investment . . .			25,000
Net present value . . .			$ (2,370)

Since the present value of the benefits, $22,630, is less than the initial outlay of $25,000, the project is not acceptable. Its **net present value** is equal to the present value of the benefits less the present value of its cost (the investment amount), which in this instance is − $2,370 ($22,630 − $25,000).

In general, a proposed investment is acceptable if it has a positive net present value. In the previous example, if the expected benefits from the investment had been $10,000 per year for four years, the present value of the benefits would have been (from Appendix C Table III):

$$\$10,000 \times 2.91371 = \$29,137$$

This yields a net present value of $4,137 ($29,137 − $25,000). Since the net present value is positive, the investment proposal is acceptable. But there may be a competing project that has an even higher net present value. In general, when the net present value method is used to screen projects, those projects that have the highest net present values should be selected.

Profitability index. When investment projects costing different amounts are being compared, the net present value method does not provide a valid means to rank the projects in order of contribution to income or desirability. A profitability index provides this additional information to management. A **profitability index** is calculated as the present value of the expected net after-tax cash inflows or benefits from an investment divided by the initial cash outlay or cost. The profitability index formula is:

$$PI = \frac{PV \text{ of net cash benefits}}{\text{Initial cost}}$$

Only those proposals having a profitability index greater than or equal to 1.00 will be considered by management. Proposals with a profitability index of less than 1.00 will not yield the minimum rate of return because the present value of the projected cash inflows will be less than the initial cost.

To illustrate, assume that a company is considering two alternative capital outlay proposals that have the following initial costs and expected net cash benefits after taxes:

	Proposal X	Proposal Y
Initial cost	$7,000	$9,500
Expected net cash benefits (after taxes):		
Year 1	$5,000	$9,000
Year 2	4,000	6,000
Year 3	6,000	3,000

Management's minimum desired rate of return is 20 percent. The net present values and profitability indices can be computed as follows (using Appendix C, Table II):

	Present Value	
	Proposal X	Proposal Y
Year 1 (cash benefit in year 1 × 0.83333) . .	$ 4,167	$ 7,500
Year 2 (cash benefit in year 2 × 0.69444) . .	2,778	4,167
Year 3 (cash benefit in year 3 × 0.57870) . .	3,472	1,736
Total	$10,417	$13,403
Initial outlay	7,000	9,500
Net present value	$ 3,417	$ 3,903

	Proposal X	Proposal Y
Profitability index:	$\frac{\$10,417}{\$7,000} = 1.49$	$\frac{\$13,403}{\$9,500} = 1.41$

When net present values are compared, proposal Y appears to be more favorable than X because the net present value is higher. But after computing the profitability indices, proposal X is found to be a more desirable investment because it has the higher profitability index. The higher the profitability index, the more profitable the project. Proposal X is earning a higher rate of return on a smaller investment than proposal Y. The effect of each proposal on such intangible factors as employee morale and the future flexibility of the firm should also be considered.

PROJECT SELECTION: THE TIME-ADJUSTED RATE OF RETURN

The time-adjusted rate of return is also called the discounted or internal rate of return. The **time-adjusted rate of return** equates the present value of future expected net after-tax cash inflows from an investment to the cost of the investment. It is the rate at which the net present value of the project is zero. If the time-adjusted rate of return equals or exceeds the cost of capital or target rate of return, then the investment should be considered further. But if the proposal's time-adjusted rate of return is less than the minimum rate, the proposal should be rejected. If management is considering several competing investments and only one can be accepted, the project with the highest time-adjusted rate of return that is over the minimum allowable rate of return should be selected.

Present value tables can be used to approximate the time-adjusted rate of return. To illustrate, assume that the Young Company is considering a $90,000 investment that is expected to last 25 years with no salvage value. The investment will yield $15,000 per year after taxes. The first step in computing rate of return is to determine the payback period. In this case, payback period is six years ($90,000 ÷ $15,000). Next, examine Appendix C, Table III, (present value of an annuity) to find the present value factor that is nearest in amount to the payback period of 6. Since the investment is expected to yield returns for 25 years, look at that row in the table. In that row, the factor nearest to 6 is 5.92745, which appears under the 16.5 percent interest column. If the annual return of $15,000 is multiplied by the 5.92745 factor, the result is $88,912 which is just below the $90,000 cost of the project. Thus, the actual rate of return is slightly less than 16.5 percent. The actual rate is less than 16.5 percent because as interest rates decrease, present values increase, since less investment is needed to generate the same income or earnings.

The above example involved level cash flows from year to year. What happens when cash flows are not level? In such instances, a trial and error procedure is necessary. For example, assume that a company is considering a $200,000 project that will last four years and yield the following returns (ignoring scrap value):

At the End of:	Net Cash Inflow (after taxes)
Year 1	$ 20,000
Year 2	40,000
Year 3	80,000
Year 4	150,000
Total	$290,000

The average annual net cash inflow is $72,500 ($290,000 ÷ 4). Based on this average net cash inflow, the payback period is 2.76 years ($200,000 ÷ $72,500). Looking in the four-year row of Appendix C, Table III, we find that the factor 2.77048 is nearest to the payback period of 2.76. But in this case, cash flows are not level. The largest returns occur in the later years of the asset's life. Since the early returns have the largest present value, it is likely that the rate of return will be less than the 16.5 percent rate that corresponds to the present value factor of 2.77048. Thus, various interest rates are tried that are less than 16.5 percent. Several attempts may be necessary before the discount rate which yields a present value closest to the initial outlay of $200,000 is found. By trial and error the rate of return is found to be slightly higher than 12 percent. The following computation reveals why this is true:

	Return	Present Value Factor at 12 Percent	Present Value of Net Cash Benefits
Year 1 . . .	$ 20,000	0.89286	$ 17,857
Year 2 . . .	40,000	0.79719	31,888
Year 3 . . .	80,000	0.71178	56,942
Year 4 . . .	150,000	0.63553	95,330
			$202,017

If the returns had been greater during the earlier years of the asset's life, the correct rate of return would have been higher than 16.5 percent.

Since the cost of capital is not a precise percentage, some financial theorists argue that the time-adjusted rate of return method is better than the net present value method. Under the time-adjusted rate of return method, the cost of capital is used only as a **cutoff point** in deciding which projects are acceptable for more consideration. Under the net present value method, the cost of capital is used in the calculation of the present value of the benefits. Thus, if the cost of capital percentage is wrong, the **ranking** of the projects will be affected. As a result, management may select projects that are really not as profitable as other projects.

No matter which of the two time value of money concepts is "better," these methods are both theoretically superior to the payback and unadjusted rate of return methods. But the time value of money methods are more difficult to compute. In reality, no single method should be used to make capital budgeting decisions. All aspects of the investment should be considered, including nonquantitative factors, such as employee morale (layoffs of workers due to higher efficiency of a new machine) and company flexibility (versatility of production of one machine over another). The firm will be committed to its investment in a capital project for a long period of time and should use the best selection techniques and judgment available.

INVESTMENTS IN WORKING CAPITAL

An investment in plant assets usually must be supported by an investment in working capital, such as accounts receivable and inventory. For example, an investment in plant assets often is expected to increase sales. The increased sales may require an increase in accounts receivable and inventory to support the higher sales level. The increases in the current assets—accounts receivable and inventory—are investments in working capital that usually are recovered in full at the end of a capital project's life. Such investments should be considered in capital budgeting decisions.

To illustrate, assume that a company is considering a capital project that will involve a $50,000 investment in machinery and a $40,000 investment in working capital. The machine, which will be used to produce a new product, has a useful life of eight years and no salvage value. The annual cash inflow (before taxes) is estimated at $25,000, with annual cash outflows (before taxes) of $5,000. The annual net cash flow from the proposal is computed below (assuming straight-line depreciation and a 40 percent tax rate):

	To Compute Tax	To Compute Cash Flows
Cash inflows	$25,000	$25,000
Cash outflows	5,000	5,000
	$20,000	$20,000
Depreciation ($50,000/8)	6,250	
Taxable income	$13,750	
Tax at 40%	$ 5,500	5,500
Annual net cash inflow, years 1–8 . . .		$14,500

In addition to the $14,500 recovered each year for eight years, the $40,000 investment in working capital will be recovered in year 8.

The net present value of the proposal is computed as follows (assuming a 14 percent minimum desired rate of return):

Net cash inflow, years 1–8 ($14,500 × 4.63886)	$67,263
Recovery of investment in working capital ($40,000 × 0.35056) . . .	14,022
Present value of net cash inflows	$81,285
Initial cash outlay ($50,000 + $40,000)	90,000
Net present value	$ (8,715)

The investment is not acceptable because it has a negative net present value. If the working capital investment had been ignored, the proposal would have had a rather large positive net present value of $17,263 ($67,263 − $50,000). Thus, it should be obvious that investments in working capital must be considered if correct capital budgeting decisions are to be made.

THE POSTAUDIT

The last step in the capital budgeting process is a postaudit review that should be performed by a person not involved in the capital budgeting decision-making process. Such a person can provide an impartial judgment on the project's worthiness. This step should be performed early in the project's life, but enough time should have passed for any operational "bugs" to have been worked out. Actual operating costs and revenues should be determined and compared with those estimated when the project was originally reviewed and accepted. This allows management to know if projections were accurate and if all items were considered in the projections.

The postaudit performs several functions. It lets management know if a particular project is performing as it was expected to in regard to costs and revenues. The review may provide additional factors for management to consider in upcoming capital budgeting decisions, such as costs which were forgotten in a particular project. Finally, since the capital budgeting process involves planning, all plans should be reviewed after implementation for control and feedback purposes under basic management principles.

SUMMARY

Capital budgeting is the term used to describe long-term capital expenditure planning for plant assets. Capital expenditure decisions differ from other expenditure decisions in several ways. They:

1. Usually involve very large sums of money.
2. Do not recur regularly.
3. Commit a firm to a long-term course of action.

The decision to invest in capital assets is affected by various pressures, external and internal to the firm. The external pressures include the effects of competition, demand, and technology. Among the internal pressures influencing capital spending are a firm's cost structure and management's expectations.

A knowledge of certain concepts is important to the understanding of the project selection techniques used in capital budgeting. One such concept is the time value of money. Another is the distinction between out-of-pocket costs and sunk costs. Since depreciation is deductible in determining federal income taxes, it forms a tax shield.

The amount of the investment proposal used in capital budgeting is the initial out-of-pocket cost of acquiring the asset and placing it in a position and condition for its intended use. This includes the cost of the asset as well as its transportation and installation cost. If any repairs are necessary to make the asset operational, these are also included.

The cost of capital, usually expressed as a rate, measures the cost of the group of all sources of capital employed by a firm. Any acceptable proposal should offer a return that exceeds the cost of capital.

Various techniques can be used to evaluate alternative proposals. Five techniques (the payback method, the unadjusted rate of return, the net present value method, the profitability index, and the time-adjusted rate of return) are discussed in the text. (Some would refer to the net present value method and the profitability index method as one method.)

The payback period is that period of time during which net cash savings or benefits from an investment must continue in order to equal the initial cash outlay. This analysis ignores the period of time beyond the payback period. The payback period also ignores the time value of money.

The unadjusted rate of return is computed by dividing the average annual earnings (after taxes) from the project by the amount of the average investment. This method does not consider the time value of money or the length of the period over which the return will be earned.

Under the net present value method, all expected cash flows (after taxes) from an investment proposal are discounted to the present, using a minimum rate of return required by management. If the amount obtained by this process exceeds or equals the investment amount, the proposal is considered acceptable for further consideration.

The profitability index method is simply a further refinement of the net present value method. The profitability index is formed by dividing the present value of the expected returns from an investment by the present value of the initial outlay. Only proposals having a profitability index equal to or greater than 1.00 will be considered for adoption.

The time-adjusted rate-of-return method involves finding a rate of return that will equate with the cost of an investment the future expected net cash benefits (after taxes) from the investment. If the time-adjusted rate equals or exceeds the minimum rate of return that management requires on investments, then the investment is acceptable for further consideration. The time-adjusted rate can be approximated with the aid of present value tables.

Ideally, a disinterested party should perform the follow-up audit early in the life of a proposal. But enough time should have elapsed for all of the operational "bugs" to be ironed out.

QUESTIONS

1. How do capital expenditures differ from ordinary expenditures?

2. What effects can capital budgeting decisions have on a firm?

3. What effect does depreciation have on cash flow?

4. Give an example of an out-of-pocket cost and a sunk cost by describing a situation in which both are encountered.

5. A machine currently is being considered for purchase. The salesperson attempting to sell the machine says that it will pay for itself in five years. What is meant by this statement?

6. Discuss the limitations of the payback method.

7 What is the profitability index and of what value is it?

8. What is the time-adjusted rate of return of a capital investment?

9. What role does the cost of capital play in the time-adjusted rate of return method and in the net present value method?

10. What is the purpose of a postaudit? When should a postaudit be performed?

EXERCISES

1. The UYB Racquet Club is considering investing $75,000 in some new athletic equipment with an estimated useful life of 10 years and no salvage value. The equipment is expected to produce $30,000 in cash inflows and $20,000 in cash outflows annually. Straight-line depreciation is used by the company, which has a 40 percent tax rate. Determine the annual estimated income and net cash flow.

2. The Stuart Manufacturing Company is considering replacing a four-year-old machine with a new, advanced model. The old machine was purchased for $40,000, has a useful life of 10 years with no salvage value, and has annual maintenance costs of $10,000. The new machine would cost $30,000 and produce the same output as the old machine. But annual maintenance costs would be only $4,000. The new machine would have

a useful life of 10 years with no salvage value. Using straight-line depreciation and a 40 percent tax rate, compute the additional annual cash inflow if the old machine is replaced.

3. Given the following annual costs, compute the payback period for the new machine if its net cost is $140,000. (Ignore income taxes.)

	Old Machine	New Machine
Depreciation . . .	$12,000	$28,000
Labor	48,000	42,000
Repairs	14,000	3,000
Other costs	8,000	2,400
	$82,000	$75,400

4. The Washington Company is considering investing $25,000 in a new machine. The machine is expected to last five years and to have no salvage value. Annual after-tax net cash inflow from the machine is expected to be $7,000. Calculate the unadjusted rate of return.

5. Compute the profitability index for each of the following two proposals assuming a desired minimum rate of return of 20 percent. Based upon the profitability indices, which proposal is better?

	Proposal R	Proposal T
Initial outlay	$16,000	$20,600
Cash flow (after taxes):		
First year	$10,000	$12,000
Second year	9,000	12,000
Third year	6,000	8,000
Fourth year	–0–	5,000
Total	$25,000	$37,000

6. The Lucky Company is considering three alternative investment proposals. Using the information presented below, rank the proposals in order of desirability using (a) the payback method and (b) the unadjusted rate of return method. Assume the net cash inflows occur evenly throughout each year.

	Proposal J	Proposal K	Proposal L
Initial outlay	$60,000	$ 60,000	$60,000
Net cash inflow (after taxes):			
First year	–0–	$ 15,000	$ 15,000
Second year	$30,000	45,000	30,000
Third year	30,000	15,000	45,000
Fourth year	15,000	30,000	75,000
Total	$75,000	$105,000	$165,000

7. The Andrew Company is considering the purchase of a new machine. The machine can be bought for $45,000. The machine is expected to

save $9,000 cash per year for 10 years, has an estimated useful life of 10 years, and an estimated salvage value of zero. Management will not make any investment unless at least an 18 percent rate of return can be earned.

Using the net present value method, determine if the proposal is acceptable.

8. Assume the same situation described in Exercise 7. Calculate the time-adjusted rate of return. (Ignore income taxes.)

9. Rank the following investments in order of their desirability using *(a)* the payback method, *(b)* the net present value method, and *(c)* the time-adjusted rate of return method. Management requires a minimum rate of return of 14 percent.

Investment	Initial Outlay	Expected After-Tax Net Cash Inflow per Year	Expected Life of Proposal
A . . .	$40,000	$6,000	8
B . . .	50,000	8,750	20
C . . .	80,000	16,000	10

PROBLEMS

20–1. Courtney Company is considering purchasing a new machine that would cost $200,000 and have a useful life of 10 years with no salvage value. The new machine is expected to have annual cash inflows of $100,000 and annual cash outflows of $40,000. The machine will be depreciated using straight-line depreciation, and the tax rate is 40 percent.

Required:

a. Determine the net after-tax cash inflow for the new machine.

b. Determine the payback period for the new machine.

20–2. The Abilene Company currently uses four machines to produce 200,000 units annually. The machines were bought three years ago for $50,000 each and have a useful life of 10 years with no salvage value. They cost a total of $28,000 a year to repair and maintain.

The company is considering replacing the four machines with one technologically superior machine that is capable of producing the 200,000 units annually by itself. The machine would cost $140,000 and have a useful life of seven years with no salvage value. Annual repair and maintenance costs are estimated at $14,000.

Required:

Assuming straight-line depreciation and a 40 percent tax rate, determine the annual additional after-tax cash inflow if the new machine is acquired.

20–3. The Alma Manufacturing Company owns five spinning machines that it uses in its manufacturing operations. Each of the machines was purchased four years ago at a cost of $80,000. Each machine has an estimated life of 10 years with no expected salvage value. A new machine has become available. One new machine has the same productive capacity as the five old machines combined. The new machine will cost $432,000, is estimated to last six years, and will have a salvage value at the end of that time of $48,000. A trade-in allowance of $16,000 is available for each of the old machines. The new machine can produce 400,000 units each year.

Operating cost per unit are compared below:

	Five Old Machines	New Machine
Repairs	$0.453	$0.057
Depreciation	0.100	0.160
Power	0.126	0.069
Other operating costs	0.108	0.033
Operating costs per unit	$0.787	$0.319

Required:

Ignore income taxes. Use the payback method for parts *(a)* and *(b)*.

a. Do you recommend replacing the old machines? Support your answer with computations. Disregard all factors except those reflected in the data given above.

b. If the old machines were already fully depreciated, would your answer be different? Why?

c. Using the net present value method with a discount rate of 20 percent, present a schedule showing whether or not the new machine should be acquired.

20–4. The Columbia Canning Company has used a particular canning machine for several years. The machine has a zero salvage value. The company is considering buying a technologically improved machine at a cost of $58,000. The new machine will save $12,500 per year after taxes in cash operating costs. If the company decides not to buy the new machine, it can use the old machine for an indefinite period of time by incurring heavy repair costs. The new machine will have a useful life of eight years.

Required:

a. Compute the time-adjusted rate of return for the new machine.

b. Management thinks the estimated useful life of the new machine may be more or less than eight years. Compute the time-adjusted rate of return for the new machine if its useful life is (1) 5 years, and (2) 12 years, instead of eight years.

c. Suppose the new machine's useful life is eight years but the annual after-tax cost savings are only $10,000. Compute the time-adjusted rate of return.

d. Assume the annual after-tax cost savings from the new machine will be $11,000 and its useful life will be 10 years. Compute the time-adjusted rate of return.

20–5. The Cougar Company is considering three different investments involving depreciable assets with no salvage value. Listed below are some data related to these investments:

Investment	Initial Outlay	Expected After-Tax Net Cash Inflow per Year	Expected Life of Proposal
1 . . .	$ 70,000	$14,000	10 years
2 . . .	120,000	24,000	20
3 . . .	180,000	34,000	10

Management requires a minimum return on investments of 12 percent.

Required:

Rank these proposals using the following selection techniques. (Ignore income taxes and salvage value.)

a. Unadjusted rate of return.

b. Payback period.

c. Time-adjusted rate of return.

d. Profitability index.

20–6. The Scottsdale Company has decided to computerize its accounting system. The company has two alternatives—it can lease a computer under a three-year contract, or it can purchase a computer outright.

If the computer is leased, the lease payment will be $18,000 each year. The first lease payment will be due on the day the lease contract is signed. The other two payments will be due at the end of the first and second years. All repairs and maintenance will be provided by the lessor.

If the computer is purchased outright the following costs will be incurred:

Acquisition cost	$42,000
Repairs and maintenance:	
First year	1,200
Second year	1,000
Third year	1,400

The computer is expected to have only a three-year useful life because of obsolescence and technological advancements. The computer will have no salvage value and will be depreciated on a double-declining-balance basis. The Scottsdale Company's cost of capital is 16 percent.

Required:

Show whether the Scottsdale Company should lease or purchase the computer. (Ignore income taxes.)

20–7. The Prescott Sports Company is trying to decide whether or not to add tennis equipment to its existing line of football, baseball, and basketball equipment. Market research studies and cost analyses have provided the following information:

1. Additional machinery and equipment will be needed to manufacture the tennis equipment. The machines and equipment will cost $600,000, have a 10-year useful life, and have a $20,000 salvage value.

2. Sales of tennis equipment for the next 10 years have been projected as follows:

Year	Sales in Dollars
1	$100,000
2	150,000
3	225,000
4	250,000
5	275,000
6–10 (each year)	300,000

3. Variable costs are 60 percent of selling price, and fixed costs and straight-line depreciation will total $118,000 per year.

4. The company will need to advertise its new product line to gain rapid entry into the market. Its advertising campaign costs will be:

Years	Advertising Cost
1–3	$100,000 (each year)
4–10	50,000 (each year)

5. The company requires a 14 percent minimum rate of return on investments.

Required:

Using the net present value method, decide whether or not the Prescott Sports Company should add the tennis equipment to its line of products. (Ignore income taxes.)

20–8. The Woodruff Company is considering purchasing new equipment that will cost $300,000. It is estimated that the useful life of the equipment will be five years and that there will be a salvage value of $100,000. The company uses straight-line depreciation. It is estimated that the new equipment will have a net cash inflow (before taxes) of $43,000 annually. Assume a tax rate of 40 percent and that management requires a minimum return of 14 percent.

Required:

Using the net present value method determine whether the equipment is an acceptable investment.

20–9. The Holland Company has an opportunity to sell some equipment for $10,000. Such a sale will result in a tax-deductible loss of $1,000. If it is not sold, the equipment is expected to produce net cash inflows after taxes of $3,000 for the next 10 years. In 10 years it is expected that the equipment can be sold for its book value of $1,000. The company's management feels that currently it has other opportunities that will yield 18 percent. Assume a 40 percent tax rate.

Required:

Should the company sell the equipment? Prepare a schedule to support your conclusion.

APPENDIX A
INTERNATIONAL
ACCOUNTING

WHY ACCOUNTING PRINCIPLES AND PRACTICES DIFFER AMONG NATIONS

In today's world we find it hardly surprising to discover a British bank in Atlanta, Coca-Cola in Paris, and French airplanes in Zaire. German auto parts are assembled in Spain and sold in the United States. Japan buys oil from Saudi Arabia and sells cameras in Italy. Soviet livestock eat American grain, and the British sip tea from Sri Lanka and China. Business has become truly international, but accounting, often described as the language of business, does not cross borders so easily. Accounting principles and reporting practices differ from country to country, and international decision making is made more difficult by the lack of a common communication system. If business is practiced at an international level, then accounting must find a way to provide its services at that level.

The problem is that accounting must first reflect the national economic and social environment in which it is practiced, and this environment is not the same in Bangkok as in Boston. Some economies, for example, are mainly agricultural. Others are based on manufacturing, trade, or service industries. Still others export natural resources, such as oil or gold, while a few derive most of their income from tourism. Accounting for inventories and natural resources, cost accounting techniques, and methods of foreign currency translation naturally have a different orientation, emphasis, and degree of refinement in these different economies.

Other accounting differences stem from the legal or political system of nations. In centrally controlled economies, for instance, the state owns all or most of the property. It makes little sense to prescribe full disclosure of accounting procedures to protect investors when there is little or no private ownership of property. Some of these countries standardize their accounting methods and incorporate them into law. But in market-oriented economies, the development of accounting principles and reporting practices is left mainly to the private sector. Where uniformity exists, it occurs more by general agreement or consensus of interested parties than by governmental decree. In these economies, accounting principles and practices must be more flexible to serve the needs of business firms which differ widely in ownership, size, and complexity. In countries where business firms are predominately family owned, disclosure practices can be less complete than in countries where large, publicly-held corporations dominate.

The degree of development of the accounting profession and the general level of education of a country also influence accounting practices and procedures. Nations which lack a well-organized accounting profession may adopt, almost wholesale, the accounting methods of other countries. Commonwealth countries, for example, tend to follow British accounting standards; the former French colonies of Africa use French systems; Bermuda follows Canadian pronouncements; and the influence of the United States is widespread. At the same time, levels of expertise vary. There is little point in advocating statistical accounting and auditing techniques in countries where there is little knowledge or understanding of statistics. Accounting systems designed for electronic data processing are not helpful in countries where few or no businesses use computers.

Even in advanced countries, genuine differences of opinion exist regarding accounting theory and appropriate accounting methods. American standards, for example, require the periodic amortization of goodwill to expense, but British, German, and Dutch standards do not. Accounting methods also differ within nations. Most countries including the United States, permit several depreciation methods and two or more inventory costing methods. Such flexibility is essential if accounting is to serve a useful purpose in economic, political, and social environments that are not uniform.

ATTEMPTED HARMONIZATION OF ACCOUNTING PRACTICES

The question arises whether financial statements that reflect the economic and social environment of, say, France, can also be useful to a potential American investor. Can some of the differences between French and American accounting be eliminated or at least explained so that French and American investors will understand each other's reports and find them useful when they make decisions?

Several organizations are working to achieve greater understanding and harmonization of different accounting practices. Examples include the United Nations Commission on Transnational Corporations, the Organization for Economic Cooperation and Development (OECD), the European Economic Community (EEC), the International Federation of Accountants (IFAC), and the International Accounting Standards Committee (IASC). These organizations study the information needs and accounting and reporting practices of different nations and issue pronouncements recommending specific practices and procedures for adoption by all members.

The IASC is making a significant contribution to the development of international accounting standards. It was founded in London in 1973 by the professional accountancy bodies of 10 countries: Australia, Canada, France, Germany, Ireland, Japan, Mexico, the Netherlands, the United Kingdom, and the United States. Since 1973, the professional bodies of more than 30 countries have joined the IASC as associate members. The IASC selects a topic for study from lists of problems submitted by the profession all over the world. After research and discussion by special committees, the IASC issues an exposure draft of a proposed standard for consideration by the profession and the business and financial communities. After about six months' further study of the topic in light of the comments received, the IASC issues the final international accounting standard. To date, 19 standards have been issued on topics as varied as *Disclosure of Accounting Policies* (IAS 1), *Depreciation Accounting* (IAS 4), *Statement of Changes in Financial Position* (IAS 7), and *Revenue Recognition* (IAS 18, effective January 1, 1984). Setting international standards is not easy. If the standards are too detailed or rigid, then the flexibility needed to reflect different national environments will be lost. On the other hand, if pronouncements are vague and allow too many alternative methods, then there is little point in setting international standards.

One major problem is the enforcement of these standards. There is no organization, nor is there likely to be, which can ensure compliance with international standards. Enforcement is left to national standard-setting bodies or legislatures, which may or may not adopt a recommended international standard. Generally, members commit themselves to support the objectives of the international body. The members promise to use their best endeavors to see that international standards are formally adopted by local professional accountancy bodies, by government departments or other authorities that control the securities markets, and by the industrial, business, and financial communities of their respective countries.

The American Institute of Certified Public Accountants (AICPA), for example, issued a revised statement in 1975 reaffirming its support for the implementation of international standards adopted by the IASC. The AICPA's position is that international accounting standards must be specifically adopted by the Financial Accounting Standards Board (FASB), which is not a member of the IASC, in order to achieve acceptance in the United States. But if there is no significant difference between an international standard and U.S. practice, compliance with U.S. generally accepted accounting principles (GAAP) constitutes compliance with the international standard. Where a significant difference exists, the AICPA publishes the IASC standard together with comments on how it differs from U.S. GAAP and undertakes to urge the FASB to give early consideration to harmonizing the differences.[1] Significant support for IASC standards has also resulted from a resolution adopted by the World Federation of Stock Exchanges in 1975. The resolution binds members to require conformance with IASC standards in securities listing agreements.[2]

Although these developments are important for international harmonization of accounting, ultimately the success of international pronouncements depends on the willingness of the members body to support them. In some cases, national legislation is required and may be slow or difficult to pass. The EEC, for example, issues "Directives" which must be accepted as compulsory objectives by the 10 member states (Belgium, Denmark, France, Germany, Greece, Ireland, Italy, Luxembourg, the Netherlands, and the United Kingdom) but which are translated into national legislation at the discretion of each member state. The EEC's inportant *Fourth Directive* was adopted in 1978 to regulate the preparation, content, presentation, audit, and publication of the accounts and reports of companies. It applies to all limited-liability companies (corporations) registered in the EEC, except for banks and insurance companies. Under the directive, member states were to introduce legislation by July 1980 so that accounts in all EEC countries would conform to the directive as of the fiscal year beginning January 1, 1982. Yet by that date, only Belgium, Denmark, and the United Kingdom had passed the necessary legislation, although most of the other member countries were close to doing so.

The general movement toward international harmonization of accounting standards is increasing in other areas of society. The accounting profession, national standard-setting bodies, universities, academic societies, and multinational corporations have all shown an increased interest in international accounting problems in recent years. The AICPA has as International Practice Division as a formal part of its line organization. The American Accounting Association officially established an International Accounting Section in 1976. The University of Lancaster (England) and the University of Illinois have international accounting research centers which support research studies and conduct international conferences and seminars. Georgia State University received a Touche Ross & Co. grant to internationalize its accounting curriculum. Many universities currently offer courses in international business and accounting.

---

[1] American Institute of Certified Public Accountants, *CPA Letter,* August 1975.
[2] *CA Magazine,* January 1975, p. 52.

All this activity helps to increase the flow of information and our understanding of the accounting and reporting practices in other parts of the world. Greater understanding improves the likelihood that unnecessary differences will be eliminated and enhances the general acceptance of international standards.

The rest of the appendix gives examples of the accounting methods used in different countries and of the concepts that underlie them to illustrate the difficulty of achieving international harmonization.

FOREIGN CURRENCY TRANSLATION

Foreign currency translation is probably the most common problem in an international business environment. Foreign currency translation has two main components: accounting for transactions in a foreign currency and translating the financial statements of foreign enterprises into a different, common currency.

Accounting for Transactions in a Foreign Currency

Suppose an American automobile dealership imports vehicles from Japan and promises to pay for them in yen 90 days after receiving them. If there is no change in the dollar-yen exchange rate between the date the goods are received and the date the invoice is paid, there is no problem. Both the purchase and the payment will be recorded at the same dollar value. But if the yen appreciates against the dollar during the 90-day period, the importer must pay more dollars for the yen needed on the settlement date.[3] Which exchange rate should the importer use to record payment of the invoice—the rate in effect on the purchase date or on the payment date?

One approach to the problem is to regard the purchase of the automobiles and settlement of the invoice as two separate transactions and record them at two different exchange rates. The difference between the amount recorded in Accounts Payable on the purchase date and the decrease in Cash on the settlement date is considered an exchange gain or loss (a loss in this case). This approach is known as the "time-of-transaction" method and was the prescribed or predominant practice in 61 of 64 countries surveyed in 1979,[4] including the United States.[5] The time-of-transaction method is also the

---

[3] This example ignores the possibility that the importer might obtain a forward exchange contract, a discussion of which is beyond the scope of this text.

[4] Price Waterhouse International, *International Survey.* Data on the different methods used and on the number of countries using each method described in these examples are derived substantially from this publication.

[5] FASB *Statement of Financial Accounting Standards No. 8,* "Accounting for the Translation of Foreign Currency Transactions and Foreign Currency Financial Statements" (Stamford, Conn., 1975). The "time-of-transaction" method is also prescribed by FASB *Statement No. 52,* "Foreign Currency Translation" (Stamford, Conn., 1981) which supersedes FASB *Statement No. 8.*

method recommended in the IASC's exposure draft, *Accounting for the Effects of Changes in Foreign Exchange Rates,* issued in March 1982.

Another approach known as the "time-of-settlement" method, regards the transaction and its settlement as a single event. If this method is used, the amount recorded on the purchase date is regarded as an estimate of the settlement amount. Any fluctuations in the exchange rate between the purchase date and the settlement date are accounted for as part of the transaction and are not treated as a separate gain or loss. Consequently there is no effect on earnings.

Although the time-of-transaction method is widely used, the treatment of resulting exchange gains and losses is not uniform. If the gains or losses are realized, that is, if settlement is made within the same accounting period as the purchase, then most countries recognize such gains and losses in the income statement for that period. If the exchange gains or losses are unrealized, that is, if they result from translating Accounts Payable (or Accounts Receivable for the vendor) at the balance sheet date, the treatment varies. Recording unrealized losses of this kind was the prescribed or predominant practice in 54 countries in 1979. But only 40 countries similarly recognized exchange gains in income, the remaining nations preferring to defer them until settlement. In the United States, under the provisions of FASB *Statement No. 52,* both realized and unrealized transaction gains and losses are recognized in earnings of the period in which the exchange rate changes.

Translating Financial Statements

Financial statements of foreign subsidiaries are translated into a single common unit of measurement, such as the dollar, for purposes of consolidation. Considerable argument has arisen in recent years as to the correct way to do this; that is, which exchange rate should be used to translate items in the balance sheet and income statement, and what treatment is appropriate for any resulting exchange gains and losses? Items that are translated at the historical rate cannot suffer exchange gains or losses. But items that are translated at the exchange rate in effect on the balance sheet date (the current rate) can suffer exchange gains and losses if the current rate differs from the rate in effect when those items were recorded (the historical rate). If the current rate is used, a related question is: should the resulting exchange gains or losses be recognized immediately in income or deferred in some way?

The several methods commonly used to translate financial statements fall basically into two groups: translation of all items at the current rate and translation of some items at the current rate and others at the historical rates. The two groups are based on different concepts of both consolidation and international business.

The current-rate approach. The current- or closing-rate method translates all assets and liabilities at the exchange rate in effect on the balance sheet date. The main advantage of this method is its simplicity; it treats all items uniformly. The approach is based on the view that a foreign subsidiary is a separate unit from the domestic parent company. The subsidiary's assets are viewed as being acquired largely out of local borrowing. Multinational groups, therefore, consist of entities which operate independently but which contribute to a central fund of resources. Consequently, in consolidation it is believed that stockholders of the parent company are interested primarily in the parent company's net investment in the foreign subsidiary.

The current/historical-rates approach. This approach regards the parent company and its foreign subsidiaries as a single business undertaking. Assets owned by a foreign subsidiary are viewed as indistinguishable from assets owned by the parent company. Foreign assets should, therefore, be reflected in consolidated statements in the same way that similar assets of the parent company are reported, that is, at historical cost in the parent company's currency.

Two translation methods are commonly used under this approach. The **current-noncurrent method** translates current assets and current liabilities at the current rate—the rate in effect on the balance sheet date—while noncurrent items are translated at their respective historical rates. Under the **monetary-nonmonetary method,** the current rate is used for monetary assets and liabilities—that is, for those that have a fixed, nominal value in terms of the foreign currency, while historical rates are applied to nonmonetary items.

Disagreement over the appropriate translation method seems likely to continue—because of the different concepts of parent-subsidiary relations on which they are founded. A recent survey conducted by Price Waterhouse International found that only six countries prescribed a single method. The United States currently uses the current-rate method (FASB *Statement No. 52*). Apart from these 6 nations, 24 countries, including Japan, Australia, and most of Europe followed predominantly the current-rate approach, while in 25 countries, including Germany, South Africa, and most of Central and South America, some variation of the current/historical-rates approach was common practice.

The treatment of exchange gains and losses produced by translating items at the current rate varies and is not strictly related to the translation method used. The predominant practice in 42 nations, including Latin America, Japan, the United States, and much of Europe was to recognize all gains and losses immediately in income. Eighteen of these countries used the current-rate-translation method and 23 followed one of the current/historical-rates methods. Alternative treatments of translation gains and losses included recording them directly in stockholders' equity (Australia), recognizing some of them immediately in income and deferring others (United Kingdom), and recognizing some in income and deferring and amortizing others over the remaining life of the items concerned (Canada and Bermuda).

Since the issuance of FASB *Statement No. 52,* the immediate recognition of translation gains and losses in income is not permitted in the United States. Instead, translation gains and losses are reported separately and accumulated in a separate component of stockhholders' equity until the parent company's investment in the foreign subsidiary is sold or liquidated, at which time they are reported as part of the gain or loss on sale or liquidation of the investment.

INVENTORIES

Variations in accounting for inventories relate principally to the basis for determining cost, whether cost once determined should be increased or decreased to reflect the market value of the inventories, and whether the variable (direct) costing or the absorption (full) costing approach should be used to allocate overhead.

Determination of Cost

Although other methods are occasionally used in some countries, this text will only discuss the three principal bases for determining inventory cost: first-in, first-out (FIFO); last-in, first-out (LIFO); and average cost.

The most frequently used methods identified in the Price Waterhouse international survey were FIFO and average cost. Each of these methods was predominant in 31 countries, although no country required the use of one method to the exclusion of the other. FIFO was more common in Europe, although Austria, France, Greece, and Portugal used an average method. FIFO also predominated in Australia, Canada, South Africa, and the United States. The average method was generally followed in Latin America, Japan, and much of Africa. LIFO was the principal method in only one country—Italy—although it was a common minority method in Japan, the United States, most of Latin America, and several European countries. LIFO was considered an unacceptable method in Australia, Brazil, France, Ireland, Malawi, Norway, Peru, and the United Kingdom. IASC's Statement No. 2, *Valuation and Presentation of Inventories in the Context of the Historical Cost System,* supports the preference of the majority of countries and recommends the use of FIFO or average cost.

Market Value of Inventories

The survey revealed that only seven countries did not require or predominantly follow the principle that inventories should be carried at the lower of cost or market value. Five of these countries, including

Japan, used cost, even when cost exceeded market value. In the other two countries—Portugal and Switzerland—most enterprises wrote down inventories to amounts below both cost and market value, a practice permitted by law.

The main difference in the countries that did use the lower of cost or market approach was in the interpretation of "market value." Forty-eight countries equated it with net realizable value, meaning estimated selling price in the ordinary course of business less costs of completion and necessary selling expenses. This view was essentially requried in 22 countries, including Australia, France, Ireland, South Africa, and the United Kingdom. IASC Statement No. 2 also requires this interpretation. Austria, Greece, Italy, and Venezuela interpreted market value as replacement cost—the current cost of replacing the inventories in their present condition and location.

The United States defines market value as replacement cost, with the stipulation that it cannot exceed net realizable value or fall below net realizable value reduced by the normal profit margin. In 1979, Chile, the Dominican Republic, Mexico, Panama, and the Philippines also used this interpretation of market value.

Allocation of Overhead

Recall from Chapter 14 that under direct (variable) costing, all variable manufacturing costs are charged to the product and all fixed costs (including fixed manufacturing costs) are charged to expense. Manufacturing overhead costs must, therefore, be separated into variable and fixed portions. The variable portion is assigned to production and included in inventory costs until the goods are sold, whereas the fixed portion is expensed immediately. In contrast, under absorption (full) costing, all manufacturing costs, including fixed overhead costs, are applied to production and included in inventories.

The survey found that fifty-one countries required or predominantly used absorption costing based on a level of normal capacity. IASC Statement No. 2 requires this approach. Ecuador, Ivory Coast, Malaysia, Morocco, and Senegal used direct costing, while in Botswana, the Netherlands, South Africa, and Switzerland there was no predominant practice. Chile, Denmark, India, and Malawi normally excluded all overhead—fixed and variable—from inventories.

In view of the importance of inventories and the wide variation in accounting for them, it is fortunate for the users of financial statements that most countries require disclosure of information relating to the valuation of inventories. Only 8 of the countries surveyed did not generally disclose whether the basis of valuation was cost, market, or the lower of cost or market, while all but 13 countries usually disclosed the basis for determining cost. IASC Statement No. 2 also recommends adequate disclosure.

**Accounting for
the Effects of
Changing Prices**

The final example of international differences illustrates an opportunity for international harmonization that is almost unique. Accounting for the effects of inflation is still in its infancy, so it may be possible to achieve a general international approach to the problem before national practices become too varied and too entrenched.

In Chapter 12 two approaches to accounting for the effects of inflation on business enterprises were discussed: general price-level accounting and current-cost accounting. The FASB, in *Statement No. 33,* requires both methods.[6] The first approach attempts to reflect the effects of changes in general purchasing power on historical-cost financial statements, while the second is concerned with the impact of specific price changes.

A number of countries are concerned about the loss of relevance of historical-cost financial reporting in inflationary environments, and several have adopted one of the two approaches. So far only the United States and Mexico have required both. Some countries, usually those with the longest history of severe inflation, have issued standards that are mandatory for all enterprises, or at least for large or publicly held entities. In other countries, the accounting profession recommends, but does not prescribe, a form of inflation-adjusted statements, usually as supplementary information. The accountancy bodies of several nations have issued exposure drafts but have not yet adopted formal standards. But few countries are prepared to abandon the historical-cost basis for their primary financial statements, at least until decision makers have had sufficient experience with inflation accounting to give an opinion on its utility. Exceptions to this view are Argentina, Brazil, and Chile, which now require incorporation of general price-level accounting in the primary financial statements of all enterprises.

The United Kingdom's standard prescribes the provision of current-cost information either in the primary financial statements or as supplementary statements or additional information. New Zealand requires a supplementary income statement and balance sheet on a current-cost basis. Australia and South Africa recommend but do not yet require similar supplementary current-cost statements. Germany recommends incorporation of current-cost information in notes to the historical-cost financial statements, while in the Netherlands, some companies prepare the primary statements on a current-cost basis, and some provide only supplementary information.

Even with something as relatively new as inflation accounting, the accountancy bodies of various nations are adopting neither a uniform approach nor a uniform application of any approach. This fact highlights the difficulty of achieving international harmoniza-

---

[6] FASB *Statement of Financial Accounting Standards No. 33,* "Financial Reporting and Changing Prices" (Stamford, Conn., FASB, 1979). As of this writing, it appears that only one method will be required in the United States as of 1985.

tion of accounting standards. Adoption of different approaches to inflation accounting by different countries will make the preparation of consolidated financial statements by multinational corporations especially difficult, while at the same time comparability of the financial reports of companies in different nations will be further reduced. But even if all countries adopted a similar approach, a major barrier to comparability would still remain: the price indices used in each country to compute adjustments for price changes are not comparable in composition, accuracy, frequency of publication, or timeliness.

Many accountants are reluctant to see inflation-adjusted statements replace historical-cost financial statements because they believe historical cost is the most objective basis of valuation. But business entities may be more likely to favor inflation accounting, once they become accustomed to it, because of its tax implications. Since inflation accounting generally leads to lower profit figures than those computed on a historical-cost basis, there is a strong incentive for companies to adopt inflation accounting in those countries where computation of the tax liability is based on reported net income. Governments, on the other hand, may decide to prohibit the use of inflation accounting for tax purposes when a decline in tax revenues becomes apparent. (The United States does not allow the use of inflation accounting for tax purposes.)

The current trend in the use of inflation-accounting approaches appears to be towards current-cost accounting and away from general price-level accounting. It has been suggested that, of the two approaches, governments prefer current-cost accounting, and this preference may influence the decisions of the accounting profession in some countries. As one British writer has pointed out,

> No government wants to have the effects of its currency debasement measured by anyone—certainly not by every business enterprise in the country. Much better to point the finger at all those individual prices moving around because of the machinations of big business, big labour and big aliens.[7]

Whether current-cost accounting will become common practice or whether some combination of current-cost and general price-level accounting will gain favor, perhaps along the lines of FASB *Statement No. 33*, should depend on the usefulness of the information provided by each approach to decision makers. One thing is clear: unless inflation abates, more countries will adopt some form of inflation accounting. The opportunity to achieve a higher level of international harmonization while national standards are still at the development stage should not be missed.

We have attempted in these few pages to provide a broad and

---

[7] P. H. Lyons, "Farewell to Historical Costs?" *CA Magazine*, February 1976, p. 23.

general picture of the variety of accounting principles and reporting practices that exist across the world. This variety is inevitable and necessary if accounting is to be useful within widely differing national business environments. At the same time, the information needs of international business must also be satisfied. It is a challenging problem and one that will receive increasing attention in the years to come.

SELECTED BIBLIOGRAPHY

Arthur Andersen & Co. (London). *European Review,* nos. 1–5 (January 1981–May 1982).

Choi, Frederick D. S. and Gerhard G. Mueller. *An Introduction to Multinational Accounting.* Englewood Cliffs, N.J.: Prentice-Hall, Inc., 1978.

Hauworth, William P., II. "A Comparison of Various International Proposals on Inflation Accounting: A Practitioner's View." Monograph, 1980.

International Centre for Research in Accounting. *International Financial Reporting Standards: Problems and Prospects. ICRA Occasional Paper No. 13.* Lancaster, England: ICRA, University of Lancaster, 1977.

Price Waterhouse International. *International Survey of Accounting Principles and Reporting Practices,* 1979.

Stamp, Edward. *The Future of Accounting and Auditing Standards. ICRA Occasional Paper No. 18.* Lancaster, England: International Centre for Research in Accounting, University of Lancaster, 1979.

Stamp, Edward, and Maurice Moonitz. "International Auditing Standards—Parts I and II." *The CPA Journal* LII, nos. 6 and 7 (June–July 1982).

APPENDIX B
FINANCIAL
STATEMENTS
CONTAINED IN
THE ANNUAL
REPORT OF THE
GENERAL MOTORS
CORPORATION

Presented in this appendix are 13 pages of the 1983 Annual Report of General Motors Corporation, and its consolidated subsidiaries. Included are (1) Statement of Consolidated Income; (2) Consolidated Balance Sheet; (3) Statement of Changes in Consolidated Financial Position; (4) Notes to Consolidated Financial Statements; (5) Report of Independent Accountants; and (6) Supplementary Financial Information and Effects of Inflation on Financial Data in which inflation-adjusted accounting information is disclosed and compared with required historical cost based data in a five-year summary. These items illustrate the financial reporting practices of a modern business corporation to its stockholders and to other external parties.

Particular attention should be paid to the rather substantial amounts of additional information and explanation presented in the Notes to Consolidated Financial Statements. For example, Note 1 discloses the accounting policies followed in developing the amounts reported in the various statements, such as the income tax and inventory methods used as well as the consolidation principles employed.

A strong trend has developed in recent years toward making more informative disclosures in corporate annual reports. Many of these added disclosures result from FASB or SEC requirements.

CONSOLIDATED FINANCIAL STATEMENTS

General Motors Corporation
and Consolidated Subsidiaries

RESPONSIBILITIES FOR FINANCIAL STATEMENTS

The following financial statements of General Motors Corporation and consolidated subsidiaries were prepared by the management which is responsible for their integrity and objectivity. The statements have been prepared in conformity with generally accepted accounting principles and, as such, include amounts based on judgments of management. Financial information elsewhere in this Annual Report is consistent with that in the financial statements.

Management is further responsible for maintaining a system of internal accounting controls, designed to provide reasonable assurance that the books and records reflect the transactions of the companies and that its established policies and procedures are carefully followed. From a stockholder's point of view, perhaps the most important feature in the system of control is that it is continually reviewed for its effectiveness and is augmented by written policies and guidelines, the careful selection and training of qualified personnel, and a strong program of internal audit.

Deloitte Haskins & Sells, independent certified public accountants, are engaged to examine the financial statements of General Motors Corporation and its subsidiaries and issue reports thereon. Their examination is conducted in accordance with generally accepted auditing standards which comprehend a review of internal accounting controls and a test of transactions. The Accountants' Report appears on page 26.

The Board of Directors, through the Audit Committee (composed entirely of non-employe Directors), is responsible for assuring that management fulfills its responsibilities in the preparation of the financial statements. The Committee selects the independent public accountants annually in advance of the Annual Meeting of Stockholders and submits the selection for ratification at the Meeting. In addition, the Committee reviews the scope of the audits and the accounting principles being applied in financial reporting. The independent public accountants, representatives of management, and the internal auditors meet regularly (separately and jointly) with the Committee to review the activities of each and to ensure that each is properly discharging its responsibilities. To ensure complete independence, Deloitte Haskins & Sells have full and free access to meet with the Committee, without management representatives present, to discuss the results of their examination, the adequacy of internal accounting controls, and the quality of the financial reporting.

Chairman

Chief Financial Officer

STATEMENT OF CONSOLIDATED INCOME

For the Years Ended December 31, 1983, 1982 and 1981
(Dollars in Millions Except Per Share Amounts)

	1983	1982	1981
Net Sales (Note 2)	$74,581.6	$60,025.6	$62,698.5
Costs and Expenses			
Cost of sales and other operating charges, exclusive of items listed below	60,718.8	51,548.3	55,185.2
Selling, general and administrative expenses	3,234.8	2,964.9	2,715.0
Depreciation of real estate, plants and equipment	2,569.7	2,403.0	1,837.3
Amortization of special tools	2,549.9	2,147.5	2,568.9
Total Costs and Expenses	69,073.2	59,063.7	62,306.4
Operating Income	5,508.4	961.9	392.1
Other income less income deductions—net (Note 4)	815.8	476.3	367.7
Interest expense (Note 1)	(1,352.7)	(1,415.4)	(897.9)
Income (Loss) before Income Taxes	4,971.5	22.8	(138.1)
United States, foreign and other income taxes (credit) (Note 6)	2,223.8	(252.2)	(123.1)
Income (Loss) after Income Taxes	2,747.7	275.0	(15.0)
Equity in earnings of nonconsolidated subsidiaries and associates (dividends received amounted to $757.3 in 1983, $412.7 in 1982 and $189.7 in 1981)	982.5	687.7	348.4
Net Income	3,730.2	962.7	333.4
Dividends on preferred stocks	12.9	12.9	12.9
Earnings on Common Stock	$ 3,717.3	$ 949.8	$ 320.5
Average number of shares of common stock outstanding (in millions)	313.9	307.4	299.1
Earnings Per Share of Common Stock (Note 7)	$11.84	$3.09	$1.07

Reference should be made to notes on pages 20 through 26.

CONSOLIDATED BALANCE SHEET

December 31, 1983 and 1982
(Dollars in Millions Except Per Share Amounts)

ASSETS	1983	1982
Current Assets		
Cash	$ 369.5	$ 279.6
United States Government and other marketable securities and time deposits—at cost, which approximates market of $5,834.6 and $2,835.5	5,847.4	2,846.6
Total cash and marketable securities	6,216.9	3,126.2
Accounts and notes receivable (including GMAC and its subsidiaries— $3,560.7 and $312.0)—less allowances (Note 8)	6,964.2	2,864.5
Inventories (less allowances) (Note 1)	6,621.5	6,184.2
Prepaid expenses and deferred income taxes	997.2	1,868.2
Total Current Assets	20,799.8	14,043.1
Equity in Net Assets of Nonconsolidated Subsidiaries and Associates (principally GMAC and its subsidiaries—Note 8)	4,450.8	4,231.1
Other Investments and Miscellaneous Assets—at cost (less allowances)	1,222.5	1,550.0
Common Stock Held for the Incentive Program (Note 3)	56.3	35.2
Property		
Real estate, plants and equipment—at cost (Note 9)	37,777.8	37,687.2
Less accumulated depreciation (Note 9)	20,116.8	18,148.9
Net real estate, plants and equipment	17,661.0	19,538.3
Special tools—at cost (less amortization)	1,504.1	2,000.1
Total Property	19,165.1	21,538.4
Total Assets	$45,694.5	$41,397.8

LIABILITIES AND STOCKHOLDERS' EQUITY		
Current Liabilities		
Accounts payable (principally trade)	$ 4,642.3	$ 3,600.7
Loans payable (principally overseas) (Note 11)	1,255.2	1,182.5
Accrued liabilities (Note 10)	9,011.5	7,601.8
Total Current Liabilities	14,909.0	12,385.0
Long-Term Debt (Note 11)	3,137.2	4,452.0
Capitalized-Leases	384.6	293.1
Other Liabilities (including GMAC and its subsidiaries—$300.0 and $876.0)	4,698.2	4,259.8
Deferred Credits (including investment tax credits—$1,281.1 and $1,158.7)	1,798.9	1,720.8
Stockholders' Equity (Notes 3 and 12)		
Preferred stocks ($5.00 series, $183.6; $3.75 series, $100.0)	283.6	283.6
Common stock (issued, 315,711,299 and 312,363,657 shares)	526.2	520.6
Capital surplus (principally additional paid-in capital)	2,136.8	1,930.4
Net income retained for use in the business	18,390.5	15,552.5
Subtotal	21,337.1	18,287.1
Accumulated foreign currency translation and other adjustments (Note 1)	(570.5)	—
Total Stockholders' Equity	20,766.6	18,287.1
Total Liabilities and Stockholders' Equity	$45,694.5	$41,397.8

Reference should be made to notes on pages 20 through 26.

STATEMENT OF CHANGES
IN CONSOLIDATED FINANCIAL POSITION

For the Years Ended December 31, 1983, 1982 and 1981
(Dollars in Millions)

	1983	1982	1981
Source of Funds			
Net income	$ 3,730.2	$ 962.7	$ 333.4
Depreciation of real estate, plants and equipment	2,569.7	2,403.0	1,837.3
Amortization of special tools	2,549.9	2,147.5	2,568.9
Deferred income taxes, undistributed earnings of nonconsolidated subsidiaries and associates, etc.—net	645.5	75.8	68.0
Total funds provided by current operations	9,495.3	5,589.0	4,807.6
Increase in long-term debt	3,177.1	2,497.4	2,172.7
Proceeds from sale of newly issued common stock	212.0	353.5	303.6
Other—net	772.8	1,459.2	1,703.3
Total	13,657.2	9,899.1	8,987.2
Use of Funds			
Dividends paid to stockholders (Note 12)	892.2	750.2	730.5
Decrease in long-term debt	4,491.9	1,846.5	257.6
Expenditures for real estate, plants and equipment	1,923.0	3,611.1	6,563.3
Expenditures for special tools	2,083.7	2,601.0	3,178.1
Increase (Decrease) in other working capital items	1,142.0	(1,306.2)	341.2
Investments in nonconsolidated subsidiaries and associates	33.7	591.0	311.0
Total	10,566.5	8,093.6	11,381.7
Increase (Decrease) in cash and marketable securities	3,090.7	1,805.5	(2,394.5)
Cash and marketable securities at beginning of the year	3,126.2	1,320.7	3,715.2
Cash and marketable securities at end of the year	$ 6,216.9	$3,126.2	$ 1,320.7
Increase (Decrease) in Other Working Capital Items by Element			
Accounts and notes receivable	$ 4,099.7	($ 778.8)	($ 125.1)
Inventories	437.3	(1,038.5)	(72.3)
Prepaid expenses and deferred income taxes	(871.0)	341.1	820.6
Accounts payable	(1,041.6)	99.0	268.0
Loans payable	(72.7)	545.3	(51.3)
Accrued liabilities	(1,409.7)	(474.3)	(498.7)
Increase (Decrease) in other working capital items	$ 1,142.0	($1,306.2)	$ 341.2

Reference should be made to notes on pages 20 through 26.

NOTES TO FINANCIAL STATEMENTS

NOTE 1. Significant Accounting Policies

Principles of Consolidation

The consolidated financial statements include the accounts of the Corporation and all domestic and foreign subsidiaries which are more than 50% owned and engaged principally in manufacturing or wholesale marketing of General Motors products. General Motors' share of earnings or losses of nonconsolidated subsidiaries and of associates in which at least 20% of the voting securities is owned is generally included in consolidated income under the equity method of accounting.

Income Taxes

Investment tax credits are deferred and amortized over the lives of the related assets. The tax effects of timing differences between pretax accounting income and taxable income (principally related to depreciation, sales and product allowances, vehicle instalment sales, undistributed earnings of subsidiaries and associates, and benefit plans expense) are deferred. Provisions are made for estimated United States and foreign taxes, less available tax credits and deductions, which may be incurred on remittance of the Corporation's share of subsidiaries' undistributed earnings less those deemed to be permanently reinvested. Possible taxes beyond those provided would not be material.

Inventories

Inventories are stated generally at cost, which is not in excess of market. The cost of substantially all domestic inventories was determined by the last-in, first-out (LIFO) method. If the first-in, first-out (FIFO) method of inventory valuation had been used by the Corporation for U.S. inventories, it is estimated they would be $2,038.6 million higher at December 31, 1983, compared with $1,886.0 million higher at December 31, 1982. As a result of decreases in unit sales and actions taken to reduce inventories, certain LIFO inventory quantities carried at lower costs prevailing in prior years, as compared with the costs of current purchases, were liquidated in 1982 and 1981. These inventory adjustments favorably affected income (loss) before income taxes by approximately $305.0 million and $89.2 million in the respective years. The cost of inventories outside the United States was determined generally by the FIFO or the average cost method.

Major Classes of Inventories

(Dollars in Millions)	1983	1982
Productive material, work in process and supplies	$4,202.2	$3,774.4
Finished product, service parts, etc.	2,419.3	2,409.8
Total	$6,621.5	$6,184.2

Depreciation and Amortization

Depreciation is provided on groups of property using, with minor exceptions, an accelerated method which accumulates depreciation of approximately two-thirds of the depreciable cost during the first half of the estimated lives of the property.

Expenditures for special tools are amortized, with the amortization applied directly to the asset account, over short periods of time because the utility value of the tools is radically affected by frequent changes in the design of the functional components and appearance of the product. Replacement of special tools for reasons other than changes in products is charged directly to cost of sales.

Pension Program

The Corporation and its subsidiaries have several pension plans covering substantially all of their employes. Benefits under the plans are generally related to an employe's length of service, wages and salaries, and, where applicable, contributions. The costs of these plans are determined on the basis of actuarial cost methods and include amortization of prior service cost over periods not in excess of 30 years from the later of October 1, 1979 or the date such costs are established. With the exception of certain overseas subsidiaries, pension costs accrued are funded within the limitations set by the Employee Retirement Income Security Act.

Product Related Expenses

Expenditures for advertising and sales promotion and for other product related expenses are charged to costs and expenses as incurred; provisions for estimated costs related to product warranty are made at the time the products are sold.

Expenditures for research and development are charged to expenses as incurred and amounted to $2,602.2 million in 1983, $2,175.1 million in 1982 and $2,249.6 million in 1981.

Interest Cost

Total interest cost incurred in 1983, 1982 and 1981 amounted to $1,401.8 million, $1,544.6 million and $995.2 million, respectively, of which $49.1 million, $129.2 million and $97.3 million related to certain real estate, plants and equipment acquired in those years was capitalized.

Accounting Changes

As required by the Financial Accounting Standards Board, effective January 1, 1983, the Corporation implemented Statement of Financial Accounting Standards (SFAS) No. 52, Foreign Currency Translation. Under SFAS No. 52, all assets and liabilities of operations outside the United States, except for operations in highly inflationary economies (principally in Latin America) or those that are highly integrated with operations of the Corporation (principally in Canada), are translated into U.S. dollars using current exchange rates and the effects of foreign currency translation adjustments are deferred and included as a component of stockholders' equity. Foreign currency translation adjustments related to operations in other countries continue to be included in income. The effect of adopting SFAS No. 52 was to reduce net income for 1983 by about $422.5 million ($1.35 per share). The financial statements for prior years have not been restated for this change.

Exchange and translation gains (losses) included in net income in 1983, 1982 and 1981 amounted to ($52.3) million, $348.4 million and $226.2 million, respectively.

The Corporation also implemented SFAS No. 60, Accounting and Reporting by Insurance Enterprises, in 1983. Under SFAS No. 60, investments of insurance subsidiaries in common and nonredeemable preferred stocks are reported at market value. The adjustment to market value is included in stockholders' equity and does not affect net income until realized.

Included in the new section of stockholders' equity titled "Accumulated foreign currency translation and other adjustments" are accumulated foreign currency translation adjustments of ($661.8) million and net unrealized gains on marketable equity securities (net of applicable income taxes) of the Corporation's insurance subsidiaries of $91.3 million.

639

Notes to Financial Statements (continued)

NOTE 2. Net Sales

(Dollars in Millions)	1983	1982	1981
Net sales includes sales to:			
Nonconsolidated sub-sidiaries and associates	$ 111.2	$ 96.3	$ 130.4
Dealerships operating under dealership assistance plans	$1,634.3	$1,253.7	$1,688.9

Unrealized intercompany profits on sales to nonconsolidated sub-sidiaries and to associates are deferred.

NOTE 3. Incentive Program

The Incentive Program consists of the General Motors Bonus Plan, the General Motors Stock Option Plans and the General Motors Perfor-mance Achievement Plan. The By-Laws provide that the Plans in which directors or officers of the Corporation may participate shall be pre-sented for action at a stockholders' meeting at least once in every five years. The Program was last approved by stockholders at the 1982 Annual Meeting.

The Corporation maintains a reserve for purposes of the Bonus Plan. For any year, a maximum credit may be made to the reserve equal to the amount which the independent public accountants of the Corpora-tion determine to be 8% of the net earnings which exceed $1 billion, but not in excess of the amount paid out as dividends on the common stock during the year. The Bonus and Salary Committee may, at its discretion, direct that for any year an amount less than the maximum amount available under the formula be credited. Further, the Commit-tee may, but is not obligated to, award as bonus in any year the full amount available in the reserve for such awards. Bonus awards under the Bonus Plan and such other amounts arising out of the operation of the Bonus Plan as the Committee may determine are charged to the reserve.

The Bonus and Salary Committee has determined to limit the credit for 1983 to the reserve to the maximum permitted under the Bonus Plan formula approved by stockholders in 1977, as determined by the independent public accountants. The credit of $180.0 million so deter-mined was less than the maximum which could have been credited to the reserve under the Bonus Plan approved by stockholders in 1982 and, as required by the Bonus Plan, less than the amount distributed as dividends to holders of General Motors common stock in 1983. On February 6, 1984, the Committee granted awards to 5,808 employes approximating the aggregate amount available for distribution, consisting of $180.0 million credited to the reserve in 1983 plus the unawarded reserve of $1.7 million carried forward from 1979. These awards consisted of 1,259,218 shares of General Motors common stock (including 586,034 unissued shares), valued at an average of $72.19 per share for award purposes in accordance with the Bonus Plan, and $90.8 million in cash. No credits were made to the Bonus Plan reserve in 1982 and 1981.

In 1982, the Committee established performance achievement levels for the initial three-year phase-in period and for the first five-year period ending in 1986 under the Performance Achievement Plan approved by stockholders in 1982. Under the Plan, the annual average of the aggre-gate final awards relating to the aggregate target awards granted in the years 1982 through 1986 shall not exceed $60 million. Payment of these awards is contingent upon achievement of earnings in relation to average worldwide industry sales volume targets over the term of the performance period related to each grant. In the future, it is anticipated that new grants will be made every two years. Employes selected to participate in the Plan are granted target awards payable in cash and/or stock which are, in general, expressed as a percentage of the participant's salary at the begin-ning of the performance period. Accruals of $15.5 million and $11.0 million were made in 1983 to recognize progress toward achieving the three-year and five-year earnings targets, respectively, through 1983. The awards for these periods will not be paid until 1985 and 1987, respectively, with

the ultimate amounts dependent on actual performance. There was no accrual in 1982 for the Plan.

Under the provisions of the Bonus Plan, participants receive their awards in instalments in as many as three years. Performance Achieve-ment Plan awards are to be paid as soon as is practicable following completion of the performance period. If participants in the Plans fail tb meet conditions precedent to receiving undelivered instalments of bonus and performance achievement awards (and contingent credits related to the Stock Option Plan prior to 1977), the amount of any such instalments is credited to income. Upon the exercise of stock options, any related contingent credits are proportionately reduced and the amount of the reduction is credited to income.

Changes during 1981, 1982 and 1983 in the status of options granted under the Stock Option Plans are shown in the following table. The option prices are 100% of the average of the highest and lowest sales prices of General Motors common stock on the dates the options were granted as reported (1) on the New York Stock Exchange for options granted prior to 1976, and (2) on the Composite Tape of transactions on all major exchanges and nonexchange markets in the U.S. for options granted in 1976 and subsequent years. Incentive stock options expire ten years from date of grant. Nonqualified stock options granted prior to 1982 expire ten years from date of grant and nonqualified stock options granted in 1982 and thereafter expire ten years and two days from date of grant. Options are subject to earlier termination under certain conditions.

The Corporation intends to deliver newly issued stock upon the exer-cise of any of the options. The maximum number of shares for which additional options might be granted under the Plans was 1,230,055 at January 1, 1981, 931,405 at December 31, 1981, 6,760,945 at December 31, 1982 and 6,195,185 at December 31, 1983.

	Years Granted	Option Prices	Shares Under Option
Outstanding at Jan. 1, 1981	1973-1980	$50.00-$73.38	1,612,613
Granted	1981	50.00	464,255
Terminated	1973-1981		(269,195)
Outstanding at Dec. 31, 1981			1,807,673
Granted:	March 1982	38.25	897,150
	Oct. 1982	46.50	740,420
Exercised	1980-1981	50.00-53.25	(1,635)
Terminated	1973-1982		(191,469)
Outstanding at Dec. 31, 1982			3,252,139
Granted	1983	72.88	586,820
Exercised	1974-1982	38.25-66.57	(627,318)
Terminated	1973-1983		(111,347)
Outstanding at Dec. 31, 1983			3,100,294

Options outstanding at December 31, 1983 consisted of:

1972 Plan	1974	$50.00	53,646
	1976	65.19	45,588
1977 Plan	1977	66.57	171,935
	1978	63.75	199,970
	1979	59.50	234,350
	1980	53.25	285,016
	1981	50.00	279,719
	1982	38.25	555,975
1982 Plan	1982	46.50	694,175
	1983	72.88	579,920
Total Shares Under Option			3,100,294

(continued)

NOTES TO FINANCIAL STATEMENTS (continued)

NOTE 3. (concluded)

Common stock held for the Incentive Program is stated substantially at cost and used exclusively for payment of Program liabilities.

(Dollars in Millions)	1983		1982	
	Shares	Amount	Shares	Amount
Balance at Jan. 1	592,207	$35.2	1,177,137	$71.5
Acquired during the year	594,680	42.6	2,039	.1
Sold to trustee of S-SPP	—	—	(2,723)	(.1)
Delivered to participants	(358,614)	(21.5)	(584,246)	(36.3)
Balance at Dec. 31	828,273	$56.3	592,207	$35.2

NOTE 4. Other Income Less Income Deductions

(Dollars in Millions)	1983	1982	1981
Other income:			
Interest	$719.5	$483.6	$427.9
Other*	161.7	174.5	123.6
Income deductions	(65.4)	(181.8)	(183.8)
Net	$815.8	$476.3	$367.7

*Includes gains of $13.9 million in 1983 and $48.7 million in 1982 from early retirements of long-term debt.

NOTE 5. Pension Program

Total pension expense of the Corporation and its consolidated subsidiaries amounted to $1,714.2 million in 1983, $1,565.9 million in 1982 and $1,493.8 million in 1981. For purposes of determining pension expense, the Corporation uses a variety of assumed rates of return on pension funds in accordance with local practice and regulations, which rates approximate 7%. The following table compares accumulated plan benefits and plan net assets for the Corporation's defined benefit plans in the United States as of October 1 (the plans' anniversary date) of both 1983 and 1982:

(Dollars in Millions)	1983	1982
Actuarial present value of accumulated plan benefits:		
Vested	$18,239.5	$16,347.8
Nonvested	3,159.9	1,754.1
Total	$21,399.4	$18,101.9
Net assets available for benefits:		
Trustees	$14,817.8	$11,381.7
Insurance companies	3,310.2	3,130.6
Total	$18,128.0	$14,512.3

The assumed rates of return used in determining the actuarial present value of accumulated plan benefits shown in the table above were based upon those published by the Pension Benefit Guaranty Corporation, a public corporation established under the Employee Retirement Income Security Act (ERISA). Such rates averaged approximately 9% for 1983 and approximately 10¼% for 1982.

The Corporation's pension plans of subsidiaries outside the United States are not required to report to governmental agencies pursuant to ERISA and the actuarial value of accumulated benefits for these plans has not been determined in the manner calculated and shown above. The total of these plans' pension funds and balance sheet accruals, less pension prepayments and deferred charges, exceeded the actuarially computed value of vested benefits by approximately $497 million at December 31, 1983 and $483 million at December 31, 1982.

NOTE 6. United States, Foreign and Other Income Taxes (Credit)

(Dollars in Millions)	1983	1982	1981
Taxes estimated to be payable (refundable) currently:			
United States Federal	$ 254.4	($168.6)	$442.9
Foreign	146.0	98.6	62.4
State and local	126.0	(8.1)	41.4
Total	526.4	(78.1)	546.7
Taxes deferred—net:			
United States Federal	1,241.3	(146.3)	(829.3)
Foreign	192.7	(35.0)	(57.9)
State and local	142.0	(40.4)	(89.6)
Total	1,576.0	(221.7)	(976.8)
Investment tax credits deferred—net:			
United States Federal	47.7	85.3	312.6
Foreign	73.7	(37.7)	(5.6)
Total	121.4	47.6	307.0
Total taxes (credit)	$2,223.8	($252.2)	($123.1)

Investment tax credits entering into the determination of taxes estimated to be payable (refundable) currently amounted to $406.2 million in 1983, $403.0 million in 1982 and $592.1 million in 1981.

The deferred taxes (credit) for timing differences consisted principally of the following: 1983—$519.2 million for benefit plans expense, ($438.0) million for sales and product allowances, $379.5 million for vehicle instalment sales and $707.5 million for depreciation; 1982—($164.0) million for benefit plans expense, ($172.0) million for sales and product allowances and $275.0 million for depreciation; and 1981—($546.3) million for benefit plans expense and ($267.2) million for sales and product allowances.

Income (loss) before income taxes included the following components:

(Dollars in Millions)	1983	1982	1981
Domestic income	$4,387.6	$170.4	$288.7
Foreign income (loss)	583.9	(147.6)	(426.8)
Total	$4,971.5	$ 22.8	($138.1)

The consolidated income tax (credit) was different than the amount computed at the United States statutory income tax rate for the reasons set forth in the table below:

	1983	1982	1981
Expected tax (credit) at U.S. statutory income tax rate	$2,286.9	$ 10.5	($ 63.5)
Investment tax credits amortized	(284.8)	(355.4)	(285.1)
Foreign tax rate differential	66.5	169.3	213.0
State and local income taxes	144.7	(26.2)	(26.0)
Other adjustments	10.5	(50.4)	38.5
Consolidated income tax (credit)	$2,223.8	($252.2)	($123.1)

NOTE 7. Earnings Per Share of Common Stock

Earnings per share of common stock are based on the average number of shares outstanding during each year. The effect on earnings per share resulting from the assumed exercise of outstanding options and delivery of bonus awards and contingent credits under the Incentive Program is not material.

NOTES TO FINANCIAL STATEMENTS (continued)

NOTE 8. General Motors Acceptance Corporation and Subsidiaries

Condensed Consolidated Balance Sheet (Dollars in Millions)

	1983	1982
Cash and investments in securities	$ 2,002.6	$ 1,674.2
Finance receivables—net (including GM and affiliates—$300.0 and $876.0)	48,124.4	41,771.1
Other assets	1,271.0	969.4
Total Assets	$51,398.0	$44,414.7
Short-term debt	$26,257.9	$22,114.1
Accounts payable and other liabilities (including GM and affiliates—$3,560.7* and $312.0)	6,216.6	2,689.0
Long-term debt	14,798.1	15,695.5
Stockholder's equity	4,125.4	3,916.1
Total Liabilities and Stockholder's Equity	$51,398.0	$44,414.7

*Includes $2,562.4 million related to dealer vehicle stocks for which payment from GMAC was due at a later date than previously had been the practice. GMAC pays interest to GM on such amounts.

Condensed Statement of Consolidated Income (Dollars in Millions)

	1983	1982	1981
Gross Revenue	$7,391.1	$7,255.4	$6,153.9
Interest and discount	4,099.1	4,482.1	4,174.7
Other expenses	2,290.0	2,085.3	1,614.0
Total Expenses	6,389.1	6,567.4	5,788.7
Net Income	$1,002.0	$ 688.0	$ 365.2

NOTE 9. Real Estate, Plants and Equipment and Accumulated Depreciation

(Dollars in Millions)	1983	1982
Real estate, plants and equipment (Note 11):		
Land	$ 347.2	$ 361.8
Land improvements	1,145.1	1,136.8
Leasehold improvements—less amortization	47.1	41.8
Buildings	8,010.2	7,921.3
Machinery and equipment	25,669.1	24,802.1
Furniture and office equipment	469.0	403.6
Capitalized leases	754.7	711.7
Construction in progress	1,335.4	2,308.1
Total	$37,777.8	$37,687.2
Accumulated depreciation:		
Land improvements	$ 628.3	$ 576.5
Buildings	3,937.0	3,650.6
Machinery and equipment	15,057.8	13,505.9
Furniture and office equipment	196.4	160.9
Capitalized leases	297.3	255.0
Total	$20,116.8	$18,148.9

NOTE 10. Accrued Liabilities

(Dollars in Millions)	1983	1982
Taxes, other than income taxes	$1,016.5	$ 885.1
Payrolls	1,633.5	1,476.7
Employe benefits	1,297.2	1,111.4
Dealer and customer allowances, claims, discounts, etc.	3,305.4	2,990.8
Other	1,758.9	1,137.8
Total	$9,011.5	$7,601.8

NOTE 11. Long-Term Debt

(Dollars in Millions)	Interest Rate	Maturity	1983	1982
GM:				
U.S. dollars:				
Notes	8.05 %	1985	$ 300.0	$ 300.0
Notes	10.00	1985-86	125.0	200.0
Notes	12.20	1986-88	200.0	200.0
Notes	10.00	1991	250.0	237.5
Debentures	8.625	2005	102.4	160.1
Adjustable Rate Notes	6.07	1985-2000	—	400.0
Other			80.1	91.9
Other currencies	7.48	1985-87	19.9	411.6
Consolidated subsidiaries:				
U.S. dollars	12.19	1985-93	821.7	931.6
Spanish pesetas	13.74	1985-90	597.9	680.0
Mexican pesos	20.00	1985-88	216.6	65.1
Australian dollars	9.57	1985-91	177.1	213.9
Austrian schillings	6.00	1985-87	132.9	150.7
German marks	6.20	1985-96	106.0	38.9
Venezuelan bolivars	17.62	1985-89	57.6	127.9
Brazilian cruzeiros			—	183.0
Other currencies	Various	1985-2004	59.0	170.0
Total			3,246.2	4,562.2
Less unamortized discount (principally on 10% notes due 1991)			109.0	110.2
Total			$3,137.2	$4,452.0

At year-end 1983, the Corporation and its consolidated subsidiaries had unused short-term credit lines of approximately $2.9 billion and unused long-term credit agreements of approximately $2.3 billion. Long-term debt at December 31, 1983 and 1982 included approximately $883 million and $2,032 million, respectively, of short-term obligations which are intended to be renewed or refinanced under long-term credit agreements. Long-term debt (including current portion) bore interest at a weighted average rate of approximately 11.8% at December 31, 1983 and 13.3% at December 31, 1982.

In 1981, the Corporation and a subsidiary arranged a private financing of $500 million in 10% notes due 1991, of which $475 million was outstanding at December 31, 1982 and $500 million at December 31, 1983. The difference between the 10% stated interest rate and the 14.7% effective rate

(continued)

NOTES TO FINANCIAL STATEMENTS (continued)

NOTE 11. (concluded)

at issuance reflects the discount which is being amortized over the lives of the notes. An option to acquire certain real estate in 1991 was also granted. The option holder may deliver the notes in payment for the real estate.

Under the sinking fund provisions of the trust indenture for the Corporation's 8⅜% Debentures due 2005, the Corporation is to make annual sinking fund payments of $3.0 million in 2002 and $11.8 million in each of the years 2003 and 2004.

Maturities of long-term debt in the years 1984 through 1988 are (in millions) $423.4 (included in loans payable at December 31, 1983), $879.9, $504.2, $425.2 and $301.6. Loans payable at December 31, 1982 included $465.4 million current portion of long-term debt.

NOTE 12. Stockholders' Equity

(Dollars in Millions Except Per Share Amounts)	1983	1982	1981
Capital Stock:			
Preferred Stock, without par value, cumulative dividends (authorized, 6,000,000 shares), no change during the year:			
$5.00 series, stated value $100 per share, redeemable at Corporation option at $120 per share (issued, 1,875,366 shares; in treasury, 39,722 shares; outstanding, 1,835,644 shares)	$ 183.6	$ 183.6	$ 183.6
$3.75 series, stated value $100 per share, redeemable at Corporation option at $100 per share (issued and outstanding, 1,000,000 shares)	100.0	100.0	100.0
Common Stock, $1⅔ par value (authorized, 500,000,000 shares):			
Issued at beginning of the year (312,363,657 shares in 1983, 304,804,228 in 1982 and 298,053,782 in 1981)	520.6	508.0	496.7
Newly issued stock sold under provisions of the Stock Option Plans, Employe Stock Ownership Plans, Savings-Stock Purchase Programs and the Dividend Reinvestment Plan (3,029,593 shares in 1983, 6,459,429 in 1982 and 6,750,446 in 1981) and exchanged for long-term debt (318,049 shares in 1983 and 1,100,000 in 1982)	5.6	12.6	11.3
Issued at end of the year (315,711,299 shares in 1983, 312,363,657 in 1982 and 304,804,228 in 1981)	526.2	520.6	508.0
Total capital stock at end of the year	809.8	804.2	791.6
Capital Surplus (principally additional paid-in capital):			
Balance at beginning of the year	1,930.4	1,589.5	1,297.2
Proceeds in excess of par value of newly issued common stock sold under provisions of the Stock Option Plans, Employe Stock Ownership Plans, Savings-Stock Purchase Programs and the Dividend Reinvestment Plan and, in 1983 and 1982, exchanged for long-term debt	206.4	340.9	292.3
Balance at end of the year	2,136.8	1,930.4	1,589.5
Net Income Retained for Use in the Business:			
Balance at beginning of the year	15,552.5	15,340.0	15,737.1
Net income	3,730.2	962.7	333.4
Total	19,282.7	16,302.7	16,070.5
Cash dividends:			
Preferred stock, $5.00 series, $5.00 per share	9.2	9.2	9.2
Preferred stock, $3.75 series, $3.75 per share	3.7	3.7	3.7
Common stock, $2.80 per share in 1983 and $2.40 in 1982 and 1981	879.3	737.3	717.6
Total cash dividends	892.2	750.2	730.5
Balance at end of the year	18,390.5	15,552.5	15,340.0
Accumulated Foreign Currency Translation and Other Adjustments (Note 1):			
Adjustments as of January 1, 1983:			
Accumulated foreign currency translation adjustments	(668.0)	—	—
Net unrealized gains on marketable equity securities	68.1	—	—
Changes during the year:			
Accumulated foreign currency translation adjustments	6.2	—	—
Net unrealized gains on marketable equity securities	23.2	—	—
Balance at end of the year	(570.5)	—	—
Total Stockholders' Equity	$20,766.6	$18,287.1	$17,721.1

The preferred stock is subject to redemption at the option of the Board of Directors on any dividend date on not less than thirty days' notice at the redemption prices stated above plus accrued dividends.

The Certificate of Incorporation provides that no cash dividends may be paid on the common stock so long as current assets (excluding prepaid expenses) in excess of current liabilities of the Corporation are less than $75 per share of outstanding preferred stock. Such current assets (with inventories calculated on the FIFO basis) in excess of current liabilities were greater than $75 in respect of each share of outstanding preferred stock at December 31, 1983.

The equity of the Corporation and its consolidated subsidiaries in the accumulated net loss, since acquisition, of associates has been included in net income retained for use in the business.

NOTES TO FINANCIAL STATEMENTS (continued)

NOTE 13. Segment Reporting

General Motors is a highly vertically-integrated business operating primarily in a single industry consisting of the manufacture, assembly and sale of automobiles, trucks and related parts and accessories classified as automotive products. Because of the high degree of integration, substantial interdivisional and intercompany transfers of materials and services are made. Consequently, any determination of income by area of operations or class of products is necessarily arbitrary because of the allocation and reallocation of costs, including Corporate costs, benefiting more than one division or product.

Substantially all of General Motors' products are marketed through retail dealers and through distributors and jobbers in the United States and Canada and through distributors and dealers overseas. To assist in the merchandising of General Motors' products, GMAC and its subsidiaries offer financial services and certain types of automobile insurance to dealers and customers.

Net sales, net income (loss), total and net assets and average number of employes in the U.S. and in locations outside the U.S. for 1983, 1982 and 1981 are summarized below. Net income (loss) is after provisions for deferred income taxes applicable to that portion of the undistributed earnings deemed to be not permanently invested, less available tax credits and deductions, and appropriate consolidating adjustments for the geographic areas set forth below. Interarea sales are made at negotiated selling prices. The financial statements for 1982 and 1981 have not been restated for the accounting changes described in Note 1.

1983	United States	Canada	Europe	Latin America	All Other	Total[1]
Net Sales:			(Dollars in Millions)			
Outside	$59,668.7	$ 3,866.4	$7,761.7	$1,742.7	$1,542.1	$74,581.6
Interarea	6,493.4	7,366.0	208.6	653.1	295.4	–
Total net sales	$66,162.1	$11,232.4	$7,970.3	$2,395.8	$1,837.5	$74,581.6
Net Income (Loss)	$ 3,469.0	$ 592.3	($ 228.3)	($ 15.0)	($ 91.1)	$ 3,730.2
Total Assets	$34,670.4	$ 2,385.5	$5,379.1	$2,834.3	$ 813.9	$45,694.5
Net Assets	$18,749.3	$ 1,332.9	($ 120.5)	$ 919.6	$ 8.9	$20,766.6
Average Number of Employes (in thousands)	463	39	123	41	25	691
1982						
Net Sales:						
Outside	$45,650.1	$ 2,621.9	$7,150.5	$2,699.5	$1,903.6	$60,025.6
Interarea	4,673.8	5,350.7	234.3	310.2	192.9	–
Total net sales	$50,323.9	$ 7,972.6	$7,384.8	$3,009.7	$2,096.5	$60,025.6
Net Income (Loss)	$ 1,079.3	($ 33.5)	$ 6.2	($ 16.5)	($ 63.2)	$ 962.7
Total Assets	$29,227.4	$ 2,299.0	$5,952.3	$2,973.3	$1,063.5	$41,397.8
Net Assets	$15,756.0	$ 774.7	$ 803.3	$ 894.3	$ 170.7	$18,287.1
Average Number of Employes (in thousands)	441	34	114	38	30	657
1981						
Net Sales:						
Outside	$47,022.4	$ 4,099.2	$6,585.2	$2,730.0	$2,261.7	$62,698.5
Interarea	5,731.1	4,747.2	265.6	129.9	128.1	–
Total net sales	$52,753.5	$ 8,846.4	$6,850.8	$2,859.9	$2,389.8	$62,698.5
Net Income (Loss)	$ 763.3	($ 35.6)	($ 426.7)	($ 62.6)	$ 129.2	$ 333.4
Total Assets	$27,510.8	$ 2,772.8	$5,208.5	$2,642.8	$ 980.3	$38,979.0
Net Assets	$15,608.7	$ 832.6	$ 505.5	$ 640.7	$ 247.3	$17,721.1
Average Number of Employes (in thousands)	522	39	113	38	29	741

[1] After elimination of interarea transactions.

NOTE 14. Profit Sharing Plans

Profit Sharing Plans were established, effective January 1, 1983, under which eligible United States hourly and salaried employes will share in the success of the Corporation's U.S. operations. Under the Plans' provisions, 10% of profits, as defined, will be shared when the Corporation's U.S. income before income taxes plus equity in U.S. earnings of nonconsolidated subsidiaries (principally GMAC) exceeds 10% of the net worth of U.S. operations plus 5% of the difference between total assets of U.S. operations and net worth of U.S. operations. Amounts applicable to subsidiaries incorporated in the U.S. that are operating outside of the U.S., as well as amounts applicable to associates, are excluded from the calculation. Ten percent of the amount in excess of the minimum annual return, less expenses of administering the Plans and a diversion for the Guaranteed Income Stream Benefit Program and Income Protection Plan, will be distributed to eligible U.S. employes by March 31 following the year earned. The calculation of the profit sharing accrual for 1983 is shown on the next page.

(continued)

Notes to Financial Statements (concluded)

NOTE 14. (concluded)

(Dollars in Millions)   1983

Minimum Annual Return	January 1, 1983	December 31, 1983	Average	
Total Assets in the U.S.	$29,295.5	$34,670.4		
Deduct assets of excluded subsidiaries and associates	1,207.4	1,329.8		
Total Assets of U.S. operations as defined in the Plans	$28,088.1	$33,340.6	$30,714.3	
Net Assets in the U.S.	$15,824.1	$18,749.3		
Deduct net assets of excluded subsidiaries and associates	933.2	1,143.6		
Net Worth of U.S. operations as defined in the Plans	$14,890.9	$17,605.7	16,248.3 X 10% =	$1,624.8
Other assets of U.S. operations			$14,466.0 X 5% =	723.3
Minimum Annual Return as defined in the Plans				$2,348.1

Profits as Defined in the Plans

Net Income in the U.S.	$3,469.0
Add (Deduct): Net income of excluded subsidiaries and associates	(40.4)
Income taxes of U.S. operations	1,796.0
Provision for the Incentive Program applicable to U.S. operations	182.9
Profit sharing accrual	322.2
Administrative expenses of the Plans	1.7
Profits as defined in the Plans	$5,731.4

Profit Sharing Accrual

Profits as defined in the Plans	$5,731.4		
Deduct Minimum Annual Return as defined in the Plans	2,348.1		
Profits in excess of Minimum Annual Return	$3,383.3 X 10% =		$ 338.3
Deduct: Administrative expenses of the Plans	$ 1.7		
Diversion for Guaranteed Income Stream Benefit Program and Income Protection Plan	14.4		16.1
Profit Sharing Accrual			$ 322.2

NOTE 15. Contingent Liabilities

There are various claims and pending actions against the Corporation and its subsidiaries with respect to commercial matters, including warranties and product liability, governmental regulations including environmental and safety matters, civil rights, antitrust, patent matters, taxes and other matters arising out of the conduct of the business. Certain of these actions purport to be class actions, seeking damages in very large amounts. The amounts of liability on these claims and actions at December 31, 1983 were not determinable but, in the opinion of management, the ultimate liability resulting will not materially affect the consolidated financial position or results of operations of the Corporation and its consolidated subsidiaries.

──────────── **ACCOUNTANTS' REPORT** ────────────

Deloitte Haskins · Sells

CERTIFIED PUBLIC ACCOUNTANTS

1114 Avenue of the Americas
New York, New York 10036

General Motors Corporation, its Directors and Stockholders: February 6, 1984

We have examined the Consolidated Balance Sheet of General Motors Corporation and consolidated subsidiaries as of December 31, 1983 and 1982 and the related Statements of Consolidated Income and Changes in Consolidated Financial Position for each of the three years in the period ended December 31, 1983. Our examinations were made in accordance with generally accepted auditing standards and, accordingly, included such tests of the accounting records and such other auditing procedures as we considered necessary in the circumstances.

In our opinion, these financial statements present fairly the financial position of the companies at December 31, 1983 and 1982 and the results of their operations and the changes in their financial position for each of the three years in the period ended December 31, 1983, in conformity with generally accepted accounting principles consistently applied during the period except for the change in 1983, with which we concur, in the method of accounting for foreign currency translation as described in Note 1 to the Financial Statements.

Deloitte Haskins & Sells

SUPPLEMENTARY INFORMATION

Selected Quarterly Data
(Dollars in Millions Except Per Share Amounts)

	1983 Quarters				1982 Quarters			
	1st	2nd	3rd	4th	1st	2nd	3rd	4th
Net sales	$16,743.8	$19,400.2	$17,619.3	$20,818.3	$14,721.4	$17,144.6	$14,282.6	$13,877.0
Operating income (loss)	692.9	1,775.2	866.0	2,174.3	(7.4)	863.3	(53.6)	159.6
Income (loss) before income taxes	518.5	1,655.7	738.7	2,058.6	(259.7)	665.4	(236.8)	(146.1)
United States, foreign and other income taxes (credit)	112.3	860.8	236.1	1,014.6	(256.8)	236.3	(151.5)	(80.2)
Income (loss) after income taxes	406.2	794.9	502.6	1,044.0	(2.9)	429.1	(85.3)	(65.9)
Equity in earnings of nonconsolidated subsidiaries and associates	246.9	248.5	234.3	252.8	131.2	130.9	214.7	210.9
Net income	653.1	1,043.4	736.9	1,296.8	128.3	560.0	129.4	145.0
Dividends on preferred stocks	3.2	3.3	3.2	3.2	3.2	3.3	3.2	3.2
Earnings on common stock	$ 649.9	$ 1,040.1	$ 733.7	$ 1,293.6	$ 125.1	$ 556.7	$ 126.2	$ 141.8
Average number of shares of common stock outstanding (in millions)	312.4	313.5	314.7	314.8	304.7	306.8	307.6	310.5
Earnings per share of common stock*	$2.08	$3.32	$2.33	$4.11	$0.41	$1.82	$0.41	$0.45
Dividends per share of common stock	$0.60	$0.60	$0.60	$1.00	$0.60	$0.60	$0.60	$0.60
Stock price range**								
High	$65.75	$75.25	$77.50	$80.00	$41.38	$47.13	$50.13	$64.50
Low	$57.38	$56.00	$65.50	$72.00	$34.00	$40.13	$39.63	$46.25

*Includes favorable (unfavorable) effects on earnings per share of foreign exchange/translation activity [1983: first quarter—$0.51, second quarter—($0.45), third quarter—($0.12), fourth quarter—($0.11); 1982: first quarter—$0.83, second quarter—$0.25, third quarter—($0.07), fourth quarter—$0.05].
**The principal market is the New York Stock Exchange and prices are based on the Composite Tape. Common stock is also listed on the Midwest, Pacific and Philadelphia stock exchanges. As of December 31, 1983, there were 983,616 holders of record of common stock.

The effective income tax rates for the 1983 quarters reflect the continuing high level of U.S. investment tax credits. The net credits for income taxes in the 1982 quarters reflect the relatively low level of earnings combined with the favorable impact of U.S. investment tax credits.

Selected Financial Data

(Dollars in Millions Except Per Share Amounts)	1983	1982	1981	1980	1979
Net sales	$74,581.6	$60,025.6	$62,698.5	$57,728.5	$66,311.2
Earnings (loss) on common stock	$ 3,717.3	$ 949.8	$ 320.5	($ 775.4)	$ 2,879.8
Dividends on common stock	879.3	737.3	717.6	861.2	1,520.3
Net income (loss) retained in the year	$ 2,838.0	$ 212.5	($ 397.1)	($ 1,636.6)	$ 1,359.5
Earnings (loss) on common stock—per share	$11.84	$3.09	$1.07	($2.65)	$10.04
Dividends on common stock—per share	2.80	2.40	2.40	2.95	5.30
Net income (loss) retained in the year—per share	$ 9.04	$0.69	($1.33)	($5.60)	$ 4.74
Average number of shares of common stock outstanding (in millions)	313.9	307.4	299.1	292.4	286.8
Dividends on capital stock as a percent of net income	23.9%	77.9%	219.1%	N.A.	53.0%
Expenditures for real estate, plants and equipment	$ 1,923.0	$ 3,611.1	$ 6,563.3	$ 5,160.5	$ 3,351.3
Expenditures for special tools	$ 2,083.7	$ 2,601.0	$ 3,178.1	$ 2,600.0	$ 2,015.0
Cash and marketable securities	$ 6,216.9	$ 3,126.2	$ 1,320.7	$ 3,715.2	$ 2,986.4
Working capital	$ 5,890.8	$ 1,658.1	$ 1,158.8	$ 3,212.1	$ 6,751.0
Total assets	$45,694.5	$41,397.8	$38,979.0	$34,581.0	$32,215.8
Long-term debt and capitalized leases	$ 3,521.8	$ 4,745.1	$ 4,044.0	$ 2,058.3	$ 1,030.8

See Note 1 to the Financial Statements concerning adoption of Statement of Financial Accounting Standards No. 52, Foreign Currency Translation, effective January 1, 1983.

EFFECTS OF INFLATION ON FINANCIAL DATA

The accompanying Schedules display the basic historical cost financial data adjusted for general inflation (constant dollar) and also for changes in specific prices (current cost) for use in the evaluation of comparative financial results. The Schedules are intended to help readers of financial data assess results in the following specific areas:

a. The erosion of general purchasing power,
b. Enterprise performance,
c. The erosion of operating capability, and
d. Future cash flows.

In reviewing these Schedules, the following comments may be of assistance in understanding the reasons for the different "income" amounts and the uses of the data.

Financial statements—historical cost method

The objective of financial statements, and the primary purpose of accounting, is to furnish, to the fullest extent practicable, objective, quantifiable summaries of the results of financial transactions to those who need or wish to judge management's ability to manage. The data are prepared by management and audited by the independent public accountants.

The present accounting system in general use in the United States and the financial statements prepared by major companies from that system were never intended to be measures of relative economic value, but instead are basically a history of transactions which have occurred and by which current and potential investors and creditors can evaluate their expectations. There are many subjective, analytical, and economic factors which must be taken into consideration when evaluating a company. Those factors cannot be quantified objectively. Just as the financial statements cannot present in reasonable, objective, quantifiable form all of the data necessary to evaluate a business, they also should not be expected to furnish all the data needed to evaluate the effects of inflation on a company.

Data adjusted for general inflation—constant dollar method

The constant dollar income statement contains two basic adjustments to the historical cost data: the provision for depreciation and amortization and the cost of sales data are recalculated. Historical dollar accounting tends to understate the economic cost of property (including special tools) consumed in production because the depreciation and amortization charges are based on the original dollar cost of assets acquired over a period of years. However, the use of accelerated methods of depreciation and amortization tends to counteract this effect. Constant dollar depreciation and amortization restates such expense based on asset values adjusted to reflect increases for inflation subsequent to acquisition or construction of the related property. Cost of sales is adjusted to reflect changes for inflation for the portion of inventories not stated on the last-in, first-out (LIFO) basis in the conventional financial statements. Other items of income and expense are not adjusted for inflation because they generally reflect trans-actions that took place in 1983 and, therefore, were recorded in average 1983 dollars.

In measuring the effects of inflation on U.S. operations, the U.S. Bureau of Labor Statistics' Consumer Price Index for Urban Consumers (CPI-U) is used. For locations outside the United States, indices which measure the general rate of inflation applicable to the operations are generally used, with the resulting amounts translated into U.S. dollars using year-end foreign currency exchange rates.

Data adjusted for changes in specific prices—current cost method

Another manner in which to analyze the effects of inflation on financial data (and thus the business) is by adjusting the historical cost data to the current costs for the major balance sheet items which have been accumulated through the accounting system over a period of years and which thus reflect different prices for the same commodities and services.

The current cost of property owned and the related depreciation and amortization expense for U.S. operations were calculated by applying (1) selected producer price indices to historical book values of machinery and equipment and (2) the Marshall Valuation Service index to buildings, and the use of assessed values for land. For locations outside the United States, such amounts were calculated generally by applying indices closely related to the assets being measured and translating the resulting amounts using year-end foreign currency exchange rates.

The purpose of this type of restatement is to furnish estimates of the effects of price increases for replacement of inventories and property on the potential future net income of the business and thus assess the probability of future cash flows. Although these data may be useful for this purpose, they do not reflect specific plans for the replacement of property. A more meaningful estimate of the effects of such costs on future earnings is the estimated level of future capital expenditures which is set forth on page 15 in the Financial Review: Management's Discussion and Analysis.

Summary

Under both the constant dollar and the current cost methods, the net income of General Motors is lower (or the net loss is higher) than that determined under the historical cost method. This means that businesses, as well as individuals, are affected by inflation and that the purchasing power of business dollars also has declined. In addition, the costs of main-taining the productive capacity, as reflected in the current cost data (and estimate of future capital expenditures), have increased, and thus man-agement must seek ways to cope with the effects of inflation through accounting methods such as the LIFO method of inventory valuation, which matches current costs with current revenues, and through accel-erated methods of depreciation and amortization.

It must be emphasized that there is a continuing need for national monetary and fiscal policies designed to control inflation and to pro-vide adequate capital for future business growth which, in turn, will mean increased productivity and employment.

647

SCHEDULE A　　Comparison of Selected Data Adjusted for Effects of Changing Prices
(Dollars in Millions Except Per Share Amounts)
Historical cost data adjusted for general inflation (constant dollar) and changes in specific prices (current cost). (A)

	1983	1982	1981	1980	1979
Net Sales—as reported	$74,581.6	$60,025.6	$62,698.5	$57,728.5	$66,311.2
—in constant 1967 dollars	24,993.8	20,762.9	23,017.1	23,390.8	30,501.9
Net Income (Loss)—as reported	$ 3,730.2	$ 962.7	$ 333.4	($ 762.5)	$ 2,892.7
—in constant 1967 dollars	1,199.2(B)	(38.9)	(305.8)	(1,023.8)	817.0
—in current cost 1967 dollars	1,144.0(B)	71.7	(252.8)	(829.5)	829.5
Net income (loss) as a percent of sales—as reported	5.0%	1.6%	0.5%	(1.3%)	4.4%
—in constant 1967 dollars	4.8	(0.2)	(1.3)	(4.4)	2.7
—in current cost 1967 dollars	4.6	0.3	(1.1)	(3.5)	2.7
Earnings (Loss) per share of common stock—as reported	$11.84	$3.09	$1.07	($2.65)	$10.04
—in constant 1967 dollars	3.80(B)	(0.14)	(1.04)	(3.52)	2.83
—in current cost 1967 dollars	3.63(B)	0.22	(0.86)	(2.86)	2.87
Dividends per share of common stock—as reported	$2.80	$2.40	$2.40	$2.95	$5.30
—in constant 1967 dollars	0.94	0.83	0.88	1.20	2.44
Net assets at year-end—as reported	$20,766.6	$18,287.1	$17,721.1	$17,814.6	$19,179.3
—in constant 1967 dollars	11,059.5	10,153.9	10,247.2	10,887.6	12,163.4
—in current cost 1967 dollars	10,635.1	9,818.3	10,450.9	11,377.2	12,982.7
Accumulated foreign currency translation adjustments —as reported	($ 661.8)				
—in constant 1967 dollars	(109.3)				
—in current cost 1967 dollars	(129.8)				
Unrealized gain from decline in purchasing power of dollars of net amounts owed	$ 86.5	$ 130.5	$ 241.3	$ 182.3	$ 83.8
Excess of increase in general price level over increase in specific prices of inventory and property	$ 78.4	$ 861.2	$ 619.0	$ 689.2	$ 221.8
Market price per common share at year-end—unadjusted	$74.38	$62.38	$38.50	$45.00	$50.00
—in constant 1967 dollars	24.93	21.58	14.13	18.23	23.00
Average Consumer Price Index	298.4	289.1	272.4	246.8	217.4

(A) Adjusted data have generally been determined by applying the Consumer Price Index—Urban to the data with 1967 (CPI-100) as the base year. Depreciation has been determined on a straight-line basis for this calculation.

(B) These amounts will differ from those shown for constant dollar and current cost in Schedule B because a different base year (1983) has been used in Schedule B in order to illustrate the effect of changing prices in an alternative form.

SCHEDULE B　　Schedule of Income Adjusted for Changing Prices
For the Year Ended December 31, 1983
(Dollars in Millions Except Per Share Amounts)

	As Reported in the Financial Statements (Historical Cost)	Adjusted for General Inflation (1983 Constant Dollar)	Adjusted for Changes in Specific Prices (1983 Current Cost)
Net Sales	$74,581.6	$74,581.6	$74,581.6
Cost of sales	60,718.8	60,870.7	60,767.0
Depreciation and amortization expense (A)	5,119.6	5,025.8	5,387.9
Other operating and nonoperating items—net	2,789.2	2,789.2	2,789.2
United States and other income taxes	2,223.8	2,223.8	2,223.8
Total costs and expenses	70,851.4	70,909.5	71,167.9
Net Income	$ 3,730.2	$ 3,672.1(B)	$ 3,413.7(B)
Earnings per share of common stock	$11.84	$11.66(B)	$10.83(B)
Accumulated foreign currency translation adjustments	($ 661.8)	($ 462.4)	($ 387.5)
Unrealized gain from decline in purchasing power of dollars of net amounts owed		$ 258.0	$ 258.0
Excess of increase in general price level over increase in specific prices of inventory and property			$ 233.9(C)

(A) The recent high level of expenditures for property (including special tools), coupled with the use of accelerated methods for computing historical cost depreciation and amortization, causes the historical cost amounts to approximate constant dollar and current cost depreciation and amortization which are calculated using the straight-line method.

(B) These amounts will differ from those shown for constant dollar and current cost in Schedule A because a different base year (1967) has been used in Schedule A in order to illustrate the effect of changing prices in an alternative form.

(C) At December 31, 1983, current cost of inventory was $8,658.8 million and current cost of property (including special tools), net of accumulated depreciation and amortization, was $28,096.4 million.

APPENDIX C

Table I
FUTURE VALUE OF $1 AT COMPOUND INTEREST: 0.5%–10%

$$F_{1,n} = (1 + i)^n$$

Period	.5%	1%	1.5%	2%	2.5%	3%	3.5%	4%	4.5%	5%
1	1.00500	1.01000	1.01500	1.02000	1.02500	1.03000	1.03500	1.04000	1.04500	1.05000
2	1.01003	1.02010	1.03023	1.04040	1.05063	1.06090	1.07123	1.08160	1.09203	1.10250
3	1.01508	1.03030	1.04568	1.06121	1.07689	1.09273	1.10872	1.12486	1.14117	1.15762
4	1.02015	1.04060	1.06136	1.08243	1.10381	1.12551	1.14752	1.16986	1.19252	1.21551
5	1.02525	1.05101	1.07728	1.10408	1.13141	1.15927	1.18769	1.21665	1.24618	1.27628
6	1.03038	1.06152	1.09344	1.12616	1.15969	1.19405	1.22926	1.26532	1.30226	1.34010
7	1.03553	1.07214	1.10984	1.14869	1.18869	1.22987	1.27228	1.31593	1.36086	1.40710
8	1.04071	1.08286	1.12649	1.17166	1.21840	1.26677	1.31681	1.36857	1.42210	1.47746
9	1.04591	1.09369	1.14339	1.19509	1.24886	1.30477	1.36290	1.42331	1.48610	1.55133
10	1.05114	1.10462	1.16054	1.21899	1.28008	1.34392	1.41060	1.48024	1.55297	1.62889
11	1.05640	1.11567	1.17795	1.24337	1.31209	1.38423	1.45997	1.53945	1.62285	1.71034
12	1.06168	1.12683	1.19562	1.26824	1.34489	1.42576	1.51107	1.60103	1.69588	1.79586
13	1.06699	1.13809	1.21355	1.29361	1.37851	1.46853	1.56396	1.66507	1.77220	1.88565
14	1.07232	1.14947	1.23176	1.31948	1.41297	1.51259	1.61869	1.73168	1.85194	1.97993
15	1.07768	1.16097	1.25023	1.34587	1.44830	1.55797	1.67535	1.80094	1.93528	2.07893
16	1.08307	1.17258	1.26899	1.37279	1.48451	1.60471	1.73399	1.87298	2.02237	2.18287
17	1.08849	1.18430	1.28802	1.40024	1.52162	1.65285	1.79468	1.94790	2.11338	2.29202
18	1.09393	1.19615	1.30734	1.42825	1.55966	1.70243	1.85749	2.02582	2.20848	2.40662
19	1.09940	1.20811	1.32695	1.45681	1.59865	1.75351	1.92250	2.10685	2.30786	2.52695
20	1.10490	1.22019	1.34686	1.48595	1.63862	1.80611	1.98979	2.19112	2.41171	2.65330
21	1.11042	1.23239	1.36706	1.51567	1.67958	1.86029	2.05943	2.27877	2.52024	2.78596
22	1.11597	1.24472	1.38756	1.54598	1.72157	1.91610	2.13151	2.36992	2.63365	2.92526
23	1.12155	1.25716	1.40838	1.57690	1.76461	1.97359	2.20611	2.46472	2.75217	3.07152
24	1.12716	1.26973	1.42950	1.60844	1.80873	2.03279	2.28333	2.56330	2.87601	3.22510
25	1.13280	1.28243	1.45095	1.64061	1.85394	2.09378	2.36324	2.66584	3.00543	3.38635
26	1.13846	1.29526	1.47271	1.67342	1.90029	2.15659	2.44596	2.77247	3.14068	3.55567
27	1.14415	1.30821	1.49480	1.70689	1.94780	2.22129	2.53157	2.88337	3.28201	3.73346
28	1.14987	1.32129	1.51722	1.74102	1.99650	2.28793	2.62017	2.99870	3.42970	3.92013
29	1.15562	1.33450	1.53998	1.77584	2.04641	2.35657	2.71188	3.11865	3.58404	4.11614
30	1.16140	1.34785	1.56308	1.81136	2.09757	2.42726	2.80679	3.24340	3.74532	4.32194

5.5%	6%	6.5%	7%	7.5%	8%	8.5%	9%	9.5%	10%
1.05500	1.06000	1.06500	1.07000	1.07500	1.08000	1.08500	1.09000	1.09500	1.10000
1.11303	1.12360	1.13423	1.14490	1.15563	1.16640	1.17723	1.18810	1.19903	1.21000
1.17424	1.19102	1.20795	1.22504	1.24230	1.25971	1.27729	1.29503	1.31293	1.33100
1.23882	1.26248	1.28647	1.31080	1.33547	1.36049	1.38586	1.41158	1.43766	1.46410
1.30696	1.33823	1.37009	1.40255	1.43563	1.46933	1.50366	1.53862	1.57424	1.61051
1.37884	1.41852	1.45914	1.50073	1.54330	1.58687	1.63147	1.67710	1.72379	1.77156
1.45468	1.50363	1.55399	1.60578	1.65905	1.71382	1.77014	1.82804	1.88755	1.94872
1.53469	1.59385	1.65500	1.71819	1.78348	1.85093	1.92060	1.99256	2.06687	2.14359
1.61909	1.68948	1.76257	1.83846	1.91724	1.99900	2.08386	2.17189	2.26322	2.35795
1.70814	1.79085	1.87714	1.96715	2.06103	2.15892	2.26098	2.36736	2.47823	2.59374
1.80209	1.89830	1.99915	2.10485	2.21561	2.33164	2.45317	2.58043	2.71366	2.85312
1.90121	2.01220	2.12910	2.25219	2.38178	2.51817	2.66169	2.81266	2.97146	3.13843
2.00577	2.13293	2.26749	2.40985	2.56041	2.71962	2.88793	3.06580	3.25375	3.45227
2.11609	2.26090	2.41487	2.57853	2.75244	2.93719	3.13340	3.34173	3.56285	3.79750
2.23248	2.39656	2.57184	2.75903	2.95888	3.17217	3.39974	3.64248	3.90i32	4.17725
2.35526	2.54035	2.73901	2.95216	3.18079	3.42594	3.68872	3.97031	4.27195	4.59497
2.48480	2.69277	2.91705	3.15882	3.41935	3.70002	4.00226	4.32763	4.67778	5.05447
2.62147	2.85434	3.10665	3.37993	3.67580	3.99602	4.34245	4.71712	5.12217	5.55992
2.76565	3.02560	3.30859	3.61653	3.95149	4.31570	4.71156	5.14166	5.60878	6.11591
2.91776	3.20714	3.52365	3.86968	4.24785	4.66096	5.11205	5.60441	6.14161	6.72750
3.07823	3.39956	3.75268	4.14056	4.56644	5.03383	5.54657	6.10881	6.72507	7.40025
3.24754	3.60354	3.99661	4.43040	4.90892	5.43654	6.01803	6.65860	7.36395	8.14027
3.42615	3.81975	4.25639	4.74053	5.27709	5.87146	6.52956	7.25787	8.06352	8.95430
3.61459	4.04893	4.53305	5.07237	5.67287	6.34118	7.08457	7.91108	8.82956	9.84973
3.81339	4.29187	4.82770	5.42743	6.09834	6.84848	7.68676	8.62308	9.66836	10.83471
4.02313	4.54938	5.14150	5.80735	6.55572	7.39635	8.34014	9.39916	10.58686	11.91818
4.24440	4.82235	5.47570	6.21387	7.04739	7.98806	9.04905	10.24508	11.59261	13.10999
4.47784	5.11169	5.83162	6.64884	7.57595	8.62711	9.81822	11.16714	12.69391	14.42099
4.72412	5.41839	6.21067	7.11426	8.14414	9.31727	10.65277	12.17218	13.89983	15.86309
4.98395	5.74349	6.61437	7.61226	8.75496	10.06266	11.55825	13.26768	15.22031	17.44940

Table I *(concluded)*
FUTURE VALUE OF $1 AT COMPOUND INTEREST: 10.5%–20%

Period	10.5%	11%	11.5%	12%	12.5%	13%	13.5%	14%	14.5%	15%
1	1.10500	1.11000	1.11500	1.12000	1.12500	1.13000	1.13500	1.14000	1.14500	1.15000
2	1.22103	1.23210	1.24323	1.25440	1.26563	1.27690	1.28822	1.29960	1.31102	1.32250
3	1.34923	1.36763	1.38620	1.40493	1.42383	1.44290	1.46214	1.48154	1.50112	1.52088
4	1.49090	1.51807	1.54561	1.57352	1.60181	1.63047	1.65952	1.68896	1.71879	1.74901
5	1.64745	1.68506	1.72335	1.76234	1.80203	1.84244	1.88356	1.92541	1.96801	2.01136
6	1.82043	1.87041	1.92154	1.97382	2.02729	2.08195	2.13784	2.19497	2.25337	2.31306
7	2.01157	2.07616	2.14252	2.21068	2.28070	2.35261	2.42645	2.50227	2.58011	2.66002
8	2.22279	2.30454	2.38891	2.47596	2.56578	2.65844	2.75402	2.85259	2.95423	3.05902
9	2.45618	2.55804	2.66363	2.77308	2.88651	3.00404	3.12581	3.25195	3.38259	3.51788
10	2.71408	2.83942	2.96995	3.10585	3.24732	3.39457	3.54780	3.70722	3.87307	4.04556
11	2.99906	3.15176	3.31149	3.47855	3.65324	3.83586	4.02675	4.22623	4.43466	4.65239
12	3.31396	3.49845	3.69231	3.89598	4.10989	4.33452	4.57036	4.81790	5.07769	5.35025
13	3.66193	3.88328	4.11693	4.36349	4.62363	4.89801	5.18736	5.49241	5.81395	6.15279
14	4.04643	4.31044	4.59037	4.88711	5.20158	5.53475	5.88765	6.26135	6.65697	7.07571
15	4.47130	4.78459	5.11827	5.47357	5.85178	6.25427	6.68248	7.13794	7.62223	8.13706
16	4.94079	5.31089	5.70687	6.13039	6.58325	7.06733	7.58462	8.13725	8.72746	9.35762
17	5.45957	5.89509	6.36316	6.86604	7.40616	7.98608	8.60854	9.27646	9.99294	10.76126
18	6.03283	6.54355	7.09492	7.68997	8.33193	9.02427	9.77070	10.57517	11.44192	12.37545
19	6.66628	7.26334	7.91084	8.61276	9.37342	10.19742	11.08974	12.05569	13.10039	14.23177
20	7.36623	8.06231	8.82058	9.64629	10.54509	11.52309	12.58686	13.74349	15.00064	16.36654
21	8.13969	8.94917	9.83495	10.80385	11.86323	13.02109	14.28608	15.66758	17.17573	18.82152
22	8.99436	9.93357	10.96597	12.10031	13.34613	14.71383	16.21470	17.86104	19.66621	21.64475
23	9.93876	11.02627	12.22706	13.55235	15.01440	16.62663	18.40369	20.36158	22.51781	24.89146
24	10.98233	12.23916	13.63317	15.17863	16.89120	18.78809	20.88818	23.21221	25.78290	28.62518
25	12.13548	13.58546	15.20098	17.00006	19.00260	21.23054	23.70809	26.46192	29.52141	32.91895
26	13.40971	15.07986	16.94910	19.04007	21.37793	23.99051	26.90868	30.16658	33.80202	37.85680
27	14.81772	16.73865	18.89824	21.32488	24.05017	27.10928	30.54135	34.38991	38.70331	43.53531
28	16.37359	18.57990	21.07154	23.88387	27.05644	30.63349	34.66443	39.20449	44.31529	50.06561
29	18.09281	20.62369	23.49477	26.74993	30.43849	34.61584	39.34413	44.69312	50.74101	57.57545
30	19.99256	22.89230	26.19667	29.95992	34.24330	39.11590	44.65559	50.95016	58.09846	66.21177

15.5%	16%	16.5%	17%	17.5%	18%	18.5%	19%	19.5%	20%
1.15500	1.16000	1.16500	1.17000	1.17500	1.18000	1.18500	1.19000	1.19500	1.20000
1.33402	1.34560	1.35722	1.36890	1.38063	1.39240	1.40422	1.41610	1.42802	1.44000
1.54080	1.56090	1.58117	1.60161	1.62223	1.64303	1.66401	1.68516	1.70649	1.72800
1.77962	1.81064	1.84206	1.87389	1.90613	1.93878	1.97185	2.00534	2.03926	2.07360
2.05546	2.10034	2.14600	2.19245	2.23970	2.28776	2.33664	2.38635	2.43691	2.48832
2.37406	2.43640	2.50009	2.56516	2.63164	2.69955	2.76892	2.83976	2.91211	2.98598
2.74204	2.82622	2.91260	3.00124	3.09218	3.18547	3.28117	3.37932	3.47997	3.58318
3.16706	3.27841	3.39318	3.51145	3.63331	3.75886	3.88818	4.02139	4.15856	4.29982
3.65795	3.80296	3.95306	4.10840	4.26914	4.43545	4.60750	4.78545	4.96948	5.15978
4.22493	4.41144	4.60531	4.80683	5.01624	5.23384	5.45989	5.69468	5.93853	6.19174
4.87980	5.11726	5.36519	5.62399	5.89409	6.17593	6.46996	6.77667	7.09654	7.43008
5.63617	5.93603	6.25045	6.58007	6.92555	7.28759	7.66691	8.06424	8.48037	8.91610
6.50977	6.88579	7.28177	7.69868	8.13752	8.59936	9.08528	9.59645	10.13404	10.69932
7.51879	7.98752	8.48326	9.00745	9.56159	10.14724	10.76606	11.41977	12.11018	12.83918
8.68420	9.26552	9.88300	10.53872	11.23487	11.97375	12.75778	13.58953	14.47167	15.40702
10.03025	10.74800	11.51370	12.33030	13.20097	14.12902	15.11797	16.17154	17.29364	18.48843
11.58494	12.46768	13.41346	14.42646	15.51114	16.67225	17.91480	19.24413	20.66590	22.18611
13.38060	14.46251	15.62668	16.87895	18.22559	19.67325	21.22904	22.90052	24.69575	26.62333
15.45460	16.77652	18.20508	19.74838	21.41507	23.21444	25.15641	27.25162	29.51143	31.94800
17.85006	19.46076	21.20892	23.10560	25.16271	27.39303	29.81035	32.42942	35.26615	38.33760
20.61682	22.57448	24.70839	27.03355	29.56618	32.32378	35.32526	38.59101	42.14305	46.00512
23.81243	26.18640	28.78527	31.62925	34.74026	38.14206	41.86043	45.92331	50.36095	55.20614
27.50335	30.37622	33.53484	37.00623	40.81981	45.00763	49.60461	54.64873	60.18134	66.24737
31.76637	35.23642	39.06809	43.29729	47.96327	53.10901	58.78147	65.03199	71.91670	79.49685
36.69016	40.87424	45.51433	50.65783	56.35684	62.66863	69.65604	77.38807	85.94045	95.39622
42.37713	47.41412	53.02419	59.26966	66.21929	73.94898	82.54240	92.09181	102.69884	114.47546
48.94559	55.00038	61.77318	69.34550	77.80767	87.25980	97.81275	109.58925	122.72511	137.37055
56.53216	63.80044	71.96576	81.13423	91.42401	102.96656	115.90811	130.41121	146.65651	164.84466
65.29464	74.00851	83.84011	94.92705	107.42321	121.50054	137.35111	155.18934	175.25453	197.81359
75.41531	85.84988	97.67373	111.06465	126.22227	143.37064	162.76106	184.67531	209.42916	237.37631

Table II
PRESENT VALUE OF $1 AT COMPOUND INTEREST: 0.5%–7%

$$P_{1,n} = \frac{1}{(1+i)^n}$$

Period	.5%	1%	1.5%	2%	2.5%	3%	3.5%	4%	4.5%	5%	5.5%	6%	6.5%	7%
1 ...	0.99502	0.99010	0.98522	0.98039	0.97561	0.97087	0.96618	0.96154	0.95694	0.95238	0.94787	0.94340	0.93897	0.93458
2 ...	0.99007	0.98030	0.97066	0.96117	0.95181	0.94260	0.93351	0.92456	0.91573	0.90703	0.89845	0.89000	0.88166	0.87344
3 ...	0.98515	0.97059	0.95632	0.94232	0.92860	0.91514	0.90194	0.88900	0.87630	0.86384	0.85161	0.83962	0.82785	0.81630
4 ...	0.98025	0.96098	0.94218	0.92385	0.90595	0.88849	0.87144	0.85480	0.83856	0.82270	0.80722	0.79209	0.77732	0.76290
5 ...	0.97537	0.95147	0.92826	0.90573	0.88385	0.86261	0.84197	0.82193	0.80245	0.78353	0.76513	0.74726	0.72988	0.71299
6 ...	0.97052	0.94205	0.91454	0.88797	0.86230	0.83748	0.81350	0.79031	0.76790	0.74622	0.72525	0.70496	0.68533	0.66634
7 ...	0.96569	0.93272	0.90103	0.87056	0.84127	0.81309	0.78599	0.75992	0.73483	0.71068	0.68744	0.66506	0.64351	0.62275
8 ...	0.96089	0.92348	0.88771	0.85349	0.82075	0.78941	0.75941	0.73069	0.70319	0.67684	0.65160	0.62741	0.60423	0.58201
9 ...	0.95610	0.91434	0.87459	0.83676	0.80073	0.76642	0.73373	0.70259	0.67290	0.64461	0.61763	0.59190	0.56735	0.54393
10 ...	0.95135	0.90529	0.86167	0.82035	0.78120	0.74409	0.70892	0.67556	0.64393	0.61391	0.58543	0.55839	0.53273	0.50835
11 ...	0.94661	0.89632	0.84893	0.80426	0.76214	0.72242	0.68495	0.64958	0.61620	0.58468	0.55491	0.52679	0.50021	0.47509
12 ...	0.94191	0.88745	0.83639	0.78849	0.74356	0.70138	0.66178	0.62460	0.58966	0.55684	0.52598	0.49697	0.46968	0.44401
13 ...	0.93722	0.87866	0.82403	0.77303	0.72542	0.68095	0.63940	0.60057	0.56427	0.53032	0.49856	0.46884	0.44102	0.41496
14 ...	0.93256	0.86996	0.81185	0.75788	0.70773	0.66112	0.61778	0.57748	0.53997	0.50507	0.47257	0.44230	0.41410	0.38782
15 ...	0.92792	0.86135	0.79985	0.74301	0.69047	0.64186	0.59689	0.55526	0.51672	0.48102	0.44793	0.41727	0.38883	0.36245
16 ...	0.92330	0.85282	0.78803	0.72845	0.67362	0.62317	0.57671	0.53391	0.49447	0.45811	0.42458	0.39365	0.36510	0.33873
17 ...	0.91871	0.84438	0.77639	0.71416	0.65720	0.60502	0.55720	0.51337	0.47318	0.43630	0.40245	0.37136	0.34281	0.31657
18 ...	0.91414	0.83602	0.76491	0.70016	0.64117	0.58739	0.53836	0.49363	0.45280	0.41552	0.38147	0.35034	0.32189	0.29586
19 ...	0.90959	0.82774	0.75361	0.68643	0.62553	0.57029	0.52016	0.47464	0.43330	0.39573	0.36158	0.33051	0.30224	0.27651
20 ...	0.90506	0.81954	0.74247	0.67297	0.61027	0.55368	0.50257	0.45639	0.41464	0.37689	0.34273	0.31180	0.28380	0.25842
21 ...	0.90056	0.81143	0.73150	0.65978	0.59539	0.53755	0.48557	0.43883	0.39679	0.35894	0.32486	0.29416	0.26648	0.24151
22 ...	0.89608	0.80340	0.72069	0.64684	0.58086	0.52189	0.46915	0.42196	0.37970	0.34185	0.30793	0.27751	0.25021	0.22571
23 ...	0.89162	0.79544	0.71004	0.63416	0.56670	0.50669	0.45329	0.40573	0.36335	0.32557	0.29187	0.26180	0.23494	0.21095
24 ...	0.88719	0.78757	0.69954	0.62172	0.55288	0.49193	0.43796	0.39012	0.34770	0.31007	0.27666	0.24698	0.22060	0.19715
25 ...	0.88277	0.77977	0.68921	0.60953	0.53939	0.47761	0.42315	0.37512	0.33273	0.29530	0.26223	0.23300	0.20714	0.18425
26 ...	0.87838	0.77205	0.67902	0.59758	0.52623	0.46369	0.40884	0.36069	0.31840	0.28124	0.24856	0.21981	0.19450	0.17220
27 ...	0.87401	0.76440	0.66899	0.58586	0.51340	0.45019	0.39501	0.34682	0.30469	0.26785	0.23560	0.20737	0.18263	0.16093
28 ...	0.86966	0.75684	0.65910	0.57437	0.50088	0.43708	0.38165	0.33348	0.29157	0.25509	0.22332	0.19563	0.17148	0.15040
29 ...	0.86533	0.74934	0.64936	0.56311	0.48866	0.42435	0.36875	0.32065	0.27902	0.24295	0.21168	0.18456	0.16101	0.14056
30 ...	0.86103	0.74192	0.63976	0.55207	0.47674	0.41199	0.35628	0.30832	0.26700	0.23138	0.20064	0.17411	0.15119	0.13137
31 ...	0.85675	0.73458	0.63031	0.54125	0.46511	0.39999	0.34423	0.29646	0.25550	0.22036	0.19018	0.16425	0.14196	0.12277
32 ...	0.85248	0.72730	0.62099	0.53063	0.45377	0.38834	0.33259	0.28506	0.24450	0.20987	0.18027	0.15496	0.13329	0.11474
33 ...	0.84824	0.72010	0.61182	0.52023	0.44270	0.37703	0.32134	0.27409	0.23397	0.19987	0.17087	0.14619	0.12516	0.10723
34 ...	0.84402	0.71297	0.60277	0.51003	0.43191	0.36604	0.31048	0.26355	0.22390	0.19035	0.16196	0.13791	0.11752	0.10022
35 ...	0.83982	0.70591	0.59387	0.50003	0.42137	0.35538	0.29998	0.25342	0.21425	0.18129	0.15352	0.13011	0.11035	0.09366
36 ...	0.83564	0.69892	0.58509	0.49022	0.41109	0.34503	0.28983	0.24367	0.20503	0.17266	0.14552	0.12274	0.10361	0.08754
37 ...	0.83149	0.69200	0.57644	0.48061	0.40107	0.33498	0.28003	0.23430	0.19620	0.16444	0.13793	0.11579	0.09729	0.08181
38 ...	0.82735	0.68515	0.56792	0.47119	0.39128	0.32523	0.27056	0.22529	0.18775	0.15661	0.13074	0.10924	0.09135	0.07646
39 ...	0.82323	0.67837	0.55953	0.46195	0.38174	0.31575	0.26141	0.21662	0.17967	0.14915	0.12392	0.10306	0.08578	0.07146
40 ...	0.81914	0.67165	0.55126	0.45289	0.37243	0.30656	0.25257	0.20829	0.17193	0.14205	0.11746	0.09722	0.08054	0.06678
41 ...	0.81506	0.66500	0.54312	0.44401	0.36335	0.29763	0.24403	0.20028	0.16453	0.13528	0.11134	0.09172	0.07563	0.06241
42 ...	0.81101	0.65842	0.53509	0.43530	0.35448	0.28896	0.23578	0.19257	0.15744	0.12884	0.10554	0.08653	0.07101	0.05833
43 ...	0.80697	0.65190	0.52718	0.42677	0.34584	0.28054	0.22781	0.18517	0.15066	0.12270	0.10003	0.08163	0.06668	0.05451
44 ...	0.80296	0.64545	0.51939	0.41840	0.33740	0.27237	0.22010	0.17805	0.14417	0.11686	0.09482	0.07701	0.06261	0.05095
45 ...	0.79896	0.63905	0.51171	0.41020	0.32917	0.26444	0.21266	0.17120	0.13796	0.11130	0.08988	0.07265	0.05879	0.04761
46 ...	0.79499	0.63273	0.50415	0.40215	0.32115	0.25674	0.20547	0.16461	0.13202	0.10600	0.08519	0.06854	0.05520	0.04450
47 ...	0.79103	0.62646	0.49670	0.39427	0.31331	0.24926	0.19852	0.15828	0.12634	0.10095	0.08075	0.06466	0.05183	0.04159
48 ...	0.78710	0.62026	0.48936	0.38654	0.30567	0.24200	0.19181	0.15219	0.12090	0.09614	0.07654	0.06100	0.04867	0.03887
49 ...	0.78318	0.61412	0.48213	0.37896	0.29822	0.23495	0.18532	0.14634	0.11569	0.09156	0.07255	0.05755	0.04570	0.03632
50 ...	0.77929	0.60804	0.47500	0.37153	0.29094	0.22811	0.17905	0.14071	0.11071	0.08720	0.06877	0.05429	0.04291	0.03395
51 ...	0.77541	0.60202	0.46798	0.36424	0.28385	0.22146	0.17300	0.13530	0.10594	0.08305	0.06518	0.05122	0.04029	0.03173
52 ...	0.77155	0.59606	0.46107	0.35710	0.27692	0.21501	0.16715	0.13010	0.10138	0.07910	0.06178	0.04832	0.03783	0.02965
53 ...	0.76771	0.59016	0.45426	0.35010	0.27017	0.20875	0.16150	0.12509	0.09701	0.07533	0.05856	0.04558	0.03552	0.02771
54 ...	0.76389	0.58431	0.44754	0.34323	0.26358	0.20267	0.15603	0.12028	0.09284	0.07174	0.05551	0.04300	0.03335	0.02590
55 ...	0.76009	0.57853	0.44093	0.33650	0.25715	0.19677	0.15076	0.11566	0.08884	0.06833	0.05262	0.04057	0.03132	0.02420
56 ...	0.75631	0.57280	0.43441	0.32991	0.25088	0.19104	0.14566	0.11121	0.08501	0.06507	0.04987	0.03827	0.02941	0.02262
57 ...	0.75255	0.56713	0.42799	0.32344	0.24476	0.18547	0.14073	0.10693	0.08135	0.06197	0.04727	0.03610	0.02761	0.02114
58 ...	0.74880	0.56151	0.42167	0.31710	0.23879	0.18007	0.13598	0.10282	0.07785	0.05902	0.04481	0.03406	0.02593	0.01976
59 ...	0.74508	0.55595	0.41544	0.31088	0.23297	0.17483	0.13138	0.09886	0.07450	0.05621	0.04247	0.03213	0.02434	0.01847
60 ...	0.74137	0.55045	0.40930	0.30478	0.22728	0.16973	0.12693	0.09506	0.07129	0.05354	0.04026	0.03031	0.02286	0.01726

Period	.5%	1%	1.5%	2%	2.5%	3%	3.5%	4%	4.5%	5%	5.5%	6%	6.5%	7%
61 ..	0.73768	0.54500	0.40325	0.29881	0.22174	0.16479	0.12264	0.09140	0.06822	0.05099	0.03816	0.02860	0.02146	0.01613
62 ..	0.73401	0.53960	0.39729	0.29295	0.21633	0.15999	0.11849	0.08789	0.06528	0.04856	0.03617	0.02698	0.02015	0.01507
63 ..	0.73036	0.53426	0.39142	0.28720	0.21106	0.15533	0.11449	0.08451	0.06247	0.04625	0.03428	0.02545	0.01892	0.01409
64 ..	0.72673	0.52897	0.38563	0.28157	0.20591	0.15081	0.11062	0.08126	0.05978	0.04404	0.03250	0.02401	0.01777	0.01317
65 ..	0.72311	0.52373	0.37993	0.27605	0.20089	0.14641	0.10688	0.07813	0.05721	0.04195	0.03080	0.02265	0.01668	0.01230
66 ..	0.71952	0.51855	0.37432	0.27064	0.19599	0.14215	0.10326	0.07513	0.05474	0.03995	0.02920	0.02137	0.01566	0.01150
67 ..	0.71594	0.51341	0.36879	0.26533	0.19121	0.13801	0.09977	0.07224	0.05239	0.03805	0.02767	0.02016	0.01471	0.01075
68 ..	0.71237	0.50833	0.36334	0.26013	0.18654	0.13399	0.09640	0.06946	0.05013	0.03623	0.02623	0.01902	0.01381	0.01004
69 ..	0.70883	0.50330	0.35797	0.25503	0.18199	0.13009	0.09314	0.06679	0.04797	0.03451	0.02486	0.01794	0.01297	0.00939
70 ..	0.70530	0.49831	0.35268	0.25003	0.17755	0.12630	0.08999	0.06422	0.04590	0.03287	0.02357	0.01693	0.01218	0.00877
71 ..	0.70179	0.49338	0.34746	0.24513	0.17322	0.12262	0.08694	0.06175	0.04393	0.03130	0.02234	0.01597	0.01143	0.00820
72 ..	0.69830	0.48850	0.34233	0.24032	0.16900	0.11905	0.08400	0.05937	0.04204	0.02981	0.02117	0.01507	0.01074	0.00766
73 ..	0.69483	0.48366	0.33727	0.23561	0.16488	0.11558	0.08116	0.05709	0.04023	0.02839	0.02007	0.01421	0.01008	0.00716
74 ..	0.69137	0.47887	0.33229	0.23099	0.16085	0.11221	0.07842	0.05490	0.03849	0.02704	0.01902	0.01341	0.00947	0.00669
75 ..	0.68793	0.47413	0.32738	0.22646	0.15693	0.10895	0.07577	0.05278	0.03684	0.02575	0.01803	0.01265	0.00889	0.00625
76 ..	0.68451	0.46944	0.32254	0.22202	0.15310	0.10577	0.07320	0.05075	0.03525	0.02453	0.01709	0.01193	0.00835	0.00585
77 ..	0.68110	0.46479	0.31777	0.21766	0.14937	0.10269	0.07073	0.04880	0.03373	0.02336	0.01620	0.01126	0.00784	0.00546
78 ..	0.67772	0.46019	0.31308	0.21340	0.14573	0.09970	0.06834	0.04692	0.03228	0.02225	0.01536	0.01062	0.00736	0.00511
79 ..	0.67434	0.45563	0.30845	0.20921	0.14217	0.09680	0.06603	0.04512	0.03089	0.02119	0.01456	0.01002	0.00691	0.00477
80 ..	0.67099	0.45112	0.30389	0.20511	0.13870	0.09398	0.06379	0.04338	0.02956	0.02018	0.01380	0.00945	0.00649	0.00446
81 ..	0.66765	0.44665	0.29940	0.20109	0.13532	0.09124	0.06164	0.04172	0.02829	0.01922	0.01308	0.00892	0.00609	0.00417
82 ..	0.66433	0.44223	0.29497	0.19715	0.13202	0.08858	0.05955	0.04011	0.02707	0.01830	0.01240	0.00841	0.00572	0.00390
83 ..	0.66102	0.43785	0.29062	0.19328	0.12880	0.08600	0.05754	0.03857	0.02590	0.01743	0.01175	0.00794	0.00537	0.00364
84 ..	0.65773	0.43352	0.28632	0.18949	0.12566	0.08350	0.05559	0.03709	0.02479	0.01660	0.01114	0.00749	0.00504	0.00340
85 ..	0.65446	0.42922	0.28209	0.18577	0.12259	0.08107	0.05371	0.03566	0.02372	0.01581	0.01056	0.00706	0.00473	0.00318
86 ..	0.65121	0.42497	0.27792	0.18213	0.11960	0.07870	0.05190	0.03429	0.02270	0.01506	0.01001	0.00666	0.00445	0.00297
87 ..	0.64797	0.42077	0.27381	0.17856	0.11669	0.07641	0.05014	0.03297	0.02172	0.01434	0.00948	0.00629	0.00417	0.00278
88 ..	0.64474	0.41660	0.26977	0.17506	0.11384	0.07419	0.04845	0.03170	0.02079	0.01366	0.00899	0.00593	0.00392	0.00260
89 ..	0.64154	0.41248	0.26578	0.17163	0.11106	0.07203	0.04681	0.03048	0.01989	0.01301	0.00852	0.00559	0.00368	0.00243
90 ..	0.63834	0.40839	0.26185	0.16826	0.10836	0.06993	0.04522	0.02931	0.01903	0.01239	0.00808	0.00528	0.00346	0.00227
91 ..	0.63517	0.40435	0.25798	0.16496	0.10571	0.06789	0.04369	0.02818	0.01821	0.01180	0.00766	0.00498	0.00324	0.00212
92 ..	0.63201	0.40034	0.25417	0.16173	0.10313	0.06591	0.04222	0.02710	0.01743	0.01124	0.00726	0.00470	0.00305	0.00198
93 ..	0.62886	0.39638	0.25041	0.15856	0.10062	0.06399	0.04079	0.02606	0.01668	0.01070	0.00688	0.00443	0.00286	0.00185
94 ..	0.62573	0.39246	0.24671	0.15545	0.09816	0.06213	0.03941	0.02505	0.01596	0.01019	0.00652	0.00418	0.00269	0.00173
95 ..	0.62262	0.38857	0.24307	0.15240	0.09577	0.06032	0.03808	0.02409	0.01527	0.00971	0.00618	0.00394	0.00252	0.00162
96 ..	0.61952	0.38472	0.23947	0.14941	0.09343	0.05856	0.03679	0.02316	0.01462	0.00924	0.00586	0.00372	0.00237	0.00151
97 ..	0.61644	0.38091	0.23594	0.14648	0.09116	0.05686	0.03555	0.02227	0.01399	0.00880	0.00555	0.00351	0.00222	0.00141
98 ..	0.61337	0.37714	0.23245	0.14361	0.08893	0.05520	0.03434	0.02142	0.01338	0.00838	0.00526	0.00331	0.00209	0.00132
99 ..	0.61032	0.37341	0.22901	0.14079	0.08676	0.05359	0.03318	0.02059	0.01281	0.00798	0.00499	0.00312	0.00196	0.00123
100 ..	0.60729	0.36971	0.22563	0.13803	0.08465	0.05203	0.03026	0.01980	0.01226	0.00760	0.00473	0.00295	0.00184	0.00115
101 ..	0.60427	0.36605	0.22230	0.13533	0.08258	0.05052	0.03098	0.01904	0.01173	0.00724	0.00448	0.00278	0.00173	0.00108
102 ..	0.60126	0.36243	0.21901	0.13267	0.08057	0.04905	0.02993	0.01831	0.01122	0.00690	0.00425	0.00262	0.00162	0.00101
103 ..	0.59827	0.35884	0.21577	0.13007	0.07860	0.04762	0.02892	0.01760	0.01074	0.00657	0.00403	0.00247	0.00152	0.00094
104 ..	0.59529	0.35529	0.21258	0.12752	0.07669	0.04623	0.02794	0.01693	0.01028	0.00626	0.00382	0.00233	0.00143	0.00088
105 ..	0.59233	0.35177	0.20944	0.12502	0.07482	0.04488	0.02699	0.01627	0.00984	0.00596	0.00362	0.00220	0.00134	0.00082
106 ..	0.58938	0.34828	0.20635	0.12257	0.07299	0.04358	0.02608	0.01565	0.00941	0.00567	0.00343	0.00208	0.00126	0.00077
107 ..	0.58645	0.34484	0.20330	0.12017	0.07121	0.04231	0.02520	0.01505	0.00901	0.00540	0.00325	0.00196	0.00118	0.00072
108 ..	0.58353	0.34142	0.20029	0.11781	0.06947	0.04108	0.02435	0.01447	0.00862	0.00515	0.00308	0.00185	0.00111	0.00067
109 ..	0.58063	0.33804	0.19733	0.11550	0.06778	0.03988	0.02352	0.01391	0.00825	0.00490	0.00292	0.00174	0.00104	0.00063
110 ..	0.57774	0.33469	0.19442	0.11324	0.06613	0.03872	0.02273	0.01338	0.00789	0.00467	0.00277	0.00165	0.00098	0.00059
111 ..	0.57487	0.33138	0.19154	0.11101	0.06451	0.03759	0.02196	0.01286	0.00755	0.00445	0.00262	0.00155	0.00092	0.00055
112 ..	0.57201	0.32810	0.18871	0.10884	0.06294	0.03649	0.02122	0.01237	0.00723	0.00423	0.00249	0.00146	0.00086	0.00051
113 ..	0.56916	0.32485	0.18592	0.10670	0.06140	0.03543	0.02050	0.01189	0.00692	0.00403	0.00236	0.00138	0.00081	0.00048
114 ..	0.56633	0.32164	0.18318	0.10461	0.05991	0.03440	0.01981	0.01143	0.00662	0.00384	0.00223	0.00130	0.00076	0.00045
115 ..	0.56351	0.31845	0.18047	0.10256	0.05845	0.03340	0.01914	0.01099	0.00633	0.00366	0.00212	0.00123	0.00072	0.00042
116 ..	0.56071	0.31530	0.17780	0.10055	0.05702	0.03243	0.01849	0.01057	0.00606	0.00348	0.00201	0.00116	0.00067	0.00039
117 ..	0.55792	0.31218	0.17518	0.09858	0.05563	0.03148	0.01786	0.01016	0.00580	0.00332	0.00190	0.00109	0.00063	0.00036
118 ..	0.55514	0.30908	0.17259	0.09665	0.05427	0.03056	0.01726	0.00977	0.00555	0.00316	0.00180	0.00103	0.00059	0.00034
119 ..	0.55238	0.30602	0.17004	0.09475	0.05295	0.02967	0.01668	0.00940	0.00531	0.00301	0.00171	0.00097	0.00056	0.00032
120 ..	0.54963	0.30299	0.16752	0.09289	0.05166	0.02881	0.01611	0.00904	0.00508	0.00287	0.00162	0.00092	0.00052	0.00030

Table II *(continued)*
PRESENT VALUE OF $1 AT COMPOUND INTEREST: 7.5%–14%

Period	7.5%	8%	8.5%	9%	9.5%	10%	10.5%	11%	11.5%	12%	12.5%	13%	13.5%	14%
1	0.93023	0.92593	0.92166	0.91743	0.91324	0.90909	0.90498	0.90090	0.89686	0.89286	0.88889	0.88496	0.88106	0.87719
2	0.86533	0.85734	0.84946	0.84168	0.83401	0.82645	0.81898	0.81162	0.80436	0.79719	0.79012	0.78315	0.77626	0.76947
3	0.80496	0.79383	0.78291	0.77218	0.76165	0.75131	0.74116	0.73119	0.72140	0.71178	0.70233	0.69305	0.68393	0.67497
4	0.74880	0.73503	0.72157	0.70843	0.69557	0.68301	0.67073	0.65873	0.64699	0.63553	0.62430	0.61332	0.60258	0.59208
5	0.69656	0.68058	0.66505	0.64993	0.63523	0.62092	0.60700	0.59345	0.58026	0.56743	0.55493	0.54276	0.53091	0.51937
6	0.64796	0.63017	0.61295	0.59627	0.58012	0.56447	0.54932	0.53464	0.52042	0.50663	0.49327	0.48032	0.46776	0.45559
7	0.60275	0.58349	0.56493	0.54703	0.52979	0.51316	0.49712	0.48166	0.46674	0.45235	0.43846	0.42506	0.41213	0.39964
8	0.56070	0.54027	0.52067	0.50187	0.48382	0.46651	0.44989	0.43393	0.41860	0.40388	0.38974	0.37616	0.36311	0.35056
9	0.52158	0.50025	0.47988	0.46043	0.44185	0.42410	0.40714	0.39092	0.37543	0.36061	0.34644	0.33288	0.31992	0.30751
10	0.48519	0.46319	0.44229	0.42241	0.40351	0.38554	0.36845	0.35218	0.33671	0.32197	0.30795	0.29459	0.28187	0.26974
11	0.45134	0.42888	0.40764	0.38753	0.36851	0.35049	0.33344	0.31728	0.30198	0.28748	0.27373	0.26070	0.24834	0.23662
12	0.41985	0.39711	0.37570	0.35553	0.33654	0.31863	0.30175	0.28584	0.27083	0.25668	0.24332	0.23071	0.21880	0.20756
13	0.39056	0.36770	0.34627	0.32618	0.30734	0.28966	0.27308	0.25751	0.24290	0.22917	0.21628	0.20416	0.19278	0.18207
14	0.36331	0.34046	0.31914	0.29925	0.28067	0.26333	0.24713	0.23199	0.21785	0.20462	0.19225	0.18068	0.16985	0.15971
15	0.33797	0.31524	0.29414	0.27454	0.25632	0.23939	0.22365	0.20900	0.19538	0.18270	0.17089	0.15989	0.14964	0.14010
16	0.31439	0.29189	0.27110	0.25187	0.23409	0.21763	0.20240	0.18829	0.17523	0.16312	0.15190	0.14150	0.13185	0.12289
17	0.29245	0.27027	0.24986	0.23107	0.21378	0.19784	0.18316	0.16963	0.15715	0.14564	0.13502	0.12522	0.11616	0.10780
18	0.27205	0.25025	0.23028	0.21199	0.19523	0.17986	0.16576	0.15282	0.14095	0.13004	0.12002	0.11081	0.10235	0.09456
19	0.25307	0.23171	0.21224	0.19449	0.17829	0.16351	0.15001	0.13768	0.12641	0.11611	0.10668	0.09806	0.09017	0.08295
20	0.23541	0.21455	0.19562	0.17843	0.16282	0.14864	0.13575	0.12403	0.11337	0.10367	0.09483	0.08678	0.07945	0.07276
21	0.21899	0.19866	0.18029	0.16370	0.14870	0.13513	0.12285	0.11174	0.10168	0.09256	0.08429	0.07680	0.07000	0.06383
22	0.20371	0.18394	0.16617	0.15018	0.13580	0.12285	0.11118	0.10067	0.09119	0.08264	0.07493	0.06796	0.06167	0.05599
23	0.18950	0.17032	0.15315	0.13778	0.12402	0.11168	0.10062	0.09069	0.08179	0.07379	0.06660	0.06014	0.05434	0.04911
24	0.17628	0.15770	0.14115	0.12640	0.11326	0.10153	0.09106	0.08170	0.07335	0.06588	0.05920	0.05323	0.04787	0.04308
25	0.16398	0.14602	0.13009	0.11597	0.10343	0.09230	0.08240	0.07361	0.06579	0.05882	0.05262	0.04710	0.04218	0.03779
26	0.15254	0.13520	0.11990	0.10639	0.09446	0.08391	0.07457	0.06631	0.05900	0.05252	0.04678	0.04168	0.03716	0.03315
27	0.14190	0.12519	0.11051	0.09761	0.08626	0.07628	0.06749	0.05974	0.05291	0.04689	0.04158	0.03689	0.03274	0.02908
28	0.13200	0.11591	0.10185	0.08955	0.07878	0.06934	0.06107	0.05382	0.04746	0.04187	0.03696	0.03264	0.02885	0.02551
29	0.12279	0.10733	0.09387	0.08215	0.07194	0.06304	0.05527	0.04849	0.04256	0.03738	0.03285	0.02889	0.02542	0.02237
30	0.11422	0.09938	0.08652	0.07537	0.06570	0.05731	0.05002	0.04368	0.03817	0.03338	0.02920	0.02557	0.02239	0.01963
31	0.10625	0.09202	0.07974	0.06915	0.06000	0.05210	0.04527	0.03935	0.03424	0.02980	0.02596	0.02262	0.01973	0.01722
32	0.09884	0.08520	0.07349	0.06344	0.05480	0.04736	0.04096	0.03545	0.03070	0.02661	0.02307	0.02002	0.01738	0.01510
33	0.09194	0.07889	0.06774	0.05820	0.05004	0.04306	0.03707	0.03194	0.02754	0.02376	0.02051	0.01772	0.01532	0.01325
34	0.08553	0.07305	0.06243	0.05339	0.04570	0.03914	0.03355	0.02878	0.02470	0.02121	0.01823	0.01568	0.01349	0.01162
35	0.07956	0.06763	0.05754	0.04899	0.04174	0.03558	0.03036	0.02592	0.02215	0.01894	0.01621	0.01388	0.01189	0.01019
36	0.07401	0.06262	0.05303	0.04494	0.03811	0.03235	0.02748	0.02335	0.01987	0.01691	0.01440	0.01228	0.01047	0.00894
37	0.06885	0.05799	0.04888	0.04123	0.03481	0.02941	0.02487	0.02104	0.01782	0.01510	0.01280	0.01087	0.00923	0.00784
38	0.06404	0.05369	0.04505	0.03783	0.03179	0.02673	0.02250	0.01896	0.01598	0.01348	0.01138	0.00962	0.00813	0.00688
39	0.05958	0.04971	0.04152	0.03470	0.02903	0.02430	0.02036	0.01708	0.01433	0.01204	0.01012	0.00851	0.00716	0.00604
40	0.05542	0.04603	0.03827	0.03184	0.02651	0.02209	0.01843	0.01538	0.01285	0.01075	0.00899	0.00753	0.00631	0.00529
41	0.05155	0.04262	0.03527	0.02921	0.02421	0.02009	0.01668	0.01386	0.01153	0.00960	0.00799	0.00666	0.00556	0.00464
42	0.04796	0.03946	0.03251	0.02680	0.02211	0.01826	0.01509	0.01249	0.01034	0.00857	0.00711	0.00590	0.00490	0.00407
43	0.04461	0.03654	0.02996	0.02458	0.02019	0.01660	0.01366	0.01125	0.00927	0.00765	0.00632	0.00522	0.00432	0.00357
44	0.04150	0.03383	0.02761	0.02255	0.01844	0.01509	0.01236	0.01013	0.00832	0.00683	0.00561	0.00462	0.00380	0.00313
45	0.03860	0.03133	0.02545	0.02069	0.01684	0.01372	0.01119	0.00913	0.00746	0.00610	0.00499	0.00409	0.00335	0.00275
46	0.03591	0.02901	0.02345	0.01898	0.01538	0.01247	0.01012	0.00823	0.00669	0.00544	0.00444	0.00362	0.00295	0.00241
47	0.03340	0.02686	0.02162	0.01742	0.01405	0.01134	0.00916	0.00741	0.00600	0.00486	0.00394	0.00320	0.00260	0.00212
48	0.03107	0.02487	0.01992	0.01598	0.01283	0.01031	0.00829	0.00668	0.00538	0.00434	0.00350	0.00283	0.00229	0.00186
49	0.02891	0.02303	0.01836	0.01466	0.01171	0.00937	0.00750	0.00601	0.00483	0.00388	0.00312	0.00251	0.00202	0.00163
50	0.02689	0.02132	0.01692	0.01345	0.01070	0.00852	0.00679	0.00542	0.00433	0.00346	0.00277	0.00222	0.00178	0.00143
51	0.02501	0.01974	0.01560	0.01234	0.00977	0.00774	0.00615	0.00488	0.00388	0.00309	0.00246	0.00196	0.00157	0.00125
52	0.02327	0.01828	0.01438	0.01132	0.00892	0.00704	0.00556	0.00440	0.00348	0.00276	0.00219	0.00174	0.00138	0.00110
53	0.02164	0.01693	0.01325	0.01038	0.00815	0.00640	0.00503	0.00396	0.00312	0.00246	0.00194	0.00154	0.00122	0.00096
54	0.02013	0.01567	0.01221	0.00953	0.00744	0.00582	0.00455	0.00357	0.00280	0.00220	0.00173	0.00136	0.00107	0.00085
55	0.01873	0.01451	0.01126	0.00874	0.00680	0.00529	0.00412	0.00322	0.00251	0.00196	0.00154	0.00120	0.00094	0.00074
56	0.01742	0.01344	0.01037	0.00802	0.00621	0.00481	0.00373	0.00290	0.00225	0.00175	0.00137	0.00107	0.00083	0.00065
57	0.01621	0.01244	0.00956	0.00736	0.00567	0.00437	0.00338	0.00261	0.00202	0.00157	0.00121	0.00094	0.00073	0.00057
58	0.01508	0.01152	0.00881	0.00675	0.00518	0.00397	0.00305	0.00235	0.00181	0.00140	0.00108	0.00083	0.00065	0.00050
59	0.01402	0.01067	0.00812	0.00619	0.00473	0.00361	0.00276	0.00212	0.00162	0.00125	0.00096	0.00074	0.00057	0.00044
60	0.01305	0.00988	0.00749	0.00568	0.00432	0.00328	0.00250	0.00191	0.00146	0.00111	0.00085	0.00065	0.00050	0.00039

Period	7.5%	8%	8.5%	9%	9.5%	10%	10.5%	11%	11.5%	12%	12.5%	13%	13.5%	14%
61 ..	0.01214	0.00914	0.00690	0.00521	0.00394	0.00299	0.00226	0.00172	0.00131	0.00099	0.00076	0.00058	0.00044	0.00034
62 ..	0.01129	0.00847	0.00636	0.00478	0.00360	0.00271	0.00205	0.00155	0.00117	0.00089	0.00067	0.00051	0.00039	0.00030
63 ..	0.01050	0.00784	0.00586	0.00439	0.00329	0.00247	0.00185	0.00140	0.00105	0.00079	0.00060	0.00045	0.00034	0.00026
64 ..	0.00977	0.00726	0.00540	0.00402	0.00300	0.00224	0.00168	0.00126	0.00094	0.00071	0.00053	0.00040	0.00030	0.00023
65 ..	0.00909	0.00672	0.00498	0.00369	0.00274	0.00204	0.00152	0.00113	0.00085	0.00063	0.00047	0.00035	0.00027	0.00020
66 ..	0.00845	0.00622	0.00459	0.00339	0.00250	0.00185	0.00137	0.00102	0.00076	0.00056	0.00042	0.00031	0.00023	0.00018
67 ..	0.00786	0.00576	0.00423	0.00311	0.00229	0.00169	0.00124	0.00092	0.00068	0.00050	0.00037	0.00028	0.00021	0.00015
68 ..	0.00732	0.00534	0.00390	0.00285	0.00209	0.00153	0.00113	0.00083	0.00061	0.00045	0.00033	0.00025	0.00018	0.00014
69 ..	0.00680	0.00494	0.00359	0.00262	0.00191	0.00139	0.00102	0.00075	0.00055	0.00040	0.00030	0.00022	0.00016	0.00012
70 ..	0.00633	0.00457	0.00331	0.00240	0.00174	0.00127	0.00092	0.00067	0.00049	0.00036	0.00026	0.00019	0.00014	0.00010
71 ..	0.00589	0.00424	0.00305	0.00220	0.00159	0.00115	0.00083	0.00061	0.00044	0.00032	0.00023	0.00017	0.00012	0.00009
72 ..	0.00548	0.00392	0.00281	0.00202	0.00145	0.00105	0.00075	0.00055	0.00039	0.00029	0.00021	0.00015	0.00011	0.00008
73 ..	0.00510	0.00363	0.00259	0.00185	0.00133	0.00095	0.00068	0.00049	0.00035	0.00026	0.00018	0.00013	0.00010	0.00007
74 ..	0.00474	0.00336	0.00239	0.00170	0.00121	0.00086	0.00062	0.00044	0.00032	0.00023	0.00016	0.00012	0.00009	0.00006
75 ..	0.00441	0.00311	0.00220	0.00156	0.00111	0.00079	0.00056	0.00040	0.00028	0.00020	0.00015	0.00010	0.00008	0.00005
76 ..	0.00410	0.00288	0.00203	0.00143	0.00101	0.00071	0.00051	0.00036	0.00026	0.00018	0.00013	0.00009	0.00007	0.00005
77 ..	0.00382	0.00267	0.00187	0.00131	0.00092	0.00065	0.00046	0.00032	0.00023	0.00016	0.00012	0.00008	0.00006	0.00004
78 ..	0.00355	0.00247	0.00172	0.00120	0.00084	0.00059	0.00041	0.00029	0.00021	0.00014	0.00010	0.00007	0.00005	0.00004
79 ..	0.00330	0.00229	0.00159	0.00110	0.00077	0.00054	0.00038	0.00026	0.00018	0.00013	0.00009	0.00006	0.00005	0.00003
80 ..	0.00307	0.00212	0.00146	0.00101	0.00070	0.00049	0.00034	0.00024	0.00017	0.00012	0.00008	0.00006	0.00004	0.00003
81 ..	0.00286	0.00196	0.00135	0.00093	0.00064	0.00044	0.00031	0.00021	0.00015	0.00010	0.00007	0.00005	0.00004	0.00002
82 ..	0.00266	0.00182	0.00124	0.00085	0.00059	0.00040	0.00028	0.00019	0.00013	0.00009	0.00006	0.00004	0.00003	0.00002
83 ..	0.00247	0.00168	0.00115	0.00078	0.00054	0.00037	0.00025	0.00017	0.00012	0.00008	0.00006	0.00004	0.00003	0.00002
84 ..	0.00230	0.00156	0.00106	0.00072	0.00049	0.00033	0.00023	0.00016	0.00011	0.00007	0.00005	0.00003	0.00002	0.00002
85 ..	0.00214	0.00144	0.00097	0.00066	0.00045	0.00030	0.00021	0.00014	0.00010	0.00007	0.00004	0.00003	0.00002	0.00001
86 ..	0.00199	0.00134	0.00090	0.00060	0.00041	0.00028	0.00019	0.00013	0.00009	0.00006	0.00004	0.00003	0.00002	0.00001
87 ..	0.00185	0.00124	0.00083	0.00055	0.00037	0.00025	0.00017	0.00011	0.00008	0.00005	0.00004	0.00002	0.00002	0.00001
88 ..	0.00172	0.00114	0.00076	0.00051	0.00034	0.00023	0.00015	0.00010	0.00007	0.00005	0.00003	0.00002	0.00001	0.00001
89 ..	0.00160	0.00106	0.00070	0.00047	0.00031	0.00021	0.00014	0.00009	0.00006	0.00004	0.00003	0.00002	0.00001	0.00001
90 ..	0.00149	0.00098	0.00065	0.00043	0.00028	0.00019	0.00013	0.00008	0.00006	0.00004	0.00002	0.00002	0.00001	0.00001
91 ..	0.00139	0.00091	0.00060	0.00039	0.00026	0.00017	0.00011	0.00008	0.00005	0.00003	0.00002	0.00001	0.00001	0.00001
92 ..	0.00129	0.00084	0.00055	0.00036	0.00024	0.00016	0.00010	0.00007	0.00004	0.00003	0.00002	0.00001	0.00001	0.00001
93 ..	0.00120	0.00078	0.00051	0.00033	0.00022	0.00014	0.00009	0.00006	0.00004	0.00003	0.00002	0.00001	0.00001	0.00001
94 ..	0.00112	0.00072	0.00047	0.00030	0.00020	0.00013	0.00008	0.00005	0.00004	0.00002	0.00002	0.00001	0.00001	0.00000
95 ..	0.00104	0.00067	0.00043	0.00028	0.00018	0.00012	0.00008	0.00005	0.00003	0.00002	0.00001	0.00001	0.00001	0.00000
96 ..	0.00097	0.00062	0.00040	0.00026	0.00016	0.00011	0.00007	0.00004	0.00003	0.00002	0.00001	0.00001	0.00001	0.00000
97 ..	0.00090	0.00057	0.00037	0.00023	0.00015	0.00010	0.00006	0.00004	0.00003	0.00002	0.00001	0.00001	0.00000	0.00000
98 ..	0.00084	0.00053	0.00034	0.00021	0.00014	0.00009	0.00006	0.00004	0.00002	0.00002	0.00001	0.00001	0.00000	0.00000
99 ..	0.00078	0.00049	0.00031	0.00020	0.00013	0.00008	0.00005	0.00003	0.00002	0.00001	0.00001	0.00001	0.00000	0.00000
100 ..	0.00072	0.00045	0.00029	0.00018	0.00011	0.00007	0.00005	0.00003	0.00002	0.00001	0.00001	0.00000	0.00000	0.00000
101 ..	0.00067	0.00042	0.00026	0.00017	0.00010	0.00007	0.00004	0.00003	0.00002	0.00001	0.00001	0.00000	0.00000	0.00000
102 ..	0.00063	0.00039	0.00024	0.00015	0.00010	0.00006	0.00004	0.00002	0.00002	0.00001	0.00001	0.00000	0.00000	0.00000
103 ..	0.00058	0.00036	0.00022	0.00014	0.00009	0.00005	0.00003	0.00002	0.00001	0.00001	0.00001	0.00000	0.00000	0.00000
104 ..	0.00054	0.00033	0.00021	0.00013	0.00008	0.00005	0.00003	0.00002	0.00001	0.00001	0.00000	0.00000	0.00000	0.00000
105 ..	0.00050	0.00031	0.00019	0.00012	0.00007	0.00005	0.00003	0.00002	0.00001	0.00001	0.00000	0.00000	0.00000	0.00000
106 ..	0.00047	0.00029	0.00018	0.00011	0.00007	0.00004	0.00003	0.00002	0.00001	0.00001	0.00000	0.00000	0.00000	0.00000
107 ..	0.00044	0.00027	0.00016	0.00010	0.00006	0.00004	0.00002	0.00001	0.00001	0.00001	0.00000	0.00000	0.00000	0.00000
108 ..	0.00041	0.00025	0.00015	0.00009	0.00006	0.00003	0.00002	0.00001	0.00001	0.00000	0.00000	0.00000	0.00000	0.00000
109 ..	0.00038	0.00023	0.00014	0.00008	0.00005	0.00003	0.00002	0.00001	0.00001	0.00000	0.00000	0.00000	0.00000	0.00000
110 ..	0.00035	0.00021	0.00013	0.00008	0.00005	0.00003	0.00002	0.00001	0.00001	0.00000	0.00000	0.00000	0.00000	0.00000
111 ..	0.00033	0.00019	0.00012	0.00007	0.00004	0.00003	0.00002	0.00001	0.00001	0.00000	0.00000	0.00000	0.00000	0.00000
112 ..	0.00030	0.00018	0.00011	0.00006	0.00004	0.00002	0.00001	0.00001	0.00001	0.00000	0.00000	0.00000	0.00000	0.00000
113 ..	0.00028	0.00017	0.00010	0.00006	0.00004	0.00002	0.00001	0.00001	0.00000	0.00000	0.00000	0.00000	0.00000	0.00000
114 ..	0.00026	0.00015	0.00009	0.00005	0.00003	0.00002	0.00001	0.00001	0.00000	0.00000	0.00000	0.00000	0.00000	0.00000
115 ..	0.00024	0.00014	0.00008	0.00005	0.00003	0.00002	0.00001	0.00001	0.00000	0.00000	0.00000	0.00000	0.00000	0.00000
116 ..	0.00023	0.00013	0.00008	0.00005	0.00003	0.00002	0.00001	0.00001	0.00000	0.00000	0.00000	0.00000	0.00000	0.00000
117 ..	0.00021	0.00012	0.00007	0.00004	0.00002	0.00001	0.00001	0.00000	0.00000	0.00000	0.00000	0.00000	0.00000	0.00000
118 ..	0.00020	0.00011	0.00007	0.00004	0.00002	0.00001	0.00001	0.00000	0.00000	0.00000	0.00000	0.00000	0.00000	0.00000
119 ..	0.00018	0.00011	0.00006	0.00004	0.00002	0.00001	0.00001	0.00000	0.00000	0.00000	0.00000	0.00000	0.00000	0.00000
120 ..	0.00017	0.00010	0.00006	0.00003	0.00002	0.00001	0.00001	0.00000	0.00000	0.00000	0.00000	0.00000	0.00000	0.00000

Table II *(concluded)*
PRESENT VALUE OF $1: 14.5%–20%

Period	14.5%	15%	15.5%	16%	16.5%	17%	17.5%	18%	18.5%	19%	19.5%	20%
1	0.87336	0.86957	0.86580	0.86207	0.85837	0.85470	0.85106	0.84746	0.84388	0.84034	0.83682	0.83333
2	0.76276	0.75614	0.74961	0.74316	0.73680	0.73051	0.72431	0.71818	0.71214	0.70616	0.70027	0.69444
3	0.66617	0.65752	0.64901	0.64066	0.63244	0.62437	0.61643	0.60863	0.60096	0.59342	0.58600	0.57870
4	0.58181	0.57175	0.56192	0.55229	0.54287	0.53365	0.52462	0.51579	0.50714	0.49867	0.49038	0.48225
5	0.50813	0.49718	0.48651	0.47611	0.46598	0.45611	0.44649	0.43711	0.42796	0.41905	0.41036	0.40188
6	0.44378	0.43233	0.42122	0.41044	0.39999	0.38984	0.37999	0.37043	0.36115	0.35214	0.34339	0.33490
7	0.38758	0.37594	0.36469	0.35383	0.34334	0.33320	0.32340	0.31393	0.30477	0.29592	0.28736	0.27908
8	0.33850	0.32690	0.31575	0.30503	0.29471	0.28478	0.27523	0.26604	0.25719	0.24867	0.24047	0.23257
9	0.29563	0.28426	0.27338	0.26295	0.25297	0.24340	0.23424	0.22546	0.21704	0.20897	0.20123	0.19381
10	0.25819	0.24718	0.23669	0.22668	0.21714	0.20804	0.19935	0.19106	0.18315	0.17560	0.16839	0.16151
11	0.22550	0.21494	0.20493	0.19542	0.18639	0.17781	0.16966	0.16192	0.15456	0.14757	0.14091	0.13459
12	0.19694	0.18691	0.17743	0.16846	0.15999	0.15197	0.14439	0.13722	0.13043	0.12400	0.11792	0.11216
13	0.17200	0.16253	0.15362	0.14523	0.13733	0.12989	0.12289	0.11629	0.11007	0.10421	0.09868	0.09346
14	0.15022	0.14133	0.13300	0.12520	0.11788	0.11102	0.10459	0.09855	0.09288	0.08757	0.08258	0.07789
15	0.13120	0.12289	0.11515	0.10793	0.10118	0.09489	0.08901	0.08352	0.07838	0.07359	0.06910	0.06491
16	0.11458	0.10686	0.09970	0.09304	0.08685	0.08110	0.07575	0.07078	0.06615	0.06184	0.05782	0.05409
17	0.10007	0.09293	0.08632	0.08021	0.07455	0.06932	0.06447	0.05998	0.05582	0.05196	0.04839	0.04507
18	0.08740	0.04081	0.07474	0.06914	0.06399	0.05925	0.05487	0.05083	0.04711	0.04367	0.04049	0.03756
19	0.07633	0.07027	0.06471	0.05961	0.05493	0.05064	0.04670	0.04308	0.03975	0.03670	0.03389	0.03130
20	0.06666	0.06110	0.05602	0.05139	0.04715	0.04328	0.03974	0.03651	0.03355	0.03084	0.02836	0.02608
21	0.05822	0.05313	0.04850	0.04430	0.04047	0.03699	0.03382	0.03094	0.02831	0.02591	0.02373	0.02174
22	0.05085	0.04620	0.04199	0.03819	0.03474	0.03162	0.02879	0.02622	0.02389	0.02178	0.01986	0.01811
23	0.04441	0.04017	0.03636	0.03292	0.02982	0.02702	0.02450	0.02222	0.02016	0.01830	0.01662	0.01509
24	0.03879	0.03493	0.03148	0.02838	0.02560	0.02310	0.02085	0.01883	0.01701	0.01538	0.01390	0.01258
25	0.03387	0.03038	0.02726	0.02447	0.02197	0.01974	0.01774	0.01596	0.01436	0.01292	0.01164	0.01048
26	0.02958	0.02642	0.02360	0.02109	0.01886	0.01687	0.01510	0.01352	0.01211	0.01086	0.00974	0.00874
27	0.02584	0.02297	0.02043	0.01818	0.01619	0.01442	0.01285	0.01146	0.01022	0.00912	0.00815	0.00728
28	0.02257	0.01997	0.01769	0.01567	0.01390	0.01233	0.01094	0.00971	0.00863	0.00767	0.00682	0.00607
29	0.01971	0.01737	0.01532	0.01351	0.01193	0.01053	0.00931	0.00823	0.00728	0.00644	0.00571	0.00506
30	0.01721	0.01510	0.01326	0.01165	0.01024	0.00900	0.00792	0.00697	0.00614	0.00541	0.00477	0.00421
31	0.01503	0.01313	0.01148	0.01004	0.00879	0.00770	0.00674	0.00591	0.00518	0.00455	0.00400	0.00351
32	0.01313	0.01142	0.00994	0.00866	0.00754	0.00658	0.00574	0.00501	0.00438	0.00382	0.00334	0.00293
33	0.01147	0.00993	0.00861	0.00746	0.00648	0.00562	0.00488	0.00425	0.00369	0.00321	0.00280	0.00244
34	0.01001	0.00864	0.00745	0.00643	0.00556	0.00480	0.00416	0.00360	0.00312	0.00270	0.00234	0.00203
35	0.00875	0.00751	0.00645	0.00555	0.00477	0.00411	0.00354	0.00305	0.00263	0.00227	0.00196	0.00169
36	0.00764	0.00653	0.00559	0.00478	0.00410	0.00351	0.00301	0.00258	0.00222	0.00191	0.00164	0.00141
37	0.00667	0.00568	0.00484	0.00412	0.00352	0.00300	0.00256	0.00219	0.00187	0.00160	0.00137	0.00118
38	0.00583	0.00494	0.00419	0.00355	0.00302	0.00256	0.00218	0.00186	0.00158	0.00135	0.00115	0.00098
39	0.00509	0.00429	0.00362	0.00306	0.00259	0.00219	0.00186	0.00157	0.00133	0.00113	0.00096	0.00082
40	0.00444	0.00373	0.00314	0.00264	0.00222	0.00187	0.00158	0.00133	0.00113	0.00095	0.00080	0.00068
41	0.00388	0.00325	0.00272	0.00228	0.00191	0.00160	0.00134	0.00113	0.00095	0.00080	0.00067	0.00057
42	0.00339	0.00282	0.00235	0.00196	0.00164	0.00137	0.00114	0.00096	0.00080	0.00067	0.00056	0.00047
43	0.00296	0.00245	0.00204	0.00169	0.00141	0.00117	0.00097	0.00081	0.00068	0.00056	0.00047	0.00039
44	0.00259	0.00213	0.00176	0.00146	0.00121	0.00100	0.00083	0.00069	0.00057	0.00047	0.00039	0.00033
45	0.00226	0.00186	0.00153	0.00126	0.00104	0.00085	0.00071	0.00058	0.00048	0.00040	0.00033	0.00027
46	0.00197	0.00161	0.00132	0.00109	0.00089	0.00073	0.00060	0.00049	0.00041	0.00033	0.00028	0.00023
47	0.00172	0.00140	0.00114	0.00093	0.00076	0.00062	0.00051	0.00042	0.00034	0.00028	0.00023	0.00019
48	0.00150	0.00122	0.00099	0.00081	0.00066	0.00053	0.00043	0.00035	0.00029	0.00024	0.00019	0.00016
49	0.00131	0.00106	0.00086	0.00069	0.00056	0.00046	0.00037	0.00030	0.00024	0.00020	0.00016	0.00013
50	0.00115	0.00092	0.00074	0.00060	0.00048	0.00039	0.00031	0.00025	0.00021	0.00017	0.00014	0.00011
51	0.00100	0.00080	0.00064	0.00052	0.00041	0.00033	0.00027	0.00022	0.00017	0.00014	0.00011	0.00009
52	0.00088	0.00070	0.00056	0.00044	0.00036	0.00028	0.00023	0.00018	0.00015	0.00012	0.00009	0.00008
53	0.00076	0.00061	0.00048	0.00038	0.00031	0.00024	0.00019	0.00015	0.00012	0.00010	0.00008	0.00006
54	0.00067	0.00053	0.00042	0.00033	0.00026	0.00021	0.00017	0.00013	0.00010	0.00008	0.00007	0.00005
55	0.00058	0.00046	0.00036	0.00028	0.00022	0.00018	0.00014	0.00011	0.00009	0.00007	0.00006	0.00004
56	0.00051	0.00040	0.00031	0.00025	0.00019	0.00015	0.00012	0.00009	0.00007	0.00006	0.00005	0.00004
57	0.00044	0.00035	0.00027	0.00021	0.00017	0.00013	0.00010	0.00008	0.00006	0.00005	0.00004	0.00003
58	0.00039	0.00030	0.00023	0.00018	0.00014	0.00011	0.00009	0.00007	0.00005	0.00004	0.00003	0.00003
59	0.00034	0.00026	0.00020	0.00016	0.00012	0.00009	0.00007	0.00006	0.00004	0.00003	0.00003	0.00002
60	0.00030	0.00023	0.00018	0.00014	0.00010	0.00008	0.00006	0.00005	0.00004	0.00003	0.00002	0.00002

Period	14.5%	15%	15.5%	16%	16.5%	17%	17.5%	18%	18.5%	19%	19.5%	20%
61	0.00026	0.00020	0.00015	0.00012	0.00009	0.00007	0.00005	0.00004	0.00003	0.00002	0.00002	0.00001
62	0.00023	0.00017	0.00013	0.00010	0.00008	0.00006	0.00005	0.00003	0.00003	0.00002	0.00002	0.00001
63	0.00020	0.00015	0.00011	0.00009	0.00007	0.00005	0.00004	0.00003	0.00002	0.00002	0.00001	0.00001
64	0.00017	0.00013	0.00010	0.00007	0.00006	0.00004	0.00003	0.00003	0.00002	0.00001	0.00001	0.00001
65	0.00015	0.00011	0.00009	0.00006	0.00005	0.00004	0.00003	0.00002	0.00002	0.00001	0.00001	0.00001
66	0.00013	0.00010	0.00007	0.00006	0.00004	0.00003	0.00002	0.00002	0.00001	0.00001	0.00001	0.00001
67	0.00011	0.00009	0.00006	0.00005	0.00004	0.00003	0.00002	0.00002	0.00001	0.00001	0.00001	0.00000
68	0.00010	0.00007	0.00006	0.00004	0.00003	0.00002	0.00002	0.00001	0.00001	0.00001	0.00001	0.00000
69	0.00009	0.00006	0.00005	0.00004	0.00003	0.00002	0.00001	0.00001	0.00001	0.00001	0.00000	0.00000
70	0.00008	0.00006	0.00004	0.00003	0.00002	0.00002	0.00001	0.00001	0.00001	0.00001	0.00000	0.00000
71	0.00007	0.00005	0.00004	0.00003	0.00002	0.00001	0.00001	0.00001	0.00001	0.00000	0.00000	0.00000
72	0.00006	0.00004	0.00003	0.00002	0.00002	0.00001	0.00001	0.00001	0.00000	0.00000	0.00000	0.00000
73	0.00005	0.00004	0.00003	0.00002	0.00001	0.00001	0.00001	0.00001	0.00000	0.00000	0.00000	0.00000
74	0.00004	0.00003	0.00002	0.00002	0.00001	0.00001	0.00001	0.00000	0.00000	0.00000	0.00000	0.00000
75	0.00004	0.00003	0.00002	0.00001	0.00001	0.00001	0.00001	0.00000	0.00000	0.00000	0.00000	0.00000
76	0.00003	0.00002	0.00002	0.00001	0.00001	0.00001	0.00000	0.00000	0.00000	0.00000	0.00000	0.00000
77	0.00003	0.00002	0.00002	0.00001	0.00001	0.00001	0.00000	0.00000	0.00000	0.00000	0.00000	0.00000
78	0.00003	0.00002	0.00001	0.00001	0.00001	0.00000	0.00000	0.00000	0.00000	0.00000	0.00000	0.00000
79	0.00002	0.00002	0.00001	0.00001	0.00001	0.00000	0.00000	0.00000	0.00000	0.00000	0.00000	0.00000
80	0.00002	0.00001	0.00001	0.00001	0.00000	0.00000	0.00000	0.00000	0.00000	0.00000	0.00000	0.00000
81	0.00002	0.00001	0.00001	0.00001˙	0.00000	0.00000	0.00000	0.00000	0.00000	0.00000	0.00000	0.00000
82	0.00002	0.00001	0.00001	0.00001	0.00000	0.00000	0.00000	0.00000	0.00000	0.00000	0.00000	0.00000
83	0.00001	0.00001	0.00001	0.00000	0.00000	0.00000	0.00000	0.00000	0.00000	0.00000	0.00000	0.00000
84	0.00001	0.00001	0.00001	0.00000	0.00000	0.00000	0.00000	0.00000	0.00000	0.00000	0.00000	0.00000
85	0.00001	0.00001	0.00000	0.00000	0.00000	0.00000	0.00000	0.00000	0.00000	0.00000	0.00000	0.00000
86	0.00001	0.00001	0.00000	0.00000	0.00000	0.00000	0.00000	0.00000	0.00000	0.00000	0.00000	0.00000
87	0.00001	0.00001	0.00000	0.00000	0.00000	0.00000	0.00000	0.00000	0.00000	0.00000	0.00000	0.00000
88	0.00001	0.00000	0.00000	0.00000	0.00000	0.00000	0.00000	0.00000	0.00000	0.00000	0.00000	0.00000
89	0.00001	0.00000	0.00000	0.00000	0.00000	0.00000	0.00000	0.00000	0.00000	0.00000	0.00000	0.00000
90	0.00001	0.00000	0.00000	0.00000	0.00000	0.00000	0.00000	0.00000	0.00000	0.00000	0.00000	0.00000
91	0.00000	0.00000	0.00000	0.00000	0.00000	0.00000	0.00000	0.00000	0.00000	0.00000	0.00000	0.00000
92	0.00000	0.00000	0.00000	0.00000	0.00000	0.00000	0.00000	0.00000	0.00000	0.00000	0.00000	0.00000
93	0.00000	0.00000	0.00000	0.00000	0.00000	0.00000	0.00000	0.00000	0.00000	0.00000	0.00000	0.00000
94	0.00000	0.00000	0.00000	0.00000	0.00000	0.00000	0.00000	0.00000	0.00000	0.00000	0.00000	0.00000
95	0.00000	0.00000	0.00000	0.00000	0.00000	0.00000	0.00000	0.00000	0.00000	0.00000	0.00000	0.00000
96	0.00000	0.00000	0.00000	0.00000	0.00000	0.00000	0.00000	0.00000	0.00000	0.00000	0.00000	0.00000
97	0.00000	0.00000	0.00000	0.00000	0.00000	0.00000	0.00000	0.00000	0.00000	0.00000	0.00000	0.00000
98	0.00000	0.00000	0.00000	0.00000	0.00000	0.00000	0.00000	0.00000	0.00000	0.00000	0.00000	0.00000
99	0.00000	0.00000	0.00000	0.00000	0.00000	0.00000	0.00000	0.00000	0.00000	0.00000	0.00000	0.00000
100	0.00000	0.00000	0.00000	0.00000	0.00000	0.00000	0.00000	0.00000	0.00000	0.00000	0.00000	0.00000
101	0.00000	0.00000	0.00000	0.00000	0.00000	0.00000	0.00000	0.00000	0.00000	0.00000	0.00000	0.00000
102	0.00000	0.00000	0.00000	0.00000	0.00000	0.00000	0.00000	0.00000	0.00000	0.00000	0.00000	0.00000
103	0.00000	0.00000	0.00000	0.00000	0.00000	0.00000	0.00000	0.00000	0.00000	0.00000	0.00000	0.00000
104	0.00000	0.00000	0.00000	0.00000	0.00000	0.00000	0.00000	0.00000	0.00000	0.00000	0.00000	0.00000
105	0.00000	0.00000	0.00000	0.00000	0.00000	0.00000	0.00000	0.00000	0.00000	0.00000	0.00000	0.00000
106	0.00000	0.00000	0.00000	0.00000	0.00000	0.00000	0.00000	0.00000	0.00000	0.00000	0.00000	0.00000
107	0.00000	0.00000	0.00000	0.00000	0.00000	0.00000	0.00000	0.00000	0.00000	0.00000	0.00000	0.00000
108	0.00000	0.00000	0.00000	0.00000	0.00000	0.00000	0.00000	0.00000	0.00000	0.00000	0.00000	0.00000
109	0.00000	0.00000	0.00000	0.00000	0.00000	0.00000	0.00000	0.00000	0.00000	0.00000	0.00000	0.00000
110 ,...	0.00000	0.00000	0.00000	0.00000	0.00000	0.00000	0.00000	0.00000	0.00000	0.00000	0.00000	0.00000
111	0.00000	0.00000	0.00000	0.00000	0.00000	0.00000	0.00000	0.00000	0.00000	0.00000	0.00000	0.00000
112	0.00000	0.00000	0.00000	0.00000	0.00000	0.00000	0.00000	0.00000	0.00000	0.00000	0.00000	0.00000
113	0.00000	0.00000	0.00000	0.00000	0.00000	0.00000	0.00000	0.00000	0.00000	0.00000	0.00000	0.00000
114	0.00000	0.00000	0.00000	0.00000	0.00000	0.00000	0.00000	0.00000	0.00000	0.00000	0.00000	0.00000
115	0.00000	0.00000	0.00000	0.00000	0.00000	0.00000	0.00000	0.00000	0.00000	0.00000	0.00000	0.00000
116	0.00000	0.00000	0.00000	0.00000	0.00000	0.00000	0.00000	0.00000	0.00000	0.00000	0.00000	0.00000
117	0.00000	0.00000	0.00000	0.00000	0.00000	0.00000	0.00000	0.00000	0.00000	0.00000	0.00000	0.00000
118	0.00000	0.00000	0.00000	0.00000	0.00000	0.00000	0.00000	0.00000	0.00000	0.00000	0.00000	0.00000
119	0.00000	0.00000	0.00000	0.00000	0.00000	0.00000	0.00000	0.00000	0.00000	0.00000	0.00000	0.00000
120	0.00000	0.00000	0.00000	0.00000	0.00000	0.00000	0.00000	0.00000	0.00000	0.00000	0.00000	0.00000

Table III
PRESENT VALUE OF AN ORDINARY ANNUITY OF $1 PER PERIOD: 0.5%–7%

$$P_{A_{1,n}} = \frac{1 - \frac{1}{(1-i)^n}}{i}$$

Period	.5%	1%	1.5%	2%	2.5%	3%	3.5%	4%	4.5%	5%	5.5%	6%	6.5%	7%
1	0.99502	0.99010	0.98522	0.98039	0.97561	0.97087	0.96618	0.96154	0.95694	0.95238	0.94787	0.94340	0.93897	0.93458
2	1.98510	1.97040	1.95588	1.94156	1.92742	1.91347	1.89969	1.88609	1.87267	1.85941	1.84632	1.83339	1.82063	1.80802
3	2.97025	2.94099	2.91220	2.88388	2.85602	2.82861	2.80164	2.77509	2.74896	2.72325	2.69793	2.67301	2.64848	2.62432
4	3.95050	3.90197	3.85438	3.80773	3.76197	3.71710	3.67308	3.62990	3.58753	3.54595	3.50515	3.46511	3.42580	3.38721
5	4.92587	4.85343	4.78264	4.71346	4.64583	4.57971	4.51505	4.45182	4.38998	4.32948	4.27028	4.21236	4.15568	4.10020
6	5.89638	5.79548	5.69719	5.60143	5.50813	5.41719	5.32855	5.24214	5.15787	5.07569	4.99553	4.91732	4.84101	4.76654
7	6.86207	6.72819	6.59821	6.47199	6.34939	6.23028	6.11454	6.00205	5.89270	5.78637	5.68297	5.58238	5.48452	5.38929
8	7.82296	7.65168	7.48593	7.32548	7.17014	7.01969	6.87396	6.73274	6.59589	6.46321	6.33457	6.20979	6.08875	5.97130
9	8.77906	8.56602	8.36052	8.16224	7.97087	7.78611	7.60769	7.43533	7.26879	7.10782	6.95220	6.80169	6.65610	6.51523
10	9.73041	9.47130	9.22218	8.98259	8.75206	8.53020	8.31661	8.11090	7.91272	7.72173	7.53763	7.36009	7.18883	7.02358
11	10.67703	10.36763	10.07112	9.78685	9.51421	9.25262	9.00155	8.76048	8.52892	8.30641	8.09254	7.88687	7.68904	7.49867
12	11.61893	11.25508	10.90751	10.57534	10.25776	9.95400	9.66333	9.38507	9.11858	8.86325	8.61852	8.38384	8.15873	7.94269
13	12.55615	12.13374	11.73153	11.34837	10.98318	10.63496	10.30274	9.98565	9.68285	9.39357	9.11708	8.85268	8.59974	8.35765
14	13.48871	13.00370	12.54338	12.10625	11.69091	11.29607	10.92052	10.56312	10.22283	9.89864	9.58965	9.29498	9.01384	8.74547
15	14.41662	13.86505	13.34323	12.84926	12.38138	11.93794	11.51741	11.11839	10.73955	10.37966	10.03758	9.71225	9.40267	9.10791
16	15.33993	14.71787	14.13126	13.57771	13.05500	12.56110	12.09412	11.65230	11.23402	10.83777	10.46216	10.10590	9.76776	9.44665
17	16.25863	15.56225	14.90765	14.29187	13.71220	13.16612	12.65132	12.16567	11.70719	11.27407	10.86461	10.47726	10.11058	9.76322
18	17.17277	16.39827	15.67256	14.99203	14.35336	13.75351	13.18968	12.65930	12.15999	11.68959	11.24607	10.82760	10.43247	10.05909
19	18.08236	17.22601	16.42617	15.67846	14.97889	14.32380	13.70984	13.13394	12.59329	12.08532	11.60765	11.15812	10.73471	10.33560
20	18.98742	18.04555	17.16864	16.35143	15.58916	14.87747	14.21240	13.59033	13.00794	12.46221	11.95038	11.46992	11.01851	10.59401
21	19.88798	18.85698	17.90014	17.01121	16.18455	15.41502	14.69797	14.02916	13.40472	12.82115	12.27524	11.76408	11.28498	10.83553
22	20.78406	19.66038	18.62082	17.65805	16.76541	15.93692	15.16712	14.45112	13.78442	13.16300	12.58317	12.04158	11.53520	11.06124
23	21.67568	20.45582	19.33086	18.29220	17.33211	16.44361	15.62041	14.85684	14.14777	13.48857	12.87504	12.30338	11.77014	11.27219
24	22.56287	21.24339	20.03041	18.91393	17.88499	16.93554	16.05837	15.24696	14.49548	13.79864	13.15170	12.55036	11.99074	11.46933
25	23.44504	22.02316	20.71961	19.52346	18.42438	17.41315	16.48151	15.62208	14.82821	14.09394	13.41393	12.78336	12.19788	11.65358
26	24.32402	22.79520	21.39863	20.12104	18.95061	17.87684	16.89035	15.98277	15.14661	14.37519	13.66250	13.00317	12.39237	11.82578
27	25.19803	23.55961	22.06762	20.70690	19.46401	18.32703	17.28536	16.32959	15.45130	14.64303	13.89810	13.21053	12.57500	11.98671
28	26.06769	24.31644	22.72672	21.28127	19.96489	18.76411	17.66702	16.66306	15.74287	14.89813	14.12142	13.40616	12.74648	12.13711
29	26.93302	25.06579	23.37608	21.84438	20.45355	19.18845	18.03577	16.98371	16.02189	15.14107	14.33310	13.59072	12.90749	12.27767
30	27.79405	25.80771	24.01584	22.39646	20.93029	19.60044	18.39205	17.29203	16.28889	15.37245	14.53375	13.76483	13.05868	12.40904
31	28.65080	26.54229	24.64615	22.93770	21.39541	20.00043	18.73628	17.58849	16.54439	15.59281	14.72393	13.92909	13.20063	12.53181
32	29.50328	27.26959	25.26714	23.46833	21.84918	20.38877	19.06887	17.87355	16.78889	15.80268	14.90420	14.08404	13.33393	12.64656
33	30.35153	27.98969	25.87895	23.98856	22.29188	20.76579	19.39021	18.14765	17.02286	16.00255	15.07507	14.23023	13.45909	12.75379
34	31.19555	28.70267	26.48173	24.49859	22.72379	21.13184	19.70068	18.41120	17.24676	16.19290	15.23703	14.36814	13.57661	12.85401
35	32.03537	29.40858	27.07559	24.99862	23.14516	21.48722	20.00066	18.66461	17.46101	16.37419	15.39055	14.49825	13.68696	12.94767
36	32.87102	30.10751	27.66068	25.48884	23.55625	21.83225	20.29049	18.90828	17.66604	16.54685	15.53607	14.62099	13.79057	13.03521
37	33.70250	30.79951	28.23713	25.96945	23.95732	22.16724	20.57053	19.14258	17.86224	16.71129	15.67400	14.73678	13.88786	13.11702
38	34.52985	31.48466	28.80505	26.44064	24.34860	22.49246	20.84109	19.36786	18.04999	16.86789	15.80474	14.84602	13.97921	13.19347
39	35.35309	32.16303	29.36458	26.90259	24.73034	22.80822	21.10250	19.58448	18.22966	17.01704	15.92866	14.94907	14.06499	13.26493
40	36.17223	32.83469	29.91585	27.35548	25.10278	23.11477	21.35507	19.79277	18.40158	17.15909	16.04612	15.04630	14.14553	13.33171
41	36.98729	33.49969	30.45896	27.79949	25.46612	23.41240	21.59910	19.99305	18.56611	17.29437	16.15746	15.13802	14.22115	13.39412
42	37.79830	34.15811	30.99405	28.23479	25.82061	23.70136	21.83488	20.18563	18.72355	17.42321	16.26300	15.22454	14.29216	13.45245
43	38.60527	34.81001	31.52123	28.66156	26.16645	23.98190	22.06269	20.37079	18.87421	17.54591	16.36303	15.30617	14.35884	13.50696
44	39.40823	35.45545	32.04062	29.07996	26.50385	24.25427	22.28279	20.54884	19.01838	17.66277	16.45785	15.38318	14.42144	13.55791
45	40.20720	36.09451	32.55234	29.49016	26.83302	24.51871	22.49545	20.72004	19.15635	17.77407	16.54773	15.45583	14.48023	13.60552
46	41.00219	36.72724	33.05649	29.89231	27.15417	24.77545	22.70092	20.88465	19.28837	17.88007	16.63292	15.52437	14.53543	13.65002
47	41.79322	37.35370	33.55319	30.28658	27.46748	25.02471	22.89944	21.04294	19.41471	17.98102	16.71366	15.58903	14.58725	13.69161
48	42.58032	37.97396	34.04255	30.67312	27.77315	25.26671	23.09124	21.19513	19.53561	18.07716	16.79020	15.65003	14.63592	13.73047
49	43.36350	38.58808	34.52468	31.05208	28.07137	25.50166	23.27656	21.34147	19.65130	18.16872	16.86275	15.70757	14.68161	13.76680
50	44.14279	39.19612	34.99969	31.42361	28.36231	25.72976	23.45562	21.48218	19.76201	18.25593	16.93152	15.76186	14.72452	13.80075
51	44.91820	39.79814	35.46767	31.78785	28.64616	25.95123	23.62862	21.61749	19.86795	18.33898	16.99670	15.81308	14.76481	13.83247
52	45.68975	40.39419	35.92874	32.14495	28.92308	26.16624	23.79576	21.74758	19.96933	18.41807	17.05848	15.86139	14.80264	13.86212
53	46.45746	40.98435	36.38300	32.49505	29.19325	26.37499	23.95726	21.87267	20.06634	18.49340	17.11705	15.90697	14.83816	13.88984
54	47.22135	41.56866	36.83054	32.83828	29.45683	26.57766	24.11330	21.99296	20.15918	18.56515	17.17255	15.94998	14.87151	13.91573
55	47.98145	42.14719	37.27147	33.17479	29.71398	26.77443	24.26405	22.10861	20.24802	18.63347	17.22517	15.99054	14.90282	13.93994
56	48.73776	42.71999	37.70588	33.50469	29.96486	26.96546	24.40971	22.21982	20.33303	18.69854	17.27504	16.02881	14.93223	13.96256
57	49.49031	43.28712	38.13387	33.82813	30.20962	27.15094	24.55045	22.32675	20.41439	18.76052	17.32232	16.06492	14.95984	13.98370
58	50.23911	43.84863	38.55554	34.14523	30.44841	27.33101	24.68642	22.42957	20.49224	18.81954	17.36712	16.09898	14.98577	14.00346
59	50.98419	44.40459	38.97097	34.45610	30.68137	27.50583	24.81780	22.52843	20.56673	18.87575	17.40960	16.13111	15.01011	14.02192
60	51.72556	44.95504	39.38027	34.76089	30.90866	27.67556	24.94473	22.62349	20.63802	18.92929	17.44985	16.16143	15.03297	14.03918

Period	.5%	1%	1.5%	2%	2.5%	3%	3.5%	4%	4.5%	5%	5.5%	6%	6.5%	7%
61 ...	52.46324	45.50004	39.78352	35.05969	31.13040	27.84035	25.06738	22.71489	20.70624	18.98028	17.48801	16.19003	15.05443	14.05531
62 ...	53.19726	46.03964	40.18080	35.35264	31.34673	28.00034	25.18587	22.80278	20.77152	19.02883	17.52418	16.21701	15.07458	14.07038
63 ...	53.92762	46.57390	40.57222	35.63984	31.55778	28.15567	25.30036	22.88729	20.83399	19.07508	17.55847	16.24246	15.09350	14.08447
64 ...	54.65435	47.10287	40.95785	35.92141	31.76369	28.30648	25.41097	22.96855	20.89377	19.11912	17.59096	16.26647	15.11127	14.09764
65 ...	55.37746	47.62661	41.33779	36.19747	31.96458	28.45289	25.51785	23.04668	20.95098	19.16107	17.62177	16.28912	15.12795	14.10994
66 ...	56.09698	48.14516	41.71210	36.46810	32.16056	28.59504	25.62111	23.12181	21.00572	19.20102	17.65096	16.31049	15.14362	14.12144
67 ...	56.81291	48.65857	42.08088	36.73343	32.35177	28.73305	25.72088	23.19405	21.05811	19.23907	17.67864	16.33065	15.15833	14.13219
68 ...	57.52529	49.16690	42.44423	36.99356	32.53831	28.86704	25.81727	23.26351	21.10824	19.27530	17.70487	16.34967	15.17214	14.14223
69 ...	58.23411	49.67020	42.80219	37.24859	32.72030	28.99712	25.91041	23.33030	21.15621	19.30981	17.72974	16.36762	15.18511	14.15162
70 ...	58.93942	50.16851	43.15487	37.49862	32.89786	29.12342	26.00040	23.39451	21.20211	19.34268	17.75330	16.38454	15.19728	14.16039
71 ...	59.64121	50.66190	43.50234	37.74374	33.07108	29.24604	26.08734	23.45626	21.24604	19.37398	17.77564	16.40051	15.20872	14.16859
72 ...	60.33951	51.15039	43.84467	37.98406	33.24008	29.36509	26.17134	23.51564	21.28808	19.40379	17.79682	16.41558	15.21945	14.17625
73 ...	61.03434	51.63405	44.18194	38.21967	33.40495	29.48067	26.25251	23.57273	21.32830	19.43218	17.81689	16.42979	15.22953	14.18341
74 ...	61.72571	52.11292	44.51422	38.45066	33.56581	29.59288	26.33092	23.62762	21.36680	19.45922	17.83591	16.44320	15.23900	14.19010
75 ...	62.41365	52.58705	44.84160	38.67711	33.72274	29.70183	26.40669	23.68041	21.40363	19.48497	17.85395	16.45585	15.24788	14.19636
76 ...	63.09815	53.05649	45.16414	38.89913	33.87584	29.80760	26.47989	23.73116	21.43888	19.50950	17.87104	16.46778	15.25623	14.20220
77 ...	63.77926	53.52127	45.48191	39.11680	34.02521	29.91029	26.55062	23.77996	21.47262	19.53285	17.88724	16.47904	15.26407	14.20767
78 ...	64.45697	53.98146	45.79498	39.33019	34.17094	30.00999	26.61896	23.82689	21.50490	19.55510	17.90260	16.48966	15.27142	14.21277
79 ...	65.13132	54.43709	46.10343	39.53940	34.31311	30.10679	26.68498	23.87201	21.53579	19.57628	17.91716	16.49968	15.27833	14.21755
80 ...	65.80231	54.88821	46.40732	39.74451	34.45182	30.20076	26.74878	23.91539	21.56534	19.59646	17.93095	16.50913	15.28482	14.22201
81 ...	66.46996	55.33486	46.70672	39.94560	34.58714	30.29200	26.81041	23.95711	21.59363	19.61568	17.94403	16.51805	15.29091	14.22617
82 ...	67.13428	55.77709	47.00170	40.14275	34.71916	30.38059	26.86996	23.99722	21.62070	19.63398	17.95643	16.52646	15.29663	14.23007
83 ...	67.79531	56.21494	47.29231	40.33603	34.84796	30.46659	26.92750	24.03579	21.64660	19.65141	17.96818	16.53440	15.30200	14.23371
84 ...	68.45304	56.64845	47.57863	40.52552	34.97362	30.55009	26.98309	24.07287	21.67139	19.66801	17.97932	16.54188	15.30704	14.23711
85 ...	69.10750	57.07768	47.86072	40.71129	35.09621	30.63115	27.03680	24.10853	21.69511	19.68382	17.98987	16.54895	15.31178	14.24029
86 ...	69.75871	57.50265	48.13864	40.89342	35.21582	30.70986	27.08870	24.14282	21.71781	19.69887	17.99988	16.55561	15.31622	14.24326
87 ...	70.40668	57.92342	48.41246	41.07198	35.33251	30.78627	27.13884	24.17579	21.73953	19.71321	18.00936	16.56190	15.32040	14.24604
88 ...	71.05142	58.34002	48.68222	41.24704	35.44635	30.86045	27.18728	24.20749	21.76032	19.72687	18.01835	16.56783	15.32431	14.24864
89 ...	71.69296	58.75249	48.94800	41.41867	35.55741	30.93248	27.23409	24.23797	21.78021	19.73987	18.02688	16.57342	15.32800	14.25106
90 ...	72.33130	59.16088	49.20985	41.58693	35.66577	31.00241	27.27932	24.26728	21.79924	19.75226	18.03495	16.57870	15.33145	14.25333
91 ...	72.96647	59.56523	49.46784	41.75189	35.77148	31.07030	27.32301	24.29546	21.81746	19.76406	18.04261	16.58368	15.33470	14.25545
92 ...	73.59847	59.96557	49.72201	41.91362	35.87462	31.13621	27.36523	24.32256	21.83489	19.77529	18.04987	16.58838	15.33774	14.25743
93 ...	74.22734	60.36195	49.97242	42.07218	35.97524	31.20021	27.40602	24.34861	21.85156	19.78599	18.05675	16.59281	15.34060	14.25928
94 ...	74.85307	60.75441	50.21913	42.22762	36.07340	31.26234	27.44543	24.37367	21.86753	19.79619	18.06327	16.59699	15.34329	14.26101
95 ...	75.47569	61.14298	50.46220	42.38002	36.16917	31.32266	27.48350	24.39776	21.88280	19.80589	18.06945	16.60093	15.34581	14.26262
96 ...	76.09522	61.52770	50.70168	42.52943	36.26261	31.38122	27.52029	24.42092	21.89742	19.81513	18.07531	16.60465	15.34818	14.26413
97 ...	76.71166	61.90862	50.93761	42.67592	36.35376	31.43808	27.55584	24.44319	21.91140	19.82394	18.08086	16.60816	15.35040	14.26555
98 ...	77.32503	62.28576	51.17006	42.81953	36.44269	31.49328	27.59018	24.46461	21.92479	19.83232	18.08612	16.61147	15.35249	14.26687
99 ...	77.93536	62.65917	51.39907	42.96032	36.52946	31.54687	27.62337	24.48520	21.93760	19.84031	18.09111	16.61460	15.35445	14.26810
100 ...	78.54264	63.02888	51.62470	43.09835	36.61411	31.59891	27.65543	24.50500	21.94985	19.84791	18.09584	16.61755	15.35629	14.26925
101 ...	79.14691	63.39493	51.84700	43.23368	36.69669	31.64942	27.68640	24.52404	21.96158	19.85515	18.10032	16.62033	15.35802	14.27033
102 ...	79.74817	63.75736	52.06601	43.36635	36.77726	31.69847	27.71633	24.54234	21.97281	19.86205	18.10457	16.62295	15.35964	14.27133
103 ...	80.34644	64.11619	52.28178	43.49642	36.85586	31.74609	27.74525	24.55995	21.98355	19.86862	18.10860	16.62542	15.36117	14.27228
104 ...	80.94173	64.47148	52.49437	43.62394	36.93255	31.79232	27.77318	24.57687	21.99382	19.87488	18.11241	16.62776	15.36260	14.27315
105 ...	81.53406	64.82325	52.70381	43.74896	37.00736	31.83720	27.80018	24.59315	22.00366	19.88083	18.11603	16.62996	15.36394	14.27398
106 ...	82.12344	65.17153	52.91016	43.87153	37.08035	31.88078	27.82626	24.60879	22.01307	19.88651	18.11946	16.63204	15.36521	14.27474
107 ...	82.70989	65.51637	53.11346	43.99170	37.15156	31.92308	27.85146	24.62384	22.02208	19.89191	18.12271	16.63400	15.36639	14.27546
108 ...	83.29342	65.85779	53.31375	44.10951	37.22104	31.96416	27.87581	24.63831	22.03070	19.89706	18.12579	16.63585	15.36750	14.27613
109 ...	83.87405	66.19583	53.51108	44.22501	37.28882	32.00404	27.89933	24.65222	22.03894	19.90196	18.12872	16.63759	15.36855	14.27676
110 ...	84.45180	66.53053	53.70550	44.33824	37.35494	32.04276	27.92206	24.66560	22.04684	19.90663	18.13148	16.63924	15.36953	14.27735
111 ...	85.02666	66.86191	53.89704	44.44926	37.41946	32.08035	27.94402	24.67846	22.05439	19.91108	18.13411	16.64079	15.37045	14.27789
112 ...	85.59867	67.19001	54.08576	44.55810	37.48240	32.11684	27.96523	24.69082	22.06162	19.91531	18.13659	16.64226	15.37131	14.27840
113 ...	86.16783	67.51486	54.27168	44.66480	37.54380	32.15227	27.98573	24.70272	22.06853	19.91934	18.13895	16.64364	15.37212	14.27888
114 ...	86.73416	67.83649	54.45486	44.76941	37.60371	32.18667	28.00554	24.71415	22.07515	19.92318	18.14119	16.64494	15.37289	14.27933
115 ...	87.29767	68.15494	54.63533	44.87197	37.66216	32.22007	28.02467	24.72514	22.08148	19.92684	18.14331	16.64617	15.37360	14.27975
116 ...	87.85838	68.47024	54.81313	44.97252	37.71918	32.25250	28.04316	24.73571	22.08754	19.93033	18.14531	16.64733	15.37428	14.28014
117 ...	88.41630	68.78242	54.98831	45.07110	37.77481	32.28398	28.06103	24.74588	22.09334	19.93364	18.14722	16.64843	15.37491	14.28050
118 ...	88.97144	69.09150	55.16089	45.16775	37.82908	32.31454	28.07829	24.75565	22.09889	19.93680	18.14902	16.64946	15.37550	14.28084
119 ...	89.52382	69.39753	55.33093	45.26250	37.88203	32.34421	28.09496	24.76505	22.10420	19.93981	18.15073	16.65043	15.37606	14.28116
120 ...	90.07345	69.70052	55.49845	45.35539	37.93369	32.37302	28.11108	24.77409	22.10929	19.94268	18.15235	16.65135	15.37658	14.28146

Table III (continued)
PRESENT VALUE OF AN ORDINARY ANNUITY OF $1 PER PERIOD: 7.5%–14%

Period	7.5%	8%	8.5%	9%	9.5%	10%	10.5%	11%	11.5%	12%	12.5%	13%	13.5%	14%
1	0.93023	0.92593	0.92166	0.91743	0.91324	0.90909	0.90498	0.90090	0.89686	0.89286	0.88889	0.88496	0.88106	0.87719
2	1.79557	1.78326	1.77111	1.75911	1.74725	1.73554	1.72396	1.71252	1.70122	1.69005	1.67901	1.66810	1.65732	1.64666
3	2.60053	2.57710	2.55402	2.53129	2.50891	2.48685	2.46512	2.44371	2.42262	2.40183	2.38134	2.36115	2.34125	2.32163
4	3.34933	3.31213	3.27560	3.23972	3.20448	3.16987	3.13586	3.10245	3.06961	3.03735	3.00564	2.97447	2.94383	2.91371
5	4.04588	3.99271	3.94064	3.88965	3.83971	3.79079	3.74286	3.69590	3.64988	3.60478	3.56057	3.51723	3.47474	3.43308
6	4.69385	4.62288	4.55359	4.48592	4.41983	4.35526	4.29218	4.23054	4.17029	4.11141	4.05384	3.99755	3.94250	3.88867
7	5.29660	5.20637	5.11851	5.03295	4.94961	4.86842	4.78930	4.71220	4.63704	4.56379	4.49230	4.42261	4.35463	4.28830
8	5.85730	5.74664	5.63918	5.53482	5.43344	5.33493	5.23919	5.14612	5.05564	4.96764	4.88205	4.79877	4.71774	4.63886
9	6.37889	6.24689	6.11906	5.99525	5.87528	5.75902	5.64632	5.53705	5.43106	5.32825	5.22848	5.13166	5.03765	4.94637
10	6.86408	6.71008	6.56135	6.41766	6.27880	6.14457	6.01477	5.88923	5.76777	5.65022	5.53643	5.42624	5.31952	5.21612
11	7.31542	7.13896	6.96898	6.80519	6.64730	6.49506	6.34821	6.20652	6.06975	5.93770	5.81016	5.68694	5.56786	5.45273
12	7.73528	7.53608	7.34469	7.16073	6.98384	6.81369	6.64996	6.49236	6.34058	6.19437	6.05348	5.91765	5.78666	5.66029
13	8.12584	7.90378	7.69095	7.48690	7.29118	7.10336	6.92304	6.74987	6.58348	6.42355	6.26976	6.12181	5.97943	5.84236
14	8.48915	8.24424	8.01010	7.78615	7.57185	7.36669	7.17018	6.98187	6.80133	6.62817	6.46201	6.30249	6.14928	6.00207
15	8.82712	8.55948	8.30424	8.06069	7.82818	7.60608	7.39382	7.19087	6.99671	6.81086	6.63289	6.46238	6.29893	6.14217
16	9.14151	8.85137	8.57533	8.31256	8.06226	7.82371	7.59622	7.37916	7.17194	6.97399	6.78479	6.60388	6.43077	6.26506
17	9.43396	9.12164	8.82519	8.54363	8.27604	8.02155	7.77939	7.54879	7.32909	7.11963	6.91982	6.72909	6.54694	6.37286
18	9.70601	9.37189	9.05548	8.75563	8.47127	8.20141	7.94515	7.70162	7.47004	7.24967	7.03984	6.83991	6.64928	6.46742
19	9.95908	9.60360	9.26772	8.95011	8.64956	8.36492	8.09515	7.83929	7.59644	7.36578	7.14652	6.93797	6.73946	6.55037
20	10.19449	9.81815	9.46334	9.12855	8.81238	8.51356	8.23091	7.96333	7.70982	7.46944	7.24135	7.02475	6.81890	6.62313
21	10.41348	10.01680	9.64363	9.29224	8.96108	8.64869	8.35376	8.07507	7.81149	7.56200	7.32565	7.10155	6.88890	6.68696
22	10.61719	10.20074	9.80980	9.44243	9.09688	8.77154	8.46494	8.17574	7.90269	7.64465	7.40058	7.16951	6.95057	6.74294
23	10.80669	10.37106	9.96295	9.58021	9.22089	8.88322	8.56556	8.26643	7.98447	7.71843	7.46718	7.22966	7.00491	6.79206
24	10.98297	10.52876	10.10410	9.70661	9.33415	8.98474	8.65662	8.34814	8.05782	7.78432	7.52638	7.28288	7.05279	6.83514
25	11.14695	10.67478	10.23419	9.82258	9.43758	9.07704	8.73902	8.42174	8.12361	7.84314	7.57901	7.32998	7.09497	6.87293
26	11.29948	10.80998	10.35409	9.92897	9.53203	9.16095	8.81359	8.48806	8.18261	7.89566	7.62578	7.37167	7.13213	6.90608
27	11.44138	10.93516	10.46460	10.02658	9.61830	9.23722	8.88108	8.54780	8.23552	7.94255	7.66736	7.40856	7.16487	6.93515
28	11.57338	11.05108	10.56645	10.11613	9.69707	9.30657	8.94215	8.60162	8.28298	7.98442	7.70432	7.44120	7.19372	6.96066
29	11.69617	11.15841	10.66033	10.19828	9.76902	9.36961	8.99742	8.65011	8.32554	8.02181	7.73717	7.47009	7.21914	6.98304
30	11.81039	11.25778	10.74684	10.27365	9.83472	9.42691	9.04744	8.69379	8.36371	8.05518	7.76638	7.49565	7.24153	7.00266
31	11.91664	11.34980	10.82658	10.34280	9.89472	9.47901	9.09271	8.73315	8.39795	8.08499	7.79234	7.51828	7.26126	7.01988
32	12.01548	11.43500	10.90008	10.40624	9.94952	9.52638	9.13367	8.76860	8.42866	8.11159	7.81541	7.53830	7.27864	7.03498
33	12.10742	11.51389	10.96781	10.46444	9.99956	9.56943	9.17074	8.80054	8.45619	8.13535	7.83592	7.55602	7.29396	7.04823
34	12.19295	11.58693	11.03024	10.51784	10.04526	9.60857	9.20429	8.82932	8.48089	8.15656	7.85415	7.57170	7.30745	7.05985
35	12.27251	11.65457	11.08778	10.56682	10.08699	9.64416	9.23465	8.85524	8.50304	8.17550	7.87036	7.58557	7.31934	7.07005
36	12.34652	11.71719	11.14081	10.61176	10.12511	9.67651	9.26213	8.87859	8.52291	8.19241	7.88476	7.59785	7.32982	7.07899
37	12.41537	11.77518	11.18969	10.65299	10.15992	9.70592	9.28700	8.89963	8.54072	8.20751	7.89757	7.60872	7.33904	7.08683
38	12.47941	11.82887	11.23474	10.69082	10.19171	9.73265	9.30950	8.91859	8.55670	8.22099	7.90895	7.61833	7.34718	7.09371
39	12.53899	11.87858	11.27625	10.72552	10.22074	9.75696	9.32986	8.93567	8.57103	8.23303	7.91906	7.62684	7.35434	7.09975
40	12.59441	11.92461	11.31452	10.75736	10.24725	9.77905	9.34829	8.95105	8.58389	8.24378	7.92806	7.63438	7.36065	7.10504
41	12.64596	11.96723	11.34979	10.78657	10.27146	9.79914	9.36497	8.96491	8.59541	8.25337	7.93605	7.64104	7.36621	7.10969
42	12.69392	12.00670	11.38229	10.81337	10.29357	9.81740	9.38006	8.97740	8.60575	8.26194	7.94316	7.64694	7.37111	7.11376
43	12.73853	12.04324	11.41225	10.83795	10.31376	9.83400	9.39372	8.98865	8.61502	8.26959	7.94947	7.65216	7.37543	7.11733
44	12.78003	12.07707	11.43986	10.86051	10.33220	9.84909	9.40608	8.99878	8.62334	8.27642	7.95509	7.65678	7.37923	7.12047
45	12.81863	12.10840	11.46531	10.88120	10.34904	9.86281	9.41727	9.00791	8.63080	8.28252	7.96008	7.66086	7.38258	7.12322
46	12.85454	12.13741	11.48877	10.90018	10.36442	9.87528	9.42739	9.01614	8.63749	8.28796	7.96451	7.66448	7.38554	7.12563
47	12.88794	12.16427	11.51038	10.91760	10.37847	9.88662	9.43656	9.02355	8.64349	8.29282	7.96846	7.66768	7.38814	7.12774
48	12.91902	12.18914	11.53031	10.93358	10.39130	9.89693	9.44485	9.03022	8.64887	8.29716	7.97196	7.67052	7.39043	7.12960
49	12.94792	12.21216	11.54867	10.94823	10.40301	9.90630	9.45235	9.03624	8.65369	8.30104	7.97508	7.67302	7.39245	7.13123
50	12.97481	12.23348	11.56560	10.96168	10.41371	9.91481	9.45914	9.04165	8.65802	8.30450	7.97785	7.67524	7.39423	7.13266
51	12.99982	12.25323	11.58119	10.97402	10.42348	9.92256	9.46529	9.04653	8.66190	8.30759	7.98031	7.67720	7.39580	7.13391
52	13.02309	12.27151	11.59557	10.98534	10.43240	9.92960	9.47085	9.05093	8.66538	8.31035	7.98250	7.67894	7.39718	7.13501
53	13.04474	12.28843	11.60882	10.99573	10.44055	9.93600	9.47588	9.05489	8.66850	8.31281	7.98444	7.68048	7.39839	7.13597
54	13.06487	12.30410	11.62103	11.00525	10.44799	9.94182	9.48043	9.05846	8.67130	8.31501	7.98617	7.68184	7.39947	7.13682
55	13.08360	12.31861	11.63229	11.01399	10.45478	9.94711	9.48456	9.06168	8.67382	8.31697	7.98771	7.68304	7.40041	7.13756
56	13.10103	12.33205	11.64266	11.02201	10.46099	9.95191	9.48829	9.06457	8.67607	8.31872	7.98907	7.68411	7.40124	7.13821
57	13.11723	12.34449	11.65222	11.02937	10.46666	9.95629	9.49166	9.06718	8.67809	8.32029	7.99029	7.68505	7.40198	7.13878
58	13.13231	12.35601	11.66104	11.03612	10.47183	9.96026	9.49472	9.06954	8.67990	8.32169	7.99137	7.68589	7.40262	7.13928
59	13.14633	12.36668	11.66916	11.04231	10.47656	9.96387	9.49748	9.07165	8.68152	8.32294	7.99232	7.68663	7.40319	7.13972
60	13.15938	12.37655	11.67664	11.04799	10.48088	9.96716	9.49998	9.07356	8.68298	8.32405	7.99318	7.68728	7.40369	7.14011

Period	7.5%	8%	8.5%	9%	9.5%	10%	10.5%	11%	11.5%	12%	12.5%	13%	13.5%	14%
61....	13.17152	12.38570	11.68354	11.05320	10.48482	9.97014	9.50225	9.07528	8.68429	8.32504	7.99394	7.68786	7.40413	7.14044
62....	13.18281	12.39416	11.68990	11.05798	10.48842	9.97286	9.50430	9.07683	8.68546	8.32593	7.99461	7.68837	7.40452	7.14074
63....	13.19331	12.40200	11.69576	11.06237	10.49171	9.97532	9.50615	9.07822	8.68651	8.32673	7.99521	7.68882	7.40487	7.14100
64....	13.20308	12.40926	11.70116	11.06640	10.49471	9.97757	9.50783	9.07948	8.68745	8.32743	7.99574	7.68922	7.40517	7.14123
65....	13.21217	12.41598	11.70614	11.07009	10.49745	9.97961	9.50935	9.08061	8.68830	8.32807	7.99621	7.68958	7.40544	7.14143
66....	13.22062	12.42221	11.71073	11.07347	10.49996	9.98146	9.51072	9.08163	8.68906	8.32863	7.99663	7.68989	7.40567	7.14160
67....	13.22848	12.42797	11.71496	11.07658	10.50224	9.98315	9.51196	9.08255	8.68974	8.32913	7.99701	7.69017	7.40588	7.14176
68....	13.23580	12.43330	11.71885	11.07943	10.50433	9.98468	9.51309	9.08338	8.69035	8.32958	7.99734	7.69042	7.40606	7.14189
69....	13.24260	12.43825	11.72245	11.08205	10.50624	9.98607	9.51411	9.08413	8.69090	8.32999	7.99764	7.69063	7.40622	7.14201
70....	13.24893	12.44282	11.72576	11.08445	10.50798	9.98734	9.51503	9.08480	8.69139	8.33034	7.99790	7.69083	7.40636	7.14211
71....	13.25482	12.44706	11.72881	11.08665	10.50957	9.98849	9.51586	9.08541	8.69183	8.33066	7.99813	7.69100	7.40648	7.14221
72....	13.26030	12.45098	11.73162	11.08867	10.51102	9.98954	9.51662	9.08595	8.69222	8.33095	7.99834	7.69115	7.40659	7.14229
73....	13.26539	12.45461	11.73421	11.09052	10.51235	9.99049	9.51730	9.08644	8.69257	8.33121	7.99852	7.69128	7.40669	7.14236
74....	13.27013	12.45797	11.73660	11.09222	10.51356	9.99135	9.51792	9.08688	8.69289	8.33143	7.99869	7.69140	7.40678	7.14242
75....	13.27454	12.46108	11.73880	11.09378	10.51467	9.99214	9.51848	9.08728	8.69318	8.33164	7.99883	7.69150	7.40685	7.14247
76....	13.27864	12.46397	11.74083	11.09521	10.51568	9.99285	9.51899	9.08764	8.69343	8.33182	7.99896	7.69160	7.40692	7.14252
77....	13.28246	12.46664	11.74270	11.09653	10.51660	9.99350	9.51945	9.08797	8.69366	8.33198	7.99908	7.69168	7.40698	7.14256
78....	13.28601	12.46911	11.74443	11.09773	10.51744	9.99409	9.51986	9.08826	8.69387	8.33213	7.99918	7.69175	7.40703	7.14260
79....	13.28931	12.47140	11.74601	11.09883	10.51821	9.99463	9.52024	9.08852	8.69405	8.33226	7.99927	7.69181	7.40707	7.14263
80....	13.29238	12.47351	11.74748	11.09985	10.51892	9.99512	9.52057	9.08876	8.69422	8.33237	7.99935	7.69187	7.40711	7.14266
81....	13.29524	12.47548	11.74883	11.10078	10.51956	9.99556	9.52088	9.08897	8.69436	8.33247	7.99942	7.69192	7.40715	7.14268
82....	13.29790	12.47729	11.75007	11.10163	10.52015	9.99597	9.52116	9.08916	8.69450	8.33257	7.99949	7.69197	7.40718	7.14270
83....	13.30037	12.47897	11.75122	11.10241	10.52068	9.99633	9.52141	9.08934	8.69462	8.33265	7.99955	7.69201	7.40721	7.14272
84....	13.30267	12.48053	11.75228	11.10313	10.52117	9.99667	9.52164	9.08949	8.69472	8.33272	7.99960	7.69204	7.40723	7.14274
85....	13.30481	12.48197	11.75325	11.10379	10.52162	9.99697	9.52185	9.08963	8.69482	8.33279	7.99964	7.69207	7.40725	7.14275
86....	13.30680	12.48331	11.75415	11.10440	10.52202	9.99724	9.52203	9.08976	8.69490	8.33285	7.99968	7.69210	7.40727	7.14277
87....	13.30865	12.48455	11.75497	11.10495	10.52240	9.99749	9.52220	9.08987	8.69498	8.33290	7.99972	7.69212	7.40729	7.14278
88....	13.31037	12.48569	11.75574	11.10546	10.52274	9.99772	9.52235	9.08998	8.69505	8.33294	7.99975	7.69214	7.40730	7.14279
89....	13.31197	12.48675	11.75644	11.10593	10.52305	9.99793	9.52249	9.09007	8.69511	8.33299	7.99978	7.69216	7.40731	7.14280
90....	13.31346	12.48773	11.75709	11.10635	10.52333	9.99812	9.52262	9.09015	8.69517	8.33302	7.99980	7.69218	7.40732	7.14280
91....	13.31485	12.48864	11.75768	11.10675	10.52359	9.99829	9.52273	9.09023	8.69522	8.33306	7.99982	7.69219	7.40733	7.14281
92....	13.31614	12.48948	11.75823	11.10711	10.52383	9.99844	9.52283	9.09029	8.69526	8.33309	7.99984	7.69221	7.40735	7.14282
93....	13.31734	12.49026	11.75874	11.10744	10.52404	9.99859	9.52293	9.09036	8.69530	8.33311	7.99986	7.69222	7.40735	7.14282
94....	13.31846	12.49098	11.75921	11.10774	10.52424	9.99871	9.52301	9.09041	8.69534	8.33314	7.99988	7.69223	7.40736	7.14283
95....	13.31949	12.49165	11.75964	11.10802	10.52442	9.99883	9.52309	9.09046	8.69537	8.33316	7.99989	7.69224	7.40736	7.14283
96....	13.32046	12.49227	11.76004	11.10827	10.52458	9.99894	9.52315	9.09050	8.69540	8.33318	7.99990	7.69225	7.40737	7.14283
97....	13.32136	12.49284	11.76040	11.10851	10.52473	9.99903	9.52322	9.09054	8.69543	8.33319	7.99991	7.69225	7.40737	7.14284
98....	13.32219	12.49337	11.76074	11.10872	10.52487	9.99912	9.52327	9.09058	8.69545	8.33321	7.99992	7.69226	7.40738	7.14284
99....	13.32297	12.49386	11.76105	11.10892	10.52500	9.99920	9.52332	9.09061	8.69547	8.33322	7.99993	7.69226	7.40738	7.14284
100....	13.32369	12.49432	11.76134	11.10910	10.52511	9.99927	9.52337	9.09064	8.69549	8.33323	7.99994	7.69227	7.40738	7.14284
101....	13.32437	12.49474	11.76160	11.10927	10.52522	9.99934	9.52341	9.09067	8.69551	8.33324	7.99995	7.69227	7.40739	7.14284
102....	13.32499	12.49513	11.76184	11.10942	10.52531	9.99940	9.52345	9.09069	8.69552	8.33325	7.99995	7.69228	7.40739	7.14285
103....	13.32557	12.49549	11.76207	11.10956	10.52540	9.99945	9.52348	9.09071	8.69553	8.33326	7.99996	7.69228	7.40739	7.14285
104....	13.32611	12.49582	11.76227	11.10969	10.52548	9.99950	9.52351	9.09073	8.69555	8.33327	7.99996	7.69228	7.40739	7.14285
105....	13.32662	12.49613	11.76246	11.10981	10.52555	9.99955	9.52354	9.09075	8.69556	8.33328	7.99997	7.69229	7.40739	7.14285
106....	13.32709	12.49642	11.76264	11.10991	10.52562	9.99959	9.52357	9.09077	8.69557	8.33328	7.99997	7.69229	7.40740	7.14285
107....	13.32752	12.49668	11.76280	11.11001	10.52568	9.99963	9.52359	9.09078	8.69558	8.33329	7.99997	7.69229	7.40740	7.14285
108....	13.32793	12.49693	11.76295	11.11010	10.52573	9.99966	9.52361	9.09079	8.69558	8.33329	7.99998	7.69229	7.40740	7.14285
109....	13.32831	12.49716	11.76309	11.11019	10.52578	9.99969	9.52363	9.09080	8.69559	8.33330	7.99998	7.69230	7.40740	7.14285
110....	13.32866	12.49737	11.76322	11.11026	10.52583	9.99972	9.52365	9.09082	8.69560	8.33330	7.99998	7.69230	7.40740	7.14285
111....	13.32898	12.49756	11.76333	11.11033	10.52587	9.99975	9.52366	9.09082	8.69560	8.33330	7.99998	7.69230	7.40740	7.14285
112....	13.32929	12.49774	11.76344	11.11040	10.52591	9.99977	9.52368	9.09083	8.69561	8.33331	7.99999	7.69230	7.40740	7.14285
113....	13.32957	12.49791	11.76354	11.11046	10.52595	9.99979	9.52369	9.09084	8.69561	8.33331	7.99999	7.69230	7.40740	7.14285
114....	13.32983	12.49807	11.76363	11.11051	10.52598	9.99981	9.52370	9.09085	8.69562	8.33331	7.99999	7.69230	7.40740	7.14285
115....	13.33008	12.49821	11.76371	11.11056	10.52601	9.99983	9.52371	9.09085	8.69562	8.33332	7.99999	7.69230	7.40740	7.14286
116....	13.33030	12.49834	11.76379	11.11060	10.52603	9.99984	9.52372	9.09086	8.69562	8.33332	7.99999	7.69230	7.40740	7.14286
117....	13.33051	12.49846	11.76386	11.11065	10.52606	9.99986	9.52373	9.09086	8.69563	8.33332	7.99999	7.69230	7.40740	7.14286
118....	13.33071	12.49858	11.76393	11.11069	10.52608	9.99987	9.52374	9.09087	8.69563	8.33332	7.99999	7.69230	7.40741	7.14286
119....	13.33089	12.49868	11.76399	11.11072	10.52610	9.99988	9.52374	9.09087	8.69563	8.33332	7.99999	7.69230	7.40741	7.14286
120....	13.33106	12.49878	11.76405	11.11075	10.52612	9.99989	9.52375	9.09088	8.69563	8.33332	7.99999	7.69230	7.40741	7.14286

Table III *(concluded)*
PRESENT VALUE OF AN ORDINARY ANNUITY OF $1 PER PERIOD: 14.5%–20%

Period	14.5%	15%	15.5%	16%	16.5%	17%	17.5%	18%	18.5%	19%	19.5%	20%
1	0.87336	0.86957	0.86580	0.86207	0.85837	0.85470	0.85106	0.84746	0.84388	0.84034	0.83682	0.83333
2	1.63612	1.62571	1.61541	1.60523	1.59517	1.58521	1.57537	1.56564	1.55602	1.54650	1.53709	1.52778
3	2.30229	2.28323	2.26443	2.24589	2.22761	2.20958	2.19181	2.17427	2.15698	2.13992	2.12309	2.10648
4	2.88410	2.85498	2.82634	2.79818	2.77048	2.74324	2.71643	2.69006	2.66412	2.63859	2.61346	2.58873
5	3.39223	3.35216	3.31285	3.27429	3.23646	3.19935	3.16292	3.12717	3.09208	3.05763	3.02382	2.99061
6	3.83600	3.78448	3.73407	3.68474	3.63645	3.58918	3.54291	3.49760	3.45323	3.40978	3.36721	3.32551
7	4.22358	4.16042	4.09876	4.03857	3.97979	3.92238	3.86631	3.81153	3.75800	3.70570	3.65457	3.60459
8	4.56208	4.48732	4.41451	4.34359	4.27449	4.20716	4.14154	4.07757	4.01519	3.95437	3.89504	3.83716
9	4.85771	4.77158	4.68789	4.60654	4.52746	4.45057	4.37578	3.30302	4.23223	4.16333	4.09627	4.03097
10	5.11591	5.01877	4.92458	4.83323	4.74460	4.65860	4.57513	4.49409	4.41538	4.33893	4.26466	4.19247
11	5.34140	5.23371	5.12951	5.02864	4.93099	4.83641	4.74479	4.65601	4.56994	4.48650	4.40557	4.32706
12	5.53834	5.42062	5.30693	5.19711	5.09098	4.98839	4.88918	4.79322	4.70037	4.61050	4.52349	4.43922
13	5.71034	5.58315	5.46055	5.34233	5.22831	5.11828	5.01207	4.90951	4.81044	4.71471	4.62217	4.53268
14	5.86056	5.72448	5.59355	5.46753	5.34619	5.22930	5.11666	5.00806	4.90333	4.80228	4.70474	4.61057
15	5.99176	5.84737	5.70870	5.57546	5.44747	5.32419	5.20567	5.09158	4.98171	4.87586	4.77384	4.67547
16	6.10634	5.95423	5.80840	5.66850	5.53422	5.40529	5.28142	5.16235	5.04786	4.93770	4.83167	4.72956
17	6.20641	6.04716	5.89472	5.74870	5.60878	5.47461	5.34589	5.22233	5.10368	4.98966	4.88006	4.77463
18	6.29381	6.12797	5.96945	5.81785	5.67277	5.53385	5.40075	5.27316	5.15078	5.03333	4.92055	4.81219
19	6.37014	6.19823	6.03416	5.87746	5.72770	5.58449	5.44745	5.31624	5.19053	5.07003	4.95443	4.84350
20	6.43680	6.25933	6.09018	5.92884	5.77485	5.62777	5.48719	5.35275	5.22408	5.10086	4.98279	4.86958
21	6.49502	6.31246	6.13868	5.97314	5.81532	5.66476	5.52101	5.38368	5.25239	5.12677	5.00652	4.89132
22	6.54587	6.35866	6.18068	6.01133	5.85006	5.69637	5.54980	5.40990	5.27628	5.14855	5.02638	4.90943
23	6.59028	6.39884	6.21704	6.04425	5.87988	5.72340	5.57430	5.43212	5.29644	5.16685	5.04299	4.92453
24	6.62907	6.43377	6.24852	6.07263	5.90548	5.74649	5.59515	5.45095	5.31345	5.18223	5.05690	4.93710
25	6.66294	6.46415	6.27577	6.09709	5.92745	5.76623	5.61289	5.46691	5.32780	5.19515	5.06853	4.94759
26	6.69252	6.49056	6.29937	6.11818	5.94631	5.78311	5.62799	5.48043	5.33992	5.20601	5.07827	4.95632
27	6.71836	6.51353	6.31980	6.13636	5.96250	5.79753	5.64084	5.49189	5.35014	5.21513	5.08642	4.96360
28	6.74093	6.53351	6.33749	6.15204	5.97639	5.80985	5.65178	5.50160	5.35877	5.22280	5.09324	4.96967
29	6.76064	6.55088	6.35281	6.16555	5.98832	5.82039	5.66109	5.50983	5.36605	5.22924	5.09894	4.97472
30	6.77785	6.56598	6.36607	6.17720	5.99856	5.82939	5.66901	5.51681	5.37219	5.23466	5.10372	4.97894
31	6.79288	6.57911	6.37755	6.18724	6.00734	5.83709	5.67576	5.52272	5.37738	5.23921	5.10771	4.98245
32	6.80601	6.59053	6.38749	6.19590	6.01489	5.84366	5.68150	5.52773	5.38175	5.24303	5.11106	4.98537
33	6.81747	6.60046	6.39609	6.20336	6.02136	5.84928	5.68638	5.53197	5.38545	5.24625	5.11386	4.98781
34	6.82749	6.60910	6.40354	6.20979	6.02692	5.85409	5.69054	5.53557	5.38856	5.24895	5.11620	4.98984
35	6.83623	6.61661	6.40999	6.21534	6.03169	5.85820	5.69407	5.53862	5.39119	5.25122	5.11816	4.99154
36	6.84387	6.62314	6.41558	6.22012	6.03579	5.86171	5.69708	5.54120	5.39341	5.25312	5.11980	4.99295
37	6.85054	6.62881	6.42041	6.22424	6.03930	5.86471	5.69965	5.54339	5.39528	5.25472	5.12117	4.99412
38	6.85637	6.63375	6.42460	6.22779	6.04232	5.86727	5.70183	5.54525	5.39686	5.25607	5.12232	4.99510
39	6.86146	6.63805	6.42823	6.23086	6.04491	5.86946	5.70368	5.54682	5.39820	5.25720	5.12328	4.99592
40	6.86590	6.64178	6.43136	6.23350	6.04713	5.87133	5.70526	5.54815	5.39932	5.25815	5.12408	4.99660
41	6.86978	6.64502	6.43408	6.23577	6.04904	5.87294	5.70660	5.54928	5.40027	5.25895	5.12475	4.99717
42	6.87317	6.64785	6.43643	6.23774	6.05068	5.87430	5.70775	5.55024	5.40107	5.25962	5.12532	4.99764
43	6.87613	6.65030	6.43847	6.23943	6.05208	5.87547	5.70872	5.55105	5.40175	5.26019	5.12579	4.99803
44	6.87872	6.65244	6.44024	6.24089	6.05329	5.87647	5.70955	5.55174	5.40232	5.26066	5.12618	4.99836
45	6.88098	6.65429	6.44176	6.24214	6.05433	5.87733	5.71026	5.55232	5.40280	5.26106	5.12651	4.99863
46	6.88295	6.65591	6.44308	6.24323	6.05522	5.87806	5.71086	5.55281	5.40321	5.26140	5.12679	4.99886
47	6.88467	6.65731	6.44423	6.24416	6.05598	5.87868	5.71137	5.55323	5.40355	5.26168	5.12702	4.99905
48	6.88618	6.65853	6.44522	6.24497	6.05664	5.87922	5.71180	5.55359	5.40384	5.26191	5.12721	4.99921
49	6.88749	6.65959	6.44608	6.24566	6.05720	5.87967	5.71217	5.55389	5.40409	5.26211	5.12738	4.99934
50	6.88864	6.66051	6.44682	6.24626	6.05768	5.88006	5.71249	5.55414	5.40429	5.26228	5.12751	4.99945
51	6.88964	6.66132	6.44746	6.24678	6.05809	5.88039	5.71275	5.55436	5.40447	5.26242	5.12762	4.99954
52	6.89052	6.66201	6.44802	6.24722	6.05845	5.88068	5.71298	5.55454	5.40461	5.26254	5.12772	4.99962
53	6.89128	6.66262	6.44850	6.24760	6.05876	5.88092	5.71318	5.55469	5.40474	5.26264	5.12780	4.99968
54	6.89195	6.66315	6.44892	6.24793	6.05902	5.88113	5.71334	5.55483	5.40484	5.26272	5.12786	4.99974
55	6.89253	6.66361	6.44928	6.24822	6.05924	5.88131	5.71348	5.55494	5.40493	5.26279	5.12792	4.99978
56	6.89304	6.66401	6.44959	6.24846	6.05944	5.88146	5.71360	5.55503	5.40500	5.26285	5.12797	4.99982
57	6.89348	6.66435	6.44987	6.24868	6.05960	5.88159	5.71370	5.55511	5.40507	5.26290	5.12801	4.99985
58	6.89387	6.66466	6.45010	6.24886	6.05974	5.88170	5.71379	5.55518	5.40512	5.26294	5.12804	4.99987
59	6.89421	6.66492	6.45030	6.24902	6.05987	5.88180	5.71386	5.55524	5.40516	5.26297	5.12807	4.99989
60	6.89451	6.66515	6.45048	6.24915	6.05997	5.88188	5.71393	5.55529	5.40520	5.26300	5.12809	4.99991

Period	14.5%	15%	15.5%	16%	16.5%	17%	17.5%	18%	18.5%	19%	19.5%	20%
61	6.89477	6.66534	6.45063	6.24927	6.06006	5.88195	5.71398	5.55533	5.40523	5.26303	5.12811	4.99993
62	6.89499	6.66552	6.45076	6.24937	6.06014	5.88200	5.71403	5.55536	5.40526	5.26305	5.12812	4.99994
63	6.89519	6.66567	6.45088	6.24946	6.06020	5.88206	5.71406	5.55539	5.40528	5.26307	5.12814	4.99995
64	6.89536	6.66580	6.45098	6.24953	6.06026	5.88210	5.71410	5.55542	5.40530	5.26308	5.12815	4.99996
65	6.89551	6.66591	6.45106	6.24960	6.06031	5.88214	5.71413	5.55544	5.40532	5.26309	5.12816	4.99996
66	6.89565	6.66601	6.45114	6.24965	6.06035	5.88217	5.71415	5.55546	5.40533	5.26310	5.12816	4.99997
67	6.89576	6.66609	6.45120	6.24970	6.06039	5.88219	5.71417	5.55547	5.40534	5.26311	5.12817	4.99997
68	6.89586	6.66617	6.45125	6.24974	6.06042	5.88222	5.71419	5.55548	5.40535	5.26312	5.12818	4.99998
69	6.89595	6.66623	6.45130	6.24978	6.06045	5.88224	5.71420	5.55549	5.40536	5.26313	5.12818	4.99998
70	6.89602	6.66629	6.45134	6.24981	6.06047	5.88225	5.71421	5.55550	5.40537	5.26313	5.12819	4.99999
71	6.89609	6.66634	6.45138	6.24983	6.06049	5.88227	5.71422	5.55551	5.40537	5.26314	5.12819	4.99999
72	6.89615	6.66638	6.45141	6.24986	6.06050	5.88228	5.71423	5.55552	5.40538	5.26314	5.12819	4.99999
73	6.89620	6.66642	6.45144	6.24988	6.06052	5.88229	5.71424	5.55552	5.40538	5.26314	5.12819	4.99999
74	6.89624	6.66645	6.45146	6.24989	6.06053	5.88230	5.71425	5.55553	5.40539	5.26314	5.12820	4.99999
75	6.89628	6.66648	6.45148	6.24991	6.06054	5.88231	5.71425	5.55553	5.40539	5.26315	5.12820	4.99999
76	6.89632	6.66650	6.45150	6.24992	6.06055	5.88231	5.71426	5.55554	5.40539	5.26315	5.12820	5.00000
77	6.89635	6.66653	6.45151	6.24993	6.06056	5.88232	5.71426	5.55554	5.40540	5.26315	5.12820	5.00000
78	6.89637	6.66654	6.45153	6.24994	6.06057	5.88232	5.71427	5.55554	5.40540	5.26315	5.12820	5.00000
79	6.89640	6.66656	6.45154	6.24995	6.06057	5.88233	5.71427	5.55554	5.40540	5.26315	5.12820	5.00000
80	6.89642	6.66657	6.45155	6.24996	6.06058	5.88233	5.71427	5.55555	5.40540	5.26315	5.12820	5.00000
81	6.89643	6.66659	6.45156	6.24996	6.06058	5.88234	5.71427	5.55555	5.40540	5.26315	5.12820	5.00000
82	6.89645	6.66660	6.45157	6.24997	6.06058	5.88234	5.71428	5.55555	5.40540	5.26315	5.12820	5.00000
83	6.89646	6.66661	6.45157	6.24997	6.06059	5.88234	5.71428	5.55555	5.40540	5.26316	5.12820	5.00000
84	6.89647	6.66661	6.45158	6.24998	6.06059	5.88234	5.71428	5.55555	5.40540	5.26316	5.12820	5.00000
85	6.89648	6.66662	6.45158	6.24998	6.06059	5.88234	5.71428	5.55555	5.40540	5.26316	5.12820	5.00000
86	6.89649	6.66663	6.45159	6.24998	6.06059	5.88234	5.71428	5.55555	5.40540	5.26316	5.12820	5.00000
87	6.89650	6.66663	6.45159	6.24998	6.06060	5.88235	5.71428	5.55555	5.40540	5.26316	5.12820	5.00000
88	6.89651	6.66664	6.45159	6.24999	6.06060	5.88235	5.71428	5.55555	5.40540	5.26316	5.12820	5.00000
89	6.89651	6.66664	6.45160	6.24999	6.06060	5.88235	5.71428	5.55555	5.40540	5.26316	5.12820	5.00000
90	6.89652	6.66664	6.45160	6.24999	·6.06060	5.88235	5.71428	5.55555	5.40540	5.26316	5.12820	5.00000
91	6.89652	6.66665	6.45160	6.24999	6.06060	5.88235	5.71428	5.55555	5.40540	5.26316	5.12820	5.00000
92	6.89652	6.66665	6.45160	6.24999	6.06060	5.88235	5.71428	5.55555	5.40540	5.26316	5.12820	5.00000
93	6.89653	6.66665	6.45160	6.24999	6.06060	5.88235	5.71428	5.55555	5.40540	5.26316	5.12820	5.00000
94	6.89653	6.66665	6.45160	6.24999	6.06060	5.88235	5.71428	5.55555	5.40540	5.26316	5.12820	5.00000
95	6.89653	6.66666	6.45161	6.25000	6.06060	5.88235	5.71428	5.55555	5.40540	5.26316	5.12820	5.00000
96	6.89654	6.66666	6.45161	6.25000	6.06060	5.88235	5.71428	5.55555	5.40540	5.26316	5.12820	5.00000
97	6.89654	6.66666	6.45161	6.25000	6.06060	5.88235	5.71428	5.55555	5.40541	5.26316	5.12820	5.00000
98	6.89654	6.66666	6.45161	6.25000	6.06060	5.88235	5.71428	5.55556	5.40541	5.26316	5.12820	5.00000
99	6.89654	6.66666	6.45161	6.25000	6.06060	5.88235	5.71429	5.55556	5.40541	5.26316	5.12821	5.00000
100	6.89654	6.66666	6.45161	6.25000	6.06060	5.88235	5.71429	5.55556	5.40541	5.26316	5.12821	5.00000
101	6.89654	6.66666	6.45161	6.25000	6.06060	5.88235	5.71429	5.55556	5.40541	5.26316	5.12821	5.00000
102	6.89654	6.66666	6.45161	6.25000	6.06061	5.88235	5.71429	5.55556	5.40541	5.26316	5.12821	5.00000
103	6.89655	6.66666	6.45161	6.25000	6.06061	5.88235	5.71429	5.55556	5.40541	5.26316	5.12821	5.00000
104	6.89655	6.66666	6.45161	6.25000	6.06061	5.88235	5.71429	5.55556	5.40541	5.26316	5.12821	5.00000
105	6.89655	6.66666	6.45161	6.25000	6.06061	5.88235	5.71429	5.55556	5.40541	5.26316	5.12821	5.00000
106	6.89655	6.66666	6.45161	6.25000	6.06061	5.88235	5.71429	5.55556	5.40541	5.26316	5.12821	5.00000
107	6.89655	6.66666	6.45161	6.25000	6.06061	5.88235	5.71429	5.55556	5.40541	5.26316	5.12821	5.00000
108	6.89655	6.66666	6.45161	6.25000	6.06061	5.88235	5.71429	5.55556	5.40541	5.26316	5.12821	5.00000
109	6.89655	6.66667	6.45161	6.25000	6.06061	5.88235	5.71429	5.55556	5.40541	5.26316	5.12821	5.00000
110	6.89655	6.66667	6.45161	6.25000	6.06061	5.88235	5.71429	5.55556	5.40541	5.26316	5.12821	5.00000
111	6.89655	6.66667	6.45161	6.25000	6.06061	5.88235	5.71429	5.55556	5.40541	5.26316	5.12821	5.00000
112	6.89655	6.66667	6.45161	6.25000	6.06061	5.88235	5.71429	5.55556	5.40541	5.26316	5.12821	5.00000
113	6.89655	6.66667	6.45161	6.25000	6.06061	5.88235	5.71429	5.55556	5.40541	5.26316	5.12821	5.00000
114	6.89655	6.66667	6.45161	6.25000	6.06061	5.88235	5.71429	5.55556	5.40541	5.26316	5.12821	5.00000
115	6.89655	6.66667	6.45161	6.25000	6.06061	5.88235	5.71429	5.55556	5.40541	5.26316	5.12821	5.00000
116	6.89655	6.66667	6.45161	6.25000	6.06061	5.88235	5.71429	5.55556	5.40541	5.26316	5.12821	5.00000
117	6.89655	6.66667	6.45161	6.25000	6.06061	5.88235	5.71429	5.55556	5.40541	5.26316	5.12821	5.00000
118	6.89655	6.66667	6.45161	6.25000	6.06061	5.88235	5.71429	5.55556	5.40541	5.26316	5.12821	5.00000
119	6.89655	6.66667	6.45161	6.25000	6.06061	5.88235	5.71429	5.55556	5.40541	5.26316	5.12821	5.00000
120	6.89655	6.66667	6.45161	6.25000	6.06061	5.88235	5.71429	5.55556	5.40541	5.26316	5.12821	5.00000

INDEX

A

Absorption costing, 433–36
Accelerated Cost Recovery System (ACRS), 585–87
Accelerated depreciation, 172–74
Accounting
 Accounting Principles Standards Board, 8
 accrual basis, defined, 69–70
 American Accounting Association, 8
 and American Institute of Public Certified Accountants (AICPA), 2, 7–8
 cash, and taxes, 584
 cash basis, 69
 and consistency, 348
 constant dollar, 358, 359, 360–65
 conventions, modified, 354–55
 current cost, 358, 365–66
 current dollar, 358, 359–60, 365–66
 defined, 2
 depreciation, 169–70
 and economic activity, 1, 197
 external users of, 5–6
 and foreign currency, 627–28
 general purpose financial statements and, 347
 going concern (continuity) and, 346
 historical cost accounting, 356–57

Accounting—*Cont.*
 and inflation, 357–60
 internal users of, 6–7
 international, 623–30
 job opportunities in
  not-for-profit sector, 4
  private accounting, 3–4
  public accounting, 2–3
 labor cost accounting, 395
 management, 3
 in manufacturing companies, 388–406
 measurement in, 348
 money measurement in, 346
 need for accounting information, 4–7
 payroll accounting, 395–96
 periodicity and, 346–47
 procedures and concepts
  accounting assumptions, 16–17
  accounting equation, 15–16
  balance sheet, 13–14
  bias effect, accounting information, 372–73
  continuity assumption, defined, 17
  dividends, 26
  financial accounting process, 15–16
  financial statements, 12–15
  income statements, 14

Accounting—*Cont.*
  questions users want answered, 6–7
  revenue and expense transactions, 21
  Securities and Exchange Commission, 8
  statement of retained earnings, 14–15
  terms defined, 13–14, 16–17
  transaction and analysis, 16–20
 purchases, 109–10
 qualities, hierarchy of, 371
 responsibility, 481–90
 and transactions approach, 348
Accounting curriculums, internationalizing, 626
Accounting equation, 15–16
Accounting methods, and taxes, 584–87
Accounting period, 70
Accounting principles
 changes in, 225–27
 differences among nations, 623–27
 generally accepted accounting principles (GAAP), 6, 368, 374
 and theory, 349–54
Accounting Principles Board, 197, 326
Accounting qualities, hierarchy of, 371

This book has been set VideoComp, in 10 and 9 point Compano, leaded 2 points. Chapter numbers are 36 point Palatino Bold. Chapter titles are 24 point Compano. The size of the type page is 35 by 46 picas.